Worlds of History

A Comparative Reader

Worlds of History

A Comparative Reader

Volume Two: Since 1400

Sixth Edition

Kevin Reilly
Raritan Valley College

bedford/st.martin's
Macmillan Learning
Boston • New York

For Bedford/St. Martin's

Vice President, Editorial, Macmillan Learning Humanities: Edwin Hill
Publisher for History: Michael Rosenberg
Acquiring Editor for History: Laura Arcari
Director of Development for History: Jane Knetzger
Developmental Editor: Tess Fletcher
Production Editor: Matt Glazer
Production Supervisor: Lisa McDowell
History Marketing Manager: Melissa Famiglietti
Assistant Editor: Mary Posman
Copy Editor: Melissa Cook
Photo Editor: Robin Fadool
Photo Researcher: Naomi Kornhauser
Permissions Editor: Jen Roach
Senior Art Director: Anna Palchik
Cover Design: William Boardman
Cover Art/Cover Photo: (Top) View of Nihonbashi in Tokyo, c.1870 (coloured woodblock), Utagawa, Kuniteru II (1830-74) / Victoria & Albert Museum, London, UK / Bridgeman Images; (Bottom) Ritual drinking vessel (kero), with Inca-Spanish colonial decoration / Werner Forman Archive / Bridgeman Images
Composition: Cenveo Publisher Services
Printing and Binding: RR Donnelley and Sons

Manufactured in the United States of America.

1   0   9   8   7   6
f   e   d   c   b   a

For information, write: Bedford/St. Martin's, 75 Arlington Street, Boston, MA 02116 (617-399-4000)

ISBN 978-1-319-04208-0

Acknowledgments

Text acknowledgments and copyrights appear at the back of the book on pages ACK-1– ACK-5, which constitute an extension of the copyright page. Art acknowledgments and copyrights appear on the same page as the art selections they cover.

Preface

The college-level world history course is undergoing another transformation: the third since I first wrote about the subject for the American Historical Association in 1984.[1] The first two were the almost contemporaneous conceptual jump from Western history to world history and the inclusion of a vast array of new subject areas, especially in social and cultural history. The third, occurring now, is a trend toward engaging students with sources rather than solely with writings about those sources, "flipping" the course from lecture to discussion, and teaching historical thinking skills rather than merely transferring information. The purpose of this book is to satisfy the needs expressed in these three revolutions. The switch to world history from courses in "Western Civilization" that rarely ventured over the Alps or the Pyrenees is an obvious need of students in the twenty-first century. So, too, is the addition of topics on gender, race, and class; migrations, trade, and encounters; religion, sexuality, and work; climate, ecology, and disease; and so many more fruits of contemporary scholarship, micro and global. Our title, *Worlds of History*, is a reflection of both these goals.

The need to teach students to think critically and independently, an often unspoken goal of history education over the past several decades, is now receiving explicit formulation and vigorous advocacy in the efforts of institutions like the American Historical Association and the College Board to answer public unease about the value of college degrees in history and the other humanities. What are the thinking skills or "habits of mind" that we teach or can teach when we teach history? This book suggests answers to that question and prepares teachers to demonstrate them.

To engage students who are not only new to the college experience but new to reading source material as well, I have continued my efforts to provide accessible readings that pique their interest. This new edition aims to maintain that high level of reader interest with new selections, like an explanation from the fourteenth-century College of Physicians in Paris for the causes of the Black Death and an image depicting Aztec education from the *Codex Mendoza*. As in previous editions, I have also included secondary as well as primary texts. In some chapters the secondary text introduces an issue that the primary sources then address, while at other times the secondary source offers a summary or suggestions for new directions. My aim in combining these two types of sources is for students to learn how texts, whether primary or secondary, talk to each other—and without having to buy separate books of each.

[1] Kevin Reilly, ed., *The Introductory History Course: Six Models* (American Historical Association), 1984.

As a framework, I've used a thematic and topical organization that also proceeds chronologically, with each chapter focusing on a captivating topic within a particular time period. I have long found a comparative approach to be a useful tool for approaching world history, and for this sixth edition, I have continued to use this tool, examining two or more cultures at a time. In some chapters students can trace parallel developments in separate regions, such as the development of society in ancient Greece and India in Chapter 3, or the advent of nationalism in Japan and India in Chapter 23. In other cases students can examine the enduring effects of contact and exchange between cultures, as in the chapter on Mongol and Viking raiding and settlements from the tenth to the fourteenth centuries, or Volume 2's chapter on the scientific revolution in Europe, the Ottoman Empire, China, Japan, and the Americas. Even the normally bipolar study of the Cold War can be expanded, as documents in Chapter 26 relating to the superpowers' fight to control the emerging "Third World" show.

I continue to include a wealth of pedagogical tools to help students unlock the readings and hone their critical thinking skills. Each chapter begins with a "Historical Context" introduction that sets the stage for directed comparisons among the chapter's readings. A "Thinking Historically" section follows, which introduces a particular critical thinking skill—such as asking about author, audience, and agenda or distinguishing causes of change—that is designed to mine the chapter's selections. Introductions preceding each selection provide additional context, while document-specific "Thinking Historically" content poses questions to encourage close analysis of the selections using the critical thinking skill introduced at the beginning of the chapter. Explanatory gloss notes and pronunciation guides throughout help ensure comprehension of the readings. A set of "Reflections" that both summarizes and extends the chapter's lessons concludes each chapter.

■ NEW TO THIS EDITION

While I am continually testing selections in my own classroom, I appreciate input from readers and adopters, and I want to thank them for their many suggestions for exciting new chapters and selections. Having incorporated some of this feedback, I think those who have used the reader previously will find the sixth edition even more geographically and topically comprehensive, interesting, and accessible to students. Close to a third of its selections are new, resulting in fresh material in almost every chapter. In addition, I have added two new chapters, an exploration of traditions of students and education across the world (Chapter 13) and a look at empire, religion, and war in Asian, Islamic, and Christian states (Chapter 17).

In my ongoing efforts to make the book more accessible, I have added new Thinking Historically skills to both new and existing chapters. Chapter 10 includes a new section on Understanding Causes; Chapter 13 asks students to think critically about Texts and Contexts; Chapter 17 deepens students' understanding of Author, Audience, and Agenda; and Chapter 25 has been reframed to encourage students to delve into World War II–era documents through the lens of Empathetic Understanding.

I am not a believer in change for its own sake; when I have discovered a successful way of teaching a subject, I am not disposed to jettison it for something new. Consequently, many of my most satisfying changes in this edition are incremental: a better translation of a document, the addition of a newly discovered source, or additional questions to further inspire critical thinking. In some cases I have been able to further edit a useful source, retaining its muscle while also providing space for a precious new find. I begin each round of revision with the conviction that the book is already as good as it can get. And, as history happens all around us in the years between editions, I end each round with a book that is not only updated but also better than it was.

What's more, *Worlds of History* is being offered in an electronic format this year for the first time. The new PDF e-book can be read on a variety of devices, including e-readers, laptops, and tablets. For more information, you or your students can visit macmillanhighered.com/ebookpartners.

■ ACKNOWLEDGMENTS

A book like this cannot be written without the help and advice of a vast army of colleagues and friends. I consider myself enormously fortunate to have met and known such a large group of gifted and generous scholars. Some were especially helpful in the preparation of this new edition. They include: Lawrence Backlund, Montgomery County Community College; Roger Deal, University of South Caroline-Aiken; Grant Hardy, University of North Carolina at Asheville; Obbe Haverkamp, Davidson Community College; Martin Kalb, Northern Arizona University; Dana Wessell Lightfoot, University of Northern British Columbia; Matthew Maher, Metropolitan State College of Denver; Kate McGrath, Central Connecticut State University; Kelli Nakamura, Kapiolani Community College; Raphael Njoku, Idaho State University; Janine Peterson, Marist College; Marynel Ryan Van Zee, University of Minnesota, Morris; and Peter Winn, Tufts University.

Over the years I have benefited from the suggestions of innumerable friends and fellow world historians. Among them: Michael Adas, Rutgers University; the late Jerry Bentley, University of Hawai'i; David

Berry, Essex County Community College; Edmund (Terry) Burke III, University of California–Santa Cruz; Catherine Clay, Shippensburg University; the late Philip Curtin, Johns Hopkins University; S. Ross Doughty, Ursinus College; Ross Dunn, San Diego State University; Marc Gilbert, Hawai'i Pacific University; Steve Gosch, University of Wisconsin–Eau Claire; Sue Gronewold, Kean University; Gregory Guzman, Bradley University; Brock Haussamen, Raritan Valley College; Allen Howard, Rutgers University; Sarah Hughes, Shippensburg University; Karen Jolly, University of Hawai'i; Stephen Kaufman, Raritan Valley College; Maghan Keita, Villanova University; Craig Lockard, University of Wisconsin–Green Bay; Pat Manning, University of Pittsburgh; Adam McKeown, Columbia University; John McNeill, Georgetown University; William H. McNeill, University of Chicago; Gyan Prakash, Princeton University; Lauren Ristvet, University of Pennsylvania; Robert Rosen, University of California–Los Angeles; Heidi Roupp, Aspen High School; John Russell-Wood, Johns Hopkins University; Lynda Shaffer, Tufts University; Ira Spar, Ramapo College; Robert Strayer, California State University–Monterey Bay; George Sussman, LaGuardia Community College; Robert Tignor, Princeton University; John Voll, Georgetown University; and Peter Winn, Tufts University.

I also want to thank the people at Bedford/St. Martin's: Michael Rosenberg, publisher for history; Jane Knetzger, director of development for history; Laura Arcari, acquiring editor for world history; Tess Fletcher, developmental editor for this edition; Mary Posman, editorial assistant; my copy editors, Susan Moore and Melissa Cook; the book's cover designer, William Boardman; and Matt Glazer, production editor. None of this would have been possible if I had not been blessed in my own introduction to history and critical thinking at Rutgers in the 1960s with teachers I still aspire to emulate. Eugene Meehan taught me how to think and showed me that I could. Traian Stoianovich introduced me to the world and an endless range of historical inquiry. Warren Susman lit up a room with more life than I ever knew existed. Donald Weinstein guided me as a young teaching assistant to listen to students and talk with them rather than at them. And Peter Stearns showed me how important and exciting it could be to understand history by making comparisons. I dedicate this book to them.

Finally, I want to thank my own institution, Raritan Valley College, for nurturing my career, allowing me to teach whatever I wanted, and entrusting me with some of the best students one could encounter anywhere. I could not ask for anything more. Except, of course, a loving wife like Pearl.

Kevin Reilly

Introduction for Students

When most people think of history books, they think of books that tell a story about the past. It may be a small part of the past, like a presidential election or the making of the atomic bomb, or a large chunk of the past like the history of China or the history of warfare. In either case, these are books that tell a continuous story from beginning to end. The story might evolve gradually or reveal a conclusion at the start. It might be dramatic or plodding. There may be quotations from various people scattered throughout or indented in long paragraphs, but the book is written by a single author (or sometimes a few who agree on what to say) and presented with a single voice. The voice of a single storyteller gives this kind of history book a strong sense of authority. The reader is not invited to question anything, much less disagree. Any doubts are met by an implicit: "Wait, let me finish," and the author's conclusions follow inevitably from the facts that he or she has determined best fit the story.

The book you are holding in your hands is a different kind of history book. It does not tell a single story, but many. And while these selections are gathered by a single editor (a not unimportant matter), they were originally crafted by hundreds of different people. These people came from various places throughout the world, lived at different times, and were addressing different subjects, often with no awareness of what any of the other authors in this book said—or even of their existence.

This book contains many different stories. But it contains much more. Most of the selections are not stories in the way that history books are. First of all, most were not written by historians. Some of the stories in this book are literary or imaginary, while others come from personal letters or diaries. And many are not even stories. There are selections from treaties, philosophy books, scientific treatises, holy books, telegrams, poems, hymns, and speeches. Further, some of the selections are not even writings. There are paintings, art works, photographs, pictures of things, and cartoons. There would be music too, if it could fit into a book.

The point is that this book contains what are called **historical sources** rather than histories. Historical sources are the raw materials that historians use to construct histories. Of course, when you think of all the possible sources available to historians, you realize that even a book of this size can contain only a miniscule number of sources. There are in fact whole libraries devoted to archiving historical sources—from presidential libraries that contain the papers of a president to the archives of government offices. In addition, museums, university libraries, film archives, and ever-expanding online collections include sources ranging from newspapers, magazines, and books to images, letters, e-mails, and more.

Historians use these collections in order to find the sources they need to tell a particular story. The sources are as varied as the questions historians ask. Say, for instance, you are studying the history of individuality and you want to see if the use of the pronoun *I* increased in the late Middle Ages. There happens to be an archive that includes every scrap of writing from a medieval Jewish community in Cairo that saved everything on the chance that a piece of paper might contain the word for God, and therefore, under Jewish tradition, could not be destroyed. With this archive, tedious work, and a good computer, you could chart the use of a single word like *I* over the hundreds of years in which these papers were gathered. It would be within one community, to be sure; but there are few, if any, comparable source collections for this period. Someday a historian may even try to figure out what college students were thinking in the last years of the Age of Reading by a study of your e-mail, essays, or other personal possessions.

This book, then, is one of the two types of books most often used in a history course. The first type is the survey textbook. This book is the second type. It is variously called a "reader," "source book," or an anthology, and it collects a variety of sources in one book. It is designed to introduce you to working with historical sources. The reason for using a reader in addition to, or instead of, a survey text is that it allows us to do those things that the text makes so difficult. It allows us to interpret sources on our own, ask questions, solve problems, and actively build our understanding. Sources can engage our minds in ways that narrative textbooks, with their sense of authority and finality, do not.

Many source books contain only what are called **primary sources,** pieces from the past that were created in the period we are studying. This book contains some **secondary sources** as well. Secondary sources are pieces *about* the period we are studying. They are usually written by scholars. Most of the secondary sources in this book were written fairly recently by modern historians. My reason for including secondary sources is to provide some context or perspective to consider the primary sources (which make up most of the selections in each chapter). Historians read and write secondary sources, continually checking and revising them to conform to primary sources — the actual evidence from the past.

Primary sources can be difficult to interpret because they were often written in a time that is not familiar to us, and the context specific to their creation may be unknown. They use funny words, address weird issues, say strange things, and are sometimes written in a language that we have to struggle to make sense of. I have tried to minimize some of these problems with footnotes, pronunciation help, and some modernization of the language.

I've also included headnotes before each source that give you some historical background about the author and the source. But I can't do too much of that because it is important for you to appreciate the unfamiliarity of these sources in order to do your own analysis. A wise novelist once said: "The past is a foreign country: They do things differently there."[1] These sources were created in a different time, which often makes them seem foreign and remote. So it is precisely this context of a different time that we have to immerse ourselves in to understand the source and the world from which it came. Primary sources require and enable a kind of time travel to knowledge in which we have to leave many of our assumptions behind as excess baggage.

Because the authors of primary sources were not writing for us, and indeed had no idea we'd ever exist, they can't lie to us (at least as they might have, had they been given the opportunity). They tell us so much more than they intended. Primary sources can also be full of deceit, based on illusion, and riddled with error. They can even seem bonkers—and by those very characteristics, tell us much. Working with primary sources is like being a fly on the wall or being able to see things while remaining invisible. It is like having a superpower—gained from the study of history.

Throughout both volumes of this reader you have chapters in world history, which deal with particular historical periods and topics. Some topics cover long periods, like the rise of civilization and patriarchy (Chapter 1) or migrations, travel, and trade from 3000 B.C.E to 1350 C.E. (Chapter 8). Some topics cover brief periods, like the First Crusade from 1095–1099 (Chapter 10) and the Black Death from 1346–1350 (Chapter 12). Most fall in between these extremes. There are, for example, chapters on the topics of women, marriage, and family in most of the large periods that divide the book, i.e., ancient, classical, medieval, and early modern. There are also chapters that compare different societies: classical India and Greece, the Roman and Chinese empires, and Mongols and Vikings. There are chapters on such conventionally defined topics as the Atlantic Slave Trade, the Scientific Revolution, the Enlightenment, the First and Second World Wars, and the Cold War. There are also chapters that pose new historical frameworks like secularization, democratization, and globalization.

As you learn about historical periods and topics, you will also be learning to explore history by analyzing primary and secondary sources systematically. The "Thinking Historically" exercises in each chapter encourage habits of mind that I associate with my own study of history. They are not necessarily intended to turn you into historians but, rather, to give you skills that will help you in all of your college courses. Indeed, these are skills for life: for jury duty and the voting booth; for writing letters or drafting memos on the job; for weighing options and making smart decisions. Hopefully these new habits of mind will also expand your interests and nourish your self-confidence.

---

[1] L. P. Hartley, *The Go-Between* (New York: NYRB Classics, 2002), 17. First published in London in 1953.

These skills are organized from the simple to the more complex. Since skill building is cumulative, your ability to understand, analyze, and use sources will become increasingly sophisticated as you read through this text. But you need not wait for the end of the course to begin your analysis of these sources. Rather, it would be useful to develop the habit of asking the basic questions that journalists are trained to ask whenever they are assigned a story: who, what, where, when, and why?

Whether the source is primary or secondary, a piece of writing or a work of art, a run-through of these basic "w" questions is a good place to start when analyzing sources:

- **Who** wrote or created the source? If the author is unknown or anonymous, what sort of person does the author appear to be? An observer, participant, or eyewitness? A later historian? This will establish whether it is a primary or secondary source. Are there any clues to the identity of the author in the source itself? Are there signs of the author's social class, political position, and attitudes toward the subject of the source?
- **What** is the source? Is it a history by a modern historian and, therefore, a secondary source? Or is it a primary source from the past? If so, what kind of primary source? Is it an engraved stone, a poem, a love letter, a diary entry, a chapter from an ancient book of philosophy, a prayer?
- **Where** does it come from? China? Ancient Mesopotamia? France? Paris? Has it traveled from one place to another, or has it always been in the same place?
- **When** was it created? If it is writing, was it revised? Was there an earlier written or oral version? Is it an example of an older style? How new is it?
- **Why** was it created? To entertain, exorcise, instruct, persuade? **What** was the purpose? **Who** was the audience?

Ultimately, our answers to these questions might help us answer the most important question of all: **What** does this source tell us about the world from which it came?

World history is nothing less than everything ever done or imagined, so we cannot possibly cover it all; we are forced to choose among different places and times in our study of the global past. Our choices do include some particular moments in time, like the one in 111 C.E. in the first half of this reader, when the Roman governor of Bithynia consulted Emperor Trajan about proper treatment of Christians. But our attention will be directed toward much longer periods as well. While we will visit particular places in time like Imperial Rome in the second century or Africa in the nineteenth century, typically we will study more than one place at a time by using a comparative approach.

Comparisons can be enormously useful in studying world history. When we compare the raiding and trading of Vikings and Mongols, the scientific revolution in Europe and Japan, and the Cold War in Cuba and Afghanistan, we learn about the general and the specific at the same time. My hope is that by comparing some of the various worlds of history, a deeper and more nuanced understanding of our global past will emerge. With that understanding, we are better equipped to make sense of the world today and to confront whatever the future holds.

Contents

15. Overseas Expansion in the Early Modern Period: Asia, Africa, Europe, and the Americas, 1400–1600 514

Both China and Europe set sail with a goal of global expansion in the fifteenth century, but China's explorations ended just as Europe's began. What were the factors that led to their similar efforts yet different outcomes? We examine primary and secondary sources in search of clues.

16. Atlantic World Encounters: Europeans, Americans, and Africans, 1500–1850 563

European encounters with Africans and Americans were similar in some ways, yet markedly different in others. The cultural clashes created a new Atlantic world that integrated, divided, and uprooted these indigenous peoples. We compare primary sources, including visual evidence, to understand these first contacts and conflicts.

17. Empire, Religion, and War: Asian, Islamic, and Christian States, 1500–1800 608

Between the years 1500 and 1800, the world saw the rise of both empires and religious conflict and war. In this chapter, we ask about the relationship between these two developments and interrogate sources to better understand author, audience, and agenda.

18. Women, Marriage, and Family: China and Europe, 1550–1700 639

With the blinds drawn on the domestic lives of our ancestors, one might assume their private worlds were uneventful and everywhere the same. By comparing artifacts from different cultures, however, we see historical variety in family and economic life and in the roles of both women and men.

19. The Scientific Revolution: Europe, the Ottoman Empire, China, Japan, and the Americas, 1600–1800 677

The scientific revolution of the seventeenth and eighteenth centuries occurred in Europe, but it had important roots in Asia, and its consequences reverberated throughout the world. In this chapter we seek to understand what changed and how. How "revolutionary" was the scientific revolution, and how do we distinguish between mere change and "revolutionary" change?

21. Capitalism and the Industrial Revolution: Europe and the World, 1750–1900 750

Modern society has been shaped dramatically by capitalism and the industrial revolution, but these two forces are not the same. Which one is principally responsible for the creation of our modern world: the economic system of the market or the technology of the industrial revolution? Distinguishing different "causes" allows us to gauge their relative effects and legacies.

25. World War II and Mass Killing: Germany, the Soviet Union, Japan, and the United States, 1926–1945 894

The rise of fascism in Europe and Asia led to total war, genocide, war crimes, and civilian massacres on an almost unimaginable scale. How could governments, armies, and ordinary people commit such unspeakable acts? How can we recognize the unbelievable and understand the inexcusable?

HISTORICAL CONTEXT *894*

THINKING HISTORICALLY: Empathetic Understanding *895*

1. BENITO MUSSOLINI, The Doctrine of Fascism, 1932 *896*

2. ADOLPH HITLER, Mein Kampf, 1926 *899*

3. HEINRICH HIMMLER, Speech to the SS, 1943 *906*

4. JEAN-FRANÇOIS STEINER, Treblinka, 1967 *908*

5. TIMOTHY SNYDER, Holocaust: The Ignored Reality, 2009 *914*

6. DR. ROBERT WILSON, Letters from Nanking, 1937–1938 *924*

7. AKIHIRO TAKAHASHI, Memory of Hiroshima, 1945/1986 *931*

REFLECTIONS *933*

26. The Cold War and the Third World: Korea, Vietnam, Cuba, the Congo, and Afghanistan, 1945–1989 935

The Cold War was not only a conflict between the United States and the Soviet Union in which both superpowers avoided direct military confrontation. It was also a series of hot wars and propaganda battles, often played out with surrogates, for the creation of a new "post-colonial" world order and the control of an emerging "Third World." A war of words is a good place to look for hidden political meanings.

HISTORICAL CONTEXT *935*

THINKING HISTORICALLY: Detecting Ideological Language *936*

1. HEONIK KWON, Origins of the Cold War, 2010 *937*

2. WINSTON CHURCHILL, Iron Curtain Speech, 1946 *942*

3. The Vietnamese Declaration of Independence, 1945 *944*

4. EDWARD LANSDALE, Report on CIA Operations in Vietnam, 1954–1955 *947*

27. New Democracy Movements: The World, 1977 to the Present 974

Demands for democracy are on the rise, challenging and sometimes sweeping away old empires, petty tyrants, military dictatorships, and one-party states. Even "old" democracies are pushed to raise the bar to include social justice, economic opportunity, and a right to education. Where are these movements coming from? Are they connected or coincidental? Are they for real?

HISTORICAL CONTEXT *974*

THINKING HISTORICALLY: **Using Connections and Context to Interpret the Past** *976*

28. Globalization: The World, 1990 to the Present 1013

Globalization is a word with many meanings and a process with many causes. What are the forces most responsible for the shrinking of the world into one global community? Do the forces of globalization unite or divide us? Do they impoverish or enrich us? We undertake the study of process to answer these questions.

Geographic Contents

South Asia

East Asia

Southeast Asia

Australasia and the Pacific

Europe and Russia

The Americas

Interregional Contacts

Worlds of History

A Comparative Reader

15

Overseas Expansion in the Early Modern Period

Asia, Africa, Europe, and the Americas, 1400–1600

■ HISTORICAL CONTEXT

Between 1400 and 1500, the balance between Chinese and European sea power changed drastically. Before 1434, Chinese shipbuilding was the envy of the world. Chinese ships were larger, more numerous, safer, and better outfitted than European ships. The Chinese navy made frequent trips through the South China Sea to the Spice Islands, through the Indian Ocean, and as far as East Africa and the Persian Gulf (see Map 15.1). Every island, port, and kingdom along the route was integrated into the Chinese system of tributaries. Goods were exchanged, marriages arranged, and princes taken to visit the Chinese emperor.

In the second half of the fifteenth century, the Chinese navy virtually disappeared. At the same time, the Portuguese began a series of explorations down the coast of Africa and into the Atlantic Ocean. In 1434 Portuguese ships rounded the treacherous Cape Bojador, just south of Morocco, and in 1498 Bartolomeu Dias rounded the Cape of Good Hope. Vasco da Gama sailed into the Indian Ocean, arriving in Calicut the following year. And in 1500 a fortuitous landfall in Brazil by Pedro Cabral gave the Portuguese a claim from the western Atlantic to the Indian Ocean. By 1512 Portuguese ships had reached the Bandas and Moluccas—the Spice Islands of what is today eastern Indonesia.

Beginning in 1492, after the defeat of the Moors (Muslims) and the voyages of Columbus, the Spanish claimed most of the Western Hemisphere until challenged by the Dutch, English, and French. European control in the Americas penetrated far deeper than in Asia, where it was limited to

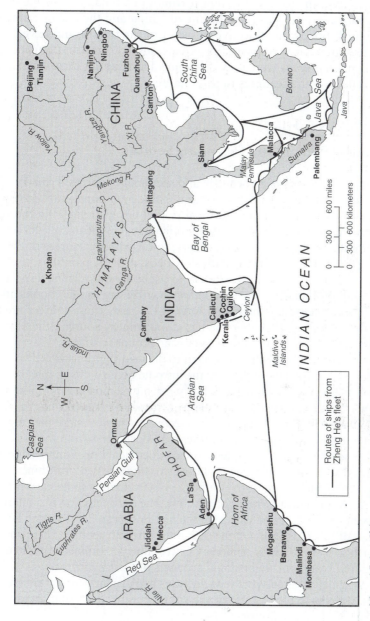

Map 15.1 Chinese Naval Expeditions, 1405–1433.

enclaves on the coast and where European nations were in an almost perpetual state of war with each other. Taken together, the nations of Western Europe dominated the seas of the world after 1500 (see Map 15.2).

What accounts for the different fortunes of China and Europe in the fifteenth century? Were the decline of China and the rise of Europe inevitable? Probably no objective observer of the time would have thought so. In what ways were the expansions of China and Europe similar? In what ways were they different? Think about these questions as you reflect on the readings in this chapter.

■ THINKING HISTORICALLY

Reading Primary and Secondary Sources

This chapter contains both primary and secondary sources. *Primary sources* are actual pieces of the past and include anything — art, letters, essays, and so on — from the historical period being studied. If a future historian were to study and research students in American colleges at the beginning of the twenty-first century, some primary sources might include diaries, letters, cartoons, music videos, posters, paintings, text messages, blogs and Web sites, class notes, school newspapers, tests, and official and unofficial records. *Secondary sources* are usually books and articles *about* the past — interpretations of the past. These sources are "secondary" because they must be based on primary sources; therefore, a history written after an event occurs is a secondary source.

In your studies, you will be expected to distinguish primary from secondary sources. A quick glance at the introductions to this chapter's selections tells you that the first article is written by a modern journalist in 1999 and the last is written by a modern environmentalist, taken from his book published in 1991. These are both secondary sources since they are modern interpretations of the past rather than documents from the past. The other selections in this chapter are such documents, or primary sources. The second selection is an account of the great fifteenth-century Chinese admiral Zheng He's* voyage to Southeast Asia written by someone who was there, Ma Huan, a member of the crew. The third selection is similarly a participant's account of the voyage of the first European fleet to reach South Asia, that of Vasco da Gama at the end of the fifteenth century. These and the fourth selection, a letter penned by Christopher Columbus more than five hundred years ago, are firsthand accounts of worlds long past.

Having determined whether selections are primary or secondary sources, we also explore some of the subtle complexities that are overlooked by such designations.

---

* jung HUH Z

Note: Pronunciations of difficult-to-pronounce terms will be given throughout the book. The emphasis goes on the syllable appearing in all capitals. [Ed.]

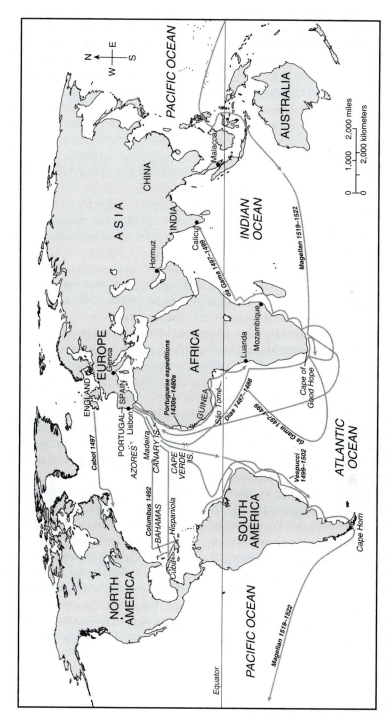

Map 15.2 European Overseas Exploration, 1430s–1530s.

1

NICHOLAS D. KRISTOF

1492: The Prequel, 1999

Almost a century before Columbus, Zheng He, a eunuch admiral in the court, sailed from China with three hundred ships and twenty-eight thousand men. His fleet stopped at ports in the Indian Ocean and journeyed as far as the east coast of Africa. Nicholas Kristof travels to the East African island of Pate to find traces of these fifteenth-century Chinese sailors. What types of evidence is he seeking? What does Kristof's brief history suggest about China, India, and Europe and their roles in the making of the modern world? How would today's world be different if Chinese ships had reached the Western Hemisphere before Columbus?

THINKING HISTORICALLY

In his secondary account of Zheng He's voyages, Kristof alludes to certain possible primary sources. What sorts of primary sources are available to historians interested in reconstructing the life and voyages of Zheng He? What primary sources are not available? Why are they not available? Has Kristof's recent voyage led to the discovery of a new primary source?

From the sea, the tiny East African island of Pate, just off the Kenyan coast, looks much as it must have in the 15th century: an impenetrable shore of endless mangrove trees. As my little boat bounced along the waves in the gray dawn, I could see no antennae or buildings or even gaps where trees had been cut down, no sign of human habitation, nothing but a dense and mysterious jungle.

The boatman drew as close as he could to a narrow black-sand beach, and I splashed ashore. My local Swahili interpreter led the way through the forest, along a winding trail scattered with mangoes, coconuts, and occasional seashells deposited by high tides. The tropical sun was firmly overhead when we finally came upon a village of stone houses with thatched roofs, its dirt paths sheltered by palm trees. The village's inhabitants, much lighter-skinned than people on the Kenyan mainland, emerged barefoot to stare at me with the same curiosity with which I was studying them. These were people I had come halfway around the world to see, in the hope of solving an ancient historical puzzle.

Source: Nicholas D. Kristof, "1492: The Prequel," *New York Times Magazine*, June 6, 1999, 6, 80:1.

"Tell me," I asked the first group I encountered, "where did the people here come from? Long ago, did foreign sailors ever settle here?" The answer was a series of shrugs. "I've never heard about that," one said. "You'll have to ask the elders."

I tried several old men and women without success. Finally the villagers led me to the patriarch of the village, Bwana Mkuu Al-Bauri, the keeper of oral traditions. He was a frail old man with gray stubble on his cheeks, head, and chest. He wore a yellow sarong around his waist; his ribs pressed through the taut skin on his bare torso. Al-Bauri hobbled out of his bed, resting on a cane and the arm of a grandson. He claimed to be 121 years old; a pineapple-size tumor jutted from the left side of his chest.

"I know this from my grandfather, who himself was the keeper of history here," the patriarch told me in an unexpectedly clear voice. "Many, many years ago, there was a ship from China that wrecked on the rocks off the coast near here. The sailors swam ashore near the village of Shanga—my ancestors were there and saw it themselves.

"The Chinese were visitors, so we helped those Chinese men and gave them food and shelter, and then they married our women. Although they do not live in this village, I believe their descendants still can be found somewhere else on this island."

I almost felt like hugging Bwana Al-Bauri. For months I had been poking around obscure documents and research reports, trying to track down a legend of an ancient Chinese shipwreck that had led to a settlement on the African coast. My interest arose from a fascination with what to me is a central enigma of the millennium: Why did the West triumph over the East?

For most of the last several thousand years, it would have seemed far likelier that Chinese or Indians, not Europeans, would dominate the world by the year 2000, and that America and Australia would be settled by Chinese rather than by the inhabitants of a backward island called Britain. The reversal of fortunes of East and West strikes me as the biggest news story of the millennium, and one of its most unexpected as well.

As a resident of Asia for most of the past thirteen years, I've been searching for an explanation. It has always seemed to me that the turning point came in the early 1400s, when Admiral Zheng He sailed from China to conquer the world. Zheng He (pronounced JUNG HUH) was an improbable commander of a great Chinese fleet, in that he was a Muslim from a rebel family and had been seized by the Chinese Army when he was still a boy. Like many other prisoners of the time, he was castrated, his sexual organs completely hacked off, a process that killed many of those who suffered it. But he was a brilliant and tenacious boy who grew up to be physically imposing. A natural leader, he had the good fortune to be assigned, as a houseboy, to the household of a great prince, Zhu Di.

In time, the prince and Zheng He grew close, and they conspired to overthrow the prince's nephew, the Emperor of China. With Zheng He as one of the prince's military commanders, the revolt succeeded and the prince became China's Yongle Emperor. One of the emperor's first acts (after torturing to death those who had opposed him) was to reward Zheng He with the command of a great fleet that was to sail off and assert China's pre-eminence in the world.

Between 1405 and 1433, Zheng He led seven major expeditions, commanding the largest armada the world would see for the next five centuries. Not until World War I did the West mount anything comparable. Zheng He's fleet included twenty-eight thousand sailors on three hundred ships, the longest of which were four hundred feet. By comparison, Columbus in 1492 had ninety sailors on three ships, the biggest of which was eighty-five feet long. Zheng He's ships also had advanced design elements that would not be introduced in Europe for another 350 years, including balanced rudders and watertight bulwark compartments.

The sophistication of Zheng He's fleet underscores just how far ahead of the West the East once was. Indeed, except for the period of the Roman Empire, China had been wealthier, more advanced, and more cosmopolitan than any place in Europe for several thousand years. Hangzhou, for example, had a population in excess of a million during the time it was China's capital (in the twelfth century), and records suggest that as early as the seventh century, the city of Guangzhou had 200,000 foreign residents: Arabs, Persians, Malays, Indians, Africans, and Turks. By contrast, the largest city in Europe in 1400 was probably Paris, with a total population of slightly more than 100,000.

A half-century before Columbus, Zheng He had reached East Africa and learned about Europe from Arab traders. The Chinese could easily have continued around the Cape of Good Hope and established direct trade with Europe. But as they saw it, Europe was a backward region, and China had little interest in the wood, beads, and wine Europe had to trade. Africa had what China wanted—ivory, medicines, spices, exotic woods, even specimens of native wildlife.

In Zheng He's time, China and India together accounted for more than half of the world's gross national product, as they have for most of human history. Even as recently as 1820, China accounted for 29 percent of the global economy and India another 16 percent, according to the calculations of Angus Maddison, a leading British economic historian.

Asia's retreat into relative isolation after the expeditions of Zheng He amounted to a catastrophic missed opportunity, one that laid the groundwork for the rise of Europe and, eventually, America. Westerners often attribute their economic advantage today to the intelligence, democratic habits, or hard work of their forebears, but a more important reason may well have been the folly of fifteenth-century Chinese rulers. That is why I came to be fascinated with Zheng He and set out earlier this year to retrace his journeys. I wanted to see what legacy, if any, remained of his achievement, and to figure out why his travels did not remake the world in the way that Columbus's did.

Zheng He lived in Nanjing, the old capital, where I arrived one day in February. Nanjing is a grimy metropolis on the Yangtze River in the heart of China. It has been five centuries since Zheng He's death, and his marks on the city have grown faint. The shipyards that built his fleet are still busy, and the courtyard of what had been his splendid seventy-two-room mansion is now the Zheng He Memorial Park, where children roller-skate and old couples totter around for exercise. But though the park has a small Zheng He museum, it was closed—for renovation, a caretaker told me, though he knew of no plans to reopen it.

I'd heard that Zheng He's tomb is on a hillside outside the city, and I set out to find it. It wasn't long before the road petered out, from asphalt to gravel to dirt to nothing. No tomb was in sight, so I approached an old man weeding a vegetable garden behind his house. Tang Yiming, seventy-two, was still lithe and strong. His hair was gray and ragged where he had cut it himself, disastrously, in front of a mirror. Evidently lonely, he was delighted to talk, and offered to show me the path to the tomb. As we walked, I mentioned that I had read that there used to be an old Ming Dynasty tablet on Zheng He's grave.

"Oh, yeah, the old tablet," he said nonchalantly. "When I was a boy, there was a Ming Dynasty tablet here. When it disappeared, the Government offered a huge reward to anyone who would return it—a reward big enough to build a new house. Seemed like a lot of money. But the problem was that we couldn't give it back. People around here are poor. We'd smashed it up to use as building materials."

A second mystery concerned what, if anything, is actually buried in Zheng He's tomb, since he is believed to have died on his last voyage and been buried at sea. So I said in passing that I'd heard tell the tomb is empty, and let my voice trail off.

"Oh, there's nothing in there," Tang said, a bit sadly. "No bones, nothing. That's for sure."

"How do you know?"

"In 1962, people dug up the grave, looking for anything to sell. We dug up the ground to one and a half times the height of a man. But there was absolutely nothing in there. It's empty."

The absence of impressive monuments to Zheng He in China today should probably come as no surprise, since his achievement was ultimately renounced. Curiously, it is not in China but in Indonesia where his memory has been most actively kept alive. Zheng He's expeditions led directly to the wave of Chinese immigration to Southeast Asia, and in some countries he is regarded today as a deity. In the Indonesia city of Semarang, for example, there is a large temple honoring Zheng He, located near a cave where he once nursed a sick friend. Indonesians still pray to Zheng He for a cure or good luck.

Not so in his native land. Zheng He was viewed with deep suspicion by China's traditional elite, the Confucian scholars, who made sure to destroy the archives of his journey. Even so, it is possible to learn something about his story from Chinese sources — from imperial archives and even the memoirs of crewmen. The historical record makes clear, for example, that it was not some sudden impulse of extroversion that led to Zheng He's achievement. It grew, rather, out of a long sailing tradition. Chinese accounts suggest that in the fifth century a Chinese monk sailed to a mysterious "far east country" that sounds very much like Mayan Mexico, and Mayan art at that time suddenly began to include Buddhist symbols. By the thirteenth century, Chinese ships regularly traveled to India and occasionally to East Africa.

Zheng He's armada was far grander, of course, than anything that came before. His grandest vessels were the "treasure ships," 400 feet long and 160 feet wide, with nine masts raising red silk sails to the wind, as well as multiple decks and luxury cabins with balconies. His armada included supply ships to carry horses, troop transports, warships, patrol boats, and as many as twenty tankers to carry fresh water. The full contingent of 28,000 crew members included interpreters for Arabic and other languages, astrologers to forecast the weather, astronomers to study the stars, pharmacologists to collect medicinal plants, ship-repair specialists, doctors, and even two protocol officers to help organize official receptions.

In the aftermath of such an incredible undertaking, you somehow expect to find a deeper mark on Chinese history, a greater legacy. But perhaps the faintness of Zheng He's trace in contemporary China is itself a lesson. In the end, an explorer makes history but does not necessarily change it, for his impact depends less on the trail he blazes than on the willingness of others to follow. The daring of a great expedition ultimately is hostage to the national will of those who remain behind.

In February I traveled to Calicut, a port town in southwestern India that was (and still is) the pepper capital of the world. The evening I arrived, I went down to the beach in the center of town to look at the coastline where Zheng He once had berthed his ships. In the fourteenth and fifteenth centuries, Calicut was one of the world's great ports, known to the Chinese as "the great country of the Western ocean." In the early fifteenth century, the sight of Zheng He's fleet riding anchor in Calicut harbor symbolized the strength of the world's two greatest powers, China and India.

On this sultry evening, the beach, framed by long piers jutting out to sea, was crowded with young lovers and ice-cream vendors. Those piers are all that remain of the port of Calicut, and you can see at a glance that they are no longer usable. The following day I visited the port offices, musty with handwritten ledgers of ship visits dating back nearly a century. The administrator of the port, Captain E. G. Mohanan, explained matter-of-factly what had happened. "The piers got old and no proper maintenance was ever carried out," he said, as a ceiling fan whirred tiredly overhead. "By the time we thought of it, it was not economical to fix it up." So in 1989, trade was halted, and one of the great ports of the world became no port at all.

The disappearance of a great Chinese fleet from a great Indian port symbolized one of history's biggest lost opportunities — Asia's failure to dominate the second half of this millennium. So how did this happen?

While Zheng He was crossing the Indian Ocean, the Confucian scholar-officials who dominated the upper echelons of the Chinese Government were at political war with the eunuchs, a group they regarded as corrupt and immoral. The eunuchs' role at court involved looking after the concubines, but they also served as palace administrators, often doling out contracts in exchange for kickbacks. Partly as a result of their legendary greed, they promoted commerce. Unlike the scholars — who owed their position to their mastery of two thousand-year-old texts — the eunuchs, lacking any such roots in a classical past, were sometimes outward-looking and progressive. Indeed, one can argue that it was the virtuous, incorruptible scholars who in the mid-fifteenth century set China on its disastrous course.

After the Yongle Emperor died in 1424, China endured a series of brutal power struggles; a successor emperor died under suspicious circumstances and ultimately the scholars emerged triumphant. They ended the voyages of Zheng He's successors, halted construction of new ships, and imposed curbs on private shipping. To prevent any backsliding, they destroyed Zheng He's sailing records and, with the backing of the new emperor, set about dismantling China's navy.

By 1500 the Government had made it a capital offense to build a boat with more than two masts, and in 1525 the Government ordered the destruction of all oceangoing ships. The greatest navy in history, which a century earlier had 3,500 ships (by comparison, the United States Navy today has 324), had been extinguished, and China set a course for itself that would lead to poverty, defeat, and decline.

Still, it was not the outcome of a single power struggle in the 1440s that cost China its worldly influence. Historians offer a host of reasons for why Asia eventually lost its way economically and was late to industrialize; two and a half reasons seem most convincing.

The first is that Asia was simply not greedy enough. The dominant social ethos in ancient China was Confucianism and in India it was caste, with the result that the elites in both nations looked down their noses at business. Ancient China cared about many things — prestige, honor, culture, arts, education, ancestors, religion, filial piety — but making money came far down the list. Confucius had specifically declared that it was wrong for a man to make a distant voyage while his parents were alive, and he had condemned profit as the concern of "a little man." As it was, Zheng He's ships were built on such a grand scale and carried such lavish gifts to foreign leaders that the voyages were not the huge money spinners they could have been.

In contrast to Asia, Europe was consumed with greed. Portugal led the age of discovery in the fifteenth century largely because it wanted spices, a precious commodity; it was the hope of profits that drove its ships steadily farther down the African coast and eventually around the Horn to Asia. The profits of this trade could be vast: Magellan's crew once sold a cargo of twenty-six tons of cloves for ten thousand times the cost.

A second reason for Asia's economic stagnation is more difficult to articulate but has to do with what might be called a culture of complacency. China and India shared a tendency to look inward, a devotion to past ideals and methods, a respect for authority, and a suspicion of new ideas. David S. Landes, a Harvard economist, has written of ancient China's "intelligent xenophobia"; the former Indian Prime Minister Jawaharlal Nehru referred to the "petrification of classes" and the "static nature" of Indian society. These are all different ways of describing the same economic and intellectual complacency.

Chinese elites regarded their country as the "Middle Kingdom" and believed they had nothing to learn from barbarians abroad. India exhibited much of the same self-satisfaction. "Indians didn't go to Portugal not because they couldn't but because they didn't want to," mused M. P. Sridharan, a historian, as we sat talking on the porch of his home in Calicut.

The fifteenth-century Portuguese were the opposite. Because of its coastline and fishing industry, Portugal always looked to the sea, yet rivalries with Spain and other countries shut it out of the Mediterranean trade. So the only way for Portugal to get at the wealth of the East was by conquering the oceans.

The half reason is simply that China was a single nation while Europe was many. When the Confucian scholars reasserted control in Beijing and banned shipping, their policy mistake condemned all of China. In contrast, European countries committed economic suicide selectively. So when Portugal slipped into a quasi-Chinese mind-set in the sixteenth century, slaughtering Jews and burning heretics, and driving astronomers and scientists abroad, Holland and England were free to take up the slack.

When I first began researching Zheng He, I never thought I'd be traveling all the way to Africa to look for traces of his voyages. Then I came across a few intriguing references to the possibility of an ancient Chinese shipwreck that might have left some Chinese stranded on the island of Pate (pronounced PAH-tay). One was a skeptical reference in a scholarly journal, another was a casual conversation with a Kenyan I met a few years ago, and the third was the epilogue of Louise Levathes's wonderful 1994 book about China's maritime adventures, "When China Ruled the Seas." Levathes had traveled to Kenya and found people who believed they were descended from survivors of a Chinese shipwreck. So, on a whim and an expense account, I flew to Lamu, an island off northern Kenya, and hired a boat and an interpreter to go to Pate and see for myself.

Pate is off in its own world, without electricity or roads or vehicles. Mostly jungle, it has been shielded from the twentieth century largely because it is accessible from the Kenyan mainland only by taking a boat through a narrow tidal channel that is passable only at high tide. Initially I was disappointed by what I found there. In the first villages I visited, I saw people who were light-skinned and had hair that was not tightly curled, but they could have been part Arab or European rather than part Chinese. The remote villages of Chundwa and Faza were more promising, for there I found people whose eyes, hair, and complexion hinted at Asian ancestry, though their background was ambiguous.

And then on a still and sweltering afternoon I strolled through the coconut palms into the village of Siyu, where I met a fisherman in his forties named Abdullah Mohammed Badui. I stopped and stared at the man in astonishment, for he had light skin and narrow eyes. Fortunately, he was as rude as I was, and we stared at each other in mutual surprise before venturing a word. Eventually I asked him about his background and appearance.

"I am in the Famao clan," he said. "There are fifty or one hundred of us Famao left here. Legend has it that we are descended from Chinese and others.

"A Chinese ship was coming along and it hit rocks and wrecked," Badui continued. "The sailors swam ashore to the village that we now call Shanga, and they married the local women, and that is why we Famao look so different."

Another Famao, with the same light complexion and vaguely Asian features, approached to listen. His name was Athman Mohammed Mzee, and he, too, told of hearing of the Chinese shipwreck from the elders. He volunteered an intriguing detail: The Africans had given giraffes to the Chinese.

Salim Bonaheri, a fifty-five-year-old Famao man I met the next day, proudly declared, "My ancestors were Chinese or Vietnamese or something like that." I asked how they had got to Pate.

"I don't know," Bonaheri said with a shrug. Most of my conversations were like that, intriguing but frustrating dead ends. I was surrounded by people whose appearance seemed tantalizingly Asian, but who had only the vaguest notions of why that might be. I kept at it, though, and eventually found people like Khalifa Mohammed Omar, a fifty-five-year-old Famao fisherman who looked somewhat Chinese and who also clearly remembered the stories passed down by his grandfather. From him and others, a tale emerged.

Countless generations ago, they said, Chinese sailors traded with local African kings. The local kings gave them giraffes to take back to China. One of the Chinese ships struck rocks off the eastern coast of Pate, and the sailors swam ashore, carrying with them porcelain and other goods from the ship. In time they married local women, converted to Islam, and named the village Shanga, after Shanghai. Later, fighting erupted among Pate's clans, Shanga was destroyed, and the Famao fled, some to the mainland, others to the village of Siyu.

Every time I heard the story about the giraffes my pulse began to race. Chinese records indicate that Zheng He had brought the first giraffes to China, a fact that is not widely known. The giraffe caused an enormous stir in China because it was believed to be the mythical qilin, or Chinese unicorn. It is difficult to imagine how African villagers on an island as remote as Pate would know about the giraffes unless the tale had been handed down to them by the Chinese sailors.

Chinese ceramics are found in many places along the east African coast, and their presence on Pate could be the result of purchases from Arab traders. But the porcelain on Pate was overwhelmingly concentrated among the Famao clan, which could mean that it had been inherited rather than purchased. I also visited some ancient Famao graves that looked less like traditional Kenyan graves than what the Chinese call "turtle-shell graves," with rounded tops.

Researchers have turned up other equally tantalizing clues. Craftsmen on Pate and the other islands of Lamu practice a kind of basket-weaving that is common in southern China but unknown on the Kenyan mainland. On Pate, drums are more often played in the Chinese than the African style, and the local dialect has a few words that may be Chinese in origin. More startling, in 1569 a Portuguese priest named Monclaro wrote that Pate had a flourishing silk-making industry—Pate, and no other place in the region. Elders in several villages on Pate confirmed to me that their island had produced silk until about half a century ago.

When I asked my boatman, Bakari Muhaji Ali, if he thought it was possible that a ship could have wrecked off the coast near Shanga, he laughed. "There are undersea rocks all over there," he said. "If you don't know exactly where you're going, you'll wreck your ship for sure."

If indeed there was a Chinese shipwreck off Pate, there is reason to think it happened in Zheng He's time. For if the shipwreck had predated him, surviving sailors would not have passed down stories of the giraffes. And if the wreck didn't occur until after Zheng He, its survivors could not have settled in Shanga, since British archeological digs indicate that the village was sacked, burned, and abandoned in about 1440—very soon after Zheng He's last voyage.

Still, there is no hard proof for the shipwreck theory, and there are plenty of holes in it. No ancient Chinese characters have been found on tombs in Pate, no nautical instruments have ever turned up on the island, and there are no Chinese accounts of an African shipwreck. This last lacuna might be explained by the destruction of the fleet's records. Yet if one of Zheng He's ships did founder on the rocks off Pate, then why didn't some other ships in the fleet come to the sailors' rescue?

As I made my way back through the jungle for the return trip, I pondered the significance of what I'd seen on Pate. In the faces of the Famao, in those bits of pottery and tantalizing hints of Chinese culture, I felt as though I'd glimpsed the shadowy outlines of one of the greatest might-have-beens of the millennium now ending. I thought about the Columbian Exchange, the swap of animals, plants, genes, germs, weapons, and peoples that utterly remade both the New World and the Old, and I couldn't help wondering about another exchange—Zheng He's—that never took place, yet could have.

If ancient China had been greedier and more outward-looking, if other traders had followed in Zheng He's wake and then continued on, Asia might well have dominated Africa and even Europe. Chinese might have settled in not only Malaysia and Singapore, but also in East Africa, the Pacific Islands, even in America. Perhaps the Famao show us what the mestizos of such a world might have looked like, the children of a hybrid culture that was never born. What I'd glimpsed in Pate was the highwater mark of an Asian push that simply stopped—not for want of ships or know-how, but strictly for want of national will.

All this might seem fanciful, and yet in Zheng He's time the prospect of a New World settled by the Spanish or English would have seemed infinitely more remote than a New World made by the Chinese. How different would history have been had Zheng He continued on to America? The mind rebels; the ramifications are almost too overwhelming to contemplate. So consider just one: This magazine would have been published in Chinese.

2

MA HUAN

On Calicut, India, 1433

Ma Huan was a Chinese Muslim who acted as an aide and interpreter on Zheng He's expeditions to Southeast Asia. In 1433 he wrote *The Overall Survey of the Ocean Shores,* a travel account of the lands he visited. This selection, taken from that account, describes his visit to Calicut on the Malabar, or southwest, coast of India. Note that Ma Huan is not always an accurate observer. More familiar with Buddhists than Hindus, for example, he mistakes the latter for the former. Nevertheless, he provides some useful information about

Source: Ma Huan, "On Calicut, India," in *Ma Huan, Ying-yai Sheng-lan: The Overall Survey of the Ocean's Shores,* ed. and trans. Feng Ch'eng-Chun with an introduction by J. V. G. Mills (Bangkok: The White Lotus Press, 1970), 137–44.

Hindu-Muslim relations; the spread of the Abrahamic religions (note the story about Moses); the vitality of Indian trade; and the variety of Indian plants, animals, and manufactures. In addition to describing Calicut, what does Ma Huan tell us about the reasons for these expeditions?

THINKING HISTORICALLY

Ma Huan's account of Zheng He's expedition does not seem to have had an official purpose, but it was probably published instead to satisfy the growing interests of a Chinese public hungry for information about foreign lands and peoples. What sorts of things are of interest to Ma Huan? What does this tell us about his audience? How are his interests similar to, or different from, those of a modern traveler? What might be Ma Huan's strengths and weaknesses as a primary source?

The Country of Ku-Li [Calicut]

[This is] the great country of the Western Ocean.

Setting sail from the anchorage in the country of Ko-chih,[1] you travel north-west, and arrive [here] after three days. The country lies beside the sea. [Travelling] east from the mountains for five hundred, or seven hundred, *li*, you make a long journey through to the country of K'an-pa-i.[2] On the west [the country of Ku-li] abuts on the great sea; on the south it joins the boundary of the country of Ko-chih; [and] on the north side it adjoins the territory of the country of Hen-nu-erh.[3]

"The great country of the Western Ocean" is precisely this country.

In the fifth year of the Yung-lo [period] the court ordered[4] the principal envoy the grand eunuch Cheng Ho and others to deliver an imperial mandate to the king[5] of this country and to bestow on him a patent conferring a title of honour, and the grant of a silver seal, [also] to

---

[1] Cochin, a city in southwest India along the Arabian Sea, 80 miles south of Calicut; Ma Huan made a very slow voyage.

[2] Koyampadi, modern Coimbatore, situated in about 11° N, 77° E, 76 miles nearly due east of Calicut. In giving the distance as 500 *li*, nearly 200 miles, Ma Huan was guilty of an exaggeration.

[3] Now called Honavar, situated in 14° 16′ N, 74° 27′ E; it is on the coast, 199 miles northward from Calicut.

[4] The order was made in October 1407; but, although in nominal command of this, the second expedition, Cheng Ho did not accompany it.

[5] A new king, Mana Vikraman, had evidently succeeded since Cheng Ho was at Calicut in 1406–1407 during the course of his first expedition.

promote all the chiefs and award them hats and girdles of various grades.

[So Cheng Ho] went there in command of a large fleet of treasure-ships, and he erected a tablet with a pavilion over it and set up a stone which said "Though the journey from this country to the Central Country is more than a hundred thousand *li*, yet the people are very similar, happy and prosperous, with identical customs. We have here engraved a stone, a perpetual declaration for ten thousand ages."[6]

The king of the country is a Nan-k'un[7] man; he is a firm believer in the Buddhist religion;[8] [and] he venerates the elephant and the ox.

The population of the country includes five classes, the Muslim people, the Nan-K'un people, the Che-ti people, the Ko-ling people, and the Mu-kua people.

The king of the country and the people of the country all refrain from eating the flesh of the ox.[9] The great chiefs are Muslim people; [and] they all refrain from eating the flesh of the pig.[10] Formerly there was a king who made a sworn compact with the Muslim people, [saying] "You do not eat the ox; I do not eat the pig; we will reciprocally respect the taboo,"[11] [and this compact] has been honoured right down to the present day.

The king has cast an image of Buddha in brass; it is named Nai-na-erh;[12] he has erected a temple of Buddha and has cast tiles of brass and covered the dais of Buddha with them; [and] beside [the dais] a well has been dug. Every day at dawn the king goes to [the well], draws water, and washes [the image of] Buddha; after worshipping, he orders men to collect the pure dung of yellow oxen; this is stirred with water in a brass basin [until it is] like paste; [then] it is smeared all over the surface of the ground and walls inside the temple. Moreover, he has given orders that the chiefs and wealthy personages shall also smear and scour themselves with ox-dung every morning.

He also takes ox-dung, burns it till it is reduced to a white ash, and grinds it to a fine powder; using a fair cloth as a small bag, he fills it with the ash, and regularly carries it on his person. Every day at dawn, after he has finished washing his face, he takes the ox-dung ash, stirs it up with water, and smears it on his forehead and between his two

---

[6] Translated "May the period Yung-lo last for ever."

[7] Probably Ma Huan wrote "Nan-p'i" and meant the upper classes consisting of Brahmans and Kshatriyas.

[8] Ma Huan is mistaken; the king was a Hindu.

[9] Detestation of cow-slaughter is the most prominent outward mark of Hinduism.

[10] It is noteworthy that a Hindu ruler was employing Muslims as great officers.

[11] Since it was the king who made the compact, it would seem reasonable to prefer, "You do not eat the pig; I do not eat the ox"; thus, they agreed to respect each others' convictions in the matter of diet. It scarcely needs to be said that the pig is anathema to Muslims.

[12] The name might be a corruption of Narayana, a name for Vishnu. All these references to Buddha, then, must be construed as references to a Hindu deity.

thighs—thrice in each [place]. This denotes his sincerity in venerating Buddha[13] and in venerating the ox.

There is a traditional story that in olden times there was a holy man named Mou-hsieh,[14] who established a religious cult; the people knew that he was a true [man of] Heaven, and all men revered and followed him. Later the holy man went away with [others] to another place, and ordered his younger brother named Sa-mo-li[15] to govern and teach the people.

[But] his younger brother began to have depraved ideas; he made a casting of a golden calf and said "This is the holy lord; everyone who worships it will have his expectations fulfilled." He taught the people to listen to his bidding and to adore the golden ox, saying "It always excretes gold." The people got the gold, and their hearts rejoiced; and they forgot the way of Heaven; all took the ox to be the true lord.

Later Mou-hsieh the holy man returned; he saw that the multitude, misled by his younger brother Sa-mo-li, were corrupting the holy way; thereupon he destroyed the ox and wished to punish his younger brother; [and] his younger brother mounted a large elephant and vanished.

Afterwards, the people thought of him and hoped anxiously for his return. Moreover, if it was the beginning of the moon, they would say "In the middle of the moon he will certainly come," and when the middle of the moon arrived, they would say once more "At the end of the moon he will certainly come"; right down to the present day they have never ceased to hope for his return.

This is the reason why the Nan-k'un[16] people venerate the elephant and the ox.

The king has two great chiefs who administer the affairs of the country; both are Muslims.

The majority of the people in the country all profess the Muslim religion. There are twenty or thirty temples of worship, and once in seven days they go to worship. When the day arrives, the whole family fast and bathe, and attend to nothing else. In the *ssu* and *wu* periods,[17] the menfolk, old and young, go to the temple to worship. When the *wei* period[18] arrives, they disperse and return home; thereupon they carry on with their trading, and transact their household affairs.

---

[13] Again, a Hindu deity.

[14] "Musa" (Moses). Ma Huan alleges that the incidents occurred at Calicut. Presumably he learnt the story of Aaron and the golden calf from Arab informants. A number of Old Testament characters, including Moses, figure prominently in the Koran.

[15] "Al-Sameri" (the Samaritan), the name appearing in the Koran.

[16] Probably Ma Huan wrote "Nan-p'i," and referred to the upper classes of Brahmans and Kshatriyas.

[17] 9 A.M. to 11 A.M., and 11 A.M. to 1 P.M., respectively.

[18] 1 P.M. to 3 P.M.

The people are very honest and trustworthy. Their appearance is smart, fine, and distinguished.

Their two great chiefs received promotion and awards from the court of the Central Country.

If a treasure-ship goes there, it is left entirely to the two men to superintend the buying and selling; the king sends a chief and a Che-ti Wei-no-chi[19] to examine the account books in the official bureau; a broker comes and joins them; [and] a high officer who commands the ships discusses the choice of a certain date for fixing prices. When the day arrives, they first of all take the silk embroideries and the openwork silks, and other such goods which have been brought there, and discuss the price of them one by one; [and] when [the price] has been fixed, they write out an agreement stating the amount of the price; [this agreement] is retained by these persons.

The chief and the Che-ti, with his excellency the eunuch, all join hands together, and the broker then says "In such and such a moon on such and such a day, we have all joined hands and sealed our agreement with a hand-clasp; whether [the price] be dear or cheap, we will never repudiate it or change it."

After that, the Che-ti and the men of wealth then come bringing precious stones, pearls, corals, and other such things, so that they may be examined and the price discussed; [this] cannot be settled in a day; [if done] quickly, [it takes] one moon; [if done] slowly, [it takes] two or three moons.[20]

Once the money-price has been fixed after examination and discussion, if a pearl or other such article is purchased, the price which must be paid for it is calculated by the chief and the Wei-no-chi who carried out the original transaction; [and] as to the quantity of the hemp-silk or other such article which must be given in exchange for it, goods are given in exchange according to [the price fixed by] the original hand-clasp—there is not the slightest deviation.[21]

In their method of calculation, they do not use a calculating-plate;[22] for calculating, they use only the two hands and two feet and the twenty digits on them; and they do not make the slightest mistake; [this is] very extraordinary.

[19] Another observer, Kung Chen, translates "accountant," and adds that the man in question was a broker; Kung Chen further notes that "they wrote out a contract in duplicate, and each [party] kept one [document]."

[20] Presumably the goods were unloaded, unless the Chinese left one or two ships behind; at any rate, on the seventh expedition the Chinese stayed only 4 days, from 10 to 14 December 1432, at Calicut.

[21] This instructive disquisition on administrative procedure illustrates the meticulous care taken to fix the rate of exchange in times prior to the advent of the Europeans.

[22] The abacus, a wooden frame in which are fixed a number of beads strung on parallel wires; used by the Chinese for all kinds of arithmetic calculations upon the decimal system; it came into use in late Sung times.

The king uses gold of sixty per cent [purity] to cast a coin for current use; it is named a *pa-nan*;[23] the diameter of the face of each coin is three *fen* eight *li* [in terms of] our official *ts'un*;[24] it has lines[25] on the face and on the reverse; [and] it weighs one *fen* on our official steelyard.[26] He also makes a coin of silver; it is named a *ta-erh*;[27] each coin weighs about three *li*;[28] [and] this coin is used for petty transactions. . . .

The people of the country also take the silk of the silk-worm, soften it by boiling, dye it in all colours, and weave it into kerchiefs with decorative stripes at intervals; the breadth is four or five *ch'ih*, and the length one *chang* two or three *ch'ih*;[29] [and] each length is sold for one hundred gold coins.[30]

As to the pepper: the inhabitants of the mountainous countryside have established gardens, and it is extensively cultivated. When the period of the tenth moon arrives, the pepper ripens; [and] it is collected, dried in the sun, and sold. Of course, big pepper-collectors come and collect it, and take it up to the official storehouse to be stored; if there is a buyer, an official gives permission for the sale; the duty is calculated according to the amount [of the purchase price] and is paid in to the authorities. Each one *po-ho* of pepper is sold for two hundred gold coins.[31]

The Che-ti mostly purchase all kinds of precious stones and pearls, and they manufacture coral beads and other such things.

Foreign ships from every place come there; and the king of the country also sends a chief and a writer and others to watch the sales; thereupon they collect the duty and pay it in to the authorities.

The wealthy people mostly cultivate coconut trees—sometimes a thousand trees, sometimes two thousand or three thousand—; this constitutes their property.

The coconut has ten different uses. The young tree has a syrup, very sweet, and good to drink; [and] it can be made into wine by fermentation, The old coconut has flesh, from which they express oil, and make sugar, and make a foodstuff for eating. From the fibre which envelops the outside [of the nut] they make ropes for ship-building. The shell of the coconut makes bowls and makes cups; it is also good for burning to

[23] Representing the sound *fanam*. The king was an independent sovereign minting his own coinage; but doubtless, as in 1443, he "lived in great fear" of Vijayanagar (Abdul Razzak).

[24] The diameter of the *fanam*, being 0.38 of the Chinese *ts'un* of 1.22 inches, equalled 0.46 of an English inch.

[25] Or "characters."

[26] The gold content weighed 3.45 grains or 0.00719 ounce troy.

[27] Representing the sound *tar* or *tare* (*tara*).

[28] If the silver was pure, the silver content weighed 0.00359 ounce troy.

[29] The equivalent of 4 *ch'ih* was 48.9 inches; 1 *chang* 2 *ch'ih* equaled 12 feet 2.9 inches.

[30] The gold content weighed 345.375 grains or 0.7195 ounce troy.

[31] The gold content of 200 *fanam* weighed 690.751 grains or 1.439 ounces troy.

ash for the delicate operation of inlaying[32] gold or silver. The trees are good for building houses, and the leaves are good for roofing houses.

For vegetables they have mustard plants, green ginger, turnips, caraway seeds, onions, garlic, bottle-gourds, egg-plants, cucumbers, and gourd-melons[33]—all these they have in [all] the four seasons [of the year]. They also have a kind of small gourd which is as large as [one's] finger, about two *ts'un*[34] long, and tastes like a green cucumber. Their onions have a purple skin; they resemble garlic; they have a large head and small leaves; [and] they are sold by the *chin*[35] weight.

The *mu-pieb-tzu*[36] tree is more than ten *chang* high; it forms a fruit which resembles a green persimmon and contains thirty or forty seeds; it falls of its own accord when ripe; [and] the bats, as large as hawks, all hang upside-down and rest on this tree.

They have both red and white rice, [but] barley and wheat are both absent; [and] their wheat-flour all comes from other places as merchandise for sale [here].

Fowls and ducks exist in profusion, [but] there are no geese. Their goats have tall legs and an ashen hue; they resemble donkey-foals. The water-buffaloes are not very large. Some of the yellow oxen weigh three or four hundred *chin*;[37] the people do not eat their flesh; [but] consume only the milk and cream. The people never eat rice without butter. Their oxen are cared for until they are old; [and] when they die, they are buried. The price of all kinds of sea-fish is very cheap. Deer and hares [from up] in the mountains are also for sale.

Many of the people rear peafowl. As to their other birds: they have crows, green hawks, egrets, and swallows; [but] of other kinds of birds besides these they have not a single one, great or small. The people of the country can also play and sing; they use the shell of a calabash to make a musical instrument, and copper wires to make the strings; and they play [this instrument] to accompany the singing of their foreign songs; the melodies are worth hearing.[38]

---

[32] *Hsiang*, "a box," used for *hsiang*, "side rooms," which in turn is used for *hsiang*, "to inlay."

[33] *Tung kua*, "eastern gourd," the same vegetable as *tung kua*, "winter gourd."

[34] That is, 2.4 inches.

[35] That is, 1.3 pounds avoirdupois.

[36] The tree is *Momordica cochinchinensis*. The editor is indebted to Dr. J. Needham, F.R.S., for the information that *Momordica* seeds were prescribed in the form of paste for abscesses, ulcers, and wounds, as well as in other ways for other affections. The equivalent of 10 *chang* was 102 feet.

[37] The equivalent of 300 *chin* was 394.6 pounds avoirdupois.

[38] Music was cultivated at the royal courts, and numbers of musicians were employed in the temples. Conti, in his account of Vijayanagar city, records solemn singing at religious festivals, and the celebration of weddings with "banquets, songs, trumpets, and instruments muche like unto ours." The instrument referred to by Ma Huan was probably the vina, a fretted instrument of the guitar kind, which was particularly favoured by Indian musicians.

As to the popular customs and the marriage- and funeral-rites, the So-li people and the Muslim people each follow the ritual forms of their own class, and these are different.

The king's throne does not descend to his son, but descends to his sister's son; descent is to the sister's son [because] they consider that the offspring of the women's body alone constitutes the legal family. If the king has no elder or younger sister, [the throne] descends to his younger brother; [and] if he has no younger brother, [the throne] is yielded up to some man of merit. Such is the succession from one generation to another.

3

Journal of the First Voyage of Vasco da Gama, 1498

In 1497 the Portuguese seaman Vasco da Gama left Portugal with a fleet of four ships, arriving in India ten months later. He benefited from the experience of Bartolomeu Dias, who ten years before had negotiated the rough waters of the South African Cape. But Dias had returned to Portugal. Da Gama continued up the African coast and sailed across the Indian Ocean to the port of Calicut, the center of a kingdom that encompassed much of the modern state of Kerala in southwest India. What seem to have been the motives of Portugal and da Gama in sailing to South Asia? How were the Portuguese intentions similar to, and different from, those of China earlier in the century? How would you compare the preparation and behavior of Chinese and Portuguese crews? How would you explain the differences between Chinese and Portuguese voyages?

THINKING HISTORICALLY

We do not know the identity of the author of this document. He was one of the officers or crewmen who sailed on this voyage, however, and many of their names are known to us. What indications do you have that they spanned a wide range of Portuguese society?

The fact that the author was a witness does not mean that he gets everything right. What does he miss? What might have caused him to be misled? Generally, primary sources get more things right than wrong. How do you know this is true for this selection? How do we determine where a primary source is reliable and where it is not?

Source: *A Journal of the First Voyage of Vasco da Gama, 1497–1499,* trans. and ed. E. G. Ravenstein (London: Hakluyt Society, 1898), 48–59, 60–63.

Calicut

[*Arrival.*][1] That night[2] [May 20] we anchored two leagues from the city of Calicut, and we did so because our pilot mistook *Capua*,[3] a town at that place, for Calicut. Still further there is another town called *Panda-rani*.[4] We anchored about a league and a half from the shore. After we were at anchor, four boats (*almadias*) approached us from the land, who asked of what nation we were. We told them, and they then pointed out Calicut to us.

On the following day [May 21] these same boats came again along-side, when the captain-major[5] sent one of the convicts[6] to Calicut, and those with whom he went took him to two Moors from Tunis,[7] who could speak Castilian and Genoese. The first greeting that he received was in these words: "May the Devil take thee! What brought you hither?" They asked what he sought so far away from home, and he told them that we came in search of Christians and of spices. They said: "Why does not the King of Castile, the King of France, or the Signoria of Venice send thither?" He said that the King of Portugal would not consent to their doing so, and they said he did the right thing. After this conversation they took him to their lodgings and gave him wheaten bread and honey. When he had eaten he returned to the ships, accompanied by one of the Moors, who was no sooner on board, than he said these words: "A lucky venture, a lucky venture! Plenty of rubies, plenty of emeralds! You owe great thanks to God, for having brought you to a country holding such riches!" We were greatly astonished to hear his talk, for we never expected to hear our language spoken so far away from Portugal.

[*A description of Calicut.*] The city of Calicut is inhabited by Christians.[8] They are of tawny complexion. Some of them have big beards and long hair, whilst others clip their hair short or shave the head, merely allowing a tuft to remain on the crown as a sign that they are Christians.

[1] Brackets enclose editorial additions of the translator, Ravenstein, unless otherwise indicated. [Ed.]

[2] Afternoon (*a tarde*), according to Glenn J. Ames, *Em Nome de Deus* (Leiden: Brill, 2009), 70. [Ed.]

[3] Kappatt, a village about 7 miles north of Calicut. [Ed.]

[4] About 14 miles north of Calicut. [Ed.]

[5] Da Gama. [Ed.]

[6] The crew included a number of "convict-exiles," men who had been convicted of a crime punishable by death who were pardoned by the king to sail as adventurers and live out their lives overseas. Da Gama wanted such people in his crew to create a permanent presence overseas. [Ed.]

[7] Likely Muslim exiles from Spain after the defeat of the last Muslim stronghold in Granada by Christians in 1492. [Ed.]

[8] There were Christians in southern India, but the population was overwhelmingly. Hindu and Muslim. Note Ma Huan's estimate (p. 530) that a majority were Muslim. [Ed.]

They also wear moustaches. They pierce the ears and wear much gold in them. They go naked down to the waist, covering their lower extremities with very fine cotton stuffs. But it is only the most respectable who do this, for the others manage as best they are able.

The women of this country, as a rule, are ugly and of small stature. They wear many jewels of gold round the neck, numerous bracelets on their arms, and rings set with precious stones on their toes. All these people are well-disposed and apparently of mild temper. At first sight they seem covetous and ignorant.

[*A messenger sent to the King.*] When we arrived at Calicut the king was fifteen leagues away. The captain-major sent two men to him with a message, informing him that an ambassador had arrived from the King of Portugal with letters, and that if he desired it he would take them to where the king then was.

The king presented the bearers of this message with much fine cloth. He sent word to the captain-major bidding him welcome, saying that he was about to proceed to Calicut. As a matter of fact, he started at once with a large retinue.

[*At Anchor at Pandarani, May 27.*] A pilot accompanied our two men, with orders to take us to a place called Pandarani, below the place [Capua] where we anchored at first. At this time we were actually in front of the city of Calicut. We were told that the anchorage at the place to which we were to go was good, whilst at the place we were then it was bad, with a stony bottom, which was quite true; and, moreover, that it was customary for the ships which came to this country to anchor there for the sake of safety. We ourselves did not feel comfortable, and the captain-major had no sooner received this royal message than he ordered the sails to be set, and we departed. We did not, however, anchor as near the shore as the king's pilot desired.

When we were at anchor, a message arrived informing the captain-major that the king was already in the city. At the same time the king sent a *bale*,[9] with other men of distinction, to Pandarani, to conduct the captain-major to where the king awaited him. This *bale* is like an *alcaide*,[10] and is always attended by two hundred men armed with swords and bucklers. As it was late when this message arrived, the captain-major deferred going.

[*Gama goes to Calicut.*] On the following morning, which was Monday, May 28th, the captain-major set out to speak to the king, and took with him thirteen men, of which I was one.[11] On landing, the captain-major was received by the *alcaide*, with whom were many men,

---

[9] Governor. [Ed.]

[10] Mayor. [Ed.]

[11] We know the names of about half of the thirteen, but not which of them is the author. [Ed.]

armed and unarmed. The reception was friendly, as if the people were pleased to see us, though at first appearances looked threatening, for they carried naked swords in their hands. A palanquin[12] was provided for the captain-major, such as is used by men of distinction in that country, as also by some of the merchants, who pay something to the king for this privilege. The captain-major entered the palanquin, which was carried by six men by turns. Attended by all these people we took the road of Calicut, and came first to another town, called Capua. The captain-major was there deposited at the house of a man of rank, whilst we others were provided with food, consisting of rice, with much butter, and excellent boiled fish. The captain-major did not wish to eat, and as we had done so, we embarked on a river close by, which flows between the sea and the mainland, close to the coast. The two boats in which we embarked were lashed together, so that we were not separated. There were numerous other boats, all crowded with people. As to those who were on the banks I say nothing; their number was infinite, and they had all come to see us. We went up that river for about a league, and saw many large ships drawn up high and dry on its banks, for there is no port here.

When we disembarked, the captain-major once more entered his palanquin. The road was crowded with a countless multitude anxious to see us. Even the women came out of their houses with children in their arms and followed us.

[*A Christian Church.*][13] When we arrived [at Calicut] they took us to a large church, and this is what we saw: —

The body of the church is as large as a monastery, all built of hewn stone and covered with tiles. At the main entrance rises a pillar of bronze as high as a mast, on the top of which was perched a bird, apparently a cock.[14] In addition to this, there was another pillar as high as a man, and very stout. In the center of the body of the church rose a chapel, all built of hewn stone, with a bronze door sufficiently wide for a man to pass, and stone steps leading up to it. Within this sanctuary stood a small image which they said represented Our Lady.[15] Along the walls, by the main entrance, hung seven small bells. In this church the captain-major said his prayers, and we with him.[16]

---

[12] An enclosed chair carried on poles front and rear. [Ed.]

[13] The translator, Ravenstein, who supplied this heading, added a note: "This 'church' was, of course, a pagoda or temple." [Ed.]

[14] Ravenstein (1898) believes the bird to be a Hindu war-god. Ames (2009) suggests it was an image of Garuda, the bird-god who carried Vishnu, the creator-god of the Hindu trinity. [Ed.]

[15] Possibly Mari, a local deity, protector from smallpox. [Ed.]

[16] Another source reports that at least one of the crew did not believe it was a Christian church. He is said to have knelt next to Vasco da Gama and said: "If this is the devil, I worship the True God" (Ames, 2009, 76). [Ed.]

We did not go within the chapel, for it is the custom that only certain servants of the church, called *quafees*,[17] should enter. These *quafees* wore some threads passing over the left shoulder and under the right arm, in the same manner as our deacons wear the stole. They threw holy water over us, and gave us some white earth,[18] which the Christians of this country are in the habit of putting on their foreheads, breasts, around the neck, and on the forearms. They threw holy water upon the captain-major and gave him some of the earth, which he gave in charge of someone, giving them to understand that he would put it on later.[19]

Many other saints were painted on the walls of the church, wearing crowns. They were painted variously, with teeth protruding an inch from the mouth, and four or five arms.

Below this church there was a large masonry tank, similar to many others which we had seen along the road.

[*Progress through the Town.*] After we had left that place, and had arrived at the entrance to the city [of Calicut] we were shown another church, where we saw things like those described above. Here the crowd grew so dense that progress along the street became next to impossible, and for this reason they put the captain-major into a house, and us with him.

The king sent a brother of the *bale*, who was a lord of this country, to accompany the captain-major, and he was attended by men beating drums, blowing *anafils* and bagpipes, and firing off matchlocks. In conducting the captain-major they showed us much respect, more than is shown in Spain to a king. The number of people was countless, for in addition to those who surrounded us, and among whom there were two thousand armed men, they crowded the roofs and houses.

[*The King's Palace.*] The further we advanced in the direction of the king's palace, the more did they increase in number. And when we arrived there, men of much distinction and great lords came out to meet the captain-major, and joined those who were already in attendance upon him. It was then an hour before sunset. When we reached the palace we passed through a gate into a courtyard of great size, and before we arrived at where the king was, we passed four doors, through which we had to force our way, giving many blows to the people. When, at last, we reached the door where the king was, there came forth from it a little old man, who holds a position resembling that of a bishop, and whose advice the king acts upon in all affairs of the church. This man embraced the captain-major when he entered the door. Several men were wounded at this door, and we only got in by the use of much force.

---

[17] Ames (2009) suggests that this term for Brahman priests was either the Arabic *quadi* (judge) or *kafir* (unbeliever). [Ed.]

[18] Possibly ash from burnt cow dung. [Ed.]

[19] Did da Gama's refusal to anoint himself with ash mean he questioned the legitimacy of ritual or church? [Ed.]

[*A Royal Audience, May 28.*] The king[20] was in a small court, reclining upon a couch covered with a cloth of green velvet, above which was a good mattress, and upon this again a sheet of cotton stuff, very white and fine, more so than any linen. The cushions were after the same fashion. In his left hand the king held a very large golden cup [spittoon], having a capacity of half an almude [8 pints]. At its mouth this cup was two palmas [16 inches] wide, and apparently it was massive. Into this cup the king threw the husks of a certain herb which is chewed by the people of this country because of its soothing effects, and which they call *atambor*.[21] On the right side of the king stood a basin of gold, so large that a man might just encircle it with his arms: this contained the herbs. There were likewise many silver jugs. The canopy above the couch was all gilt.

The captain, on entering, saluted in the manner of the country: by putting the hands together, then raising them towards Heaven, as is done by Christians when addressing God, and immediately afterwards opening them and shutting fists quickly. The king beckoned to the captain with his right hand to come nearer, but the captain did not approach him, for it is the custom of the country for no man to approach the king except only the servant who hands him the herbs, and when anyone addresses the king he holds his hand before the mouth, and remains at a distance. When the king beckoned to the captain he looked at us others, and ordered us to be seated on a stone bench near him, where he could see us. He ordered that water for our hands should be given us, as also some fruit, one kind of which resembled a melon, except that its outside was rough and the inside sweet, whilst another kind of fruit resembled a fig, and tasted very nice. There were men who prepared these fruits for them; and the king looked at them eating, and smiled; and talked to the servant who stood near him supplying him with the herbs referred to.

Then, throwing his eyes on the captain, who sat facing him, he invited him to address himself to the courtiers present, saying they were men of much distinction, that he could tell them whatever he desired to say, and they would repeat it to him (the king). The captain-major replied that he was the ambassador of the King of Portugal, and the bearer of a message which he could only deliver to him personally. The king said this was good, and immediately asked him to be conducted to a chamber. When the captain had entered, the king, too, rose and joined him, whilst we remained where we were. All this happened about sunset. An old man who was in the court took away the couch as soon as the king rose, but allowed the plate to remain. The king, when he joined

[20] Manivikraman Raja. [Ed.]
[21] Betel-nut. [Ed.]

the captain, threw himself upon another couch, covered with various stuffs embroidered in gold, and asked the captain what he wanted.

And the captain told him he was the ambassador of a King of Portugal, who was Lord of many countries and the possessor of great wealth of every description, exceeding that of any king of these parts; that for a period of sixty years his ancestors had annually sent out vessels to make discoveries in the direction of India, as they knew that there were Christian kings there like themselves. This, he said, was the reason which induced them to order this country to be discovered, not because they sought for gold or silver, for of this they had such abundance that they needed not what was to be found in this country. He further stated that the captains sent out traveled for a year or two, until their provisions were exhausted, and then returned to Portugal, without having succeeded in making the desired discovery. There reigned a king now whose name was Dom Manuel, who had ordered him to build three vessels, of which he had been appointed captain-major, and who had ordered him not to return to Portugal until he should have discovered this King of the Christians, on pain of having his head cut off. That two letters had been intrusted to him to be presented in case he succeeded in discovering him, and that he would do so on the ensuing day; and, finally, he had been instructed to say by word of mouth that he [the King of Portugal] desired to be his friend and brother.

In reply to this the king said that he was welcome; that, on his part, he held him as a friend and brother, and would send ambassadors with him to Portugal. This latter had been asked as a favor, the captain pretending that he would not dare to present himself before his king and master unless he was able to present, at the same time, some men of this country.

These and many other things passed between the two in this chamber, and as it was already late in the night, the king asked the captain with whom he desired to lodge, with Christians or with Moors? And the captain replied, neither with Christians nor with Moors, and begged as a favor that he be given a lodging by himself. The king said he would order it thus, upon which the captain took leave of the king and came to where the men were, that is, to a veranda lit up by a huge candlestick. By that time four hours of the night had already gone.[22] . . .

[*Presents for the King.*] On Tuesday, May 29, the captain-major got ready the following things to be sent to the king, viz., twelve pieces of *lambel*,[23] four scarlet hoods, six hats, four strings of coral, a case containing six wash-hand basins, a case of sugar, two casks of oil, and two of honey.[24] And as it is the custom not to send anything to the king

---

[22] Four hours after sunset, or about 10 P.M. [Ed.]

[23] Striped cloth. [Ed.]

[24] The ships had been loaded by Bartolomeu Dias (1451–1500), who used such goods effectively in trading with Africans. [Ed.]

without the knowledge of the Moor, his factor, and of the *bale*, the captain informed them of his intention. They came, and when they saw the present they laughed at it, saying that it was not a thing to offer to a king, that the poorest merchant from Mecca, or any other part of India, gave more, and that if he wanted to make a present it should be in gold, as the king would not accept such things. When the captain heard this he grew sad, and said that he had brought no gold, that, moreover, he was no merchant, but an ambassador; that he gave of that which he had, which was his own [private gift] and not the king's; that if the King of Portugal ordered him to return he would intrust him with far richer presents; and that if King Camolim[25] would not accept these things he would send them back to the ships. Upon this they declared that they would not forward his presents, nor consent to his forwarding them himself. When they had gone there came certain Moorish merchants, and they all depreciated the present which the captain desired to be sent to the king.

When the captain saw that they were determined not to forward his present, he said, that as they would not allow him to send his present to the palace he would go to speak to the king, and would then return to the ships. They approved of this, and told him that if he would wait a short time they would return and accompany him to the palace. And the captain waited all day, but they never came back. The captain was very wroth at being among so phlegmatic and unreliable a people, and intended, at first, to go to the palace without them. On further consideration, however, he thought it best to wait until the following day. The men diverted themselves, singing and dancing to the sound of trumpets, and enjoyed themselves much.

[*A Second Audience, May 30.*] On Wednesday morning the Moors returned, and took the captain to the palace, and others with him. The palace was crowded with armed men. Our captain was kept waiting with his conductors for fully four long hours, outside a door, which was only opened when the king sent word to admit him, attended by two men only, whom he might select. The captain-major said that he desired to have Fernão Martins with him, who could interpret, and his secretary. It seemed to him, as it did to us, that this separation portended no good.

When he had entered, the king said that he had expected him on Tuesday. The captain-major said that the long road had tired him, and that for this reason he had not come to see him. The king then said that he had told him that he came from a very rich kingdom, and yet had brought him nothing; that he had also told him that he was the bearer of

[25] Camorim (with a soft *c*) is a version of the king's title, more often written as Zamorin or Samorin, meaning ruler of the coasts or king of the seas. [Ed.]

a letter, which had not yet been delivered. To this the captain rejoined that he had brought nothing, because the object of his voyage was merely to make discoveries, but that when other ships came he would then see what they brought him; as to the letter, it was true that he had brought one, and would deliver it immediately.

The king then asked what it was he had come to discover: stones or men? If he came to discover men, as he said, why had he brought nothing? Moreover, he had been told that he carried with him the golden image of a Santa Maria. The captain-major said that the Santa Maria was not of gold, and that even if she were he would not part with her, as she had guided him across the ocean, and would guide him back to his own country. The king then asked for the letter. The captain said that he begged as a favor, that as the Moors wished him ill and might misinterpret him, a Christian able to speak Arabic should be sent for. The king said this was well, and at once sent for a young man, of small stature, whose name was Quaram. The captain-major then said that he had two letters, one written in his own language and the other in that of the Moors;[26] that he was able to read the former, and knew that it contained nothing but what would prove acceptable; but that as to the other he was unable to read it, and it might be good, or contain something that was erroneous. As the Christian was unable to *read* Moorish, four Moors took the letter and read it between them, after which they translated it to the king, who was well satisfied with its contents.

The king then asked what kind of merchandise was to be found in his country. The captain said there was much corn,[27] cloth, iron, bronze, and many other things. The king asked whether he had any merchandise with him. The captain-major replied that he had a little of each sort, as samples, and that if permitted to return to the ships he would order it to be landed, and that meantime four or five men would remain at the lodgings assigned them. The king said no! He might take all his people with him, securely moor his ships, land his merchandise, and sell it to the best advantage. Having taken leave of the king the captain-major returned to his lodgings, and we with him. As it was already late no attempt was made to depart that night.

---

[26] Arabic. [Ed.]

[27] Corn had already been transplanted from the Americas by this time, but the author more likely meant wheat (Ames, 2009, 83). [Ed.]

4

CHRISTOPHER COLUMBUS

Letter to King Ferdinand and Queen Isabella, 1493

Christopher Columbus sent this letter to his royal backers, King Ferdinand and Queen Isabella of Spain, on his return in March 1493 from his first voyage across the Atlantic. (See Map 15.3.)

An Italian sailor from Genoa, Columbus, in 1483–1484, tried to convince King John II of Portugal to underwrite his plan to sail across the western ocean to the spice-rich East Indies. Relying on a Florentine map that used Marco Polo's overstated distance from Venice to Japan across Asia and an understated estimate of the circumference of the globe, Columbus believed that Japan lay only 2,500 miles west of the Portuguese Azores. King John II rejected the proposal because he had more accurate estimates indicating that sailing around Africa was the shorter route, as the voyages of Bartolomeu Dias in 1488 and Vasco da Gama in 1497–1499 proved.

Less knowledgeable about navigation, the new Spanish monarchs, Ferdinand and Isabella, supported Columbus and financed his plan to sail west to Asia. In four voyages, Columbus touched a number of Caribbean islands and the coast of Central America, settled Spaniards on Hispaniola (Española), and began to create one of the largest empires in world history for Spain — all the while thinking he was near China and Japan, in the realm of the Great Khan whom Marco Polo had met and who had died hundreds of years earlier.

In what ways was the voyage of Columbus similar to that of da Gama? In what ways was it similar to that of Zheng He? In what ways was it different from both of these voyages? Taking the voyages of da Gama and Columbus together, what were the differences between Chinese and European expansion?

THINKING HISTORICALLY

Because this document comes from the period we are studying and is written by Columbus himself, it is a primary source. Primary sources have a great sense of immediacy and can often seem to transport us directly into the past. However, involvement when reading does not always lead to understanding, so it is important

Source: "First Voyage of Columbus," in *The Four Voyages of Columbus*, ed. Cecil Jane (New York: Dover, 1988), 1–18.

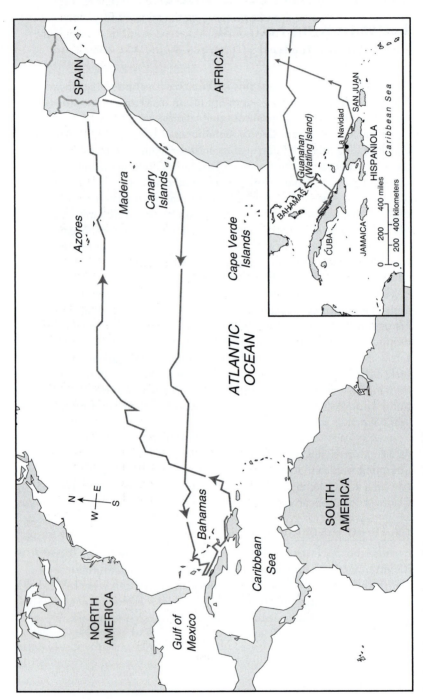

Map 15.3 Columbus's First Voyage, 1492–1493.

to think critically about the source and the writer's intended audience as we read. First we must determine the source of the document. Where does it come from? Is it original? If not, is it a copy or a translation? Next, we must determine who wrote it, when it was written, and for what purpose. After answering these questions, we are able to read the document with a critical eye, which leads to greater understanding.

The original letter by Columbus has been lost. This selection is an English translation based on three different printed Spanish versions of the letter. So this text is a reconstruction, not an original, though it is believed to be quite close to the original.

The original letter was probably composed during a relaxed time on the return voyage before its date of February 15, 1493 — possibly as early as the middle of January — and sent to the Spanish monarchs from Lisbon in order to reach them by the time Columbus arrived in Barcelona.

What does Columbus want to impart to Ferdinand and Isabella? First and foremost, he wants them to know that he reached the Indies, that the voyage was a success. And so, the letter's opening sentence tells us something that Columbus certainly did not intend or know. We learn that on his return in 1493, Columbus thought he had been to the Indies when in fact he had not. (It is due to Columbus's confusion that we call the islands he visited the West Indies and Native Americans "Indians.")

Knowing what the author wants a reader to believe is useful information because it serves as a point of reference for other statements the author makes. The success of Columbus's voyage is a case in point. Columbus does not admit to the loss of one of his ships in his letter, nor does he explain fully why he had to build a fort at Navidad and leave some of his crew there, returning home without them. Clearly, Columbus had reason to worry that his voyage would be viewed as a failure. He had not found the gold mines he sought or the Asian cities described by Marco Polo. He thought he had discovered many spices, though only the chili peppers were new. Notice, as you read this letter, how Columbus presents his voyage in the best light.

Aside from what Columbus intends, what facts do you learn from the letter about Columbus, his first voyage, and his encounter with the New World? What seems to drive Columbus to do what he does? What is Columbus's attitude toward the "Indians"? What does Columbus's letter tell us about the society and culture of the Taino* — the people he met in the Caribbean?

* TY noh

Sir, As I know that you will be pleased at the great victory with which Our Lord has crowned my voyage, I write this to you, from which you will learn how in thirty-three days, I passed from the Canary Islands to the Indies with the fleet which the most illustrious king and queen, our sovereigns, gave to me. And there I found very many islands filled with people innumerable, and of them all I have taken possession for their highnesses, by proclamation made and with the royal standard unfurled, and no opposition was offered to me. To the first island which I found, I gave the name *San Salvador*, in remembrance of the Divine Majesty, Who has marvellously bestowed all this; the Indians call it "Guanahani."* To the second, I gave the name *Isla de Santa María de Concepción*; to the third, *Fernandina*; to the fourth, *Isabella*; to the fifth, *Isla Juana*, and so to each one I gave a new name.

When I reached Juana, I followed its coast to the westward, and I found it to be so extensive that I thought that it must be the mainland, the province of Catayo. And since there were neither towns nor villages on the seashore, but only small hamlets, with the people which I could not have speech, because they all fled immediately, I went forward on the same course, thinking that I should not fail to find great cities and towns. And, at the end of many leagues, seeing that there was no change and that the coast was bearing me northwards, which I wished to avoid, since winter was already beginning and I proposed to make from it to the south, and as moreover the wind was carrying me forward, I determined not to wait for a change in the weather and retraced my path as far as a certain harbour known to me. And from that point, I sent two men inland to learn if there were a king or great cities. They travelled three days' journey and found an infinity of small hamlets and people without number, but nothing of importance. For this reason, they returned.

I understood sufficiently from other Indians, whom I had already taken, that this land was nothing but an island. And therefore I followed its coast eastwards for one hundred and seven leagues to the point where it ended. And from that cape, I saw another island, distant eighteen leagues from the former, to the east, to which I at once gave the name "Española." And I went there and followed its northern coast, as I had in the case of Juana, to the eastward for one hundred and eighty-eight great leagues in a straight line. This island and all the others are very fertile to a limitless degree, and this island is extremely so. In it there are many harbours on the coast of the sea, beyond comparison with others which I know in Christendom, and many rivers, good and large, which is marvellous. Its lands are high, and there are in it very many sierras and very lofty mountains, beyond comparison with the island of Teneriffe. All are most beautiful, of a thousand shapes, and all are accessible and

* gwah nah HAH nee

filled with trees of a thousand kinds and tall, and they seem to touch the sky. And I am told that they never lose their foliage, as I can understand, for I saw them as green and as lovely as they are in Spain in May, and some of them were flowering, some bearing fruit, and some in another stage, according to their nature. And the nightingale was singing and other birds of a thousand kinds in the month of November there where I went. There are six or eight kinds of palm, which are a wonder to behold on account of their beautiful variety, but so are the other trees and fruits and plants. In it are marvellous pine groves, and there are very large tracts of cultivatable lands, and there is honey, and there are birds of many kinds and fruits in great diversity. In the interior are mines of metals, and the population is without number. Española is a marvel.

The sierras and mountains, the plains and arable lands and pastures, are so lovely and rich for planting and sowing, for breeding cattle of every kind, for building towns and villages. The harbours of the sea here are such as cannot be believed to exist unless they have been seen, and so with the rivers, many and great, and good waters, the majority of which contain gold. In the trees and fruits and plants, there is a great difference from those of Juana. In this island, there are many spices and great mines of gold and of other metals.

The people of this island, and of all the other islands which I have found and of which I have information, all go naked, men and women, as their mothers bore them, although some women cover a single place with the leaf of a plant or with a net of cotton which they make for the purpose. They have no iron or steel or weapons, nor are they fitted to use them, not because they are not well built men and of handsome stature, but because they are very marvellously timorous. They have no other arms than weapons made of canes, cut in seeding time, to the ends of which they fix a small sharpened stick. And they do not dare to make use of these, for many times it has happened that I have sent ashore two or three men to some town to have speech, and countless people have come out to them, and as soon as they have seen my men approaching they have fled, even a father not waiting for his son. And this, not because ill has been done to anyone; on the contrary, at every point where I have been and have been able to have speech, I have given to them of all that I had, such as cloth and many other things, without receiving anything for it; but so they are, incurably timid. It is true that, after they have been reassured and have lost their fear, they are so guileless and so generous with all they possess, that no one would believe it who has not seen it. They never refuse anything which they possess, if it be asked of them; on the contrary, they invite anyone to share it, and display as much love as if they would give their hearts, and whether the thing be of value or whether it be of small price, at once with whatever trifle of whatever kind it may be that is given to them, with that they are content. I forbade that they should be given things so worthless as fragments of broken crockery and scraps of broken glass, and ends of straps, although when they were able to get them, they fancied that they possessed the best jewel in the world. So it was found that a sailor for a strap received gold to the weight of two and a half *castellanos*, and others much more for other things which were worth much less. As for new *blancas*,[1] for them they would give everything which they had, although it might be two or three *castellanos'* weight of gold or an *arroba*[2] or two of spun cotton. . . . They took even the pieces of the broken hoops of the wine barrels and, like savages, gave what they had, so that it seemed to me to be wrong and I forbade it. And I gave a thousand handsome good things, which I had brought, in order that they might conceive affection, and more than that, might become Christians and be inclined to the love and service of their highnesses and of the whole Castilian nation, and strive to aid us and to give us of the things which they have in abundance and which are necessary to us. And they do not know any creed and are not idolaters; only they all believe that power and good are in the heavens, and they are very firmly convinced that I, with these ships and men, came from the heavens, and in this belief they everywhere received me, after they had overcome their fear. And this does not come because they are ignorant; on the contrary, they are of a very acute intelligence and are men who navigate all those seas, so that it is amazing how good an account they give of everything, but it is because they have never seen people clothed or ships of such a kind.

And as soon as I arrived in the Indies, in the first island which I found, I took by force some of them, in order that they might learn and give me information of that which there is in those parts, and so it was that they soon understood us, and we them, either by speech or signs, and they have been very serviceable. I still take them with me, and they are always assured that I come from Heaven, for all the intercourse which they have had with me; and they were the first to announce this wherever I went, and the others went running from house to house and to the neighbouring towns, with loud cries of, "Come! Come to see the people from Heaven!" So all, men and women alike, when their minds were set at rest concerning us, came, so that not one, great or small, remained behind, and all brought something to eat and drink, which they gave with extraordinary affection. In all the island, they have very many canoes, like rowing *fustas*,[3] some larger, some smaller, and some are larger than a *fusta* of eighteen benches. They are not so broad, because they are made of a single log of wood, but a *fusta* would not keep up with them in rowing, since their speed is a thing incredible. And in these they navigate among all those islands, which are innumerable,

---

[1] Spanish copper coins. [Ed.]

[2] A unit of weight (about 25 pounds) indicated by the @ symbol. [Ed.]

[3] Fast ships with oars and sails, probably of Arab origin. [Ed.]

and carry their goods. One of these canoes I have seen with seventy and eighty men in her, and each one with his oar.

In all these islands, I saw no great diversity in the appearance of the people or in their manners and language. On the contrary, they all understand one another, which is a very curious thing, on account of which I hope that their highnesses will determine upon their conversion to our holy faith, towards which they are very inclined.

I have already said how I have gone one hundred and seven leagues in a straight line from west to east along the seashore of the island Juana, and as a result of that voyage, I can say that this island is larger than England and Scotland together, for, beyond these one hundred and seven leagues, there remain to the westward two provinces to which I have not gone. One of these provinces they call "Avan," and there the people are born with tails; and these provinces cannot have a length of less than fifty or sixty leagues, as I could understand from those Indians whom I have and who know all the islands.

The other, Española, has a circumference greater than all Spain, from Colibre, by the sea-coast, to Fuenterabia in Vizcaya, since I voyaged along one side one hundred and eighty-eight great leagues in a straight line from west to east. It is a land to be desired and, seen, it is never to be left. And in it, although of all I have taken possession for their highnesses and all are more richly endowed than I know how, or am able, to say, and I hold them all for their highnesses, so that they may dispose of them as, and as absolutely as, of the kingdoms of Castile, in this Española, in the situation most convenient and in the best position for the mines of gold and for all intercourse as well with the mainland here as with that there, belonging to the Grand Khan, where will be great trade and gain, I have taken possession of a large town, to which I gave the name *Villa de Navidad*, and in it I have made fortifications and a fort, which now will by this time be entirely finished, and I have left in it sufficient men for such a purpose with arms and artillery and provisions for more than a year, and a *fusta*, and one, a master of all seacraft, to build others, and great friendship with the king of that land, so much so, that he was proud to call me, and to treat me as, a brother. And even if he were to change his attitude to one of hostility towards these men, he and his do not know what arms are and they go naked, as I have already said, and are the most timorous people that there are in the world, so that the men whom I have left there alone would suffice to destroy all that land, and the island is without danger for their persons, if they know how to govern themselves.

In all these islands, it seems to me that all men are content with one woman, and to their chief or king they give as many as twenty. It appears to me that the women work more than the men. And I have not been able to learn if they hold private property; what seemed to me to appear was that, in that which one had, all took a share, especially of eatable things.

In these islands I have so far found no human monstrosities, as many expected, but on the contrary the whole population is very well-formed, nor are they negros as in Guinea, but their hair is flowing, and they are not born where there is intense force in the rays of the sun; it is true that the sun has there great power, although it is distant from the equinoctial line twenty-six degrees. In these islands, where there are high mountains, the cold was severe this winter, but they endure it, being used to it and with the help of meats which they eat with many and extremely hot spices. As I have found no monsters, so I have had no report of any, except in an island "Quaris," the second at the coming into the Indies, which is inhabited by a people who are regarded in all the islands as very fierce and who eat human flesh. They have many canoes with which they range through all the islands of India and pillage and take as many as they can. They are no more malformed than the others, except that they have the custom of wearing their hair long like women, and they use bows and arrows of the same cane stems, with a small piece of wood at the end, owing to lack of iron which they do not possess. They are ferocious among these other people who are cowardly to an excessive degree, but I make no more account of them than of the rest. These are those who have intercourse with the women of "Matinino," which is the first island met on the way from Spain to the Indies, in which there is not a man. These women engage in no feminine occupation, but use bows and arrows of cane, like those already mentioned, and they arm and protect themselves with plates of copper, of which they have much.

In another island, which they assure me is larger than Española, the people have no hair. In it, there is gold incalculable, and from it and from the other islands, I bring with me Indians as evidence.

In conclusion, to speak only of that which has been accomplished on this voyage, which was so hasty, their highnesses can see that I will give them as much gold as they may need, if their highnesses will render me very slight assistance; moreover, spice and cotton, as much as their highnesses shall command; and mastic, as much as they shall order to be shipped and which, up to now, has been found only in Greece, in the island of Chios, and the Seignory sells it for what it pleases; and aloe wood, as much as they shall order to be shipped, and slaves, as many as they shall order to be shipped and who will be from the idolaters. And I believe that I have found rhubarb and cinnamon, and I shall find a thousand other things of value, which the people whom I have left there will have discovered, for I have not delayed at any point, so far as the wind allowed me to sail, except in the town of Navidad, in order to leave it secured and well established, and in truth, I should have done much more, if the ships had served me, as reason demanded.

This is enough . . . and the eternal God, our Lord, Who gives to all those who walk in His way triumph over things which appear to be impossible, and this was notably one; for, although men have talked or have written of these lands, all was conjectural, without suggestion of ocular evidence, but amounted only to this, that those who heard for the most part listened and judged it to be rather a fable than as having any vestige of truth. So that, since Our Redeemer has given this victory to our most illustrious king and queen, and to their renowned kingdoms, in so great a matter, for this all Christendom ought to feel delight and make great feasts and give solemn thanks to the Holy Trinity with many solemn prayers for the great exaltation which they shall have, in the turning of so many peoples to our holy faith, and afterwards for temporal benefits, for not only Spain but all Christians will have hence refreshment and gain.

This, in accordance with that which has been accomplished, thus briefly.

Done in the caravel,[4] off the Canary Islands, on the fifteenth of February, in the year one thousand four hundred and ninety-three.

At your orders.   El Almirante.

After having written this, and being in the sea of Castile, there came on me so great a south-south-west wind, that I was obliged to lighten ship. But I ran here to-day into this port of Lisbon, which was the greatest marvel in the world, whence I decided to write to their highnesses. In all the Indies, I have always found weather like May; where I went in thirty-three days and I had returned in twenty-eight, save for these storms which have detained me for fourteen days, beating about in this sea. Here all the sailors say that never has there been so bad a winter nor so many ships lost.

Done on the fourth day of March.

[4] A ship, in this case the *Niña* or *Pinta*, not the larger *Santa Maria* which had run aground off Haiti on Christmas Eve, and its timber was then used for the building of Navidad, a fort to settle its crew. [Ed.]

5

KIRKPATRICK SALE

The Conquest of Paradise, 1991

In this selection from his popular study of Columbus, Sale is concerned with Columbus's attitude toward nature in the New World. Sale regards Columbus as a symbol of European expansion. If Columbus is distinctly European, what is Sale saying about European expansion? How and what does Sale add to your understanding of the similarities and differences between Chinese and European expansion?

Source: Kirkpatrick Sale, *The Conquest of Paradise* (New York: Penguin, 1991), 92–104.

Was Columbus much different from Zheng He? Or were the areas and peoples they visited causes for different responses? Vasco da Gama visited the same areas as Zheng He. How similar, or different, were da Gama and Zheng He? If da Gama was a better symbol of European expansion, how different was the European experience from the Chinese?

THINKING HISTORICALLY

Clearly, this selection is a secondary source; Sale is a modern writer, not a fifteenth-century contemporary of Columbus. Still, you will not have to read very far into the selection to realize that Sale has a distinct point of view. Secondary sources, like primary ones, should be analyzed for bias and perspective, and the author's interpretation should be identified.

Sale is an environmentalist and a cultural critic. Do his beliefs and values hinder his understanding of Columbus, or do they inform and illuminate aspects of Columbus that might otherwise be missed? Does Sale help you recognize things you would not have seen on your own, or does he persuade you to see things that might not truly be there?

Notice how Sale uses primary sources in his text. He quotes from Columbus's journal and his letter to King Ferdinand and Queen Isabella. Do these quotes help you understand Columbus, or do they simply support Sale's argument? What do you think about Sale's use of the Spanish *Colón** for *Columbus*? Does Sale "take possession" of Columbus by, in effect, "renaming" him for modern readers? Is the effect humanizing or debunking?

Notice how Sale sometimes calls attention to what the primary source did *not* say rather than what it did say. Is this a legitimate way to understand someone, or is Sale projecting a twentieth-century perspective on Columbus to make a point?

Toward the end of the selection, Sale extends his criticism beyond Columbus to include others. Who are the others? What is the effect of this larger criticism?

Admiral Colón spent a total of ninety-six days exploring the lands he encountered on the far side of the Ocean Sea—four rather small coralline islands in the Bahamian chain and two substantial coastlines of what he finally acknowledged were larger islands—every one of which he "took possession of" in the name of his Sovereigns.

The first he named San Salvador, no doubt as much in thanksgiving for its welcome presence after more than a month at sea as for the Son

* koh LOHN

of God whom it honored; the second he called Santa María de la Concepcíon, after the Virgin whose name his flagship bore; and the third and fourth he called Fernandina and Isabela, for his patrons, honoring Aragon before Castile for reasons never explained (possibly protocol, possibly in recognition of the chief sources of backing for the voyage). The first of the two large and very fertile islands he called Juana, which Fernando [Columbus's son] says was done in honor of Prince Juan, heir to the Castilian throne, but just as plausibly might have been done in recognition of Princess Juana, the unstable child who eventually carried on the line; the second he named la Ysla Española, the "Spanish Island," because it resembled (though he felt it surpassed in beauty) the lands of Castile.

It was not that the islands were in need of names, mind you, nor indeed that Colón was ignorant of the names that native peoples had already given them, for he frequently used those original names before endowing them with his own. Rather, the process of bestowing new names went along with "taking possession of" those parts of the world he deemed suitable for Spanish ownership, showing the royal banners, erecting various crosses, and pronouncing certain oaths and pledges. If this was presumption, it had an honored heritage: It was Adam who was charged by his Creator with the task of naming "every living creature," including the product of his own rib, in the course of establishing "dominion over" them.

Colón went on to assign no fewer than sixty-two other names on the geography of the islands—capes, points, mountains, ports—with a blithe assurance suggesting that in his (and Europe's) perception the act of name-giving was in some sense a talisman of conquest, a rite that changed raw neutral stretches of far-off earth into extensions of Europe. The process began slowly, even haltingly—he forgot to record, for example, until four days afterward that he named the landfall island San Salvador—but by the time he came to Española at the end he went on a naming spree, using more than two-thirds of all the titles he concocted on that one coastline. On certain days it became almost a frenzy: on December 6 he named six places, on the nineteenth six more, and on January 11 no fewer than ten—eight capes, a point, and a mountain. It is almost as if, as he sailed along the last of the islands, he was determined to leave his mark on it the only way he knew how, and thus to establish his authority—and by extension Spain's—even, as with baptism, to make it thus sanctified, and real, and official. . . .

This business of naming and "possessing" foreign islands was by no means casual. The Admiral took it very seriously, pointing out that "it was my wish to bypass no island without taking possession" (October 15) and that "in all regions [I] always left a cross standing" (November 16) as a mark of Christian dominance. There even seem to have been certain prescriptions for it (the instructions from the Sovereigns speak of "the administering of the oath and the performing of the rites prescribed in such cases"), and Rodrigo de Escobedo was sent along as secretary of the fleet explicitly to witness and record these events in detail.

But consider the implications of this act and the questions it raises again about what was in the Sovereigns' minds, what in Colón's. Why would the Admiral assume that these territories were in some way *un*possessed—even by those clearly inhabiting them—and thus available for Spain to claim? Why would he not think twice about the possibility that some considerable potentate—the Grand Khan of China, for example, whom he later acknowledged (November 6) "must be" the ruler of Española—might descend upon him at any moment with a greater military force than his three vessels commanded and punish him for his territorial presumption? Why would he make the ceremony of possession his very first act on shore, even before meeting the inhabitants or exploring the environs, or finding out if anybody there objected to being thus possessed—particularly if they actually owned the great treasures he hoped would be there? No European would have imagined that anyone—three small boatloads of Indians, say—could come up to a European shore or island and "take possession" of it, nor would a European imagine marching up to some part of North Africa or the Middle East and claiming sovereignty there with impunity. Why were these lands thought to be different?

Could there be any reason for the Admiral to assume he had reached "unclaimed" shores, new lands that lay far from the domains of any of the potentates of the East? Can that really have been in his mind—or can it all be explained as simple Eurocentrism, or Eurosuperiority, mixed with cupidity and naiveté? . . .

Once safely "possessed,"[1] San Salvador was open for inspection. Now the Admiral turned his attention for the first time to the "naked people" staring at him on the beach—he did not automatically give them a name, interestingly enough, and it would be another six days before he decided what he might call them—and tried to win their favor with his trinkets.

> They all go around as naked as their mothers bore them; and also the women, although I didn't see more than one really young girl. All that I saw were young people [*mancebos*], none of them more than 30 years old. They are very well built, with very handsome bodies and very good faces; their hair [is] coarse, almost like the silk of a horse's tail, and short. They wear their hair over their eyebrows, except for a little in the back that they wear long and never cut. Some of them paint themselves black (and they are the color of the Canary Islanders, neither black nor white), and some paint themselves white, and some red, and some with what they find. And some paint their faces, and some of them the whole body, and some the eyes only, and some of them only the nose.

It may fairly be called the birth of American anthropology.

[1] Given Spanish names. [Ed.]

A crude anthropology, of course, as superficial as Colón's descriptions always were when his interest was limited, but simple and straightforward enough, with none of the fable and fantasy that characterized many earlier (and even some later) accounts of new-found peoples. There was no pretense to objectivity, or any sense that these people might be representatives of a culture equal to, or in any way a model for, Europe's. Colón immediately presumed the inferiority of the natives, not merely because (a sure enough sign) they were naked, but because (his society could have no surer measure) they seemed so technologically backward. "It appeared to me that these people were very poor in everything," he wrote on that first day, and, worse still, "they have no iron." And they went on to prove their inferiority to the Admiral by being ignorant of even such a basic artifact of European life as a sword: "They bear no arms, nor are they acquainted with them," he wrote, "for I showed them swords and they grasped them by the blade and cut themselves through ignorance." Thus did European arms spill the first drops of native blood on the sands of the New World, accompanied not with a gasp of compassion but with a smirk of superiority.

Then, just six sentences further on, Colón clarified what this inferiority meant in his eyes:

> They ought to be good servants and of good intelligence [*ingenio*]. . . . I believe that they would easily be made Christians, because it seemed to me that they had no religion. Our Lord pleasing, I will carry off six of them at my departure to Your Highnesses, in order that they may learn to speak.

No clothes, no arms, no possessions, no iron, and now no religion—not even speech: hence they were fit to be servants, and captives. It may fairly be called the birth of American slavery.

Whether or not the idea of slavery was in Colón's mind all along is uncertain, although he did suggest he had had experience as a slave trader in Africa (November 12) and he certainly knew of Portuguese plantation slavery in the Madeiras and Spanish slavery of Guanches in the Canaries. But it seems to have taken shape early and grown ever firmer as the weeks went on and as he captured more and more of the helpless natives. At one point he even sent his crew ashore to kidnap "seven head of women, young ones and adults, and three small children"; the expression of such callousness led the Spanish historian Salvador de Madariaga to remark, "It would be difficult to find a starker utterance of utilitarian subjection of man by man than this passage [whose] form is no less devoid of human feeling than its substance."

To be sure, Colón knew nothing about these people he encountered and considered enslaving, and he was hardly trained to find out very much, even if he was moved to care. But they were in fact members of an extensive, populous, and successful people whom Europe, using its own peculiar taxonomy, subsequently called "Taino" (or "Taíno"), their own word for "good" or "noble," and their response when asked who they were. They were related distantly by both language and culture to the Arawak people of the South American mainland, but it is misleading (and needlessly imprecise) to call them Arawaks, as historians are wont to do, when the term "Taino" better establishes their ethnic and historical distinctiveness. They had migrated to the islands from the mainland at about the time of the birth of Christ, occupying the three large islands we now call the Greater Antilles and arriving at Guanahani (Colón's San Salvador) and the end of the Bahamian chain probably sometime around A.D. 900. There they displaced an earlier people, the Guanahacabibes (sometimes called Guanahatabeys), who by the time of the European discovery occupied only the western third of Cuba and possibly remote corners of Española; and there, probably in the early fifteenth century, they eventually confronted another people moving up the islands from the mainland, the Caribs, whose culture eventually occupied a dozen small islands of what are called the Lesser Antilles.

The Tainos were not nearly so backward as Colón assumed from their lack of dress. (It might be said that it was the Europeans, who generally kept clothed head to foot during the day despite temperatures regularly in the eighties, who were the more unsophisticated in garmenture—especially since the Tainos, as Colón later noted, also used their body paint to prevent sunburn.) Indeed, they had achieved a means of living in a balanced and fruitful harmony with their natural surroundings that any society might well have envied. They had, to begin with, a not unsophisticated technology that made exact use of their available resources, two parts of which were so impressive that they were picked up and adopted by the European invaders: *canoa* (canoes) that were carved and fire-burned from large silk-cotton trees, "all in one piece, and wonderfully made" (October 13), some of which were capable of carrying up to 150 passengers; and *hamaca* (hammocks) that were "like nets of cotton" (October 17) and may have been a staple item of trade with Indian tribes as far away as the Florida mainland. Their houses were not only spacious and clean—as the Europeans noted with surprise and appreciation, used as they were to the generally crowded and slovenly hovels and huts of south European peasantry—but more apropos, remarkably resistant to hurricanes; the circular walls were made of strong cane poles set deep and close together ("as close as the fingers of a hand," Colón noted), the conical roofs of branches and vines tightly interwoven on a frame of smaller poles and covered with heavy palm leaves. Their artifacts and jewelry, with the exception of a few gold trinkets and ornaments, were based largely on renewable materials, including bracelets and necklaces of coral, shells, bone, and stone, embroidered cotton belts, woven baskets, carved statues and chairs, wooden and shell utensils, and pottery of variously intricate decoration depending on period and place.

Perhaps the most sophisticated, and most carefully integrated, part of their technology was their agricultural system, extraordinarily productive and perfectly adapted to the conditions of the island environment. It was based primarily on fields of knee-high mounds, called *conucos*, planted with *yuca* (sometimes called manioc), *batata* (sweet potato), and various squashes and beans grown all together in multicrop harmony: The root crops were excellent in resisting erosion and producing minerals and potash, the leaf crops effective in providing shade and moisture, and the mound configurations largely resistant to erosion and flooding and adaptable to almost all topographic conditions including steep hillsides. Not only was the *conuco* system environmentally appropriate—"conuco agriculture seems to have provided an exceptionally ecologically well-balanced and protective form of land use," according to David Watts's recent and authoritative *West Indies*—but it was also highly productive, surpassing in yields anything known in Europe at the time, with labor that amounted to hardly more than two or three hours a week, and in continuous yearlong harvest. The pioneering American geographical scholar Carl Sauer calls Taino agriculture "productive as few parts of the world," giving the "highest returns of food in continuous supply by the simplest methods and modest labor," and adds, with a touch of regret, "The white man never fully appreciated the excellent combination of plants that were grown in conucos."

In their arts of government the Tainos seem to have achieved a parallel sort of harmony. Most villages were small (ten to fifteen families) and autonomous, although many apparently recognized loose allegiances with neighboring villages, and they were governed by a hereditary official called a *kaseke* (*cacique*,* in the Spanish form), something of a cross between an arbiter and a prolocutor, supported by advisers and elders. So little a part did violence play in their system that they seem, remarkably, to have been a society without war (at least we know of no war music or signals or artifacts, and no evidence of intertribal combats) and even without overt conflict (Las Casas reports that no Spaniard ever saw two Tainos fighting). And here we come to what was obviously the Tainos' outstanding cultural achievement, a proficiency in the social arts that led those who first met them to comment unfailingly on their friendliness, their warmth, their openness, and above all—so striking to those of an acquisitive culture—their generosity.

"They are the best people in the world and above all the gentlest," Colón recorded in his *Journal* (December 16), and from first to last he was astonished at their kindness:

> They became so much our friends that it was a marvel. . . . They traded and gave everything they had, with good will [October 12].

---

* kah SEEK

I sent the ship's boat ashore for water, and they very willingly showed my people where the water was, and they themselves carried the full barrels to the boat, and took great delight in pleasing us [October 16].

They are very gentle and without knowledge of what is evil; nor do they murder or steal [November 12].

Your Highnesses may believe that in all the world there can be no better or gentler people . . . for neither better people nor land can there be. . . . All the people show the most singular loving behavior and they speak pleasantly [December 24].

I assure Your Highnesses that I believe that in all the world there is no better people nor better country. They love their neighbors as themselves, and they have the sweetest talk in the world, and are gentle and always laughing [December 25].

Even if one allows for some exaggeration—Colón was clearly trying to convince Ferdinand and Isabella that his Indians could be easily conquered and converted, should that be the Sovereigns' wish—it is obvious that the Tainos exhibited a manner of social discourse that quite impressed the rough Europeans. But that was not high among the traits of "civilized" nations, as Colón and Europe understood it, and it counted for little in the Admiral's assessment of these people. However struck he was with such behavior, he would not have thought that it was the mark of a benign and harmonious society, or that from it another culture might learn. For him it was something like the wondrous behavior of children, the naive guilelessness of prelapsarian[2] creatures who knew no better how to bargain and chaffer and cheat than they did to dress themselves: "For a lacepoint they gave good pieces of gold the size of two fingers" (January 6), and "They even took pieces of the broken hoops of the wine casks and, like beasts [*como besti*], gave what they had" (Santangel Letter).[3] Like beasts; such innocence was not human.

It is to be regretted that the Admiral, unable to see past their nakedness, as it were, knew not the real virtues of the people he confronted. For the Tainos' lives were in many ways as idyllic as their surroundings, into which they fit with such skill and comfort. They were well fed and well housed, without poverty or serious disease. They enjoyed considerable leisure, given over to dancing, singing, ballgames, and sex, and expressed themselves artistically in basketry, woodworking, pottery, and jewelry. They lived in general harmony and peace, without greed or covetousness or theft. . . .

---

[2] Before the Fall. In other words, before the time, according to the Old Testament, when Adam and Eve sinned and were banished by God from the Garden of Eden. [Ed.]

[3] A version of the letter to Ferdinand and Isabella. Santangel was the minister of Ferdinand and Isabella who received the letter. [Ed.]

It is perhaps only natural that Colón should devote his initial attention to the handsome, naked, naive islanders, but it does seem peculiar that he pays almost no attention, especially in the early days, to the spectacular scenery around them. Here he was, in the middle of an old-growth tropical forest the likes of which he could not have imagined before, its trees reaching sixty or seventy feet into the sky, more varieties than he knew how to count much less name, exhibiting a lushness that stood in sharp contrast to the sparse and denuded lands he had known in the Mediterranean, hearing a melodious multiplicity of bird songs and parrot calls—why was it not an occasion of wonder, excitement, and the sheer joy at nature in its full, arrogant abundance? But there is not a word of that: He actually said nothing about the physical surroundings on the first day, aside from a single phrase about "very green trees" and "many streams," and on the second managed only that short sentence about a big island with a big lake and green trees. Indeed, for the whole two weeks of the first leg of his voyage through the Bahamas to Cuba, he devoted only a third of the lines of description to the phenomena around him. And there are some natural sights he seems not to have noticed at all: He did not mention (except in terms of navigation) the nighttime heavens, the sharp, glorious configurations of stars that he must have seen virtually every night of his journey, many for the first time.

Eventually Colón succumbed to the islands' natural charms as he sailed on—how could he not?—and began to wax warmly about how "these islands are very green and fertile and the air very sweet" (October 15), with "trees which were more beautiful to see than any other thing that has ever been seen" (October 17), and "so good and sweet a smell of flowers or trees from the land" (October 19). But his descriptions are curiously vapid and vague, the language opaque and lifeless:

> The other island, which is very big [October 15] . . . this island is very large [October 16] . . . these islands are very green and fertile [October 15] . . . this land is the best and most fertile [October 17] . . . in it many plants and trees . . . if the others are very beautiful, this is more so [October 19] . . . here are some great lagoons . . . big and little birds of all sorts . . . if the others already seen are very beautiful and green and fertile, this one is much more so [October 21] . . . full of very good harbors and deep rivers [October 28].

You begin to see the Admiral's problem: He cares little about the features of nature, at least the ones he doesn't use for sailing, and even when he admires them he has little experience in assessing them and less acquaintance with a vocabulary to describe them. To convey the lush density and stately grandeur of those tropical forests, for example, he had little more than the modifiers "green" and "very": "very green trees" (October 12), "trees very green" (October 13), "trees . . . so green and with leaves like those of Castile" (October 14), "very green and very big trees" (October 19), "large groves are very green" (October 21), "trees . . . beautiful and green" (October 28). And when he began to be aware of the diversity among those trees, he was still unable to make meaningful distinctions: "All the trees are as different from ours as day from night" (October 17), "trees of a thousand kinds" (October 21), "a thousand sorts of trees" (October 23), "trees . . . different from ours" (October 28), "trees of a thousand sorts" (November 14), "trees of a thousand kinds" (December 6).

Such was his ignorance—a failing he repeatedly bemoaned ("I don't recognize them, which gives me great grief," October 19)—that when he did stop to examine a species he often had no idea what he was looking at. "I saw many trees very different from ours," he wrote on October 16, "and many of them have branches of many kinds, and all on one trunk, and one twig is of one kind and another of another, and so different that it is the greatest wonder in the world how much diversity there is of one kind from the other. That is to say, one branch has leaves like a cane, and another like mastic, and thus on one tree five or six kinds, and all so different." There is no such tree in existence, much less "many of them," and never was: Why would anyone imagine, or so contrive, such a thing to be?

Colón's attempts to identify species were likewise frequently wrong-headed, usually imputing to them commercial worth that they did not have, as with the worthless "aloes" he loaded such quantities of. The "amaranth" he identified on October 28 and the "oaks" and "arbutus" of November 25 are species that do not grow in the Caribbean; the "mastic" he found on November 5 and loaded on board to sell in Spain was gumbo-limbo, commercially worthless. (On the other hand, one of the species of flora he deemed of no marketable interest—"weeds [tizon] in their hands to drink in the fragrant smoke" [November 6]—was tobacco.) Similarly, the "whales" he spotted on October 16 must have been simply large fish, the "geese" he saw on November 6 and again on December 22 were ducks, the "nightingales" that kept delighting him (November 6; December 7, 13) do not exist in the Americas, and the skulls of "cows" he identified on October 29 were probably not those of land animals but of manatees.

This all seems a little sad, revealing a man rather lost in a world that he cannot come to know, a man with a "geographic and naturalistic knowledge that doesn't turn out to be very deep or nearly complete," and "a limited imagination and a capacity for comparisons conditioned by a not very broad geographic culture," in the words of Gaetano Ferro, a Columbus scholar and professor of geography at the University of Genoa. One could not of course have expected that an adventurer and sailor of this era would also be a naturalist, or necessarily even have some genuine interest in or curiosity about the natural world, but it is a disappointment nonetheless that the Discoverer of the New World turns out to be quite so simple, quite so inexperienced, in the ways of discovering his environment.

Colón's limitations, I hasten to say, were not his alone; they were of his culture, and they would be found in the descriptions of many others — Vespucci, Cortés, Hawkins, Juet, Cartier, Champlain, Raleigh — in the century of discovery to follow. They are the source of what the distinguished English historian J. H. Elliott has called "the problem of description" faced by Europeans confronting the uniqueness of the New World: "So often the physical appearance of the New World is either totally ignored or else described in the flattest and most conventional phraseology. This off-hand treatment of nature contrasts strikingly with the many precise and acute descriptions of the native inhabitants. It is as if the American landscape is seen as no more than a backcloth against which the strange and perennially fascinating peoples of the New World are dutifully grouped." The reason, Elliott thinks, and this is telling, may be "a lack of interest among sixteenth-century Europeans, and especially those of the Mediterranean world, in landscape and in nature." This lack of interest was reflected in the lack of vocabulary, the lack of that facility common to nature-based peoples whose cultures are steeped in natural imagery. Oviedo, for example, setting out to write descriptions for his *Historia General* in the next century, continually threw his hands up in the air: "Of all the things I have seen," he said at one point, "this is the one which has most left me without hope of being able to describe it in words"; or at another, "It needs to be painted by the hand of a Berruguete or some other excellent painter like him, or by Leonardo da Vinci or Andrea Mantegna, famous painters whom I knew in Italy." Like Colón, visitor after visitor to the New World seemed mind-boggled and tongue-tied trying to convey the wonders before them, and about the only color they seem to have eyes for is green — and not very many shades of that, either. . . .

■ REFLECTIONS

It is difficult to ignore moral issues when considering explorations and explorers. The prefix *great* is used liberally, and words like *discovery* and *courage* readily fit when describing "firsts" and "unknowns." However, celebratory images, national myths, and heroic biographies inevitably breed skepticism. Sometimes the result is an opposite assessment. Kirkpatrick Sale charges Columbus with arrogance, ignorance, and insufficient curiosity. Chinese historians of the last twenty years have swung from ignoring to celebrating the voyages of Zheng He, and some more recently have criticized Zheng He for military suppression of those in the lands his fleet visited.

On the matter of preparation, the difference between the Chinese and European voyages is especially striking. Da Gama at least brought an Arabic interpreter, though the absence of valuable gifts undermined the success of the voyage. The floating Chinese scientific laboratories, traveling experts, sages, and interpreters contrast starkly with the lack of a single artist or naturalist on board Columbus's ships. But the inability to distinguish shades of green is not a moral failure. We might say that Columbus's voyage was premature, Zheng He's meticulously planned and prepared. Like the designers of a modern aircraft, the Chinese built in redundancies: separate compartments that could fill with water without sinking the ship, more rice and fresh water than they would need, experts to find plants that might cure diseases yet unknown. By contrast, Columbus seems like a loose cannon, unaware of where he was going or where he had been, capable of lighting a match inside a dark powder shed.

These were, and in many ways still are, the differences between Chinese and European (now Western) scientific innovation. No European king could organize an enterprise on the scale of Zhu Di, Zheng He's emperor. No Chinese emperor had reason to sanction an experimental voyage into the unknown. The domain of the emperor was the known world, of which he was the center. In the Europe of closely competing princes, a Columbus could hatch a personal scheme with minimal supervision and barely sufficient funding and the consequences could still be — indeed, were — momentous. (See Chapter 16.) Was such a system irresponsible? Today, as we begin to probe the heavens around us, even as we tamper with technologies that change the balance of natural forces on Earth, we might consider whether the Confucian scholars of six hundred years ago were on to something when they burned the ships and destroyed all the records of their age of great discovery.

Primary sources are not limited to artifacts, images, and old written records, however. In the recent phase of celebrating the memory of Zheng He, the Chinese claimed as their own a young woman from Kenya, Mwamaka Sharifu, who looked like some of the people Kristof saw in 1999. Chinese-African faces on the coast of East Africa are evidence of contact, but not of contact in 1421. Combined, however, with family stories, DNA tests, local histories, and archaeological finds, a single living primary source may become the basis for a new interpretation of a broader history. In the case of Mwamaka Sharifu, members of her family, and other residents of coastal Somalia and Kenya, the evidence has proved convincing.

16

Atlantic World Encounters

Europeans, Americans, and Africans,
1500–1850

■ HISTORICAL CONTEXT

European expansion in the Atlantic that began with Portuguese voyages along the African coast in the 1440s and Columbus's discovery of the Americas in 1492 created a new Atlantic zone of human contact and communication that embraced four continents and one ocean. Nothing prior — neither the Chinese contacts with Africa in the early fifteenth century, nor the expansion of Islam throughout Eurasia in the almost thousand years since the Prophet Muhammad's death in 632 — had so thoroughly and so permanently changed the human and ecological balance of the world.

Sub-Saharan Africa had already been integrated into the world of Eurasia by 1450. African populations became more mixed as peoples from the Niger River area migrated east and south throughout the continent during the fifteen hundred years before the arrival of the Portuguese. Muslims from North Africa and the Middle East aided or established Muslim states and trading ports south of the Sahara in East and West Africa after 1000. Cultural and technical innovations of the Middle East, like the literacy that came with Islam, penetrated slowly, and the spread of the many plants and animals of the Northern Hemisphere was slowed by the Sahara and equator. However, microbes traveled swiftly and easily from Eurasia to Africa, creating a single set of diseases and immunities for the peoples of the Afro-Eurasian Old World.

The peoples of the Americas, having been isolated ecologically for more than ten thousand years, were not so fortunate. The arrival of Europeans and Africans in the Americas after 1492 had devastating consequences for Native American populations. Old World diseases like

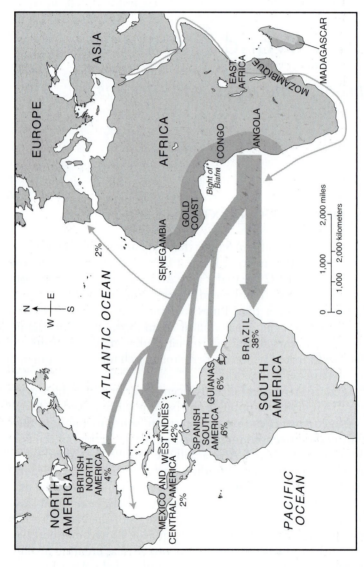

Map 16.1 The Atlantic Slave Trade.

smallpox were responsible for millions of Native American deaths—a tragedy of far greater scope than the casualties caused by wars. To work the mines and plantations of the New World, Europeans used Indian labor, but increasingly, especially for lowland plantations, they used African slaves (see Map 16.1). By 1850 the combination of Indian "die-off" and African and European migration resulted in vastly different populations in the Americas. On some Caribbean islands and in plantation areas like northeastern Brazil, Indian populations were entirely replaced by Africans. At the same time, European animals (for example, goats, cattle, horses) multiplied in the absence of natural predators.

The new Atlantic ecological system was not a uniform zone, however. Coastal regions in Western Europe and towns on the eastern seaboard of the Americas prospered, while American interiors and African populations in Africa stagnated or declined. The Atlantic Ocean became a vast lake that united port cities and plantations with sailing ships that carried African slaves to the Caribbean, Caribbean sugar and rum to North American and European industrial ports, and guns, pots, and liquor to the African "Slave Coast."

Thus, the Atlantic world was integrated with the Old World. Trade routes that began in Boston or Bahia, Brazil, stretched across Eurasia and around southern Africa into the Indian Ocean and the China Sea. Crops that had previously been known only to Native Americans—corn, potatoes, and tomatoes—fueled population explosions from Ireland to China and graced the tables of peasants and princes in between. What began as an effort by European merchants to import Asian spices directly became after 1650 (as European tastes for pepper and Asian spices moderated) a new global pantry of possibilities.

In this chapter, we will read selections that describe this new global dynamic. We will read of Europeans in the Americas and in West Africa and examine European depictions of natives from both North and South America. We will also explore some of the African and American responses to this European expansion. When studying these accounts and images, notice how individuals at the frontier of a new age understood and treated each other. Consider how these exchanges, so apparently fortuitous and transitory at the time, changed the face of the world.

■ THINKING HISTORICALLY

Comparing Primary Sources

By comparing and contrasting one thing with another, we learn more about each, and by examining related works in their proper context, we learn more about the whole of which they are part. In the first chapter we compared China and Europe or Chinese and European expansion in the fifteenth century. In this chapter we look at the Atlantic world, especially at Europeans in Africa and the Americas. We begin with three views of the Spanish conquest of Mexico — separate accounts by the Spanish conquistadors, by the Mexicans, and by a Dominican friar. The fourth selection juxtaposes two European depictions of Native Americans.

The final five selections examine encounters between Europeans and Africans and the development of the Atlantic slave trade. Did Europeans treat Africans differently from the way they treated Native Americans? If so, why? How were the African reactions to Europeans different from the Native American reactions? What accounts for those differences?

1

BERNAL DÍAZ

The Conquest of New Spain, c. 1560

Bernal Díaz del Castillo was born in Spain in 1492, the year Columbus sailed to America. After participating in two explorations of the Mexican coast, Díaz joined the expedition of Hernán Cortés to Mexico City in 1519. He wrote this history of the conquest much later, when he was in his seventies; he died circa 1580, a municipal official with a small estate in Guatemala.

The conquest of Mexico did not automatically follow from the first Spanish settlements in Santo Domingo, Hispaniola, and then Cuba in the West Indies. The Spanish crown had given permission for trade and exploration, not colonization. But many Spaniards, from fortune-seeking peasant-soldiers to minor nobility, were eager to conquer their own lands and exploit the populations of dependent Indians.

Cortés, of minor noble descent, at the age of nineteen sailed to the Indies, where he established a sizeable estate on the island of Hispaniola. When he heard stories of Montezuma's gold, he was deter-mined to find the fabled capital of the Aztec Empire, Tenochtitlán* (modern Mexico City). He gathered more than five hundred amateur soldiers, eleven ships, sixteen horses, and several pieces of artillery, then sailed across the Caribbean and Gulf of Mexico, and there began the long march from the coast up to the high central plateau of Mexico.

* teh NOHCH teet LAHN

Source: Bernal Díaz, *The Conquest of New Spain*, trans. J. M. Cohen (Baltimore: Penguin Books, 1963), 217–19, 221–25, 228–38, 241–43.

The Aztecs were new to central Mexico, arriving from the North American desert only about two hundred years before the Spanish, around 1325. By 1500 they had established dominion over almost all other city-states of Mexico, ruling an empire that stretched as far south as Guatemala and as far east as the Maya lands of the Yucatan Peninsula.

Aztec power relied on a combination of old and new religious ideas and a military system that conquered through terror. The older religious tradition that the Aztecs adopted from Toltec culture centered on Quetzalcoatl* — the feathered serpent, god of creation and brotherhood, whose nurturing forces continued in Aztec society in a system of universal education and in festivals dedicated to life, creativity, and procreation. But the Aztecs also worshiped Huitzilopochtli,[†] a warrior-god primed for death and sacrifice, who was given dominant status in the Aztec pantheon. Huitzilopochtli (rendered "Huichilobos"[‡] in this selection) was a force for building a powerful Aztec Empire. Drawing on the god's need for human sacrifice — a need not unknown among religions of central Mexico (or Christians) — Montezuma's predecessors built altars to Huitzilopochtli at Tenochtitlán, Cholula, and other sites. The war-god required a never-ending supply of human hearts, a need that prompted armies to ever-more remote sections of Central America in search of sacrificial victims and that created an endless supply of enemies of the Aztecs, among them, the Tlaxcalans.

With the help of his Indian captive and companion Doña Marina — called La Malinche[§] by some of the Indians (thus, Montezuma sometimes calls Cortés "Lord Malinche" in the selection) — Cortés was able to communicate with the Tlaxcalans and other Indians who were tired of Aztec domination. On his march toward Tenochtitlán, Cortés stopped to join forces with the Tlaxcalans, perhaps cementing the relationship and demonstrating his resolve through a brutal massacre of the people of Cholula, an Aztec ally and archenemy of the Tlaxcalans. By the time Cortés arrived at Tenochtitlán, Montezuma knew of the defeat of his allies at Cholula.

This selection from Bernal Díaz begins with the Spanish entry into Tenochtitlán. What impresses Díaz, and presumably other Spanish conquistadors, about the Mexican capital city? What parts of the city attract his attention the most? What conclusions does he draw about Mexican (or Aztec) civilization? Does he think Spanish civilization is equal, inferior, or superior to that of Mexico?

* keht zahl koh AH tuhl
[†] wheat zee loh po ACHT lee
[‡] wee chee LOH bohs
[§] lah mah LEEN cheh   A variation on "Marina." In contemporary Mexico a traitor is often called a "Malinchisto."

Díaz gives us a dramatic account of the meeting of Cortés and Montezuma. What do you think each is thinking and feeling? Do you see any signs of tension in their elaborate greetings? Why are both behaving so politely? What do they want from each other?

Notice how the initial hospitality turns tense. What causes this? Is either side more to blame for what happens next? Was conflict inevitable? Could the encounter have ended in some sort of peaceful resolution?

THINKING HISTORICALLY

Remember, we are going to compare Díaz's view with a Mexican view of these events. From your reading of Díaz, does he seem able to understand the Mexican point of view? Would you call him a sympathetic observer?

When Cortes saw, heard, and was told that the great Montezuma was approaching, he dismounted from his horse, and when he came near to Montezuma each bowed deeply to the other. Montezuma welcomed our Captain, and Cortes, speaking through Doña Marina, answered by wishing him very good health. Cortes, I think, offered Montezuma his right hand, but Montezuma refused it and extended his own. Then Cortes brought out a necklace which he had been holding. It was made of those elaborately worked and coloured glass beads called *margaritas*, . . . and was strung on a gold cord and dipped in musk to give it a good odour. This he hung round the great Montezuma's neck, and as he did so attempted to embrace him. But the great princes who stood round Montezuma grasped Cortes' arm to prevent him, for they considered this an indignity.

Then Cortes told Montezuma that it rejoiced his heart to have seen such a great prince, and that he took his coming in person to receive him and the repeated favours he had done him as a high honour. After this Montezuma made him another complimentary speech, and ordered two of his nephews who were supporting him, the lords of Texcoco and Coyoacan, to go with us and show us our quarters. Montezuma returned to the city with the other two kinsmen of his escort, the lords of Cuitlahuac and Tacuba; and all those grand companies of *Caciques*[1] and dignitaries who had come with him returned also in his train. . . .

On our arrival we entered the large court, where the great Montezuma was awaiting our Captain. Taking him by the hand, the prince led him

---

[1] kah SEEK Chiefs. [Ed.]

to his apartment in the hall where he was to lodge, which was very richly furnished in their manner. Montezuma had ready for him a very rich necklace, made of golden crabs, a marvellous piece of work, which he hung round Cortes' neck. His captains were greatly astonished at this sign of honour.

After this ceremony, for which Cortes thanked him through our interpreters, Montezuma said: "Malinche, you and your brothers are in your own house. Rest a while." He then returned to his palace, which was not far off.

We divided our lodgings by companies, and placed our artillery in a convenient spot. Then the order we were to keep was clearly explained to us, and we were warned to be very much on the alert, both the horsemen and the rest of us soldiers. We then ate a sumptuous dinner which they had prepared for us in their native style.

So, with luck on our side, we boldly entered the city of Tenochtitlán or Mexico on 8 November in the year of our Lord 1519.

The Stay in Mexico

. . . Montezuma had ordered his stewards to provide us with everything we needed for our way of living: maize, grindstones, women to make our bread, fowls, fruit, and plenty of fodder for the horses. He then took leave of us all with the greatest courtesy, and we accompanied him to the street. However, Cortes ordered us not to go far from our quarters for the present until we knew better what conduct to observe.

Next day Cortes decided to go to Montezuma's palace. But first he sent to know whether the prince was busy and to inform him of our coming. He took four captains with him: Pedro de Alvarado, Juan Velazquez de Leon, Diego de Ordaz, and Gonzalo de Sandoval, and five of us soldiers.

When Montezuma was informed of our coming, he advanced into the middle of the hall to receive us, closely surrounded by his nephews, for no other chiefs were allowed to enter his palace or communicate with him except upon important business. Cortes and Montezuma exchanged bows, and clasped hands. Then Montezuma led Cortes to his own dais, and setting him down on his right, called for more seats, on which he ordered us all to sit also.

Cortes began to make a speech through our interpreters, saying that we were all now rested, and that in coming to see and speak with such a great prince we had fulfilled the purpose of our voyage and the orders of our lord the King. The principal things he had come to say on behalf of our Lord God had already been communicated to Montezuma through his three ambassadors, on that occasion in the sandhills when he did us the favour of sending us the golden moon and sun. We had then told him that we were Christians and worshipped one God alone, named

Jesus Christ, who had suffered His passion and death to save us; and that what they worshipped as gods were not gods but devils, which were evil things, and if they were ugly to look at, their deeds were uglier. But he had proved to them how evil and ineffectual their gods were, as both the prince and his people would observe in the course of time, since, where we had put up crosses such as their ambassadors had seen, they had been too frightened to appear before them.

The favour he now begged of the great Montezuma was that he should listen to the words he now wished to speak. Then he very carefully expounded the creation of the world, how we are all brothers, the children of one mother and father called Adam and Eve; and how such a brother as our great Emperor, grieving for the perdition of so many souls as their idols were leading to hell, where they burnt in living flame, had sent us to tell him this, so that he might put a stop to it, and so that they might give up the worship of idols and make no more human sacrifices—for all men are brothers—and commit no more robbery or sodomy. He also promised that in the course of time the King would send some men who lead holy lives among us, much better than our own, to explain this more fully, for we had only come to give them warning. Therefore he begged Montezuma to do as he was asked.

As Montezuma seemed about to reply, Cortes broke off his speech, saying to those of us who were with him: "Since this is only the first attempt, we have now done our duty."

"My lord Malinche," Montezuma replied, "these arguments of yours have been familiar to me for some time. I understand what you said to my ambassadors on the sandhills about the three gods and the cross, also what you preached in the various towns through which you passed. We have given you no answer, since we have worshipped our own gods here from the beginning and know them to be good. No doubt yours are good also, but do not trouble to tell us any more about them at present. Regarding the creation of the world, we have held the same belief for many ages, and for this reason are certain that you are those who our ancestors predicted would come from the direction of the sunrise. As for your great King, I am in his debt and will give him of what I possess. For, as I have already said, two years ago I had news of the Captains who came in ships, by the road that you came, and said they were servants of this great king of yours. I should like to know if you are all the same people."

Cortes answered that we were all brothers and servants of the Emperor, and that they had come to discover a route and explore the seas and ports, so that when they knew them well we could follow, as we had done. Montezuma was referring to the expeditions of Francisco Hernandez de Cordoba and of Grijalva, the first voyages of discovery. He said that ever since that time he had wanted to invite some of these men to visit the cities of his kingdom, where he would receive them and do them honour, and that now his gods had fulfilled his desire, for we were in his house, which we might call our own. Here we might rest and enjoy ourselves, for we should receive good treatment. If on other occasions he had sent to forbid our entrance into his city, it was not of his own free will, but because his vassals were afraid. For they told him we shot out flashes of lightning, and killed many Indians with our horses, and that we were angry *Teules*,[2] and other such childish stories. But now that he had seen us, he knew that we were of flesh and blood and very intelligent, also very brave. Therefore he had a far greater esteem for us than these reports had given him, and would share with us what he had.

We all thanked him heartily for his . . . good will, and Montezuma replied with a laugh, because in his princely manner he spoke very gaily: "Malinche, I know that these people of Tlascala with whom you are so friendly have told you that I am a sort of god or *Teule*, and keep nothing in any of my houses that is not made of silver and gold and precious stones. But I know very well that you are too intelligent to believe this and will take it as a joke. See now, Malinche, my body is made of flesh and blood like yours, and my houses and palaces are of stone, wood, and plaster. It is true that I am a great king, and have inherited the riches of my ancestors, but the lies and nonsense you have heard of us are not true. You must take them as a joke, as I take the story of your thunders and lightnings."

Cortes answered also with a laugh that enemies always speak evil and tell lies about the people they hate, but he knew he could not hope to find a more magnificent prince in that land, and there was good reason why his fame should have reached our Emperor.

While this conversation was going on, Montezuma quietly sent one of his nephews, a great *Cacique*, to order his stewards to bring certain pieces of gold, which had apparently been set aside as a gift for Cortes, and ten loads of fine cloaks which he divided: the gold and cloaks between Cortes and the four captains, and for each of us soldiers two gold necklaces, each worth ten pesos, and two loads of cloaks. The gold that he then gave us was worth in all more than a thousand pesos, and he gave it all cheerfully, like a great and valiant prince.

As it was now past midday and he did not wish to be importunate, Cortes said to Montezuma: "My lord, the favours you do us increase, load by load, every day, and it is now the hour of your dinner." Montezuma answered that he thanked us for visiting him. We then took our leave with the greatest courtesy, and returned to our quarters, talking as we went of the prince's fine breeding and manners and deciding to show him the greatest respect in every way, and to remove our quilted caps in his presence, which we always did.

[2] Gods. [Ed.]

The great Montezuma was about forty years old, of good height, well proportioned, spare and slight, and not very dark, though of the usual Indian complexion. He did not wear his hair long but just over his ears, and he had a short black beard, well-shaped and thin. His face was rather long and cheerful, he had fine eyes, and in his appearance and manner could express geniality or, when necessary, a serious composure. He was very neat and clean, and took a bath every afternoon. He had many women as his mistresses, the daughters of chieftains, but two legitimate wives who were *Caciques* in their own right, and when he had intercourse with any of them it was so secret that only some of his servants knew of it. He was quite free from sodomy. The clothes he wore one day he did not wear again till three or four days later. He had a guard of two hundred chieftains lodged in rooms beside his own, only some of whom were permitted to speak to him. When they entered his presence they were compelled to take off their rich cloaks and put on others of little value. They had to be clean and walk barefoot, with their eyes downcast, for they were not allowed to look him in the face, and as they approached they had to make three obeisances, saying as they did so, "Lord, my lord, my great lord!" Then, when they had said what they had come to say, he would dismiss them with a few words. They did not turn their backs on him as they went out, but kept their faces towards him and their eyes downcast, only turning round when they had left the room. Another thing I noticed was that when other great chiefs came from distant lands about disputes or on business, they too had to take off their shoes and put on poor cloaks before entering Montezuma's apartments; and they were not allowed to enter the palace immediately but had to linger for a while near the door, since to enter hurriedly was considered disrespectful. . . .

Montezuma had two houses stocked with every sort of weapon; many of them were richly adorned with gold and precious stones. There were shields large and small, and a sort of broadsword, and two-handed swords set with flint blades that cut much better than our swords, and lances longer than ours, with five-foot blades consisting of many knives. Even when these are driven at a buckler or a shield they are not deflected. In fact they cut like razors, and the Indians can shave their heads with them. They had very good bows and arrows, and double and single-pointed javelins as well as their throwing-sticks and many slings and round stones shaped by hand, and another sort of shield that can be rolled up when they are not fighting, so that it does not get in the way, but which can be opened when they need it in battle and covers their bodies from head to foot. There was also a great deal of cotton armour richly worked on the outside with different coloured feathers, which they used as devices and distinguishing marks, and they had casques and helmets made of wood and bone which were also highly decorated with feathers on the outside. They had other arms of different kinds which I will not mention through fear of prolixity, and workmen skilled in the manufacture of such things, and stewards who were in charge of these arms. . . .

I have already described the manner of their sacrifices. They strike open the wretched Indian's chest with flint knives and hastily tear out the palpitating heart which, with the blood, they present to the idols in whose name they have performed the sacrifice. Then they cut off the arms, thighs, and head, eating the arms and thighs at their ceremonial banquets. The head they hang up on a beam, and the body of the sacrificed man is not eaten but given to the beasts of prey. They also had many vipers in this accursed house, and poisonous snakes which have something that sounds like a bell in their tails. These, which are the deadliest snakes of all, they kept in jars and great pottery vessels full of feathers, in which they laid their eggs and reared their young. They were fed on the bodies of sacrificed Indians and the flesh of the dogs that they bred. We know for certain, too, that when they drove us out of Mexico and killed over eight hundred and fifty of our soldiers, they fed those beasts and snakes on their bodies for many days, as I shall relate in due course. These snakes and wild beasts were dedicated to their fierce idols, and kept them company. As for the horrible noise when the lions and tigers roared, and the jackals and foxes howled, and the serpents hissed, it was so appalling that one seemed to be in hell. . . .

When our Captain and the Mercedarian friar realized that Montezuma would not allow us to set up a cross at Huichilobos' *cue*[3] or build a church there, it was decided that we should ask his stewards for masons so that we could put up a church in our own quarters. For every time we had said mass since entering the city of Mexico we had had to erect an altar on tables and dismantle it again.

The stewards promised to tell Montezuma of our wishes, and Cortes also sent our interpreters to ask him in person. Montezuma granted our request and ordered that we should be supplied with all the necessary material. We had our church finished in two days, and a cross erected in front of our lodgings, and mass was said there each day until the wine gave out. For as Cortes and some other captains and a friar had been ill during the Tlascalan campaign, there had been a run on the wine that we kept for mass. Still, though it was finished, we still went to church every day and prayed on our knees before the altar and images, firstly because it was our obligation as Christians and a good habit, and secondly so that Montezuma and all his captains should observe us and, seeing us worshipping on our knees before the cross — especially when we intoned the Ave Maria — might be inclined to imitate us.

It being our habit to examine and inquire into everything, when we were all assembled in our lodging and considering which was the best place for an altar, two of our men, one of whom was the carpenter

[3] The temple of the sun-god, who demanded human sacrifice. [Ed.]

Alonso Yañez, called attention to some marks on one of the walls which showed that there had once been a door, though it had been well plastered up and painted. Now as we had heard that Montezuma kept his father's treasure in this building, we immediately suspected that it must be in this room, which had been closed up only a few days before. Yañez made the suggestion to Juan Velazquez de Leon and Francisco de Lugo, both relatives of mine, to whom he had attached himself as a servant; and they mentioned the matter to Cortes. So the door was secretly opened, and Cortes went in first with certain captains. When they saw the quantity of golden objects—jewels and plates and ingots—which lay in that chamber they were quite transported. They did not know what to think of such riches. The news soon spread to the other captains and soldiers, and very secretly we all went in to see. The sight of all that wealth dumbfounded me. Being only a youth at the time and never having seen such riches before, I felt certain that there could not be a store like it in the whole world. We unanimously decided that we could not think of touching a particle of it, and that the stones should immediately be replaced in the doorway, which should be blocked again and cemented just as we had found it. We resolved also that not a word should be said about this until times changed, for fear Montezuma might hear of our discovery.

Let us leave this subject of the treasure and tell how four of our most valiant captains took Cortes aside in the church, with a dozen soldiers who were in his trust and confidence, myself among them, and asked him to consider the net or trap in which we were caught, to look at the great strength of the city and observe the causeways and bridges, and remember the warnings we had received in every town we had passed through that Huichilobos had counselled Montezuma to let us into the city and kill us there. We reminded him that the hearts of men are very fickle, especially among the Indians, and begged him not to trust the good will and affection that Montezuma was showing us, because from one hour to another it might change. If he should take it into his head to attack us, we said, the stoppage of our supplies of food and water, or the raising of any of the bridges, would render us helpless. Then, considering the vast army of warriors he possessed, we should be incapable of attacking or defending ourselves. And since all the houses stood in the water, how could our Tlascalan allies come in to help us? We asked him to think over all that we had said, for if we wanted to preserve our lives we must seize Montezuma immediately, without even a day's delay. We pointed out that all the gold Montezuma had given us, and all that we had seen in the treasury of his father Axayacatl, and all the food we ate was turning to poison in our bodies, for we could not sleep by night or day or take any rest while these thoughts were in our minds. If any of our soldiers gave him less drastic advice, we concluded, they would be senseless beasts charmed by the gold and incapable of looking death in the eye.

When he had heard our opinion, Cortes answered: "Do not imagine, gentlemen, that I am asleep or that I do not share your anxiety. You must have seen that I do. But what strength have we got for so bold a course as to take this great lord in his own palace, surrounded as he is by warriors and guards? What scheme or trick can we devise to prevent him from summoning his soldiers to attack us at once?"

Our captains (Juan Velazquez de Leon, Diego de Ordaz, Gonzalo de Sandoval, and Pedro de Alvarado) replied that Montezuma must be got out of his palace by smooth words and brought to our quarters. Once there, he must be told that he must remain as a prisoner, and that if he called out or made any disturbance he would pay for it with his life. If Cortes was unwilling to take this course at once, they begged him for permission to do it themselves. With two very dangerous alternatives before us, the better and more profitable thing, they said, would be to seize Montezuma rather than wait for him to attack us. Once he did so, what chance would we have? Some of us soldiers also remarked that Montezuma's stewards who brought us our food seemed to be growing insolent, and did not serve us as politely as they had at first. Two of our Tlascalan allies had, moreover, secretly observed to Jeronimo de Aguilar that for the last two days the Mexicans had appeared less well disposed to us. We spent a good hour discussing whether or not to take Montezuma prisoner, and how it should be done. But our final advice, that at all costs we should take him prisoner, was approved by our Captain, and we then left the matter till next day. All night we prayed God to direct events in the interests of His holy service. . . .

2

The Broken Spears: The Aztec Account of the Conquest of Mexico, c. 1540s

This Aztec account, one of several written by native priests and wise men of the encounter between the Spanish and the Indians of Mexico, was written some years after the events described. Spanish Christian monks helped a postconquest generation of Aztec Nahuatl* speakers translate the illustrated manuscripts of the conquest period. According to this account, how did Montezuma respond to Cortés?

*nah WAH tuhl

Source: *The Broken Spears: The Aztec Account of the Conquest of Mexico*, ed. Miguel Leon-Portilla (Boston: Beacon Press, 1990), 64–76.

Was Montezuma's attitude toward the Spanish shared by other Aztecs? How reliable is this account, do you think, in describing Montezuma's thoughts, motives, and behavior?

THINKING HISTORICALLY

How does the Aztec account of the conquest differ from that of the Spanish, written by Díaz? Is this difference merely a matter of perspective, or do the authors disagree about what happened? To the extent to which there are differences, how do you decide which account to believe and accept?

Speeches of Motecuhzoma and Cortes

When Motecuhzoma[1] had given necklaces to each one, Cortes asked him: "Are you Motecuhzoma? Are you the king? Is it true that you are the king Motecuhzoma?"

And the king said: "Yes, I am Motecuhzoma." Then he stood up to welcome Cortes; he came forward, bowed his head low and addressed him in these words: "Our lord, you are weary. The journey has tired you, but now you have arrived on the earth. You have come to your city, Mexico. You have come here to sit on your throne, to sit under its canopy.

"The kings who have gone before, your representatives, guarded it and preserved it for your coming. The kings Itzcoatl, Motecuhzoma the Elder, Axayacatl, Tizoc, and Ahuitzol ruled for you in the City of Mexico. The people were protected by their swords and sheltered by their shields.

"Do the kings know the destiny of those they left behind, their posterity? If only they are watching! If only they can see what I see!

"No, it is not a dream. I am not walking in my sleep. I am not seeing you in my dreams. . . . I have seen you at last! I have met you face to face! I was in agony for five days, for ten days, with my eyes fixed on the Region of the Mystery. And now you have come out of the clouds and mists to sit on your throne again.

"This was foretold by the kings who governed your city, and now it has taken place. You have come back to us; you have come down from the sky. Rest now, and take possession of your royal houses. Welcome to your land, my lords!"

When Motecuhzoma had finished, La Malinche translated his address into Spanish so that the Captain could understand it. Cortes replied in his strange and savage tongue, speaking first to La Malinche: "Tell

---

[1] Montezuma (earlier spelling). [Ed.]

Motecuhzoma that we are his friends. There is nothing to fear. We have wanted to see him for a long time, and now we have seen his face and heard his words. Tell him that we love him well and that our hearts are contented."

Then he said to Motecuhzoma: "We have come to your house in Mexico as friends. There is nothing to fear."

La Malinche translated this speech and the Spaniards grasped Motecuhzoma's hands and patted his back to show their affection for him.

Attitudes of the Spaniards and the Native Lords

The Spaniards examined everything they saw. They dismounted from their horses, and mounted them again, and dismounted again, so as not to miss anything of interest.

The chiefs who accompanied Motecuhzoma were: Cacama, king of Tezcoco; Tetlepanquetzaltzin, king of Tlacopan; Itzcuauhtzin the Tlacochcalcatl, lord of Tlatelolco; and Topantemoc, Motecuhzoma's treasurer in Tlatelolco. These four chiefs were standing in a file.

The other princes were: Atlixcatzin [chief who has taken captives];[2] Tepeoatzin, the Tlacochcalcatl; Quetzalaztatzin, the keeper of the chalk; Totomotzin; Hecateupatiltzin; and Cuappiatzin.

When Motecuhzoma was imprisoned, they all went into hiding. They ran away to hide and treacherously abandoned him!

The Spaniards Take Possession of the City

When the Spaniards entered the Royal House, they placed Motecuhzoma under guard and kept him under their vigilance. They also placed a guard over Itzcuauhtzin, but the other lords were permitted to depart.

Then the Spaniards fired one of their cannons, and this caused great confusion in the city. The people scattered in every direction; they fled without rhyme or reason; they ran off as if they were being pursued. It was as if they had eaten the mushrooms that confuse the mind, or had seen some dreadful apparition. They were all overcome by terror, as if their hearts had fainted. And when night fell, the panic spread through the city and their fears would not let them sleep.

In the morning the Spaniards told Motecuhzoma what they needed in the way of supplies: tortillas, fried chickens, hens' eggs, pure water, firewood, and charcoal. Also: large, clean cooking pots, water jars, pitchers, dishes, and other pottery. Motecuhzoma ordered that it be sent to them.

[2] Military title given to a warrior who had captured four enemies.

The chiefs who received this order were angry with the king and no longer revered or respected him. But they furnished the Spaniards with all the provisions they needed—food, beverages, and water, and fodder for the horses.

The Spaniards Reveal Their Greed

When the Spaniards were installed in the palace, they asked Motecuhzoma about the city's resources and reserves and about the warriors' ensigns and shields. They questioned him closely and then demanded gold.

Motecuhzoma guided them to it. They surrounded him and crowded close with their weapons. He walked in the center, while they formed a circle around him.

When they arrived at the treasure house called Teucalco, the riches of gold and feathers were brought out to them: ornaments made of quetzal feathers, richly worked shields, disks of gold, the necklaces of the idols, gold nose plugs, gold greaves,[3] and bracelets and crowns.

The Spaniards immediately stripped the feathers from the gold shields and ensigns. They gathered all the gold into a great mound and set fire to everything else, regardless of its value. Then they melted down the gold into ingots. As for the precious green stones, they took only the best of them; the rest were snatched up by the Tlaxcaltecas. The Spaniards searched through the whole treasure house, questioning and quarreling, and seized every object they thought was beautiful.

The Seizure of Motecuhzoma's Treasures

Next they went to Motecuhzoma's storehouse, in the place called Totocalco [Place of the Palace of the Birds],[4] where his personal treasures were kept. The Spaniards grinned like little beasts and patted each other with delight.

When they entered the hall of treasures, it was as if they had arrived in Paradise. They searched everywhere and coveted everything; they were slaves to their own greed. All of Motecuhzoma's possessions were brought out: fine bracelets, necklaces with large stones, ankle rings with little gold bells, the royal crowns, and all the royal finery—everything that belonged to the king and was reserved to him only. They seized these treasures as if they were their own, as if this plunder were merely a stroke of good luck. And when they had taken all the gold, they heaped up everything else in the middle of the patio.

[3] Leg armour. [Ed.]
[4] The zoological garden attached to the royal palaces.

La Malinche called the nobles together. She climbed up to the palace roof and cried: "Mexicanos, come forward! The Spaniards need your help! Bring them food and pure water. They are tired and hungry; they are almost fainting from exhaustion! Why do you not come forward? Are you angry with them?"

The Mexicans were too frightened to approach. They were crushed by terror and would not risk coming forward. They shied away as if the Spaniards were wild beasts, as if the hour were midnight on the blackest night of the year. Yet they did not abandon the Spaniards to hunger and thirst. They brought them whatever they needed, but shook with fear as they did so. They delivered the supplies to the Spaniards with trembling hands, then turned and hurried away.

The Preparations for the Fiesta

The Aztecs begged permission of their king to hold the fiesta of Huitzilopochtli.[5] The Spaniards wanted to see this fiesta to learn how it was celebrated. A delegation of the celebrants came to the palace where Motecuhzoma was a prisoner, and when their spokesman asked his permission, he granted it to them.

As soon as the delegation returned, the women began to grind seeds of the *chicalote*.[6] These women had fasted for a whole year. They ground the seeds in the patio of the temple.

The Spaniards came out of the palace together, dressed in armor and carrying their weapons with them. They stalked among the women and looked at them one by one; they stared into the faces of the women who were grinding seeds. After this cold inspection, they went back into the palace. It is said that they planned to kill the celebrants if the men entered the patio.

The Statue of Huitzilopochtli

On the evening before the fiesta of Toxcatl, the celebrants began to model a statue of Huitzilopochtli. They gave it such a human appearance that it seemed the body of a living man. Yet they made the statue with nothing but a paste made of the ground seeds of the chicalote, which they shaped over an armature of sticks.

When the statue was finished, they dressed it in rich feathers, and they painted crossbars over and under its eyes. They also clipped on its earrings of turquoise mosaic; these were in the shape of serpents, with

[5] Aztec war-god. [Ed.]
[6] Edible plants also used in medicines. [Ed.]

gold rings hanging from them. Its nose plug, in the shape of an arrow, was made of gold and was inlaid with fine stones.

They placed the magic headdress of hummingbird feathers on its head. They also adorned it with an *anecuyotl*, which was a belt made of feathers, with a cone at the back. Then they hung around its neck an ornament of yellow parrot feathers, fringed like the locks of a young boy. Over this they put its nettle-leaf cape, which was painted black and decorated with five clusters of eagle feathers.

Next they wrapped it in its cloak, which was painted with skull and bones, and over this they fastened its vest. The vest was painted with dismembered human parts: skulls, ears, hearts, intestines, torsos, breasts, hands, and feet. They also put on its *maxtlatl*, or loincloth, which was decorated with images of dissevered limbs and fringed with amate paper. This *maxtlatl* was painted with vertical stripes of bright blue.

They fastened a red paper flag at its shoulder and placed on its head what looked like a sacrificial flint knife. This too was made of red paper; it seemed to have been steeped in blood.

The statue carried a *tehuehuelli*, a bamboo shield decorated with four clusters of fine eagle feathers. The pendant of this shield was blood-red, like the knife and the shoulder flag. The statue also carried four arrows.

Finally, they put the wristbands on its arms. These bands, made of coyote skin, were fringed with paper cut into little strips.

The Beginning of the Fiesta

Early the next morning, the statue's face was uncovered by those who had been chosen for that ceremony. They gathered in front of the idol in single file and offered it gifts of food, such as round seedcakes or perhaps human flesh. But they did not carry it up to its temple on top of the pyramid.

All the young warriors were eager for the fiesta to begin. They had sworn to dance and sing with all their hearts, so that the Spaniards would marvel at the beauty of the rituals.

The procession began, and the celebrants filed into the temple patio to dance the Dance of the Serpent. When they were all together in the patio, the songs and the dance began. Those who had fasted for twenty days and those who had fasted for a year were in command of the others; they kept the dancers in file with their pine wands. (If anyone wished to urinate, he did not stop dancing, but simply opened his clothing at the hips and separated his clusters of heron feathers.)

If anyone disobeyed the leaders or was not in his proper place they struck him on the hips and shoulders. Then they drove him out of the patio, beating him and shoving him from behind. They pushed him so hard that he sprawled to the ground, and they dragged him outside by the ears. No one dared to say a word about this punishment, for those who had fasted during the year were feared and venerated; they had earned the exclusive title "Brothers of Huitzilopochtli."

The great captains, the bravest warriors, danced at the head of the files to guide the others. The youths followed at a slight distance. Some of the youths wore their hair gathered into large locks, a sign that they had never taken any captives. Others carried their headdresses on their shoulders; they had taken captives, but only with help.

Then came the recruits, who were called "the young warriors." They had each captured an enemy or two. The others called to them: "Come, comrades, show us how brave you are! Dance with all your hearts!"

The Spaniards Attack the Celebrants

At this moment in the fiesta, when the dance was loveliest and when song was linked to song, the Spaniards were seized with an urge to kill the celebrants. They all ran forward, armed as if for battle. They closed the entrances and passageways, all the gates of the patio: the Eagle Gate in the lesser palace, the Gate of the Canestalk and the Gate of the Serpent of Mirrors. They posted guards so that no one could escape, and then rushed into the Sacred Patio to slaughter the celebrants. They came on foot, carrying their swords and their wooden or metal shields.

They ran in among the dancers, forcing their way to the place where the drums were played. They attacked the man who was drumming and cut off his arms. Then they cut off his head, and it rolled across the floor.

They attacked all the celebrants, stabbing them, spearing them, striking them with their swords. They attacked some of them from behind, and these fell instantly to the ground with their entrails hanging out. Others they beheaded: they cut off their heads, or split their heads to pieces.

They struck others in the shoulders, and their arms were torn from their bodies. They wounded some in the thigh and some in the calf.

They slashed others in the abdomen, and their entrails all spilled to the ground. Some attempted to run away, but their intestines dragged as they ran; they seemed to tangle their feet in their own entrails. No matter how they tried to save themselves, they could find no escape.

Some attempted to force their way out, but the Spaniards murdered them at the gates. Others climbed the walls, but they could not save themselves. Those who ran into the communal houses were safe there for a while; so were those who lay down among the victims and pretended to be dead. But if they stood up again, the Spaniards saw them and killed them.

The blood of the warriors flowed like water and gathered into pools. The pools widened, and the stench of blood and entrails filled the air. The Spaniards ran into the communal houses to kill those who were hiding. They ran everywhere and searched everywhere; they invaded every room, hunting and killing.

3

European Views of Native Americans,
Sixteenth and Seventeenth Centuries

Many Europeans harbored fantastical and negative notions about the inhabitants of the "New World," envisioning them as wild and cannibalistic, savage and ruthless toward their enemies. Reinforcing this impression were images that circulated throughout Europe during the sixteenth and seventeenth centuries, such as this engraving from 1564, part of a series by Flemish engraver Theodore de Bry, based on paintings by an artist who had accompanied a French expedition to Florida a few decades earlier. Figure 16.1 shows the alleged cannibalistic practices by natives supposedly witnessed by the explorers. What is going on in this picture? It is likely that de Bry made adjustments to his engravings from the originals to please potential buyers. If so, what does this tell us about the expectations of European audiences about the Americas and their inhabitants?

Figure 16.1   Cannibalism, engraving by Theodore de Bry.

Source: Service Historique de la Marine, Vincennes, France / Bridgeman Images.

Almost seventy-five years later, a very different set of no less remarkable images emerged from a Dutch colony in northeastern Brazil. Count Johan Maurits, the humanist governor general of the colony from 1636 to 1644, brought several artists and scientists with him to observe and record the region's flora and fauna as well as its inhabitants. He commissioned from artist Albert Eckhout a number of still-lifes and group and individual portraits, including one showing a female Tapuya Indian (see Figure 16.2). According to Dutch accounts,

Figure 16.2   Tapuya Indian, by Albert Eckhout.
Source: Granger, NYC.

the Tapuya were more warlike and less "civilized" than some of the other local peoples—for example, they sometimes consumed their dead instead of burying them. Aside from the body parts this woman carries in her hand and in her bag, what other signs of this warlike tendency do you see in Figure 16.2? Look closely at the many interesting details in this painting. What does the artist seem to be interested in showing?

THINKING HISTORICALLY

What are the differences in style and content between Figures 16.1 and 16.2, and how do you account for them? Which of the following factors do you think is most important in explaining their differences: chronology, agenda of the artist, the potential audience for the image, the setting in which they were produced? What might be the pitfalls for students of history in comparing these two images? Consider how women are depicted in these works. What differences and similarities do you see? What might that tell us about European notions of women and gender in the New World?

4

NZINGA MBEMBA

Appeal to the King of Portugal, 1526

Although Europeans conquered the Americas beginning in the fifteenth century, they were unable to conquer the African continent until the nineteenth and twentieth centuries. Rivers that fell steeply to the sea, military defenses, and diseases like malaria proved insurmountable to Europeans before the age of the steamship, the machine gun, and antimalarial quinine. Before the last half of the nineteenth century, Europeans had to be content with alliances with African kings and rulers. The Portuguese had been the first to meet Africans in the towns and villages along the Atlantic coast, and they became the first European missionaries and trading partners.

Nzinga Mbemba, whose Christian name was Affonso, was king of the West African state of Congo (comprising what is today parts of Angola as well as the two Congo states) from about 1506 to 1543. He succeeded his father, King Nzinga, a Kuwu who, shortly after his first contact with the Portuguese in 1483, sent officials to Lisbon to learn European ways. In 1491 father and son were baptized, and

Source: Basil Davidson, *The African Past* (Boston: Little, Brown, and Company, 1964), 191–94.

Portuguese priests, merchants, artisans, and soldiers were provided with a coastal settlement.

What exactly is the complaint of the king of Congo? What seems to be the impact of Portuguese traders (called "factors") in the Congo? What does King Affonso want the king of Portugal to do?

THINKING HISTORICALLY

This selection offers an opportunity to compare European expansion in the Americas and Africa. Portuguese contact with Nzinga Mbemba of the Congo was roughly contemporaneous with Spanish colonialism in the Americas. What differences do you see between these two cases of early European expansion? Can you think of any reasons that Congo kings converted to Christianity whereas Mexican kings did not?

Compare the Europeans' treatment of Africans with their treatment of Native Americans. Why did Europeans enslave Africans and not, for the most part, American Indians?

Sir, Your Highness [of Portugal] should know how our Kingdom is being lost in so many ways that it is convenient to provide for the necessary remedy, since this is caused by the excessive freedom given by your factors and officials to the men and merchants who are allowed to come to this Kingdom to set up shops with goods and many things which have been prohibited by us, and which they spread throughout our Kingdoms and Domains in such an abundance that many of our vassals, whom we had in obedience, do not comply because they have the things in greater abundance than we ourselves; and it was with these things that we had them content and subjected under our vassalage and jurisdiction, so it is doing a great harm not only to the service of God, but to the security and peace of our Kingdoms and State as well.

And we cannot reckon how great the damage is, since the mentioned merchants are taking every day our natives, sons of the land and the sons of our noblemen and vassals and our relatives, because the thieves and men of bad conscience grab them wishing to have the things and wares of this Kingdom which they are ambitious of; they grab them and get them to be sold; and so great, Sir, is the corruption and licentiousness that our country is being completely depopulated, and Your Highness should not agree with this nor accept it as in your service. And to avoid it we need from those [your] Kingdoms no more than some priests and a few people to teach in schools, and no other goods except wine and flour for the holy sacrament. That is why we beg of Your Highness to help and assist us in this matter, commanding your factors that they should not send here either merchants or wares, because it is *our will that in these Kingdoms there should not be any trade of slaves nor outlet for them.*[1] Concerning what is referred above, again we beg of Your Highness to agree with it, since otherwise we cannot remedy such an obvious damage. Pray Our Lord in His mercy to have Your Highness under His guard and let you do for ever the things of His service. I kiss your hands many times.

> At our town of Congo, written on the sixth day of July.
> João Teixeira did it in 1526.
> The King. Dom Affonso.
> [On the back of this letter the following can be read:
> To the most powerful and excellent prince Dom João, King our Brother.]

Moreover, Sir, in our Kingdoms there is another great inconvenience which is of little service to God, and this is that many of our people [*naturaes*], keenly desirous as they are of the wares and things of your Kingdoms, which are brought here by your people, and in order to satisfy their voracious appetite, seize many of our people, freed and exempt men; and very often it happens that they kidnap even noblemen and the sons of noblemen, and our relatives, and take them to be sold to the white men who are in our Kingdoms; and for this purpose they have concealed them; and others are brought during the night so that they might not be recognized.

And as soon as they are taken by the white men they are immediately ironed and branded with fire, and when they are carried to be embarked, if they are caught by our guards' men the whites allege that they have bought them but they cannot say from whom, so that it is our duty to do justice and to restore to the freemen their freedom, but it cannot be done if your subjects feel offended, as they claim to be.

And to avoid such a great evil we passed a law so that any white man living in our Kingdoms and wanting to purchase goods in any way should first inform three of our noblemen and officials of our court whom we rely upon in this matter, and these are Dom Pedro Manipanza and Dom Manuel Manissaba, our chief usher, and Gonçalo Pires our chief freighter, who should investigate if the mentioned goods are captives or free men, and if cleared by them there will be no further doubt nor embargo for them to be taken and embarked. But if the white men do not comply with it they will lose the aforementioned goods. And if we do them this favor and concession it is for the part Your Highness has in it, since we know that it is in your service too that these goods are taken from our Kingdom, otherwise we should not consent to this. . . .

Sir, Your Highness has been kind enough to write to us saying that we should ask in our letters for anything we need, and that we shall be

---

[1] Emphasis in the original.

provided with everything, and as the peace and the health of our Kingdom depend on us, and as there are among us old folks and people who
have lived for many days, it happens that we have continuously many
and different diseases which put us very often in such a weakness that
we reach almost the last extreme; and the same happens to our children,
relatives, and natives owing to the lack in this country of physicians and
surgeons who might know how to cure properly such diseases. And as
we have got neither dispensaries nor drugs which might help us in this
forlornness, many of those who had been already confirmed and
instructed in the holy faith of Our Lord Jesus Christ perish and die;
and the rest of the people in their majority cure themselves with herbs
and breads and other ancient methods, so that they put all their faith
in the mentioned herbs and ceremonies if they live, and believe that
they are saved if they die; and this is not much in the service of God.

And to avoid such a great error and inconvenience, since it is from
God in the first place and then from your Kingdoms and from Your
Highness that all the goods and drugs and medicines have come to save
us, we beg of you to be agreeable and kind enough to send us two physicians and two apothecaries and one surgeon, so that they may come with
their drug-stores and all the necessary things to stay in our kingdoms,
because we are in extreme need of them all and each of them. We shall
do them all good and shall benefit them by all means, since they are sent
by Your Highness, whom we thank for your work in their coming. We
beg of Your Highness as a great favor to do this for us, because besides
being good in itself it is in the service of God as we have said above.

5

CAPTAIN THOMAS PHILLIPS

Buying Slaves in 1693

Phillips, the captain of the English ship *Hannibal*, arrived at the
African port of Ouidah (Whydah) in what is today Benin to purchase
slaves for transport and sale in the West Indian islands of St. Thomas
and Barbados. From this part of his journal, we can see that the
captain is well versed in the procedures for buying slaves on the African
coast. What sorts of preparations has he made for the purchase?

Source: Capt. Thomas Phillips' Journal, in *Churchill's Collection of Voyages*, vol. 6, London,
1746. Reprinted in George Francis Dow, *Slave Ships and Slaving*, originally published by the
Marine Research Society, Salem, MA, 1927. Reprinted by Dover Press, 2002, 58–64.

How does he go about making the purchase? What does this selection tell you about the African slave trade?

THINKING HISTORICALLY

The circumstances by which Europeans encountered Africans were clearly different from those by which they encountered Native Americans. What are these differences, and how do they account for differences in their attitudes toward Africans and Indians?

This day got our canoos and all things else ready, in order to go ashore to-morrow to purchase our slaves.

May the 21st. This morning I went ashore at Whidaw, accompany'd by my doctor and purser, Mr. Clay, the present captain of the *East India Merchant*, his doctor and purser, and about a dozen of our seamen for our guard, arm'd, in order here to reside till we could purchase 1300 negro slaves, which was the number we both wanted, to compleat 700 for the *Hannibal*, and 650 for the *East India Merchant*, according to our agreement in our charter-parties with the Royal African Company; in procuring which quantity of slaves we spent about nine weeks, during which time what observations my indisposition with convulsions in my head, &c. would permit me to make on this country, its trade, manners, &c. are as follows, viz. . . .

Our factory, built by Captain Wiburne, Sir John Wiburne's brother, stands low near the marshes, which renders it a very unhealthy place to live in; the white men the African Company send there, seldom returning to tell their tale; 'tis compass'd round with a mud wall, about six foot high, and on the south-side is the gate; within is a large yard, a mud thatch'd house, where the factor[1] lives, with the white men; also a store-house, a trunk for slaves, and a place where they bury their dead white men, call'd, very improperly, the hog-yard; there is also a good forge, and some other small houses: To the east are two small flankers of mud, with a few popguns and harquebusses,[2] which serve more to terrify the poor ignorant negroes than to do any execution. . . .

This factory, feared as 'tis, proved very beneficial to us, by housing our goods which came ashore late, and could not arrive at the king's town where I kept my warehouse, ere it was dark, when they would be very incident to be pilfer'd by the negro porters which carry them, at which they are most exquisite; for in the day-time they would steal the cowries,[3] altho' our white

[1] Manager or agent. [Ed.]
[2] Firearms with a long barrel and a cord to ignite powder. [Ed.]
[3] Shells used as currency. [Ed.]

men that attended the goods from the marine watched them, they having instruments like wedges, made on purpose to force asunder the staves of the barrels, that contain'd the cowries, whereby the shells dropt out; and when any of our seamen that watch'd the goods came near such porters, they would take out their machine, and the staves would insensibly close again, so that no hole did appear, having always their wives and children running by them to carry off the plunder; which with all our threats and complaints made to the king, we could not prevent, tho' we often beat them cruelly, and piniar'd some, but it was all one, what was bred in the bone, &c. whatever we could do would not make them forbear.

The factory prov'd beneficial to us in another kind; for after we had procured a parcel of slaves, and sent them down to the sea-side to be carry'd off, it sometimes proved bad weather, and so great a sea, that the canoos could not come ashore to fetch them, so that they returned to the factory, where they were secured and provided for till good weather presented, and then were near to embrace the opportunity, we some-times shipping off a hundred of both sexes at a time.

We had our cook ashore, and eat as well as we could, provisions being plenty and cheap; but we soon lost our stomachs by sickness, most of my men having fevers, and myself such convulsions and aches in my head, that I could hardly stand or go to the trunk without assistance, and there often fainted with the horrid stink of the negroes, it being an old house where all the slaves are kept together, and evacuate nature where they lie, so that no jakes[4] can stink worse; there being forced to sit three or four hours at a time, quite ruin'd my health, but there was no help.

When we were at the trunk, the king's slaves, if he had any, were the first offer'd to sale, which the cappasheirs[5] would be very urgent with us to buy, and would in a manner force us to it ere they would shew us any other, saying they were the Reys Cosa,[6] and we must not refuse them, tho' as I observed they were generally the worst slaves in the trunk, and we paid more for them than any others, which we could not remedy, it being one of his majesty's prerogatives. Then the cappasheirs each brought out his slaves according to his degree and quality, the greatest first, &c. and our surgeon examined them well in all kinds, to see that they were sound wind and limb, making them jump, stretch out their arms swiftly, looking in their mouths to judge of their age; for the cappasheirs are so cunning, that they shave them all close before we see them, so that let them be never so old we can see no grey hairs in their heads or beards; and then having liquor'd them well and sleeked with palm oil, 'tis no easy matter to know an old one from a middle-aged one, but by the teeths decay. But our greatest care of all is to buy none that are pox'd, lest they should infect the rest aboard; for

---

[4] British slang for a latrine. [Ed.]
[5] Slave handlers appointed by the African king. [Ed.]
[6] The African king's special slaves. [Ed.]

tho' we separate the men and women aboard by partitions and bulk-heads, to prevent quarrels and wranglings among them, yet do what we can they will come together, and that distemper which they call the yaws, is very common here, and discovers itself by almost the same symptoms as the *Lues Venerea*[7] or clap does with us; therefore our surgeon is forc'd to examine the privities of both men and women with the nicest scrutiny, which is a great slavery, but what can't be omitted. When we had selected from the rest such as we liked, we agreed in what goods to pay for them, the prices being already stated before the king, how much of each sort of merchandize we were to give for a man, woman, and child, which gave us much ease, and saved abundance of disputes and wranglings, and gave the owner a note, signifying our agreement of the sorts of goods; upon delivery of which the next day he receiv'd them; then we mark'd the slaves we had bought in the breast, or shoulder, with a hot iron, having the letter of the ship's name on it, the place being before anointed with a little palm oil, which caused but little pain, the mark being usually well in four or five days, appearing very plain and white after.

When we had purchased to the number of 50 or 60, we would send them aboard, there being a cappasheir, intitled the captain of the slaves, whose care it was to secure them to the waterside, and see them all off; and if in carrying to the marine any were lost, he was bound to make them good to us, the captain of the trunk being oblig'd to do the like, if any run away while under his care, for after we buy them we give him charge of them till the captain of the slaves comes to carry them away: There are two officers appointed by the king for this purpose, to each of which every ship pays the value of a slave in what goods they like best for their trouble, when they have done trading. . . .

There is likewise a captain of the sand, who is appointed to take care of the merchandise we have come ashore to trade with, that the negroes do not plunder them. . . .

When our slaves were come to the sea-side, our canoos were ready to carry them off to the longboat, if the sea permitted, and he convey'd them aboard ship, where the men were all put in irons, two and two shackl'd together, to prevent their mutiny, or swimming ashore.

The negroes are so wilful and loth to leave their own country, that they have often leap'd out of the canoos, boat and ship, into the sea, and kept under water till they were drowned, to avoid being taken up and saved by our boats, which pursued them; they having a more dreadful apprehension of Barbadoes than we can have of hell, tho' in reality they live much better there than in their own country; but home is home, &c. . . . We had about 12 negroes did wilfully drown themselves, and others starv'd themselves to death; for 'tis their belief that when they die they return home to their own country and friends again.

[7] Venereal disease (STD). [Ed.]

The best goods to purchase slaves here are cowries, the smaller the more esteemed; for they pay them all by tale, the smallest being as valuable as the biggest, but take them from us by measure or weight, of which about 100 pounds for a good man-slave. The next in demand are brass neptunes or basons, very large, thin, and flat; for after they have bought them they cut them in pieces to make anilias or bracelets, and collars for their arms, legs and necks. The other preferable goods are blue paper sletias, cambricks or lawns, caddy chints, broad ditto, coral, large, smooth, and of a deep red, rangoes large and red, iron bars, powder and brandy.[8]

With the above goods a ship cannot want slaves here, and may purchase them for about three pounds fifteen shillings a head, but near half the cargo value must be cowries or booges, and brass basons, to set off the other goods that we buy cheaper, as coral, rangoes, iron, &c. else they will not take them; for if a cappasheir sells five slaves, he will have two of them paid for in cowries, and one in brass, which are dear slaves; for a slave in cowries costs us above four pounds in England; whereas a slave in coral, rangoes, or iron, does not cost fifty shillings; but without the cowries and brass they will take none of the last goods, and but small quantities at best, especially, if they can discover that you have good store of cowries and brass aboard . . . therefore every man that comes here, ought to be very cautious in making his report to the king at first, of what sorts and quantities of goods he has, and be sure to say his cargo consists mostly in iron, coral, rangoes, chints, &c. so that he may dispose of those goods as soon as he can. . . .

[8] Sletias were cloths, also called silesias, after their probable origin; cambricks were fine white linens from Cambray, Flanders; chints referred to chintz, an Indian cotton with brightly colored design, usually flowers; broad referred to broad cloths; lawns were linens from Laorn, France; rangoes were beads. [Ed.]

6

J. B. ROMAIGNE

Journal of a Slave Ship Voyage, 1819

The French slave ship *Le Rodeur* sailed from the Guinea coast of Africa to the French Caribbean island of Guadeloupe in April, 1819. The ship carried twenty-two crewmen and a cargo of 160 African slaves.

Source: Capt. Ernest H. Pentecost, RNR, "Introduction" to George Francis Dow, *Slave Ships and Slaving*, originally published by the Marine Research Society, Salem, MA, 1927. Reprinted by Dover Press, 2002, xxvii–xxxv.

J. B. Romaigne, the twelve-year-old son of a Guadeloupe planter, was a passenger under the special care of the captain. This is his journal of the voyage, written for his mother. What happened on that voyage? How were the slaves treated? What does this account tell you about the transatlantic slave trade?

THINKING HISTORICALLY

Both this and the previous selection are taken from journals, or diaries. What unique characteristics and common elements of diaries should enhance their reliability for the historian? Is the journal of a twelve-year-old likely to be more or less reliable than that of a sea captain like Phillips? What aspects of this document make it seem more, or less, reliable to you?

I

"It is now just a week since we sailed; but, indeed, it is not my fault that I have not sooner sat down to write. The first two days I was sick, and the other five were so stormy that I could not sit at the table without holding. Even now we are rolling like a great porpoise yet I can sit very well and keep the pen steady. Since I am to send you what I do without copying it over again at the end of the voyage, I shall take what pains I can; but I hope, my dear mother, you will consider that my fingers are grown hard and tarry with hauling all day on the ropes, the Captain being determined, as he says, to make me a sailor. The Captain is very fond of me and is very good-tempered; he drinks a great deal of brandy; he is a fine, handsome man and I am sure I shall like him very much.

II

"I enquired of the Captain today, how long it would be before we should get to Guadaloupe; and he told me we had a great distance to go before we should steer that way at all. He asked how I should like to have a little black slave and I said very well; that I was to have plenty of them at Guadaloupe. He asked me what I could do with them. 'Feed them,' I said. 'That is right,' said the Captain; 'it will make them strong. But you will make them work won't you?' added he. 'Yes, to be sure,' said I. 'Then I can tell you you must flog them as well as feed them.' 'I will,' said I, 'it is what I intend, but I must not hurt them very much.' 'Of course not maim them,' returned he, 'for then they could not work; but if you do not make them feel to the marrow, you might as well throw them into the sea.'

III

"Since we have been at this place, Bonny Town in the Bonny river, on the coast of Africa, I have become more accustomed to the howling of these negroes. At first, it alarmed me, and I could not sleep. The Captain says that if they behave well they will be much better off at Guadaloupe; and I am sure, I wish the ignorant creatures would come quietly and have it over. Today, one of the blacks whom they were forcing into the hold, suddenly knocked down a sailor and attempted to leap overboard. He was caught, however, by the leg by another of the crew, and the sailor, rising up in a passion, hamstrung him with a cutlass. The Captain, seeing this, knocked the butcher flat upon the deck with a handspike. 'I will teach you to keep your temper,' said he, with an oath. 'He was the best slave in the lot.' I ran to the main chains and looked over; for they had dropped the black into the sea when they saw that he was useless. He continued to swim, even after he had sunk under water, for I saw the red track extending shoreward; but by and by, it stopped, widened, faded, and I saw it no more.

IV

"We are now fairly at sea again, and I am sure my dear Mother, I am heartily glad of it. The Captain is in the best temper in the world; he walks the deck, rubbing his hands and humming a tune. He says he has six dozen slaves on board, men, women and children, and all in prime marketable condition. I have not seen them, however, since we set sail. Their cries are so terrible that I do not like to go and look down into the hold. . . .

V

"Today, word was brought to the Captain, while we were at breakfast, that two of the slaves were dead, suffocated, as was supposed, by the closeness of the hold; and he immediately ordered the rest should be brought up, gang by gang, to the forecastle, to give them air. I ran up on deck to see them. They did not appear to me to be very unwell; but these blacks, who are not distinguished from one another by dress, are so much alike one can hardly tell.

"However, they had no sooner reached the ship's side, than first one, then another, then a third, sprang up on the gunwale, and darted into the sea, before the astonished sailors could tell what they were about. Many more made the attempt, but without success; they were all knocked flat to the deck, and the crew kept watch over them with handspikes and cutlasses till the Captain's pleasure should be known with regard to the revolt.

"The negroes, in the meantime, who had got off, continued dancing about among the waves, yelling with all their might, what seemed to me a song of triumph, in the burden of which they were joined by some of their companions on deck. Our ship speedily left the ignorant creatures behind; their voices came fainter and fainter upon the wind; the black head, first of one, then of another, disappeared; and then the sea was without a spot; and the air without a sound.

"When the Captain came up on deck, having finished his breakfast, and was told of the revolt, his face grew pale, and he gnashed his teeth. 'We must make an example,' said he, 'or our labour will be lost.' He then ordered the whole of the slaves in the ship to be tied together in gangs and placed upon the forecastle, and having selected six, who were known to have joined in the chorus of the revolters and might thus be considered as the ringleaders, he caused three of them to be shot, and the other three hanged, before the eyes of their comrades. . . .

VII

"The negroes, ever since the revolt, were confined closely to the lower hold and this brought on a disease called ophthalmia, which produced blindness. The sailors, who sling down the provisions from the upper hold, report that the disease is spreading frightfully and today, at dinner, the Captain and the surgeon held a conference on the subject. The surgeon declared that, from all he could learn, the cases were already so numerous as to be beyond his management; but the Captain insisted that every slave cured was worth his value and that it was better to lose a part than all. The disease, it seems, although generally fatal to the negro, is not always so. The patient is at first blind; but some escape, eventually, with the loss of one eye or a mere dimness of vision. The result of the conversation was, that the infected slaves were to be transferred to the upper hold and attended by the surgeon the same as if they were white men.

VIII

"All the slaves and some of the crew are blind. The Captain, the surgeon, and the mate are blind. There is hardly enough men left, out of our twenty-two, to work the ship. The Captain preserves what order he can and the surgeon still attempts to do his duty, but our situation is frightful.

IX

"All the crew are now blind but one man. The rest work under his orders like unconscious machines; the Captain standing by with a thick rope, which he sometimes applies, when led to any recreant by the man who can see. My own eyes begin to be affected; in a little while, I shall see nothing but death. I asked the Captain if he would not allow the blacks to come up on deck. He said it was of no use; that the crew, who were always on deck, were as blind as they; that if brought up, they would only drown themselves, whereas, if they remained where they were, there would, in all probability, be at least a portion of them salable, if we had ever the good fortune to reach Guadaloupe. . . .

X

"Mother, your son was blind for ten days, although now so well as to be able to write. I can tell you hardly anything of our history during that period. Each of us lived in a little dark world of his own, peopled by shadows and phantasms. . . .

"Then there came a storm. No hand was upon the helm, not a reef upon the sails. On we flew like a phantom ship of old, that cared not for wind or weather, our masts straining and cracking; . . . the furious sea one moment devouring us up, stem and stern, and the next casting us forth again, as if with loathing and disgust. . . . The wind, at last, died moaningly away, and we found ourselves rocking, without progressive motion, on the sullen deep. We at length heard a sound upon the waters, unlike that of the smooth swell which remained after the storm, and our hearts beat with a hope which was painful from its suddenness and intensity. We held our breath. The sound was continued; it was like the splashing of a heavy body in smooth water; and a simultaneous cry arose from every lip on deck and was echoed by the men in their hammocks below and by the slaves in the hold. . . .

"The Captain was the first to recover his self-possession, and our voices sank into silence when we heard him speak the approaching vessel with the usual challenge.

"'Ship Ahoy! Ahoy! What ship?'

"'The *Saint Leon* of Spain. Help us for God's sake!'

"'We want help ourselves,' replied our Captain.

"'We are dying of hunger and thirst. Send us on board some provisions and a few hands to work the ship and name your own terms.'

"'We can give you food, but we are in want of hands. Come on board of us and we will exchange provisions with you for men,' answered our Captain.

"'Dollars! dollars! We will pay you in money, a thousand fold; but we cannot send. We have negroes on board; they have infected us with ophthalmia, and we are all stone-blind.'

"At the announcement of this horrible coincidence, there was a silence among us, for some moments, like that of death. It was broken by a fit of laughter, in which I joined myself; and, before our awful merriment was over, we could hear, by the sound of the curses which the Spaniards shouted against us, that the *St. Leon* had drifted away.

"This vessel, in all probability, foundered at sea, as she never reached any port.

<h2 style="text-align:center">XI</h2>

"The man who preserved his sight the longest, recovered the soonest; and to his exertions alone, under the providence of God and the mercy of the blessed saints, is it owing that we are now within a few leagues of Guadaloupe, this twenty-first day of June 1819. I am myself almost well. The surgeon and eleven more are irrecoverably blind; the Captain has lost one eye; four others have met with the same calamity; and five are able to see, though dimly, with both. Among the slaves, thirty-nine are completely blind and the rest blind of one eye or their sight otherwise injured.

"This morning the Captain called all hands on deck, negroes and all. The shores of Guadaloupe were in sight. I thought he was going to return God thanks publicly for our miraculous escape.

"'Are you quite certain,' said the mate, 'that the cargo is insured?'

"'I am,' said the Captain. 'Every slave that is lost must be made good by the underwriters. Besides, would you have me turn my ship into a hospital for the support of blind negroes? They have cost us enough already. Do your duty.'

"The mate picked out thirty-nine negroes who were completely blind, and, with the assistance of the rest of the crew, tied a piece of ballast to the legs of each. The miserable wretches were then thrown into the sea."

7

Images of African-American Slavery,
Eighteenth and Nineteenth Centuries

The visual record of slavery in the Americas is dominated by images rendered by members of the slave-owning societies; few images by slaves themselves exist. Nevertheless, much can be learned about the circumstances of slavery from the illustrations that do exist. Figure 16.3

Figure 16.3 Buying slaves in Africa, late 1700s or early 1800s.
Source: Rue des Archives / Granger, NYC.

shows a sale of slaves in Africa that was not atypical. Who are the slaves? Who is selling them? Who is buying them?

The work and living conditions of slaves varied among countries and slaveholders. Many slaves were put to work on large plantations to help with large-scale production, while others worked in smaller operations or as house servants and were sometimes hired out to work in other locations by their masters. A fortunate few were eventually granted their freedom after years of dedicated labor. Figure 16.4 depicts plantation work in Martinique in the early nineteenth century. Published in a traveler's account of the Americas, the text accompanying this image reads: "The slaves are called to work by the plantation bell at 6 in the morning, each person takes his hoe to the field under the supervision of overseers, either European or Creole; in a single line, they work in unison while chanting some African work song; the overseers occasionally use the whip to increase the work pace; at 11 the bell sounds, they take a meal, then resume their work until 6 in the evening." What does this image tell you that you might not have known about slavery?

Slaves were sold at auction both upon arrival from Africa and sometimes when being sold by their owners. Figure 16.5 illustrates a slave auction in Brazil in the 1830s. Do slaves appear to be in high demand here? What does this image suggest to you about the cost and care of slaves in Brazil? Figure 16.6 offers a contrasting scene from a British

Figure 16.4   Plantation work, Martinique, 1826.

Source: *Voyage pittoresque dans les deux Amériques*, Albert and Shirley Small Special Collections Library, University of Virginia.

Figure 16.5   Slave market, Rio de Janeiro, Brazil, 1830s.

Source: Snark / Art Resource, NY.

Figure 16.6 Slaves awaiting sale, New Orleans, 1861.

Source: Private Collection / Bridgeman Images.

newspaper of slaves awaiting sale in the United States. The article from the *Illustrated London News* reads: "The accompanying engraving represents a gang of Negroes exhibited in the city of New Orleans, previous to an auction, from a sketch made on the spot by our artist. The men and women are well clothed, in their Sunday best—the men in blue cloth . . . with beaver hats; and the women in calico dresses, of more or less brilliancy, with silk bandana handkerchiefs bound round their heads. . . . they stand through a good part of the day, subject to the inspection of the purchasing or non-purchasing passing crowd. . . . An orderly silence is preserved as a general rule at these sales, although conversation does not seem to be altogether prohibited." What does this image suggest to you about slavery in New Orleans in 1861?

THINKING HISTORICALLY

These four images of African slavery in the Americas are selected out of thousands of paintings, engravings, and drawings, almost all done by Europeans who held varying attitudes toward slavery. Even if they accurately depict what the European artist saw at a particular moment in a particular place, we should be careful to avoid making generalizations based on a single image. Nevertheless, often a primary source, written or visual, prompts new questions rather than answers to old ones. What questions occur to you when you view these images?

8

VENTURE SMITH

Life and Adventures, 1798

Most of the approximately twelve million slaves who were taken to the Americas were sent to Brazil and the Caribbean. Only about six and a half percent were taken to British North America. A majority in all three destinations were made to work on plantations, where the production of sugar, cotton, rice, and other agricultural commodities was normally carried out under punishing conditions. Nevertheless, conditions in the lives of slaves in the Americas varied. In certain urban environments like Rio de Janeiro or North American cities, some slaves had relatively more freedom of movement than others. This is the account of one of those slaves.

Venture Smith (c. 1729–1805), born Broteer Furro, oldest child of the first wife of a prince living near Lake Chad (in west-central Africa), was captured and marched to what is today Ghana, where he was sold to a Rhode Island merchant who called him a business "venture" and brought him to Rhode Island.

In this excerpt, Venture Smith looks back at his life both in Connecticut and on Long Island in the 1750s. Our selection comes from *A Narrative of the Life and Adventures of Venture, a Native of Africa, but Resident above Sixty Years in the United States of America, Related by Himself,* published in 1798. How are the experiences of Venture Smith different from what you might expect of a plantation slave? What does this account tell you about how the conditions of slavery varied throughout the Americas?

THINKING HISTORICALLY

Compare this source with that of J. B. Romaigne. What are the differences in the behavior of the slave owners? What might have caused these differences? Which, if any, of the illustrations in the preceding selection brings to mind the experiences described by Venture Smith?

After I had lived with my master thirteen years, being then about twenty two years old, I married Meg, a slave of his who was about my age. My master owned a certain Irishman, named Heddy, who about that time

---

Source: Venture Smith, *A Narrative of the Life and Adventures of Venture, a Native of Africa, but Resident above Sixty Years in the United States of America, Related by Himself* (New London: 1798).

formed a plan of secretly leaving his master. After he had long had this plan in meditation he suggested it to me. At first I cast a deaf ear to it, and rebuked Heddy for harboring in his mind such a rash undertaking. But after he had persuaded and much enchanted me with the prospect of gaining my freedom by such a method, I at length agreed to accompany him. Heddy next inveigled two of his fellow servants to accompany us. The place to which we designed to go was the Mississippi. Our next business was to lay in a sufficient store of provisions for our voyage. We privately collected out of our master's store, six great old cheeses, two firkins of butter, and one whole batch of new bread. When we had gathered all our own clothes and some more, we took them all about midnight, and went to the water side. We stole our master's boat, embarked, and then directed our course for the Mississippi river.

We mutually confederated not to betray or desert one another on pain of death. We first steered our course for Montauk point, the east end of Long-Island. After our arrival there we landed, and Heddy and I made an incursion into the island after fresh water, while our two comrades were left at a little distance from the boat, employed at cooking. When Heddy and I had sought some time for water, he returned to our companions, and I continued on looking for my object. When Heddy had performed his business with our companions who were engaged in cooking, he went directly to the boat, stole all the clothes in it, and then travelled away for East-Hampton, as I was informed. I returned to my fellows not long after. They informed me that our clothes were stolen, but could not determine who was the thief, yet they suspected Heddy as he was missing. After reproving my two comrades for not taking care of our things which were in the boat, I advertised Heddy and sent two men in search of him. They pursued and overtook him at Southampton and returned him to the boat. I then thought it might afford some chance for my freedom, or at least a palliation for my running away, to return Heddy immediately to his master, and inform him that I was induced to go away by Heddy's address. Accordingly I set off with him and the rest of my companions for our master's, and arrived there without any difficulty. I informed my master that Heddy was the ringleader of our revolt, and that he had used us ill. He immediately put Heddy into custody, and myself and companions were well received and went to work as usual.

Not a long time passed after that, before Heddy was sent by my master to New-London gaol. At the close of that year I was sold to a Thomas Stanton, and had to be separated from my wife and one daughter, who was about one month old. He resided at Stonington-point. To this place I brought with me from my late master's, two johannes, three old Spanish dollars, and two thousand of coppers, besides five pounds of my wife's money. This money I got by cleaning gentlemen's shoes and drawing boots, by catching musk-rats and minks, raising potatoes and carrots, &c. and by fishing in the night, and at odd spells.

All this money amounting to near twenty-one pounds York currency, my master's brother, Robert Stanton, hired of me, for which he gave me his note. About one year and a half after that time, my master purchased my wife and her child, for seven hundred pounds old tenor. One time my master sent me two miles after a barrel of molasses, and ordered me to carry it on my shoulders. I made out to carry it all the way to my master's house. When I lived with Captain George Mumford, only to try my strength, I took up on my knees a tierce of salt containing seven bushels, and carried it two or three rods. Of this fact there are several eye witnesses now living.

Towards the close of the time that I resided with this master, I had a falling out with my mistress. This happened one time when my master was gone to Long-Island a gunning. At first the quarrel began between my wife and her mistress. I was then at work in the barn, and hearing a racket in the house, induced me to run there and see what had broken out. When I entered the house, I found my mistress in a violent passion with my wife, for what she informed me was a mere trifle; such a small affair that I forbear to put my mistress to the shame of having it known. I earnestly requested my wife to beg pardon of her mistress for the sake of peace, even if she had given no just occasion for offence. But whilst I was thus saying my mistress turned the blows which she was repeating on my wife to me. She took down her horse-whip, and while she was glutting her fury with it, I reached out my great black hand, raised it up and received the blows of the whip on it which were designed for my head. Then I immediately committed the whip to the devouring fire.

When my master returned from the island, his wife told him of the affair, but for the present he seemed to take no notice of it, and mentioned not a word about it to me. Some days after his return, in the morning as I was putting on a log in the fire-place, not suspecting harm from any one, I received a most violent stroke on the crown of my head with a club two feet long and as large round as a chair-post. This blow very badly wounded my head, and the scar of it remains to this day. The first blow made me have my wits about me you may suppose, for as soon as he went to renew it, I snatched the club out of his hands and dragged him out of the door. He then sent for his brother to come and assist him, but I presently left my master, took the club he wounded me with, carried it to a neighboring Justice of the Peace, and complained of my master. He finally advised me to return to my master, and live contented with him till he abused me again, and then complain. I consented to do accordingly. But before I set out for my master's, up he come and his brother Robert after me. The Justice improved this convenient opportunity to caution my master. He asked him for what he treated his slave thus hastily and unjustly, and told him what would be the consequence if he continued the same treatment towards me. After the Justice had ended his discourse with my master, he and his brother set out with me for home, one before and the other behind me. When they had come to a bye place, they both dismounted their respective horses, and fell to beating me with great violence. I became enraged at this and immediately turned them both under me, laid one of them across the other, and stamped both with my feet what I would.

This occasioned my master's brother to advise him to put me off. A short time after this I was taken by a constable and two men. They carried me to a blacksmith's shop and had me hand-cuffed. When I returned home my mistress enquired much of her waiters, whether VENTURE was hand-cuffed. When she was informed that I was, she appeared to be very contented and was much transported with the news. In the midst of this content and joy, I presented myself before my mistress, shewed her my hand-cuffs, and gave her thanks for my gold rings. For this my master commanded a negro of his to fetch him a large ox chain. This my master locked on my legs with two padlocks. I continued to wear the chain peaceably for two or three days, when my master asked me with contemptuous hard names whether I had not better be freed from my chains and go to work. I answered him, No. Well then, said me, I will send you to the West-Indies or banish you, for I am resolved not to keep you. I answered him I crossed the waters to come here, and I am willing to cross them to return.

For a day or two after this not any one said much to me, until one Hempsted Miner, of Stonington, asked me if I would live with him. I answered him that I would. He then requested me to make myself discontented and to appear as unreconciled to my master as I could before that he bargained with him for me; and that in return he would give me a good chance to gain my freedom when I came to live with him. I did as he requested me. Not long after Hempsted Miner purchased me of my master for fifty-six pounds lawful. He took the chain and padlocks from off me immediately after.

It may here be remembered, that I related a few pages back, that I hired out a sum of money to Mr. Robert Stanton, and took his note for it. In the fray between my master Stanton and myself, he broke open my chest containing his brother's note to me, and destroyed it. Immediately after my present master bought me, he determined to sell me at Hartford. As soon as I became apprized of it, I bethought myself that I would secure a certain sum of money which lay by me, safer than to hire it out to a Stanton. Accordingly I buried it in the earth, a little distance from Thomas Stanton's, in the road over which he passed daily. A short time after my master carried me to Hartford, and first proposed to sell me to one William Hooker of that place. Hooker asked whether I would go to the German Flats with him. I answered, No. He said I should, if not by fair means I should by foul. If you will go by no other measures, I will tie you down in my sleigh. I replied to him, that if he carried me in that manner, no person would purchase me, for it would be thought that he had a murderer for sale. After this he tried no more, and said he would not have me as a gift.

My master next offered me to Daniel Edwards, Esq. of Hartford, for sale. But not purchasing me, my master pawned me to him for ten pounds, and returned to Stonington. After some trial of my honesty, Mr. Edwards placed considerable trust and confidence in me. He put me to serve as his cup-bearer and waiter. When there was company at his house, he would send me into his cellar and other parts of his house to fetch wine and other articles occasionally for them. When I had been with him some time, he asked me why my master wished to part with such an honest negro, and why he did not keep me himself. I replied that I could not give him the reason, unless it was to convert me into cash, and speculate with me as with other commodities. I hope that he can never justly say it was on account of my ill conduct that he did not keep me himself. Mr. Edwards told me that he should be very willing to keep me himself, and that he would never let me go from him to live, if it was not unreasonable and inconvenient for me to be parted from my wife and children; therefore he would furnish me with a horse to return to Stonington, if I had a mind for it. As Miner did not appear to redeem me I went, and called at my old master Stanton's first to see my wife, who was then owned by him. As my old master appeared much ruffled at my being there, I left my wife before I had spent any considerable time with her, and went to Colonel O. Smith's. Miner had not as yet wholly settled with Stanton for me, and had before my return from Hartford given Col. Smith a bill of sale of me. These men once met to determine which of them should hold me, and upon my expressing a desire to be owned by Col. Smith, and upon my master's settling the remainder of the money which was due to Stanton for me, it was agreed that I should live with Col. Smith. This was the third time of my being sold, and I was then thirty-one years old. As I never had an opportunity of redeeming myself whilst I was owned by Miner, though he promised to give me a chance, I was then very ambitious of obtaining it. I asked my master one time if he would consent to have me purchase my freedom. He replied that he would. I was then very happy, knowing that I was at that time able to pay part of the purchase money, by means of the money which I some time since buried. This I took out of the earth and tendered to my master, having previously engaged a free negro man to take his security for it, as I was the property of my master, and therefore could not safely take his obligation myself. What was wanting in redeeming myself, my master agreed to wait on me for, until I could procure it for him. I still continued to work for Col. Smith. There was continually some interest accruing on my master's note to my friend the free negro man above named, which I received, and with some besides which I got by fishing, I laid out in land adjoining my old master Stanton's. By cultivating this land with the greatest diligence and economy, at times when my master did not require my labor, in two years I laid up ten pounds. This my friend tendered my master for myself, and received his note for it.

Being encouraged by the success which I had met in redeeming myself, I again solicited my master for a further chance of completing it. The chance for which I solicited him was that of going out to work the ensuing winter. He agreed to this on condition that I would give him one quarter of my earnings. On these terms I worked the following winter, and earned four pounds sixteen shillings, one quarter of which went to my master for the privilege, and the rest was paid him on my own account. This added to the other payments made up forty four pounds, eight shillings, which I had paid on my own account. I was then about thirty five years old. The next summer I again desired he would give me a chance of going out to work. But he refused and answered that he must have my labor this summer, as he did not have it the past winter. I replied that I considered it as hard that I could not have a chance to work out when the season became advantageous, and that I must only be permitted to hire myself out in the poorest season of the year. He asked me after this what I would give him for the privilege per month. I replied that I would leave it wholly with his own generosity to determine what I should return him a month. Well then, said he, if so two pounds a month. I answered him that if that was the least he would take I would be contented.

Accordingly I hired myself out at Fisher's Island, and earned twenty pounds; thirteen pounds six shillings of which my master drew for the privilege, and the remainder I paid him for my freedom. This made fifty-one pounds two shillings which I paid him. In October following I went and wrought six months at Long Island. In that six month's time I cut and corded four hundred cords of wood, besides threshing out seventy-five bushels of grain, and received of my wages down only twenty pounds, which left remaining a larger sum. Whilst I was out that time, I took up on my wages only one pair of shoes. At night I lay on the hearth, with one coverlet over and another under me. I returned to my master and gave him what I received of my six months labor. This left only thirteen pounds eighteen shillings to make up the full sum for my redemption. My master liberated me, saying that I might pay what was behind if I could ever make it convenient, otherwise it would be well. The amount of the money which I had paid my master towards redeeming my time, was seventy-one pounds two shillings. The reason of my master for asking such an unreasonable price, was he said, to secure himself in case I should ever come to want. Being thirty-six years old, I left Col. Smith once for all. I had already been sold three different times, made considerable money with seemingly nothing to derive it from, been cheated out of a large sum of money, lost much by misfortunes, and paid an enormous sum for my freedom.

■ REFLECTIONS

This chapter asks you to compare European encounters with Native Americans and Africans. Why did Europeans enslave Africans and not, for the most part, American Indians? Because so many Africans were taken to the Americas to work on plantations, this topic is especially compelling.

Initially, of course, Indians *were* enslaved. Recall the letter of Columbus (Chapter 15, selection 4). Part of the reason this enslavement did not continue was the high mortality of Native Americans exposed to smallpox and other Old World diseases. In addition, Native Americans who survived the bacterial onslaught had the "local knowledge" and support needed to escape from slavery.

Above and beyond this were the humanitarian objections of Spanish priests and the concerns of the Spanish monarchy that slavery would increase the power of the conquistadors at the expense of the Crown. In 1542 the enslavement of Indians was outlawed in Spanish dominions of the New World. Clearly, these "New Laws" were not always obeyed by Spaniards in the Americas or by the Portuguese subjects of the unified Spanish-Portuguese crown between 1580 and 1640. Still, the different legal positions of Africans and Indians in the minds of Europeans require further explanation.

Some scholars have suggested that the difference in treatment lies in the differing needs of the main European powers involved in the encounter. The anthropologist Marvin Harris makes the argument this way:

> The most plausible explanation of the New Laws [of 1542] is that they represented the intersection of the interests of three power groups: the Church, the Crown, and the colonists. All three of these interests sought to maximize their respective control over the aboriginal populations. Outright enslavement of the Indians was the method preferred by the colonists. But neither the Crown nor the Church could permit this to happen without surrendering their own vested and potential interests in the greatest resource of the New World—its manpower.[1]

Why then did Europeans permit and even encourage the enslavement of Africans? In this matter all three power groups stood to gain. Africans who remained in Africa were of no use to any of the three groups, since effective military and political domination of that continent by Europeans was not achieved until the middle of the nineteenth century. To make use of African manpower, Africans had to be removed from their homelands. The only way to accomplish this

[1] Marvin Harris, *Patterns of Race in the Americas* (New York: W. W. Norton, 1964), 17.

was to buy them as slaves from dealers on the coast. For both the Crown and the Church, it was better to have Africans under the control of the New World colonists than to leave Africans under the control of Africans.

But of course the Atlantic world slave trade was just one of the lasting outcomes of Atlantic world encounters. Toward the end of his dramatic account of the Spanish conquest of Mexico (selection 1), Bernal Díaz describes a grizzly discovery made by the victorious conquistadors:

> I solemnly swear that all the houses and stockades in the lake were full of heads and corpses. I do not know how to describe it but it was the same in the streets and courts of Tlatelolco. We could not walk without treading on the bodies and heads of dead Indians. (Díaz, 1963, 405)

After two years of continual and heavy warfare, the fortunes of the Spanish turned in their favor and they seized a ravaged city where, according to Bernal Díaz, "the stench was so bad, no one could endure it." Díaz assumed that the Mexicans had been starved and denied fresh water, but we now know that at least part of the cause was the spread of smallpox, a disease that the Spanish carried from the Old World and for which the Native Americans had no immunities. Because of thousands of years of contact, Africans shared many of the same immunities as Europeans, but Native Americans, having inhabited a separate biological realm for over ten thousand years, were completely vulnerable to the new diseases and perished in droves.

Ultimately, slavery came to an end, even if in some cases—the work of Italians on Brazilian sugar plantations, Chinese rail workers, or free African day laborers—it was hard to see a difference in working conditions. In any case, the long-term impact of the "Columbian exchange" was more ecological than economic. The potatoes of South America and the corn of Mexico fed more families in Afro-Eurasia than had ever existed in the Americas. Conversely, the flora and fauna of the Americas were transformed through the introduction of the grasses, trees, fruits, grains, horses, cattle, pigs, and chickens that had nourished the ancestors of the conquistadors.

17

Empire, Religion, and War

Asian, Islamic, and Christian States, 1500–1800

■ HISTORICAL CONTEXT

The period between 1500 and 1800 in world history, often called the Early Modern Period, began with the rise of empires, as we have seen in the two previous chapters, and religious conflict and war. In this chapter, we ask about the relationship between these two developments.

Neither empires nor religions were new in 1500. Empires had existed for more than 4,000 years, some major religions for almost half that time. But before 1500, empires were rarely driven by a desire to win religious conversions. The Arab conquests of the seventh to tenth centuries and the Christian crusades that followed were exceptions, but even the Arab conquests that vastly expanded the world of Islam were traditionally predatory in nature, benefiting more from the taxation of the conquered than from their conversion. The Mongol Empire of the thirteenth and fourteenth centuries was entirely predatory, its leaders often adopting the religion of those they conquered (Islam or Buddhism). The Chinese Ming naval empire of the early fifteenth century, as we saw, was commanded by a Muslim admiral serving a Buddhist emperor. During his naval expeditions, Zheng He dedicated prayer monuments for Hindu, Buddhist, Taoist, and Muslim worshipers.

It would not be correct, however, to say that empires were secular or tolerant before 1500: Mongol animism included religious beliefs and practices, Romans had their civic and imperial deities, and the Chinese worshiped deities and revered the emperor. Explicit rejections of these beliefs or practices were often punished. But otherwise, empires were more indifferent to religion than either hostile or tolerant toward it. Why after 1500 (or thereabouts) did many emperors and kings insist on the religious conversions of conquered peoples? Did they all? If not, what accounts for the new kind of religious empire that appeared in this period?

We focus on two of its religious empires: the Christian and Islamic. We will pay particular attention to Spain's Christian empire in the Americas and the Muslim empire in India. Both began about 1500, both were powered by religious fervor, and both confronted peoples of different religions: Native Americans and Hindus.

■ THINKING HISTORICALLY

Understanding Author, Audience, and Agenda

Sources cannot be taken at face value. They have to be interrogated. Even when they are reasonably reliable, we can always understand them better by asking about their author, audience, and agenda. First, who is the author or creator of the source? What do we know of the author's background, interests, positions, other works, and so on? Second, who or what is the intended audience for the source? For whom was it written or created? Third, what was the author's likely agenda? Why was the source created? We will be asking variants of these questions for each of the following selections.

1

BARTOLOMÉ DE LAS CASAS

The Devastation of the Indies, 1555

Bartolomé de Las Casas (1484–1566) emigrated with his father from Spain to the island of Hispaniola in 1502. Eight years later, he became a priest, served as a missionary to the Taino of Cuba, and attempted to create a utopian society for the Indians of Venezuela, becoming a Dominican friar in 1522. Repelled by his early experience among the conquistadors, Las Casas then devoted his adult life to aiding the Indians in the Americas and in the Spanish court. This selection is drawn from his brief history, *The Devastation of the Indies*, published in 1555. The work for this book and a larger volume, *In Defense of the Indians*, presented his case against Indian slavery in the great debate at the Spanish court at Valladolid in 1550. Along with his monumental *History of the Indies*, the writings of Las Casas constituted such an indictment of Spanish colonialism that Protestant enemies were able to

Source: Bartolomé de Las Casas, *The Devastation of the Indies: A Brief Account*, trans. Herma Briffault (Baltimore: Johns Hopkins University Press, 1992), 32–35, 40–41.

argue that Catholic Spain was uniquely barbaric, a dubious proposition that became known as the "Black Legend." What does Las Casas suggest about the nature of Christian expansion?

THINKING HISTORICALLY

Who was Las Casas, and for what audience is he writing? What does this suggest about Las Casas's agenda? How effective is he here in advancing his agenda? Notice that Las Casas continually refers to the settlers as "Christians" rather than "settlers" or "Spaniards." How might calling them "Christians" contribute to his agenda? How might this unfairly depict their behavior as religiously motivated?

This [Hispaniola][1] was the first land in the New World to be destroyed and depopulated by the Christians, and here they began their subjection of the women and children, taking them away from the Indians to use them and ill use them, eating the food they provided with their sweat and toil. The Spaniards did not content themselves with what the Indians gave them of their own free will, according to their ability, which was always too little to satisfy enormous appetites, for a Christian eats and consumes in one day an amount of food that would suffice to feed three houses inhabited by ten Indians for one month. And they committed other acts of force and violence and oppression which made the Indians realize that these men had not come from Heaven. And some of the Indians concealed their foods while others concealed their wives and children and still others fled to the mountains to avoid the terrible transactions of the Christians.

And the Christians attacked them with buffets and beatings, until finally they laid hands on the nobles of the villages. Then they behaved with such temerity and shamelessness that the most powerful ruler of the islands had to see his own wife raped by a Christian officer.

From that time onward the Indians began to seek ways to throw the Christians out of their lands. They took up arms, but their weapons were very weak and of little service in offense and still less in defense. (Because of this, the wars of the Indians against each other are little more than games played by children.) And the Christians, with their horses and swords and pikes began to carry out massacres and strange cruelties against them. They attacked the towns and spared neither the children nor the aged nor pregnant women nor women in childbed, not only stabbing them and dismembering them but cutting them to pieces as if dealing with sheep in the slaughter house. They laid bets as to who, with one stroke of the sword, could split a man in two or could cut off his head or spill out his entrails with a single stroke of the pike. They took infants from their mothers'

---

[1] The island that today includes the Dominican Republic and Haiti. [Ed.]

breasts, snatching them by the legs and pitching them headfirst against the crags or snatched them by the arms and threw them into the rivers, roaring with laughter and saying as the babies fell into the water, "Boil there, you offspring of the devil!" Other infants they put to the sword along with their mothers and anyone else who happened to be nearby. They made some low wide gallows on which the hanged victim's feet almost touched the ground, stringing up their victims in lots of thirteen, in memory of Our Redeemer and His twelve Apostles, then set burning wood at their feet and thus burned them alive. To others they attached straw or wrapped their whole bodies in straw and set them afire. With still others, all those they wanted to capture alive, they cut off their hands and hung them round the victim's neck, saying, "Go now, carry the message," meaning, Take the news to the Indians who have fled to the mountains. They usually dealt with the chieftains and nobles in the following way: they made a grid of rods which they placed on forked sticks, then lashed the victims to the grid and lighted a smoldering fire underneath, so that little by little, as those captives screamed in despair and torment, their souls would leave them.

I once saw this, when there were four or five nobles lashed on grids and burning; I seem even to recall that there were two or three pairs of grids where others were burning, and because they uttered such loud screams that they disturbed the captain's sleep, he ordered them to be strangled. And the constable, who was worse than an executioner, did not want to obey that order (and I know the name of that constable and know his relatives in Seville), but instead put a stick over the victims' tongues, so they could not make a sound, and he stirred up the fire, but not too much, so that they roasted slowly, as he liked. I saw all these things I have described, and countless others.

And because all the people who could do so fled to the mountains to escape these inhuman, ruthless, and ferocious acts, the Spanish captains, enemies of the human race, pursued them with the fierce dogs they kept which attacked the Indians, tearing them to pieces and devouring them. And because on few and far between occasions, the Indians justifiably killed some Christians, the Spaniards made a rule among themselves that for every Christian slain by the Indians, they would slay a hundred Indians. . . .

Because the particulars that enter into these outrages are so numerous they could not be contained in the scope of much writing, for in truth I believe that in the great deal I have set down here I have not revealed the thousandth part of the sufferings endured by the Indians, I now want only to add that, in the matter of these unprovoked and destructive wars, and God is my witness, all these acts of wickedness I have described, as well as those I have omitted, were perpetrated against the Indians without cause, without any more cause than could give a community of good monks living together in a monastery. And still more strongly I affirm that until the multitude of people on this island of Hispaniola were killed and their lands devastated, they committed no sin against the Christians that would be punishable by man's laws, and as to those sins punishable by God's law, such as vengeful feelings against such powerful enemies as the Christians have been, those sins would be committed by the very few Indians who are hardhearted and impetuous. And I can say this from my great experience with them: their hardness and impetuosity would be that of children, of boys ten or twelve years old. I know by certain infallible signs that the wars waged by the Indians against the Christians have been justifiable wars and that all the wars waged by the Christians against the Indians have been unjust wars, more diabolical than any wars ever waged anywhere in the world. This I declare to be so of all the many wars they have waged against the peoples throughout the Indies.

After the wars and the killings had ended, when usually there survived only some boys, some women, and children, these survivors were distributed among the Christians to be slaves. The *repartimiento* or distribution was made according to the rank and importance of the Christian to whom the Indians were allocated, one of them being given thirty, another forty, still another, one or two hundred, and besides the rank of the Christian there was also to be considered in what favor he stood with the tyrant they called Governor. The pretext was that these allocated Indians were to be instructed in the articles of the Christian Faith. As if those Christians who were as a rule foolish and cruel and greedy and vicious could be caretakers of souls! And the care they took was to send the men to the mines to dig for gold, which is intolerable labor, and to send the women into the fields of the big ranches to hoe and till the land, work suitable for strong men. Nor to either the men or the women did they give any food except herbs and legumes, things of little substance. The milk in the breasts of the women with infants dried up and thus in a short while the infants perished.

2

FRANCISCUS DE VICTORIA

On the Indians, or on the Law of War Made by the Spaniards on the Barbarians, 1557

Franciscus de Victoria (c. 1483–1546) was a Spanish Dominican theologian and philosopher. In 1532, he was asked by the Spanish King Charles, who was alarmed by Las Casas's reports of atrocities, to advise the king on Spain's rights to the Indian lands in the Americas. Victoria responded by preparing a series of lectures at the University of

Source: Franciscus de Victoria, *De Indis et de Ivre Belli Reflectiones*, ed. Ernest Nys, in *The Classics of International Law*, ed. James Brown Scott (Washington, DC: Carnegie Institution of Washington, 1917), 170–73.

Salamanca on the rights of nations, which was later published in 1557, after his death. Remembered today as one of the fathers of international law and human rights (though these terms were not yet used), he spoke of the "republic of the whole world" and the "freedom of the seas" and, after the Italian priest and philosopher Thomas Aquinas, furthered ideas of "the law of nations" and "the law of war."

Notice how Victoria uses both Christian and Greek authorities to make his argument. Does he use legal principles based on reason, moral judgments based on faith, or a combination of the two?

THINKING HISTORICALLY

Unlike his contemporary, Bartolomé de Las Casas, who lived in Spain and the Americas and knew the lives of conquistadors and Indians personally, Victoria lived the life of an intellectual in Paris and Salamanca, Spain, never traveled to the Americas, and knew only a few Indians who had been brought to Spain. Despite a lack of personal experience, Victoria used the writings of Aquinas and Aristotle to construct a systematic philosophy and legal principles that would persuade many of the illegality of all slavery and unjust wars.

Victoria carved out ideas of law, war, justice, and personal responsibility that were clearly ahead of his time. Some in fact may still be ahead of the consensus of our own time. Which of these ideas are part of our modern consensus? Which, if any, are controversial even today? What does his argument's reliance on the writings of Aquinas, Aristotle, and others suggest about his audience?

10. What may be a reason and cause of just war? It is particularly necessary to ask this in connection with the case of the Indian aborigines, which is now before us. Here my first proposition is: Difference of religion is not a cause of just war. This was shown at length in the preceding Reflection, when we demolished the fourth alleged title for taking possession of the Indians, namely, their refusal to accept Christianity. And it is the opinion of St. Thomas and the common opinion of the doctors—indeed, I know of no one of the opposite way of thinking.

11. Second proposition: Extension of empire is not a just cause of war. This is too well known to need proof, for otherwise each of the two belligerents might have an equally just cause and so both would be innocent. This in its turn would involve the consequence that it would not be lawful to kill them and so imply a contradiction, because it would be a just war.

12. Third proposition: Neither the personal glory of the prince nor any other advantage to him is a just cause of war. This, too is notorious. For a prince ought to subordinate both peace and war to the common

weal of his State and not spend public revenues in quest of his own glory or gain, much less expose his subjects to danger on that account. Herein, indeed, is the difference between a lawful king and a tyrant, that the latter directs his government towards his individual profit and advantage, but a king to the public welfare, as Aristotle says. Also, the prince derives his authority from the State. Therefore he ought to use it for the good of the State. Also, laws ought "not to be enacted for the private good of any individual, but in the common interest of all the citizens," as is ruled in can. 2, Dist. 4, a citation from Isadore. Therefore the rules relating to war ought to be for the common good of all and not for the private good of the prince. Again, this is the difference between freemen and slaves, as Aristotle says that masters exploit slaves for their own good and not for the good of the slaves, while freemen do not exist in the interest of others, but in their own interest. And so, were a prince to misuse his subjects by compelling them to go soldiering and to contribute money for his campaigns, not for the public good, but for his own private gain, this would be to make slaves of them.

13. Fourth proposition: There is a single and only just cause for commencing a war, namely, a wrong received. . . .

14. Fifth proposition: Not every kind and degree of wrong can suffice for commencing a war. The proof of this is that not even upon one's own fellow-countrymen is it lawful for every offense to exact atrocious punishments, such as death or banishment or confiscation of property. As, then, the evils inflicted in war are all of a severe and atrocious character, such as slaughter and fire and devastation, it is not lawful for slight wrongs to pursue the authors of the wrongs with war, seeing that the degree of the punishment ought to correspond to the measure of the offence. . . .

20. Many doubts are suggested by what has just been said. In the first place, there is a doubtful point in connection with the justice of a war, whether it be enough for a just war that the prince believes himself to have a just cause. On this point let my first proposition be: This belief is not always enough. And for proof I rely, first, on the fact that in some matters of less moment it is not enough either for a prince or for private persons to believe that they are acting justly. This is notorious, for their error may be vincible and deliberate, and the opinion of the individual is not enough to render an act good, but it must come up to the standard of a wise man's judgment, as appears from Ethics, bk. 2. Also the result would otherwise be that very many wars would be just on both sides, for although it is not a common occurrence for princes to wage war in bad faith, they nearly always think theirs is a just cause. In this way all belligerents would be innocent and it would not be lawful to kill them. Also, were it otherwise, even Turks and Saracens might wage just wars against Christians, for they think they are thus rendering God service.

21. Second proposition: It is essential for a just war that an exceedingly careful examination be made of the justice and causes of the war and that the reasons of those who on grounds of equity oppose it be listened to. For (as the comic poet says) "A wise man must make trial of everything by words before resorting to force," and he ought to consult the good and wise and those who speak with freedom and without anger or bitterness or greed, seeing that (as Sallust says) "where these vices hold sway, truth is not easily distinguished." This is self-evident. For truth and justice in moral questions are hard of attainment and so any careless treatment of them easily leads to error, an error which will be inexcusable, especially in a concern of great moment, involving danger and calamity to many, and they our neighbors, too, whom we are bound to love as ourselves.

22. Second doubt: Whether subjects are bound to examine the cause of a war or whether they may serve in the war without any careful scrutiny thereof, just as the lictors had to enforce the praetor's decree without questioning. On this doubt let my first proposition be: If a subject is convinced of the injustice of a war, he ought not to serve in it, even on the command of his prince. This is clear, for no one can authorize the killing of an innocent person. But in the case before us the enemy are innocent. Therefore they may not be killed. Again, a prince sins when he commences a war in such a case. But "not only are they who commit such things worthy of death, but they, too, who consent to the doing thereof." Therefore soldiers also are not excused when they fight in bad faith. Again, it is not lawful to kill innocent citizens at the prince's command. Therefore not aliens either.

23. Hence flows the corollary that subjects whose conscience is against the justice of a war may not engage in it whether they be right or wrong. This is clear, for "whatever is not of faith is sin."

3

MARTIN LUTHER

Hymns, 1523–1529

The Spanish Christian empire was driven by religious zeal to wage war, but in the process, it also raised a new moral challenge to religious war. Another challenge to the empire came in the form of

Source: *The Handbook to the Lutheran Hymnal* (St. Louis, MO: Concordia Publishing House, 1942), 189–90, and *The Methodist Hymnal*, trans. Frederick Hedge (Nashville, TN: The Methodist Book Concern, 1939), Hymn 67.

the Protestant Reformation. But while critics like Martin Luther challenged the power, the materialism, and even the militancy of the Catholic Church and the Holy Roman Empire, they did not challenge the phenomena of Christian soldiers, religious war, or holy martyrdom themselves. The Protestant Reformation split Europe into two opposing camps at a moment when princes and kings were looking for belief systems to consolidate power and secure the allegiance of the subjects within their newly created states. In 1618, Protestant states in north and central Europe erupted against the Catholic Holy Roman Empire, largely devastating its authority by 1648 (though it limped along until 1806).

Martin Luther (1483–1546), an exact contemporary of Franciscus de Victoria and just a year older than Bartolomé de Las Casas, was a German and an Augustinian monk (the Augustinians were a Catholic teaching order like the Dominicans, but a bit less zealous). Luther criticized the corruption and arrogance of the church, displayed in such acts as funding improvements to St. Peter's Cathedral by selling what were known as indulgences that promised God's mercy for a price. He believed the Catholic Church inflated its importance with its grand bureaucracy, material splendor, and disdain for princes and the German people. In a revolutionary break from Catholic teachings, he believed that God sanctified only baptism and the Lord's Supper as sacraments, that only God chose who would be saved and who could be a priest, that priests could marry, that ordinary people should read the Bible for themselves, and that one could not bargain with God for salvation by doing "good works."

While none of these core ideas dealt with war, struggle, or martyrdom, they set Protestants on a collision course with the most powerful forces in Europe. Essentially, Protestantism declared that 1,500 years of church history were at best irrelevant, certainly full of error, and likely the work of the devil.

Breaking with Catholic traditions, Luther simplified the church service and made it more accessible to the people. He translated the Bible into German and explained it in his sermons and writings. (His collected works fill fifty-five large volumes today.) Recognizing the power of rhyme and song to teach the illiterate as well as those who could read, he set out in 1523 to find or commission hymns to be sung by the congregation at services. From December 1523 until late summer of 1524, he wrote twenty-four of these himself. "Flung to the Heedless Winds" is thought to be the first. "A Mighty Fortress Is Our God," the most popular of Luther's hymns, is thought to have been composed in 1529.

What ideas and values do these hymns express? What do they suggest about the idea of a just war? How is Luther's attitude toward religious war different from that of Victoria?

THINKING HISTORICALLY

Luther's agenda in writing these hymns was sometimes quite specific. In the case of the first hymn, "Flung to the Heedless Winds" (a two-stanza summary of a ten-stanza poem), Luther wanted to memorialize two young Augustinian friars who were burned at the stake for their Lutheran beliefs in Brussels on July 1, 1523. Luther was particularly eager to extinguish the rumor spread by Catholics that the young martyrs had recanted just before they died. "A Mighty Fortress" may have originated as a martial song to inspire Christian soldiers fighting the forces of the Muslim Ottoman Empire.

Who was the audience for these hymns? Clearly it was the members of the new Lutheran congregations. But they were both the audience and the performers. Luther's innovation was not only to present contemporary music in the people's own language but also to have the people sing it themselves. How might churchgoers have been affected by the singing of these hymns? Notice in particular the frequent use of words like *our*, *us*, and *we* in "A Mighty Fortress." How do you imagine congregation members might have felt after singing this hymn loudly, as a group? How might the act of singing these hymns link to Luther's agenda for writing them?

"Flung to the Heedless Winds," 1523

1. Flung to the heedless winds
Or on the waters cast,
The martyrs' ashes, watched,
Shall gathered be at last.
And from that scattered dust,
Around us and abroad,
Shall spring a plenteous seed
Of witnesses for God.

2. The Father hath received
Their latest living breath,
And vain is Satan's boast
Of victory in their death.
Still, still, though dead, they speak,
And, trumpet-tongued, proclaim
To many a wakening land
The one availing Name.

"A Mighty Fortress Is Our God," 1529

1. A mighty fortress is our God,
A bulwark never failing;
Our helper He, amid the flood
Of mortal ills prevailing;
For still our ancient foe
Doth seek to work us woe;
His craft and power are great,
And, armed with cruel hate,
On Earth is not his equal.

2. Did we in our own strength confide,
Our striving would be losing;
Were not the right Man on our side,
The Man of God's own choosing;
Dost ask who that may be?
Christ Jesus, it is He;
Lord Sabaoth, His name,
From age to age the same,
And He must win the battle.

3. And though this world, with devils filled,
Should threaten to undo us,
We will not fear, for God hath willed
His truth to triumph through us;
The Prince of Darkness grim—
We tremble not for him;
His rage we can endure,
For lo, his doom is sure,
What little word shall fell him.

4. That word above all earthly powers,
No thanks to them, abideth.
The Spirit and the gifts are ours
Through Him who with us sideth;
Let goods and kindred go,
This mortal life also;
The body they may kill;
God's truth abideth still,
His kingdom is forever.

BENJAMIN J. KAPLAN

European Faiths and States, 2007

In Europe, the state emerged as a major force after 1500. But the rise of the European state was preceded by an equally volatile revolution: the creation of self-conscious, faith-based communities, spurred by the Protestant Reformation and the Catholic response to it. In this selection, Benjamin J. Kaplan, a modern historian, shows the novelty and intolerance of this combination of confessional community and state power. Why was this combination so volatile? Did it make European society and European governments more intolerant than other societies?

THINKING HISTORICALLY

Kaplan is a modern historian writing for a general audience. "Agenda" may be too pointed a word to describe why a historian chooses a particular topic to examine, but interest in the present century in the subjects of religion and toleration is not without context. What might be the "agenda" (besides discovery and understanding) in arguing, as Kaplan does, that Europeans became increasingly intolerant, rather than tolerant, from 1550 to 1750?

No religion is static, and over its two millennia of existence the Roman Catholic Church has transformed itself several times. The so-called Investiture Controversy[1] of the eleventh century precipitated one such transformation; in the 1960s, Vatican II[2] decreed another. So too in the sixteenth century, partly in response to the Protestant challenge, partly driven by internal impulses for renewal and reform, the Catholic Church initiated sweeping changes in everything from ecclesiastic administration and the training of priests to liturgy and forms of private devotion. Conventionally, the drive to enact these changes is referred to as either the Counter-Reformation or the Catholic Reformation, the first term emphasizing its reactive quality, the second its self-generation. Both

---

[1] A struggle in Europe in the eleventh and twelfth centuries over whether kings or the pope had authority to appoint church officials. [Ed.]

[2] An important series of changes under Pope John XXIII said to modernize the Catholic Church (1962–1965). [Ed.]

Source: Benjamin J. Kaplan, *Divided by Faith: Religious Conflict and the Practice of Toleration in Early Modern Europe* (Cambridge, MA: Harvard University Press, 2007), 28–32, 100–103.

terms, however, obscure a crucial fact: that changes in Catholicism resembled in some respects the reforms instituted by Protestants. That is, for all the differences and points of contention that bitterly divided them, in some respects the churches of early modern Europe were developing in parallel to one another. Christianity was changing, irrespective of church. The new type of Christianity that resulted from this process is known as "confessional." Its emergence, also called the "rise of confessionalism" or the "formation of confessions," can be charted beginning in the sixteenth century and continuing through the seventeenth.

To dispel any confusion, it must be explained that the term *confession* and its derivatives do not refer in this context to the Catholic sacrament of penance. Rather they refer to a type of document, the "confession of faith," a declaration of the fundamental doctrines held by a church. Perhaps the most famous was the Augsburg Confession of 1530, which came to define Lutheran orthodoxy. All early modern churches issued such documents, which embodied three of the most basic trends then in Christianity: the internalization of church teaching, the drawing of sharp dichotomies, and the quest for "holy uniformity." Each fueled intolerance.

The timing and modalities of these trends varied greatly by church and by region, and in Ireland they had hardly affected the vast majority of peasants (who remained loyal to Catholicism) by the 1660s. According to Englishman Jeremy Taylor, the Irish peasantry could "give no account of their religion what it is: only they believe as their priest bids them and go to mass which they understand not, and reckon their beads to tell the number and the tale of their prayers, and abstain from eggs and flesh in Lent, and visit St. Patrick's well, and leave pins and ribbons, yarn or thread in their holy wells, and pray to God, S. Mary and S. Patrick, S. Columbanus and S. Bridget, and desire to be buried with S. Francis cord about them, and to fast on Saturdays in honour of our Lady."[3]

Granted that Taylor was a hostile outsider, his description not only matches what we know about seventeeth-century Ireland, it captures a state of affairs that was quite the norm across Europe prior to the Reformation. For medieval Christians, religion was as much a set of ritual practices as a set of beliefs. It entailed feasting and fasting on prescribed days; attending mass; reciting prayers in a language (Latin) they scarcely understood; making pilgrimages to holy places, where they offered sacrifices to wonder-working saints; and a wide array of other "works." These had merit, according to theologians, only if performed in a devout frame of mind. In practice, though, priests and laity attributed to them an efficacy as reliable as transubstantiation, the miracle of the mass whereby wafer and wine became Christ's body and blood. The more

---

[3] Keith Thomas, *Religion and the Decline of Magic* (New York, 1971), 76–77.

frequently they were performed, it was said, the more divine grace they conveyed and the better your chances of going to heaven. Many religious acts, in any event, were directed less toward attaining salvation after death than toward escaping misfortune in life. Making the sign of the cross, wearing an amulet containing the words from the Gospel of John, parading images of saints through parish streets: such acts were believed to ward off evil, offering protection from disease, accident, war, and famine.

In medieval Europe, ordinary laypeople knew little church doctrine. They received no formal religious instruction, and their pastors rarely preached. Like Taylor's peasants, they could establish their orthodoxy simply by declaring they "believe as their priest bids them." Such ignorance did not matter greatly in a world where everyone was by default Catholic. It did after Europe split into competing "confessions," each propounding a rival truth. As each church began to define its identity in terms of its unique teachings, doctrine took on an unprecedented importance, and the expectation, echoed in Taylor's disdain, began to build that church members know what their church taught and how it differed from other churches. For Protestants, this expectation was built into the very definition of their religion, which taught that salvation is "by faith alone." All the Protestant churches accepted it as their mission to teach Christians what they needed to believe to be saved. At the same time, a more general dynamic operated: the very existence of alternatives created pressure for Christians to be better informed and more self-conscious in their commitments. Catholic reformers too began to demand that ordinary church members internalize the teachings of their church. Religion itself thus came increasingly to mean belief in a particular creed, and a life lived in accordance with it.

It was easy for churches to enunciate such dramatically raised standards. Implementing them required decades, in some regions as much as two centuries, of strenuous effort. The churches had to undertake massive pedagogic campaigns, which they conducted via preaching, education, printed propaganda, church discipline, and revamped rituals. In all these areas Protestant reformers broke new ground. They made the sermon the centerpiece of Protestant worship. They required that children receive elementary religious instruction, either at school or through special catechism[4] classes. They released torrents of printed propaganda and encouraged ordinary Christians to read scripture. They established new institutions and procedures to supervise parish life. . . .

Facing many of the same challenges as Protestant reformers, Catholic reformers had no qualms about adopting the former's pedagogic methods (and vice versa). The Jesuits in particular engaged in a range of

---

[4] Indoctrination; memorizing doctrine. [Ed.]

activities that show striking parallels to those of their enemies. They became renowned preachers, wrote catechisms (that of Peter Canisius was the most popular in Catholic Europe), and founded hundreds of new schools, mostly at the secondary and college level. Using the *Spiritual Exercises* written by their founder, Ignatius of Loyola, they taught people how to examine their own consciences and achieve pious goals through a remarkable self-discipline. As confessors, chaplains, and organizers of a new type of club, the Marian sodality, they encouraged frequent confession and Communion. This disciplinary routine encouraged the internalization of norms even as it provided an external mechanism for enforcing them. . . .

Just as the welfare of towns and villages depended on God's favor, Europeans believed, so did that of countries. . . . In 1663, when Ottoman armies launched an offensive into central Europe, prayers went up across the Continent. One pietist preacher warned his Dutch congregation that the Turks would conquer all unless lax, indifferent Christians put into practice the teachings they mouthed. Two decades later the Turks attacked again, this time reaching the walls of Vienna. At this critical juncture, Pope Innocent XI marshaled an international alliance to relieve the imperial capital. Protestant as well as Catholic princes of Germany sent troops to fight alongside Poles and Austrians. After the combined Christian army broke the Turks' siege, Innocent organized a "Holy League" whose forces drove the Turks once and for all back to the Balkans. This crusade was the last hurrah for the medieval concept of a united Christendom led by pope and emperor.

By then, two developments had made the concept almost completely anachronistic. One we have already examined: the division of Christendom into competing confessions. The other was the emergence of political units resembling modern nation-states. Particularism[5] did not disappear, either as a set of power relationships or as a mentality. Increasingly, though, Europe's rulers asserted an impersonal authority that can be called sovereignty, rather than (or, perhaps better, in addition to) the personal suzerainty[6] of the feudal Middle Ages. They codified laws, issued regulations, raised taxes, formalized institutions, and mobilized networks of officials, casting in this way a tighter net of control over society. One must not exaggerate the control rulers achieved, for early modern governments never had the tools of law enforcement modern ones take for granted. More than is often realized, their authority depended on the consent of the governed. Nevertheless, by the late seventeenth century some princes had achieved what at the time was called "absolute" authority: they could wage war, issue laws, and

---

[5] Local, personal, and decentralized politics, as in medieval feudalism. [Ed.]
[6] Dependence. [Ed.]

impose taxes without the approval of representative institutions, or with sure knowledge of their rubber stamp. "Absolutism" vested all sovereign power in a single individual, but even in polities that remained fragmented, like those of the Dutch and Swiss, there developed "a more encompassing, more systematic, and more literate articulation of power and authority."[7] The development took as many forms as there were forms of polity, but across Europe it was clear: the state grew stronger as an institution and more cohesive as a political community.

The fusion of these two developments, confessionalism and state formation, was explosive. The fictional Irishman Dooley, creation of modern humorist Finley Peter Dunne, once observed: "Rellijon is a quare thing. Be itself it's all right. But sprinkle a little pollyticks into it an' dinnymit is bran flour compared with it. Alone it prepares a man f'r a better life. Combined with polyticks it hurries him to it."[8] The observation has a special ring of truth in the mouth of an Irishman, for in modern Ireland, religious and political causes—Protestantism and Union with Britain, Catholicism and Irish Nationalism—have become inseparable. In the sixteenth century, religion and politics combined similarly across Europe. Religious enemies, their hatreds fanned by confessional ideology, became political enemies, and vice versa, as people at odds with one another for social or political reasons tended to choose opposing sides religiously as well. In this way, Europe's religious divisions not only created new conflicts, they threw ideological fuel on the fires of existing ones. Competitions for power, wealth, or land became cosmic struggles between the forces of God and Satan. Inversely, the bonds of a common confession brought people together in equally powerful ways. When they cut across social or political lines, they could make friends of strangers or even former enemies. On every level, from the local to the international, co-religionists felt an impulse to make common cause with one another.

To Europe's rulers, then, the rise of confessionalism held out both perils and promises. A difference in religion could alienate their subjects from them and undermine their authority. As the French Wars of Religion demonstrated, to the horror of contemporaries, it could set citizen against fellow citizen and tear states apart in civil war. A shared religion, on the other hand, could bolster rulers' authority, binding their subjects to them and to one another more firmly. Given these starkly contrasting possibilities, it is no wonder rulers tried to impose religious uniformity on their territories. Their personal piety impelled many to do the same. Since the thirteenth century, the Catholic Church had asked them to

---

[7] So characterized by Randolph C. Head in "Fragmented Dominion, Fragmented Churches: The Institutionalization of the *Landfrieden* in the Thurgau, 1531–1610," *Archiv fur Reformationsgeschichte* 96 (2005): 119.

[8] Leonard W. Levy, *The Establishment Clause: Religion and the First Amendment* (New York, 1986), ix.

swear they would "strive in good faith and to the best of their ability to exterminate in the territories subject to their jurisdiction all heretics pointed out by the Church."[9] The division of Western Christendom gave them compelling new reasons to do so.

In its wake, Europe's rulers tried to make their personal choice of faith official for their state. Most succeeded, though, as we shall see, not all. Either way, the resulting confessional allegiance eventually became a defining aspect of political identity. Whether or not it initially had wide support, the allegiance was institutionalized and sank popular roots. In some essential and irreversible way, England became a Protestant country, Poland a Catholic one, Sweden Lutheran, the Dutch Republic Calvinist, and so forth. This fusion of religious and political identity, piety and patriotism, was (after confessionalism and the communal quest for holiness) the third great cause of religious intolerance in early modern Europe. Forged in the course of Europe's religious wars, it led both rulers and ordinary people to equate orthodoxy with loyalty and religious dissent with sedition. It gave national politics and even foreign affairs the power to spark waves of religious riots as well as official persecution.

[9] Robert I. Moore, *The Formation of a Persecuting Society: Power and Deviance in Western Europe, 950–1250* (Oxford, 1987), 7.

5

ABU-L-FAZL

The Akbarnama, 1596

At the same time that Europe was conquering and Christianizing the Americas, undergoing religious reformation and division within its own borders, and developing competitive, faith-based national states, descendants of the Turks and Mongols were pressing their power and beliefs on former empires of western and southern Asia. Three new empires were formed by waves of these Central Asian Muslim tribal armies: Ottoman Turkey (1299–1923), Safavid Persia (1502–1736), and Mughal India (1526–1707). In India, the Persian-speaking Mughals (from "Mongols") came out of Afghanistan to conquer what is today Pakistan and northern India. Their conquest

---

Source: *The Akbarnama of Abu-l-Fazl*, Vol. III, trans. H. Beveridge (Calcutta: The Asiatic Society, 1897), 157–59, 364–72.

of various Hindu kingdoms and tribal groups provides the best parallel to the European conquest of the Americas. Like the European Christians, the Muslim Mughals saw their new territories as unenlightened civilizations in need of religious conversion.

Akbar, the third Mughal emperor, reigned from 1556 to 1605. He consolidated Mughal control over all of north India and created a capital city, Fatehpur Sikri, from which he administered the vast empire. This selection from the *Akbarnama* (Akbar Book) by Akbar's counsel, biographer, and historian, Abu-I-Fazl, describes some of Akbar's interests and activities in Fatehpur Sikri. What do these activities suggest about Akbar's ideas about religious conflict or tolerance? Based on this selection, how would you compare Muslim rule in India with European rule in the Americas in the 1500s?

THINKING HISTORICALLY

How would you characterize the language that Abu-I-Fazl uses to refer to Akbar? What does it tell you about the relationship of author and subject? What does this language suggest about the author's purpose or agenda in writing the book?

At this time when the capital was illuminated by his glorious advent, His Majesty ordered that a house of worship should be built in order to the adornment of the spiritual kingdom, and that it should have four verandahs. Though the Divine bounty always has an open door and searches for the fit person, and the inquirer, yet as the lord of the universe, from his general benevolence, conducts his measures according to the rules of the superficial, he chose the eve of Friday, which bears on its face the colouring of the announcement of auspiciousness, for the out-pouring. A general proclamation was issued that, on that night of illumination, all orders and sects of mankind—those who searched after spiritual and physical truth, and those of the common public who sought for an awakening, and the inquirers of every sect—should assemble in the precincts of the holy edifice, and bring forward their spiritual experiences, and their degrees of knowledge of the truth in various and contradictory forms in the bridal chamber of manifestation.

Wisdom and deeds would be tested, and the essence of manhood would be exhibited. Those who were founded on truth entered the hall of acceptance, while those who were only veneered with gold went hastily to the pit of base metal. There was a feast of theology and worship. The vogue of creature-worship was reduced. The dust-stained ones of the pit of contempt became adorners of dominion, and the smooth-tongued, empty-headed rhetoricians lost their rank. To the delightful precincts of that mansion founded upon Truth, thousands upon thousands of inquirers from the seven climes came with heartfelt respect and waited for the advent of the S̲h̲āhin_s̲h̲ah.[1] The world's lord would, with open brow, a cheerful countenance, a capacious heart and an understanding soul, pour the limpid waters of graciousness on those thirsty-lipped ones of expectation's desert, and act as a refiner. He put them into currency, sect by sect, and tested them company by company. He got hold of every one of the miserable and dust-stained ones, and made them successful in their desires,—to say nothing of the be-cloaked and the be-turbaned. From that general assemblage H.M. selected by his far-reaching eye a chosen hand from each class, and established a feast of truth. . . .

Ṣūfī, philosopher, orator, jurist, Sunnī, S̲h̲īa, Brahman, Jatī, Sīūrā Cārbāk, Nazarene, Jew, Ṣābī, Zoroastrian,[2] and others enjoyed exquisite pleasure by beholding the calmness of the assembly, the sitting of the world-lord in the lofty pulpit, and the adornment of the pleasant abode of impartiality. The treasures of secrets were opened out without fear of hostile seekers after battle. The just and truth-perceiving ones of each sect emerged from haughtiness and conceit, and began their search anew. They displayed profundity and meditation, and gathered eternal bliss on the divan of greatness. The conceited and quarrelsome from evilness of disposition and shortness of thought descended into the mire of presumption and sought their profit in loss. Being guided by ignorant companions, and from the predominance of a somnolent fortune, they went into disgrace. The conferences were excellently arranged by the acuteness and keen quest of truth of the world's Khedive.[3] . . .

One night, the assembly in the 'Ibādatk̲h̲āna was increasing the light of truth. Padre Radīf, one of the Nazarene sages, who was singular for his understanding and ability, was making points in that feast of intelligence. Some of the untruthful bigots came forward in a blundering way to answer him. Owing to the calmness of the august assembly, and the increasing light of justice, it became clear that each of these was weaving a circle of old acquisitions, and was not following the highway of proof, and that the explanation of the riddle of truth was not present to their thoughts. The veil was nearly being stripped, once for all, from their procedure. They were ashamed, and abandoned such discourse, and applied themselves to perverting the words of the Gospels. But they could not silence their antagonist by such arguments. The Padre quietly and with an air of conviction said, "Alas, that such things should be thought to be true! In fact, if this faction have such an opinion of our Book, and regard the *Furqān*[4] as the pure word of God, it is proper that

---

[1] King of Kings. [Ed.]

[2] The point of this list is the great variety of sects and faiths; including not only different Muslims, Hindus, and Jains, but also Christians, Jews, and Zoroastrians. [Ed.]

[3] Ruler. [Ed.]

[4] Quran. [Ed.]

a heaped fire be lighted. We shall take the Gospels in our hands, and the 'Ulamā[5] of that faith shall take their book, and then let us enter that testing-place of truth. The escape of any one will be a sign of his truthfulness." The liverless and black-hearted fellows wavered, and in reply to the challenge had recourse to bigotry and wrangling. This cowardice and effrontery displeased [Akbar's] equitable soul, and the banquet of enlightenment was made resplendent by acute observations. Continually, in those day-like nights, glorious subtleties and profound words dropped from his pearl-filled mouth. Among them was this: "Most persons, from intimacy with those who adorn their outside, but are inwardly bad, think that outward semblance, and the letter of Muḥammadanism, profit without internal conviction. Hence we by fear and force compelled many believers in the Brahman[6] religion to adopt the faith of our ancestors. Now that the light of truth has taken possession of our soul, it has become clear that in this distressful place of contrarities, where darkness of comprehension and conceit are heaped up, fold upon fold, a single step cannot be taken without the torch of proof, and that that creed is profitable which is adopted with the approval of wisdom. To repeat the creed, to remove a piece of skin and to place the end of one's bones on the ground from dread of the Sultan, is not seeking after God."[7] . . .

The acute sovereign gave no weight to common talk, and praised whatever was good in any religion. He often adorned the tablet of his tongue by saying "He is a man who makes Justice the guide of the path of inquiry, and takes from every sect what is consonant to reason. Perhaps in this way the lock, whose key has been lost, may be opened." In this connexion, he praised the truth-seeking of the natives of India, and eloquently described the companionship of the men of that country in the day of disaster, and how they played away for the sake of Fidelity, Property, Life, Reputation, and Religion, which are reckoned as comprising the four goods of the world's market. He also dwelt upon the wonderful way in which the women of that country become ashes whenever the day of calamity arrives.[8]

This bliss-collecting class has several divisions. Some protagonists of the path of righteousness yield up their lives merely on hearing of the inevitable lot of their husbands. Many sensualists of old times were, from ignorance and irreflection, unable to read such exquisite creatures by the lines of the forehead, or the record of their behaviour, and entered

---

[5] Those recognized as scholars or authorities in the religious hierarchy of the Islamic religious sciences. [Ed.]

[6] Hindu. [Ed.]

[7] Christian recitation of belief, Jewish circumcision, and Muslim touching of the head to the ground are acts that may be performed without feeling. [Ed.]

[8] Sati: sacrifice of widow on husband's funeral pyre. [Ed.]

with loss the ravine of experiment, and cast away recklessly the priceless jewel! Some deliberately and with open brow enter the flames along with their husband's corpse, or with some token of him who hath gone to the land of annihilation.

Verse.

Being saturated with love, they burn together,
Like two wicks caught by one flame.

Some whom sacrifice of life and fellowship do not make happy, yet, from fear of men's reproach, observe the letter of love, and descend into the mouth of the fire. He said to the learned Christians, "Since you reckon the reverencing of women as part of your religion, and allow not more than one wife to a man, it would not be wonderful if such fidelity and life-sacrifice were found among your women. The extraordinary thing is that it occurs among those of the Brahman religion. There are numerous concubines, and many of them are neglected and unappreciated and spend their days unfructuously in the privy chamber of chastity, yet in spite of such bitterness of life they are flaming torches of love and fellowship." On hearing such noble recitals those present remained silent in the hall of reply, and their tongues reddened with surprise. The Divine message filled with joy all the seekers after wisdom in the august assemblage.

6

JAHANGIR

Memoirs of the Emperor Jahangueir, c. 1625

Jahangir, eldest surviving son of Akbar, reigned as fourth Mughal Emperor from 1605 to 1627. Like his father, he was known for his military exploits, extending and pacifying the empire, and for helping to bring about (though even more than Akbar) the cultural achievements of Mughal India at its greatest. By the time of Jahangir, composing an emperor's memoir had become a well-established tradition among Mughal rulers. Written in Persian, though demonstrating some knowledge of Hindi, Jahangir's memoir was the

Source: Jahangir, *Memoirs of the Emperor Jahangueir*, trans. Major David Price (London: The Oriental Translation Committee, 1829), 14–15, 28–29, 44–45, 49, 94.

latest of several generations of memoirs, going as far back as Timur's fourteenth-century Turkic-Mongol memoir, that were read, translated, poured over, discussed, and cross-referenced by successive generations.

This selection from Jahangir's memoir focuses on two themes: religion and war. How was his treatment of non-Muslims similar to, and different from, that of his father, Akbar? Would you call Jahangir a peaceful man? Would you call him tolerant?

THINKING HISTORICALLY

Jahangir's writings on the first nineteen years of his reign were eventually melded by others into a *Jahangir Nama*, or official biography, in the tradition of his father's *Akbar Nama* and his grandfather Babur's *Babur Nama*, all written by official historians. Notice the language in the following selection compared with the language describing Akbar in *Akbar Nama*. How do the differences in language confirm the likelihood that, in contrast to the *Akbar Nama*, Jahangir wrote this himself? How was his agenda probably different from that of Abu-l-Fazl?

I am here led to relate that at the city of Banaras a temple had been erected by Rajah Maun Sing, which cost him the sum of nearly thirty-six laks of five methkaly ashrefies. The principal idol in this temple had on its head a tiara or cap, enriched with jewels to the amount of three laks of ashrefies. He had placed in this temple moreover, as the associates and ministering servants of the principal idol, four other images of solid gold, each crowned with a tiara, in the like manner enriched with precious stones. It was the belief of these Jehennemites that a dead Hindû, provided when alive he had been a worshipper, when laid before this idol would be restored to life. As I could not possibly give credit to such a pretence, I employed a confidential person to ascertain the truth; and, as I justly supposed, the whole was detected to be an impudent imposture. Of this discovery I availed myself, and I made it my plea for throwing down the temple which was the scene of this imposture; and on the spot, with the very same materials, I erected the great mosque, because the very name of Islam was proscribed at Banaras, and with God's blessing it is my design, if I live, to fill it full with true believers.

On this subject I must however acknowledge, that having on one occasion asked my father the reason why he had forbidden any one to prevent or interfere with the building of these haunts of idolatry, his reply was in the following terms: "My dear child," said he, "I find myself a puissant monarch, the shadow of God upon earth. I have seen that he bestows the blessings of his gracious providence upon all his creatures without distinction. Ill should I discharge the duties of my exalted station, were I to withhold my compassion and indulgence from any of those entrusted to my charge. With all of the human race, with all of God's creatures, I am at peace: why then should I permit myself under any consideration, to be the cause of molestation or aggression to any one? Besides, are not five parts in six of mankind either Hindûs or aliens to the faith; and were I to be governed by motives of the kind suggested in your inquiry, what alternative can I have but to put them all to death! I have thought it therefore my wisest plan to let these men alone. Neither is it to be forgotten, that the class of whom we are speaking, in common with the other inhabitants of Agrah, are usefully engaged, either in the pursuits of science or the arts, or of improvements for the benefit of mankind, and have in numerous instances arrived at the highest distinctions in the state, there being, indeed, to be found in this city men of every description, and of every religion on the face of the earth." . . .

In the practice of being burnt on the funeral pyre of their husbands, as sometimes exhibited among the widows of the Hindûs, I had previously directed, that no woman who was the mother of children should be thus made a sacrifice, however willing to die; and I now further ordained, that in no case was the practice to be permitted, when compulsion was in the slightest degree employed, whatever might be the opinions of the people. In other respects they were in no wise to be molested in the duties of their religion, nor exposed to oppression or violence in any manner whatever. For when I consider that the Almighty has constituted me the shadow of his beneficence on earth, and that his gracious providence is equally extended to all existence, it would but ill accord with the character thus bestowed, to contemplate for an instant the butchery of nearly a whole people; for of the whole population of Hindûstaun, it is notorious that five parts in six are composed of Hindûs, the adorers of images, and the whole concerns of trade and manufactures, weaving, and other industrious and lucrative pursuits, are entirely under the management of these classes. Were it, therefore, ever so much my desire to convert them to the true faith, it would be impossible, otherwise than through the excision of millions of men. Attached as they thus are to their religion, such as it is, they will be snared in the web of their own inventions: they cannot escape the retribution prepared for them; but the massacre of a whole people can never be any business of mine. . . .

In conversation one evening with certain Pundits, the appellation by which their divines and learned men are distinguished by the Hindûs, I took occasion to demand, supposing it to be their intention, in the images which were the objects of their worship, in some sense or other to represent the nature or essence of the Deity, what could be a greater absurdity, or more revolting to the understanding, since we all knew that the Almighty is eternally exempt from change or decay, has neither length nor breadth, and must therefore be totally invisible; how then could it be possible to bring him in any shape under the imperfect scope of human vision? "If, on the other hand," continued I, "your idea is the descent or manifestation of the light divine in such bodies, we already know that the power of the divinity pervades all existence; this was announced to the legislator of Israel from the midst of the burning bush! If, again, it be your design to delineate by affinity (*qu.*) any of the attributes of the Supreme Being, we must confess that here below there cannot in reality exist any affinity, otherwise we might have expected some such manifestation by the hands of those whom, in any religion, we believe to have possessed the faculty of working miracles, and who surpassed all other men in knowledge, in power, and every human perfection. But if you consider these figures as the immediate objects of adoration, and as the source from which you may derive support and assistance in these designs, this is a most fearful conclusion, since adoration is due to God alone, supreme in glory, who has neither equal nor associate." After a variety of arguments for and against, the most intelligent of these Pundits seemed convinced of the weakness of their cause, finally confessing, once for all, that without the intervention of these images they found it impossible to settle their minds to a steady contemplation of the perfections of the Supreme Being. To which, in reply, I could only observe, in what manner, after all, was it that these images of theirs could contribute to the attainment of such an object.

With these pundits my father Akbar was in the constant habit of familiar conversation on every subject. He associated, indeed, with the learned among the Hindûs of every description; and although he might not have derived any particular advantage from the attainment, he had acquired such a knowledge of the elegance of composition, both in prose and verse, that a person not acquainted with the circumstances of his elevated character and station, might have set him down as profoundly learned in every branch of science. . . .

But in his character one prominent feature was, that with every religion he seems to have entered, through life, into terms of unreserved concord, and with the virtuous and enlightened of every class, of every sect and profession of faith, he did not scruple to associate, as opportunities occurred; for the most part devoting the live-long night to this species of social enjoyment. . . .

It had been made known to me that the roads about Kandahar were grievously infested by the Afghans, who by their vexatious exactions rendered the communication in that quarter extremely unsafe for travellers of every description. I had it therefore in contemplation to employ a competent force for the extirpation of these lawless marauders. But while I was yet deliberating on the subject, an individual of the nation of distinguished eminence in his tribe, and who now enjoys in my court the title of Allahdaud Khaun, communicated to me such convincing reasons, that I determined to appoint an imperial foujdaur for the province, under whose management, should they again set at nought the imperial authority, they might then be exterminated without further caution. I did not hesitate to vest the appointment in himself, and he still retains the office under my authority.

Another arrangement in the same quarter was not accomplished with quite as little difficulty. Lushker Khaun, who originally bore the name of Khaujah Abûl Hussun, and who had from an early period been attached to the service of the house of Teymûr, had recently been dignified with his title, and was despatched by my orders towards Kabûl for the purpose of clearing the roads in that direction, which had been also rendered unsafe by the outrages of a licentious banditti. It so happened that when this commander had nearly reached the point for which he was destined he found opposed to him a body of mountaineers, in manners and intellect not much better than wild beasts or devils, who had assembled to the number of forty thousand, horse and foot and matchlock-men, had shut up the approaches against him, and prevented his further advance. Confiding, nevertheless, in the goodness of God and my unwarring fortune, he did not hesitate, with whatever disparity of force, to precipitate himself upon such superior numbers. A conflict thus commenced, which continued with unabated obstinacy from dawn of day until nearly sunset. The enemy were however finally defeated, with the loss of seventeen thousand killed, a number taken prisoners, and a still greater proportion escaping to their hiding-places among the mountains. The prisoners were conducted to my presence yoked together, with the heads of the seventeen thousand slain in the battle suspended from their necks. *After some deliberation as to the destiny of these captives, I resolved that their lives should be spared, and that they should be employed in bringing forage for my elephants.*

7

ABDULLAH WAHHAB

Doctrine of Wahhabis, c. 1800

When one thinks of religious intolerance, one thinks of conquistadors rather than Las Casas and Victoria, and of Wahhabis rather than Akbar and Jahangir. A strict and intolerant interpretation of Islam that subordinates everything to an extreme idea of monotheism, Wahhabism, in fact, is often said to have been or to be the root of

Source: "Translation of an Arabic Pamphlet on the history and doctrines of the Wahhabis, written by the grandson of 'Abdul Wahhab,' founder of the sect, by J. O. Kinealy, C.S.," in *Journal of the Asiatic Society of Bengal*, Vol. XLIII, Part I (Calcutta: Lewis, Baptist Mission Press, 1874), 68–82.

the religious intolerance of Osama bin Laden, Al-Qaeda, the Islamic State, and other militant Islamist organizations. Wahhabism comes from the doctrines of Muhammad ibn 'Abd al-Wahhab (1703–1792), an Arabian preacher who helped establish the kingdom of Saudi Arabia. In the following selection, the grandson of the founder describes the Wahhabi conquest of the holy city of Mecca in 1803 during the annual pilgrimage. What does his account tell you about Wahhabi beliefs and actions? Why, according to this account, did the Wahhabis behave as they did? In what ways were the Wahhabis like the Protestants?

THINKING HISTORICALLY

While the Wahhabis enjoyed the support of Abdul-Azis al-Saud, an alliance that created the Saudi state that exists today, they faced opposition not only from the Ottoman government that was in control of Mecca at that time but also from the many Muslims who did not take to their strict monotheism. What signs do you see in the following selection that the author was addressing this Muslim audience? What criticisms did the Wahhabis feel they had to answer?

Praise be to God, the Lord of the Universe, and blessing and peace be upon our prophet Muhammad, the faithful, and on his people and his companions, and those who lived after them, and their successors of the next generation! Now I was engaged in the holy war, carried on by those who truly believe in the Unity of God, when God, praised be He, graciously permitted us to enter Makkah, the holy, the exalted, at midday, on the 6th day of the week on the 8th of the month (Muharram), 1218, Hijrí. Before this, Sa'úd, our leader in the holy war, whom the Lord protect, had summoned the nobles, the divines, and the common people of Makkah; for indeed the leaders of the pilgrims and the rulers of Makkah had resolved on battle, and had risen up against us in the holy place (haram), to exclude us from the house of God. But when the army of the true believers advanced, the Lord filled their hearts with terror, and they fled hither and thither. Then our commander gave protection to every one within the holy place, while we, with shaven heads and hair cut short, entered with safety, crying "Labbaika," without fear of any created being, and only of the Lord God. Now, though we were more numerous, better armed and disciplined than the people of Makkah, yet we did not cut down their trees, neither did we hunt, nor shed any blood except the blood of victims, and of those four-footed beasts which the Lord has made lawful by his commands.

When our pilgrimage was over, we gathered the people together on the forenoon of the first day of the week, and our leader, whom the

Lord save, explained to the divines what we required of the people, and for which we would slay them, *viz.*, a pure belief in the Unity of God Almighty. He pointed out to them that there was no dispute between us and them except on two points, and that one of these was a sincere belief in the unity of God, and a knowledge of the different kinds of prayer of which *du'á* was one. He added that to shew the significance of 'shirk,' the prophet (may he be blessed!) had put people to death on account of it; that he had continued to call upon them to believe in the Unity of God for some time after he became inspired, and that he had abandoned shirk before the Lord had declared to him the remaining four pillars of Islám. The second point related to actions lawful and unlawful as prohibited. He said that as regards these they retained but the name, while the use, nay any vestige of them, had altogether disappeared.

Then they jointly and severally admitted that our belief was best, and promised the Amír to be guided by the Qorán and the Sunnat. He accepted their promise and pardoned them. Neither did he give any of them the least annoyance, nor cease to treat them with the greatest friendship, especially the divines. And he spoke to them of our faith, publicly and privately giving them proofs of what he believed. We, too, asked them to discourse and confer with us and to speak the truth without reservation. . . .

When this was over, we razed all the large tombs in the city which the people generally worshipped and believed in, and by which they hoped to obtain benefits or ward off evil, so that there did not remain an idol to be adored in that pure city, for which God be praised. Then the taxes and customs we abolished, all the different kinds of instruments for using tobacco we destroyed, and tobacco itself we proclaimed forbidden. Next we burned the dwellings of those selling *hashish*, and living in open wickedness, and issued a proclamation, directing the people to constantly exercise themselves in prayer. They were not to pray in separate groups according to the different Imáms; but all were directed to arrange themselves at each time of prayer behind any Imám who is a (muqallid) follower of any of the four Imáms (may the Lord be pleased with them!). For in this way the Lord would be worshipped by as it were one voice, the faithful of all sects would become friendly disposed towards each other, and all dissensions would cease.

We appointed a ruler over them, 'Abd ul-Mu'ír, the Sharíf, and his rule was established without shedding of blood, and without dishonoring or annoying any person. Praised be the Lord of the Universe! . . .

We believe, our sect holds the real true religion, is the sect of the Ahl-us-Sunnat and al-Jamá'at, and that our way to salvation is that of the pious ancient departed, most easy and excellent, and opposed to the doctrines of those who hold that the modern way is the best. We construe the Qorán and Hadíses according to the meaning apparent on the face of them, and leave the interpretation of them to God, for He is the Ruler. And for this reason that the divines who have passed away, so acted in answering the question as to whether the highest heaven is level or not, which arose out of the words of the merciful God, "The 'Arsh is level;" they held that "level" was well known, and as it was predicated of 'Arsh, it was lawful to believe in it, and heretical to question it. We believe that good and evil proceed from God, the exalted; that nothing happens in His kingdom, but what He commands; that created beings do not possess free will, and are not accountable for their own acts; but on the contrary they obtain rank and spiritual reward, merely as an act of grace, and suffer punishment justly, for God is not bound to do any-thing for His slaves. We believe that the faithful will see Him in the end, but we do not know under what form, as it was beyond our comprehen-sion. And in the same way we follow Imám Ahmad Ibn Hanbal in mat-ters of detail; but we do not reject any one who follows any of the four Imáms, as we do the Shi'ahs, the Zaidiyyahs, and the Imámiyyahs, &c., who belong to no regular churches. . . .

As to those liars and concealers of the truth who say, that we explain the Qorán according to our own views and only hold those traditions which agree with our opinions, without having recourse to the well known commentaries on the one or taking into consideration the narra-tors of the other; that we lower the dignity of our prophet Muhammad (may, &c.) and say that he has rotted in his grave, and that any one of us would derive more advantage from his staff than from him; that he can-not intercede for us; that pilgrimage to his tomb is improper; and that he was so ignorant, as not to know positively "There is no God except God" until he became inspired;—we answer, 'only consider that this sentence "There is no God but God" was given forth in Madínah.' Moreover, they say, we do not attend to the sayings of the learned and destroy the writ-ings of those adhering to any one sect, because though partly true, they are also partly false; that being numerous, we proclaim as infidels not only the people of our time, but all since the beginning of the tenth cen-tury (Hijrah), except those who hold as we do; that we do not enrol any person in our sect until he admits that he was a Mushrik, and his father died one; that we prohibit the invocation of our prophet (may, &c.) and pilgrimage to his grave even in cases where it is lawful; that whoever joins us, is considered as free of all incumbrances, *even his debts*; that we do not allow the Ahl-ul-bait (may the Lord be pleased with them!) any superior rights; that we compel them to marry inferiors, and that we force those who are old to put away their young wives, in order to marry them to young men among us, although no suit for a divorce has been instituted before us, nor is it desired by the parties. All this is simple nonsense, and when we are asked about them, we only answer in the words of the Qorán, "Praised be you. These are great calumnies." In short, whoever asserts any such thing of us, lies against us. He who has seen how we order our lives, has visited our meetings, or knows what we hold, can affirm that all these have been made up, and that the disseminators of them are enemies of religion, brothers of the devil, who lure men away from offering up their prayers to God, the exalted, in perfect accord with His Unity, and prevent them from abandoning those different kinds of shirk of which the Lord has declared that He will never forgive, though He will forgive whatever else He wishes. We believe that whoever commits a mortal sin, such as putting a Muslim to death, fornication, taking interest, drinking wines, or whoever repeats such, does not cease to be a Muslim, nor will he suffer eternal punishment, provided he dies entertaining a true belief in the Unity of God. . . .

We prohibit those forms of Bid'at that affect religion or pious works. Thus drinking coffee, reciting poetry, praising kings, do not affect religion or pious works and are not prohibited, so long as they are not mixed up with acts of the nature above described, neither do we prohibit I'tikáf in a mosque in the belief that it is a pious act. Thus Hasan told 'Omar ibn al Khattáb, Commander of the Faithful, that he had sung before one who was better than he, and 'Omar allowed him to sing.

All games are lawful. Our prophet (may, &c.) allowed Al-Habshí to play in his mosque on the 'I'd day. So it is lawful to chide and punish persons in various ways; to train them in the use of different weapons; or to use anything which tends to encourage warriors in battle, such as a war-drum. But it must not be accompanied with musical instruments. These are forbidden, and indeed the difference between them and a war drum is clear. However the Daff is allowed at marriages. The prophet (may, &c.) has said, "Impurity has descended to us with purity." And again, "tell the Jews that our faith is not difficult." . . .

■ REFLECTIONS

Reports from the self-proclaimed Islamic State of Iraq and Syria (ISIS), at this writing the ugliest example of a Wahhabi-like scourge, feature an often-noticed dichotomy between unspeakable terror and honeyed recruitment. Its propaganda celebrates mass beheadings in order to terrorize other Muslims into submission at the same time that it advertises improved municipal government, schools, and hospitals— improvements that may or may not materialize but whose mention shows a desire to at least appear friendly and supportive. We might see an early instance of this dichotomy in Abdullah Wahhab's account of the Wahhabi conquest of Mecca: "the Lord filled their hearts with terror" but "we didn't cut down their trees . . . nor shed any blood except the blood of the victims." Part of this dichotomy is the difference between the propaganda of conquest and that of governance; another is the difference between the groups' treatment of the "good people" and its acts against the "bad people."

We noticed the same dichotomy in Christianity: the actions of the conquistadors versus the idea of human rights. We do not find either extreme outside of the monotheistic tradition, except in borrowed form. Chinese, Mongol, and Roman soldiers could be every bit as brutal, vengeful, or bloodthirsty as their monotheistic counterparts, but the societies on whose part they battled rarely, if ever, fought for something as absolute and eternal as loyalty to the Creator. Nor, however, did they develop ideas of intrinsic human worth or the brotherhood of man.

We used to think extreme religious views were becoming a thing of the past. Since the eighteenth-century Enlightenment, philosophers and historians have described an increasingly secular world. But if God is dead, religion is not. The nineteenth century witnessed a global religious revival that in many ways has continued into the present. But ironically, religious toleration has also evolved—not as a reaction to religion in a wave of secularism, but within the context of religious revival and competition itself.

Luther, John Calvin, Henry VIII, and most early Protestants were vigorous proponents of state religions, the legislation of Christian morality, and the censorship and proscription of contrary beliefs and behavior. Benjamin Kaplan shows how both the Protestant Reformation and the similar Catholic Counter-Reformation created robustly intolerant religious communities. New kings and parliaments put religious doctrines into the service of national states as if they were badges of identity or flags to be saluted.

It is a modern conceit that religious tolerance has gradually increased since the "dark ages." Kaplan shows us, however, how intolerance increased in Europe with the rise of confessional faiths and the state. A similar transition occurred in India, from the rule of Akbar to that of Aurangzeb, the sixth Mughal emperor. In both cases, religious fundamentalists made government less tolerant of diversity or heterodoxy. The religious leaders who suffered most under the Mughals were not Hindus, but rather the reformers who attempted to unite Hinduism and Islam under a new monotheism, the Sikhs. European Catholics sometimes sided with Turks against Protestants. As often happens, the reformers closest to home smelled the foulest to those in power.

Neither the Chinese nor Hindu traditions held religious orthodoxies, but both required proper observance of certain social and political proprieties. Strong governments, as in most of Chinese history, turned principles like Confucian filial piety into virtual religions that had the force of law and made little appeal to the conscience or individual choice. Daoism and Buddhism appealed to the inner lives of Chinese devotees, but normally posed no conflict to state power. Only in periods of unrest, feudalism, or the breakdown of the state did Daoist or Buddhist monks and priests exercise political power. Even then, however, they did not challenge the state as much as they filled the vacuum left by its weakness or disappearance. In both Japan and Europe, the post-feudal age was one in which the state's rise depended, in part, on the reclamation and monopolization of powers previously exercised by religious institutions.

There are many pasts, but increasingly one present. As many cultural differences meld with the force of rockets and the speed of the Internet, one might well ask to what extent separate histories will still matter to a common present. Increasingly, principles of toleration are enshrined by international organizations in declarations of human rights and the proceedings of international tribunals. Whether we see the roots of modern principles of tolerance in Confucian secularism, Christian separation of church and state, or Muslim cosmopolitanism, we now live in a world where intolerance is widely condemned and legitimately prosecuted.

And yet, fanaticism and intolerance have not disappeared. Religious fundamentalists of various stripes declare their missions to take over governments, convert or even eliminate whole populations, and bring about what they see as the rule of God. History has shown that tolerance is not guaranteed in secular societies, either. Indeed, even the aggressively secular regimes of the twentieth and twenty-first centuries have demonstrated and continue to demonstrate a capacity for brutal persecution of dissidents, religious and otherwise.

The study of the past may be more proficient at revealing what we want for the future than showing us how we can achieve it. But the knowledge of how to get there from here begins with the knowledge of where we are and where we have been. At the very least, the knowledge of how things have changed from the past to the present holds a key to unlocking the future.

18

Women, Marriage, and Family
China and Europe, 1550–1700

■ HISTORICAL CONTEXT

The family is the oldest and most important social institution. For those who marry, marriage can be one of the most important passages in one's life. Yet up until the last few decades these subjects rarely registered as important topics in world history. There were at least three reasons for this. One was the tendency to think of history as the story of public events only — the actions of political officials, governments, and their representatives — instead of the private and domestic sphere. The second was the assumption that the private or domestic sphere had no history, that it had always been the same. As the documents in this chapter will show, nothing could be further from the truth. The third is that most history was written by men until about forty years ago.

Since the urban revolution five thousand years ago, most societies have been patriarchal. The laws, social codes, and dominant ideas have enshrined the power and prestige of men over women, husbands over wives, fathers over children, gods over goddesses, even brothers over sisters. Double standards for adultery, inheritance laws that favor sons, and laws that deny women property or political rights all attest to the power of patriarchal culture and norms. Almost everywhere patriarchies have limited women to the domestic sphere while granting men public and political power.

To better focus our investigation, we will concentrate on two of the important patriarchal civilizations of the Early Modern period: China and Europe. We will study a variety of sources from each, including laws, diaries, poetry, and paintings. Our goal will be to notice and characterize customs and ideas about marriage and family life in these two civilizations.

■ THINKING HISTORICALLY

Making Comparisons

We learn by making comparisons. Every new piece of knowledge we acquire leads to a comparison with what we already know. For example, we arrive in a new town and we are struck by something that we have not seen before. The town has odd street lamps, flowerpots on the sidewalks, or lots of trucks on the street. We start to formulate a theory about the differences between what we observe in the new town and what we already know about our old town. We think we're on to something, but our theory falls apart when we make more observations by staying in the new town another day, or traveling on to the next town, or going halfway across the world. As we gain more experience and make more observations, our original theory explaining an observed difference is supplanted by a much more complex theory about *types* of towns.

History is very much like travel. We learn by comparison, one step at a time, and the journey is never ending. On this trip we begin in China and then move on to Europe. We begin with primary sources and then conclude with a secondary source that will allow us to draw upon our previous readings to make increasingly informed and complex comparisons. Welcome aboard. Next stop, China.

1

Family Instructions for the Miu Lineage, Late Sixteenth Century

Chinese families in Ming times (1368–1644) often organized themselves into groups by male lineage. These groups often shared common land, built ancestral halls, published genealogies, honored their common ancestors, and ensured the success and well-being of future generations. To accomplish the last of these, lineage groups frequently compiled lists of family rules or instructions. This particular example, from the various lines of the Miu family of the Guangdong province in the south, shows how extensive these instructions could be. What values did these family instructions encourage? What activities did the Miu lineage regulate? What kind of families, and what kind of individuals, were these rules intended to produce? How would these rules have had a different impact on women and men?

Source: "Family Instructions for the Miu Lineage, Late Sixteenth Century," trans. Clara Yu, in *Chinese Civilization: A Sourcebook,* 2nd ed., ed. Patricia Ebrey (New York: Free Press, 1993), 238–40, 241–43.

THINKING HISTORICALLY

It is difficult to read this selection without thinking of one's own family and of families in one's own society. How many of the Miu lineage's concerns are concerns of families you know? Family instructions and lineage organizations are not common features of modern American society, even among Chinese Americans who may have a sense of their lineage and family identity. What institutions in modern American society regulate the activities addressed by these family instructions? Or are these activities left for self-regulation or no regulation at all? From reading this document, what do you think are some of the differences between Ming-era Chinese families and modern American families?

Work Hard at One of the Principal Occupations

1. To be filial to one's parents, to be loving to one's brothers, to be diligent and frugal—these are the first tenets of a person of good character. They must be thoroughly understood and faithfully carried out.

One's conscience should be followed like a strict teacher and insight should be sought through introspection. One should study the words and deeds of the ancients to find out their ultimate meanings. One should always remember the principles followed by the ancients, and should not become overwhelmed by current customs. For if one gives in to cruelty, pride, or extravagance, all virtues will be undermined, and nothing will be achieved.

Parents have special responsibilities. *The Book of Changes*[1] says: "The members of a family have strict sovereigns." The "sovereigns" are the parents. Their position in a family is one of unique authority, and they should utilize their authority to dictate matters to maintain order, and to inspire respect, so that the members of the family will all be obedient. If the parents are lenient and indulgent, there will be many troubles which in turn will give rise to even more troubles. Who is to blame for all this? The elders in a family must demand discipline of themselves, following all rules and regulations to the letter, so that the younger members emulate their good behavior and exhort each other to abide by the teachings of the ancient sages. Only in this way can the family hope to last for generations. If, however, the elders of a family should find it difficult to abide by these regulations, the virtuous youngsters of the family should help them along. Because the purpose of my work is to make such work easier, I am not afraid of giving many small details. . . .

2. Those youngsters who have taken Confucian scholarship as their hereditary occupation should be sincere and hard-working, and try to

[1] The *I Ching*, a Chinese classic. [Ed.]

achieve learning naturally while studying under a teacher. Confucianism is the only thing to follow if they wish to bring glory to their family. Those who know how to keep what they have but do not study are as useless as puppets made of clay or wood. Those who study, even if they do not succeed in the examinations, can hope to become teachers or to gain personal benefit. However, there are people who study not for learning's sake, but as a vulgar means of gaining profit. These people are better off doing nothing.

Youngsters who are incapable of concentrating on studying should devote themselves to farming; they should personally grasp the ploughs and eat the fruit of their own labor. In this way they will be able to support their families. If they fold their hands and do nothing, they will soon have to worry about hunger and cold. If, however, they realize that their forefathers also worked hard and that farming is a difficult way of life, they will not be inferior to anyone. In earlier dynasties, officials were all selected because they were filial sons, loving brothers, and diligent farmers. This was to set an example for all people to devote themselves to their professions, and to ensure that the officials were familiar with the hardships of the common people, thereby preventing them from exploiting the commoners for their own profit.

3. Farmers should personally attend to the inspection, measurement, and management of the fields, noting the soil as well as the terrain. The early harvest as well as the grain taxes and the labor service obligations should be carefully calculated. Anyone who indulges in indolence and entrusts these matters to others will not be able to distinguish one kind of crop from another and will certainly be cheated by others. I do not believe such a person could escape bankruptcy.

4. The usual occupations of the people are farming and commerce. If one tries by every possible means to make a great profit from these occupations, it usually leads to loss of capital. Therefore it is more profitable to put one's energy into farming the land; only when the fields are too far away to be tilled by oneself should they be leased to others. One should solicit advice from old farmers as to one's own capacity in farming.

Those who do not follow the usual occupations of farming or business should be taught a skill. Being an artisan is a good way of life and will also shelter a person from hunger and cold. All in all, it is important to remember that one should work hard when young, for when youth expires one can no longer achieve anything. Many people learn this lesson only after it is too late. We should guard against this mistake.

5. Fish can be raised in ponds by supplying them with grass and manure. Vegetables need water. In empty plots one can plant fruit trees such as the pear, persimmon, peach, prune, and plum, and also beans, wheat, hemp, peas, potatoes, and melons. When harvested, these vegetables and fruits can sustain life. During their growth, one should give them constant care, nourishing them and weeding them. In this way, no labor is wasted and no fertile land is left uncultivated. On the contrary,

to purchase everything needed for the morning and evening meals means the members of the family will merely sit and eat. Is this the way things should be?

6. Housewives should take full charge of the kitchen. They should make sure that the store of firewood is sufficient, so that even if it rains several days in succession, they will not be forced to use silver or rice to pay for firewood, thereby impoverishing the family. Housewives should also closely calculate the daily grocery expenses, and make sure there is no undue extravagance. Those who simply sit and wait to be fed only are treating themselves like pigs and dogs, but also are leading their whole households to ruin. . . .

Exercise Restraint

1. Our young people should know their place and observe correct manners. They are not permitted to gamble, to fight, to engage in lawsuits, or to deal in salt[2] privately. Such unlawful acts will only lead to their own downfall.

2. If land or property is not obtained by righteous means, descendants will not be able to enjoy it. When the ancients invented characters, they put gold next to two spears to mean "money," indicating that the danger of plunder or robbery is associated with it. If money is not accumulated by good means, it will disperse like overflowing water; how could it be put to any good? The result is misfortune for oneself as well as for one's posterity. This is the meaning of the saying: "The way of Heaven detests fullness, and only the humble gain." Therefore, accumulation of great wealth inevitably leads to great loss. How true are the words of Laozi![3]

A person's fortune and rank are predestined. One can only do one's best according to propriety and one's own ability; the rest is up to Heaven. If one is easily contented, then a diet of vegetables and soups provides a lifetime of joy. If one does not know one's limitations and tries to accumulate wealth by immoral and dishonest means, how can one avoid disaster? To be able to support oneself through life and not leave one's sons and grandsons in hunger and cold is enough; why should one toil so much?

3. Pride is a dangerous trait. Those who pride themselves on wealth, rank, or learning are inviting evil consequences. Even if one's accomplishments are indeed unique, there is no need to press them on anyone else. "The way of Heaven detests fullness, and only the humble gain." I have seen the truth of this saying many times.

---

[2] Get involved in the salt trade, a state monopoly. Salt was used as a preservative for fish, meat, and other foods. [Ed.]

[3] Lao Tzu, legendary Chinese philosopher and author of the *Dao de Jing*, the Daoist classic. [Ed.]

4. Taking concubines in order to beget heirs should be a last resort, for the sons of the legal wife and the sons of the concubine are never of one mind, causing innumerable conflicts between half brothers. If the parents are in the least partial, problems will multiply, creating misfortune in later generations. Since families have been ruined because of this, it should not be taken lightly.

5. Just as diseases are caused by what goes into one's mouth, misfortunes are caused by what comes out of one's mouth. Those who are immoderate in eating and unrestrained in speaking have no one else to blame for their own ruin.

6. Most men lack resolve and listen to what their women say. As a result, blood relatives become estranged and competitiveness, suspicion, and distance arise between them. Therefore, when a wife first comes into a family, it should be made clear to her that such things are prohibited. "Start teaching one's son when he is a baby; start teaching one's daughter-in-law when she first arrives." That is to say, preventive measures should be taken early.

7. "A family's fortune can be foretold from whether its members are early risers" is a maxim of our ancient sages. Everyone, male and female, should rise before dawn and should not go to bed until after the first drum. Never should they indulge themselves in a false sense of security and leisure, for such behavior will eventually lead them to poverty.

8. Young family members who deliberately violate family regulations should be taken to the family temple, have their offenses reported to the ancestors, and be severely punished. They should then be taught to improve themselves. Those who do not accept punishment or persist in their wrongdoings will bring harm to themselves.

9. As a preventive measure against the unpredictable, the gates should be closed at dusk, and no one should be allowed to go out. Even when there are visitors, dinner parties should end early, so that there will be no need for lighting lamps and candles. On very hot or very cold days, one should be especially considerate of the kitchen servants.

10. For generations this family had dwelt in the country, and everyone has had a set profession; therefore, our descendants should not be allowed to change their place of residence. After living in the city for three years, a person forgets everything about farming; after ten years, he does not even know his lineage. Extravagance and leisure transform people, and it is hard for anyone to remain unaffected. I once remarked that the only legitimate excuse to live in a city temporarily is to flee from bandits.

11. The inner and outer rooms, halls, doorways, and furniture should be swept and dusted every morning at dawn. Dirty doorways and courtyards and haphazardly placed furniture are sure signs of a declining family. Therefore, a schedule should be followed for cleaning them, with no excuses allowed.

12. Those in charge of cooking and kitchen work should make sure that breakfast is served before nine o'clock in the morning and dinner

before five o'clock in the afternoon. Every evening the iron wok and other utensils should be washed and put away, so that the next morning, after rising at dawn, one can expect tea and breakfast to be prepared immediately and served on time. In the kitchen no lamps are allowed in the morning or at night. This is not only to save the expense, but also to avoid harmful contamination of food. Although this is a small matter, it has a great effect on health. Furthermore, since all members of the family have their regular work to do, letting them toil all day without giving them meals at regular hours is no way to provide comfort and relief for them. If these rules are deliberately violated, the person in charge will be punished as an example to the rest.

13. On the tenth and twenty-fifth days of every month, all the members of this branch, from the honored aged members to the youngsters, should gather at dusk for a meeting. Each will give an account of what he has learned, by either calling attention to examples of good and evil, or encouraging diligence, or expounding his obligations, or pointing out tasks to be completed. Each member will take turns presenting his own opinions and listening attentively to others. He should examine himself in the matters being discussed and make efforts to improve himself. The purpose of these meetings is to encourage one another in virtue and to correct each other's mistakes.

The members of the family will take turns being the chairman of these meetings, according to schedule. If someone is unable to chair a meeting on a certain day, he should ask the next person in line to take his place. The chairman should provide tea, but never wine. The meetings may be canceled on days of ancestor worship, parties, or other such occasions, or if the weather is severe. Those who are absent from these meetings for no reason are only doing themselves harm.

There are no set rules for where the meeting should be held, but the place should be convenient for group discussions. The time of the meeting should always be early evening, for this is when people have free time. As a general precaution the meeting should never last until late at night.

14. Women from lower-class families who stop at our houses tend to gossip, create conflicts, peek into the kitchens, or induce our women to believe in prayer and fortune-telling, thereby cheating them out of their money and possessions. Consequently, one should question these women often and punish those who come for no reason, so as to put a stop to the traffic.

15. Blood relatives are as close as the branches of a tree, yet their relationships can still be differentiated according to importance and priority: Parents should be considered before brothers, and brothers should be considered before wives and children. Each person should fulfill his own duties and share with others profit and loss, joy and sorrow, life and death. In this way, the family will get along well and be blessed by Heaven. Should family members fight over property or end up treating each other like enemies, then when death or misfortune strikes they will

be of even less use than strangers. If our ancestors have consciousness, they will not tolerate these unprincipled descendants who are but animals in man's clothing. Heaven responds to human vices with punishments as surely as an echo follows a sound. I hope my sons and grandsons take my words seriously.

16. To get along with patrilineal relatives, fellow villages, and relatives through marriage, one should be gentle in speech and mild in manners. When one is opposed by others, one may remonstrate with them; but when others fall short because of their limitations, one should be tolerant. If one's youngsters or servants get into fights with others, one should look into oneself to find the blame. It is better to be wronged than to wrong others. Those who take affront and become enraged, who conceal their own shortcomings and seek to defeat others, are courting immediate misfortune. Even if the other party is unbearably unreasonable, one should contemplate the fact that the ancient sages had to endure much more. If one remains tolerant and forgiving, one will be able to curb the other party's violence.

2

Qing Law Code on Marriage, 1644–1810

The Chinese law code of the Qing dynasty was essentially the same as that of the preceding Ming dynasty. The entire code covered no more than about 600 pages. Implementation was left up to judges who seemed to have based decisions more on the facts of the case than legal precedent. This selection contains sections from the code on the subject of marriage. Keep in mind that these are only selections from the code, so the absence of an issue does not mean that the code did not cover it.

Try to determine the reasons for these laws. What purpose did each of these serve? What do these laws tell you about Qing China?

THINKING HISTORICALLY

How would you compare this document with the previous selection? Which of these laws are similar to those in your own society? Which are not? For those that are not similar, does your society have a different way of solving the problem or is the issue not a problem?

Source: Ta Tsing leu lee, *Being the Fundamental Laws, and a Selection from the Supplementary Statutes, of the Penal Code of China,* trans. George Thomas Staunton (London: T. Cadell & W. Davies, 1810), 107–08, 110–12, 116–18, 120. Spelling modernized.

Section 101

Marriages: How Regulated

When a marriage is intended to be contracted, it shall be, in the first instance reciprocally explained to, and clearly understood by, the families interested, whether the parties who design to marry are or are not, diseased, infirm, aged, or under age; and whether they are the children of their parents by blood, or only by adoption; if either of the contracting families then object, the proceedings shall be carried no further; if they still approve, they shall then in conjunction with the negotiators of the marriage, if such there be, draw up the marriage-articles.

If, after the woman is thus regularly affianced by the recognition of the marriage-articles, or by a personal interview and agreement between the families, the family of the intended bride should repent having entered into the contract, and refuse to execute it, the person amongst them who had authority to give her away shall be punished with 50 blows, and the marriage shall be completed agreeably to the original contract.—Although the marriage-articles should not have been drawn up in writing, the acceptance of the marriage-presents shall be sufficient evidence of the agreement between the parties. . . .

Section 102

Lending Wives or Daughters on Hire

Whoever lends any one of his wives, to be hired as a temporary wife, shall be punished with 80 blows,—whoever lends his daughter in like manner, shall be punished with 60 blows; the wife or daughter in such cases, shall not be held responsible.

Whoever, falsely representing any of his wives as his sister, gives her away in marriage, shall receive 100 blows, and the wife consenting thereto, shall be punished with 80 blows.

Those who knowingly receive in marriage the wives, or hire for a limited time the wives or daughters of others, shall participate equally in the aforesaid punishment, and the parties thus unlawfully connected, shall be separated; the daughter shall be returned to her parents, and the wife to the family to which she originally belonged; the pecuniary confederation in each case shall be forfeited to government. Those who ignorantly receive such persons in marriage, contrary to the laws, shall be excused, and recover the amount of the marriage-presents.

Section 103

Regard to Rank and Priority among Wives

Whoever degrades his first or principal wife to the condition of an inferior wife or concubine, shall be punished with 100 blows. Whoever, during the life-time of his first wife, raises an inferior wife to the rank and condition of a first wife, shall be punished with 90 blows, and in both the cases, each of the several wives shall be replaced in the rank to which she was originally entitled upon her marriage.

Whoever, having a first wife living, enters into marriage with another female as a first wife, shall likewise be punished with 90 blows; and the marriage being considered null and void, the parties shall be separated, and the woman returned to her parents.

Section 105

Marriage During the Legal Period of Mourning

If any man or woman enters into an equal marriage during the legal period of mourning for a deceased parent, or any widow enters into a second and equal marriage within the legal period of mourning for her deceased husband, the offending party shall be punished with 100 blows.

If it is not an equal match, that is to say, if a man takes an inferior wife from a subordinate rank, or a woman connects herself in marriage as one of the inferior wives of her husband, the punishment attending a breach of this law shall be less by two degrees.

If a widow who, during the life of her husband, had received honorary rank from the Emperor, ever marries again, she shall suffer punishment as above described, and moreover lose her rank, as well as be separated from her second husband. . . .

Section 110

Marriage of Officers of Government into Families Subject to Their Jurisdiction

If any officer belonging to the government of a city of the first, second, or third order, marries, while in office, the wife or daughter of any inhabitant of the country under his jurisdiction, he shall be punished with 80 blows.

If any officer of government marries the wife or daughter of any person having an interest in the legal proceedings at the same time under his investigation, he shall be punished with 100 blows, and the member of the family of the bride, who gave her away, shall be equally punishable.

The woman, whether previously married or not, shall be restored to her parents, and the marriage-present forfeited in every case to government.

If the officer of government accomplishes the marriage by the force or influence of his authority, his punishment shall be increased two degrees, and the family of the female, being in such a case exempt from responsibility, she shall, if previously single, be restored to her parents; and if previously married, to her former husband; the marriage-present shall, not in either case be forfeited. . . .

Section 113

Marriage with Female Musicians and Comedians

If any officer or clerk of government, either in the civil or military department, marries, as his first or other wife, a female musician or comedian, he shall be punished with 60 blows, and the marriage being null and void, the female shall be sent back to her parents and rendered incapable of returning to her profession. The marriage-present shall be forfeited to government.

If the son or grand-son, being the heir of any officer of government having hereditary rank, commits this offence; he shall suffer the same punishment, and whenever he succeeds to the inheritance, his parental honours shall descend to him under a reduction of one degree.

Section 116

Law of Divorce

If a husband repudiates his first wife, without her having broken the matrimonial connection by the crime of adultery, or otherwise; and without her having furnished him with any of the seven justifying causes of divorce, he shall in every such case be punished with 80 blows. Moreover, although one of the seven justifying causes of divorce should be chargeable upon the wife, namely, (1) barrenness; (2) lasciviousness;. (3) disregard of her husband's parents; (4) talkativeness; (5) thievish propensities; (6) envious and suspicious temper; and, lastly, (7) inveterate infirmity; yet, if any of the three reasons against a divorce should exist, namely, (1) the wife's having mourned three years for her husband's parents; (2) the family's having become rich after having been poor previous to, and at the time of, marriage; and, (3) the wife's having no parents living to receive her back again; in these cases, none of the seven aforementioned causes will justify a divorce, and the husband who puts away his wife upon such grounds, shall suffer punishment two degrees less than that last stated, and be obliged to receive her again.

If the wife shall have broken the matrimonial connection by an act of adultery, or by any other act, which by law not only authorizes but requires that the parties should be separated, the husband shall receive a punishment of 80 blows, if he retains her.

When the husband and wife do not agree, and both parties are desirous of separation, the law limiting the right of divorce shall not be enforced to prevent it. . . .

3

ANNA BIJNS

"Unyoked Is Best! Happy the Woman without a Man," 1567

Anna Bijns* (1494–1575) was a Flemish nun and poet who lived in Antwerp, taught in a Catholic school in that city, wrote biting criticism of Martin Luther and the Protestant Reformation, and in her many works helped shape the Dutch language. The impact of Luther, and Protestantism more generally, on the lives of women has been the subject of much debate. Luther opposed nunneries and monasticism, believing that it was the natural duty of all women to marry and bear children. At the same time, he encouraged a level of reciprocal love and respect in marriage that was less emphasized in Catholicism. The Protestant translations of the Bible from Latin also opened a pathway for individuals, including educated women, to participate in the religious life, though not as nuns. Whether or not the sentiments of this poem are more Catholic than Protestant, are they more European than Chinese? Why or why not?

THINKING HISTORICALLY

No one should imagine that the ideas conveyed in this poem were typical or representative of European thought in the sixteenth century. This was obviously an extreme view that ran counter to traditional and commonly accepted ideas. Note how some phrases of the poem convey the recognition that most people will disagree with the sentiments being expressed.

When we are comparing documents from different cultures, we must always try to understand how representative they are of the

* bynz

Source: Anna Bijns, "Unyoked Is Best," trans. Kristiaan P. G. Aercke, in *Women and Writers of the Renaissance and Reformation*, ed. Katharina M. Wilson (Athens: The University of Georgia Press, 1987), 382–83.

views of the larger population. The Miu family document (selection 1) expresses the views of a single family, but lineage regulations were common in sixteenth-century China, and their ubiquity reflected an even greater consensus on the importance of the family. Anna Bijns's poem is a personal view that expresses a minority opinion. But in what sense is this a European, rather than a Chinese, minority view? Do you think Anna Bijns's view might appeal to more people today than it did in the sixteenth century? If so, why?

How good to be a woman, how much better to be a man!
Maidens and wenches, remember the lesson you're about to hear.
Don't hurtle yourself into marriage far too soon.
The saying goes: "Where's your spouse? Where's your honor?"
But one who earns her board and clothes
Shouldn't scurry to suffer a man's rod.
So much for my advice, because I suspect—
Nay, see it sadly proven day by day—
'T happens all the time!
However rich in goods a girl might be,
Her marriage ring will shackle her for life.
If however she stays single
With purity and spotlessness foremost,
Then she is lord as well as lady, Fantastic, not?
Though wedlock I do not decry:
Unyoked is best! Happy the woman without a man.

Fine girls turning into loathly hags—
'Tis true! Poor sluts! Poor tramps! Cruel marriage!
Which makes me deaf to wedding bells.
Huh! First they marry the guy, luckless dears,
Thinking their love just too hot to cool.
Well, they're sorry and sad within a single year.
Wedlock's burden is far too heavy.
They know best whom it harnessed.
So often is a wife distressed, afraid.
When after troubles hither and thither he goes
In search of dice and liquor, night and day,
She'll curse herself for that initial "yes."
So, beware ere you begin.
Just listen, don't get yourself into it.
Unyoked is best! Happy the woman without a man.

A man oft comes home all drunk and pissed
Just when his wife had worked her fingers to the bone
(So many chores to keep a decent house!),
But if she wants to get in a word or two,
She gets to taste his fist—no more.

And that besotted keg she is supposed to obey?
Why, yelling and scolding is all she gets,
Such are his ways—and hapless his victim.
And if the nymphs of Venus he chooses to frequent,
What hearty welcome will await him home.
Maidens, young ladies: learn from another's doom,
Ere you, too, end up in fetters and chains,
Please don't argue with me on this,
No matter who contradicts, I stick to it:
Unyoked is best! Happy the woman without a man.

A single lady has a single income,
But likewise, isn't bothered by another's whims.
And I think: that freedom is worth a lot.
Who'll scoff at her, regardless what she does,
And though every penny she makes herself,
Just think of how much less she spends!
An independent lady is an extraordinary prize—
All right, of a man's boon she is deprived,
But she's lord and lady of her very own hearth.
To do one's business and no explaining sure is lots of fun!
Go to bed when she list,[1] rise when she list, all as she will,
And no one to comment! Grab tight your independence then.
Freedom is such a blessed thing.
To all girls: though the right Guy might come along:
Unyoked is best! Happy the woman without a man.

Regardless of the fortune a woman might bring,
Many men consider her a slave, that's all.
Don't let a honeyed tongue catch you off guard,
Refrain from gulping it all down. Let them rave,
For, I guess, decent men resemble white ravens.
Abandon the airy castles they will build for you.
Once their tongue has limed[2] a bird:
Bye bye love—and love just flies away.
To women marriage comes to mean betrayal
And the condemnation to a very awful fate.
All her own is spent, her lord impossible to bear.
It's *peine forte et dure*[3] instead of fun and games.
Oft it was the money, and not the man
Which goaded so many into their fate.
Unyoked is best! Happy the woman without a man.

[1] Wants. [Ed.]

[2] Caught. [Ed.]

[3] Long and forceful punishment; a form of torture whereby the victim was slowly crushed by heaping rocks on a board laid over his or her body. [Ed.]

A European Family from Flanders, c. 1610

This is a painting of a family in Flanders (now north Belgium) by an artist of the Flemish School around 1610. Flanders was a particularly prosperous cloth-producing and shipping center from the thirteenth century to the early 1600s. The painting is called "Portrait of a Family at Midday Meal." At the time, the midday meal was traditionally the largest meal of the day.

What signs suggest that this is a successful middle-class family? What does the painting tell you about the eating habits of the middle class in Flanders? Notice how the artist frames the family between the mother and the father. The painting also includes members of the household who were not family members. Based on the selection by Mary Jo Maynes and Ann Waltner (selection 9), who are likely the nonfamily members, and what functions did they perform?

THINKING HISTORICALLY

Compare this view of marriage and family life with that of Anna Bijns, who was also from Flanders. How does Bijns's view of marriage and the family differ from this artist's depiction of family life?

Figure 18.1 "Portrait of a Family at Midday Meal," c. 1610.
Source: Private Collection / © Lawrence Steigrad Fine Arts, New York / Bridgeman Images.

5

A Chinese Family, Eighteenth Century

This painting, called "Portrait of an Unidentified Man and His Son," was painted on a hanging scroll of silk in the eighteenth century during the Chinese Qing dynasty. The artist is unknown. We see the man in the center with various rolled scrolls and printed books at his

Figure 18.2 "Portrait of an Unidentified Man and His Son," Qing dynasty, eighteenth century.

Source: Freer Gallery of Art, Smithsonian Institution, USA / Purchase—Smithsonian Collections Acquisition Program and partial gift of Richard G. Pritzlaff / Bridgeman Images.

side. To the left is his son. Behind them are a woman who is placing peonies in a vase and another woman, under Chinese tulip tree blossoms, who seems to be carrying a cup of tea. While we do not have enough information to decipher all of these symbols, and we cannot be sure of the identities of the women, what can we say about how the picture captures Chinese ideas of the family?

THINKING HISTORICALLY

Compare this image with the previous one of a family from Flanders in Europe. How is this family's economic status similar to or different from that of the family from Flanders? How are the positions of men in relation to women similar, and what does this suggest about women's roles in the family during these periods?

6

The Autobiography of Mrs. Alice Thornton, 1645–1657

Alice Thornton (1626–1706/7) had a comfortable childhood in Ireland where her father was Lord Deputy, the king's representative. After her father's death in 1640, family circumstances declined, but despite the eruption of the English Civil War and the family's loyalty to the deposed King Charles and the Church of England, they managed an upper-middle-class standard of living in England.

Our selections from Alice Thornton's autobiography are drawn from events that occurred between 1645 and 1657. What happened in 1645 that might have influenced her idea of marriage? How did she feel about marriage when the idea was proposed in 1651? How would you characterize her married life?

THINKING HISTORICALLY

How were the author's family circumstances different from those of a woman born into the Miu lineage (selection 1)? What differences between European and Chinese marriage are revealed in this account?

Source: *The Autobiography of Mrs. Alice Thornton, of East Norton, Co., York* (London: The Surtees Society, 1875), 49–50, 75–77, 81–88, 91, 94–95. For ease of reading, the spelling has been modernized in some instances. [Ed.]

The Death of My Sister Danby, Sept. 30, 1645

About this year, my dear and only sister, the Lady Danby, drew near her time for delivery of her sixteenth child. Ten whereof had been baptized, the other six were stillborn, when she was above half gone with them, she having miscarried of them all upon frights by fire in her chamber, falls, and such like accidents happening. . . .

She had been very ill long time before her delivery, and much altered in the heat of her body, being feverish. After exceeding sore travail she was delivered of a goodly son about August 3rd, by one dame Sworre. This boy was named Francis, after another of that name, a sweet child that died that summer of the smallpox. This child came double into the world, with such extremity that she was exceedingly tormented with pains, so that she was deprived of the benefit of sleep for fourteen days, except a few frightful slumbers; neither could she eat anything for her nourishment as usual. Yet still did she spend her time in discourse of goodness excellently pious, godly, and religious, instructing her children and servants, and preparing her soul for her dear Redeemer, as it was her saying she should not be long from Him. . . .

The Marriage of Alice Wandesforde, December 15, 1651

After many troubles and afflictions under which it pleased God to exercise my mother and self in since the death of my father, she was desirous to see me comfortably settled in the estate of marriage, in which she hoped to receive some satisfaction, finding age and weakness to seize more each year, which added a spur to her desires for the future well-being of her children, according to every one of their capacities. As to myself, I was exceedingly satisfied in that happy and free condition, wherein I enjoyed my time with delight abundantly in the service of my God, and the obedience I owed to such an excellent parent, in whose enjoyment I accounted my days spent with great content and comfort; the only fears which possessed me was least I should be deprived of that great blessing I had in her life. Nor could I, without much reluctance, draw my thoughts to the change of my single life, knowing too much of the cares of this world sufficiently without the addition of such incident to the married estate. As to the fortune left by my father, it was fair, and more then competent, so that I needed not fear (by God's blessing) to have been troublesome to my friends, but to be rather in a condition to assist them if need had required. . . .

Nevertheless, such was my dear mother's affection to the family for its preservation, that she harkened to the proposal made for Mr. Thornton's marriage, albeit therein she disobliged some persons of very good worth and quality which had solicited her earnestly in my behalf, and such as were of large and considerable estates of her neighbors about her. And, after the first and second view betwixt us, she closed so far with him that she was willing he should proceed in his suit, and that cordially, if I should see cause to accept. For my own particular, I was not hasty to change my free estate without much consideration, both as to my present and future, the first inclining me rather to continue so still, wherein none could be more satisfied. The second would contract much more trouble, twisted inseparably with those comforts God gave in that estate. Yet might I be hopeful to serve God in those duties incumbent on a wife, a mother, a mistress, and governess in a family. And if it pleased God so to dispose of me in marriage, making me a more public instrument of good to those several relations, I thought it rather duty in me to accept my friends' desires for a joint benefit, then my own single retired content, so that Almighty God might receive the glory of my change, and I more capacitated to serve Him in this generation, in what He thus called me unto. Therefore it highly concerned me to enter into this greatest change of my life with abundance of fear and caution, not lightly, nor unadvisedly, nor, as I may take my God to witness that knows the secrets of hearts, I did it not to fulfill the lusts of the flesh, but in chastity and singleness of heart, as marrying in the Lord. And to that end that I might have a blessing upon me, in all my undertakings, I powered out my petitions before the God of my life to direct, strengthen, lead, and counsel me what to do in this concern, which so much tended to my future comfort or discomfort. . . . After which petitions to my God, I was the more inclined to accept of this proposition of my friends' finding; also that the gentleman seemed to be a very godly, sober, and discreet person, free from all manner of vice, and of a good conversation. . . .

Alice Wandesforde, the daughter of Christopher Wandesford, Esq., late Lord Deputy of Ireland, was married to William Thornton, esquire, of Easte Newton, at my mother's house in Hipswell, by Mr. Siddall, December the 15th, 1651. Mr. Siddall made a most pious and profitable exhortation to us, showing our duties, and teaching us the fear of the Lord in this our new estate of life, with many zealous prayers for us. My dear and honored mother gave me in marriage, in the presence of my own brother John Wandesforde; my uncle Norton, my uncle Darley (Francis), my cousin Dodsworth of Wattlosse, George Lightfoote, and Dafeny, Robert Webster, Martha Richison, Ralfe Ianson, Robert Loftus the elder. . . .

A Deliverance from Death That Day on Which I Was Married, December 15th, 1651

That very day on which I was married, having been in health and strength for many years before, I fell suddenly so ill and sick after two o'clock in the afternoon that I thought, and all that saw me did believe, it would have been my last night, being surprised with a violent pain in my head and stomach, causing a great vomiting and sickness at my heart, which lasted eight hours before I had any intermission; but, blessed be the Lord our God, the Father of mercies, Which had compassion on me, and by the means that was used I was strengthened wonderfully beyond expectation, being pretty well about ten o'clock at night. My dear husband, with my mother, was exceeding tender over me, which was a great comfort to my spirits. What the cause of this fit was I could not conjecture, save that I might have brought it upon me by cold taken the night before, when I sat up late in preparing for the next day, and washing my feet at that time of the year, which my mother did believe was the cause of that dangerous fit the next day. But, however it was, or from what cause it proceeded, I received a great mercy in my preservation from God, and shall ever acknowledge the same in humble gratitude for His infinite loving kindness forever. I looked upon this first business of my new condition to be a little discouragement, although God was able to turn all things for the best and to my good, that I might not build too much hopes of happiness in things of this world, nor in the comforts of a loving husband, whom God had given me, but set my desires more upon the love of my Lord and God.

Meditations upon My Deliverance of My First Child, and of the Great Sickness Followed for Three-Quarters of a Year; August 6, 1652, Lasted til May 12, 1653

About seven weeks after I married it pleased God to give me the blessing of conception. The first quarter I was exceeding sickly in breeding, till I was with quick childe; after which I was very strong and healthy, I bless God, only much hotter than formerly, as is usual in such cases from a natural cause, insomuch that my nose bled much when I was about half gone, by reason of the increase of heat. Mr. Thornton had a desire that I should visit his friends, in which I freely joined, his mother living about fifty miles from Hipswell, and all at Newton and Buttercrambe. In my passage thither I sweat exceedingly, and was much inclining to be feverish, wanting not eight weeks of my time, so that Dr. Wittie said that I should go near to fall into a fever, or some desperate sickness, if I did not cool my blood, by taking some away, and if I had stayed but two days longer, I had followed his advice. In his return home from Newton, his own estate, I was carried over Hambleton towards Sir William Askough's house, where I passed down on foot a very high wall betwixt Hudhill and Whitsoncliffe, which is above a mile steep down, and indeed so bad that I could not scarce tread the narrow steps, which was exceeding bad for me in that condition, and sore to endure, the way so straight and none to lead me but my maid [Susan

Gosling], which could scarce make shift to get down herself, all our company being gone down before. Each step did very much strain me, being so big with child, nor could I have got down if I had not then been in my full strength and nimble on foot. But, I bless God, I got down safe at last, though much tired, and hot and weary, finding myself not well, but troubled with pains after my walk. Mr. Thornton would not have brought me that way if he had known it so dangerous, and I was a stranger in that place; but he was advised by some to go that way before we came down the hill. This was the first occasion which brought me a great deal of misery, and killed my sweet infant in my womb. . . . The doctor came post the next day, when he found me very weak, and durst not let me blood that night, but gave me cordials, etc., till the next day, and if I got but one hour's rest that night, he would do it the morning following. That night the two doctors had a dispute about the letting me bleed. Mr. Mahum was against it, and Dr. Wittie for it; but I soon decided that dispute, and told them, if they would save my life, I must bleed. So the next day I had six or seven ounces taken which was turned very bad by my sickness, but I found a change immediately in my sight, which was exceeding dim before, and then I see as well as ever clearly, and my strength began a little to return; these things I relate that I may set forth the mercy of my ever gracious God, Who had blessed the means in such manner. Who can sufficiently extol His Majesty for His boundless mercies to me His weak creature, for from that time I was better, and he had hopes of my life. The doctor stayed with me seven days during my sickness; my poor infant within me was greatly forced with violent motions perpetually, till it grew so weak that it had left stirring, and about the 27th of August I found myself in great pains as it were the colic, after which I began to be in travail, and about the next day at night I was delivered of a goodly daughter, who lived not so long as that we could get a minister to baptize it, though we presently sent for one. This my sweet babe and first child departed this life half an hour after its birth, being received, I hope, into the arms of Him that gave it. She was buried that night, being Friday, the 27th of August, 1652, at Easby church. The effects of this fever remained by several distempers successively, first, after the miscarriage I fell into a most terrible shaking ague, lasting one quarter of a year, by fits each day twice, in much violence, so that the sweat was great with faintings, being thereby weakened till I could not stand or go. The hair on my head came off, my nails of my fingers and toes came off, my teeth did shake, and ready to come out and grew black. After the ague left me, upon a medicine of London treacle, I fell into the jaundice, which vexed me very hardly one full quarter and a half more. I finding Dr. Wittie's judgment true, that it would prove a chronic distemper; but blessed be the Lord, upon great and many means used and all remedies, I was at length cured of all distempers and weaknesses, which, from its beginning, had lasted three-quarters of a year full out. Thus had I a sad entertainment and beginning of my change of life, the comforts thereof being turned into much discomforts and weaknesses, but still I was upheld by an Almighty Power, therefore will I praise the Lord my God. Amen. . . .

Upon the Birth of My Second Child and Daughter, Born at Hipswell on the 3rd of January in the Year 1654

Alice Thornton, my second child, was born at Hipswell near Richmond in Yorkshire the 3rd day of January, 1654, baptized the 5th of the same. Witnesses, my mother the Lady Wandesforde, my uncle Mr. Major Norton, and my cousin Yorke his daughter, at Hipswell, by Mr. Michell Siddall, minister then of Caterick.

It was the pleasure of God to give me but a week time after my daughter Alice her birth, and she had many preservations from death in the first year, being one night delivered from being overlaid by her nurse, who laid in my dear mother's chamber a good while. One night my mother was writing pretty late, and she heard my dear child make a groaning troublesomely, and stepping immediately to nurse's bedside she saw the nurse fallen asleep, with her breast in the child's mouth, and lying over the child; at which she, being affrighted, pulled the nurse suddenly off from her, and so preserved my dear child from being smothered. . . .

Elizabeth Thornton's Death, the 5th of September, 1656

It pleased God to take from me my dear child Betty, which had been long in the rickets and consumption, gotten at first by an ague, and much gone in the rickets, which I conceived was caused by ill milk at two nurses. And notwithstanding all the means I used, and had her with Naly at St. Mungno's Well for it, she grew weaker, and at the last, in a most desperate cough that destroyed her lungs, she died. . . .

Elizabeth Thornton, my third child, died the 5th of September, 1656, betwixt the hours of five and six in the morning. Her age was one year six months and twenty-one days. Was buried the same day at Catterick by Mr. Siddall.

Meditations on the Deliverance of My First Son and Fifth Child at Hipswell the 10th of December, 1657

It pleased God, in much mercy, to restore me to strength to go to my full time, my labor beginning three days; but upon the Wednesday, the ninth of December, I fell into exceeding sharp travail in great extremity, so that the midwife did believe I should be delivered soon. But lo! it fell out contrary, for the child stayed in the birth, and came cross with his feet first, and in this condition continued till Thursday morning between two and three o'clock, at which time I was upon the rack in bearing my child with such exquisite torment, as if each lime were divided from other, for the space of two hours; when at length, being speechless and breathless, I was, by the infinite providence of God, in great mercy delivered. But I having had such sore travail in danger of my life so long, and the child coming into the world with his feet first, caused the child to be almost strangled in the birth, only living about half an hour, so died before we could get a minister to baptize him, although he was sent for.

7

Diary of the Countess de Rochefort, 1689

The Countess de Rochefort was an aristocrat in the court of Louis XIV. She lived on an estate in Avignon in the south of France. A good deal of the time, her husband[1] was away on military campaigns. To do so in 1689 he needed most of the family's available cash for expenses, leaving the countess to manage the estate under financial pressure. These selections from her diary for 1689 give us an idea of the daily life of a woman of the aristocracy who still is quite busy.

How does she spend her days? How dependent or independent does she seem? Does this source tell you anything about the lives of aristocratic women in Europe? If so, what?

THINKING HISTORICALLY

In both China and Europe, aristocrats lived very different lives from the middle classes. How different was the world of the countess from that of Alice Thornton? In what ways might the author's life have been different from a noble's wife in China? What would account for those differences?

---

[1] Comte de Rochefort (1630–1712), younger son of Louis de Rohan, duc de Montbazon.

Source: Julia O'Faolain and Lauro Martines, eds., *Not in God's Image: Women in History from the Greeks to the Victorians* (New York: Harper & Row, 1973), 234–37. From *Une Grande Dame dans son ménage au temps de Louis XIV, D'apres le journal de la comtesse de Rochefort* (1689).

25 May, 1689. I wrote to M. Carretier, my attorney at the Court of Toulouse, to ask for news. . . . I wrote to M. Penaut, my attorney at Montpellier, to proceed with our suit against the community of Beaucaire. The same day I wrote also to M. Belot, attorney at the Court of Toloze, for news of M. Brocardy's case.

M. Odoacre, the community's arbiter arrived today. He and the royal attorney began discussing things after dinner. It does not look to me as though we can hope for an amicable settlement. . . . Today I also went to Mormont to look at the woods. I found that far too much had been cut, but what is left is growing back very well. The part that is for sale is worth more than 40 écus, for the wood is thicker there. . . .

1 June. I ordered that on all our lands prayers be offered for M. de Rochefort until he returns.

The butcher from Roche paid me 34 livres, 10 sols of what he owes me, plus 71 pounds of mutton at 2 sols and 4 deniers per pound, and 15 pounds of beef at 18 deniers. Adding it all up, he has paid off 43 livres, 10 sols of his debt. . . .

Toward evening, being at Bégude, I inspected my crops and found them very fine. However, the tenant tells me that if he had sowed earlier the wheat would be finer and more plentiful. I decided therefore to let him follow his own judgment as to when he should sow. He also told me that the ditches need scouring, and I admitted that they did.

I got the carders in today to work on a hundredweight of washed wool from which I aim to make 8 cannes [1 canne = between 2 and 3 meters] of crépon, 14 of light wool, 13 of floss serge, and 30 of caddis.

3 June. I forgot to note that on the first of the month I had work started on one of the two mill stones at the Rochefort mill. It was very urgent because the wheat was coming out unground. I am giving the mason his food while he works on it.

10 June. M. Jean Artaud came to see me to offer to lease the small farm house at Beaujeu. . . .

13 June. We began reeling the silk today. . . . Nine pounds of cocoons produced fifteen ounces of fine silk.

14 June. I got up early to supervise the storing of the casks in the cellar. I had the vats made and the small cellars got ready for the fair. I'm having a large wooden vat made for pressing the grapes. . . .

A small pewter carafe I had made has been delivered. I have also had dishes and two dozen plates remade. All my pewter has been reworked and I have had it marked as well.

I sent 4 lbs. of soap to Pernes, where I'm having thread bleached. . . .

The same day I sent to M. Patron, the trimmer, to ask how much braid would be needed for my livery. He said I would need 80 cannes [160 meters] of the wide and 30 [60 meters] of the narrow and that to make that much would take 10 lbs. of heavy silk and 8 lbs. of fine floss silk. . . . I sent 2 cannes of red caddis to T. to make the footmen's jackets. . . .

Catin came from Rochefort today where she had been supervising the carders. She brought 100 chickens which were left of those I had bought; adding the 28 I had here, that makes 128. I have over 40 hens as well, one cock and 10 turkeys. . . .

15 June. I ordered the guard at Rochefort to sell my wine. He sold two casks to the butcher and is keeping the third one for the harvest.

I have arranged to have the Gazette sent and held for me twice a week at Tarascon.

20 June. I got up early and heard Mass, then went to see my meadow at Maubuisson. I have had all the wines in my cellar tasted; they were pronounced to be excellent. There are 22 casks altogether. I have decided to keep three and sell the rest.

I spent the rest of the day cutting out and having underclothes made up for my children.

21 June. I got up early as usual to write to M. de Rochefort and to M. Sicard. After Mass, I had the attics prepared for the new wheat; what's left of the old will be ground into flour for the servants. Next I gave orders to have my old skirts cut up to make dresses for my son, the chevalier.

M. Treven de Villeneuve came to see me to tell me that . . . he was obliged to ask me for money owed for two pensions, which amounts to 733 livres, 6 sols, 8 deniers. I answered that it was not too good a time to ask me for money, that M. de Rochefort had taken all I had to pay for his campaign and that I even had letters from the government dispensing me from paying any money out before his return. . . .

27 June. I got up early to prepare for the bleeding I am to have done on my ankle because of the bad headaches I have been suffering for some time. . . .

5 July . . . the Sisters of Mercy wrote from Avignon asking for their pension and back payments. I wrote asking them to wait until the harvest, when I would pay them; otherwise I would use my *lettres d'Etat* to stop their suit.

6 July . . . I spent the rest of the day making an inventory of the furniture, beds, chairs and so forth to make sure that nothing gets damaged during the fair.

I had good news from M. de Rochefort.

12 July. I spent the morning having beds made up in the rooms that are to be let during the fair.

I wrote to my attorney. . . .

I went down to the cellar and tasted my wines. I had the three best casks marked; they will be kept for Monsieur, and three others for the commonalty.

27 July. I spent the day doing my accounts. . . .

17 September. I sent M. Trevenin the rest of what I owed him. . . . The tenant at Jonquieres says . . . the owner of a neighboring farmhouse

has been encroaching on our land. This will have to be looked into at once. . . .

26 September. M. de Rochefort came home. . . .

30 May, 1690. From November 10 until February I was so depressed with melancholy at the bad state in which I saw my business that I was neither eating nor sleeping; . . . melancholy is good for neither the body nor the soul. . . . Now I'm partly over it. . . . I am getting back to work. . . . God has remedied my affairs when I was least expecting it. With His grace, I hope to get things into shape in a few years. But the house will have to be carefully run; I must economize all I can or else in a bad year it is impossible to make ends meet. And then we must deprive ourselves of a lot so as to be able to help the poor. . . .

8

Court Case on Marriage in High Court of Aix, 1689

At the same time as the Countess of Rochefort was managing her estate in Avignon without the help of her husband, Joseph Cabassol and his wife, Anne Geniere, were called to the High Court of Aix, France, 42 miles away. The couple's marriage was being challenged by some of the members of Cabassol's family. Who were these people? What was the reason for the suit? What was the reasoning of the court? What does this case tell you about social class and marriage in France at this time?

THINKING HISTORICALLY

Compare this document to the Qing law code (document 2). How do you think judges in Qing China might have handled a case like this? To what extent were the Chinese interests in this sort of case similar to, and different from, those of Louis XIV's France? How is our U.S. law similar or different?

C ase tried before the High Court of Aix in 1689. Joseph Cabassol . . . was the eldest of the seven children of a lawyer at the High Court of Aix. . . . [After his parent's death he succeeded to his inheritance. Then some years later] he fell in love with the woman Anne Geniere, a widow [who]

Source: Julia O'Faolain and Lauro Martines, eds., *Not in God's Image: Women in History from the Greeks to the Victorians* (New York: Harper & Row, 1973), 222–24.

had been brought before the Provost of Marseille because of her scandalous life. Convicted of prostitution and pimping, she had been sentenced by the judge to three years' banishment. . . . This sentence was confirmed, after appeal, by a decision of the High Court of Aix in 1683.

On 19 April 1688, Joseph Cabassol and Anne Geniere appeared before the bishop of Avignon, told him they were inhabitants of that town, that they wanted to get married, and that there was no canonical impediment. In proof of this, they brought three witnesses . . . and asked to be dispensed from publishing banns [request granted]. . . . They were married the following day . . . and returned to Aix on the following fourth of May. . . .

On the fourteenth of that same month of May, Joseph Cabassol's family, hearing of his marriage, his uncle, two brothers, and a sister put in a petition to have it annulled.

In Joseph Cabassol's defense, it was said that an adult of thirty years of age is free according to all the laws of God and man to choose his own wife. . . . Joseph Cabassol said that neither his uncle nor his brothers and sister were entitled to attack his marriage.

Monsieur de Saint-Martin, Director of Public Prosecutions . . . admitted that the consent of brothers and uncles is not necessary in the case of the marriage of an adult. . . .

One could not, however, conclude that such persons are never entitled to oppose the marriage of an adult. . . . The grounds for attacking this marriage were essentially two: that it was celebrated without publishing the banns and that it was not celebrated by the parties' own parish priest. . . . It was claimed that Anne Geniere had rented two furnished rooms, paying for three years rent in advance, in the town of Avignon. But we can state right away that this pretended domicile is not of the sort required by the holy decretals and the statutes . . . [which demand] that one should have lived a year or the best part of a year in a parish before one becomes really a parishioner. But the defendants had lived neither a year nor anything like it in Avignon when they got married there. . . . And so they did not satisfy the first condition. . . . If it were enough to change house for a while in order to establish domicile in order to get married, then the forethought of the Council of Trent would be illusory and that of the Royal Statute would be useless. One could make a parish priest for oneself according to one's needs, and where then could parents turn to get their authority respected? . . . Would this not be authorizing the worst license and covering it with a specious veil of marriage? . . . In order to determine whether the plaintiffs are entitled to petition for the invalidation of the marriage we must decide whether . . . the defendants' marriage is prejudicial to their honor. . . . If Anne Geniere had no other faults but those of her low rank and fortune, we would find the plaintiffs too fastidious. . . . But this is a woman who, over and above the inequality . . . has led a scandalous life. She has been stigmatized by a sentence which is a perpetual monument to her infamy. . . . If a man who wastes his patrimony can be declared incapable of managing his affairs, does it not seem that since Cabassol is wasting his honor, and managing his true interests so badly, we should listen to the voice of his relatives? . . . When the vapors with which mad passion have confused his mind withdraw . . . he will approve what he condemns today. . . .

For these reasons we believe that the petition to invalidate the marriage should be allowed . . . and that the defendants be condemned to give alms to the amount of ten pounds each to the hospitals of this town and forbidden to frequent each other, yet that they be allowed the recourse of taking any steps they think fit toward lodging an appeal in an ecclesiastical court. . . . Judgment given in conformity with these conclusions on the 14th March, 1689.

9

MARY JO MAYNES AND ANN WALTNER

Women and Marriage in Europe and China, 2001

This article is the product of a rich collaboration between historians of China and Europe who show us how a study of women and marriage is anything but peripheral to a study of these areas. What is their thesis about European and Chinese marriage patterns? What do marriage patterns tell us about a society? How do the other readings in this chapter support or challenge their thesis?

THINKING HISTORICALLY

The authors begin by comparing the role of religion, the state, and the family in setting marriage patterns in both China and Europe. Did Christianity allow European women more independence than Confucianism allowed women in China? In which society was the patriarchal family more powerful, and what was the relative impact of patriarchy on women in both societies? How do the age and rate at which people married in each society compare? What was the importance of Chinese concubinage and Christian ideals of chastity?

Source: Mary Jo Maynes and Ann Waltner, "Childhood, Youth, and the Female Life Cycle: Women's Life-Cycle Transitions in a World-Historical Perspective: Comparing Marriage in China and Europe," *Journal of Women's History* 12, no. 4 (Winter 2001): 11–19.

The authors' questions about marriage in Europe and China lead finally to a consideration of one of the most frequently asked comparative questions: Why did Europe industrialize before China? Do the different European and Chinese marriage patterns answer this question? What other comparative questions would we have to ask to arrive at a full answer?

Comparing Marriage Cross-Culturally

. . . Beginning in the late 1500s, women in northern Italy began to appeal to legal courts run by the Catholic Church when they got into disputes with their families over arranged marriages. Within the early modern Italy family system the father held a great deal of authority over his children and it was usual for the parents to determine when and whom sons and daughters married. Women and children held little power in comparison with adult men. But the Catholic Church's insistence that both parties enter into the marriage willingly gave some women an out—namely, an appeal to the Church court, claiming that the marriage their family wanted was being forced upon them without their consent. Surprisingly, these young women often won their cases against their fathers. In early modern China, by way of contrast, state, religion, and family were bound together under the veil of Confucianism. Paternal authority echoed and reinforced the political and the moral order. Religious institutions could rarely be called upon to intervene in family disputes. Therefore, young women (or young men, for that matter) had no clearly established institutional recourse in situations of unwanted marriage. So, despite the fact that paternal power was very strong in both early modern Italy and early modern China, specific institutional differences put young women at the moment of marriage in somewhat different positions.

We began with the presumption that however different the institution of "marriage" was in Italy and China, it nevertheless offered enough similarities that it made sense to speak comparatively about a category called "marriage." Parallels in the two cultures between the institution of marriage and the moment in the woman's life course that it represented make comparison useful. Nevertheless, this particular comparison also isolates some of the variable features of marriage systems that are especially significant in addressing gender relations in a world-historical context. In China, the rules of family formation and family governance were generally enforced within the bounds of each extended family group. State and religious influences were felt only indirectly through family leaders as mediators or enforcers of state and religious law. Throughout Europe, beginning in the Middle Ages, the institution of marriage was altered first by the effort of the Catholic Church to wrest some control over marriage from the family by defining it as a sacrament, and then eventually by the struggle between churches and state authorities to regulate families.

This contest among church, state, and family authorities over marriage decisions turns out to have been a particular feature of European history that had consequences for many aspects of social life. A focus on the moment of marriage presents special opportunities for understanding connections between the operation of gender relations in everyday life and in the realm of broader political developments. Marriage is a familial institution, of course, but, to varying degrees, political authorities also have a stake in it because of its implications for property transfer, reproduction, religion, and morality—in short, significant aspects of the social order. In this essay, we compare one dimension of marriage—its timing in a woman's life cycle—in two contexts, Europe and China. We argue that variations in marriage timing have world-historical implications. We examine how a woman's status and situation shifted at marriage and then suggest some implications of comparative differences in the timing and circumstances of this change of status.

The Moment of Marriage in European History

One striking peculiarity of Central and Western European history between 1600 and 1850 was the relatively late age at first marriage for men and women compared with other regions of the world. The so-called "Western European marriage pattern" was marked by relatively late marriage—that is, relative to other regions of the world where some form of marriage usually occurred around the time of puberty. In much of Europe, in contrast, men did not typically marry until their late twenties and women their mid-twenties. This practice of relatively late marriage was closely connected with the custom of delaying marriage until the couple commanded sufficient resources to raise a family. For artisans this traditionally meant having a shop and master status. For merchants it entailed saving capital to begin a business. In the case of peasant couples, this meant having a house and land and basic farming equipment. It was the responsibility of the family and the community to oversee courtship, betrothal, and marriage to assure that these conditions were met. This phenomenon was also rooted in the common practice of neolocality—the expectation that a bride and groom would set up their own household at or soon after marriage. This "delayed" marriage has attracted the attention of European historical demographers. The delay of marriage meant, quite significantly, that most European women did not begin to have children until their twenties. But this marriage pattern also has significance in other realms as well. In particular, young people of both sexes experienced a relatively long hiatus between puberty and marriage.

Unmarried European youth played a distinctive role in economic, social, cultural, and political life through such institutions as guilds, village youth groups, and universities. For the most part, historians' attention to European youth has centered on young men. Major works on the history of youth in Europe, like theories of adolescent development, tend to center on the male experience as normative. Only when gender differences in youth are recognized and the history of young women is written will the broad historical significance of the European marriage pattern become clear. Contrast between European demographic history and that of other world regions suggests a comparative pattern of particular significance for girls: Delayed marriage and childbearing meant that teenage girls were available for employment outside the familial household (either natal or marital) to a degree uncommon elsewhere. Household divisions of labor according to age and gender created constant demand for servants on larger farms; typically, unmarried youth who could be hired in from neighboring farms as servants filled this role. A period of service in a farm household, as an apprentice, or as a domestic servant in an urban household characterized male and female European youth in the life-cycle phase preceding marriage. Historians have noted but never fully explored the role young women played in European economic development, and in particular their role in the early industrial labor force.

Late marriage had gender-specific cultural ramifications as well. Whereas it was considered normal and even appropriate for teenage men to be initiated into heterosexual intercourse at brothels, in most regions of Europe, young women were expected to remain chaste until marriage. Delay of marriage heightened anxiety over unmarried women's sexuality, especially the dangers to which young women were increasingly exposed as the locus of their labor shifted from home and village to factory and city. Premarital or extramarital sexuality was uncommon, and was rigorously policed especially in the period following the religious upheavals of the Reformation in the sixteenth century. In rural areas, church and community, in addition to the family, exerted control over sexuality. Moreover, the unmarried male youth cohort of many village communities often served, in effect, as "morals police," enforcing local customs. These young men regulated courtship rituals, organized dances that young people went to, and oversaw the formation of couples. Sometimes, judging and public shaming by the youth group was the fate of couples who were mismatched by age or wealth or who violated sexual taboos. Some customs, at least symbolically, punished young men from far away who married local women, removing them from the marriage pool. Often, such a bridegroom had to pay for drinks in each village that the bridal couple passed through as they moved from the bride's parish church to their new abode—the longer the distance, the more expensive his bill.

Once married, a couple would usually begin having children immediately. Demographic evidence suggests that for most of Central and Western Europe there was virtually no practice of contraception among lower classes prior to the middle of the nineteenth century. Women had babies about every two years (more or less frequently according to region and depending on such local customs as breast-feeding length and intercourse taboos). Even though completed family sizes could be large by modern standards, the number of children most women bore was still less than if they had married in their teens. And prevailing high mortality rates further reduced the number of children who survived to adulthood.

The Moment of Marriage in Chinese History

The Chinese marriage system was traditionally characterized by early age at marriage, nearly universal marriage for women, virilocal residence (a newly married couple resided with the groom's parents), concubinage for elite men, and norms that discouraged widow remarriage. From the sixteenth through twentieth centuries, Chinese men and women married much younger on average than did their European counterparts—late teens or early twenties for women and a bit later for men. A bride typically moved to her husband's family home, which was often in a different village from her own. The moment of marriage not only meant that a girl would leave her parents but that she would also leave her network of kin and friends, all that was familiar. Families chose marriage partners, and a matchmaker negotiated the arrangements. Nothing resembling courtship existed; the bride and groom would often first meet on their wedding day.

Because a newly married Chinese couple would typically reside in an already-existing household, it was not necessary for an artisan to become established, a merchant to accumulate capital, or a peasant to own a farm before marrying. Newly married couples participated in ongoing domestic and economic enterprises that already supported the groom's family. New households were eventually established by a process of household division, which typically happened at the death of the father rather than the moment of marriage (although it could happen at other points in the family cycle as well).

Daughters were groomed from birth for marriage. They were taught skills appropriate to their social class or the social class into which their parents aspired to marry them. (In the ideal Chinese marriage, the groom was in fact supposed to be of slightly higher social status than the bride.) The feet of upper-class girls (and some who were not upper class) were bound, since Chinese men found this erotic.

Bound feet also symbolically, if not actually, restricted upper-class women's movement. Thus bound feet simultaneously enhanced the sexual desirability of upper-class women and served to contain their sexuality within domestic bounds.

Virtually all Chinese girls became brides, though not all of them married as principal wives. (This contrasts with the European pattern where a substantial minority of women in most regions never married.) Upper-class men might take one or more concubines in addition to a principal wife. The relationship between a man and his concubine was recognized legally and ritually, and children born of these unions were legitimate. A wife had very secure status: divorce was almost nonexistent. A concubine's status, in contrast, was much more tenuous. She could be expelled at the whim of her "husband"; her only real protection was community sentiment. Although only a small percentage of Chinese marriages (no more than 5 percent) involved concubines, the practice remained an important structural feature of the Chinese marriage system until the twentieth century. Concubinage also provides a partial explanation of why, despite the fact that marriage was nearly universal for women, a substantial proportion of men (perhaps as high as 10 percent) never married. Also contributing to this apparent anomaly was the practice of sex-selective infanticide, a common practice that discriminated against girl babies and, ultimately, reduced the number of potential brides.

Once married, Chinese couples began to have children almost immediately, generally spacing births at longer intervals than did European couples. The reasons for this are not yet completely understood, although infanticide, extended breast-feeding, and the fairly large number of days on which sexual intercourse was forbidden all seem to have played a role in lowering Chinese family size.

Early marriage in China meant that the category of "youth," which has been so significant for European social and economic history, has no precise counterpart in Chinese history. Young Chinese women labored, to be sure, but the location of their work was domestic—either in the household of their father or husband. Female servants existed in China, but their servitude was normally of longer duration than the life-cycle servitude common in Europe. The domestic location of young women's labor in the Chinese context also had implications for the particular ways in which Chinese industries were organized, as we suggest below.

Patterns of Marriage in Europe and China

To sum up, then, there are differences of both timing of and residency before and after marriage that are particularly germane to the comparative history of young women. As demographic historians James Z. Lee and Wang Feng also have argued, "in China, females have always married universally and early . . . in contrast to female marriage in Western Europe, which occurred late or not at all." Whereas, in the nineteenth century, all but 20 percent of young Chinese women were married by age twenty, among European populations, between 60 and 80 percent of young women remained single at this age. In traditional China, only 1 or 2 percent of women remained unmarried at age thirty, whereas between 15 and 25 percent of thirty-year-old Western European women were still single. (For men, the differences though in the same direction are far less stark.) As for residence, in the Western European neolocal pattern, norms and practices in many regions resulted in a pattern whereby newly married couples moved into a separate household at marriage; but concomitant with this was their delaying marriage until they could afford a new household. In China, newly married couples generally resided in the groom's father's household. In Western Europe, the majority of postpubescent young men and many young women left home in their teenage years for a period of employment. In the early modern era, such employment was often as a servant or apprentice in either a craft or a farm household, but, over time, that employment was increasingly likely to be in a nondomestic work setting, such as a factory, store, or other urban enterprise. "Youth" was a distinctive phase in the life course of young men and increasingly of young women in Europe, although there were important gender distinctions. Such a period of postpubescent semiautonomy from parental households did not exist for Chinese youth, especially not for young women in traditional China. Young men more typically remained in their father's household and young women moved at marriage in their late teens from their own father's household to that of their husband's father.

Comparing the Moment of Marriage: Implications and Cautions

We would now like to discuss some of the world-historical implications of this important (if crude) comparison in the marriage systems of China and Western Europe. There are obviously many possible realms for investigation. For example, these patterns imply differences in young women's education, intergenerational relationships among women (especially between mothers and daughters and mothers-in-law and daughters-in-law), and household power relations. Here, we restrict our discussion to two areas of undoubted world-historical significance, namely economic development, on the one hand, and sexuality and reproduction, on the other.

The question of why the Industrial Revolution, or, alternatively, the emergence of industrial capitalism, occurred first in Europe, has been and remains salient for both European and world historians. R. Bin Wong explores this question in his innovative comparative study of economic development in Europe and China. Wong argues that there were rough parallels in the dynamics linking demographic expansion and economic growth in China and Europe until the nineteenth century. Both economies were expanding on the basis of growth of rural industrial enterprises in which peasant families supplemented agricultural work and income with part-time industrial production. What the Chinese case demonstrates, Wong argues, is that this so-called protoindustrial form of development may be viewed as an alternative route to industrialization rather than merely a precursor of factory production. Indeed, Charles Tilly has suggested that a prescient contemporary observer of the European economy in 1750 would likely have predicted such a future—that is "a countryside with a growing proletariat working in both agriculture and manufacturing."

While Wong's study is devoted to comparative examination of the economic roots and implications of varying paths to industrial development, he also connects economic and demographic growth. In particular, Wong mentions the link between marriage and economic opportunity: "in both China and Europe, rural industry supported lower age at marriage and higher proportions of ever married than would have been plausible in its absence. This does not mean that ages at marriage dropped in Europe when rural industry appeared, but the possibility was present. For China, the development of rural industry may not have lowered ages at marriage or raised proportions married as much as it allowed previous practices of relatively low ages at marriage and high proportions of women ever married to continue." What Wong does not explore is the way in which these "previous practices" that connected the low age at marriage with both virilocality and a relatively high commitment to the domestic containment of daughters and wives also had implications for patterns of economic development. In a comparative account of why Chinese industrial development relied heavily on domestic production, the fact that the young female labor force in China was to an extent far greater than that of Europe both married and "tied" to the male-headed household needs to be part of the story. This pattern of female marriage and residency held implications for entrepreneurial choice that helped to determine the different paths toward industrialization in Europe and China. World-historical comparison, taking into account aspects of gender relations and marriage and kinship systems, highlights their possible significance for economic development, a significance that has not been given proper attention by economic historians. Indeed, it is arguable that the family and marital status of the young women who played so significant a role in the workforce (especially those employed in the textile industry, which was key to early industrial development in both Europe and China) were major factors in the varying paths to development followed in China and Europe in the centuries of protoin-dustrial growth and industrialization.

A second set of implications concerns sexuality and reproduction. Again, we are aided by another recent study, which, in a fashion parallel to Wong's, uses Chinese historical evidence to call into question general-izations about historical development based on a European model. In their book on Chinese demographic history, Lee and Wang argue against the hegemonic Malthusian (mis)understandings according to which the family and population history of China has been seen as an example of a society's failure to curb population growth by any means other than recur-rent disaster (by "positive" rather than "preventive" checks in Malthusian terms). They note the important difference in marriage systems that we have just described, but they dispute conclusions too often drawn from the Chinese historical pattern concerning overpopulation. Instead, according to Lee and Wang "persistently high nuptiality . . . did not inflate Chinese fer-tility, because of . . . the low level of fertility within marriage."

This second example points to another important realm for which the age at which women marry has great consequences. But the findings reported by Lee and Wang also caution scholars against leaping to com-parative conclusions about one society on the basis of models established in another, even while their claims still suggest the value of comparison. We should not presume that since Chinese women were married univer-sally and young, they therefore had more children or devoted a greater proportion of their time and energy to childbearing and child rearing than did their later married counterparts in Europe. Although the evi-dence is far from definitive, it nevertheless indicates that total marital fertility may have been somewhat lower in China than in Europe until the late nineteenth or early twentieth centuries. The factors in China that produced this pattern included relatively high rates of infanticide, espe-cially of female infants, as well as different beliefs and practices about child care and sexuality. For example, babies were apparently breast-fed longer in China than in Europe (a pattern in turn related to the domestic location of women's work), which would have both increased infants' chances of survival and also lengthened the intervals between births.[1] In the realm of sexuality, pertinent factors include both prescriptions for men against overly frequent intercourse, and coresidence with a parental generation whose vigilance included policing young couples' sexual behavior.

These two examples are meant to suggest how looking at women's life cycles comparatively both enhances our understanding of the impli-cations of varying patterns for women's history and also suggests the very broad ramifications, indeed world-historical significance, of differ-ent ways of institutionalizing the female life cycle.

---

[1] Breastfeeding temporarily lowers female fertility. [Ed.]

■ REFLECTIONS

Women's history has entered the mainstream during the last few decades. An older view, still pervasive in the academic world forty years ago, assumed that women's history was adequately covered by general history, which was largely the story of the exploits of men. Political, military, and diplomatic history took precedence over historical fields seen as less resolutely masculine, such as social and cultural history.

Today, women's history not only stands independently in college and university curriculums but has also helped open doors to a wide range of new fields in social history—gender, family, childhood, sexuality, domesticity, and health, to name but a few. These new research fields have contributed significantly to issues of general history, as the authors of the last reading show. In fact, the growth and development of new fields of research and teaching in social and cultural history have had the effect of relegating the study of presidents, wars, and treaties to the periphery of the profession. A recent meeting of the American Historical Association, where historians came together to talk about their work, had more sessions on women, gender, and sexuality than on politics, diplomacy, military, war, World War I, World War II, and the American Civil War combined.

Some more traditional historians complain that this is a fad, and that sooner or later the profession will get back to the more "important" topics. But others respond that it is hard to think of anything more important than the history of half of humanity. This debate leads to questions about the importance of particular individuals in history. Who had a greater impact, for instance, thirtieth U.S. president Calvin Coolidge (1872–1933) or Marie Curie (1867–1934), who won the Nobel Prize for isolating radium for therapeutic purposes?

What role do individuals play on the historical canvas anyway? A president or Nobel laureate works according to social norms, available resources, supporting institutions, and the work of hundreds or thousands of others, living and dead. Forty years ago, historians put greater stress on institutions, movements, and perceived forces than they do today. In recent years, historians have looked for the "agency" of individuals and groups, perhaps in an effort to see how people can have an impact on their world. The power of slavery and the impact of imperialism have been balanced with the tales of slave revolts; the stories of successful collaborators, adapters, and resisters; and the voices of slaves and indigenous and colonized peoples. We see this in the study of women's history as well.

We began this chapter with the observation that we live in a patriarchy. Even if we are dismantling it in the twenty-first century, it was a powerful force between 1500 and 1800: a historical force, not natural, but a product of the urban revolution, perhaps, beginning about five thousand years ago. It is useful to understand its causes, describe its workings, and relate its history. But does doing so only hamper our capacity for change? Does it ignore the stories of women who have made a difference? Conversely, are women empowered, humanity enriched, by knowing how individual women were able to work within the system, secure their needs, engage, negotiate, compromise? Do the poems of an Anna Bijns inspire us? Or do they misrepresent the past and, by consequence, delude us?

Perhaps there are no easy answers to those questions, but our exercise in comparison might come in handy. The rich and varied detail of the human past should warn us against absolute declarations. We may emphasize patriarchy or emphasize women's power, but we would be foolish to deny either. In consequence, it may be most useful to ask more specific questions and to compare. Can women own property here? Is there more restriction on women's movement in this society or that one? Only then can we begin to understand why here and not there, why then and not now. And only then can we use our understanding of the past to improve the present.

19

The Scientific Revolution

Europe, the Ottoman Empire, China, Japan, and the Americas, 1600–1800

■ HISTORICAL CONTEXT

Modern life is unthinkable apart from science. We surround ourselves with its products, from cars and computers to telephones and televisions; we are dependent on its institutions—hospitals, universities, and research laboratories; and we have internalized the methods and procedures of science in every aspect of our daily lives, from balancing checkbooks to counting calories. Even on social and humanitarian questions, the scientific method has become almost the exclusive model of knowledge in modern society.

We can trace the scientific focus of modern society to what is often called the "scientific revolution" of the seventeenth century. The seventeenth-century scientific revolution was a European phenomenon, marked by the work of such notables as Nicolas Copernicus (1473–1543) in Poland, Galileo Galilei (1564–1642) in Tuscany, and Isaac Newton (1642–1727) in England. But it was also a global event, prompted initially by Europe's new knowledge from Asia, Africa, and the Americas, and ultimately spread as a universal method for understanding and manipulating the world.

What was the scientific revolution? How revolutionary was it? How similar, or different, was European science from that practiced elsewhere in the world? And how much did the European revolution affect scientific traditions elsewhere? These are some of the issues we will study in this chapter.

■ THINKING HISTORICALLY

Distinguishing Change from Revolution

The world is always changing; it always has been changing. Sometimes, however, the change seems so formidable, extensive, important, or quick that we use the term *revolution*. In fact, we will use the term in this and the next two chapters. In this chapter we will examine what historians call the scientific revolution. The next chapter will deal with political revolutions and the chapter following with the industrial revolution. In each of these cases there are some historians who object that the changes were not really revolutionary, that they were more gradual or limited. Thus, we ask the question, how do we distinguish between mere change and revolutionary change?

In this chapter you will be asked, how revolutionary were the changes that are often called the scientific revolution? The point, however, is not to get your vote, pro or con, but to get you to think about how you might answer such a question. Do we, for instance, compare "the before" with "the after" and then somehow divide by the time it took to get from one to the other? Do we look at what people said at the time about how things were changing? Are we gauging speed of change or extent of change? What makes things change at different speeds? What constitutes a revolution?

1

JACK GOLDSTONE

Why Europe? 2009

This selection is drawn from a book by a modern historian who asks one of the enduring questions of modern history: Why was it that people in Europe pioneered the breakthroughs in modern scientific thought in the seventeenth century that led to an industrial revolution? This is a particularly intriguing question when you realize, as Goldstone points out, that between 1000 and 1500 China, India, and the Muslim world made far greater strides in science than Europe. What were the obstacles to advancement in scientific thought in most societies before 1500? What happened in Europe between 1500 and 1650 to change the way people thought about

---

Source: Jack Goldstone, *Why Europe? The Rise of the West in World History 1500–1850* (New York: McGraw-Hill, 2009), 144–53.

nature, and how did that thinking change? How did rationalism and empiricism change European science after 1650? How does a combination of rationalism and empiricism produce better science than either separately or than the other two sources of authority: tradition and religion?

THINKING HISTORICALLY

Goldstone does not use the term *scientific revolution* in this selection, but he discusses a number of changes in European society, politics, and beliefs that might be called revolutionary. What are these changes? What would make them revolutionary changes? Is it a matter of how fast they occurred, how widespread they were, what impact they had, or how unusual or uniquely European they were? Which of these measures makes them more revolutionary?

One must ask, given the glorious achievements of Islamic and other scientific traditions that were sustained over many centuries: Why did they not develop the same kind of advances leading to industrialization as did the modern European sciences?

Varieties of World Science and Different Approaches to Understanding Nature

Approaches to natural science varied across time and across different civilizations. Some traditions, such as that of China, made enormous advances in herbal medicine but remained weak in basic anatomy. Other traditions, like that of the Mayan Indians of Central America, were extremely accurate in observational astronomy but very weak in physics and chemistry.

Nonetheless, most premodern scientific traditions shared several common elements. First, their scientific understanding of nature was generally embedded in the framework for understanding the universe laid out in their society's major religious or philosophical traditions. Although there was potential for great conflict if scientific studies of nature should contradict elements of religion, this was usually avoided by making the religious views dominant, so that scientific findings would have to be reconciled with or subordinated to religious beliefs. This does *not* mean that religions were opposed to science—quite the opposite! Most political and religious leaders sponsored both scientific and religious studies, believing that each supported the other. Many distinguished Confucian scholars, Islamic judges, and Catholic priests were also outstanding mathematicians and scientists. For the most part, detailed observations of nature, including accurate measurements of planetary motions and natural phenomena, were considered valuable as privileged knowledge to political and religious elites or socially useful for improving architecture, farming, and medicine.

However, science generally remained intermingled with religious and philosophical beliefs, and any inconsistencies were generally resolved in favor of preserving the established religion. This meant that truly novel work risked being suppressed by political and religious authorities, especially during periods of religious conservatism or state enforcement of orthodox religious views.

Second, most premodern sciences maintained a separation between mathematics and natural philosophy (the study of nature). Mathematics was considered useful for exploring the properties of numbers (arithmetic) and relationships in space (geometry). It was also useful for a host of practical problems, such as surveying; compiling tables of planetary positions in the skies for navigation, calendars, and astrology; and accounting. But most premodern scientific traditions—including those of the ancient Greeks, medieval Europeans, Arabs, and the Chinese—held that mathematics was *not* useful for studying the basic constitution of the universe. This was the main subject matter of natural philosophy (the study of the natural world) and theology (the study of religious issues, including the relationship of humans and the natural world to the creator).

If one wanted to know the nature of God or the soul, or the relations between humankind and God, or the purpose of animals, or the nature of the stuff that composed the world—plants, stones, fire, air, liquids, gases, crystals—well, these were problems for reasoning based on experience and logic, not on mathematical equations. The task of philosophy was to comprehend the essential nature of things and their relationships. Measurement was a practical matter, useful but best left to surveyors, craftspeople, moneylenders, and other practical folks.

Thus the Chinese and Indian traditions believed in a basic hidden force of nature—*qi* in China and *prana* in India—that animated and infused the world. For Chinese scientists, the world was always changing, and these changes formed complex cycles and flows of opposing forces that operated to maintain an overall harmony. Thus despite their enormous skill and use of detailed mathematics and observation in areas from canals and irrigation works to astronomy and clocks, it never occurred to orthodox Chinese scientists to regard the universe as a mechanical clockwork or to apply mathematical equations to understand why natural processes occurred. What mattered was understanding signs of the ever-shifting flows of *qi* between opposing conditions—*yin* and *yang*—to avoid excesses and to maintain the harmony of the whole.

The Greeks too, since the time of Aristotle, similarly maintained a separation of mathematics from natural philosophy. Aristotle's philosophy of nature, which by the Middle Ages had become the dominant natural philosophy in Europe, analyzed nature by identifying the basic elements that composed all things. For Aristotle, there were four basic elements—earth, fire, air, and water—which were defined in terms of how they behaved. Things made of earth are solid and naturally tend to fall to the center of the universe, which is why the solid earth beneath us consists of a sphere, and all solid things fall toward it. Fire naturally rises, so things infused with fire rise. Air is transparent and moves across the surface of the Earth as winds; water flows and moves in currents and puddles and fills the seas and oceans. Since the Moon and Sun and stars and planets neither move up nor down but remain in the heavens, moving in circles in the skies, they must be composed of yet another, distinct element that was perfect and unchanging, which the Greeks called the "aether."

The way these principles were discovered and proved was through logic and argument based on experience, not through mathematics. Although mathematical forms and principles could help identify and measure relationships in nature, the true "essence" of reality was set by philosophy. For example, even though the planets actually move at varying speeds in elliptical orbits around the Sun, for over 1,000 years Islamic and European astronomers sought to describe their orbits solely in terms of combinations of uniform and circular motions, because Aristotle's natural philosophy had decreed that this was the only way that heavenly bodies could move.

In the Middle Ages, European scholars continued to treat mathematics as mainly a practical field, while focusing their attention on logic and argument as the keys to advancing knowledge. Although medieval scholars in Europe did make significant advances in the study of motion and absorbed much of the critical commentary on Greek science and philosophy from the Islamic world, they did not reject or replace the major tenets of classical Greek science or their own religious theology. Rather, much of the effort of European thought in the Middle Ages consisted of efforts to reconcile and synthesize the writings of the Greek authors on science and politics with the precepts of the Christian Bible and other religious texts, culminating in the work of St. Thomas Aquinas.

The Islamic scientific tradition went further than any other in using experiments and mathematical reasoning to challenge the arguments of Ptolemy, Galen, and others of the ancient Greeks, creating new advances in medicine, chemistry, physics, and astronomy. Yet within Islam, the discussion of the fundamental relationships and characteristics of nature was separated into the teachings of the Islamic sciences, based on classical religious texts, and the teachings of the foreign sciences, including all the works of Greek and Indian authors. After the writings of the philosophical critic Al-Ghazali in the eleventh century, who championed the value of the Islamic sciences on truly fundamental issues, this division was generally maintained, and even the most remarkable advances and findings with regard to revisions of Greek learning were not permitted to challenge the fundamental views of the universe as expressed in Islamic religious works.

Thus in all the major scientific traditions, whereas precise measurement and sophisticated mathematics were widely used, mathematical reasoning was not used to challenge the fundamental understanding of nature that was expressed in natural philosophy and religious thought.

Third, in most places, the dominant assumptions and traditions of science were so distinctive and so well established that they could hardly be shaken even by encounters with different notions and ideas. These scientific traditions tended to grow incrementally, with each successive generation modifying yet building on the works of their predecessors, so that over time a rich and longstanding tradition of scientific methods and findings grew up, intertwined with an established religious tradition. These structures of thought tended to resist wholesale change or replacement and to marginalize heterodox or conflicting views.

Thus by 1500, there were many different varieties of science in the world, each with their own strengths and distinctive characteristics. Most had developed precise observations of the Earth and heavens and had systematized a great number and variety of discoveries about nature. Most had developed a classification of essential relationships or characteristics of natural things. Most were linked in some fashion to one of the great axial age religions and over many centuries had worked to accumulate knowledge while building frameworks that were compatible with those religions. And in the next century or two, most scientific traditions would be driven to greater subordination to classical and religious orthodoxy by rulers who were responding to the political and social conflicts that struck over almost all of Europe and Asia.

How then was it possible that any culture could develop . . . technical innovations, based on new instruments and mathematical natural science . . . ? To understand this, we have to grasp the unusual events and discoveries that led to unexpected changes in Europe's approach to science.

Europe's Unusual Trajectory: From Embracing to Escaping Its Classical Tradition, 1500–1650

The study of ancient schools of thought was given a new direction by the realization, by the early 1500s, that the Spanish voyages to the west had discovered not just an alternate route to India, but in fact a whole new continent, a "New World" unknown to ancient geographers and scientists. Navigators came to realize that practically all of Greek geography was badly mistaken. Also in the early 1500s, the research of the Belgian anatomist Andreas Vesalius (who was building on the prior work of Arab scholars) demonstrated to Europeans that Galen's knowledge of human anatomy was, in many respects, inaccurate or deficient because it was based on deductions from animal dissections rather than on empirical study of human cadavers. Vesalius showed that many of Galen's (and Aristotle's) statements about the heart, the liver, the blood vessels, and the skeleton were wrong.

Then in 1543, Copernicus published his new methods for calculating the movements of the planets based on a solar system with a moving Earth circling the Sun. Although some supporters, trying to avoid conflict with the church, argued that his work should only be taken as a new method of predicting planetary positions, Copernicus argued quite forcefully that the structure and dynamics of the solar system made more sense, logically and aesthetically, if the Earth and all other planets revolved around the Sun. If so, then the system of Ptolemy and Aristotle, with the Earth as the center of all motion, was in error.

In 1573, the Danish astronomer Tycho Brahe published his account of the supernova that had suddenly appeared near the constellation of Cassiopeia in 1572. This was a phenomenon that had never been recorded in European astronomy. Indeed, since the time of Aristotle, it was assumed that the skies were unchanging and constant in their perfection. Comets and meteors were known, of course, but they were considered weather phenomena, like lightning that occurred close to the Earth rather than in the celestial heavens. But the supernova was not a comet or meteorite, because it showed no motion: It was a new body that behaved like a fixed star—something that was, according to Aristotle's philosophy, impossible.

Five years later, Brahe showed by careful observation of the movements of the great comet of 1577 that this comet must be farther away from the Earth than the Moon and thus was moving through the celestial heavens, not the atmosphere, striking yet another blow against Aristotle's cosmic system. Supernovae that can be observed from Earth by the naked eye are rare, but as chance would have it, in 1604, yet another supernova made its appearance, thus showing conclusively that the heavens were not unchanging after all.

By the late 1500s and early 1600s, therefore, the wisdom of Aristotle, Galen, and Ptolemy, which had been accepted for over 1,000 years, was coming under widespread attack. European scholars sought out new observations and new instruments for studying nature that could help determine who was correct, or incorrect, in their description of nature and the universe.

In 1609, Galileo used the new spyglass or telescope—invented by Dutch lens-grinders and then improved by Galileo himself—to observe the heavens. Looking at the Moon through a telescope rather than only the unaided eye, Galileo saw what looked like giant mountains and craters on the surface, which through the telescope looked positively Earth-like! Jupiter was found to have its own moons circling it, implying that the Earth could not be the center of all celestial motions. In every direction were previously unknown stars, and even the Milky Way was revealed to consist of thousands of tiny stars. Though many critics at first dismissed the views through the telescope as false magic, enough people acquired their own telescopes and confirmed Galileo's discoveries that they were widely accepted. People came to realize that the universe in which they lived was nothing like that described by the ancient Greek authorities.

Copernicus was not the first astronomer to suggest that the Earth revolved on its axis and moved around the Sun, instead of being the fixed center of the universe; a few ancient Greek and Islamic astronomers had also suggested that this was possible. However, until telescopic observations of the moons of Jupiter demonstrated the fact of motion around a body other than the Earth, there was no evidence on which to base a successful overthrow of Aristotle's views. It was only after 1600, with so many new observations that contradicted the ancient Greeks' knowledge—of geography, of anatomy, and of astronomy—piling up in all directions, that it became possible, even imperative, to adopt alternatives to Aristotle in particular and to Greek science and philosophy as a whole.

From 1600 to 1638, a series of books presenting new knowledge or proclaiming the need for a "new science" made a compelling case that the knowledge of the ancients was seriously flawed.

> 1600: William Gilbert, *On the Magnet*
> 1620: Francis Bacon, *The New Organon, or True Directions Concerning the Interpretation of Nature*
> 1620: Johannes Kepler, *The New Astronomy*
> 1626: Francis Bacon, *The New Atlantis*
> 1628: William Harvey, *On the Motion of the Heart and Blood*
> 1638: Galileo, *Discourses on Two New Sciences*

Gilbert argued that compass needles pointed north because the whole earth acted as a giant magnet. Francis Bacon argued that Aristotle's mainly deductive logic (collected under the title *Organon*—which means "instrument or tool") could not be trusted as a guide to understanding nature; instead Bacon argued for the use of inductive logic, based on a program of experiment and observation, as a superior method for discovering knowledge of the world. Kepler showed that the planets actually traveled in elliptical orbits around the sun, not in circles. And William Harvey showed that, contrary to Galen's teachings, the supposedly separate veins and arteries were in fact one system through which the blood was circulated by the beating of the heart.

By the mid-1600s, therefore, European philosophers and scientists found themselves in a world where the authority of ancient texts was clearly no longer a secure foundation for knowledge. Other major civilizations did not suffer such blows. For the Chinese, Indians, and Muslims—accustomed to operating in a vast intercontinental trade sphere from China to Europe and generally seeing themselves at the center of all that mattered—the discovery of new, lightly peopled lands far to the west made little difference. But for Europeans—who had long seen themselves on the literal edge of the civilized world with all that mattered lying to the east—the discovery of new and wholly unknown lands to the west changed their fundamental position in the world.

Similarly, Chinese and Indian astronomers had observed supernovae before (accurately recording observations of the heavens for thousands of years) and had long ago developed philosophies of nature that were built around ideas of continuous change as the normal course of things in the universe. Unlike the Greeks and Europeans, they had no rigid notions of perfect and unchanging heavens, separate from the Earth, that would cause their classical traditions to be fundamentally challenged by new observations of comets and stars.

Moreover, just when Europeans started their impassioned debates over these new observations and put forth their alternative ideas, the Ottoman, Mughal, and Chinese Empires were focused on internal concerns, seeking to recover from internal rebellions by closing off outside influences and strengthening traditional orthodox beliefs.

Thus the Europeans, more than any other major civilization, suddenly found that the classical tradition that they had sought to embrace now had to be escaped if they were going to understand the true nature of their world and their universe. This led Europeans to undertake a search for new systems of philosophy and new ways of studying and describing nature.

Searching for New Directions in European Science: Cartesian Reasoning and British Empiricism, 1650–1750

Prior to 1650, all major civilizations drew on four basic sources to justify knowledge and authority (which were generally closely connected). These were:

1. Tradition—knowledge that was revered for its age and long use
2. Religion or revelation—knowledge that was based on sacred texts or the sayings of prophets, saints, and other spiritual leaders
3. Reason—knowledge that was obtained from logical demonstration, either in arithmetic and geometry or by deductive reasoning from basic premises

4. Repeated observation and experience—knowledge that was
    confirmed by widely shared and repeated observations and
    everyday experience, such as that day follows night, the sun
    rises in the east, objects fall, heat rises. This also includes various
    agricultural and manufacturing techniques that were proven
    in use.

We have noted that in Europe by the early 1600s new discoveries,
observations, and concepts about the Earth and the universe had already
started to chip away at tradition and religious belief as guides to knowledge about the natural world. In addition, the seventeenth century was a
period of sharp religious schism and conflict in Europe, capped by the
Thirty Years' War (1618–1648). During these years Catholics, Lutherans,
Calvinists, and other sects all claimed to be correcting the errors of
others' interpretation of Christian faith, and various religious groups
rebelled and embroiled Europe in massive civil and international wars.
The lack of accepted religious authority and of any way to choose
between competing claims seemed to offer nothing but the prospect of
endless conflict.

The same problems, as we have noted, led Asian empires to promote a return to their traditional orthodox beliefs to suppress these
conflicts. Some European states tried to do the same thing. In Spain and
Italy and part of Germany and Poland, the counter-Reformation led to
the suppression of heresies and unorthodox views and enforcement of
traditional Catholic beliefs. These states banned books that threatened
Catholic orthodoxy and sought to curtail the actions of "dangerous"
authors, such as Giordano Bruno and Galileo (Bruno was burned at the
stake for his heresies; Galileo, more prudent and better connected, was
allowed to live under house arrest). France and the Netherlands, though
less severe, and Britain through 1640, also tried to restore uniform state
religions and force dissenters underground or into exile. However, in a
few states—including Britain after 1689, Denmark, and Prussia—
religious tolerance remained, and throughout western Europe, there
was a checkerboard of different states following different varieties of
religion—Catholic, Calvinist, Lutheran. Throughout Europe, the result
of the rise and spread of Protestantism in the sixteenth and seventeenth
centuries was that the authority of the Catholic Church—and of the
philosophical and scientific work that was closely associated with the
church's teachings—was seriously weakened. This provided an additional reason for philosophers to struggle to find a new basis for more
certain knowledge.

European thinkers therefore turned away from the first and second
major sources of knowledge and authority—tradition and religion—to
seek new systems of knowledge. After 1650, two major directions were
proposed to deal with this dilemma—rationalism and empiricism.

One way to set aside traditional and revelation-based assumptions was to try to get down to bedrock conclusions by reasoning purely from logic. The critical figure leading this approach was the French philosopher and mathematician René Descartes, who resolved to begin by doubting everything—the teaching of the ancients, the teachings of the church, and even his own experience. He extended his doubt until only one thing remained certain—the fact of his own doubt! This fact could then be the basis for logical deductions. After all, if Descartes could not escape the fact of his own doubt, he—as a doubting, thinking entity—must exist! This conclusion was rendered in his famous statement "I think, therefore I am."

Descartes continued this argument further. If he doubted, he could not be perfect. But if he was aware of his imperfection, this could only be because a perfect entity existed, thus there must be a perfect being, or God. And because we can only conceive of God as perfect, and hence perfectly logical, the universe constructed by God must also follow perfect logic. Descartes further argued that we can only logically perceive space if something is there, extending through space (empty space, Descartes argued, was a logical contradiction). What must fill space, then, are invisible particles whose motions and interactions must cause all that we see.

In this fashion, Descartes built up a logically consistent model of a mechanical universe in which all phenomena are to be explained by the movements and collisions of moving particles. This led Descartes to numerous valuable insights, such as the notion that we see things because invisible particles of light move from the objects we see to strike our eyes. But it also led him to deduce things that we now know are simply not true, such as the idea that the planets travel around the Sun because they are caught up in vortexes or whirlpools of swirling invisible particles.

This Cartesian rationalism provided a very attractive alternative to Aristotelian philosophy, which was now in disrepute. It seemed to have the power of purely logical demonstration behind its ideas. Also, because all phenomena were reduced to the motions of particles, it held the promise of applying mathematical principles—already worked out by Galileo for many kinds of particle motion—to all of nature. Finally, it allowed one to explain almost anything by coming up with some characteristics of particles. For example, one could suggest that spicy or sweet flavors were the respective results of sharp or smooth particles hitting the tongue or that different colors of light were produced by particles of light spinning at different speeds.

However, Cartesian rationalism also had its defects. In putting reason above experience, Cartesians disdained experiments. This limited what could be learned or discovered and often led to significant errors. Descartes' assumptions led him to misjudge the way bodies acted in collisions and turned his followers away from studying the properties of vacuums (since empty space could not exist, they must be tricks or errors by experimenters). Descartes also flatly ruled out the possibility of forces acting directly across space between objects, such as gravity. For all of its virtues, Cartesian rationalism therefore saddled its followers with a variety of errors and false explanations of the mechanics of motion in nature.

The motion of the Earth, the weight of the atmosphere, and the properties of vacuums were all discoveries whose proof rested on the use of scientific instruments (telescopes, barometers, vacuum pumps) to capture information not ordinarily available to the senses. The use of such instruments was a prime feature of the Baconian plan of developing scientific knowledge by experiments.

The experimental program reached its most systematic organization in the work of the Royal Society of London, led by Robert Boyle and later by Isaac Newton. The Royal Society based its research on experiments with scientific instruments and apparatus publicly performed at meetings of the society, and accounts of those experiments were widely published. The Royal Society used air pumps, telescopes, microscopes, electrostatic generators, prisms, lenses, and a variety of other tools to carry out its investigations. Indeed, the society came to rely on specially trained craftspeople to supply the growing demand for scientific instruments for its members.

The fame of the Royal Society in Britain skyrocketed with the achievements of Isaac Newton. Newton was the first to demonstrate that both motion on the Earth—whether the movement of falling apples, cannonballs, or the tides—and the motions of the planets through the heavens could *all* be explained by the action of a universal force of gravity. This force acted to attract objects to each other with a strength that increased with their mass but decreased with the inverse square of the distance between them. Newton's theory of gravity made it possible, for the first time, to explain the precise path and speed that the planets followed through the skies, as well as the movement of the Moon and the tides.

Newton also discovered the correct laws of mechanical force—that force was needed for all changes in the direction or speed of motion of an object, in proportion to the mass of the object and the magnitude of the change. Newton's laws of force made it possible to easily figure out the amount of work provided by, for example, a volume of falling water based on the height that it fell, or the amount of work it would take to raise a certain weight a desired distance. Newton further discovered the key principle of optics: that white light was composed of a number of different colors of light, each of which bent slightly differently when moving through water or a glass lens, thus creating rainbows in the sky and color patterns in prisms and lenses. . . .

2

Images of Anatomy, Fourteenth and Sixteenth Centuries

Andreas Vesalius (1514–1564), like generations of physicians before him, learned anatomy from the writings of Galen (129–216 C.E.), a Greek-born Roman. Because of Galen's authority, and subsequent Christian and Muslim strictures against conducting dissections, very little was learned about human anatomy for the next thousand years. Only gradually after 1200 were dissections performed again, and yet most physicians still read Galen while surgeons (formerly barbers) did the cutting. Vesalius himself began as a defender of Galen, until he moved from his native Belgium to teach at the University of Padua in Italy in 1537. There he was able to secure enough cadavers of executed criminals to perform multiple dissections and discover that Galen (who had only been able to dissect animals) had been wrong about elements of human anatomy. A facile artist himself, Vesalius engaged leading Italian draftsmen for the publication of his findings in *De humani corporis fabrica* (On the Structure of the Human Body), published in 1543.

An image from the fourteenth century (Figure 19.1) is followed by an image from the *Fabrica*, showing bones of the human skeleton (Figure 19.2). How would you describe the differences between the drawing in the *Fabrica* and the one from the fourteenth century?

THINKING HISTORICALLY

The actual mistakes that Vesalius found in Galen might seem relatively trivial. For instance, Vesalius realized that the human jaw was one bone, not two as Galen claimed after dissecting monkeys. He also saw that the sternum (which protects the chest) is three bones instead of seven and that, also contrary to Galen, the fibula and tibia of the human leg were longer than the arm. In this regard we might think of his work as evolutionary rather than revolutionary. Yet when we compare the images of the fourteenth century with those of Vesalius, barely more than a hundred years later, the differences strike us as revolutionary. Why do you think that is? Was this a revolution? If so, in what?

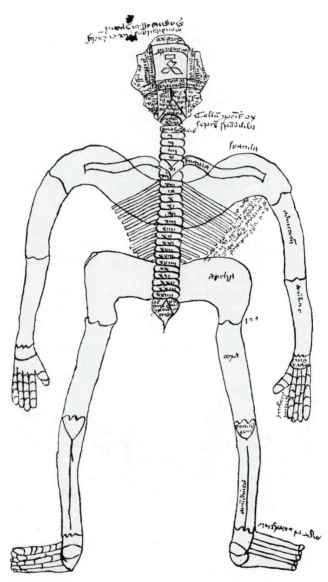

Figure 19.1   Skeleton drawing, from the Latin Munich MS Codex, fourteenth century.
Source: Wellcome Library, London.

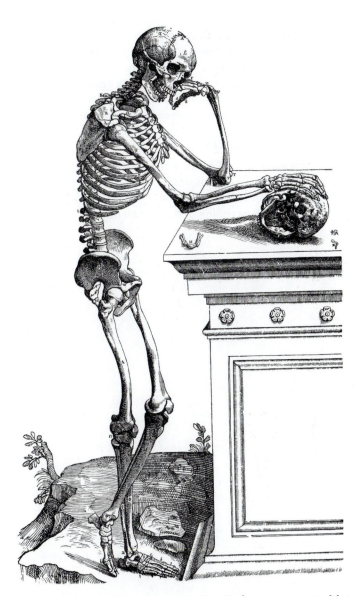

Figure 19.2   Woodcut of a skeleton, from Vesalius, *De humani corporis fabrica*,1543.
Source: Granger, NYC.

Image of Anatomy in China, Early Eighteenth Century

This image is from an eighteenth-century Chinese study of acupuncture called the Jing Guan Qi Zhi. Acupuncture designates particular points on the body where the insertion of needles is to have therapeutic results and has been documented as a practice in China from as early as 100 B.C.E. How is the Chinese study of acupuncture similar to, and different from, developments of European science and medicine?

THINKING HISTORICALLY

How does this evidence of Chinese anatomical and medical knowledge compare with the previous images from Europe? Consider how the developments in both the West and the East were important steps toward an understanding of the human body.

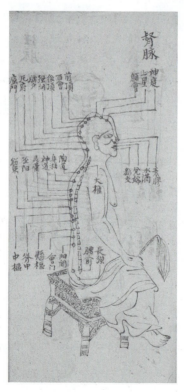

Figure 19.3 Acupuncture points along the spine and head, early eighteenth century.
Source: Private Collection / The Stapleton Collection / Bridgeman Images.

4

FRANCIS BACON

The New Organon or True Directions Concerning the Interpretation of Nature, 1620

Francis Bacon (1561–1626) was England's Renaissance man. Often called the father of science, the scientific method, induction, and empiricism, he was also a philosopher, statesman, poet, parliamentarian, and diplomat. Although frequently in debt, Bacon managed to move from prison to power, serving as attorney general and chancellor under Queen Elizabeth and King James I. Between ventures establishing colonies in Virginia and Newfoundland; keeping steps ahead of the executioner on charges of treason; and, as attorney general, convicting, torturing, and executing his enemies, Sir Francis Bacon pioneered the methods and theoretical underpinnings of modern science. That part of his work was recognized mainly in the century after his death. What problem did he see with the practice of science in his day? What did he mean by the methods of ants, spiders, and bees? What did he mean by the need for writing as well as thinking? What did he mean by "middle axioms," and why did he prefer them?

THINKING HISTORICALLY

Where does Bacon seem to be calling for a compromise or middle ground between then-current methods, and where does he seem to be calling for a revolutionary change in how science was done? In what ways was his method revolutionary?

XCV

Those who have handled sciences have been either men of experiment or men of dogmas. The men of experiment are like the ant; they only collect and use: the reasoners resemble spiders, who make cobwebs out of their own substance. But the bee takes a middle course; it gathers its material from the flowers of the garden and of the field, but transforms and digests it by a power of its own. Not unlike this is the true business of philosophy; for it neither relies solely or chiefly on the powers of the mind, nor does it take the matter which it gathers from natural history and mechanical experiments and lay it up in the memory whole, as it

Source: James Spedding, Robert Leslie Ellis, Douglas Denon Heath, eds., *The Works of Francis Bacon*, Vol. IV (London: Longman and Co., 1858), 92, 94, 96–97.

finds it; but lays it up in the understanding altered and digested. Therefore from a closer and purer league between these two faculties, the experimental and the rational, (such as has never yet been made) much may be hoped. . . .

XCVIII

Now for grounds of experience—since to experience we must come—we have as yet had either none or very weak ones; no search has been made to collect a store of particular observations sufficient either in number, or in kind, or in certainty, to inform the understanding, or in any way adequate. On the contrary, men of learning, but easy withal and idle, have taken for the construction or for the confirmation of their philosophy certain rumours and vague fames or airs of experience, and allowed to these the weight of lawful evidence. And just as if some kingdom or state were to direct its counsels and affairs, not by letters and reports from ambassadors and trustworthy messengers, but by the gossip of the streets; such exactly is the system of management introduced into philosophy with relation to experience. Nothing duly investigated, nothing verified, nothing counted, weighed, or measured, is to be found in natural history: and what in observation is loose and vague, is in information deceptive and treacherous.

CI

But even after such a store of natural history and experience as is required for the work of the understanding, or of philosophy, shall be ready at hand, still the understanding is by no means competent to deal with it off hand and by memory alone; no more than if a man should hope by force of memory to retain and make himself master of the computation of an ephemeris. And yet hitherto more has been done in matter of invention by thinking than by writing; and experience has not yet learned her letters. Now no course of invention can be satisfactory unless it be carried on in writing. But when this is brought into use, and experience has been taught to read and write, better things may be hoped.

CII

Moreover, since there is so great a number and army of particulars, and that army so scattered and dispersed as to distract and confound the understanding, little is to be hoped for from the skirmishings and slight attacks and desultory movements of the intellect, unless all the particulars which pertain to the subject of inquiry shall, by means of Tables of

Discovery, apt, well arranged, and as it were animate, be drawn up and marshalled; and the mind be set to work upon the helps duly prepared and digested which these tables supply. . . .

CIV

The understanding must not however be allowed to jump and fly from particulars to remote axioms and of almost the highest generality (such as the first principles, as they are called, of arts and things), and taking stand upon them as truths that cannot be shaken, proceed to prove and frame the middle axioms by reference to them; which has been the practice hitherto; the understanding being not only carried that way by a natural impulse, but also by the use of syllogistic demonstration trained and inured to it. But then, and then only, may we hope well of the sciences, when in a just scale of ascent, and by successive steps not interrupted or broken, we rise from particulars to lesser axioms; and then to middle axioms, one above the other; and last of all to the most general. For the lowest axioms differ but slightly from bare experience, while the highest and most general (which we now have) are notional and abstract and without solidity. But the middle are the true and solid and living axioms, on which depend the affairs and fortunes of men; and above them again, last of all, those which are indeed the most general; such I mean as are not abstract, but of which those intermediate axioms are really limitations.

The understanding must not therefore be supplied with wings, but rather hung with weights, to keep it from leaping and flying. Now this has never yet been done; when it is done, we may entertain better hopes of the sciences.

5

BONNIE S. ANDERSON
AND JUDITH P. ZINSSER

Women and Science, 1988

This selection from a history of European women shows how some women, especially the better educated, could participate in the scientific revolution of the seventeenth and eighteenth centuries. But Anderson

Source: Bonnie S. Anderson and Judith P. Zinsser, *A History of Their Own: Women in Europe from Prehistory to the Present* (New York: Harper & Row, 1988) 2:87–89, 96–99.

and Zinsser also demonstrate how much of the scientific revolution endowed male prejudices with false scientific respectability. What factors seem to have enabled women to participate in the scientific revolution? In what ways was the scientific revolution a new bondage for women?

THINKING HISTORICALLY

What do the authors mean when they say that for women "there was no Scientific Revolution"? In what ways were women's lives different after the scientific revolution? In what ways were they the same? Were the differences caused by the scientific revolution?

Women Scientists

In the same way that women responded to and participated in Humanism,[1] so they were drawn to the intellectual movement known as the Scientific Revolution. The excitement of the new discoveries of the seventeenth and eighteenth centuries, in particular, inspired a few gifted women scientists to formulate their own theories about the natural world, to perform their own experiments, and to publish their findings. In contrast to those educated strictly and formally according to Humanist precepts, these women had little formal training, and chose for themselves what they read and studied. Rather than encouraging them, their families at best left them to their excitement with the wonders of the "Scientific Revolution"; at worst, parents criticized their daughters' absorption in such inappropriate, inelegant, and unfeminine endeavors.

All across Europe from the sixteenth to the eighteenth centuries these women found fascination in the natural sciences. They corresponded and studied with the male scientists of their day. They observed, and they formulated practical applications from their new knowledge of botany, horticulture, and chemistry. The Countess of Chinchon, wife of the Viceroy to Peru, brought quinine bark to Spain from Latin America because it had cured her malaria. Some noblewomen, like the German Anna of Saxony (1532–1582), found medical uses for the plants they studied. The most gifted of these early naturalists is remembered not as a scientist but as an artist. Maria Sibylla Merian (1647–1717) learned drawing and probably acquired her interest in plants and insects from her stepfather, a Flemish still-life artist. As a little girl she went with him into the fields to collect specimens. Though she married, bore two daughters, and ran a household, between 1679 and her death in 1717 she also

---

[1] A faith in the capacities of humans that reached religious dimensions in the sixteenth century. Renaissance humanism valued reason, classical culture and literature, and civic engagement. [Ed.]

managed to complete and have published six collections of engravings of European flowers and insects. These were more than artist's renderings. For example, her study of caterpillars was unique for the day. Unlike the still life done by her contemporaries, the drawings show the insect at every stage of development as observed from the specimens that she collected and nursed to maturity. She explained:

> From my youth I have been interested in insects, first I started with silkworms in my native Frankfurt-am-Main. After that . . . I started to collect all the caterpillars I could find to observe their changes.

Merian's enthusiasm, patience, and skill brought her to the attention of the director of the Amsterdam Botanical Gardens and other male collectors. When her daughter married and moved to the Dutch colony of Surinam, their support was important when she wanted to raise the money for a new scientific project. In 1699, at the age of fifty-two, Maria Sibylla Merian set off on what became a two-year expedition into the interior of South America. She collected, made notations and sketches. Only yellow fever finally forced her to return to Amsterdam in 1701. The resulting book of sixty engravings established her contemporary reputation as a naturalist.

Mathematics, astronomy, and studies of the universe also interested these self-taught women scientists. In 1566 in Paris Marie de Coste Blanche published *The Nature of the Sun and Earth*. Margaret Cavendish (1617–1673), the seventeenth-century Duchess of Newcastle, though haphazard in her approach to science, produced fourteen books on everything from natural history to atomic physics.

Even more exceptional in the eighteenth century was the French noblewoman and courtier, Emilie du Châtelet (1706–1749). She gained admission to the discussions of the foremost mathematicians and scientists of Paris, earned a reputation as a physicist and as an interpreter of the theories of Leibnitz and Newton. Emilie du Châtelet showed unusual intellectual abilities even as a child. By the age of ten she had read Cicero, studied mathematics and metaphysics. At twelve she could speak English, Italian, Spanish, and German and translated Greek and Latin texts like Aristotle and Virgil. Presentation at court and life as a courtier changed none of her scientific interests and hardly modified her studious habits. She seemed to need no sleep, read incredibly fast, and was said to appear in public with ink stains on her fingers from her notetaking and writing. When she took up the study of Descartes, her father complained to her uncle: "I argued with her in vain; she would not understand that no great lord will marry a woman who is seen reading every day." Her mother despaired of a proper future for such a daughter who "flaunts her mind, and frightens away the suitors her other excesses have not driven off." It was her lover and lifelong friend, the Duke de Richelieu, who encouraged her to continue and to formalize her studies by hiring professors in mathematics and physics from the Sorbonne to tutor her. In 1733 she stormed her way into the Café Gradot, the Parisian coffee-house where the scientists, mathematicians, and philosophers regularly met. Barred because she was a woman, she simply had a suit of men's clothes made for herself and reappeared, her long legs now in breeches and hose, to the delight of cheering colleagues and the consternation of the management....

Châtelet made her reputation as a scientist with her three-volume work on the German mathematician and philosopher Leibnitz, *The Institutions of Physics,* published in 1740. Contemporaries also knew of her work from her translation of Newton's *Principles of Mathematics,* her book on algebra, and her collaboration with Voltaire on his treatise about Newton.

From the fifteenth to the eighteenth centuries privileged women participated in the new intellectual movements. Like the men of their class, they became humanist scholars, naturalists, and scientists. Unfortunately, many of these women found themselves in conflict with their families and their society. A life devoted to scholarship conflicted with the roles that women, however learned, were still expected to fulfill.

Science Affirms Tradition

In the sixteenth and seventeenth centuries Europe's learned men questioned, altered, and dismissed some of the most hallowed precepts of Europe's inherited wisdom. The intellectual upheaval of the Scientific Revolution caused them to examine and describe anew the nature of the universe and its forces, the nature of the human body and its functions. Men used telescopes and rejected the traditional insistence on the smooth surface of the moon. Galileo, Leibnitz, and Newton studied and charted the movement of the planets, discovered gravity and the true relationship between the earth and the sun. Fallopio dissected the human body, Harvey discovered the circulation of the blood, and Leeuwenhoek found spermatozoa with his microscope.

For women, however, there was no Scientific Revolution. When men studied female anatomy, when they spoke of female physiology, of women's reproductive organs, of the female role in procreation, they ceased to be scientific. They suspended reason and did not accept the evidence of their senses. Tradition, prejudice, and imagination, not scientific observation, governed their conclusions about women. The writings of the classical authors like Aristotle and Galen continued to carry the same authority as they had when first written, long after they had been discarded in other areas. Men spoke in the name of the new "science" but mouthed words and phrases from the old misogyny. In the name of "science" they gave a supposed physiological basis to the traditional views of women's nature, function, and role. Science affirmed what men had always known, what custom, law, and religion had postulated and justified. With the authority of their "objective," "rational" inquiry they restated ancient premises and arrived at the same traditional conclusions: the innate superiority of the male and the justifiable subordination of the female.

In the face of such certainty, the challenges of women like Lucrezia Marinella and María de Zayas had little effect. As Marie de Gournay, the French essayist, had discovered at the beginning of the seventeenth century, those engaged in the scientific study of humanity viewed the female as if she were of a different species—less than human, at best; nature's mistake, fit only to "play the fool and serve [the male]."

The standard medical reference work, *Gynaecea*, reprinted throughout the last decades of the sixteenth century, included the old authorities like Aristotle and Galen, and thus the old premises about women's innate physical inferiority. A seventeenth-century examination for a doctor in Paris asked the rhetorical question "Is woman an imperfect work of nature?" All of the Aristotelian ideals about the different "humors" of the female and male survived in the popular press even after they had been rejected by the medical elite. The colder and moister humors of the female meant that women had a passive nature and thus took longer to develop in the womb. Once grown to maturity, they were better able to withstand the pain of childbirth.

Even without reference to the humors, medical and scientific texts supported the limited domestic role for women. Malebranche, a French seventeenth-century philosopher, noted that the delicate fibers of the woman's brain made her overly sensitive to all that came to it; thus she could not deal with ideas or form abstractions. Her body and mind were so relatively weak that she must stay within the protective confines of the home to be safe.

No amount of anatomical dissection dispelled old bits of misinformation or changed the old misconceptions about women's reproductive organs. Illustrations continued to show the uterus shaped like a flask with two horns, and guides for midwives gave the principal role in labor to the fetus. As in Greek and Roman medical texts these new "scientific" works assumed that women's bodies dictated their principal function, procreation. Yet even this role was devalued. All of the evidence of dissection and deductive reasoning reaffirmed the superiority of the male's role in reproduction. Men discovered the spermatazoon, but not the ovum. They believed that semen was the single active agent. Much as Aristotle had done almost two millennia earlier, seventeenth-century scientific study hypothesized that the female supplied the "matter," while the life and essence of the embryo came from the sperm alone.

These denigrating and erroneous conclusions were reaffirmed by the work of the seventeenth-century English scientist William Harvey. Having discovered the circulation of the blood, Harvey turned his considerable talents to the study of human reproduction and published his conclusions in 1651. He dissected female deer at all stages of their cycle, when pregnant and when not. He studied chickens and roosters. With all of this dissection and all of this observation he hypothesized an explanation for procreation and a rhapsody to male semen far more extreme than anything Aristotle had reasoned. The woman, like the hen with her unfertilized egg, supplies the matter, the man gives it form and life. The semen, he explained, had almost magical power to "elaborate, concoct"; it was "vivifying . . . endowed with force and spirit and generative influence," coming as it did from "vessels so elaborate, and endowed with such vital energy." So powerful was this fluid that it did not even have to reach the woman's uterus or remain in the vagina. Rather he believed it gave off a "fecundating power," leaving the woman's body to play a passive, or secondary, role. Simple contact with this magical elixir of life worked like lightning, or—drawing on another set of his experiments—"in the same way as iron touched by the magnet is endowed with its powers and can attract other iron to it." The woman was but the receiver and the receptacle.

Anatomy and physiology confirmed the innate inferiority of woman and her limited reproductive function. They also proved as "scientific truth" all of the traditional negative images of the female nature. A sixteenth-century Italian anatomist accepted Galen's view and believed the ovaries to be internal testicles. He explained their strange placement so "as to keep her from perceiving and ascertaining her sufficient perfection," and to humble her "continual desire to dominate." An early-seventeenth-century French book on childbirth instructed the midwife to tie the umbilical cord far from the body to assure a long penis and a well-spoken young man for a male child and close to the body to give the female a straighter form and to ensure that she would talk less.

No one questioned the equally ancient and traditional connection between physiology and nature: the role of the uterus in determining a woman's behavior. The organ's potential influence confirmed the female's irrationality and her need to accept a subordinate role to the male. The sixteenth-century Italian anatomist Fallopio repeated Aristotle's idea that the womb lusted for the male in its desire to procreate. The French sixteenth-century doctor and writer Rabelais took Plato's view of the womb as insatiable, like an animal out of control when denied sexual intercourse, the cause of that singularly female ailment, "hysteria." Other sixteenth- and seventeenth-century writers on women and their health adopted all of the most misogynistic explanations of the traditional Greek and Roman authorities. No menstruation meant a diseased womb, an organ suffocating in a kind of female excrement. Only intercourse with a man could prevent or cure the condition. Left untreated the uterus would put pressure on other organs, cause convulsions, or drive the woman crazy. Thus, the male remained the key agent in the woman's life. She was innately inferior, potentially irrational, and lost to ill-health and madness without his timely intervention.

So much changed from the fifteenth to the eighteenth centuries in the ways in which women and men perceived their world, its institutions and attitudes. The Renaissance offered the exhilaration of a society in which the individual could be freed from traditional limitations. In the spirit of Humanistic and scientific inquiry men questioned and reformulated assumptions about the mind's capabilities and the description of the natural universe. New methods of reasoning and discourse, of observation and experimentation, evolved and led to the reorientation of the natural universe and more accurate descriptions of the physical world, including man's own body. Yet when it came to questions and assumptions about women's function and role and to descriptions of her nature and her body, no new answers were formulated. Instead, inspired by the intellectual excitement of the times and the increasing confidence in their own perceptions of the spiritual and material world, men argued even more strongly from traditional premises, embellishing and revitalizing the ancient beliefs. Instead of breaking with tradition, descriptions of the female accumulated traditions: the classical, the religious, the literary, the customary, and the legal—all stated afresh in the secular language of the new age. Instead of being freed, women were ringed with yet more binding and seemingly incontrovertible versions of the traditional attitudes about their inferior nature, their proper function and role, and their subordinate relationship to men.

With the advent of printing, men were able to disseminate these negative conclusions about women as they never could before. From the sixteenth century on the printing presses brought the new tracts, pamphlets, treatises, broadsides, and engravings to increasing numbers of Europeans: pictures of the sperm as a tiny, fully formed infant; works by scholars and jurists explaining the female's "natural" physical and legal incapacity; romances and ballads telling of unchaste damsels and vengeful wives set to plague man.

Although these misogynistic attitudes about women flourished and spread, the defense of women had also begun. In her *Book of the City of Ladies* Christine de Pizan, the fifteenth-century writer, asks why no one had spoken on their behalf before, why the "accusations and slanders" had gone uncontradicted for so long? Her allegorical mentor, "Rectitude," replies, "Let me tell you that in the long run, everything comes to a head at the right time."

The world of the courts had widened the perimeters of women's expectations and given some women increased opportunities. However, for the vast majority of women, still not conscious of their disadvantaged and subordinate status, changes in material circumstances had a far greater impact. From the seventeenth to the twentieth centuries more women were able to live the life restricted in previous ages to the few. In Europe's salons and parlors they found increased comfort, greater security, and new ways to value their traditional roles and functions. For these women, "the right time"—the moment for questioning and rejecting the ancient premises of European society—lay in the future.

6

LADY MARY WORTLEY MONTAGUE

Letter on Turkish Smallpox Inoculation, 1717

Lady Mary Wortley Montague, an English aristocrat, came down with smallpox in 1715. She survived, but was badly scarred by the rash that accompanied the often-fatal disease. Her younger brother died from smallpox, one of the tens of thousands who succumbed in epidemics across Europe and around the world in the eighteenth and nineteenth centuries. Two years after her recovery Montague traveled to Istanbul with her husband, who was the British ambassador to the Ottoman Empire. There, she witnessed a new approach to warding off smallpox infections, as she described in the following letter to a friend in England. What process does Montague describe in her letter? What was her response to the events she witnessed in Turkey?

THINKING HISTORICALLY

This letter provides a clear example of how scientific observation can change the material world in which we live. After observing the Turkish smallpox inoculation, Montague had her son and daughter inoculated. In fact, she became an advocate for smallpox inoculation in England and played an important role in persuading the English medical profession to support the innovative procedure. Montague paved the way for a safer vaccine, developed by Edward Jenner in 1796, that would eventually eradicate the disease from the planet.

Despite her admirable efforts, it was difficult to convince Europeans to embrace smallpox inoculation, which had been practiced in Asia

Source: *Letters of Lady Mary Wortley Montague, written during her travels in Europe, Asia, and Africa, to which are added poems by the same author* (Bordeaux: J. Pinard, 1805). The UCLA Louis M. Darling Biomedical Library, History and Special Collections Division. Also available from Gutenberg E-Books at Lady Mary Wortley Montague, Her Life and Letters (1689–1762). Author: Lewis Melville. Release Date: January 4, 2004 [EBook #10590].

for centuries. Even though the effectiveness of this technology came to be recognized in England during Montague's lifetime, the French and other Europeans, according to Voltaire, thought that the English were "fools and madmen" for experimenting with inoculation. What does this suggest about the nature of scientific discovery? Besides lack of knowledge, what other obstacles need to be overcome? What does this resistance say about how revolutionary the "scientific revolution" was?

To Mrs. S. C., Adrianople, April 1, O.S.

A Propos of distempers, I am going to tell you a thing, that will make you wish yourself here. The small pox, so fatal, and so general amongst us, is here entirely harmless, by the invention of ingrafting, which is the term they give it. There is a set of old women, who make it their business to perform the operation, every autumn, in the month of September, when the great heat is abated. People send to one another to know if any of their family has a mind to have the small-pox; they make parties for this purpose, and when they are met (commonly fifteen or sixteen together) the old woman comes with a nut-shell full of the matter of the best sort of small pox, and asks what vein you please to have opened. She immediately rips open that you offer to her, with a large needle (which gives you no more pain than a common scratch), and puts into the vein as much matter as can lie upon the head of her needle, and after that, binds up the little wound with a hollow bit of shell, and in this manner opens four or five veins. The Grecians have commonly the superstition of opening one in the middle of the forehead, one in each arm, and one in the breast, to mark the sign of the cross; but this has a very ill effect, all these wounds leaving little scars, and is not done by those that are not superstitious, who choose to have them in the legs, or that part of the arm that is concealed. The children or young patients play together all the rest of the day, and are in perfect health to the eighth.

Then the fever begins to seize them, and they keep their beds two days, very seldom three. They have very rarely above twenty or thirty in their faces, which never mark, and in eight days time they are as well as before their illness. Where they are wounded, there remains running sores during the distemper, which I don't doubt is a great relief to it. Every year thousands undergo this operation, and the French ambassador says pleasantly that they take the small-pox here by way of diversion, as they take the waters in other countries. There is no example of any one that has died in it, and you may believe I am well satisfied of the safety of this experiment, since I intend to try it on my dear little son. I am patriot enough to take pains to bring this useful invention into fashion in England, and I should not fail to write to some of our doctors very particularly about it, if I knew any one of them that I thought had virtue enough to destroy such a considerable branch of their revenue, for the good of mankind. But that distemper is too beneficial to them, not to expose to all their resentment the hardy wight[1] that should undertake to put an end to it. Perhaps if I live to return, I may, however have the courage to war with them. Upon this occasion, admire the heroism in the heart of

Your friend, etc. etc.

[1] Creature. [Ed.]

7

LYNDA NORENE SHAFFER

China, Technology, and Change, 1986–1987

In this essay an important contemporary world historian asks us to compare the revolutionary consequences of scientific and technological changes that occurred in China and Europe before the seventeenth century. What is Shaffer's argument? In what ways was the European scientific revolution different from the changes in China she describes here?

THINKING HISTORICALLY

What exactly was the impact of printing, the compass, and gunpowder in Europe? What was the "before" and "after" for each of these innovations? What, according to Shaffer, was the situation in China before and after each of these innovations? Were these innovations as revolutionary in China as they were in Europe?

Francis Bacon (1561–1626), an early advocate of the empirical method, upon which the scientific revolution was based, attributed Western Europe's early modern take-off to three things in particular: printing, the compass, and gunpowder. Bacon had no idea where these things had come from, but historians now know that all three were invented in China. Since, unlike Europe, China did not take off onto a path leading from the scientific to the Industrial Revolution, some historians are now

Source: Lynda Norene Shaffer, "China, Technology, and Change," *World History Bulletin* 4, no. 1 (Fall/Winter 1986–1987): 1–6.

asking why these inventions were so revolutionary in Western Europe and, apparently, so unrevolutionary in China.

In fact, the question has been posed by none other than Joseph Needham, the foremost English-language scholar of Chinese science and technology. It is only because of Needham's work that the Western academic community has become aware that until Europe's take-off, China was the unrivaled world leader in technological development. That is why it is so disturbing that Needham himself has posed this apparent puzzle. The English-speaking academic world relies upon him and repeats him; soon this question and the vision of China that it implies will become dogma. Traditional China will take on supersociety qualities—able to contain the power of printing, to rein in the potential of the compass, even to muffle the blast of gunpowder.

The impact of these inventions on Western Europe is well known. Printing not only eliminated much of the opportunity for human copying errors, it also encouraged the production of more copies of old books and an increasing number of new books. As written material became both cheaper and more easily available, intellectual activity increased. Printing would eventually be held responsible, at least in part, for the spread of classical humanism and other ideas from the Renaissance. It is also said to have stimulated the Protestant Reformation, which urged a return to the Bible as the primary religious authority.

The introduction of gunpowder in Europe made castles and other medieval fortifications obsolete (since it could be used to blow holes in their walls) and thus helped to liberate Western Europe from feudal aristocratic power. As an aid to navigation the compass facilitated the Portuguese- and Spanish-sponsored voyages that led to Atlantic Europe's sole possession of the Western Hemisphere, as well as the Portuguese circumnavigation of Africa, which opened up the first all-sea route from Western Europe to the long-established ports of East Africa and Asia.

Needham's question can thus be understood to mean, Why didn't China use gunpowder to destroy feudal walls? Why didn't China use the compass to cross the Pacific and discover America, or to find an all-sea route to Western Europe? Why didn't China undergo a Renaissance or Reformation? The implication is that even though China possessed these technologies, it did not change much. Essentially Needham's question is asking, What was wrong with China?

Actually, there was nothing wrong with China. China was changed fundamentally by these inventions. But in order to see the changes, one must abandon the search for peculiarly European events in Chinese history, and look instead at China itself before and after these breakthroughs.

To begin, one should note that China possessed all three of these technologies by the latter part of the Tang dynasty (618–906)—between four and six hundred years before they appeared in Europe. And it was during just that time, from about 850, when the Tang dynasty began to falter, until 960, when the Song dynasty (960–1279) was established, that China underwent fundamental changes in all spheres. In fact, historians are now beginning to use the term *revolution* when referring to technological and commercial changes that culminated in the Song dynasty, in the same way that they refer to the changes in eighteenth- and nineteenth-century England as the Industrial Revolution. And the word might well be applied to other sorts of changes in China during this period.

For example, the Tang dynasty elite was aristocratic, but that of the Song was not. No one has ever considered whether the invention of gunpowder contributed to the demise of China's aristocrats, which occurred between 750 and 960, shortly after its invention. Gunpowder may, indeed, have been a factor although it is unlikely that its importance lay in blowing up feudal walls. Tang China enjoyed such internal peace that its aristocratic lineages did not engage in castle-building of the sort typical in Europe. Thus, China did not have many feudal fortifications to blow up.

The only wall of significance in this respect was the Great Wall, which was designed to keep steppe nomads from invading China. In fact, gunpowder may have played a role in blowing holes in this wall, for the Chinese could not monopolize the terrible new weapon, and their nomadic enemies to the north soon learned to use it against them. The Song dynasty ultimately fell to the Mongols, the most formidable force ever to emerge from the Eurasian steppe. Gunpowder may have had a profound effect on China—exposing a united empire to foreign invasion and terrible devastation—but an effect quite opposite to the one it had on Western Europe.

On the other hand, the impact of printing on China was in some ways very similar to its later impact on Europe. For example, printing contributed to a rebirth of classical (that is, preceding the third century A.D.) Confucian learning, helping to revive a fundamentally humanistic outlook that had been pushed aside for several centuries.

After the fall of the Han dynasty (206 B.C.–A.D. 220), Confucianism had lost much of its credibility as a world view, and it eventually lost its central place in the scholarly world. It was replaced by Buddhism, which had come from India. Buddhists believed that much human pain and confusion resulted from the pursuit of illusory pleasures and dubious ambitions: Enlightenment and, ultimately, salvation would come from a progressive disengagement from the real world, which they also believed to be illusory. This point of view dominated Chinese intellectual life until the ninth century. Thus the academic and intellectual comeback of classical Confucianism was in essence a return to a more optimistic literature that affirmed the world as humans had made it.

The resurgence of Confucianism within the scholarly community was due to many factors, but printing was certainly one of the most important. Although it was invented by Buddhist monks in China, and at first benefited Buddhism, by the middle of the tenth century, printers were turning out innumerable copies of the classical Confucian corpus. This return of scholars to classical learning was part of a more general movement that shared not only its humanistic features with the later Western European Renaissance, but certain artistic trends as well.

Furthermore, the Protestant Reformation in Western Europe was in some ways reminiscent of the emergence and eventual triumph of Neo-Confucian philosophy. Although the roots of Neo-Confucianism can be found in the ninth century, the man who created what would become its most orthodox synthesis was Zhu Xi (Chu Hsi, 1130–1200). Neo-Confucianism was significantly different from classical Confucianism, for it had undergone an intellectual (and political) confrontation with Buddhism and had emerged profoundly changed. It is of the utmost importance to understand that not only was Neo-Confucianism new, it was also heresy, even during Zhu Xi's lifetime. It did not triumph until the thirteenth century, and it was not until 1313 (when Mongol conquerors ruled China) that Zhu Xi's commentaries on the classics became the single authoritative text against which all academic opinion was judged.

In the same way that Protestantism emerged out of a confrontation with the Roman Catholic establishment and asserted the individual Christian's autonomy, Neo-Confucianism emerged as a critique of Buddhist ideas that had taken hold in China, and it asserted an individual moral capacity totally unrelated to the ascetic practices and prayers of the Buddhist priesthood. In the twelfth century Neo-Confucianists lifted the work of Mencius (Meng Zi, 370–290 B.C.) out of obscurity and assigned it a place in the corpus second only to that of the *Analects of Confucius*. Many facets of Mencius appealed to the Neo-Confucianists, but one of the most important was his argument that humans by nature are fundamentally good. Within the context of the Song dynasty, this was an assertion that morality could be pursued through an engagement in human affairs, and that the Buddhist monks' withdrawal from life's mainstream did not bestow upon them any special virtue.

The importance of these philosophical developments notwithstanding, printing probably had its greatest impact on the Chinese political system. The origin of the civil service examination system in China can be traced back to the Han dynasty, but in the Song dynasty government-administered examinations became the most important route to political power in China. For almost a thousand years (except the early period of Mongol rule), China was governed by men who had come to power simply because they had done exceedingly well in examinations on the Neo-Confucian canon. At any one time thousands of students were studying for the exams, and thousands of inexpensive books were required. Without printing such a system would not have been possible.

The development of this alternative to aristocratic rule was one of the most radical changes in world history. Since the examinations were ultimately open to 98 percent of all males (actors were one of the few groups excluded), it was the most democratic system in the world prior to the development of representative democracy and popular suffrage in Western Europe in the eighteenth and nineteenth centuries. (There were some small-scale systems, such as the classical Greek city-states, which might be considered more democratic, but nothing comparable in size to Song China or even the modern nation-states of Europe.)

Finally we come to the compass. Suffice it to say that during the Song dynasty, China developed the world's largest and most technologically sophisticated merchant marine and navy. By the fifteenth century its ships were sailing from the north Pacific to the east coast of Africa. They could have made the arduous journey around the tip of Africa and on into Portuguese ports; however, they had no reason to do so. Although the Western European economy was prospering, it offered nothing that China could not acquire much closer to home at much less cost. In particular, wool, Western Europe's most important export, could easily be obtained along China's northern frontier.

Certainly, the Portuguese and the Spanish did not make their unprecedented voyages out of idle curiosity. They were trying to go to the Spice Islands, in what is now Indonesia, in order to acquire the most valuable commercial items of the time. In the fifteenth century these islands were the world's sole suppliers of the fine spices, such as cloves, nutmeg, and mace, as well as a source for the more generally available pepper. It was this spice market that lured Columbus westward from Spain and drew Vasco Da Gama around Africa and across the Indian Ocean.

After the invention of the compass, China also wanted to go to the Spice Islands and, in fact, did go, regularly—but Chinese ships did not have to go around the world to get there. The Atlantic nations of Western Europe, on the other hand, had to buy spices from Venice (which controlled the Mediterranean trade routes) or from other Italian city-states; or they had to find a new way to the Spice Islands. It was necessity that mothered those revolutionary routes that ultimately changed the world.

Gunpowder, printing, the compass—clearly these three inventions changed China as much as they changed Europe. And it should come as no surprise that changes wrought in China between the eighth and tenth centuries were different from changes wrought in Western Europe between the thirteenth and fifteenth centuries. It would, of course, be unfair and ahistorical to imply that something was wrong with Western Europe because the technologies appeared there later. It is equally unfair to ask why the Chinese did not accidentally bump into the Western Hemisphere while sailing east across the Pacific to find the wool markets of Spain.

8

SUGITA GEMPAKU

A Dutch Anatomy Lesson in Japan, 1771

Sugita Gempaku* (1733–1817) was a Japanese physician who, as he tells us here in his memoir, suddenly discovered the value of Western medical science when he chanced to witness a dissection shortly after he obtained a Dutch anatomy book.

What was it that Sugita Gempaku learned on that day in 1771? What were the differences between the treatments of anatomy in the Chinese *Book of Medicine* and the Dutch medical book? What accounts for these differences?

THINKING HISTORICALLY

How might the Dutch book have changed the way the author practiced medicine? How did it change his knowledge of the human body? How did it change the relevance of his knowledge of the human body to the medicine he practiced? How revolutionary was the new knowledge for Sugita Gempaku?

Whenever I met Hiraga Gennai (1729–1779), we talked to each other on this matter: "As we have learned, the Dutch method of scholarly investigation through field work and surveys is truly amazing. If we can directly understand books written by them, we will benefit greatly. However, it is pitiful that there has been no one who has set his mind on working in this field. Can we somehow blaze this trail? It is impossible

* SOO gee tah   gehm PAH koo

Source: Sugita Gempaku, *Ranto Kotohajime* (The Beginning of Dutch Studies in the East), in *Japan: A Documentary History*, ed. David J. Lu (Armonk, NY: M. E. Sharpe, 2005), 1:264–66. Iwanami Shoten, *Nihon Koten Bunka Taikei* (Major Compilation of Japanese Classics) (Tokyo: Iwanami Shoten, 1969), 95:487–93.

to do it in Edo. Perhaps it is best if we ask translators in Nagasaki to make some translations. If one book can be completely translated, there will be an immeasurable benefit to the country." Every time we spoke in this manner, we deplored the impossibility of implementing our desires. However, we did not vainly lament the matter for long.

Somehow, miraculously I obtained a book on anatomy written in that country. It may well be that Dutch studies in this country began when I thought of comparing the illustrations in the book with real things. It was a strange and even miraculous happening that I was able to obtain that book in that particular spring of 1771. Then at the night of the third day of the third month, I received a letter from a man by the name of Tokuno Bambei, who was in the service of the then Town Commissioner, Magaribuchi Kai-no-kami. Tokuno stated in his letter that "A post-mortem examination of the body of a condemned criminal by a resident physician will be held tomorrow at Senjukotsukahara. You are welcome to witness it if you so desire." At one time my colleague by the name of Kosugi Genteki had an occasion to witness a post-mortem dissection of a body when he studied under Dr. Yamawaki Tōyō of Kyoto. After seeing the dissection firsthand, Kosugi remarked that what was said by the people of old was false and simply could not be trusted. "The people of old spoke of nine internal organs, and nowadays, people divide them into five viscera and six internal organs. That [perpetuates] inaccuracy," Kosugi once said. Around that time (1759) Dr. Tōyō published a book entitled *Zōshi* (*On Internal Organs*). Having read that book, I had hoped that some day I could witness a dissection. When I also acquired a Dutch book on anatomy, I wanted above all to compare the two to find out which one accurately described the truth. I rejoiced at this unusually fortunate circumstance, and my mind could not entertain any other thought. However, a thought occurred to me that I should not monopolize this good fortune, and decided to share it with those of my colleagues who were diligent in the pursuit of their medicine. . . . Among those I invited was one [Maeno] Ryōtaku (1723–1803). . . .

The next day, when we arrived at the location . . . Ryōtaku reached under his kimono to produce a Dutch book and showed it to us. "This is a Dutch book of anatomy called *Tabulae Anatomicae*. I bought this a few years ago when I went to Nagasaki, and kept it." As I examined it, it was the same book I had and was of the same edition. We held each other's hands and exclaimed: "What a coincidence!" Ryōtaku continued by saying: "When I went to Nagasaki, I learned and heard," and opened his book. "These are called *long* in Dutch, they are lungs," he taught us. "This is *hart*, or the heart. When it says *maag* it is the stomach, and when it says *milt* it is the spleen." However, they did not look like the heart given in the Chinese medical books, and none of us were sure until we could actually see the dissection.

Thereafter we went together to the place which was especially set for us to observe the dissection in Kotsukahara. . . . The regular man who performed the chore of dissection was ill, and his grandfather, who was ninety years of age, came in his place. He was a healthy old man. He had experienced many dissections since his youth, and boasted that he dissected a number of bodies. Those dissections were performed in those days by men of the *eta*[1] class. . . . That day, the old butcher pointed to this and that organ. After the heart, liver, gall bladder, and stomach were identified, he pointed to other parts for which there were no names. "I don't know their names. But I have dissected quite a few bodies from my youthful days. Inside of everyone's abdomen there were these parts and those parts." Later, after consulting the anatomy chart, it became clear to me that I saw an arterial tube, a vein, and the suprarenal gland. The old butcher again said, "Every time I had a dissection, I pointed out to those physicians many of these parts, but not a single one of them questioned 'what was this?' or 'what was that?'" We compared the body as dissected against the charts both Ryōtaku and I had, and could not find a single variance from the charts. The Chinese *Book of Medicine* (*Yi Jing*) says that the lungs are like the eight petals of the lotus flower, with three petals hanging in front, three in back, and two petals forming like two ears and that the liver has three petals to the left and four petals to the right. There were no such divisions, and the positions and shapes of intestines and gastric organs were all different from those taught by the old theories. The official physicians, Dr. Okada Yōsen and Dr. Fujimoto Rissen, have witnessed dissection seven or eight times. Whenever they witnessed the dissection, they found that the old theories contradicted reality. Each time they were perplexed and could not resolve their doubts. Every time they wrote down what they thought was strange. They wrote in their books. "The more we think of it, there must be fundamental differences in the bodies of Chinese and of the eastern barbarians [i.e., Japanese]." I could see why they wrote this way.

That day, after the dissection was over, we decided that we also should examine the shape of the skeletons left exposed on the execution ground. We collected the bones, and examined a number of them. Again, we were struck by the fact that they all differed from the old theories while conforming to the Dutch charts.

The three of us, Ryōtaku, [Nakagawa] Junan (1739–1786), and I went home together. On the way home we spoke to each other and felt the same way. "How marvelous was our actual experience today. It is a shame that we were ignorant of these things until now. As physicians who serve their masters through medicine, we performed our duties in complete ignorance of the true form of the human body. How disgraceful it is. Somehow, through this experience, let us investigate further the

---

[1]The *eta* were an untouchable caste in Japan, defined by their restriction to certain occupations associated with death: tanning or working with hides, cremating the dead, butchering meat, and, thus, doing autopsies. They could not be physicians. The term is derogatory. Their descendants today are called Burakumin. [Ed.]

truth about the human body. If we practice medicine with this knowledge behind us, we can make contributions for people under heaven and on this earth." Ryōtaku spoke to us. "Indeed, I agree with you wholeheartedly." Then I spoke to my two companions. "Somehow if we can translate anew this book called *Tabulae Anatomicae*, we can get a clear notion of the human body inside out. It will have great benefit in the treatment of our patients. Let us do our best to read it and understand it without the help of translators." Ryōtaku responded: "I have been wanting to read Dutch books for some time, but there has been no friend who would share my ambitions. I have spent days lamenting it. If both of you wish, I have been in Nagasaki before and have retained some Dutch. Let us use it as a beginning to tackle the book together." After hearing it, I answered, "This is simply wonderful. If we are to join our efforts, I shall also resolve to do my very best." . . .

The next day, we assembled at the house of Ryōtaku and recalled the happenings of the previous day. When we faced that *Tabulae Anatomicae*, we felt as if we were setting sail on a great ocean in a ship without oars or a rudder. With the magnitude of the work before us, we were dumbfounded by our own ignorance. However, Ryōtaku had been thinking of this for some time, and he had been in Nagasaki. He knew some Dutch through studying and hearing, and knew some sentence patterns and words. He was also ten years older than I, and we decided to make him head of our group and our teacher. At that time I did not know the twenty-five letters of the Dutch alphabet. I decided to study the language with firm determination, but I had to acquaint myself with letters and words gradually.

9

BENJAMIN FRANKLIN

Letter on a Balloon Experiment in 1783

Benjamin Franklin (1706–1790) was the preeminent statesman, diplomat, and spokesman for the British colonies that became the United States during his long lifetime. Trained as a candle maker and printer, he became a journalist, publisher, merchant, homespun philosopher, and inveterate inventor. He invented the lightning rod, the Franklin stove, bifocals, and the medical catheter, among other

Source: Nathan G. Goodman, ed., *The Ingenious Dr. Franklin, Selected Scientific Letters of Benjamin Franklin* (Philadelphia: University of Pennsylvania Press, 1931), 99–102.

things. His inventions sprang from a gift of immense curiosity and an exhaustive reading in the science of his day.

Franklin, sometimes called "the first American," represented the fledging Republic in France during the Revolution, ensuring French participation against the British. In 1783 he signed the second Treaty of Paris, by which the British recognized the independence of the United States. Franklin was the only founding father to sign the Declaration of Independence (1776), the Treaty of Paris (1783), and the Constitution of the United States (1789). Throughout his life Franklin furthered his interest in scientific experiment and invention. In December of 1783, he wrote to a friend in England about a recent invention that he had witnessed in Paris: an early experiment in air travel in a balloon. What did Franklin see, and what did it mean to him?

THINKING HISTORICALLY

What evidence do you see in this letter that the scientific revolution was a genuinely revolutionary change? What was revolutionary about it? What evidence do you see that the people of the time thought they were living in a revolutionary age? How would you compare their attitudes with those of people today toward modern technological innovations?

To Sir Joseph Banks[1]

Passy, Dec. 1, 1783.

Dear Sir:—

In mine of yesterday I promised to give you an account of Messrs. Charles & Robert's experiment, which was to have been made this day, and at which I intended to be present. Being a little indisposed, and the air cool, and the ground damp, I declined going into the garden of the Tuileries, where the balloon was placed, not knowing how long I might be obliged to wait there before it was ready to depart, and chose to stay in my carriage near the statue of Louis XV, from whence I could well see it rise, and have an extensive view of the region of air through which, as the wind sat, it was likely to pass. The morning was foggy, but about one o'clock the air became tolerably clear, to the great satisfaction of the spectators, who were infinite, notice having been given of the intended experiment several days before in the papers, so that all Paris was out,

---

[1] Banks (1743–1820) was a leading British botanist and naturalist. He sailed to the South Pacific with Captain James Cook and served as president of the Royal Society, trustee of the British Museum, and advisor to George III, whom he encouraged to fund numerous scientific expeditions. (He was also an early British recipient of a smallpox vaccination, in 1760.) [Ed.]

either about the Tuileries, on the quays and bridges, in the fields, the streets, at the windows, or on the tops of houses, besides the inhabitants of all the towns and villages of the environs. Never before was a philosophical experiment so magnificently attended. Some guns were fired to give notice that the departure of the balloon was near, and a small one was discharged, which went to an amazing height, there being but little wind to make it deviate from its perpendicular course, and at length the sight of it was lost. Means were used, I am told, to prevent the great balloon's rising so high as might endanger its bursting. Several bags of sand were taken on board before the cord that held it down was cut, and the whole weight being then too much to be lifted, such a quantity was discharged as to permit its rising slowly. Thus it would sooner arrive at that region where it would be in equilibrio with the surrounding air, and by discharging more sand afterwards, it might go higher if desired. Between one and two o'clock, all eyes were gratified with seeing it rise majestically from among the trees, and ascend gradually above the buildings, a most beautiful spectacle. When it was about two hundred feet high, the brave adventurers held out and waved a little white pennant, on both sides [of] their car, to salute the spectators, who returned loud claps of applause. The wind was very little, so that the object though moving to the northward, continued long in view; and it was a great while before the admiring people began to disperse. The persons embarked were Mr. Charles, professor of experimental philosophy, and a zealous promoter of that science; and one of the Messieurs Robert, the very ingenious constructors of the machine. When it arrived at its height, which I suppose might be three or four hundred toises,[2] it appeared to have only horizontal motion. I had a pocket-glass, with which I followed it, till I lost sight first of the men, then of the car, and when I last saw the balloon, it appeared no bigger than a walnut. I write this at seven in the evening. What became of them is not yet known here. I hope they descended by daylight, so as to see and avoid falling among trees or on houses, and that the experiment was completed without any mischievous accident, which the novelty of it and the want of experience might well occasion. I am the more anxious for the event, because I am not well informed of the means provided for letting themselves down, and the loss of these very ingenious men would not only be a discouragement to the progress of the art, but be a sensible loss to science and society.

I shall inclose one of the tickets of admission, on which the globe was represented, as originally intended, but is altered by the pen to show its real state when it went off. When the tickets were engraved the car was to have been hung to the neck of the globe, as represented by a little drawing I have made in the corner.

---

[2] twaz   A height rod equal to 1.949 meters (or about 2 yards). [Ed.]

I suppose it may have been an apprehension of danger in straining too much the balloon or tearing the silk, that induced the constructors to throw a net over it, fixed to a hoop which went round its middle, and to hang the car to that hoop.

Tuesday morning, December 2d.—I am relieved from my anxiety by hearing that the adventurers descended well near L'Isle Adam before sunset. This place is near seven leagues from Paris. Had the wind blown fresh they might have gone much farther.

If I receive any further particulars of importance, I shall communicate them hereafter.

With great esteem, I am, dear sir, your most obedient and most humble servant,

FRANKLIN

P.S. *Tuesday evening.*—Since writing the above I have received the printed paper and the manuscript containing some particulars of the experiment, which I enclose. I hear further that the travellers had perfect command of their carriage, descending as they pleased by letting some of the inflammable air escape, and rising again by discharging some sand; that they descended over a field so low as to talk with the labourers in passing, and mounted again to pass a hill. The little balloon falling at Vincennes shows that mounting higher it met with a current of air in a contrary direction, an observation that may be of use to future aerial voyagers.

■ REFLECTIONS

Was there a scientific revolution in the seventeenth and eighteenth centuries? By most measures we would have to say "yes." There were new polished-glass instruments with which to observe and measure; books, theories, diagrams, debates, and discoveries emerged at a dizzying pace. Age-old authorities—Aristotle, Ptolemy, even the Bible—were called into question. The wisdom of the ages was interrogated for evidence and forced to submit to tests by experiment.

There was a revolution in the way Europeans looked at their surroundings. In the words of Shakespeare, the great English dramatist, the world became a stage, a spectacle apart that could be viewed and analyzed by objective observers. Nature no longer displayed its forces as omens or metaphors. The rainbow was no longer a sign of hope, the comet a harbinger of divine disapproval. Heavenly events might be explained in the same way as were events on Earth. Newton's rules underline the simplicity of assumptions that nature is uniform and not unnecessarily complex. We can assume that the fire in the fireplace has the same qualities as the fire of the sun, that unchanging qualities of hardness, mobility, or gravity would apply to objects too distant to measure as they do to those within our grasp. Nature follows laws that humans can derive by experiment and induction.

Goldstone reminds us that many of the scientific developments in Europe sprang from foreign innovations, and in some fields Europe was not as advanced as other societies. Lady Mary Montague provides a dramatic example of that fact. Yet the scientific revolution's unique combination of observation and generalization, experimentation and mathematics, induction and deduction established a body of knowledge and a method for research that proved lasting and irreversible.

Why was it that China, so scientifically and technologically adept during the Sung dynasty, pictured hearts and lungs as flower petals in the late-Ming and early-Qing seventeenth century? Was it that Chinese science lost momentum or changed direction? Or does such a question, as Lynda Shaffer warns, judge China unfairly by Western standards? Do the petal hearts reflect a different set of interests rather than a failure of Chinese science?

Chinese scientists excelled in acupuncture, massage, and herbal medicine, while European scientists excelled in surgery. It turned out that the inner workings of the human body were better revealed in surgical dissection than in muscle manipulation or pharmacology. And, as Sugita Gempaku reminds us, the Europeans not only cut and removed, but they also named what they found and tried to understand how it worked. Perhaps the major difference between science in Europe and that in India, China, and Japan in the seventeenth century was one of perspective: Europeans were beginning to imagine the human body as a machine and asking how it worked. In some respects, the metaphor of man as a machine proved more fruitful than organic metaphors of humans as plants or animals.

Asking probing questions and testing the answers also changed our understanding of the heavens. If mathematical calculations indicated that a star would appear at a particular spot in the heavens and it did not, Galileo might just as soon have questioned the observation as the math. From the seventeenth century on, scientists would check one or the other on the assumption that observation and mathematics could be brought together to understand the same event, that they would have to be in agreement, and that such agreement could lead to laws that could then be tested and proved or disproved.

It is this method of inquiry, not the discoveries, that was new. For the scientific method that emerged during this period constituted a systematic means of inquiry based on agreed-upon rules of hypothesis, experimentation, theory testing, law, and dissemination. This scientific inquiry was a social process in two important ways: First, any scientific discovery had to be reproducible and recognized by other scientists to gain credence. Second, a community of scientists was needed to question, dismiss, or validate the work of its members.

Europe in the seventeenth century saw the proliferation of numerous scientific associations, academies, institutes, and public experiments. These numerous organizations testified not only to a growing interest in science but also to a continuing public conversation. Science in Europe thus became a matter of public concern, a popular endeavor. Compare the masses of Parisians Ben Franklin described who turned out to view the balloon experiment with the few physicians gathered around Sugita Gempaku who could learn from the expertise of outcast butchers.

Ultimately, then, the difference between European science and that of India or China in the seventeenth century may have had more to do with society than with culture. The development of modern scientific methods relied on the numerous debates and discussions of a self-conscious class of gentlemen scientists in a Europe where news traveled quickly and ideas could be translated and tested with confidence across numerous borders. To what extent does science everywhere today demonstrate the hallmarks of the seventeenth-century scientific revolution?

20

Enlightenment and Revolution

Europe and the Americas, 1650–1850

■ **HISTORICAL CONTEXT**

Much of the modern world puts its faith in science, reason, and democracy. The seventeenth-century scientific revolution established reason as the key to understanding nature. During the eighteenth century, philosophy, social organization, and government all came under the critical light of reason. Historians call this movement the "Enlightenment," and its consequences were revolutionary. Most— though, as we shall see, not all—people believed that reason would eventually lead to freedom. Freedom of thought, religion, and association, and political liberties and representative governments were hailed as hallmarks of the Age of Enlightenment.

For some, enlightened society meant a more controlled rather than a more democratic society. Philosophers like Immanuel Kant and Jean Jacques Rousseau wanted people to become free but thought most people were incapable of achieving such a state. Rulers who were called "enlightened despots" believed that the application of reason to society would make people happier, but not necessarily freer.

Ultimately, however, the Enlightenment's faith in reason led to calls for political revolution as well as for schemes of order. In England in the seventeenth century, in America and France at the end of the eighteenth century, and in Latin America shortly thereafter, revolutionary governments were created according to rational principles of liberty and equality that dispatched monarchs and enshrined the rule of the people. In this chapter we will concentrate on the heritage of the Enlightenment, examining competing tendencies toward order and revolution, stability and liberty, equality and freedom. We will also compare the American and the French revolutions, and these with the later revolutions in Latin America.

Map 20.1 Latin American Independence, 1804–1830.

■ **THINKING HISTORICALLY**

Close Reading and Interpretation of Texts

At the core of the Enlightenment was a trust in reasoned discussion, a belief that people could understand each other, even if they were not in agreement. Such understanding demanded clear and concise communication in a world where the masses were often swayed by fiery sermons and flamboyant rhetoric. But the Enlightenment also put its faith in the written word and a literate public. Ideas were debated face to face in the salons and coffeehouses of Europe and its colonies, but it was through letters, diaries, the new world of newspapers, and the burgeoning spread of printed books that the people of the Enlightenment learned what they and their neighbors thought.

It is appropriate, then, for us to read the selections in this chapter—all primary sources—in the spirit in which they were written. We will pay special attention to the words and language that the authors use and will attempt to understand exactly what they meant, even why they chose the words they did. Such explication is a twofold process: We must understand the words first and foremost; then we must strive to understand the words in their proper context, as they were intended by the author. To achieve our first goal, we will paraphrase, a difficult task because the eighteenth-century writing style differs greatly from our own: Sentences are longer and arguments are often complex. Vocabularies were broad during this period, and we may encounter words that are used in ways unknown to us and out of usage today. As to our latter goal, we must try to make the vocabulary and perspective of the authors our own. Grappling with what makes the least sense to us and trying to understand why it was said is the challenge.

1

DAVID HUME

On Miracles, 1748

The European Enlightenment of the eighteenth century was the expression of a new class of intellectuals, independent of the clergy but allied with the rising middle class. Their favorite words were *reason, nature,* and *progress.* They applied the systematic doubt of René Descartes (1596–1650) and the reasoning method of the scientific revolution to human affairs, including religion and politics. With caustic wit and good humor, they asked new questions and popularized new points of view that would eventually revolutionize Western politics and culture. While the French *philosophes* and Voltaire (1694–1778) may be the best known, the Scottish philosopher David Hume (1711–1776) may have been the most brilliant. What does Hume argue in this selection? Does he prove his point to your satisfaction? How does he use reason and nature to make his case? Is reason incompatible with religion?

THINKING HISTORICALLY

The first step in understanding what Hume means in this essay must come from a careful reading—a sentence-by-sentence exploration. Try to paraphrase each sentence, putting it into your own words. For example, you might paraphrase the first sentence like this: "I've found a way to disprove superstition; this method should be useful as long as superstition exists, which may be forever." Notice the context of such words as *just* and *check.* What does Hume mean by these words and by *prodigies?*

Source: *The Philosophical Works of David Hume* (Edinburgh: A. Black and W. Tait, 1826).

The second sentence is a concise definition of the scientific method. How would you paraphrase it? The second and third sentences summarize the method Hume has discovered to counter superstition. What is the meaning of the third sentence?

In the rest of the essay, Hume offers four proofs, or reasons, why miracles do not exist. How would you paraphrase each of these? Do you find these more or less convincing than his more general opening and closing arguments? What does Hume mean by *miracles*?

I flatter myself that I have discovered an argument . . . , which, if just, will, with the wise and learned, be an everlasting check to all kinds of superstitious delusion, and consequently will be useful as long as the world endures; for so long, I presume, will the accounts of miracles and prodigies be found in all history, sacred and profane. . . .

A wise man proportions his belief to the evidence. . . .

A miracle is a violation of the laws of nature; and as a firm and unalterable experience has established these laws, the proof against a miracle, from the very nature of the fact, is as entire as any argument from experience can possibly be imagined. . . . Nothing is esteemed a miracle, if it ever happens in the common course of nature. It is no miracle that a man, seemingly in good health, should die on a sudden; because such a kind of death, though more unusual than any other, has yet been frequently observed to happen. But it is a miracle that a dead man should come to life; because that has never been observed in any age or country. There must, therefore, be an uniform experience against every miraculous event, otherwise the event would not merit that appellation. And as an uniform experience amounts to a proof, there is here a direct and full *proof*, from the nature of the fact, against the existence of any miracle. . . .

(Further) there is not to be found, in all history, any miracle attested by a sufficient number of men, of such unquestioned good sense, education, and learning, as to secure us against all delusion in themselves; of such undoubted integrity, as to place them beyond all suspicion of any design to deceive others; of such credit and reputation in the eyes of mankind, as to have a great deal to lose in case of their being detected in any falsehood. . . .

Secondly, We may observe in human nature a principle which, if strictly examined, will be found to diminish extremely the assurance, which we might, from human testimony, have in any kind of prodigy. . . . The passion of *surprise* and *wonder*, arising from miracles, being an agreeable emotion, gives a sensible tendency towards the belief of those events from which it is derived. . . .

With what greediness are the miraculous accounts of travellers received, their descriptions of sea and land monsters, their relations of wonderful adventures, strange men, and uncouth manners? But if the spirit of religion join itself to the love of wonder, there is an end of common sense; and human testimony, in these circumstances, loses all pretensions to authority. A religionist may be an enthusiast, and imagine he sees what has no reality: He may know his narrative to be false, and yet persevere in it, with the best intentions in the world, for the sake of promoting so holy a cause: Or even where this delusion has not place, vanity, excited by so strong a temptation, operates on him more powerfully than on the rest of mankind in any other circumstances; and self-interest with equal force. . . .

The many instances of forged miracles and prophecies and supernatural events, which, in all ages, have either been detected by contrary evidence, or which detect themselves by their absurdity, prove sufficiently the strong propensity of mankind to the extraordinary and marvellous, and ought reasonably to beget a suspicion against all relations of this kind.[1] . . .

Thirdly, It forms a strong presumption against all supernatural and miraculous relations, that they are observed chiefly to abound among ignorant and barbarous nations; or if a civilized people has ever given admission to any of them, that people will be found to have received them from ignorant and barbarous ancestors, who transmitted them with that inviolable sanction and authority which always attend received opinions. . . .

I may add, as a *fourth* reason, which diminishes the authority of prodigies, that there is no testimony for any, even those which have not been expressly detected, that is not opposed by any infinite number of witnesses; so that not only the miracle destroys the credit of testimony, but the testimony destroys itself. To make this the better understood, let us consider, that in matters of religion, whatever is different is contrary; and that it is impossible the religions of ancient Rome, of Turkey, of Siam, and of China, should all of them be established on any solid foundation. Every miracle, therefore, pretended to have been wrought in any of these religions (and all of them abound in miracles), as its direct scope is to establish the particular system to which it is attributed; so has it the same force, though more indirectly, to overthrow every other system. In destroying a rival system, it likewise destroys the credit of those miracles on which that system was established, so that all the prodigies of different religions are to be regarded as contrary facts, and the evidences of these prodigies, whether weak or strong, as opposite to each other. . . .

Upon the whole, then, it appears, that no testimony for any kind of miracle has ever amounted to a probability, much less to a proof; and that, even supposing it amounted to proof, it would be opposed by another proof, derived from the very nature of the fact which it would endeavour to establish. It is experience only which gives authority to human testimony; and it is the same experience which assures us of the

---

[1] Accounts of miracles. [Ed.]

laws of nature. When, therefore, these two kinds of experience are contrary, we have nothing to do but to subtract the one from the other, and embrace an opinion either on one side or the other, with that assurance which arises from the remainder. But according to the principle here explained, this subtraction with regard to all popular religions amounts to an entire annihilation; and therefore we may establish it as a maxim, that no human testimony can have such force as to prove a miracle, and make it a just foundation for any such system of religion.

2

JEAN JACQUES ROUSSEAU
The Social Contract, 1762

Jean Jacques Rousseau (1712–1778) was one of the leading thinkers of the Enlightenment, whose ideas were as central as those of Diderot (with whom he studied and quarreled), Voltaire (next to whom he is buried in the Pantheon), and Hume (who sheltered him in England toward the end of his life). Rousseau's indifference to formal religion both reflected and influenced French Enlightenment thought, and his political ideas affected the radicals of the French Revolution, though he died eleven years before its outbreak. In both his native Geneva and France, where he spent most of his life, Rousseau's work was often banned. In fact, most of his work was not published until after his death.

The Social Contract, Or Principles of Political Right (1762) challenged the monarchy and called for a government of the people, a force Rousseau saw not in individuals or the competing classes of a society of unequals, but in a "general will" that was greater than any institution or the sum of the people. Which ideas expressed here would be a threat to the French monarchy or establishment? Why would Rousseau's writing appeal to people who wanted to overthrow the regime?

THINKING HISTORICALLY

The power of Enlightenment thought was its radical willingness to ask, and try to answer, fundamental questions. What are some of the fundamental questions this selection grapples with? What does Rousseau mean by such phrases as the "state of nature," the "social compact," and the "general will"?

Source: Jean Jacques Rousseau, *The Social Contract, Or Principles of Political Right*, trans. G. D. H. Cole. Rendered into HTML and text by Jon Roland of the Constitution Society. Available at www. constitution.org/jjr/socon.htm.

Book I

I mean to inquire if, in the civil order,[1] there can be any sure and legitimate rule of administration, men being taken as they are and laws as they might be. In this inquiry I shall endeavor always to unite what right sanctions with what is prescribed by interest, in order that justice and utility may in no case be divided.

I enter upon my task without proving the importance of the subject. I shall be asked if I am a prince or a legislator, to write on politics. I answer that I am neither, and that is why I do so. If I were a prince or a legislator, I should not waste time in saying what wants doing; I should do it, or hold my peace.

As I was born a citizen of a free State, and a member of the Sovereign,[2] I feel that, however feeble the influence my voice can have on public affairs, the right of voting on them makes it my duty to study them: and I am happy, when I reflect upon governments, to find my inquiries always furnish me with new reasons for loving that of my own country.

1. Subject of the First Book

Man is born free; and everywhere he is in chains. One thinks himself the master of others, and still remains a greater slave than they. How did this change come about? I do not know. What can make it legitimate? That question I think I can answer.

If I took into account only force, and the effects derived from it, I should say: "As long as a people is compelled to obey, and obeys, it does well; as soon as it can shake off the yoke, and shakes it off, it does still better; for, regaining its liberty by the same right as took it away, either it is justified in resuming it, or there was no justification for those who took it away." But the social order is a sacred right which is the basis of all other rights. Nevertheless, this right does not come from nature, and must therefore be founded on conventions. . . .

4. Slavery

Since no man has a natural authority over his fellow, and force creates no right, we must conclude that conventions[3] form the basis of all legitimate authority among men. . . .

So, from whatever aspect we regard the question, the right of slavery is null and void, not only as being illegitimate, but also because it is

---

[1] Civil order: opposed to the state of nature; civic society, the world of citizens. [Ed.]
[2] The ultimate authority, which Rousseau says should be the General Will. [Ed.]
[3] Agreements, compacts. [Ed.]

absurd and meaningless. The words *slave* and *right* contradict each other, and are mutually exclusive. It will always be equally foolish for a man to say to a man or to a people: "I make with you a convention wholly at your expense and wholly to my advantage; I shall keep it as long as I like, and you will keep it as long as I like."

6. *The Social Compact*

I suppose men to have reached the point at which the obstacles in the way of their preservation in the state of nature[4] show their power of resistance to be greater than the resources at the disposal of each individual for his maintenance in that state. That primitive condition can then subsist no longer; and the human race would perish unless it changed its manner of existence.

But, as men cannot engender new forces, but only unite and direct existing ones, they have no other means of preserving themselves than the formation, by aggregation, of a sum of forces great enough to overcome the resistance. These they have to bring into play by means of a single motive power, and cause to act in concert.

This sum of forces can arise only where several persons come together: but, as the force and liberty of each man are the chief instruments of his self-preservation, how can he pledge them without harming his own interests, and neglecting the care he owes to himself? This difficulty, in its bearing on my present subject, may be stated in the following terms:

"*The problem is to find a form of association which will defend and protect with the whole common force the person and goods of each associate, and in which each, while uniting himself with all, may still obey himself alone, and remain as free as before.*" This is the fundamental problem of which the *Social Contract* provides the solution. . . .

. . . [F]or, in the first place, as each gives himself absolutely, the conditions are the same for all; and, this being so, no one has any interest in making them burdensome to others. Moreover, the alienation being without reserve,[5] the union is as perfect as it can be, and no associate has anything more to demand: for, if the individuals retained certain rights, as there would be no common superior to decide between them and the public, each, being on one point his own judge, would ask to be so on all; the state of nature would thus continue, and the association would necessarily become inoperative or tyrannical.

Finally, each man, in giving himself to all, gives himself to nobody; and as there is no associate over whom he does not acquire the same right as he yields others over himself, he gains an equivalent for everything he loses, and an increase of force for the preservation of what he has.

---

[4] A hypothetical or primitive existence before government; a frequent starting point in Enlightenment thinking about government. [Ed.]

[5] Each gives his freedom to the whole freely and completely. [Ed.]

If then we discard from the social compact what is not of its essence, we shall find that it reduces itself to the following terms:

"Each of us puts his person and all his power in common under the supreme direction of the general will, and, in our corporate capacity, we receive each member as an indivisible part of the whole."

3

The American Declaration of Independence, 1776

If anyone had taken a poll of Americans in the thirteen colonies as late as 1775, independence would not have won a majority vote anywhere. Massachusetts might have come close, perhaps, but nowhere in the land was there a definitive urge to separate from the British Empire. Still, three thousand miles was a long way for news, views, appointees, and petitions to travel, and tensions between the colonies and Britain had been growing.

Of course, each side looked at the cost of colonial administration differently. The British believed that they had carried a large part of the costs of migration, administration of trade, and control of the sea, while the colonists resented the humiliation resulting from their lack of political representation and the often inept royal officials and punitive legislation imposed on them from afar by the Parliament and the king.

By the spring of 1775, events were rapidly pushing the colonies toward independence. In April, British troops engaged colonial forces at Lexington and Concord, instigating a land war that was to last until 1781. In the midst of other urgent business, most notably raising an army, the Continental Congress asked a committee that included Thomas Jefferson, Benjamin Franklin, and John Adams to compose a statement outlining these and other reasons for separation from Britain. Jefferson wrote the first draft, the bulk of which became the final version accepted by the Continental Congress on July 4, 1776.

The Declaration of Independence was preeminently a document of the Enlightenment. Its principal author, Thomas Jefferson, exemplified the Enlightenment intellectual. Conversant in European literature, law, and political thought, he made significant contributions to

---

Source: *A Documentary History of the United States*, ed. Richard D. Heffner (New York: Penguin Books, 1991), 15–18.

eighteenth-century knowledge in natural science and architecture. Benjamin Franklin and other delegates to the Congress in Philadelphia were similarly accomplished.

It is no wonder, then, that the Declaration and the establishment of an independent United States of America should strike the world as the realization of the Enlightenment's basic tenets. That a wholly new country could be created by people with intelligence and foresight, according to principles of reason, and to realize human liberty, was heady stuff.

What were the goals of the authors of this document? In what ways was the Declaration a call for democracy? In what ways was it not?

THINKING HISTORICALLY

Before interpreting any document, we must read it carefully and put it into context—that is, determine the what, where, and why. Some of this information may be available in the text itself. For instance, to whom is the Declaration addressed? What is the reason given for writing it?

The urgency and immediate purpose of the Declaration of Independence separate it from the more theoretical *Social Contract* by Rousseau. But the age of Enlightenment enshrined similar concerns, and therefore similar ideas and language. What words or phrases are similar in both documents? How is their meaning similar or different?

Consider also the disparity between the lofty sentiments of liberty and independence and the existence of slavery in the Americas. How is Rousseau's treatment of slavery different from Jefferson's? How is it possible that Jefferson and some of the signers of the Declaration could own slaves while declaring it "self-evident that all men are created equal"? To whom did this statement apply?

In Congress, July 4, 1776, the Unanimous Declaration of the Thirteen United States of America

When in the course of human events, it becomes necessary for one people to dissolve the political bands which have connected them with another, and to assume among the powers of the earth, the separate and equal station to which the Laws of Nature and of Nature's God entitle them, a decent respect to the opinions of mankind requires that they should declare the causes which impel them to the separation.

We hold these truths to be self-evident, that all men are created equal, that they are endowed by their Creator with certain unalienable rights, that among these are life, liberty, and the pursuit of happiness. That to secure these rights, governments are instituted among men, deriving their just powers from the consent of the governed. That whenever any form of government becomes destructive of these ends, it is the right of the people to alter or to abolish it, and to institute new government, laying its foundation on such principles and organizing its powers in such form, as to them shall seem most likely to effect their safety and happiness. Prudence, indeed, will dictate that governments long established should not be changed for light and transient causes; and accordingly all experience hath shown, that mankind are more disposed to suffer, while evils are sufferable, than to right themselves by abolishing the forms to which they are accustomed. But when a long train of abuses and usurpations, pursuing invariably the same object evinces a design to reduce them under absolute despotism, it is their right, it is their duty, to throw off such government, and to provide new guards for their future security. Such has been the patient sufferance of these Colonies; and such is now the necessity which constrains them to alter their former systems of government. The history of the present King of Great Britain is a history of repeated injuries and usurpations, all having in direct object the establishment of an absolute tyranny over these States. To prove this, let facts be submitted to a candid world.

He has refused his assent to laws, the most wholesome and necessary for the public good.

He has forbidden his Governors to pass laws of immediate and pressing importance, unless suspended in their operation till his assent should be obtained; and when so suspended, he has utterly neglected to attend to them.

He has refused to pass other laws for the accommodation of large districts of people, unless those people would relinquish the right of representation in the Legislature, a right inestimable to them and formidable to tyrants only.

He has called together legislative bodies at places unusual, uncomfortable, and distant from the depository of their public records, for the sole purpose of fatiguing them into compliance with his measures.

He has dissolved representative houses repeatedly, for opposing with manly firmness his invasions on the rights of the people.

He has refused for a long time, after such dissolutions, to cause others to be elected; whereby the legislative powers, incapable of annihilation, have returned to the people at large for their exercise; the State remaining in the meantime exposed to all the dangers of invasion from without and convulsions within.

He has endeavoured to prevent the population of these states; for that purpose obstructing the laws of naturalization of foreigners; refusing to pass others to encourage their migration hither, and raising the conditions of new appropriations of lands.

He has obstructed the administration of justice, by refusing his assent to laws for establishing judiciary powers.

He has made judges dependent on his will alone, for the tenure of their offices, and the amount and payment of their salaries.

He has erected a multitude of new offices, and sent hither swarms of officers to harass our people, and eat out their substance.

He has kept among us, in times of peace, standing armies without the consent of our legislatures.

He has affected to render the military independent of and superior to the civil power.

He has combined with others to subject us to a jurisdiction foreign to our constitution, and unacknowledged by our laws; giving his assent to their acts of pretended legislation:

For quartering large bodies of armed troops among us:

For protecting them, by a mock trial, from punishment for any murders which they should commit on the inhabitants of these States:

For cutting off our trade with all parts of the world:

For imposing taxes on us without our consent:

For depriving us in many cases, of the benefits of trial by jury:

For transporting us beyond seas to be tried for pretended offences:

For abolishing the free system of English laws in a neighbouring Province, establishing therein an arbitrary government, and enlarging its boundaries so as to render it at once an example and fit instrument for introducing the same absolute rule into these Colonies:

For taking away our Charters, abolishing our most valuable laws, and altering fundamentally the forms of our governments:

For suspending our own Legislatures, and declaring themselves invested with power to legislate for us in all cases whatsoever.

He has abdicated government here, by declaring us out of his protection and waging war against us.

He has plundered our seas, ravaged our coasts, burnt our towns, and destroyed the lives of our people.

He is at this time transporting large armies of foreign mercenaries to complete the works of death, desolation, and tyranny, already begun with circumstances of cruelty and perfidy scarcely parallelled in the most barbarous ages, and totally unworthy the head of a civilized nation.

He has constrained our fellow citizens taken captive on the high seas to bear arms against their country, to become the executioners of their friends and brethren, or to fall themselves by their hands.

He has excited domestic insurrections amongst us, and has endeavoured to bring on the inhabitants of our frontiers, the merciless Indian savages, whose known rule of warfare, is an undistinguished destruction of all ages, sexes, and conditions.

In every state of these oppressions we have petitioned for redress in the most humble terms: our repeated petitions have been answered only by repeated injury. A prince whose character is thus marked by every act which may define a tyrant is unfit to be the ruler of a free people.

Nor have we been wanting in attention to our British brethren. We have warned them from time to time of attempts by their legislature to extend an unwarrantable jurisdiction over us. We have reminded them of the circumstances of our emigration and settlement here. We have appealed to their native justice and magnanimity, and we have conjured them by the ties of our common kindred to disavow these usurpations, which would inevitably interrupt our connections and correspondence. They too have been deaf to the voice of justice and of consanguinity. We must, therefore, acquiesce in the necessity, which denounces our separation, and hold them, as we hold the rest of mankind, enemies in war, in peace friends.

We, therefore, the Representatives of the United States of America, in General Congress assembled, appealing to the Supreme Judge of the world for the rectitude of our intentions, do, in the name, and by authority of the good people of these Colonies, solemnly publish and declare, That these United Colonies are, and of right ought to be Free and Independent States; that they are absolved from all allegiance to the British Crown, and that all political connection between them and the State of Great Britain, is and ought to be totally dissolved; and that as Free and Independent States, they have full power to levy war, conclude peace, contract alliances, establish commerce, and to do all other acts and things which Independent States may of right do. And for the support of this declaration, with a firm reliance on the protection of Divine Province, we mutually pledge to each other our lives, our fortunes, and our sacred honor.

4

ABIGAIL ADAMS AND JOHN ADAMS
Remember the Ladies, 1776

As a delegate to the Second Continental Congress, future American president John Adams was in Philadelphia in the spring of 1776, collaborating on writing the Declaration of Independence. In the meantime his wife, Abigail, assumed the role of the head of the household, caring for their children and managing the family farm in Braintree,

Source: Letters from Abigail Adams to John Adams, 31 March–5 April 1776, John Adams to Abigail Adams, 14 April 1776, Abigail Adams to John Adams, 7–9 May 1776 [electronic editions]. *Adams Family Papers: An Electronic Archive* (Boston: Massachusetts Historical Society, 2002), http://www.masshist.org/digitaladams/.

Massachusetts. Their relationship had always been characterized by robust intellectual debate, and John even referred to his wife as "Sister Delegate." In their famous correspondence during this period, Abigail urged her husband to "remember the ladies" as he and his fellow revolutionaries constructed the basis for the new American government. What did she mean by this? How did her husband respond? What did she think of his response?

THINKING HISTORICALLY

Enlightenment thinkers often employed grand abstractions like "all men are created equal" for both their rational simplicity and their dramatic revolutionary claim. As a consequence, such abstractions were often more sweeping in their implications than even the revolutionaries of the era intended. For example, John and Abigail Adams, both of whom opposed slavery, did not intend for "all men" to include blacks, either enslaved or free. But men like Adams might not have seriously considered how women would respond to the proclamation of universal equality. What in Adams's response to his wife reveals that he did not intend to extend universal equality to women? Does his response somehow undermine the Declaration of Independence?

Letter from Abigail Adams to John Adams, 31 March–5 April 1776

. . . I long to hear that you have declared an independency — and by the way in the new Code of Laws which I suppose it will be necessary for you to make I desire you would Remember the Ladies, and be more generous and favourable to them than your ancestors. Do not put such unlimited power into the hands of the Husbands. Remember all Men would be tyrants if they could. If perticuliar care and attention is not paid to the Ladies we are determined to foment a Rebellion, and will not hold ourselves bound by any Laws in which we have no voice, or Representation.

That your Sex is Naturally Tyrannical is a Truth so thoroughly established as to admit of no dispute, but such of you as wish to be happy willingly give up the harsh title of Master for the more tender and endearing one of Friend. Why then, not put it out of the power of the vicious and the Lawless to use us with cruelty and indignity [with impunity]. Men of Sense in all Ages abhor those customs which treat us only as the vassals of your Sex. Regard us then as Beings placed by providence under your protection and in imitation of the Supreme Being make use of the power only for our happiness.

Letter from John Adams to Abigail Adams, 14 April 1776

. . . As to Declarations of Independency, be patient. Read our Privateering Laws, and our Commercial Laws. What signifies a Word.

As to your extraordinary Code of Laws, I cannot but laugh. We have been told that our Struggle has loosened the bands of Government every where. That Children and Apprentices were disobedient—that schools and Colleges were grown turbulent—that Indians slighted their Guardians and Negroes grew insolent to their Masters.

But your Letter was the first Intimation that another Tribe more numerous and powerfull than all the rest were grown discontented.—This is rather too coarse a Compliment but you are so saucy, I wont blot it out.

Depend upon it, We know better than to repeal our Masculine systems. Altho they are in full Force, you know they are little more than Theory. We dare not exert our Power in its full Latitude. We are obliged to go fair, and softly, and in Practice you know We are the subjects. We have only the Name of Masters, and rather than give up this, which would compleatly subject Us to the Despotism of the Peticoat, I hope General Washington, and all our brave Heroes would fight. I am sure every good Politician would plot, as long as he would against Despotism, Empire, Monarchy, Aristocracy, Oligarchy, or Ochlocracy. . . .

Letter from Abigail Adams to John Adams, 7–9 May 1776

. . . I can not say that I think you very generous to the Ladies, for whilst you are proclaiming peace and good will to Men, Emancipating all Nations, you insist upon retaining an absolute power over Wives. But you must remember that Arbitary power is like most other things which are very hard, very liable to be broken—and notwithstanding all your wise Laws and Maxims we have it in our power not only to free ourselves but to subdue our Masters, and without violence throw both your natural and legal authority at our feet. . . .

The French Declaration of the Rights of Man and Citizen, 1789

The founding of the Republic of the United States of America provided a model for other peoples chafing under oppressive rule to emulate. Not surprisingly then, when the French movement to end political injustices turned to revolution in 1789 and the revolutionaries convened at the National Assembly, the Marquis de Lafayette (1757–1834), hero of the American Revolution, proposed a Declaration of the Rights of Man and Citizen. Lafayette had the American Declaration in mind, and he had the assistance of Thomas Jefferson, present in Paris as the first United States ambassador to France.

While the resulting document appealed to the French revolutionaries, the French were not able to start afresh as the Americans had done. In 1789 Louis XVI was still king of France: He could not be made to leave by a turn of phrase. Nor were men created equal in France in 1789. Those born into the nobility led lives different from those born into the Third Estate (the 99 percent of the population who were not nobility or clergy), and they had different legal rights as well. This disparity was precisely what the revolutionaries and the Declaration sought to change. Inevitably, though, such change would prove to be a more violent and revolutionary proposition than it had been in the American colonies.

In what ways did the Declaration of the Rights of Man and Citizen resemble the American Declaration of Independence? In what ways was it different? Which was more democratic?

THINKING HISTORICALLY

Compare the language of the Declaration of the Rights of Man and Citizen with that of Rousseau and that of Jefferson. In what ways does it borrow from each? Like both prior documents, the French Declaration is full of abstract, universal principles. But notice how such abstractions can claim our consent by their rationality without informing us as to how they will be implemented. What is meant by the first right, for instance? What does it mean to say that men are "born free"? Why is it necessary to distinguish between "born" and "remain"? What is meant by the phrase "general usefulness"? Do statements like these increase people's liberties, or are they intentionally vague so they can be interpreted at will?

The slogan of the French Revolution was "Liberty, Equality, Fraternity." Which of the rights in the French Declaration emphasize liberty, which equality? Can these two goals be opposed to each other? Explain how.

Source: *A Documentary History of the French Revolution*, ed. John Hall Stewart (London: Macmillan, 1979), 113–15.

The representatives of the French people, organized in National Assembly, considering that ignorance, forgetfulness, or contempt of the rights of man are the sole causes of public misfortunes and of the corruption of governments, have resolved to set forth in a solemn declaration the natural, inalienable, and sacred rights of man, in order that such declaration, continually before all members of the social body, may be a perpetual reminder of their rights and duties; in order that the acts of the legislative power and those of the executive power may constantly be compared with the aim of every political institution and may accordingly be more respected; in order that the demands of the citizens, founded henceforth upon simple and incontestable principles, may always be directed towards the maintenance of the Constitution and the welfare of all.

Accordingly, the National Assembly recognizes and proclaims, in the presence and under the auspices of the Supreme Being, the following rights of man and citizen.

1. Men are born and remain free and equal in rights; social distinctions may be based only upon general usefulness.

2. The aim of every political association is the preservation of the natural and inalienable rights of man; these rights are liberty, property, security, and resistance to oppression.

3. The source of all sovereignty resides essentially in the nation; no group, no individual may exercise authority not emanating expressly therefrom.

4. Liberty consists of the power to do whatever is not injurious to others; thus the enjoyment of the natural rights of every man has for its limits only those that assure other members of society the enjoyment of those same rights; such limits may be determined only by law.

5. The law has the right to forbid only actions which are injurious to society. Whatever is not forbidden by law may not be prevented, and no one may be constrained to do what it does not prescribe.

6. Law is the expression of the general will; all citizens have the right to concur personally, or through their representatives, in its formation; it must be the same for all, whether it protects or punishes. All citizens, being equal before it, are equally admissible to all public offices, positions, and employments, according to their capacity, and without other distinction than that of virtues and talents.

7. No man may be accused, arrested, or detained except in the cases determined by law, and according to the forms prescribed thereby. Whoever solicit, expedite, or execute arbitrary orders, or have them executed, must be punished; but every citizen summoned or apprehended in pursuance of the law must obey immediately; he renders himself culpable by resistance.

8. The law is to establish only penalties that are absolutely and obviously necessary; and no one may be punished except by virtue of a law established and promulgated prior to the offence and legally applied.

9. Since every man is presumed innocent until declared guilty, if arrest be deemed indispensable, all unnecessary severity for securing the person of the accused must be severely repressed by law.

10. No one is to be disquieted because of his opinions, even religious, provided their manifestation does not disturb the public order established by law.

11. Free communication of ideas and opinions is one of the most precious of the rights of man. Consequently, every citizen may speak, write, and print freely, subject to responsibility for the abuse of such liberty in the cases determined by law.

12. The guarantee of the rights of man and citizen necessitates a public force; therefore, is instituted for the advantage of all and not for the particular benefit of those to whom it is entrusted.

13. For the maintenance of the public force and for the expenses of administration a common tax is indispensable; it must be assessed equally on all citizens in proportion to their means.

14. Citizens have the right to ascertain, by themselves or through their representatives, the necessity of the public tax, to consent to it freely, to supervise its use, and to determine its quota, assessment, payment, and duration.

15. Society has the right to require of every public agent an accounting of his administration.

16. Every society in which the guarantee of rights is not assured or the separation of powers not determined has no constitution at all.

17. Since property is a sacred and inviolate right, no one may be deprived thereof unless a legally established public necessity obviously requires it, and upon condition of a just and previous indemnity.

6

OLYMPE DE GOUGES

French Declaration of Rights for Women, 1791

Olympe de Gouges (1748–1793) was a French playwright whose writings became increasingly political as the French Revolution progressed after 1789. When the revolutionary government of the National Assembly passed a new constitution in 1791 with the Declaration of the Rights of Man and Citizen of 1789 as the preamble, and still did not give women the vote, de Gouges wrote the following document.

Source: http://fr.wikisource.org/wiki/D%C3%A9claration_des_droits_de_la_femme_et_de_la_citoyenne. Translated from the French by the editor.

What was de Gouges's argument? What specific rights for women was she seeking?

THINKING HISTORICALLY

Compare this document with the Declaration of the Rights of Man and Citizen. What are the similarities and differences? What is the purpose of the similarities? What is the significance of the differences?

Mankind, are you capable of being just? It is a woman who asks the question; you will not deprive her of that right at least. Tell me? Who has given you the soverign empire to oppress my sex? Your strength? Your talents? Observe the creator in his wisdom; survey nature in all its grandeur, with which you seem to want to be in harmony, and give me, if you dare, an example of this tyrannical empire.

Go back to animals. Consult the elements, study plants, finally glance at all the modifications of organic matter; and surrender to the evidence as I offer you the means; search, probe, and distinguish, if you can, the sexes in the administration of nature. Everywhere you will find them mingled, everywhere they cooperate in the harmonious unity of this immortal masterpiece.

Man alone has raised his exception to a principle. Bizarre, blind, bloated with science and degenerated, in a century of enlightenment and wisdom, in the crassest ignorance, he wants to command as a despot a sex which has received all intellectual faculties; he pretends to be revolutionary, and claims his rights to equality, in order to say nothing more about it.

Preamble

Mothers, daughters, sisters, representatives of the nation, demand to be constituted a national assembly. Considering that ignorance, forgetfulness or contempt of the rights of women are the only causes of public misfortunes and government corruption, they resolve to expose in a solemn declaration, the natural, inalienable, and sacred rights of women, so that this declaration, being constantly before the public, reminds them constantly of their rights and their duties, so that the authoritative acts of men and women are always comparable to the goals of every political institution, and deserving of respect, so that citizens' demands, from now on based on simple and incontestable principles, will always support the constitution, good morals, and the happiness of all.

Consequently, the sex that is as superior in beauty as in the courage of maternity recognizes and declares, in the presence and under the auspices of the Supreme Being, the following Rights of Woman as Citizen.

I. Woman is born free and remains equal to man in rights. Social distinctions may be founded only on general usefulness.

II. The aim of every political association is the preservation of the natural and inalienable rights of Women and Men: these are the rights to liberty, property, security, and especially the resistance to oppression.

III. The source of all sovereignty resides essentially in the Nation, which is the meeting of women and men: no body, no individual, may exercise authority not emanating expressly therefrom.

IV. Liberty and Justice consist of restoring the rights of others; since the exercise of the rights of women has no limits other than those imposed by perpetual male tyranny, these limits must be made to conform to natural law and reason.

V. Laws of nature and reason forbid all acts harmful to society; everything which is not prohibited by these wise and divine laws cannot be prevented, and no one can be constrained to do what they do not prescribe.

VI. Law is to be the expression of the general will; all citizens, male and female, have the right to concur personally or through their representatives in its formation; it must be the same for all; all citizens being equal before it, are equally admissable to all public offices, positions, and employments, according to their capacity and without other distinction than that of virtues and talents. . . .

X. No one is to be disquieted because of his opinions; woman has the right to mount the scaffold; she must equally have the right to mount the rostrum, provided that her demonstrations do not disturb the legally established public order.

XI. The free communication of thoughts and opinions is one of the most precious rights of woman, since that liberty assures recognition of children by their fathers. Any female citizen thus may say freely, I am the mother of a child which belongs to you, without being forced by a barbarous prejudice to hide the truth; subject to responsibility for the abuse of this liberty in cases determined by law. . . .

XIII. For the maintenance of the public force and the expenses of administration, the contributions of woman and man are equal; she shares all the duties and all the painful tasks; therefore, she must have the same share in the distribution of positions, employment, offices, honors, and jobs. . . .

XVI. Every society in which the guarantee of rights is not assured or the separation of powers not determined has no constitution at all; the constitution is void if the majority of individuals comprising the nation have not cooperated in drafting it.

XVII. Property belongs to both sexes whether united or separate; for each it is an inviolable and sacred right; no one may be deprived thereof unless a legally established public necessity obviously requires it, and upon condition of a just and previous indemnity.

7

TOUSSAINT L'OUVERTURE
Letter to the Directory, 1797

When the French revolutionaries proclaimed the Declaration of the Rights of Man and Citizen in 1789, the French colony of Saint-Domingue[1] (now Haiti) contained a half million African slaves, most of whom worked on the sugar plantations that made France one of the richest countries in the world. Thus, the French were confronted with the difficult problem of reconciling their enlightened principles with the extremely profitable, but fundamentally unequal, institution of slavery.

French revolutionaries remained locked in debate about this issue when in 1791, the slaves of Saint-Domingue organized a revolt that culminated in establishing Haiti's national independence twelve years later. François Dominique Toussaint L'Ouverture,* a self-educated Haitian slave, led the revolt and the subsequent battles against the French planter class and French armies, as well as the Spanish forces of neighboring Santo Domingo — the eastern side of the island now known as the Dominican Republic — and the antirevolutionary forces of Britain, all of whom vied for control of the island at the end of the eighteenth century.

---

* too SAN   loo vehr TUR
[1] san doh MANG   *Santo Domingo* was the Spanish name for the eastern half of Hispaniola (now the Dominican Republic). *Saint-Domingue* was the French name for the western half of the island, now Haiti. *San Domingo*, which is used in the text, is a nineteenth-century abbreviation for *Saint-Domingue*. To further complicate matters, both the Spanish and French sometimes used their term for the whole island of Hispaniola. Spain controlled the entire island until 1697, when the Spanish recognized French control of the west.

Source: Toussaint L'Ouverture, "Letter to the Directory, November 5, 1797," in *The Black Jacobins*, ed. C. L. R. James (New York: Vintage Books, 1989), 195–97.

At first Toussaint enjoyed the support of the revolutionary government in Paris; in the Decree of 16 Pluviôse[2] (1794) the National Convention abolished slavery in the colonies. But after 1795 the revolution turned on itself, and Toussaint feared that the new conservative government, called the Directory, might send troops to restore slavery on the island.

In 1797 he wrote the Directory the letter that follows. Notice how Toussaint negotiated a difficult situation. How did he try to reassure the government of his allegiance to France? At the same time, how did he attempt to convince the Directory that a return to slavery was unthinkable?

THINKING HISTORICALLY

Notice how Toussaint defines different groups of people. What does he mean, for instance, by "the proprietors of San Domingo" as opposed to "the people of San Domingo"? What does he mean by "the colonists" and "our common enemies"? How does the use of these terms aid his cause?

... The impolitic and incendiary discourse of Vaublanc[3] has not affected the blacks nearly so much as their certainty of the projects which the proprietors of San Domingo are planning: insidious declarations should not have any effect in the eyes of wise legislators who have decreed liberty for the nations. But the attempts on that liberty which the colonists propose are all the more to be feared because it is with the veil of patriotism that they cover their detestable plans. We know that they seek to impose some of them on you by illusory and specious promises, in order to see renewed in this colony its former scenes of horror. Already perfidious emissaries have stepped in among us to ferment the destructive leaven prepared by the hands of liberticides. But they will not succeed. I swear it by all that liberty holds most sacred. My attachment to France, my knowledge of the blacks, make it my duty not to leave you ignorant either of the crimes which they meditate or the oath that we renew, to bury ourselves under the ruins of a country revived by liberty rather than suffer the return of slavery.

It is for you, Citizens Directors, to turn from over our heads the storm which the eternal enemies of our liberty are preparing in the shades of

---

[2] PLOO vee ohs   Rainy; the name of the second winter month according to the revolutionary calendar.

[3] Vincent-Marie Viénot, Count of Vaublanc (1756–1845). Born into an aristocratic family in San Domingo, he was a French royalist politician. In Paris in September 1797, he gave a speech intended to impeach republican directors and trigger a royalist coup. [Ed.]

silence. It is for you to enlighten the legislature, it is for you to prevent the enemies of the present system from spreading themselves on our unfortunate shores to sully it with new crimes. Do not allow our brothers, our friends, to be sacrificed to men who wish to reign over the ruins of the human species. But no, your wisdom will enable you to avoid the dangerous snares which our common enemies hold out for you. . . .

I send you with this letter a declaration which will acquaint you with the unity that exists between the proprietors of San Domingo who are in France, those in the United States, and those who serve under the English banner. You will see there a resolution, unequivocal and carefully constructed, for the restoration of slavery; you will see there that their determination to succeed has led them to envelop themselves in the mantle of liberty in order to strike it more deadly blows. You will see that they are counting heavily on my complacency in lending myself to their perfidious views by my fear for my children. It is not astonishing that these men who sacrifice their country to their interests are unable to conceive how many sacrifices a true love of country can support in a better father than they, since I unhesitatingly base the happiness of my children on that of my country, which they and they alone wish to destroy.

I shall never hesitate between the safety of San Domingo and my personal happiness; but I have nothing to fear. It is to the solicitude of the French Government that I have confided my children. . . . I would tremble with horror if it was into the hands of the colonists that I had sent them as hostages; but even if it were so, let them know that in punishing them for the fidelity of their father, they would only add one degree more to their barbarism, without any hope of ever making me fail in my duty. . . . Blind as they are! They cannot see how this odious conduct on their part can become the signal of new disasters and irreparable misfortunes, and that far from making them regain what in their eyes liberty for all has made them lose, they expose themselves to a total ruin and the colony to its inevitable destruction. Do they think that men who have been able to enjoy the blessing of liberty will calmly see it snatched away? They supported their chains only so long as they did not know any condition of life more happy than that of slavery. But to-day when they have left it, if they had a thousand lives they would sacrifice them all rather than be forced into slavery again. But no, the same hand which has broken our chains will not enslave us anew. France will not revoke her principles, she will not withdraw from us the greatest of her benefits. She will protect us against all our enemies; she will not permit her sublime morality to be perverted, those principles which do her most honour to be destroyed, her most beautiful achievement to be degraded, and her Decree of 16 Pluviôse which so honours humanity to be revoked. *But if, to re-establish slavery in San Domingo, this was done, then I declare to you it would be to attempt the impossible: we have known how to face dangers to obtain our liberty, we shall know how to brave death to maintain it.*

This, Citizens Directors, is the morale of the people of San Domingo, those are the principles that they transmit to you by me.

My own you know. It is sufficient to renew, my hand in yours, the oath that I have made, to cease to live before gratitude dies in my heart, before I cease to be faithful to France and to my duty, before the god of liberty is profaned and sullied by the liberticides, before they can snatch from my hands that sword, those arms, which France confided to me for the defence of its rights and those of humanity, for the triumph of liberty and equality.

8

SIMÓN BOLÍVAR

Reply of a South American to a Gentleman of This Island (Jamaica), 1815

Simón Bolívar (1783–1830), known as "the Liberator," defeated the Spanish and won independence for Venezuela, Colombia, Ecuador, Panama, Bolivia, and (with Jose St. Martin, the Liberator of Argentina and Chile) also Peru. Bolívar was born into an aristocratic military family in Caracas and educated in Spain, where he was influenced by the ideas of the Enlightenment. This selection is from a letter he wrote to a Jamaican in 1815.

How does Bolívar view the Spanish conquest of the Americas? How does he describe the condition of South America in 1815? What does he mean when he says "we are . . . neither Indian nor European," and what is the significance of that sense of identity? In what way was this Bolívarian struggle for independence different from that in North America?

THINKING HISTORICALLY

Much of the language Bolívar employs is similar to other Enlightenment writings, but some of it seems strange. When, for instance, he writes "we are in a position lower than slavery" and "we have even been deprived of an active tyranny," what does he mean?

Source: Simón Bolívar, *Selected Writings of Bolivar*, Vol. I, ed. Harold A. Bierck (New York: The Colonial Press Inc., 1951), 103–21.

Kingston, Jamaica, September 6, 1815

My dear Sir:

I hasten to reply to the letter of the 29th ultimo which you had the honor of sending me and which I received with the greatest satisfaction.

Sensible though I am of the interest you desire to take in the fate of my country, and of your commiseration with her for the tortures she has suffered from the time of her discovery until the present at the hands of her destroyers, the Spaniards, I am no less sensible of the obligation which your solicitous inquiries about the principal objects of American policy place upon me. Thus, I find myself in conflict between the desire to reciprocate your confidence, which honors me, and the difficulty of rewarding it, for lack of documents and books and because of my own limited knowledge of a land so vast, so varied, and so little known as the New World. In my opinion it is impossible to answer the questions that you have so kindly posed. Baron von Humboldt himself; with his encyclopedic theoretical and practical knowledge, could hardly do so properly, because, although some of the facts about America and her development are known, I dare say the better part are shrouded in mystery. Accordingly, only conjectures that are more or less approximate can be made, especially with regard to her future and the true plans of the Americans, inasmuch as our continent has within it potentialities for every facet of development revealed in the history of nations, by reason of its physical characteristics and because of the hazards of war and the uncertainties of politics.

As I feel obligated to give due consideration to your esteemed letter and to the philanthropic intentions prompting it, I am impelled to write you these words, wherein you will certainly not find the brilliant thoughts you seek but rather a candid statement of my ideas.

"Three centuries ago," you say, "began the atrocities committed by the Spaniards on this great hemisphere of Columbus." Our age has rejected these atrocities as mythical, because they appear to be beyond the human capacity for evil. Modern critics would never credit them were it not for the many and frequent documents testifying to these horrible truths. The humane Bishop of Chiapas, that apostle of America, Las Casas, has left to posterity a brief description of these horrors, extracted from the trial records in Sevilla relating to the cases brought against the *conquistadores*, and containing the testimony of every respectable person then in the New World, together with the charges, which the tyrants made against each other. All this is attested by the foremost historians of that time. Every impartial person has admitted the zeal, sincerity, and high character of that friend of humanity, who so fervently and so steadfastly denounced to his government and to his contemporaries the most horrible acts of sanguinary frenzy.

With what a feeling of gratitude I read that passage in your letter in which you say to me: "I hope that the success which then followed

Spanish arms may now turn in favor of their adversaries, the badly oppressed people of South America." I take this hope as a prediction, if it is justice that determines man's contests. Success will crown our efforts, because the destiny of America has been irrevocably decided; the tie that bound her to Spain has been severed. Only a concept maintained that tie and kept the parts of that immense monarchy together. That which formerly bound them now divides them. The hatred that the Peninsula has inspired in us is greater than the ocean between us. It would be easier to have the two continents meet than to reconcile the spirits of the two countries. The habit of obedience; a community of interest, of understanding, of religion; mutual goodwill; a tender regard for the birthplace and good name of our forefathers; in short, all that gave rise to our hopes, came to us from Spain. As a result there was born principle of affinity that seemed eternal, notwithstanding the misbehavior of our rulers which weakened that sympathy, or, rather, that bond enforced by the domination of their rule. At present the contrary attitude persists: we are threatened with the fear of death, dishonor, and every harm; there is nothing we have not suffered at the hands of that unnatural stepmother-Spain. The veil has been torn asunder. We have already seen the light, and it is not our desire to be thrust back into darkness. The chains have been broken; we have been freed, and now our enemies seek to enslave us anew. For this reason America fights desperately, and seldom has desperation failed to achieve victory.

Because successes have been partial and spasmodic, we must not lose faith. In some regions the Independents triumph, while in others the tyrants have the advantage. What is the end result? Is not the entire New World in motion, armed for defense? We have but to look around us on this hemisphere to witness a simultaneous struggle at every point.

The war-like state of the La Plata River provinces has purged that territory and led their victorious armies to Upper Perú, arousing Arequipa and worrying the royalists in Lima. Nearly one million inhabitants there now enjoy liberty.

The territory of Chile, populated by 800,000 souls, is fighting the enemy who is seeking her subjugation; but to no avail, because those who long ago put an end to the conquests of this enemy, the free and indomitable Araucanians, are their neighbors and compatriots. Their sublime example is proof to those fighting in Chile that a people who love independence will eventually achieve it.

The viceroyalty of Perú, whose population approaches a million and a half inhabitants, without doubt suffers the greatest subjection and is obliged to make the most sacrifices for the royal cause; and, although the thought of cooperating with that part of America may be vain, the fact remains that it is not tranquil, nor is it capable of restraining the torrent that threatens most of its provinces.

New Granada, which is, so to speak, the heart of America, obeys a general government, save for the territory of Quito which is held only with the greatest difficulty by its enemies, as it is strongly devoted to the country's cause; and the provinces of Panamá and Santa Marta endure, not without suffering, the tyranny of their masters. Two and a half million people inhabit New Granada and are actually defending that territory against the Spanish army under General Morillo, who will probably suffer defeat at the impregnable fortress of Cartagena. But should he take that city, it will be at the price of heavy casualties, and he will then lack sufficient forces to subdue the unrestrained and brave inhabitants of the interior.

With respect to heroic and hapless Venezuela, events there have moved so rapidly and the devastation has been such that it is reduced to frightful desolation and almost absolute indigence, although it was once among the fairest regions that are the pride of America. Its tyrants govern a desert, and they oppress only those unfortunate survivors who, having escaped death, lead a precarious existence. A few women, children, and old men are all that remain. Most of the men have perished rather than be slaves; those who survive continue to fight furiously on the fields and in the inland towns, until they expire or hurl into the sea those who, insatiable in their thirst for blood and crimes, rival those first monsters who wiped out America's primitive race. Nearly a million persons formerly dwelt in Venezuela, and it is no exaggeration to say that one out of four has succumbed either to the land, sword, hunger, plague, flight, or privation, all consequences of the war, save the earthquake.

According to Baron von Humboldt, New Spain, including Guatemala, had 7,800,000 inhabitants in 1808. Since that time, the insurrection, which has shaken virtually all of her provinces, has appreciably reduced that apparently correct figure, for over a million men have perished, as you can see in the report of Mr. Walton, who describes faithfully the bloody crimes committed in that abundant kingdom. There the struggle continues by dint of human and every other type of sacrifice, for the Spaniards spare nothing that might enable them to subdue those who have had the misfortune of being born on this soil, which appears to be destined to flow with the blood of its offspring. In spite of everything, the Mexicans will be free. They have embraced the country's cause, resolved to avenge their forefathers or follow them to the grave. Already they say with Raynal: The time has come at last to repay the Spaniards torture for torture and to drown that race of annihilators in its own blood or in the sea.

The islands of Puerto Rico and Cuba, with a combined population of perhaps 700,000 to 800,000 souls, are the most tranquil possessions of the Spaniards, because they are not within range of contact with the Independents. But are not the people of those islands Americans? Are they not maltreated? Do they not desire a better life?

This picture represents, on a military map, an area of 2,000 longitudinal and 900 latitudinal leagues at its greatest point, wherein 16,000,000 Americans either defend their rights or suffer repression at the hands of Spain, which, although once the world's greatest empire, is now too weak, with what little is left her, to rule the new hemisphere or even to maintain herself in the old. And shall Europe, the civilized, the merchant, the lover of liberty allow an aged serpent, bent only on satisfying its venomous rage, devour the fairest part of our globe? What! Is Europe deaf to the clamor of her own interests? Has she no eyes to see justice? Has she grown so hardened as to become insensible? The more I ponder these questions, the more I am confused. I am led to think that America's disappearance is desired; but this is impossible because all Europe is not Spain. What madness for our enemy to hope to reconquer America when she has no navy, no funds, and almost no soldiers! Those troops which she has are scarcely adequate to keep her own people in a state of forced obedience and to defend herself from her neighbors. On the other hand, can that nation carry on the exclusive commerce of one-half the world when it lacks manufactures, agricultural products, crafts and sciences, and even a policy? Assume that this mad venture were successful, and further assume that pacification ensued, would not the sons of the Americans of today, together with the sons of the European *reconquistadores* twenty years hence, conceive the same patriotic designs that are now being fought for?

Europe could do Spain a service by dissuading her from her rash obstinacy, thereby at least sparing her the costs she is incurring and the blood she is expending. And if she will fix her attention on her own precincts she can build her prosperity and power upon more solid foundations than doubtful conquests, precarious commerce, and forceful exactions from remote and powerful peoples. Europe herself, as a matter of common sense policy, should have prepared and executed the project of American independence, not alone because the world balance of power so necessitated, but also because this is the legitimate and certain means through which Europe can acquire overseas commercial establishments. A Europe which is not moved by the violent passions of vengeance, ambition, and greed, as is Spain, would seem to be entitled, by all the rules of equity, to make clear to Spain where her best interests lie.

All of the writers who have treated this matter agree on this point. Consequently, we have had reason to hope that the civilized nations would hasten to our aid in order that we might achieve that which must prove to be advantageous to both hemispheres. How vain has been this hope! Not only the Europeans but even our brothers of the North have been apathetic bystanders in this struggle which, by its very essence, is the most just, and in its consequences the most noble and vital of any which have been raised in ancient or in modern times. Indeed, can the far-reaching effects of freedom for the hemisphere which Columbus discovered ever be calculated? . . .

I have listed the population, which is based on more or less exact data, but which a thousand circumstances render deceiving. This inaccuracy cannot easily be remedied, because most of the inhabitants live in rural areas and are often nomadic; they are farmers, herders, and migrants, lost amidst thick giant forests, solitary plains, and isolated by lakes and mighty streams. Who is capable of compiling complete statistics of a land like this! Moreover, the tribute paid by the Indians, the punishments of the slaves, the first fruits of the harvest, tithes, and taxes levied on farmers, and other impositions have driven the poor Americans from their homes. This is not to mention the war of extermination that has already taken a toll of nearly an eighth part of the population and frightened another large part away. All in all, the difficulties are insuperable, and the tally is likely to show only half the true count. . . .

[W]e are, moreover, neither Indian nor European, but a species midway between the legitimate proprietors of this country and the Spanish usurpers. In short, though Americans by birth we derive our rights from Europe, and we have to assert these rights against the rights of the natives, and at the same time we must defend ourselves against the invaders. This places us in a most extraordinary and involved situation. Notwithstanding that it is a type of divination to predict the result of the political course which America is pursuing, I shall venture some conjectures which, of course, are colored by my enthusiasm and dictated by rational desires rather than by reasoned calculations.

The role of the inhabitants of the American hemisphere has for centuries been purely passive. Politically they were nonexistent. We are still in a position lower than slavery, and therefore it is more difficult for us to rise to the enjoyment of freedom. . . .

We have been harassed by a conduct which has not only deprived us of our rights but has kept us in a sort of permanent infancy with regard to public affairs. If we could at least have managed our domestic affairs and our internal administration, we could have acquainted ourselves with the processes and mechanics of public affairs. We should also have enjoyed a personal consideration, thereby commanding a certain unconscious respect from the people, which is so necessary to preserve amidst revolutions. That is why I say we have even been deprived of an active tyranny, since we have not been permitted to exercise its functions.

Americans today, and perhaps to a greater extent than ever before, who live within the Spanish system occupy a position in society no better than that of serfs destined for labor, or at best they have no more status than that of mere consumers. Yet even this status is surrounded with galling restrictions, such as being forbidden to grow European crops, or to store products which are royal monopolies, or to establish factories of a type the Peninsula itself does not possess. To this add the exclusive trading privileges, even in articles of prime necessity, and the barriers between American provinces, designed to prevent all exchange of trade, traffic, and understanding. In short, do you wish to know what our future held?—simply the cultivation of the fields of indigo, grain, coffee, sugar cane, cacao, and cotton; cattle raising on the broad plains; hunting wild game in the jungles; digging in the earth to mine its gold—but even these limitations could never satisfy the greed of Spain.

So negative was our existence that I can find nothing comparable in any other civilized society, examine as I may the entire history of time and the politics of all nations. Is it not an outrage and a violation of human rights to expect a land so splendidly endowed, so vast, rich, and populous, to remain merely passive?

As I have just explained, we were cut off and, as it were, removed from the world in relation to the science of government and administration of the state. We were never viceroys or governors, save in the rarest of instances; seldom archbishops and bishops; diplomats never; as military men, only subordinates; as nobles, without royal privileges. In brief, we were neither magistrates nor financiers and seldom merchants—all in flagrant contradiction to our institutions. . . .

The Americans have risen rapidly without previous knowledge of, and, what is more regrettable, without previous experience in public affairs, to enact upon the world stage the eminent roles of legislator, magistrate, minister of the treasury, diplomat, general, and every position of authority, supreme or subordinate, that comprises the hierarchy of a fully organized state. . . .

More than anyone, I desire to see America fashioned into the greatest nation in the world, greatest not so much by virtue of her area and wealth as by her freedom and glory. Although I seek perfection for the government of my country, I cannot persuade myself that the New World can, at the moment, be organized as a great republic. Since it is impossible, I dare not desire it; yet much less do I desire to have all America a monarchy because this plan is not only impracticable but also impossible. Wrongs now existing could not be righted, and our emancipation would be fruitless. The American states need the care of paternal governments to heal the sores and wounds of despotism and war. The parent country, for example, might be Mexico, the only country fitted for the position by her intrinsic strength, and without such power there can be no parent country. . . .

It is a grandiose idea to think of consolidating the New World into a single nation, united by pacts into a single bond. It is reasoned that, as these parts have a common origin, language, customs, and religion, they ought to have a single government to permit the newly formed states to unite in a confederation. But this is not possible. Actually, America is separated by climatic differences, geographic diversity, conflicting interests, and dissimilar characteristics. How beautiful it would be if the Isthmus of Panamá could be for us what the Isthmus of Corinth was for the Greeks! Would to God that someday we may have the good fortune to convene there an august assembly of representatives of republics, kingdoms, and empires to deliberate upon the high interests of peace and war with the nations of the other three-quarters of the globe. This type of organization may come to pass in some happier period of our regeneration. But any other plan, such as that of Abbí St. Pierre, who in laudable delirium conceived the idea of assembling a European congress to decide the fate and interests of those nations, would be meaningless. . . .

I shall tell you with what we must provide ourselves in order to expel the Spaniards and to found a free government. It is *union*, obviously; but such union will come about through sensible planning and well-directed actions rather than by divine magic. America stands together because it is abandoned by all other nations. It is isolated in the center of the world. It has no diplomatic relations, nor does it receive any military assistance; instead, America is attacked by Spain, which has more military supplies than any we can possibly acquire through furtive means.

When success is not assured, when the state is weak, and when results are distantly seen, all men hesitate; opinion is divided, passions rage, and the enemy fans these passions in order to win an easy victory because of them. As soon as we are strong and under the guidance of a liberal nation which will lend us her protection, we will achieve accord in cultivating the virtues and talents that lead to glory. Then will we march majestically toward that great prosperity for which South America is destined. Then will those sciences and arts which, born in the East, have enlightened Europe, wing their way to a free Colombia, which will cordially bid them welcome.

Such, Sir, are the thoughts and observations that I have the honor to submit to you, so that you may accept or reject them according to their merit. I beg you to understand that I have expounded them because I do not wish to appear discourteous and not because I consider myself competent to enlighten you concerning these matters.

I am, Sir, etc., etc.
Simón Bolívar

■ REFLECTIONS

The Enlightenment and its political legacies — secular order and revolutionary republicanism — were European in origin but global in impact. In this chapter, we have touched on just a few of the crosscurrents of what some historians call an "Atlantic Revolution." A tide of revolutionary fervor swept through France, the United States, and Latin America, found sympathy in Russia in 1825, and echoed in the Muslim heartland, resulting in secular, modernizing regimes in Turkey and Egypt in the next century.

The political appeal of the Enlightenment, of rationally ordered society, and of democratic government continues. Some elements of this eighteenth-century revolution—the rule of law; regular, popular elections of representatives; the separation of church and state, of government and politics, and of civil and military authority—are widely recognized ideals and emerging global realities. Like science, the principles of the Enlightenment are universal in their claims and often seem universal in their appeal. Nothing is simpler, more rational, or easier to follow than a call to reason, law, liberty, justice, or equality. And yet every society has evolved its own guidelines under different circumstances, often with lasting results. France had its king and still has a relatively centralized state. The United States began with slavery and still suffers from racism. South American states became free of Europe only to dominate Native Americans, and they continue to do so. None of the enlightened or revolutionary societies of the eighteenth century extended the "rights of man" to women. One democratic society had a king, another a House of Lords, another a national church. Are these different adaptations of the Enlightenment ideal? Or are these examples of incomplete revolution, cases of special interests allowing their governments to fall short of principle?

The debate continues today as more societies seek to realize responsive, representative government and the rule of law while oftentimes respecting conflicting traditions. Muslim countries and Israel struggle with the competing demands of secular law and religion, citizenship and communalism. Former communist countries adopt market economies and struggle with traditions of collective support and the appeal of individual liberty.

Perhaps these are conflicts within the Enlightenment tradition itself. How is it possible to have both liberty and equality? How can we claim inalienable rights on the basis of a secular, scientific creed? How does a faith in human reason lead to revolution? And how can ideas of order or justice avoid the consequences of history and human nature?

The great revolutionary declarations of the Enlightenment embarrass the modern skeptic with their naïve faith in natural laws, their universal prescriptions to cure all ills, and their hypocritical avoidance of slaves, women, and the colonized. The selections by Toussaint, de Gouges, and Abigail Adams, however, remind us that Enlightenment universalism was based not only on cool reason and calculation and the blind arrogance of the powerful. At least some of the great Enlightenment thinkers based their global prescription on the *felt* needs, even the sufferings, of others. For Toussaint, Adams, and Olympe de Gouges, the recognition of human commonality began with a reasoned capacity for empathy that the Enlightenment may have bequeathed to the modern world, even shaping modern sensibility.

21

Capitalism and the Industrial Revolution

Europe and the World, 1750–1900

■ HISTORICAL CONTEXT

Two principal forces have shaped the modern world: capitalism
and the industrial revolution. As influential as the transformations
discussed in Chapters 19 and 20 (the rise of science and the democratic
revolution), these two forces are sometimes considered to be one and
the same because the industrial revolution occurred first in capitalist
countries such as England, Belgium, and the United States. In fact, the
rise of capitalism preceded the industrial revolution by centuries.

Capitalism denotes a particular economic organization of a society,
whereas *industrial revolution* refers to a particular transformation of
technology. Specifically, in capitalism market forces (supply and demand)
set money prices that determine how goods are distributed. Before 1500,
most economic behavior was regulated by family, religion, tradition, and
political authority rather than by markets. Increasingly after 1500 in
Europe, feudal dues were converted into money rents, periodic fairs
became institutionalized, banks were established, modern bookkeeping
procedures were developed, and older systems of inherited economic
status were loosened. After 1800, new populations of urban workers had
to work for money to buy food and shelter; after 1850 in urban areas,
even clothing was usually purchased in the new "department stores." By
1900, the market had become the operating metaphor of society: One
sold oneself; everything had its price. Viewed positively, a capitalist
society is one in which buyers and sellers, who together compose the
market, make most decisions about the production and distribution of
resources. Viewed less favorably, it is the capitalists—those who own the

"capital" (resources, stores, factories, and money)—who make the decisions about production and distribution.

The industrial revolution made mass production possible with the use of power-driven machines. Mills driven by waterwheels existed in ancient times, but the construction of identical, replaceable machinery—the machine production of machines—revolutionized industry and enabled the coordination of production on a vast scale, occurring first in England's cotton textile mills at the end of the eighteenth century. The market for such textiles was capitalist, though the demand for many early mass-produced goods, such as muskets and uniforms, was government-driven.

The origins of capitalism are hotly debated among historians. Because the world's first cities, five thousand years ago, created markets, merchants, money, and private ownership of capital, some historians refer to an ancient capitalism. In this text, *capitalism* refers to those societies whose markets, merchants, money, and private ownership became central to the way society operated. As such, ancient Mesopotamia, Rome, and Sung dynasty China, which had extensive markets and paper money a thousand years ago, were not among the first capitalist societies. Smaller societies in which commercial interests and merchant classes took hold to direct political and economic matters were the capitalist forerunners. Venice, Florence, Holland, and England, the mercantile states of the fifteenth to seventeenth centuries, exemplify *commercial capitalism* or mercantile capitalism. Thus, the shift to industrial capitalism was more than a change in scale; it was also a transition from a trade-based economy to a manufacturing-based economy, a difference that meant an enormous increase in productivity, profits, and prosperity.

■ THINKING HISTORICALLY

Distinguishing Historical Processes

When two distinct historical processes occur simultaneously and in mutually reinforcing ways, like the spread of agriculture and languages—or capitalism and industrialization—we might confuse one process of change with the other. This confusion makes it difficult to see exactly what causes what. Here you will be encouraged to distinguish between the latter two historical processes. As you read these selections, keep in mind that capitalism is an economic system that spreads markets, commerce, and the interests of private capital; the industrial revolution was a transformation in technology. How did these two very different processes coincide in the nineteenth century? In what ways were they moving toward different ends, causing different effects, or benefiting different interests?

1

ARNOLD PACEY

Asia and the Industrial Revolution, 1990

Here a modern historian of technology demonstrates how Indian and East Asian manufacturing techniques were assimilated by Europeans, particularly by the English successors of the Mughal Empire, providing a boost to the industrial revolution in Britain. In what ways was Indian technology considered superior prior to the industrial revolution? How did European products gain greater markets than those of India?

THINKING HISTORICALLY

Notice how the author distinguishes between capitalism and the industrial revolution. Was India more industrially advanced than capitalistic? Did the British conquest of India benefit more from capitalism, industry, or something else?

Deindustrialization

During the eighteenth century, India participated in the European industrial revolution through the influence of its textile trade, and through the investments in shipping made by Indian bankers and merchants. Developments in textiles and shipbuilding constituted a significant industrial movement, but it would be wrong to suggest that India was on the verge of its own industrial revolution. There was no steam engine in India, no coal mines, and few machines. . . . [E]xpanding industries were mostly in coastal areas. Much of the interior was in economic decline, with irrigation works damaged and neglected as a result of the breakup of the Mughal Empire and the disruption of war. Though political weakness in the empire had been evident since 1707, and a Persian army heavily defeated Mughal forces at Delhi in 1739, it was the British who most fully took advantage of the collapse of the empire. Between 1757 and 1803, they took control of most of India except the Northwest. The result was that the East India Company now administered major sectors of the economy, and quickly reduced the role of the big Indian bankers by changes in taxes and methods of collecting them.

Meanwhile, India's markets in Europe were being eroded by competition from machine-spun yarns and printed calicoes made in Lancashire, and high customs duties were directed against Indian imports into

---

Source: Arnold Pacey, *Technology in World Civilization* (Cambridge: MIT Press, 1990), 128–35.

Britain. Restrictions were also placed on the use of Indian-built ships for voyages to England. From 1812, there were extra duties on any imports they delivered, and that must be one factor in the decline in shipbuilding. A few Indian ships continued to make the voyage to Britain, however, and there was one in Liverpool Docks in 1839 when Herman Melville arrived from America. It was the *Irrawaddy* from Bombay and Melville commented: "Forty years ago, these merchantmen were nearly the largest in the world; and they still exceed the generality." They were "wholly built by the native shipwrights of India, who . . . surpassed the European artisans." . . .

Attitudes to India changed markedly after the subcontinent had fallen into British hands. Before this, travellers found much to admire in technologies ranging from agriculture to metallurgy. After 1803, however, the arrogance of conquest was reinforced by the rapid development of British industry. This meant that Indian techniques which a few years earlier seemed remarkable could now be equalled at much lower cost by British factories. India was then made to appear rather primitive, and the idea grew that its proper role was to provide raw materials for western industry, including raw cotton and indigo dye, and to function as a market for British goods. This policy was reflected in 1813 by a relaxation of the East India Company's monopoly of trade so that other British companies could now bring in manufactured goods freely for sale in India. Thus the textile industry, iron production, and shipbuilding were all eroded by cheap imports from Britain, and by handicaps placed on Indian merchants.

By 1830, the situation had become so bad that even some of the British in India began to protest. One exclaimed, "We have destroyed the manufactures of India," pleading that there should be some protection for silk weaving, "the last of the expiring manufactures of India." Another observer was alarmed by a "commercial revolution" which produced "so much present suffering to numerous classes in India."

The question that remains is the speculative one of what might have happened if a strong Mughal government had survived. Fernand Braudel argues that although there was no lack of "capitalism" in India, the economy was not moving in the direction of home-grown industrialization. The historian of technology inevitably notes the lack of development of machines, even though there had been some increase in the use of water-wheels during the eighteenth century both in the iron industry and at gunpowder mills. However, it is impossible not to be struck by the achievements of the shipbuilding industry, which produced skilled carpenters and a model of large-scale organizations. It also trained up draughtsmen and people with mechanical interests. It is striking that one of the Wadia shipbuilders installed gas lighting in his home in 1834 and built a small foundry in which he made parts for steam engines. Given an independent and more prosperous India, it is difficult not to believe that a response to British industrialization might well have taken the form of a spread of skill and innovation from the shipyards into other industries.

As it was, such developments were delayed until the 1850s and later, when the first mechanized cotton mill opened. It is significant that some of the entrepreneurs who backed the development of this industry were from the same Parsi families as had built ships in Bombay and invested in overseas trade in the eighteenth century.

Guns and Rails: Asia, Britain, and America

Britain's "conquest" of India cannot be attributed to superior armaments. Indian armies were also well equipped. More significant was the prior breakdown of Mughal government and the collaboration of many Indians. Some victories were also the result of good discipline and bold strategy, especially when Arthur Wellesley, the future Duke of Wellington, was in command. Wellesley's contribution also illustrates the distinctive western approach to the organizational aspect of technology. Indian armies might have had good armament, but because their guns were made in a great variety of different sizes, precise weapons drill was impossible and the supply of shot to the battlefield was unnecessarily complicated. By contrast, Wellesley's forces standardized on just three sizes of field gun, and the commander himself paid close attention to the design of gun carriages and to the bullocks which hauled them, so that his artillery could move as fast as his infantry, and without delays due to wheel breakages.

Significantly, the one major criticism regularly made of Indian artillery concerned the poor design of gun carriages. Many, particularly before 1760, were little better than four-wheeled trolleys. But the guns themselves were often of excellent design and workmanship. Whilst some were imported and others were made with the assistance of foreign craftworkers, there was many a brass cannon and mortar of Indian design, as well as heavy muskets for camel-mounted troops. Captured field guns were often taken over for use by the British, and after capturing ninety guns in one crucial battle, Wellesley wrote that seventy were "the finest brass ordnance I have ever seen." They were probably made in northern India, perhaps at the great Mughal arsenal at Agra.

Whilst Indians had been making guns from brass since the sixteenth century, Europeans could at first only produce this alloy in relatively small quantities because they had no technique for smelting zinc. By the eighteenth century, however, brass was being produced in large quantities in Europe, and brass cannon were being cast at Woolwich Arsenal near London. Several European countries were importing metallic zinc from China for this purpose. However, from 1743 there was a smelter near Bristol in England producing zinc, using coke[1] as fuel, and zinc smelters were also developed in Germany. At the end of the century, Britain's imports of zinc from the Far East were only about forty tons per year. Nevertheless, a British party which visited China in 1797 took particular note of zinc smelting methods. These were similar to the process used in India, which involved vaporizing the metal and then condensing it. There is a suspicion that the Bristol smelting works of 1743 was based on Indian practice, although the possibility of independent invention cannot be excluded.

A much clearer example of the transfer of technology from India occurred when British armies on the subcontinent encountered rockets, a type of weapon of which they had no previous experience. The basic technology had come from the Ottoman Turks or from Syria before 1500, although the Chinese had invented rockets even earlier. In the 1790s, some Indian armies included very large infantry units equipped with rockets. French mercenaries in Mysore had learned to make them, and the British Ordnance Office was enquiring for somebody with expertise on the subject. In response, William Congreve, whose father was head of the laboratory at Woolwich Arsenal, undertook to design a rocket on Indian lines. After a successful demonstration, about two hundred of his rockets were used by the British in an attack on Boulogne in 1806. Fired from over a kilometre away, they set fire to the town. After this success, rockets were adopted quite widely by European armies, though some commanders, notably the Duke of Wellington, frowned on such imprecise weapons, and they tended to drop out of use later in the century. What happened next, however, was typical of the whole British relationship with India. William Congreve set up a factory to manufacture the weapons in 1817, and part of its output was exported to India to equip rocket troops operating there under British command.

Yet another aspect of Asian technology in which eighteenth-century Europeans were interested was the design of farm implements. Reports on seed drills and ploughs were sent to the British Board of Agriculture from India in 1795. A century earlier the Dutch had found much of interest in ploughs and winnowing machines of a Chinese type which they saw in Java. Then a Swedish party visiting Guangzhou (Canton) took a winnowing machine back home with them. Indeed, several of these machines were imported into different parts of Europe, and similar devices for cleaning

---

[1] Fuel from soft coal. [Ed.]

threshed grain were soon being made there. The inventor of one of them, Jonas Norberg, admitted that he got "the initial idea" from three machines "brought here from China," but had to create a new type because the Chinese machines "do not suit our kinds of grain." Similarly, the Dutch saw that the Chinese plough did not suit their type of soil, but it stimulated them to produce new designs with curved metal mould-boards in contrast to the less efficient flat wooden boards used in Europe hitherto.

In most of these cases, and especially with zinc smelting, rockets, and winnowing machines, we have clear evidence of Europeans studying Asian technology in detail. With rockets and winnowers, though perhaps not with zinc, there was an element of imitation in the European inventions which followed. In other instances, however, the more usual course of technological dialogue between Europe and Asia was that European innovation was challenged by the quality or scale of Asian output, but took a different direction, as we have seen in many aspects of the textile industry. Sometimes, the dialogue was even more limited, and served mainly to give confidence in a technique that was already known. Such was the case with occasional references to China in the writings of engineers designing suspension bridges in Britain. The Chinese had a reputation for bridge construction, and before 1700 Peter the Great had asked for bridge-builders to be sent from China to work in Russia. Later, several books published in Europe described a variety of Chinese bridges, notably a long-span suspension bridge made with iron chains.

Among those who developed the suspension bridge in the West were James Finley in America, beginning in 1801, and Samuel Brown and Thomas Telford in Britain. About 1814, Brown devised a flat, wrought-iron chain link which Telford later used to form the main structural chains in his suspension bridges. But beyond borrowing this specific technique, what Telford needed was evidence that the suspension principle was applicable to the problem he was then tackling. Finley's two longest bridges had spanned seventy-four and ninety-three metres, over the Merrimac and Schuylkill Rivers in the eastern United States. Telford was aiming to span almost twice the larger distance with his 176-metre Menai Bridge. Experiments at a Shropshire ironworks gave confidence in the strength of the chains. But Telford may have looked for reassurance even further afield. One of his notebooks contains the reminder, "Examine Chinese bridges." It is clear from the wording which follows that he had seen a recent booklet advocating a "bridge of chains," partly based on a Chinese example, to cross the Firth of Forth in Scotland.

2

KAIHO SEIRYO

Lessons of the Past, 1813

Kaiho Seiryo (1755–1817) was born in Edo (now Tokyo) to a family of administrators of a noble lord's large household. While Seiryo was a child, his father lost an effort to reform the lord's finances and retired to become a *ronin*, a samurai without obligation to a particular lord. Seiryo went to school, studied Confucianism and political thought, and became a tutor for a lord's children. After seven years of such service, he set out to travel throughout Japan to gain the knowledge and experience he wanted to become a writer. He supported himself by lecturing and tutoring, and settled finally in Kyoto. *Lessons of the Past* draws on the wide knowledge of different members of Japanese society—lords, their retainers, samurai merchants, and peasants—whom he met, and it is written in the style of someone at home with many different audiences.

What economic ideas and behavior is Seiryo advocating? Who and what is he arguing against?

THINKING HISTORICALLY

What does this selection tell you about the popularity of markets and private profit in Seiryo's Japan? What parts of Japanese society opposed enterprise, and why? To what extent is Seiryo advocating capitalism? If people followed these ideas, would that society be likely to industrialize?

It is ridiculous that the aristocracy and military class in Japan should disdain profit or that they should say that they disdain profit. When a man does not disdain profit, he is called a bad person. Such is the perverse practice of the times. In China it is the same. A man who is clever at making profits is called a sharp enterpriser or some such bad name. But if collecting taxes from those beneath you is to be a sharp enterpriser, then the *Rites of Zhou* is a book for sharp enterprisers; and if lending rice and money to the people and extracting interest from them is to be a sharp enterpriser, then the duke of Zhou himself was a sharp enterpriser. Let us first make a general case of this, go to the root of it, and examine it close at hand.

What sort of thing was it when rice fields were originally handed over to the people and rice was collected from them in return? By what

Source: *Sources of Japanese Tradition*, 2nd ed., Vol. Two: 1600–2000, ed. Wm. Theodore de Bary et al. (New York: Columbia University Press, 2005), 434–35.

logic was rice taken from the people? If we recognize only the natural principle by which this was done, we shall understand it completely. Rice fields, mountains, the sea, gold, rice, and everything between Heaven-and-earth are commodities. The gathering of rice from rice fields is no different from the gathering of profit from gold. The gathering of timber from mountain land, the gathering of fish and salt from the sea, and the gathering of profit from gold and rice are the natural principle of Heaven-and-earth. If one lets a field go uncultivated, nothing will be grown on it; if one lets gold go unused, nothing will be produced from it. But if one lends a rice field to the people and exacts an annual tribute [tax] of one-tenth on it, then one will make a profit of 10 percent. . . . Of course, the realization of profit is fast or slow depending on the case, so the rate of interest should vary accordingly. Taxes on the rice fields and taxes on mountain land are similar forms of interest, levied on commodities that have been lent. Such commodities are things on which interest must be levied. This is not sharp enterprise or anything of the sort; it is the natural principle of Heaven-and-earth.

Bo Gui was an economist in ancient times. He said to Mencius: "I think I shall take a twentieth of the produce as a land tax." He boasted that since the state had become wealthy, even a tax that small would be enough for its needs. Then Mencius said: "You had better exact a tax of one-tenth. A tax of one-twentieth would be the way of the barbarians, but the barbarians have no fortifications, no palaces, and no rites or music, so even that little is sufficient for the needs of the state. However, China has a splendid way of life, so a tax of one-tenth must be levied." . . . From ancient times it has been said that the relationship between lord and subject is according to the way of the marketplace. . . . A stipend is offered for the service of a retainer, and the retainer is a seller. It is simply a business transaction, but business transactions are good, not bad. When it is said that business transactions are not things for a superior man to worry about, this is a misunderstanding that comes from everyone's having swallowed whole the idea that Confucius despised profit. Much parasitism and wasted labor have resulted from the notion that the relationship between lord and subject is not a trade relationship. . . .

Heaven-and-earth consist of principle; buying, selling, and paying interest are inherent principles. If one wishes to enrich the country, one should return to principle. The ruler is the landlord who owns the land as a commodity. The feudal houses also are landlords who own the commodities known as feudal domains. They lend these commodities to the people and live on the interest from them; ministers and high officials sell their knowledge and abilities to the ruler and live off the daily wages he pays. Porters carry a sedan chair, and for each *ri* they carry it, they get paid so much money, with which [in their own turn] they can buy some rice cakes or wine. . . .

3

ADAM SMITH
The Wealth of Nations, 1776

An Inquiry into the Nature and Causes of the Wealth of Nations might justly be called the bible of free-market capitalism. Written in 1776 in the context of the British (and European) debate over the proper role of government in the economy, Smith's work takes aim at *mercantilism*, or government supervision of the economy. Mercantilists believed that national economies required government assistance and direction to prosper.

Smith argues that free trade will produce greater wealth than mercantilist trade and that free markets allocate resources more efficiently than the government. His notion of *laissez-faire* (literally "let do") capitalism assumes neither that capitalists are virtuous nor that governments should absent themselves entirely from the economy. However, Smith does believe that the greed of capitalists generally negates itself and produces results that are advantageous to, but unimagined by, the individual. "It is not from the benevolence of the butcher, the brewer, or the baker, that we expect our dinner," Smith writes, "but from their regard of their own interest. We address ourselves not to their humanity, but to their self-love, and never talk to them of our own necessities, but of their advantage."[1] Each person seeks to maximize his or her own gain, thereby creating an efficient market in which the cost of goods is instantly adjusted to exploit changes in supply and demand, while the market provides what is needed at the price people are willing to pay "as if by an invisible hand."

According to Smith, what is the relationship between money and industry, and which is more important? What would Smith say to a farmer or manufacturer who wanted to institute tariffs or quotas to limit the number of cheaper imports entering the country and to minimize competition? What would he say to a government official who wanted to protect an important domestic industry? What would he say to a worker who complained about low wages or boring work? What would Smith think about a "postindustrial" or "service" economy in which few workers actually make products? What would he think of a prosperous country that imported more than it exported?

THINKING HISTORICALLY

The Wealth of Nations was written in defense of free capitalism at a moment when the industrial revolution was just beginning. Some elements

[1] Book I, chapter 2.

Source: Adam Smith, *An Inquiry into the Nature and Causes of the Wealth of Nations* (Indianapolis, IN: Liberty Fund, 1981, a reprint of the Oxford University Press edition of 1976), 1:13–15, 31, 47, 73–74, 449–50, 455–57.

of Smith's writing suggest a preindustrial world, as in the quotation about the butcher, brewer, and baker mentioned earlier. Still, Smith was aware how new industrial methods were transforming age-old labor relations and manufacturing processes. In some respects, Smith recognized that capitalism could create wealth, not just redistribute it, because he appreciated the potential of industrial technology.

As you read this selection, note when Smith is discussing capitalism, the economic system, and the power of the new industrial technology. In his discussion of the division of labor, what relationship does Smith see between the development of a capitalistic market and the rise of industrial technology? To what extent could the benefits that Smith attributes to a free market be attributed to the new system of industrial production?

Book I
Of the Causes of Improvement in the Productive Powers of Labour, and of the Order According to Which Its Produce Is Naturally Distributed among the Different Ranks of the People

Chapter 1: Of the Division of Labour

The greatest improvement in the productive powers of labour, and the greater part of the skill, dexterity, and judgment with which it is anywhere directed, or applied, seem to have been the effects of the division of labour.

The effects of the division of labour, in the general business of society, will be more easily understood by considering in what manner it operates in some particular manufactures. . . .

To take an example, therefore, from a very trifling manufacture; but one in which the division of labour has been very often taken notice of, the trade of the pin-maker; a workman not educated to this business (which the division of labour has rendered a distinct trade), nor acquainted with the use of the machinery employed in it (to the invention of which the same division of labour has probably given occasion), could scarce, perhaps, with his utmost industry, make one pin in a day, and certainly could not make twenty. But in the way in which this business is now carried on, not only the whole work is a peculiar trade, but it is divided into a number of branches, of which the greater part are likewise peculiar trades. One man draws out the wire, another straights it, a third cuts it, a fourth points it, a fifth grinds it at the top for receiving the head; to make the head requires two or three distinct operations; to put it on is a peculiar business, to whiten the pins is another; it is even a trade by itself to put them into the paper; and the important business of making a pin is, in this manner, divided into about eighteen distinct operations, which, in some manufactories, are all performed by distinct hands, though in others the same man will sometimes perform two or three of them. I have seen a small manufactory of this kind where ten men only were employed, and where some of them consequently performed two or three distinct operations. But though they were very poor, and therefore but indifferently accommodated with the necessary machinery, they could, when they exerted themselves, make among them about twelve pounds of pins in a day. There are in a pound upwards of four thousand pins of a middling size. Those ten persons, therefore, could make among them upwards of forty-eight thousand pins in a day. Each person, therefore, making a tenth part of forty-eight thousand pins, might be considered as making four thousand eight hundred pins in a day. But if they had all wrought separately and independently, and without any of them having been educated to this peculiar business, they certainly could not each of them have made twenty, perhaps not one pin in a day; that is, certainly, not the two hundred and fortieth, perhaps not the four thousand eight hundredth part of what they are at present capable of performing, in consequence of a proper division and combination of their different operations.

In every other art and manufacture, the effects of the division of labour are similar to what they are in this very trifling one; though, in many of them, the labour can neither be so much subdivided, nor reduced to so great a simplicity of operation. . . .

Chapter 3: That the Division of Labour Is Limited by the Extent of the Market

As it is the power of exchanging that gives occasion to the division of labour, so the extent of this division must always be limited by the extent of that power, or, in other words, by the extent of the market. When the market is very small, no person can have any encouragement to dedicate himself entirely to one employment, for want of the power to exchange all that surplus part of the produce of his own labour, which is over and above his own consumption, for such parts of the produce of other men's labour as he has occasion for.

There are some sorts of industry, even of the lowest kind, which can be carried on nowhere but in a great town. A porter, for example, can find employment and subsistence in no other place. A village is by much too narrow a sphere for him. . . .

Chapter 5: Of the Real and Nominal Price of Commodities, or Their Price in Labour, and Their Price in Money

Every man is rich or poor according to the degree in which he can afford to enjoy the necessaries, conveniences, and amusements of human life. But after the division of labour has once thoroughly taken place, it is but a very small part of these with which a man's own labour can supply him. The far greater part of them he must derive from the labour of other people, and he must be rich or poor according to the quantity of that labour which he can command, or which he can afford to purchase. The value of any commodity, therefore, to the person who possesses it, and who means not to use or consume it himself, but to exchange it for other commodities, is equal to the quantity of labour which it enables him to purchase or command. Labour, therefore, is the real measure of the exchangeable value of all commodities. . . .

Chapter 7: Of the Natural and Market Price of Commodities

. . . When the quantity of any commodity which is brought to market falls short of the effectual demand, all those who are willing to pay the whole value of the rent, wages, and profit, which must be paid in order to bring it thither, cannot be supplied with the quantity which they want. Rather than want[2] it altogether, some of them will be willing to give more. A competition will immediately begin among them, and the market price will rise more or less above the natural price, according as either the greatness of the deficiency, or the wealth and wanton luxury of the competitors, happen to animate more or less the eagerness of the competition. Among competitors of equal wealth and luxury the same deficiency will generally occasion a more or less eager competition, according as the acquisition of the commodity happens to be of more or less importance to them. Hence the exorbitant price of the necessaries of life during the blockade of a town or in a famine.

When the quantity brought to market exceeds the effectual demand, it cannot be all sold to those who are willing to pay the whole value of the rent, wages, and profit, which must be paid in order to bring it thither. Some part must be sold to those who are willing to pay less, and the low price which they give for it must reduce the price of the whole. The market price will sink more or less below the natural price, according as the greatness of the excess increases more or less the competition of the sellers, or according as it happens to be more or less important to them to get immediately rid of the commodity. The same excess in the importation of perishables will occasion a much greater competition than in that of durable commodities; in the importation of oranges, for example, than in that of old iron.

When the quantity brought to market is just sufficient to supply the effectual demand, and no more, the market price naturally comes to be either exactly, or as nearly as can be judged of, the same with the natural price. The whole quantity upon hand can be disposed of for this price,

---

[2] Be without it. [Ed.]

and cannot be disposed of for more. The competition of the different dealers obliges them all to accept of this price, but does not oblige them to accept of less.

The quantity of every commodity brought to market naturally suits itself to the effectual demand. It is the interest of all those who employ their land, labour, or stock, in bringing any commodity to market, that the quantity never should exceed the effectual demand; and it is the interest of all other people that it never should fall short of that demand.

Book IV
Of Systems of Political Economy

Chapter 1: Of the Principle of the Commercial or Mercantile System

. . . I thought it necessary, though at the hazard of being tedious, to examine at full length this popular notion that wealth consists in money, or in gold and silver. Money in common language, as I have already observed, frequently signifies wealth, and this ambiguity of expression has rendered this popular notion so familiar to us that even they who are convinced of its absurdity are very apt to forget their own principles, and in the course of their reasonings to take it for granted as a certain and undeniable truth. Some of the best English writers upon commerce set out with observing that the wealth of a country consists, not in its gold and silver only, but in its lands, houses, and consumable goods of all different kinds. In the course of their reasonings, however, the lands, houses, and consumable goods seem to slip out of their memory, and the strain of their argument frequently supposes that all wealth consists in gold and silver, and that to multiply those metals is the great object of national industry and commerce. . . .

Chapter 2: Of Restraints upon the Importation from Foreign Countries of Such Goods as Can Be Produced at Home

. . . The produce of industry is what it adds to the subject or materials upon which it is employed. In proportion as the value of this produce is great or small, so will likewise be the profits of the employer. But it is only for the sake of profit that any man employs a capital in the support of industry; and he will always, therefore, endeavour to employ it in the support of that industry of which the produce is likely to be of the greatest value, or to exchange for the greatest quantity either of money or of other goods.

But the annual revenue of every society is always precisely equal to the exchangeable value of the whole annual produce of its industry, or rather is precisely the same thing with that exchangeable value. As every individual, therefore, endeavours as much as he can both to employ his capital in the support of domestic industry, and so to direct that industry that its produce may be of the greatest value; every individual necessarily labours to render the annual revenue of the society as great as he can. He generally, indeed, neither intends to promote the public interest, nor knows how much he is promoting it. By preferring the support of domestic to that of foreign industry, he intends only his own security; and by directing that industry in such a manner as its produce may be of the greatest value, he intends only his own gain, and he is in this, as in many other cases, led by an invisible hand to promote an end which was no part of his intention. Nor is it always the worse for the society that it was no part of it. By pursuing his own interest he frequently promotes that of the society more effectually than when he really intends to promote it. I have never known much good done by those who affected to trade for the public good. It is an affectation, indeed, not very common among merchants, and very few words need be employed in dissuading them from it.

What is the species of domestic industry which his capital can employ, and of which the produce is likely to be of the greatest value, every individual, it is evident, can, in his local situation, judge much better than any statesman or lawgiver can do for him. The statesman who should attempt to direct private people in what manner they ought to employ their capitals would not only load himself with a most unnecessary attention, but assume an authority which could safely be trusted, not only to no single person, but to no council or senate whatever, and which would nowhere be so dangerous as in the hands of a man who had folly and presumption enough to fancy himself fit to exercise it.

To give the monopoly of the home market to the produce of domestic industry, in any particular art or manufacture, is in some measure to direct private people in what manner they ought to employ their capitals, and must, in almost all cases, be either a useless or a hurtful regulation. If the produce of domestic can be brought there as cheap as that of foreign industry, the regulation is evidently useless. If it cannot, it must generally be hurtful. It is the maxim of every prudent master of a family never to attempt to make at home what it will cost him more to make than to buy. The tailor does not attempt to make his own shoes, but buys them of the shoemaker. The shoemaker does not attempt to make his own clothes, but employs a tailor. The farmer attempts to make neither the one nor the other, but employs those different artificers. All of them find it for their interest to employ their whole industry in a way in which they have some advantage over their neighbours, and to purchase with a part of its produce, or what is the same thing, with the price of a part of it, whatever else they have occasion for.

What is prudence in the conduct of every private family can scarce be folly in that of a great kingdom. If a foreign country can supply us with a commodity cheaper than we ourselves can make it, better buy it of them with some part of the produce of our own industry employed in a way in which we have some advantage. The general industry of the country, being always in proportion to the capital which employs it, will not thereby be diminished, no more than that of the abovementioned artificers; but only left to find out the way in which it can be employed with the greatest advantage. It is certainly not employed to the greatest advantage when it is thus directed towards an object which it can buy cheaper than it can make. . . .

4

The Sadler Report of the House of Commons, 1832

Although, for many factory owners, children were among the ideal workers in the factories of the industrial revolution, increasingly their exploitation became a concern of the British Parliament. One important parliamentary investigation, chaired by Michael Sadler, took volumes of testimony from child workers and older people who had worked as children in the mines and factories. The following is a sample of that testimony: an interview with a former child worker named Matthew Crabtree who had worked in a textile factory. The Sadler Commission report led to child-labor reform in the Factory Act of 1833.

What seem to be the causes of Crabtree's distress? How could it have been alleviated? If the factory owner had been asked why he didn't pay more, shorten the workday, provide more time for meals, or provide medical assistance when it was needed, how do you think he would have responded? Do you think Crabtree would have been in favor of reduced hours if it meant reduced wages?

THINKING HISTORICALLY

To what extent are the problems faced by Crabtree the inevitable results of machine production? To what extent are his problems caused by capitalism? How might the owner of this factory have addressed these issues?

Source: From *The Sadler Report: Report from the Committee on the Bill to Regulate the Labour of Children in the Mills and Factories of the United Kingdom* (London: The House of Commons, Parliamentary Papers, 1831–1832), 15:95–97.

Friday, 18 May 1832—Michael Thomas Sadler, Esquire, in the Chair

Mr. Matthew Crabtree, *called in; and Examined.*

What age are you?—Twenty-two.

What is your occupation?—A blanket manufacturer.

Have you ever been employed in a factory?—Yes.

At what age did you first go to work in one?—Eight.

How long did you continue in that occupation?—Four years.

Will you state the hours of labour at the period when you first went to the factory, in ordinary times?—From 6 in the morning to 8 at night.

Fourteen hours?—Yes.

With what intervals for refreshment and rest?—An hour at noon.

Then you had no resting time allowed in which to take your breakfast, or what is in Yorkshire called your "drinking"?—No.

When trade was brisk what were your hours?—From 5 in the morning to 9 in the evening.

Sixteen hours?—Yes.

With what intervals at dinner[1]?—An hour.

How far did you live from the mill?—About two miles.

Was there any time allowed for you to get your breakfast in the mill?—No.

Did you take it before you left your home?—Generally.

During those long hours of labour could you be punctual; how did you awake?—I seldom did awake spontaneously; I was most generally awoke or lifted out of bed, sometimes asleep, by my parents.

Were you always in time?—No.

What was the consequence if you had been too late?—I was most commonly beaten.

Severely?—Very severely, I thought.

In whose factory was this?—Messrs. Hague & Cook's, of Dewsbury.

Will you state the effect that those long hours had upon the state of your health and feelings?—I was, when working those long hours, commonly very much fatigued at night, when I left my work; so much so that I sometimes should have slept as I walked if I had not stumbled and started awake again; and so sick often that I could not eat, and what I did eat I vomited.

Did this labour destroy your appetite?—It did.

In what situation were you in that mill?—I was a piecener.

Will you state to this Committee whether piecening is a very laborious employment for children, or not?—It is a very laborious employment. Pieceners are continually running to and fro, and on their feet the whole day.

---

[1] The main meal, in the afternoon. Not the evening supper. [Ed.]

The duty of the piecener is to take the cardings from one part of the machinery, and to place them on another? — Yes.

So that the labour is not only continual, but it is unabated to the last? — It is unabated to the last.

Do you not think, from your own experience, that the speed of the machinery is so calculated as to demand the utmost exertions of a child supposing the hours were moderate? — It is as much as they could do at the best; they are always upon the stretch, and it is commonly very difficult to keep up with their work.

State the condition of the children toward the latter part of the day, who have thus to keep up with the machinery. — It is as much as they can do when they are not very much fatigued to keep up with their work, and toward the close of the day, when they come to be more fatigued, they cannot keep up with it very well, and the consequence is that they are beaten to spur them on.

Were you beaten under those circumstances? — Yes.

Frequently? — Very frequently.

And principally at the latter end of the day? — Yes.

And is it your belief that if you had not been so beaten, you should not have got through the work? — I should not if I had not been kept up to it by some means.

Does beating then principally occur at the latter end of the day, when the children are exceedingly fatigued? — It does at the latter end of the day, and in the morning sometimes, when they are very drowsy, and have not got rid of the fatigue of the day before.

What were you beaten with principally? — A strap.

Anything else? — Yes, a stick sometimes; and there is a kind of roller which runs on the top of the machine called a billy, perhaps two or three yards in length, and perhaps an inch and a half, or more in diameter; the circumference would be four or five inches; I cannot speak exactly.

Were you beaten with that instrument? — Yes.

Have you yourself been beaten, and have you seen other children struck severely with that roller? — I have been struck very severely with it myself, so much so as to knock me down, and I have seen other children have their heads broken with it.

You think that it is a general practice to beat the children with the roller? — It is.

You do not think then that you were worse treated than other children in the mill? — No, I was not, perhaps not so bad as some were.

In those mills is chastisement towards the latter part of the day going on perpetually? — Perpetually.

So that you can hardly be in a mill without hearing constant crying? — Never an hour, I believe.

Do you think that if the overlooker were naturally a humane person it would be still found necessary for him to beat the children, in order to keep up their attention and vigilance at the termination of those extraordinary days of labour?—Yes, the machine turns off a regular quantity of cardings, and of course they must keep as regularly to their work the whole of the day; they must keep with the machine, and therefore however humane the slubber may be, as he must keep up with the machine or be found fault with, he spurs the children to keep up also by various means but that which he commonly resorts to is to strap them when they become drowsy.

At the time when you were beaten for not keeping up with your work, were you anxious to have done it if you possibly could?—Yes; the dread of being beaten if we could not keep up with our work was a sufficient impulse to keep us to it if we could.

When you got home at night after this labour, did you feel much fatigued?—Very much so.

Had you any time to be with your parents, and to receive instruction from them?—No.

What did you do?—All that we did when we got home was to get the little bit of supper that was provided for us and go to bed immediately. If the supper had not been ready directly, we should have gone to sleep while it was preparing.

Did you not, as a child, feel it a very grievous hardship to be roused so soon in the morning?—I did.

Were the rest of the children similarly circumstanced?—Yes, all of them; but they were not all of them so far from their work as I was.

And if you had been too late you were under the apprehension of being cruelly beaten?—I generally was beaten when I happened to be too late; and when I got up in the morning the apprehension of that was so great, that I used to run, and cry all the way as I went to the mill.

That was the way by which your punctual attendance was secured?—Yes.

And you do not think it could have been secured by any other means?—No.

Then it is your impression from what you have seen, and from your own experience, that those long hours of labour have the effect of rendering young persons who are subject to them exceedingly unhappy?—Yes.

You have already said it had a considerable effect upon your health?—Yes.

Do you conceive that it diminished your growth?—I did not pay much attention to that; but I have been examined by some persons who said they thought I was rather stunted, and that I should have been taller if I had not worked at the mill.

What were your wages at that time?—Three shillings (per week).

And how much a day had you for overwork when you were worked so exceedingly long?—A halfpenny a day.

Did you frequently forfeit that if you were not always there to a moment? — Yes; I most frequently forfeited what was allowed for those long hours.

You took your food to the mill; was it in your mill, as is the case in cotton mills, much spoiled by being laid aside? — It was very frequently covered by flues from the wool; and in that case they had to be blown off with the mouth, and picked off with the fingers before it could be eaten.

So that not giving you a little leisure for eating your food, but obliging you to take it at the mill, spoiled your food when you did get it? — Yes, very commonly.

And that at the same time that this over-labour injured your appetite? — Yes.

Could you eat when you got home? — Not always.

What is the effect of this piecening upon the hands? — It makes them bleed; the skin is completely rubbed off, and in that case they bleed in perhaps a dozen parts.

The prominent parts of the hand? — Yes, all the prominent parts of the hand are rubbed down till they bleed; every day they are rubbed in that way.

All the time you continue at work? — All the time we are working. The hands never can be hardened in that work, for the grease keeps them soft in the first instance, and long and continual rubbing is always wearing them down, so that if they were hard they would be sure to bleed.

It is attended with much pain? — Very much.

Do they allow you to make use of the back of the hand? — No; the work cannot be so well done with the back of the hand, or I should have made use of that.

5

KARL MARX AND FRIEDRICH ENGELS

The Communist Manifesto, 1848

The Communist Manifesto was written in 1848 in the midst of European upheaval, a time when capitalist industrialization had spread from England to France and Germany. Marx and Engels were Germans who studied and worked in France and England. In the *Manifesto*, they

Source: Karl Marx and Friedrich Engels, *The Communist Manifesto* (1888; Boston: Bedford/ St. Martin's, 1999), 65–72.

imagine a revolution that will transform all of Europe. What do they see as the inevitable causes of this revolution? How, according to their analysis, is the crisis of "modern" society different from previous crises? Were Marx and Engels correct?

THINKING HISTORICALLY

Notice how Marx and Engels describe the notions of capitalism and industrialization without using those words. The term *capitalism* developed later from Marx's classic *Das Kapital* (1859), but the term *bourgeoisie*,* as Engels notes in this selection, stands for the capitalist class. For Marx and Engels, the industrial revolution (another later phrase) is the product of a particular stage of capitalist development. Thus, if Marx and Engels were asked whether capitalism or industry was the principal force that created the modern world, what would their answer be?

   The Communist Manifesto is widely known as the classic critique of capitalism, but a careful reading reveals a list of achievements of capitalist or "bourgeois civilization." What are these achievements? Did Marx and Engels consider them to be achievements? How could Marx and Engels both praise and criticize capitalism?

Bourgeois and Proletarians[1]

The history of all hitherto existing society is the history of class struggles.

   Freeman and slave, patrician and plebeian, lord and serf, guildmaster and journeyman, in a word, oppressor and oppressed, stood in constant opposition to one another, carried on an uninterrupted, now hidden, now open fight, a fight that each time ended, either in a revolutionary reconstitution of society at large, or in the common ruin of the contending classes.

   In the earlier epochs of history, we find almost everywhere a complicated arrangement of society into various orders, a manifold gradation of social rank. In ancient Rome we have patricians, knights, plebeians, slaves; in the Middle Ages, feudal lords, vassals, guildmasters, journeymen, apprentices, serfs; in almost all of these classes, again, subordinate gradations.

---

* bohr zhwah ZEE

[1] In French *bourgeois* means a town-dweller. *Proletarian* comes from the Latin *proletarius*, which meant a person whose sole wealth was his offspring (*proles*). [Ed.] [Note by Engels] By "bourgeoisie" is meant the class of modern capitalists, owners of the means of social production and employers of wage labor; by "proletariat," the class of modern wage-laborers who, having no means of production of their own, are reduced to selling their labor power in order to live.

The modern bourgeois society that has sprouted from the ruins of feudal society, has not done away with class antagonisms. It has but established new classes, new conditions of oppression, new forms of struggle in place of the old ones.

Our epoch, the epoch of the bourgeoisie, possesses, however, this distinctive feature: It has simplified the class antagonisms. Society as a whole is more and more splitting up into the two great hostile camps, into two great classes directly facing each other—bourgeoisie and proletariat.

From the serfs of the Middle Ages sprang the chartered burghers of the earliest towns. From these burgesses the first elements of the bourgeoisie were developed.

The discovery of America, the rounding of the Cape, opened up fresh ground for the rising bourgeoisie. The East-Indian and Chinese markets, the colonization of America, trade with the colonies, the increase in the means of exchange and in commodities generally, gave to commerce, to navigation, to industry, an impulse never before known, and thereby, to the revolutionary element in the tottering feudal society, a rapid development.

The feudal system of industry, in which industrial production was monopolized by closed guilds, now no longer sufficed for the growing wants of the new markets. The manufacturing system took its place. The guildmasters were pushed aside by the manufacturing middle class; division of labor between the different corporate guilds vanished in the face of division of labor in each single workshop.

Meantime the markets kept ever growing, the demand ever rising. Even manufacture[2] no longer sufficed. Thereupon, steam and machinery revolutionized industrial production. The place of manufacture was taken by the giant, modern industry, the place of the industrial middle class, by industrial millionaires—the leaders of whole industrial armies, the modern bourgeois.

Modern industry has established the world market, for which the discovery of America paved the way. This market has given an immense development to commerce, to navigation, to communication by land. This development has, in its turn, reacted on the extension of industry; and in proportion as industry, commerce, navigation, railways extended, in the same proportion the bourgeoisie developed, increased its capital, and pushed into the background every class handed down from the Middle Ages.

We see, therefore, how the modern bourgeoisie is itself the product of a long course of development, of a series of revolutions in the modes of production and of exchange.

---

[2]By *manufacture* Marx meant the system of production that succeeded the guild system but that still relied mainly on direct human labor for power. He distinguished it from modern industry, which arose when machinery driven by water and steam was introduced. [Ed.]

Each step in the development of the bourgeoisie was accompanied by a corresponding political advance of that class. An oppressed class under the sway of the feudal nobility, it became an armed and self-governing association in the medieval commune; here independent urban republic (as in Italy and Germany), there taxable "third estate" of the monarchy (as in France); afterwards, in the period of manufacture proper, serving either the semifeudal or the absolute monarchy as a counterpoise against the nobility, and, in fact, cornerstone of the great monarchies in general—the bourgeoisie has at last, since the establishment of modern industry and of the world market, conquered for itself, in the modern representative state, exclusive political sway. The executive of the modern state is but a committee for managing the common affairs of the whole bourgeoisie.

The bourgeoisie has played a most revolutionary role in history.

The bourgeoisie, wherever it has got the upper hand, has put an end to all feudal, patriarchal, idyllic relations. It has pitilessly torn asunder the motley feudal ties that bound man to his "natural superiors," and has left no other bond between man and man than naked self-interest, than callous "cash payment." It has drowned the most heavenly ecstasies of religious fervor, of chivalrous enthusiasm, of philistine sentimentalism, in the icy water of egotistical calculation. It has resolved personal worth into exchange value, and in place of the numberless indefensible chartered freedoms, has set up that single, unconscionable freedom—Free Trade. In one word, for exploitation, veiled by religious and political illusions, it has substituted naked, shameless, direct, brutal exploitation.

The bourgeoisie has stripped of its halo every occupation hitherto honored and looked up to with reverent awe. It has converted the physician, the lawyer, the priest, the poet, the man of science, into its paid wage-laborers.

The bourgeoisie has torn away from the family its sentimental veil, and has reduced the family relation to a mere money relation.

The bourgeoisie has disclosed how it came to pass that the brutal display of vigor in the Middle Ages, which reactionaries so much admire, found its fitting complement in the most slothful indolence. It has been the first to show what man's activity can bring about. It has accomplished wonders far surpassing Egyptian pyramids, Roman aqueducts, and Gothic cathedrals; it has conducted expeditions that put in the shade all former migrations of nations and crusades.

The bourgeoisie cannot exist without constantly revolutionizing the instruments of production, and thereby the relations of production, and with them the whole relations of society. Conservation of the old modes of production in unaltered form, was, on the contrary, the first condition of existence for all earlier industrial classes. Constant revolutionizing of production, uninterrupted disturbance of all social conditions, everlasting uncertainty and agitation distinguished the bourgeois epoch from all earlier ones. All fixed, fast-frozen relations, with their train of ancient and venerable prejudices and opinions, are swept away, all new-formed ones become antiquated before they can ossify. All that is solid melts into air, all that is holy is profaned, and man is at last compelled to face with sober senses his real conditions of life and his relations with his kind.

The need of a constantly expanding market for its products chases the bourgeoisie over the whole surface of the globe. It must nestle everywhere, settle everywhere, establish connections everywhere.

The bourgeoisie has through its exploitation of the world market given a cosmopolitan character to production and consumption in every country. To the great chagrin of reactionaries, it has drawn from under the feet of industry the national ground on which it stood. All old-established national industries have been destroyed or are daily being destroyed. They are dislodged by new industries, whose introduction becomes a life and death question for all civilized nations, by industries that no longer work up indigenous raw material, but raw material drawn from the remotest zones; industries whose products are consumed, not only at home, but in every quarter of the globe. In place of the old wants, satisfied by the production of the country, we find new wants, requiring for their satisfaction the products of distant lands and climes. In place of the old local and national seclusion and self-sufficiency, we have intercourse in every direction, universal interdependence of nations. And as in material, so also in intellectual production. The intellectual creations of individual nations become common property. National one-sidedness and narrow-mindedness become more and more impossible, and from the numerous national and local literatures there arises a world literature.

The bourgeoisie, by the rapid improvement of all instruments of production, by the immensely facilitated means of communication, draws all nations, even the most barbarian, into civilization. The cheap prices of its commodities are the heavy artillery with which it batters down all Chinese walls, with which it forces the barbarians' intensely obstinate hatred for foreigners to capitulate. It compels all nations, on pain of extinction, to adopt the bourgeois mode of production; it compels them to introduce what it calls civilization into their midst, i.e., to become bourgeois themselves. In a word, it creates a world after its own image.

The bourgeoisie has subjected the country to the rule of the towns. It has created enormous cities, has greatly increased the urban population as compared with the rural, and has thus rescued a considerable part of the population from the idiocy of rural life. Just as it has made the country dependent on the towns, so it has made barbarian and semi-barbarian countries dependent on the civilized ones, nations of peasants on nations of bourgeois, the East on the West.

More and more the bourgeoisie keeps doing away with the scattered state of the population, of the means of production, and of property. It has agglomerated population, centralized means of production, and has concentrated property in a few hands. The necessary consequence of this was political centralization. Independent, or but loosely connected provinces, with separate interests, laws, governments and systems of taxation, became lumped together into one nation, with one government, one code of laws, one national class interest, one frontier and one customs tariff.

The bourgeoisie, during its rule of scarce one hundred years, has created more massive and more colossal productive forces than have all preceding generations together. Subjection of nature's forces to man, machinery, application of chemistry to industry and agriculture, steam-navigation, railways, electric telegraphs, clearing of whole continents for cultivation, canalization of rivers, whole populations conjured out of the ground—what earlier century had even a presentiment that such productive forces slumbered in the lap of social labor?

We see then that the means of production and of exchange, which served as the foundation for the growth of the bourgeoisie, were generated in feudal society. At a certain stage in the development of these means of production and of exchange, the conditions under which feudal society produced and exchanged, the feudal organization of agriculture and manufacturing industry, in a word, the feudal relations of property became no longer compatible with the already developed productive forces; they became so many fetters. They had to be burst asunder; they were burst asunder.

Into their place stepped free competition, accompanied by a social and political constitution adapted to it, and by the economic and political sway of the bourgeois class.

A similar movement is going on before our own eyes. Modern bourgeois society with its relations of production, of exchange and of property, a society that has conjured up such gigantic means of production and exchange, is like the sorcerer who is no longer able to control the powers of the nether world whom he has called up by his spells. For many a decade past the history of industry and commerce is but the history of the revolt of modern productive forces against modern conditions of production, against the property relations that are the conditions for the existence of the bourgeoisie and of its rule. It is enough to mention the commercial crises that by their periodical return put the existence of the entire bourgeoisie society on trial, each time more threateningly. In these crises a great part not only of the existing products, but also of the previously created productive forces, are periodically destroyed. In these crises there breaks out an epidemic that, in all earlier epochs, would have seemed an absurdity—the epidemic of overproduction. Society suddenly finds itself put back into a state of momentary barbarism; it appears as if a famine, a

universal war of devastation had cut off the supply of every means of subsistence; industry and commerce seem to be destroyed. And why? Because
there is too much civilization, too much means of subsistence, too much
industry, too much commerce. The productive forces at the disposal of society no longer tend to further the development of the conditions of bourgeois property; on the contrary, they have become too powerful for these
conditions, by which they are fettered, and no sooner do they overcome
these fetters than they bring disorder into the whole of bourgeois society,
endanger the existence of bourgeois property. The conditions of bourgeois
society are too narrow to comprise the wealth created by them. And how
does the bourgeoisie get over these crises? On the one hand by enforced
destruction of a mass of productive forces; on the other, by the conquest of
new markets, and by the more thorough exploitation of the old ones. That
is to say, by paving the way for more extensive and more destructive crises,
and by diminishing the means whereby crises are prevented.

The weapons with which the bourgeoisie felled feudalism to the
ground are now turned against the bourgeoisie itself.

But not only has the bourgeoisie forged the weapons that bring
death to itself; it has also called into existence the men who are to wield
those weapons—the modern working class—the proletarians.

In proportion as the bourgeoisie, i.e., capital, is developed, in the same
proportion is the proletariat, the modern working class, developed—a
class of labourers, who live only so long as they find work, and who
find work only so long as their labour increases capital. These labourers,
who must sell themselves piece-meal, are a commodity, like every other
article of commerce, and are consequently exposed to all the vicissitudes
of competition, to all the fluctuations of the market.

Owing to the extensive use of machinery and to division of labour,
the work of the proletarians has lost all individual character, and consequently, all charm for the workman. He becomes an appendage of the
machine, and it is only the most simple, most monotonous, and most
easily acquired knack, that is required of him. Hence, the cost of production of a workman is restricted, almost entirely, to the means of subsistence that he requires for his maintenance, and for the propagation of
his race. But the price of a commodity, and therefore also of labour, is
equal to its cost of production. In proportion therefore, as the repulsive-
ness of the work increases, the wage decreases. Nay more, in proportion
as the use of machinery and division of labour increases, in the same
proportion the burden of toil also increases, whether by prolongation of
the working hours, by increase of the work exacted in a given time or by
increased speed of the machinery, etc.

Modern industry has converted the little workshop of the patriarchal master into the great factory of the industrial capitalist. Masses
of labourers, crowded into the factory, are organised like soldiers.
As privates of the industrial army they are placed under the command of

a perfect hierarchy of officers and sergeants. Not only are they slaves of the bourgeois class, and of the bourgeois State; they are daily and hourly enslaved by the machine, by the over-looker, and, above all, by the individual bourgeois manufacturer himself. The more openly this despotism proclaims gain to be its end and aim, the more petty, the more hateful and the more embittering it is.

The less the skill and exertion of strength implied in manual labour, in other words, the more modern industry becomes developed, the more is the labour of men superseded by that of women. Differences of age and sex have no longer any distinctive social validity for the working class. All are instruments of labour, more or less expensive to use, according to their age and sex.

No sooner is the exploitation of the labourer by the manufacturer, so far, at an end, that he receives his wages in cash, than he is set upon by the other portions of the bourgeoisie, the landlord, the shopkeeper, the pawnbroker, etc.

The lower strata of the middle class—the small tradespeople, shopkeepers, retired tradesmen generally, the handicraftsmen and peasants—all these sink gradually into the proletariat, partly because their diminutive capital does not suffice for the scale on which Modern Industry is carried on, and is swamped in the competition with the large capitalists, partly because their specialized skill is rendered worthless by the new methods of production. Thus the proletariat is recruited from all classes of the population.

6

SERGE WITTE

Secret Memo to Nicholas II, 1899

Count Serge Witte (1849–1915) was a Russian noble who, after an early career as a railroad executive, became Russian finance minister and one of the most influential advisors to Czar Nicholas II. The memo excerpted here was addressed to the czar, but kept secret because of the forces in Russian society who would have opposed Witte's proposals. Judging from his advice, what groups would have opposed his proposals? What does Witte see as the strengths and weaknesses of the Russian economy in 1899? How does he propose to make that economy stronger?

Source: T. H. Von Laue, "A Secret Memorandum of Sergei Witte on the Industrialization of Imperial Russia," *The Journal of Modern History*, Vol. 26, No. 1, March 1954 (Chicago: The University of Chicago Press), 60–74.

THINKING HISTORICALLY

What aspects of Witte's proposals would you characterize as a capitalist plan? What aspects would you call noncapitalist? Notice that Witte's memo heading calls this a "commercial and industrial" policy. How are commerce and industry related in his view?

Report of the minister of finance to His Majesty on the necessity of formulating and thereafter steadfastly adhering to a definite program of a commercial and industrial policy of the empire. Extremely secret.

The measures taken by the government for the promotion of national trade and industry have at present a far deeper and broader significance than they had at any time before. Indeed, the entire economic structure of the empire has been transformed in the course of the second half of the current century, so that now the market and its price structure represent the collective interest of all private enterprises which constitute our national economy. Buying and selling and wage labor penetrate now into much deeper layers of our national existence than was the case at the time of serf economy, when the landlord in his village constituted a self-sufficient economic little world, leading an independent life, almost without relation to the market. The division of labor; the specialization of skills; the increased exchange of goods among a population increasingly divided among towns, villages, factories, and mines; the greater complexity of the demands of the population—all these processes rapidly developed in our fatherland under the influence of the emancipation of the serfs, the construction of a railroad network, the development of credit, and the extraordinary growth of foreign trade. Now all organs and branches of our national economy are drawn into a common economic life, and all its individual units have become far more sensitive and responsive to the economic activities of the government. Because of the extremely interlaced network of contemporary economic relationships, any change in the conditions of one or the other industry, of one or the other branch of trade, credit, or communications, touches and influences, often in hidden ways, the fate of a considerable majority of our enterprises.

As a result of such fundamental transformation of the economic interests of the country, every major measure of the government more or less affects the life of the entire economic organism. The solicitude shown to various branches of industry, a new railroad, the discovery of a new field for Russian enterprise, these and other measures, even if partial and of local application only, touch the entire ever more complicated network and upset the established equilibrium. Every measure of the government in regard to trade and industry now affects almost the entire economic organism and influences the course of its further development.

In view of these facts, the minister of finance concludes that the country, which in one way or the other is nurtured by the commercial and industrial policy of the government, requires above all that this policy be carried out according to a definite plan, with strict system and continuity. . . .

In taking over the ministry of finance in 1892 1 felt obliged to make clear to myself the foundations of the commercial and industrial policy of my predecessors and to bend all efforts toward continuing and finishing what they had begun or had taken over from their predecessors. The necessity of such succession and continuity seemed to me so paramount that I relinquished my own personal views. I realized, of course, that there were very weighty arguments against the protectionist system and against high tariffs. But I supposed that even the proponents of free trade must be aware that it would be extremely harmful from the government view point to repudiate the protective system before those industries had been securely established for whose creation whole generations had paid by a high tariff. . . .

Now, as the attacks on the existing commercial and industrial policy continue and even increase in bitterness, I consider it my duty to review once more its chief foundations and to submit them to Your Imperial Highness. In order to be the true executor of Your Imperial Majesty's will, I must have instruction not for individual measures but for a comprehensive commercial and industrial policy. The country needs, above all, a firm and strict economic system.

In Russia at the present moment the protectionist system is in force. Its principal foundations were laid down in the tariff of 1891.

What are the tasks of the protectionist system?

Russia remains even at the present essentially an agricultural country. It pays for all its obligations to foreigners by exporting raw materials, chiefly of an agricultural nature, principally grain. It meets its demand for finished goods by imports from abroad. The economic relations of Russia with western Europe are fully comparable to the relations of colonial countries with their metropolises. The latter consider their colonies as advantageous markets in which they can freely sell the products of their labor and of their industry and from which they can draw with a powerful hand the raw materials necessary for them. This is the basis of the economic power of the governments of western Europe, and chiefly for that end do they guard their existing colonies or acquire new ones. Russia was, and to a considerable extent still is, such a hospitable colony for all industrially developed states, generously providing them with the cheap products of her soil, and buying dearly the products of their labor. But there is a radical difference between Russia and a colony: Russia is an independent and strong power. She has the right and the strength not to want to be the eternal handmaiden of states which are more developed economically. She should know the price of her raw materials and of the natural riches hidden in the womb of her abundant territories, and she is conscious of the great, not yet fully displayed, capacity for work among her people. She is proud of her great might, by which she jealously guards not only the political but also the economic independence of her empire. She wants to be a metropolis herself. On the basis of the people's labor, liberated from the bonds of serfdom, there began to grow our own national economy, which bids fair to become a reliable counterweight to the domination of foreign industry.

The creation of our own national industry — that is the profound task, both economic and political, from which our protectionist system arises. The advantages derived from the successful completion of this system are so numerous that I select here only the principal ones.

National labor, which at present is intensively employed only for a short agricultural season, will find full application and consequently become more productive. That, in turn, will increase the wages of the entire working population; and that again will cause an improvement of the physical and spiritual energy of the people. The welfare of Your Empire is based on national labor. The increase of its productivity and the discovery of new fields for Russian enterprise will always serve as the most reliable way for making the entire nation more prosperous.

The demand not only for raw materials but also for other articles will be met to a considerable extent by the work of the people themselves. And consequently the payment to foreigners, which at present consumes a considerable part of our national revenue, will be reduced. The import of foreign goods will then be determined not by the weakness of our industry but by the natural division of labor between nations, by which an industrially developed nation buys abroad only what it cannot advantageously produce at home; purchase abroad then enriches rather than exhausts it. Thanks to that, the accumulation of new capital from national savings is considerably facilitated, and that, in turn, promotes a further growth of productivity. . . .

It must be stated first of all that the system, because it is coherently carried out, is already beginning to show results. Industry numbers now more than 30,000 factories and mills, with an annual production surpassing 2,000,000,000 rubles. That by itself is a big figure. A widespread and tight net of economic interests is linked to the welfare of that industry. To upset it by a shift to free trade would undermine one of the most reliable foundations of our national well-being; such a shock would adversely affect its general level. In several branches, our industry grew very rapidly. . . .

It is obvious that our domestic industry, no matter how extensively it has developed, is quantitatively still small. It has not yet reached such proportions as to give birth to the creative forces of knowledge, the mobility of capital, and the spirit of enterprise. It has not yet attained the pitch of healthy competition which would enable it to produce cheaply and repay the population for its sacrifices by the cheapness and abundance of its products. It is not yet an equal partner of agriculture in providing goods for export and bearing the tax burden. But that partnership must be accomplished, and in the shortest time possible. . . .

We must give the country such industrial perfection as has been reached by the United States of America, which firmly bases its prosperity on two pillars—agriculture and industry. In order to reach these ultimate goals, we must still pass through the most difficult stretch of the road we have chosen. We have not only to direct the flow of capital into this or that field or to find new spheres for its investment, but we have to have above all a great abundance of capital, so that by its natural competition it undermines its own present monopoly position. But not even the most powerful government can create capital.

What, then, must, we do? . . .

The influx of foreign capital is, in the considered opinion of the minister of finance, the sole means by which our industry can speedily furnish our country with abundant and cheap goods. Each new wave of capital, swept in from abroad, knocks down the immoderately high level of profits to which our monopolistic entrepreneurs are accustomed and forces them to seek compensation in technical improvements, which, in turn, will lead to price reductions. Replenishing the poor store of popular savings by foreign capital makes it possible for all capital in the country to flow more freely over a broader field and to work up not only the fat but also the leaner sources of profit. Hence the natural riches of the Russian land and the productive energies of its population will be utilized to a considerably greater extent; our economy will begin to work with greater intensity. It will be difficult to say then whether foreign capital or our own productive forces, invigorated and given a chance by foreign capital, will have the greater influence over the further growth of our industries.

But in recent times objections have been raised against the influx of foreign capital. It is said that this influx is detrimental to basic national interests, that it tries to siphon off all profits from our growing Russian industries, that it will lead to the sale of our rich productive forces to foreigners. It is no secret, of course, to the minister of finance that the influx of foreign capital is disadvantageous primarily to entrepreneurs, who are harmed by any kind of competition. Not only our own, but also foreign capitalists who have already obtained an advantageous place in Russian industry join in these heart-rending complaints and thus try to guard their monopolistic profits. But, as frequently happens in the public discussion of economic problems, the interested voices are hiding behind impartial but little-informed representatives of public interests; and what is undesirable for private groups is, by a misunderstanding, eagerly interpreted as harmful to our economy as a whole. . . .

Considering the fact that the influx of foreign capital is the chief means for Russia in her present economic condition to speed up the accumulation of native capital, one should rather wish that our legislation concerning foreigners might be simplified. Historical experience shows that those human energies which accompany foreign capital are a useful creative ferment in the mass of the population of the most powerful nation and that they become gradually assimilated: mere economic ties change into organic ones. The imported cultural forces thus become an insurable part of the country itself. Only a disintegrating nation has to fear foreign enslavement. Russia, however, is not China!

I have now analyzed the chief bases of the economic system which has been followed in Russia since the reign of Alexander III.

Its starting point is the protective tariff of 1891, somewhat lowered by the subsequent trade treaties with France, Germany, Austria-Hungary, and other governments. . . .

Your Imperial Highness may see from the foregoing that the economic policy which the Russian government has followed for the last eight years is a carefully planned system, in which all parts are inseparably interconnected. Other persons, perhaps, can devise a better system to establish the needed equilibrium more successfully in a different way. Upon assuming the direction of the ministry of finance, I found a protective system almost in full operation. This system seemed to me then, and still seems to me now, completely justified. I bent all my efforts to speed its beneficial results and to alleviate, principally with the help of foreign capital, the hardships of the transition period. It is possible that we could have pursued a different policy. But in following the directives of Your Imperial Highness in such an intimately interdependent matter as our national economy, I believed it my duty as minister of finance to ask Your Majesty to consider this point: even if it were possible to follow a different economic policy, it would, no matter how beneficial its ultimate result, produce in the immediate future a sharp break. Such an unnecessary shock would aggravate the hardships now existing. Only by a system strictly sustained, and not by isolated measures, can a healthy development be guaranteed to our national economy.

Pledging all my efforts to fulfil still better the will of my sovereign, I make bold to ask that it may please your Imperial Highness to lend your firm support to the foundations of our economic system as I have analyzed them. They form, in essence, the following program:

1. To keep the tariff of 1891 unchanged until the renewal of our trade treaties.

2. To work in the meantime by all means for reducing the prices of industrial goods, not by increasing the import of goods from abroad but by the development of our domestic production, which makes mandatory the influx of foreign capital.

3. To postpone a lowering of our tariff until the time of the renewal of our trade treaties, so that, in turn, we can insist upon favorable terms for our agricultural exports.

4. Not to impose in the meantime new restraints on the influx of foreign capital, either through new laws or new interpretations of existing laws or, *especially, through administrative decrees.*

5. To maintain unchanged our present policy toward foreign capital until 1904, so that with its help our domestic industries can develop in the meantime to a position of such strength that in the renewal of trade treaties we may be able to make genuine reductions on several of our tariff rates.

6. To review in 1904, at the time of the renewal of the trade treaties, the problem of foreign capital and to decide then whether new safeguards should be added to existing legislation.

In submitting this program to favorable consideration by Your Imperial Highness, I respectfully ask that it may please you, my sovereign, to make certain that it may not be endangered henceforth by waverings and changes, because our industries, and our national economy in general, require a firm and consistent system carried to its conclusion.

If this program does not find the support of Your Imperial Highness, then, pray, tell me which economic policy I am to pursue.

STATE SECRETARY S. IU. WITTE

7

MARY ANTIN

The Promised Land, 1894/1912

The industrial revolution moved huge capital fortunes and millions of laborers across continents and oceans to places where they could be combined to further new and ever larger capitalist and industrial ventures. Not everyone, however, became a major capitalist or industrial worker. Some like Mary Antin's father played barely supporting roles in the new infrastructure.

Mary Antin (1881–1949) grew up in a Jewish family in Polotzk, Russia (now in Bellarus). In 1891 her father sailed to America, three years later calling the rest of the family (Mary, her siblings, and their mother) to join him in Boston. This selection from Antin's memoir contains part of her account of that first year in the United States, initially in Boston and then nearby in Crescent Beach and Chelsea.

Source: Mary Antin, *The Promised Land* (Houghton Mifflin, 1912; Penguin Classics, 1997), 146–49, 153–57.

How did the lives of the Antins change from Polotzk to their first year in the United States? How did they view that change? What connection do you see between immigration and nationalism?

THINKING HISTORICALLY

This selection has numerous references to the material world, capitalism, and the products of the industrial revolution. What are these references? In what ways were the Antins' lives in the United States more or less material, capitalist, or industrial than they were in Polotzk?

In our days of affluence in Russia we had been accustomed to upholstered parlors, embroidered linen, silver spoons and candlesticks, goblets of gold, kitchen shelves shining with copper and brass. We had featherbeds heaped halfway to the ceiling; we had clothes presses dusky with velvet and silk and fine woollen. The three small rooms into which my father now ushered us, up one flight of stairs, contained only the necessary beds, with lean mattresses; a few wooden chairs; a table or two; a mysterious iron structure, which later turned out to be a stove; a couple of unornamental kerosene lamps; and a scanty array of cooking-utensils and crockery. And yet we were all impressed with our new home and its furniture. It was not only because we had just passed through our seven lean years, cooking in earthen vessels, eating black bread on holidays and wearing cotton; it was chiefly because these wooden chairs and tin pans were American chairs and pans that they shone glorious in our eyes. And if there was anything lacking for comfort or decoration we expected it to be presently supplied—at least, we children did. Perhaps my mother alone, of us newcomers, appreciated the shabbiness of the little apartment, and realized that for her there was as yet no laying down of the burden of poverty.

Our initiation into American ways began with the first step on the new soil. My father found occasion to instruct or correct us even on the way from the pier to Wall Street, which journey we made crowded together in a rickety cab. He told us not to lean out of the windows, not to point, and explained the word "greenhorn." We did not want to be "greenhorns," and gave the strictest attention to my father's instructions. I do not know when my parents found opportunity to review together the history of Polotzk in the three years past, for we children had no patience with the subject; my mother's narrative was constantly interrupted by irrelevant questions, interjections, and explanations.

The first meal was an object lesson of much variety. My father produced several kinds of food, ready to eat, without any cooking, from little tin cans that had printing all over them. He attempted to introduce us to a queer, slippery kind of fruit, which he called "banana," but had to give it up for the time being. After the meal, he had better luck with a curious piece of furniture on runners, which he called "rocking-chair." There were five of us newcomers, and we found five different ways of getting into the American machine of perpetual motion, and as many ways of getting out of it. One born and bred to the use of a rocking-chair cannot imagine how ludicrous people can make themselves when attempting to use it for the first time. We laughed immoderately over our various experiments with the novelty, which was a wholesome way of letting off steam after the unusual excitement of the day.

In our flat we did not think of such a thing as storing the coal in the bathtub. There was no bathtub. So in the evening of the first day my father conducted us to the public baths. As we moved along in a little procession, I was delighted with the illumination of the streets. So many lamps, and they burned until morning, my father said, and so people did not need to carry lanterns. In America, then, everything was free, as we had heard in Russia. Light was free; the streets were as bright as a synagogue on a holy day. Music was free; we had been serenaded, to our gaping delight, by a brass band of many pieces, soon after our installation on Union Place.

Education was free. That subject my father had written about repeatedly, as comprising his chief hope for us children, the essence of American opportunity, the treasure that no thief could touch, not even misfortune or poverty. It was the one thing that he was able to promise us when he sent for us; surer, safer than bread or shelter. On our second day I was thrilled with the realization of what this freedom of education meant. A little girl from across the alley came and offered to conduct us to school. My father was out, but we five between us had a few words of English by this time. We knew the word school. We understood. This child, who had never seen us till yesterday, who could not pronounce our names, who was not much better dressed than we, was able to offer us the freedom of the schools of Boston! No application made, no questions asked, no examinations, rulings, exclusions; no machinations, no fees. The doors stood open for every one of us. The smallest child could show us the way.

This incident impressed me more than anything I had heard in advance of the freedom of education in America. It was a concrete proof— almost the thing itself. One had to experience it to understand it.

It was a great disappointment to be told by my father that we were not to enter upon our school career at once. It was too near the end of the term, he said, and we were going to move to Crescent Beach in a week or so. We had to wait until the opening of the schools in September. What a loss of precious time—from May till September!

Not that the time was really lost. Even the interval on Union Place was crowded with lessons and experiences. We had to visit the stores and be dressed from head to foot in American clothing; we had to learn the mysteries of the iron stove, the washboard, and the speaking-tube; we had to learn to trade with the fruit peddler through the window, and not to be afraid of the policeman; and, above all, we had to learn English. . . .

I am forgetting the more serious business which had brought us to Crescent Beach. While we children disported ourselves like mermaids and mermen in the surf, our respective fathers dispensed cold lemonade, hot peanuts, and pink popcorn, and piled up our respective fortunes, nickel by nickel, penny by penny. I was very proud of my connection with the public life of the beach. I admired greatly our shining soda fountain, the rows of sparkling glasses, the pyramids of oranges, the sausage chains, the neat white counter, and the bright array of tin spoons. It seemed to me that none of the other refreshment stands on the beach — there were a few — were half so attractive as ours. I thought my father looked very well in a long white apron and shirt sleeves. He dished out ice cream with enthusiasm, so I supposed he was getting rich. It never occurred to me to compare his present occupation with the position for which he had been originally destined; or if I thought about it, I was just as well content, for by this time I had by heart my father's saying, "America is not Polotzk." All occupations were respectable, all men were equal, in America.

If I admired the soda fountain and the sausage chains, I almost worshipped the partner, Mr. Wilner. I was content to stand for an hour at a time watching him make potato chips. In his cook's cap and apron, with a ladle in his hand and a smile on his face, he moved about with the greatest agility, whisking his raw materials out of nowhere, dipping into his bubbling kettle with a flourish, and bringing forth the finished product with a caper. Such potato chips were not to be had anywhere else on Crescent Beach. Thin as tissue paper, crisp as dry snow, and salt as the sea — such thirst-producing, lemonade-selling, nickel-bringing potato chips only Mr. Wilner could make. On holidays, when dozens of family parties came out by every train from town, he could hardly keep up with the demand for his potato chips. And with a waiting crowd around him our partner was at his best. He was as voluble as he was skilful, and as witty as he was voluble; at least so I guessed from the laughter that frequently drowned his voice. I could not understand his jokes, but if I could get near enough to watch his lips and his smile and his merry eyes, I was happy. That any one could talk so fast, and in English, was marvel enough, but that this prodigy should belong to *our* establishment was a fact to thrill me. I had never seen anything like Mr. Wilner, except a wedding jester; but then he spoke common Yiddish. So proud was I of the talent and good taste displayed at our stand that if my father beckoned to me in the crowd and sent me on an errand, I hoped the people noticed that I, too, was connected with the establishment.

And all this splendor and glory and distinction came to a sudden end. There was some trouble about a license—some fee or fine—there was a storm in the night that damaged the soda fountain and other fixtures—there was talk and consultation between the houses of Antin and Wilner—and the promising partnership was dissolved. No more would the merry partner gather the crowd on the beach; no more would the twelve young Wilners gambol like mermen and mermaids in the surf. And the less numerous tribe of Antin must also say farewell to the jolly seaside life, for men in such humble business as my father's carry their families, along with their other earthly goods, wherever they go, after the manner of the gypsies. We had driven a feeble stake into the sand. The jealous Atlantic, in conspiracy with the Sunday law, had torn it out. We must seek our luck elsewhere.

In Polotzk we had supposed that "America" was practically synonymous with "Boston." When we landed in Boston, the horizon was pushed back, and we annexed Crescent Beach. And now, espying other lands of promise, we took possession of the province of Chelsea, in the name of our necessity.

In Chelsea, as in Boston, we made our stand in the wrong end of the town. Arlington Street was inhabited by poor Jews, poor Negroes, and a sprinkling of poor Irish. The side streets leading from it were occupied by more poor Jews and Negroes. It was a proper locality for a man without capital to do business. My father rented a tenement with a store in the basement. He put in a few barrels of flour and of sugar, a few boxes of crackers, a few gallons of kerosene, an assortment of soap of the "save the coupon" brands; in the cellar, a few barrels of potatoes, and a pyramid of kindling-wood; in the showcase, an alluring display of penny candy. He put out his sign, with a gilt-lettered warning of "Strictly Cash," and proceeded to give credit indiscriminately. That was the regular way to do business on Arlington Street. My father, in his three years' apprenticeship, had learned the tricks of many trades. He knew when and how to "bluff." The legend of "Strictly Cash" was a protection against notoriously irresponsible customers; while none of the "good" customers, who had a record for paying regularly on Saturday, hesitated to enter the store with empty purses.

If my father knew the tricks of the trade, my mother could be counted on to throw all her talent and tact into the business. Of course she had no English yet, but as she could perform the acts of weighing, measuring, and mental computation of fractions mechanically, she was able to give her whole attention to the dark mysteries of the language, as intercourse with her customers gave her opportunity. In this she made such rapid progress that she soon lost all sense of disadvantage, and conducted herself behind the counter very much as if she were back in her old store in Polotzk. It was far more cosey than Polotzk—at least, so it seemed to me; for behind the store was the kitchen, where, in the intervals of slack trade, she did her cooking and washing. Arlington Street customers were used to waiting while the storekeeper salted the soup or rescued a loaf from the oven.

Once more Fortune favored my family with a thin little smile, and my father, in reply to a friendly inquiry, would say, "One makes a living," with a shrug of the shoulders that added "but nothing to boast of." It was characteristic of my attitude toward bread-and-butter matters that this contented me, and I felt free to devote myself to the conquest of my new world. Looking back to those critical first years, I see myself always behaving like a child let loose in a garden to play and dig and chase the butterflies. Occasionally, indeed, I was stung by the wasp of family trouble; but I knew a healing ointment — my faith in America. My father had come to America to make a living. America, which was free and fair and kind, must presently yield him what he sought. I had come to America to see a new world, and I followed my own ends with the utmost assiduity, only, as I ran out to explore, I would look back to see if my house were in order behind me — if my family still kept its head above water.

In after years, when I passed as an American among Americans, if I was suddenly made aware of the past that lay forgotten, — if a letter from Russia, or a paragraph in the newspaper, or a conversation overheard in the street-car, suddenly reminded me of what I might have been, — I thought it miracle enough that I, Mashke, the granddaughter of Raphael the Russian, born to a humble destiny, should be at home in an American metropolis, be free to fashion my own life, and should dream my dreams in English phrases. But in the beginning my admiration was spent on more concrete embodiments of the splendors of America; such as fine houses, gay shops, electric engines and apparatus, public buildings, illuminations, and parades. My early letters to my Russian friends were filled with boastful descriptions of these glories of my new country. No native citizen of Chelsea took such pride and delight in its institutions as I did. It required no fife and drum corps, no Fourth of July procession, to set me tingling with patriotism. Even the common agents and instruments of municipal life, such as the letter carrier and the fire engine, I regarded with a measure of respect. I know what I thought of people who said that Chelsea was a very small, dull, unaspiring town, with no discernible excuse for a separate name or existence.

The apex of my civic pride and personal contentment was reached on the bright September morning when I entered the public school. That day I must always remember, even if I live to be so old that I cannot tell my name. To most people their first day at school is a memorable occasion. In my case the importance of the day was a hundred times magnified, on account of the years I had waited, the road I had come, and the conscious ambitions I entertained.

I am wearily aware that I am speaking in extreme figures, in superlatives. I wish I knew some other way to render the mental life of the immigrant child of reasoning age. I may have been ever so much an exception in acuteness of observation, powers of comparison, and abnormal self-consciousness; none the less were my thoughts and conduct typical of the attitude of the intelligent immigrant child toward American institutions. And what the child thinks and feels is a reflection of the hopes, desires, and purposes of the parents who brought him overseas, no matter how precocious and independent the child may be. Your immigrant inspectors will tell you what poverty the foreigner brings in his baggage, what want in his pockets. Let the overgrown boy of twelve, reverently drawing his letters in the baby class, testify to the noble dreams and high ideals that may be hidden beneath the greasy caftan of the immigrant. Speaking for the Jews, at least, I know I am safe in inviting such an investigation.

8

Italians in Two Worlds: An Immigrant's Letters from Argentina, 1901

One of the distinctive features of the capitalist industrial revolution was the globalization of capital and labor. The capital for the British industrial revolution, beginning toward the end of the eighteenth century, filtered in from the treasures of the Indies — East and West — and owed much to the labor of slaves and legally free workers who were shipped from one end of the world to the other. By the second half of the nineteenth century, the owners of farms, factories, mines, and railroads called for many more laborers.

Millions of these workers came from Italy alone. From 1860 to 1885, most traveled from northern Italy to South America, mainly Argentina. Between 1890 and 1915, Italian immigration to Argentina continued, but even more came from southern Italy to the United States. By the beginning of the twentieth century, New York City and Buenos Aires each had larger Italian populations than many Italian cities.

This selection contains the first few letters sent back home by one of those Italian immigrants, Oreste Sola, who arrived in Buenos Aires in 1901 from northern Italy. What do these letters tell you about this immigrant's expectations? What sort of work did he do? How did he

Source: *One Family, Two Worlds: An Italian Family's Correspondence across the Atlantic*, ed. Samuel L. Baily and Franco Ramella, trans. John Lenaghan (New Brunswick, NJ: Rutgers University Press, 1988), 34–42.

manage to navigate his new world? What were his challenges? How would you describe his strengths? Based on the few hints of events in Italy, how was his life in Argentina different from what it would have likely been in Italy?

THINKING HISTORICALLY

What signs do you see in these letters of industrialization in Argentina? What signs do you see of a capitalist economic system? How is the life of Oreste shaped by the needs of capitalists? How is it shaped by a capitalist economic system? How is his life shaped by industrialization?

Letter 1

Buenos Ayres, 17 August 1901

Dearest parents,

I have been here since the 5th of this month; I am in the best of health as are my two companions. As soon as we got here, we went to the address of Godfather Zocco, who then introduced us to several people from Valdengo who have been in America for some years and all are doing well more or less. The language here is Castilian, quite similar to Spanish, but you don't hear anyone speaking it. Wherever you go, whether in the hotel or at work, everyone speaks either Piedmontese or Italian, even those from other countries, and the Argentines themselves speak Italian.[1]

This city is very beautiful. There is an enormous amount of luxury. All the streets—they call them *calle* [sic] here—are paved either with hard wood or in cement as smooth as marble, even too smooth since the horses, tram horses as well as carriage horses, which run here, keep slipping constantly. It is not unusual to see twenty or more of them fall in one day. . . .

The piazza Victoria (Plaza de Mayo) is also beautiful, where all around on two sides there are only banks. They are of all nations: English, French, Italian, Spanish, North American, etc., etc. On another side is the government building where the president of the Argentine Republic resides. He is Italian, Rocca by name, the third Italian president

---

[1] He does not speak or understand Spanish and therefore does not realize that Spanish and Castilian are the same thing. Although 25 percent of the total population and an even higher percentage of the adult population of Buenos Aires was Italian-born, and therefore the Italian language was indeed spoken in many places, Oreste obviously exaggerates when he claims that everyone speaks it.

in a row who sits on the Argentine throne.[2] There is also the railway station of the south, which is something colossal. With workshops, offices, and the station itself it will cover one million square meters. Now they are at work on a government building for the Congress (Parliament). The architect was an Italian, as is the chief contractor, who is supervising all the work. It is a job which in the end will cost more than 700 million lire. It will occupy an area of a block which is 10,000 square meters and will be surrounded by a square, which, along with the building, will constitute an area of about 100,000 square meters. This work will be better than the first [the railway station], but perhaps I shall not be able to see it finished.

All of this is inside the city, but if you should go outside for a few hours, it's worse than a desert. You only find houses made solely out of mortar, with only a ground floor and a door you have to enter on all fours. Outside you don't see a plant; everything is desert. The plains stretch as far as the eye can see; it takes hours on the train before you come to the mountains. There are a few tracts of land, sort of green, where they may let a few horses loose to graze. Here they let the animals go out no matter what the weather might be. Here you can't find a rock, though you pay its weight in gold for it. All the ground is black like manure, thick and muddy. When it doesn't rain, it gets hard, and if you try to dig, it shoots out as if it were rock.

The food here is pretty good, but it doesn't have much flavor. This is true for all Argentina.

All the guys here are jolly as crazy men. In the evening when we get together before going to bed we split our sides laughing. They would all like to go back to Italy, but they don't ever budge. Perhaps I will do the same. Here we eat, drink, and laugh and enjoy ourselves; we are in America. . . .

Take one last loving kiss and hug

from your always loving son,

Oreste

Letter 2

Mendoza, 18 September 1901

Dearest parents,

I am still in good spirits and happy that I am in America. I am now at Mendoza instead of Buenos Ayres. I didn't like Buenos Ayres too much because you don't get good wine there; and then every day the temperature changes twenty times, and I was always chilly. Otherwise it was fine.

---

[2] Oreste is in error here. The president to whom he refers, Julio Roca, was Argentine not Italian. The preceding president, José Uriburu, also was not Italian. However, Carlos Pelligrini, president from 1890 to 1892, was the son of a French-Italian father from Savoy.

One day I got the idea, knowing that Secondino's brother-in-law and sister were in Mendoza. Since the boss advanced me the money for the trip,[3] I made up my mind to come here, where you see nothing but hills and mountains in the distance, like at home. You drink very well here; the wine costs half what it does in Buenos Ayres and is pure and delicious. I am living here with Carlo and his wife and a man by the name of Luigi Ferraro from Chiavazza, who has been here for seven years traveling around in America. There are few people here from Biella, but there is no shortage of Italians. I still haven't learned a word of Castilian because, everywhere you go, they speak Italian or Piedmontese.

I am better off here than in Buenos Ayres. I am only sorry to be so far from my friends—they didn't want to come—and from Godfather and the rest.

This city is ugly; it never rains even though it is close to the mountains. I have written a friend to send me the address of my schoolmate Berretta, and I might just go and see him in Peru; it takes four days or more on the train. From Buenos Ayres to Mendoza takes two nights and a day on the railroad without ever changing trains or getting off. The longest stop is a half hour. In the entire journey you don't see a plant. [There are] two or three rivers about 400 meters wide. They are all in the plain, so calm that you can't tell which way the water is going, and yet they flow on in an imperceptible way.

Throughout the journey one meets only horses, cows, and goats, none of which have stables. On the rail line you don't see a house for three hours or more, and everything is like that. . . .

Everyone, Carlo, Cichina, and Luigi, give their regards to you. Tell Secondino to come and see America, to drink and eat and travel.

Time is pressing since I have to work every evening until ten. I work at home after work.

You should write me at:

El Taller del Ferro Carril G.O.A.
Mendoza

Goodbye everybody. Kisses to Abele and Narcisa. Tell Abele to study hard and to learn to work. Send him to the technical schools; I imagine he has been promoted. Goodbye, Mom and Dad. Be in good spirits as I am.

Yours always,
Orestes

---

[3] The government of the province of Mendoza and many individual employers made a major effort to attract European immigrants during the two decades preceding World War I. It was not unusual for an employer to advance money to pay for the trip from Buenos Aires to Mendoza.

Letter 3

Mendoza, 13 November 1901

Dearest Father, Mother, brother, and sister,

This morning Secondino arrived as you had already indicated he would in your letter of 14 October. He had a very good trip, and he made everyone happy to see him healthy and cheerful—as we are, Carlo, Cichina, and Luigi. He gave me the trousers which you gave him to bring me and the letter written by Dad and Narcisa.

I have been here in Mendoza for about three months, and I am happy that Secondino is here now too. But I don't plan to stay fixed here. I would like to go to Peru with Berretta or to Cuba, where dear Cousin Edvino is staying, since I know that those who are there are doing well now. It wouldn't be bad here except you aren't sure about employment or about anything, especially for the type of work I do. So you can't even be sure of staying in one place. Before leaving I am waiting to get the address of Berretta.

I thought that I could send something, instead I had to make some purchases. Be patient. I think of our family conditions too often to be able to think of anything else. Excuse me if I have been slow in writing. It's because I hoped to get a particular job, and I wanted to let you know. I was waiting for the decision of the company. The job went to another, also Italian, with whom nobody could compete. But let's leave the subject of work because here there are so many professions and so many trades that you can't say what you are doing. Today it's this and tomorrow it's that. I tried to go into the construction business for myself, but it didn't work out. So much effort and expense. Now I am doing something else, and I shall change again soon.

My friends as well as Godfather are still in Buenos Aires. They are fine and want to be remembered to you. I receive news (from Buenos Aires) almost every week.

Pardon me, dear parents, brother, and sister, if I am sometimes slow in writing. It is not that I forget, quite the contrary. Only please don't reproach me the way Narcisa does because, if you knew how painful these reproaches are to us here, especially when they come from the family, you would not believe it. I shall try to write more often.

Narcisa asks me for postcards, Abele for stamps. I cannot satisfy anyone since they don't sell illustrated postcards here even though there would be many beautiful things [to show], like, for example, the ruins of Mendoza of 1860 caused by the earthquake, which often happens here six or seven times a year.[4] If it is a special earthquake, you seem to be in a boat, rocking like at sea. But if it gets a bit strong, you have to lie down so as not to fall. Some attribute it to the various volcanoes,

---

[4] The earthquake to which he refers occurred on March 20, 1861. It destroyed the entire city of Mendoza and killed much of its population.

mostly extinct however, which are in the mountains here. Others say it is because of the huge storms of the Pacific meeting the winds that come from the Atlantic. However, no one can verify it.

From what I make out from Dad's letter, he says that he was planning to send me some clothes when I get established here. Excuse me, dear parents, your sacrifices are already excessive. Now it is my job to pay them back at least in part, and I shall do everything possible to that end. But excuse me, I am old enough now to earn my bread. I beg you not to be offended about this. If later I shall be in a position to, I shall send you money and everything. But for now, first of all, I have clothes to wear. I have already purchased here two suits and four pairs of trousers. So don't be upset then. Rather, I repeat, as soon as I am able, I'll see that you get something. Now I cannot; it has gone badly for me before I got started. When I shall again be the way I was in the beginning—but I don't know when because here [in] America [things] can change from one day to the next—you will have some repayment.

I have received your newspapers and bulletins, letters and all, because the telegraph and postal service here is something very precise. I was very pleased to get them. I read also in the bulletin of the professional school that they are asking for the address of members who are living outside the country. If I should send it and then, before publication, I should move, I would be in the same situation I was before. Also they want you to indicate the kind of work you are doing for publication in the bulletin because it will be, I believe, an issue with all the graduates of the professional school, and I can't tell them that. I change from one day to the next. At that moment I was a draftsman second grade in the workshop of the Trans Andes railway. It is a direct railway to Chile now under construction. But I am not doing it anymore because the section that the four of us were assigned to work on has been finished.

Now I am working as a smith and various things for the Great Western Railway of Argentina. But since they don't pay me as I want and I have to be first a blacksmith, then work as a planer, then at the lathe, I don't like it. At the first other job that comes along, I'm off. When I find something better, I don't want to work as a laborer for low wages anymore. . . .

Your most loving son and
brother,
Oreste Sola

Letter 4

Mendoza, 25 November 1901

Dearest ones,

A few days before this letter you will have received another written on the day of Secondino's arrival; a few days later he received some newspapers which indicated that you were on strike.[5] I understand that in this season such a big strike will be very distressing. I, however, right now absolutely cannot, for the moment, help you in any way. If I had been able to get that damned construction job, I assure you I would have "hit the jackpot." From one day to the next another bit of bad luck could come my way; but everything is in doubt, there is then no certainty nor prospect.

Now they are coming here every day on the emigration train, about 600 persons a week. They are then sent out of the city in great numbers; but many remain, and we are beginning to see some unemployment but only in a small way. It's just that working in such conditions you only earn a bare living and with difficulty at that. If I have bad luck, I'm not staying here any longer. I want to go to Cuba with Boffa and the rest since Berretta doesn't answer. Nothing is certain however. The ideas come in crowds, but the execution is just miserable. Still I am not losing heart ever. I have been through a good period at first, then an excellent one, and now I am in a third one that is very tough. But I'll get back on my feet. We are in America.

Be patient then. I too am aware that Mom is working at night, that you are working on Sundays, etc.—things that don't happen here. Here in every profession and everywhere you work nine hours a day and only 'til noon on Saturday. You don't work on Sunday nor after midday meal on Saturday, and you get more respect. When you ask for some improvement in pay, the owners don't say that they will show up with a rifle and fire at the first one who makes trouble, as the famous Giovanni Rivetti used to say.[6] Here, if they don't want to give it to you, they look into it, they review it; but generally they give it to you, and all this without unions or anything. They are capitalists who are more aware; that's all there is to it.

Think always of your loving son who is in America, always in good spirits, even when things are going badly for him.

Oreste Sola

Secondino, like me, is always in good spirits, and we are always together. He sends you his warmest greetings and so does Carlo's family. Secondino would like you to say hello to his wife if it is not too much trouble.

---

[5] Oreste is referring to the major strike at the Biella textile factory in which [his parents] Luigi and Margherita worked. The strike, which ended in defeat for the workers, was provoked when the owners increased the work load without increasing salaries.

[6] Giovanni Rivetti was one of the owners of the Biella textile factory in which Luigi and Margherita worked. Given the size and importance of the factory, Rivetti's conduct greatly influenced that of the other owners in the entire area.

■ REFLECTIONS

> It was because of certain traits in private capitalism that the machine—which was a neutral agent—has often seemed, and in fact has sometimes been, a malicious element in society, careless of human life, indifferent to human interests. The machine has suffered for the sins of capitalism; contrariwise, capitalism has often taken credit for the virtues of the machine.[1]

Our chapter turns the above proposition by writer Lewis Mumford into a series of questions: What has been the impact of capitalism? Is the machine only neutral, or does it have its own effects? How can we distinguish between the economic and the technological chains of cause and effect?

Capitalism and industrialization are difficult concepts to distinguish. Adam Smith illustrated the power of the market and the division of labor by imagining their impact not on a shop or trading firm but on a pin factory, an early industrial enterprise. Karl Marx summarized the achievements of the capitalist age by enumerating "wonders far surpassing Egyptian pyramids," which included chemical industries, steam navigation, railroads, and electric telegraphs. Neither Smith nor Marx used the terms *capitalism* or *industrial revolution,* although such variants as *capitalist* and *industrial* were already in circulation. Modern historians fought over their meaning and relevance as explanations of change through most of the last century. To understand the great transformation into modernity, some emphasized the expansion of market capitalism; others emphasized the power of the machine. The rise of state-capitalist and communist industrial societies politicized the debate, but even after the fall of communism, the historical questions remained. The letters of Oreste Sola support the argument of some historians of Latin America that the continent was modernized more by trade and capital than by industrialization.

After 1900 the industrial revolution spread throughout the world, but its pace was not always revolutionary. Even today some societies are still largely rural, with a majority of workers engaged in subsistence farming or small-scale manufacturing by hand. But over the long course of history people have always tried to replace human labor with machines and increase the production of machine-made goods. In some cases, the transformation has been dramatic. Malaysia, once a languid land of tropical tea and rubber plantations, sprouted enough microchip and electronics factories after 1950 to account for 60 percent of its exports by the year 2000. By the 1990s an already highly industrialized country like Japan could produce luxury cars in factories that needed only a handful of

---

[1] Lewis Mumford, *Technics and Civilization* (New York: Harcourt Brace, 1963), 27.

humans to monitor the work of computer-driven robots. Despite occasional announcements of the arrival of a "postindustrial" society, the pressure to mechanize continues unabated in the twenty-first century.

The fate of capitalism in the twentieth century was more varied. The second wave of industrial revolutions—beginning with Germany after 1850 and Japan after 1880—was directed by governments as much as capitalists. Socialist parties won large support in industrial countries in the first half of the twentieth century, creating welfare states in some after World War II. In Russia after 1917, the Communist Party pioneered a model of state-controlled industrialization that attracted imitators from China to Chile and funded anticapitalist movements throughout the world.

The Cold War (1947–1991) between the United States and the Soviet Union, though largely a power struggle between two superpowers, was widely seen as an ideological contest between capitalism and socialism. Thus the demise of the Soviet Union and its Communist Party in 1991 was heralded as the victory of capitalism over socialism. As Russia, China, and other previously communist states embraced market economies, socialism was declared dead.

But could proclaiming the death of socialism be as premature as heralding the end of industrial society? *The Communist Manifesto* of 1848 long predates the Russian Revolution of 1917. Karl Marx died in 1883. Socialists like Rosa Luxembourg criticized Lenin and the Russian communists for misinterpreting Marxism in their impatience to transform Russian society. Socialists, even Marxists, continue to write, advise, and govern today, often urging restraints on the spread of global capital markets and the threat of unregulated capitalism for the global environment. Rarely are they willing to relinquish the advantages of industrial technology; rather, they seek to release the "virtues of the machine."

22

Colonized and Colonizers

Europeans in Africa and Asia, 1850–1930

■ HISTORICAL CONTEXT

The first stage of European colonialism, beginning with Columbus, was a period in which Europeans—led by the Spanish and Portuguese—settled in the Western Hemisphere and created plantations with African labor. From 1492 to 1776, European settlement in Asia was limited to a few coastal port cities where merchants and missionaries operated. The second stage—the years between 1776, when Britain lost most of its American colonies, and 1880, when the European scramble for African territory began—has sometimes been called a period of *free-trade imperialism*. This term refers to the desire by European countries in general and by Britain in particular to expand their zones of free trade. It also refers to a widespread opposition to the expense of colonization, a conviction held especially among the British, who garnered all of the advantages of political empire without the costs of occupation and outright ownership.

The British used to quip that their second global empire was created in the nineteenth century "in a fit of absentmindedness." But colonial policy in Britain and the rest of Europe was more planned and continuous than that comment might suggest. British control of India (including Burma) increased throughout the nineteenth century, as did British control of South Africa, Australia, the Pacific, and parts of the Americas. At the same time, France, having lost most of India to the British, began building an empire that included parts of North Africa, Southeast Asia, and the Pacific.

Thus, a third stage of colonialism, beginning in the mid-nineteenth century, reached a fever pitch with the partition of Africa after 1880. The period between 1888 and 1914 spawned renewed settlement and massive population transfers, with most European migrants settling in the older colonies of the Americas (as well as in South Africa and Australia), where indigenous populations had been reduced. Even where settlement remained light, however, Europeans took political control of large areas of the Earth's surface (see Map 22.1).

■ THINKING HISTORICALLY

Using Literature in History

This chapter also explores how literature can be used in the quest to better understand history. We examine a number of fictional accounts of colonialism, some written by the colonizers, others by the colonized or their descendants, in addition to a critical study of a historical novel and a poem. How do these pieces of literature add to, or detract from, a historical understanding of colonialism? We explore this question because the European colonial experience produced a rich, evocative literature, which, used carefully, can offer a wide range of detail and insight about the period and colonialism.

Historical novels are particularly tricky. The structure of a novel bears certain similarities to history—a description of a place, proper names and biographies, descriptions of human interactions, an accounting of change, and a story. There are also structural differences in a novel—a lot of dialogue, greater attention to physical appearance and character, and a more prominent narrative. These fictional elements are often unattainable for historians. Dialogue, a person's actual words, especially thoughts, are often absent from the historical sources. A good novelist creates these elements based on historical research and familiarity with the time and place. Such details provide a great sense of verisimilitude (resemblance to reality). We feel as if we are there, a feeling that further reinforces our sense of the novel's truth. But in this regard we are captives of the novelist, caught in the web of his or her imagination. In good hands we may see what would otherwise be invisible. In bad hands, we may vividly see what was never there.

A good novel, like a good history, shows us something we did not know, something unexpected, even surprising. But the problem is that we are most easily seduced by what is most familiar to us. Thus, in the hands of the uninformed, we are most likely to believe we have seen the historical truth when we have only projected our own world onto the past. How successfully do the authors of these fictional pieces show you something about the past that is likely true?

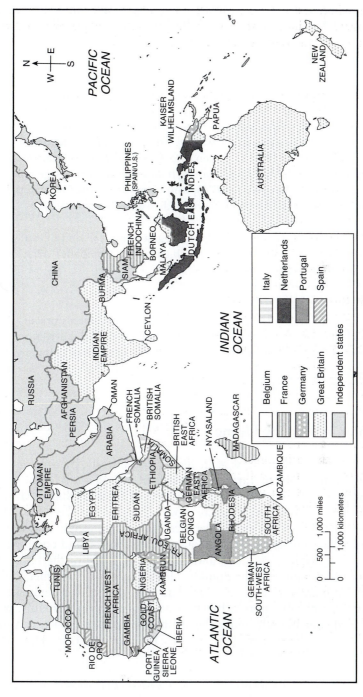

Map 22.1 European Colonialism in Africa and Asia, 1880–1914.

1

GEORGE ALFRED HENTY

With Clive in India: Or, the Beginnings of an Empire, 1884

George Alfred Henty (1832–1902) was a war correspondent and popular British novelist, especially of young adult fiction for boys. He practically invented the imperialist adventure story with its celebration of colonial conquests and its patronizing and often racist views of "natives." This type of tale was the first course of instruction for generations of British young men who would fight for and rule the British Empire. In this story, a young man serves under the legendary Major Robert Clive (1725–1774), who commanded the forces of the British East India Company against Indian and French armies to secure eastern India.

What does this opening chapter suggest about the kind of young men who went to work for the British East India Company? What does it suggest about their motivations?

THINKING HISTORICALLY

Historical novels often obscure or embroider on actual historical incidents and institutions. What historical facts does this selection convey? For example, we learn that the British East India Company played a significant role in English colonization of India. What else do we learn?

Chapter 1: Leaving Home

A lady in deep mourning was sitting, crying bitterly, by a fire in small lodgings in the town of Yarmouth. Beside her stood a tall lad of sixteen. He was slight in build, but his schoolfellows knew that Charlie Marryat's muscles were as firm and hard as those of any boy in the school. In all sports requiring activity and endurance, rather than weight and strength, he was always conspicuous. Not one in the school could compete with him in long-distance running, and when he was one of the hares there was but little chance for the hounds. He was a capital swimmer, and one of the best boxers in the school. He had a reputation for being a leader in every mischievous prank; but he was honourable and manly, would scorn to shelter himself under the semblance of a lie, and was a prime favourite with his masters, as well as his schoolfellows. His mother

---

Source: G. A. Henty, *With Clive in India: Or, the Beginnings of an Empire* (New York: Charles Scribner's Sons, 1894), 9–13, 24–25.

bewailed the frequency with which he returned home with blackened eyes and bruised face; for between Dr. Willet's school and the fisher lads of Yarmouth there was a standing feud, whose origin dated so far back that none of those now at school could trace it. Consequently, fierce fights often took place in the narrow rows, and sometimes the fisher boys would be driven back on to the broad quay shaded by trees, by the river, and there being reinforced from the craft along the side, would reassume the offensive and drive their opponents back into the main street.

It was but six months since Charlie had lost his father, who was the officer in command at the coast guard station, and his scanty pension was now all that remained for the support of his widow and children. His mother had talked his future prospects over, many times, with Charlie. The latter was willing to do anything, but could suggest nothing. His father had but little naval interest, and had for years been employed on coast guard service. Charlie agreed that, although he should have liked of all things to go to sea, it was useless to think of it now, for he was past the age at which he could have entered as a midshipman.

The matter had been talked over four years before, with his father; but the latter had pointed out that a life in the navy, without interest, is in most cases a very hard one. If a chance of distinguishing himself happened, promotion would follow; but if not, he might be for years on shore, starving on half pay and waiting in vain for an appointment, while officers with more luck and better interest went over his head.

Other professions had been discussed, but nothing determined upon, when Lieutenant Marryat suddenly died. Charlie, although an only son, was not an only child, as he had two sisters both younger than himself. After a few months of effort, Mrs. Marryat found that the utmost she could hope to do, with her scanty income, was to maintain herself and daughters, and to educate them until they should reach an age when they could earn their own living as governesses; but that Charlie's keep and education were beyond her resources. She had, therefore, very reluctantly written to an uncle, whom she had not seen for many years, her family having objected very strongly to her marriage with a penniless lieutenant in the navy. She informed him of the loss of her husband, and that, although her income was sufficient to maintain herself and her daughters, she was most anxious to start her son, who was now sixteen, in life; and therefore begged him to use his influence to obtain for him a situation of some sort. The letter which she now held in her hand was the answer to the appeal.

"My dear Niece," it began, "Since you, by your own foolish conduct and opposition to all our wishes, separated yourself from your family, and went your own way in life, I have heard little of you, as the death of your parents so shortly afterwards deprived me of all sources of information. I regret to hear of the loss which you have suffered. I have already taken the necessary steps to carry out your wishes. I yesterday dined with a friend, who is one of the directors of the Honorable East India Company, and at my request he has kindly placed a writership in the Company at your son's service. He will have to come up to London to see the board, next week, and will probably have to embark for India a fortnight later. I shall be glad if he will take up his abode with me, during the intervening time. I shall be glad also if you will favour me with a statement of your income and expenses, with such details as you may think necessary. I inclose four five-pound bank notes, in order that your son may obtain such garments as may be immediately needful for his appearance before the board of directors, and for his journey to London. I remain, my dear niece, yours sincerely,

"Joshua Tufton."

"It is cruel," Mrs. Marryat sobbed, "cruel to take you away from us, and send you to India, where you will most likely die of fever, or be killed by a tiger, or stabbed by one of those horrid natives, in a fortnight."

"Not so bad as that, Mother, I hope," Charlie said sympathizingly, although he could not repress a smile; "other people have managed to live out there, and have come back safe."

"Yes," Mrs. Marryat said, sobbing; "I know how you will come back. A little, yellow, shrivelled up old man with no liver, and a dreadful temper, and a black servant. I know what it will be."

This time Charlie could not help laughing.

"That's looking too far ahead altogether, Mother. You take the two extremes. If I don't die in a fortnight, I am to live to be a shrivelled old man. I'd rather take a happy medium, and look forward to coming back before my liver is all gone, or my temper all destroyed, with lots of money to make you and the girls comfortable.

"There is only one thing. I wish it had been a cadetship, instead of a writership."

"That is my only comfort," Mrs. Marryat said. "If it had been a cadetship, I should have written to say that I would not let you go. It is bad enough as it is; but if you had had to fight, I could not have borne it."

Charlie did his best to console his mother, by telling her how everyone who went to India made fortunes, and how he should be sure to come back with plenty of money; and that, when the girls grew up, he should be able to find rich husbands for them; and at last he succeeded in getting her to look at matters in a less gloomy light.

"And I'm sure, Mother," he said, "Uncle means most kindly. He sends twenty pounds, you see, and says that that is for immediate necessities; so I have no doubt he means to help to get my outfit, or at any rate to advance money, which I can repay him out of my salary. The letter is rather stiff and businesslike, of course, but I suppose that's his way; and you see he asks about your income, so perhaps he means to help for the girls' education. I should go away very happy, if I knew that you would be able to get on comfortably. Of course it's a long way off, Mother, and I should have liked to stay at home, to be a help to you and the girls; but one can't have all one wishes. As far as I am concerned, myself, I would rather go out as a writer there, where I shall see strange sights and a strange country, than be stuck all my life at a desk in London." . . .

The remainder of Charlie's stay in London passed most pleasantly. They visited all the sights of town, Mr. Tufton performing what he called his duty with an air of protest, but showing a general thoughtfulness and desire to please his visitors, which was very apparent even when he grunted and grumbled the most.

On the evening before he started, he called Charlie down into his counting house.

"Tomorrow you are going to sail," he said, "and to start in life on your own account, and I trust that you will, as far as possible, be steady, and do your duty to your employers. You will understand that, although the pay of a writer is not high, there are opportunities for advancement. The Company have the monopoly of the trade of India, and in addition to their great factories at Bombay, Calcutta, and Madras, they have many other trading stations. Those who, by their good conduct, attract the attention of their superiors, rise to positions of trust and emolument. There are many who think that the Company will, in time, enlarge its operations; and as they do so, superior opportunities will offer themselves; and since the subject of India has been prominently brought before my notice, I have examined the question, and am determined to invest somewhat largely in the stock of the Company, a step which will naturally give me some influence with the board. That influence I shall, always supposing that your conduct warrants it, exercise on your behalf.

"As we are now at war with France, and it is possible that the vessel in which you are proceeding may be attacked by the way, I have thought it proper that you should be armed. You will, therefore, find in your cabin a brace of pistols, a rifle, and a double-barrel shotgun: which last, I am informed, is a useful weapon at close quarters. Should your avocations in India permit your doing so, you will find them useful in the pursuit of game. I hope that you will not be extravagant; but as a matter of business I find that it is useful to be able to give entertainments, to persons who may be in a position to benefit or advance you. I have, therefore, arranged that you will draw from the factor at Madras the sum of two hundred pounds, annually, in addition to your pay. It is clearly my duty to see that my nephew has every fair opportunity for making his way.

"Now, go upstairs at once to your mother. I have letters to write, and am too busy for talking."

So saying, with a peremptory wave of his hand he dismissed his nephew.

GEORGE ORWELL

Burmese Days, 1934

George Orwell, the pen name of Eric Arthur Blair (1903–1950), is best known for such novels as *Animal Farm* (1945) and *Nineteen Eighty-Four* (1949), from which the term *Orwellian* has come to define totalitarianism. *Burmese Days* (1934) was Orwell's first novel, based on his experience in the British police in Burma from 1922 to 1927.

This selection from the novel captures the life of the British colonial class in a remote "upcountry" town in Burma in the 1920s, a hundred years after British conquest and settlement had begun and fifty years after all of Burma had been integrated into the British Indian empire.

The central character is Flory, the only Englishman at all sympathetic to the Burmese. Though he has befriended the Indian physician, Dr. Veraswami, Flory is too weak to propose him as the first "native" member of the club. The other main characters are Westfield, district superintendent of police; Ellis, local company manager and the most racist of the group; Lackersteen, local manager of a timber company who is usually drunk; Maxwell, a forest officer; and Macgregor, deputy commissioner and secretary of the club.

Why does the club loom so large in the lives of these Englishmen? If they complain so much, why are they in Burma? How do you account for the virulent racism of these men? Why does Ellis "correct" the butler's English? What does this story suggest about women in the colonial world?

THINKING HISTORICALLY

Orwell knew Burma quite well. He was born in India in 1903, and his father worked in the Opium Department of the Indian Civil Service. After attending school at Eton in England, Orwell spent five years as a member of the Indian Imperial Police in Burma. Orwell's mother had grown up in Burma, and his grandmother continued to live there in the 1920s. In his various postings, Orwell no doubt spent time in British social clubs like the one that serves as the setting for this chapter. Orwell, therefore, had a broad knowledge of Burma on which to base his story. Is there any way to determine what Orwell invented and what he merely described in this account?

Orwell was politically engaged throughout his life. Would political ideas make him better or worse as a historian or novelist? How so?

Source: George Orwell, *Burmese Days* (1934; reprint, San Diego: Harcourt Brace, 1962), 17–27.

Flory's house was at the top of the maidan,[1] close to the edge of the jungle. From the gate the maidan sloped sharply down, scorched and khaki-coloured, with half a dozen dazzling white bungalows scattered round it. All quaked, shivered in the hot air. There was an English cemetery within a white wall half-way down the hill, and nearby a tiny tin-roofed church. Beyond that was the European Club, and when one looked at the Club—a dumpy one-storey wooden building—one looked at the real centre of the town. In any town in India the European Club is the spiritual citadel, the real seat of the British power, the Nirvana for which native officials and millionaires pine in vain. It was doubly so in this case, for it was the proud boast of Kyauktada Club that, almost alone of Clubs in Burma, it had never admitted an Oriental[2] to membership. Beyond the Club, the Irrawaddy flowed huge and ochreous, glittering like diamonds in the patches that caught the sun; and beyond the river stretched great wastes of paddy fields, ending at the horizon in a range of blackish hills.

The native town, and the courts and the jail, were over to the right, mostly hidden in green groves of peepul trees. The spire of the pagoda rose from the trees like a slender spear tipped with gold. Kyauktada[3] was a fairly typical Upper Burma town, that had not changed greatly between the days of Marco Polo and 1910, and might have slept in the Middle Ages for a century more if it had not proved a convenient spot for a railway terminus. In 1910 the Government[4] made it the headquarters of a district and a seat of Progress—interpretable as a block of law courts, with their army of fat but ravenous pleaders, a hospital, a school, and one of those huge, durable jails which the English have built everywhere between Gibraltar and Hong Kong. The population was about four thousand, including a couple of hundred Indians, a few score Chinese and seven Europeans. There were also two Eurasians named Mr. Francis and Mr. Samuel, the sons of an American Baptist missionary and a Roman Catholic missionary respectively. The town contained no curiosities of any kind, except an Indian fakir[5] who had lived for twenty years in a tree near the bazaar, drawing his food up in a basket every morning.

[1] Parade-ground. [Ed.]

[2] The term *Oriental* included all Asians or people of the "East" as opposed to Occidentals or Westerners, as in Rudyard Kipling's *Barrack-room Ballads*: "East is East and West is West, and never the twain [two] shall meet" (1892). But in this case, Orwell means Indians and Burmese as well as the few Chinese. [Ed.]

[3] Fictional name for Katha or Kathar, a town on the Irrawaddy (or Ayeyarwady) River and the railroad, in northern Burma, where Orwell lived from 1926 to 1927. [Ed.]

[4] The British government eliminated the Burmese monarchy, exiling the king to India, and abolished the traditional role of the Buddhist monks, imposing instead the kind of bureaucracy they used to rule India. [Ed.]

[5] Originally a term for a Muslim Sufi mystic, here used to mean any ascetic, Hindu or Muslim, or even a beggar. [Ed.]

Flory yawned as he came out of the gate. He had been half drunk the night before, and the glare made him feel liverish. "Bloody, bloody hole!" he thought, looking down the hill. And, no one except the dog being near, he began to sing aloud, "Bloody, bloody, bloody, oh, how thou art bloody" to the tune of "Holy, holy, holy, oh how Thou art holy," as he walked down the hot red road, switching at the dried-up grasses with his stick. It was nearly nine o'clock and the sun was fiercer every minute. The heat throbbed down on one's head with a steady, rhythmic thumping, like blows from an enormous bolster. Flory stopped at the Club gate, wondering whether to go in or to go farther down the road and see Dr. Veraswami. Then he remembered that it was "English mail day" and the newspapers would have arrived. He went in, past the big tennis screen, which was overgrown by a creeper with starlike mauve flowers.

In the borders beside the path swathes of English flowers, phlox and larkspur, hollyhock and petunia, not yet slain by the sun, rioted in vast size and richness. The petunias were huge, like trees almost. There was no lawn, but instead a shrubbery of native trees and bushes—gold mohur trees like vast umbrellas of blood-red bloom, frangipanis with creamy, stalkless flowers, purple bougainvillea, scarlet hibiscus, and the pink, Chinese rose, bilious-green crotons, feathery fronds of tamarind. The clash of colours hurt one's eyes in the glare. A nearly naked *mali*,[6] watering-can in hand, was moving in the jungle of flowers like some large nectar-sucking bird.

On the Club steps a sandy-haired Englishman, with a prickly moustache, pale grey eyes too far apart, and abnormally thin calves to his legs, was standing with his hands in the pockets of his shorts. This was Mr. Westfield, the District Superintendent of Police. With a very bored air he was rocking himself backwards and forwards on his heels and pouting his upper lip so that his moustache tickled his nose. He greeted Flory with a slight sideways movement of his head. His way of speaking was clipped and soldierly, missing out every word that well could be missed out. Nearly everything he said was intended for a joke, but the tone of his voice was hollow and melancholy.

"Hullo, Flory me lad. Bloody awful morning, what?"

"We must expect it at this time of year, I suppose," Flory said. He had turned himself a little sideways, so that his birthmarked cheek was away from Westfield.

"Yes, dammit. Couple of months of this coming. Last year we didn't have a spot of rain till June. Look at that bloody sky, not a cloud in it. Like one of those damned great blue enamel saucepans. God! What'd you give to be in Piccadilly now, eh?"

"Have the English papers come?"

---

[6] Gardener. [Ed.]

"Yes. Dear old *Punch, Pink'un,* and *Vie Parisienne.* Makes you homesick to read 'em, what? Let's come in and have a drink before the ice all goes. Old Lackersteen's been fairly bathing in it. Half pickled already."

They went in, Westfield remarking in his gloomy voice, "Lead on, Macduff." Inside, the Club was a teak-walled place smelling of earthoil, and consisting of only four rooms, one of which contained a forlorn "library" of five hundred mildewed novels, and another an old and mangy billiard-table—this, however, seldom used, for during most of the year hordes of flying beetles came buzzing round the lamps and littered themselves over the cloth. There were also a card-room and a "lounge" which looked towards the river, over a wide veranda; but at this time of day all the verandas were curtained with green bamboo chicks. The lounge was an unhomelike room, with coco-nut matting on the floor, and wicker chairs and tables which were littered with shiny illustrated papers. For ornament there were a number of "Bonzo" pictures,[7] and the dusty skulls of sambhur.[8] A punkah,[9] lazily flapping, shook dust into the tepid air.

There were three men in the room. Under the punkah a florid, fine-looking, slightly bloated man of forty was sprawling across the table with his head in his hands, groaning in pain. This was Mr. Lackersteen, the local manager of a timber firm. He had been badly drunk the night before, and he was suffering for it. Ellis, local manager of yet another company, was standing before the notice board studying some notice with a look of bitter concentration. He was a tiny wiry-haired fellow with a pale, sharp-featured face and restless movements. Maxwell, the acting Divisional Forest Officer, was lying in one of the long chairs reading the *Field,* and invisible except for two large-boned legs and thick downy forearms.

"Look at this naughty old man," said Westfield, taking Mr. Lackersteen half affectionately by the shoulders and shaking him. "Example to the young, what? There, but for the grace of God and all that. Gives you an idea what you'll be like at forty."

Mr. Lackersteen gave a groan which sounded like "brandy."

"Poor old chap," said Westfield; "regular martyr to booze, eh? Look at it oozing out of his pores. Reminds me of the old colonel who used to sleep without a mosquito net. They asked his servant why and the servant said: 'At night, master too drunk to notice mosquitoes; in the morning, mosquitoes too drunk to notice master.' Look at him—boozed last night and then asking for more. Got a little niece coming to stay with him, too. Due tonight, isn't she, Lackersteen?"

---

[7] Bulldog puppy cartoons created by G. E. Studdy in the 1920s for magazines like *Punch*. [Ed.]

[8] Large South Asian deer, like elk. [Ed.]

[9] Large cloth panel fan hanging from the ceiling, usually pulled by a rope to move the air. [Ed.]

"Oh, leave that drunken sot alone," said Ellis without turning round. He had a spiteful cockney voice. Mr. Lackersteen groaned again, "—the niece! Get me some brandy, for Christ's sake."

"Good education for the niece, eh? Seeing uncle under the table seven times a week.—Hey, butler! Bringing brandy for Lackersteen master!"

The butler, a dark, stout Dravidian[10] with liquid, yellow-irised eyes like those of a dog, brought the brandy on a brass tray. Flory and West-field ordered gin. Mr. Lackersteen swallowed a few spoonfuls of brandy and sat back in his chair, groaning in a more resigned way. He had a beefy, ingenuous face, with a toothbrush moustache. He was really a very simple-minded man, with no ambitions beyond having what he called "a good time." His wife governed him by the only possible method, namely, by never letting him out of her sight for more than an hour or two. Only once, a year after they were married, she had left him for a fortnight, and had returned unexpectedly a day before her time, to find Mr. Lackersteen, drunk, supported on either side by a naked Burmese girl, while a third up-ended a whisky bottle into his mouth. Since then she had watched him, as he used to complain, "like a cat over a bloody mousehole." However, he managed to enjoy quite a number of "good times," though they were usually rather hurried ones.

"My Christ, what a head I've got on me this morning," he said. "Call that butler again, Westfield. I've got to have another brandy before my missus gets here. She says she's going to cut my booze down to four pegs a day when our niece gets here. God rot them both!" he added gloomily.

"Stop playing the fool, all of you, and listen to this," said Ellis sourly. He had a queer wounding way of speaking, hardly ever opening his mouth without insulting somebody. He deliberately exaggerated his cockney accent, because of the sardonic tone it gave to his words. "Have you seen this notice of old Macgregor's? A little nosegay for everyone. Maxwell, wake up and listen!"

Maxwell lowered the *Field*. He was a fresh-coloured blond youth of not more than twenty-five or six—very young for the post he held. With his heavy limbs and thick white eyelashes he reminded one of a carthorse colt. Ellis nipped the notice from the board with a neat, spiteful little movement and began reading it aloud. It had been posted by Mr. Mac-gregor, who, besides being Deputy Commissioner, was secretary of the Club.

"Just listen to this. 'It has been suggested that as there are as yet no Oriental members of this club, and as it is now usual to admit officials of gazetted rank, whether native or European, to membership of most European Clubs, we should consider the question of following this prac-tice in Kyauktada. The matter will be open for discussion at the next

---

[10] Dated racial term used to refer to darker-skinned inhabitants of southern India. [Ed.]

general meeting. On the one hand it may be pointed out'—oh, well, no need to wade through the rest of it. He can't even write out a notice without an attack of literary diarrhoea. Anyway, the point's this. He's asking us to break all our rules and take a dear little nigger-boy into this Club. *Dear* Dr. Veraswami, for instance. Dr. Very-slimy, I call him. That *would* be a treat, wouldn't it? Little pot-bellied niggers breathing garlic in your face over the bridge-table. Christ, to think of it! We've got to hang together and put our foot down on this at once. What do you say, Westfield? Flory?"

Westfield shrugged his thin shoulders philosophically. He had sat down at the table and lighted a black, stinking Burma cheroot.

"Got to put up with it, I suppose," he said. "B_____s of natives are getting into all the Clubs nowadays. Even the Pegu Club, I'm told. Way this country's going, you know. We're about the last Club in Burma to hold out against 'em."

"We are; and what's more, we're damn well going to go on holding out. I'll die in the ditch before I'll see a nigger in here." Ellis had produced a stump of pencil. With the curious air of spite that some men can put into their tiniest action, he re-pinned the notice on the board and pencilled a tiny, neat "B. F." against Mr. Macgregor's signature—"There, that's what I think of his idea. I'll tell him so when he comes down. What do *you* say, Flory?"

Flory had not spoken all this time. Though by nature anything but a silent man, he seldom found much to say in Club conversations. He had sat down at the table and was reading G. K. Chesterton's article in the *London News*, at the same time caressing [his dog] Flo's head with his left hand. Ellis, however, was one of those people who constantly nag others to echo their own opinions. He repeated his question, and Flory looked up, and their eyes met. The skin round Ellis's nose suddenly turned so pale that it was almost grey. In him it was a sign of anger. Without any prelude he burst into a stream of abuse that would have been startling, if the others had not been used to hearing something like it every morning.

"My God, I should have thought in a case like this, when it's a question of keeping those black, stinking swine out of the only place where we can enjoy ourselves, you'd have the decency to back me up. Even if that pot-bellied, greasy little sod of a nigger doctor *is* your best pal. *I* don't care if you choose to pal up with the scum of the bazaar. If it pleases you to go to Veraswami's house and drink whisky with all his nigger pals, that's your look-out. Do what you like outside the Club. But, by God, it's a different matter when you talk of bringing niggers in here. I suppose you'd like little Veraswami for a Club member, eh? Chipping into our conversation and pawing everyone with his sweaty hands and breathing his filthy garlic breath in our faces. By God, he'd go out with my boot behind him if ever I saw his black snout inside that door. Greasy, pot-bellied little———!" etc.

This went on for several minutes. It was curiously impressive, because it was so completely sincere. Ellis really did hate Orientals—hated them with a bitter, restless loathing as of something evil or unclean. Living and working, as the assistant of a timber firm must, in perpetual contact with the Burmese, he had never grown used to the sight of a black face. Any hint of friendly feeling towards an Oriental seemed to him a horrible perversity. He was an intelligent man and an able servant of his firm, but he was one of those Englishmen—common, unfortunately—who should never be allowed to set foot in the East.

Flory sat nursing Flo's head in his lap, unable to meet Ellis's eyes. At the best of times his birthmark made it difficult for him to look people straight in the face. And when he made ready to speak, he could feel his voice trembling—for it had a way of trembling when it should have been firm; his features, too, sometimes twitched uncontrollably.

"Steady on," he said at last, sullenly and rather feebly. "Steady on. There's no need to get so excited. *I* never suggested having any native members in here."

"Oh, didn't you? We all know bloody well you'd like to, though. Why else do you go to that oily little babu's house every morning, then? Sitting down at table with him as though he was a white man, and drinking out of glasses his filthy black lips have slobbered over—it makes me spew to think of it."

"Sit down, old chap, sit down," Westfield said. "Forget it. Have a drink on it. Not worth while quarrelling. Too hot."

"My God," said Ellis a little more calmly, taking a pace or two up and down, "my God, I don't understand you chaps. I simply don't. Here's that old fool Macgregor wanting to bring a nigger into this Club for no reason whatever, and you all sit down under it without a word. Good God, what are we supposed to be doing in this country? If we aren't going to rule, why the devil don't we clear out? Here we are, supposed to be governing a set of damn black swine who've been slaves since the beginning of history, and instead of ruling them in the only way they understand, we go and treat them as equals. And all you silly b———s take it for granted. There's Flory, makes his best pal of a black babu who calls himself a doctor because he's done two years at an Indian so-called university. And you, Westfield, proud as Punch of your knock-kneed, bribe-taking cowards of policemen. And there's Maxwell, spends his time running after Eurasian tarts. Yes, you do, Maxwell; I heard about your goings-on in Mandalay with some smelly little bitch called Molly Pereira. I supposed you'd have gone and married her if they hadn't transferred you up here? You all seem to *like* the dirty black brutes. Christ, I don't know what's come over us all. I really don't."

"Come on, have another drink," said Westfield. "Hey, butler! Spot of beer before the ice goes, eh? Beer, butler!"

The butler brought some bottles of Munich beer. Ellis presently sat down at the table with the others, and he nursed one of the cool bottles between his small hands. His forehead was sweating. He was sulky, but not in a rage any longer. At all times he was spiteful and perverse, but his violent fits of rage were soon over, and were never apologised for. Quarrels were a regular part of the routine of Club life. Mr. Lackersteen was feeling better and was studying the illustrations in *La Vie Parisienne*. It was after nine now, and the room, scented with the acrid smoke of Westfield's cheroot, was stifling hot. Everyone's shirt stuck to his back with the first sweat of the day. The invisible *chokra*[11] who pulled the punkah rope outside was falling asleep in the glare.

"Butler!" yelled Ellis, and as the butler appeared, "go and wake that bloody *chokra* up!"

"Yes, master."

"And butler!"

"Yes, master?"

"How much ice have we got left?"

"'Bout twenty pounds, master. Will only last to-day, I think. I find it very difficult to keep ice cool now."

"Don't talk like that, damn you—'I find it very difficult!' Have you swallowed a dictionary? 'Please, master, can't keeping ice cool'—that's how you ought to talk. We shall have to sack this fellow if he gets to talk English too well. I can't stick servants who talk English. D'you hear, butler?"

"Yes, master," said the butler, and retired.

"God! No ice till Monday," Westfield said. "You going back to the jungle, Flory?"

"Yes. I ought to be there now. I only came in because of the English mail."

"Go on tour myself, I think. Knock up a spot of Travelling Allowance. I can't stick my bloody office at this time of year. Sitting there under the damned punkah, signing one chit after another. Paperchewing. God, how I wish the war was on again!"

"I'm going out the day after to-morrow," Ellis said. "Isn't that damned padre coming to hold his service this Sunday? I'll take care not to be in for that, anyway. Bloody knee-drill."

"Next Sunday," said Westfield. "Promised to be in for it myself. So's Macgregor. Bit hard on the poor devil of a padre, I must say. Only gets here once in six weeks. Might as well get up a congregation when he does come."

"Oh, hell! I'd snivel psalms to oblige the padre, but I can't stick the way these damned native Christians come shoving into our church. A

---

[11] Person who pulls the punkah rope that moves a large panel to let in a breeze. [Ed.]

pack of Madrassi servants and Karen[12] school-teachers. And then those two yellow-bellies, Francis and Samuel—they call themselves Christians too. Last time the padre was here they had the nerve to come up and sit on the front pews with the white men. Someone ought to speak to the padre about that. What bloody fools we were ever to let those missionaries loose in this country! Teaching bazaar sweepers they're as good as we are. 'Please, sir, me Christian same like master.' Damned cheek."

[12] An ethnic minority group in Burma. [Ed.]

3

JOSEPH CONRAD

Heart of Darkness, 1899

Although his native tongue was Polish (and French his second language), Joseph Conrad (1857–1924) became one of the leading English novelists of the era of British imperialism. Drawing on his experience as a mariner and ship captain, he secured a post as an officer on river steamboats on the Congo River in 1890. Nine years later he published *Heart of Darkness*, a novel that has introduced generations since to Africa, the Congo, the era of colonialism, and European ideas of "the other."

In this selection from the novel, Conrad's narrator, Marlow, tells of his voyage up the Congo to meet the enigmatic European Kurtz, who has secured prodigious amounts of ivory for his Belgian employer but (we learn at the end of the novel) has lost his mind in the process.

What impression does *Heart of Darkness* give of Africa and Africans? What does it suggest were the motives or intentions of European explorers and traders in Africa? What feeling does this selection convey about European colonization of Africa?

THINKING HISTORICALLY

Like many novels, *Heart of Darkness* is based on the actual experiences of the author. Despite the basis in fact, however, it is very different from historical writing. Imagine Conrad writing a history of the events described in this selection. How would it be different? Would one account be truer, or merely reveal different truths?

Source: Joseph Conrad, *Heart of Darkness*, A Norton Critical Edition (New York: Norton, 1988), 35–39. Originally published by *Blackwood's Magazine* (London, 1899, 1902).

Going up that river was like travelling back to the earliest beginnings of the world, when vegetation rioted on the earth and the big trees were kings. An empty stream, a great silence, an impenetrable forest. The air was warm, thick, heavy, sluggish. There was no joy in the brilliance of sunshine. The long stretches of the waterway ran on, deserted, into the gloom of overshadowed distances. On silvery sandbanks hippos and alligators sunned themselves side by side. The broadening waters flowed through a mob of wooded islands. You lost your way on that river as you would in a desert and butted all day long against shoals trying to find the channel till you thought yourself bewitched and cut off for ever from everything you had known once—somewhere—far away—in another existence perhaps. There were moments when one's past came back to one, as it will sometimes when you have not a moment to spare to yourself; but it came in the shape of an unrestful and noisy dream remembered with wonder amongst the overwhelming realities of this strange world of plants and water and silence. And this stillness of life did not in the least resemble a peace. It was the stillness of an implacable force brooding over an inscrutable intention. It looked at you with a vengeful aspect. I got used to it afterwards. I did not see it any more. I had no time. I had to keep guessing at the channel; I had to discern, mostly by inspiration, the signs of hidden banks; I watched for sunken stones; I was learning to clap my teeth smartly before my heart flew out when I shaved by a fluke some infernal sly old snag that would have ripped the life out of the tin-pot steamboat and drowned all the pilgrims; I had to keep a look-out for the signs of dead wood we could cut up in the night for next day's steaming. When you have to attend to things of that sort, to the mere incidents of the surface, the reality—the reality I tell you—fades. The inner truth is hidden—luckily, luckily. But I felt it all the same; I felt often its mysterious stillness watching me at my monkey tricks. . . .

I managed not to sink that steamboat on my first trip. It's a wonder to me yet. Imagine a blindfolded man set to drive a van over a bad road. I sweated and shivered over that business considerably, I can tell you. After all, for a seaman, to scrape the bottom of the thing that's supposed to float all the time under his care is the unpardonable sin. No one may know of it, but you never forget the thump—eh? A blow on the very heart. You remember it, you dream of it, you wake up at night and think of it—years after—and go hot and cold all over. I don't pretend to say that steamboat floated all the time. More than once she had to wade for a bit, with twenty cannibals splashing around and pushing. We had enlisted some of these chaps on the way for a crew. Fine fellows—cannibals—in their place. They were men one could work with, and I am grateful to them. And, after all, they did not eat each other before my face: they had brought along a provision of hippo-meat which went rotten and made the mystery of the wilderness stink in my nostrils. Phoo! I can sniff it now. I had the Manager on board and three or four pilgrims with their staves—all complete. Sometimes we came upon a station close by the bank clinging to the skirts of the unknown, and the white men rushing out of a tumbledown hovel with great gestures of joy and surprise and welcome seemed very strange, had the appearance of being held there captive by a spell. The word "ivory" would ring in the air for a while—and on we went again into the silence, along empty reaches, round the still bends, between the high walls of our winding way, reverberating in hollow claps the ponderous beat of the stern-wheel. Trees, trees, millions of trees, massive, immense, running up high, and at their foot, hugging the bank against the stream, crept the little begrimed steamboat like a sluggish beetle crawling on the floor of a lofty portico. It made you feel very small, very lost, and yet it was not altogether depressing, that feeling. After all, if you were small, the grimy beetle crawled on—which was just what you wanted it to do. Where the pilgrims imagined it crawled to I don't know. To some place where they expected to get something, I bet! For me it crawled towards Kurtz—exclusively; but when the steam-pipes started leaking we crawled very slow. The reaches opened before us and closed behind, as if the forest had stepped leisurely across the water to bar the way for our return. We penetrated deeper and deeper into the heart of darkness. It was very quiet there. At night sometimes the roll of drums behind the curtain of trees would run up the river and remain sustained faintly, as if hovering in the air high over our heads till the first break of day. Whether it meant war, peace, or prayer we could not tell. The dawns were heralded by the descent of a chill stillness. The woodcutters slept, their fires burned low, the snapping of a twig would make you start. We were wanderers on a prehistoric earth, on an earth that wore the aspect of an unknown planet. We could have fancied ourselves the first of men taking possession of an accursed inheritance, to be subdued at the cost of profound anguish and of excessive toil. But suddenly as we struggled round a bend there would be a glimpse of rush walls, of peaked grass-roofs, a burst of yells, a whirl of black limbs, a mass of hands clapping, of feet stamping, of bodies swaying, of eyes rolling under the droop of heavy and motionless foliage. The steamer toiled along slowly on the edge of a black and incomprehensible frenzy. The prehistoric man was cursing us, praying to us, welcoming us—who could tell? We were cut off from the comprehension of our surroundings; we glided past like phantoms, wondering and secretly appalled, as sane men would be before an enthusiastic outbreak in a madhouse. We could not understand because we were too far and could not remember because we were travelling in the night of first ages, of those ages that are gone, leaving hardly a sign—and no memories.

The earth seemed unearthly. We are accustomed to look upon the shackled form of a conquered monster, but there—there you could look at a thing monstrous and free. It was unearthly and the men were. . . . No they were not inhuman. Well, you know that was the worst of it—this suspicion of their not being inhuman. It would come slowly to one. They howled and leaped and spun and made horrid faces, but what thrilled you was just the thought of their humanity—like yours—the thought of your remote kinship with this wild and passionate uproar. Ugly. Yes, it was ugly enough, but if you were man enough you would admit to yourself that there was in you just the faintest trace of a response to the terrible frankness of that noise, a dim suspicion of there being a meaning in it which you—you so remote from the night of first ages—could comprehend. And why not? The mind of man is capable of anything—because everything is in it, all the past as well as all the future. What was there after all? Joy, fear, sorrow, devotion, valour, rage—who can tell?—but truth—truth stripped of its cloak of time. Let the fool gape and shudder—the man knows and can look on without a wink. But he must at least be as much of a man as these on the shore. He must meet that truth with his own true stuff—with his own inborn strength. Principles? Principles won't do. Acquisitions, clothes, pretty rags—rags that would fly off at the first good shake. No. You want a deliberate belief. An appeal to me in this fiendish row—is there? Very well. I hear, I admit, but I have a voice too, and for good or evil mine is the speech that cannot be silenced. Of course, a fool, what with sheer fright and fine sentiments, is always safe. Who's that grunting? You wonder I didn't go ashore for a howl and a dance? Well, no—I didn't. Fine sentiments, you say? Fine sentiments be hanged! I had no time. I had to mess about with whitelead and strips of woollen blanket helping to put bandages on those leaky steam-pipes—tell you. I had to watch the steering and circumvent those snags and get the tin-pot along by hook or by crook. There was surface-truth enough in these things to save a wiser man. And between whiles I had to look after the savage who was fireman. He was an improved specimen; he could fire up a vertical boiler. He was there below me and, upon my word, to look at him was as edifying as seeing a dog in a parody of breeches and a feather hat walking on his hind legs. A few months of training had done for that really fine chap. He squinted at the steam-gauge and at the water-gauge with an evident effort of intrepidity—and he had filed teeth too, the poor devil, and the wool of his pate shaved into queer patterns, and three ornamental scars on each of his cheeks. He ought to have been clapping his hands and stamping his feet on the bank, instead of which he was hard at work, a thrall to strange witchcraft, full of improving knowledge. He was useful because he had been instructed; and what he knew was this—that should the water in that transparent thing disappear the evil spirit inside the boiler would get angry through the greatness of his thirst and take a terrible vengeance. So he sweated and fired up and watched the glass fearfully (with an impromptu charm, made of rags, tied to his arm and a piece of polished bone as big as a watch stuck flatways through his lower lip) while the wooded banks slipped past us slowly, the shore noise was left behind, the interminable miles of silence—and we crept on, towards Kurtz.

4

FRANCIS BEBEY

King Albert, 1981

Francis Bebey (1929–2001) was an African writer, artist, and musician from Cameroon. In this novel, he carries the reader to a village called Effidi in the twilight of European imperialism after World War II but before the late 1950s and early 1960s, when Cameroon and other former colonies became independent states. In this brief selection from the novel, the young Bikounou, whom everyone calls Vespasian because he rides a Vespa Motor Scooter, has returned to Effidi to speak with Chief Ndengué. What is his message? What do his message and his manner of delivery tell you about the chief, the village, and the larger world of which it is a part at this time?

THINKING HISTORICALLY

The dialogue between Bikounou and the chief tells a story about how parts of Africa changed in the period leading up to independence. What are these changes? Where and how did they occur? In a few paragraphs, write a brief history that summarizes these changes. How is your history different from the section in the novel?

The next day, a Sunday, Bikounou went to see Chief Ndengué while the other villagers were at Mass.

"I have come to thank you for the welcome which you permitted the people of Effidi to extend to us, myself and my friend Féfé."

"My son, I permitted nothing. The village spoke for itself. As you could see yourself, nobody bears you any grudge. On the contrary,

Source: Francis Bebey, *King Albert*, trans. Joyce A. Hutchinson (Westport, CT: Lawrence Hill & Co., 1981), 109–18.

everybody is very fond of you. But, as a matter of interest, where is your friend Féfé?"

"I wanted to see you alone, Chief Ndengué, to talk to you while the others are not around."

"And what is so important that you need this secrecy?" . . .

"The whites are going to ask us to choose a person to represent us."

"A person to represent us? But, my son, why do we have to choose someone to represent us? . . .

"I am saying, Chief Ndengué, that you will remain at the head of our community until the day when you are no longer with us. So it's not a question of choosing someone to replace you among us."

"Then what is it about?"

"I will explain. You know that our country is governed by the whites?"

"I know, I know. But what have they done now, these whites?"

"Nothing, except that they now realize the need to let us govern our country ourselves."

"What? What country are you talking about, my son?"

"This one, where we live, the country which takes in Effidi, Zaabat, Nkool, Palmtree Village, and even Ngala, as well as other towns."

"My son, what you have just told me is perhaps important, but you can't make me believe that Effidi, Nkool, Zaabat, Palmtree Village, and even Ngala are part of one and the same country and that they will let themselves be governed by one man, one single great Chief! For if you tell me that I shall remain at the head of the community of Effidi, then another chief will be needed to be responsible for governing the whole country, isn't that so?"

"Chief Ndengué, for a long time the whites have occupied our country and governed it in their own way. We, the educated men, have told them that we've had enough and that we wish to govern ourselves, since we are now capable of doing so."

"And the whites agreed?"

"Yes, they have agreed. . . . yes. . . . that is to say that—"

"My son, tell me the exact truth."

"That is to say that they don't believe we are capable of governing ourselves all alone."

"That is exactly what I think, too."

"But, Chief Ndengué, don't take their side! They think we can't govern ourselves alone, but *we* want to prove the opposite. We want to show them that we can live without them and govern ourselves." . . .

"Bikounou, you're mixing everything up—the country, the whites, ourselves, elections. How do you expect me to understand anything in all that?"

"Let me explain it to you, Chief Ndengué. The whites have a way of governing a country which is different from ours. With us, there is a

Chief—that's to say, somebody like you—to govern the whole community. But *they* put several people at the head of the country. . . . It is this new way of governing the country that the whites wish to teach us, and that is why there is going to be an election." . . .

"Now, it's becoming clearer," he added. "If I understand correctly, each community like ours will have to choose someone to represent it—"

"In an assembly which will therefore represent the whole country," Bikounou continued.

"Yes, yes, I see."

He thought for a few more moments, then suggested:

"Naturally, if Effidi is asked to choose, I don't see who our brothers will elect to represent them other than myself, do you?" . . .

"That is how things will turn out, isn't it?"

"Chief, when you talk about elections, you must not say in advance which man or woman is going to win."

"Which man or woman? What do you mean? Are the women also invited to stand for election? And to represent whom? The men?"

"Chief Ndengué, you must not get carried away. There may well not be a woman presumptuous enough to stand as a candidate in the election. But in the new system that the whites wish to teach us, the women have the right to stand, just like the men."

"What, what are you saying? Is that the kind of thing they wish to introduce here, and for what purpose?"

"Chief Ndengué, times change. Even in this village, which lives in closer proximity to the town than others on account of the road passing through it, people are not sufficiently informed about the evolution of the country."

"Our country is here!" Chief Ndengué shouted. "If you young people and those others educated by the whites wish to sell it, that's different. But, my son, I warn you that there are still enough people at Effidi to oppose such an idea should it ever cross your mind one day. The evolution of the country . . . the evolution of what country? Do you think you know better than old Ndengué what is our country and what it means?"

"Chief Ndengué," said Bikounou, trying to appease him, "you are right. Our country exists inasmuch as you exist as our Chief. All that is built on the tradition of our ancestors."

"Then why have you come back to the village to tell me what other people want, people who have nothing to do with what our ancestors wished this country to be? Why do you all obey these foreigners?" . . .

Bikounou wondered what answer he could possibly give to all that. He had come with the firm intention of being submissive, and you, too, must have noticed how diplomatic he was being in order not to shock Chief Ndengué. That is understandable, for it must be realized that, however innocent he might seem, on this Sunday morning when the other inhabitants of Effidi had gone to sing Mass in Latin—too bad for Father Bonsot if he hears about it—the Vespasian had the difficult job of explaining to the old chief that his period of glory and prestige based on tradition was over, and worse still, that new leaders would take his place, chosen with no reference to the law of bygone days. The young man knew what this would mean for this old man accustomed to considering as his personal property what some people would pompously call "power." He therefore decided to introduce into the conversation as much subtlety as was desirable or indeed necessary to lead Chief Ndengué gradually to accept the very principle of an election during which the people of Effidi would be free to choose him or to elect some other candidate.

"If I mentioned an allowance, Chief Ndengué, you must forgive me. You know the village people are not always aware what an unpleasant task the Administration expects you to carry out, and we have all come more or less to believe that you are paid for doing it. I confess that I personally should know something about it, since I work in a government office. In any case, I was joking when I said that, but I'm already at fault for joking with my elder. You must forgive me, Chief Ndengué. I came to see you as an obedient son comes to see his father and not to presume to make you angry."

"Now you're talking sense, my son. So, you inform me there is going to be an election. But tell me, if *I* am not elected, then who will be?"

"I have no idea, Chief Ndengué. What matters now is to know who else at Effidi might intend to stand at this election when you consider all the qualities and the knowledge a person needs to have to represent our community successfully."

"What do you mean?"

"Well, how can I explain it? It must first be understood that the elected representative will have to go to Ngala."

"Each village will have to send someone to Ngala?"

"That is where all the representatives will meet to discuss the measures to be taken concerning the country."

"Then I shall have to go to Ngala?"

"If you are elected by our community, yes."

"That's true. It's true that the community, according to your system, could very well decide that it didn't want me to represent them at Ngala. In any case, I must tell you from the start that, if things really turn out as you have just explained, I am not interested in your story of an election. I have no intention of going to sit at the side of the road every morning and wait for a truck to be kind enough to stop and take me to the town."

Bikounou gave an almost imperceptible sigh of relief. But Chief Ndengué was a crafty old man, who missed no detail of the attitude of those speaking with him. He noticed the suppressed satisfaction of the young man.

"What's the matter? Did I say something unpleasant?"

"No, Chief Ndengué, it's not that. I was in fact wondering whether you realized how difficult it would be for you to make frequent visits to the town if you were elected to represent Effidi."

"I realize it perfectly well. I also realize that in future—if your system works as you have said—it will be someone else who will go to the town to bring back orders to be passed on to the community. Yes, my son, I understand what you were saying just now: times change."

The pathos of these last words was perfectly clear to Bikounou. Nevertheless, he kept his poise, trying to allay the old man's fears:

"Oh, Chief Ndengué, don't take it like that. It's possible that someone else will go to the town to represent our community in the assembly which will meet there, but not to bring back orders, as long as you remain our Chief."

"My son, you are trying to calm me down, but since you began talking to me, I have a feeling that there is to be a change much greater than that suffered by our fathers when the whites arrived."

"There can't be any change more important for our country than when the whites arrived."

"You mean it's a continuation of the same change?"

"Yes and no, Chief Ndengué. Yes, because if the whites had not come, we should perhaps never have felt the need to prove that we are capable of governing ourselves. As a result, there would have been no need to talk of elections. But, on the other hand, we now have to choose from among us people to whom we shall entrust the conduct of our affairs."

"And you believe that, my son? You believe that one day the whites will leave us to manage our own affairs?"

"That is what the younger generation is asking them more and more urgently. They will simply be forced to leave us alone one day."

"Forced? Forced? Who can force them to do anything? These people who manufacture guns and arms who would kill us all if we refused to obey them, who can force them?"

"Chief Ndengué, these people are doubtless very intelligent. They manufacture guns, arms, motor cars, airplanes, the good Lord gives them all they desire. But they overlooked one thing."

"What thing, my son?"

"They overlooked that they shouldn't have taught us to read and write."

"I don't understand what you mean by that."

"You see, by teaching us to read, they gave us the key to their own knowledge, and there we discovered that they spoke of liberty, equality and fraternity."

"So?"

"So they are obliged to give us liberty, equality and fraternity. That's what we're asking for, Chief Ndengué."

"And that is really why there is going to be an election?"

"Actually, this election will not give us liberty, but the assembly which will be established will pave the way for the independence of the whole country."

"My son, I tell you that our country is Effidi!" the Chief growled again.

"You are right, Chief Ndengué, but I tell you that times change. And since times began to change, our country has grown bigger."

"You mean that those savages of Palmtree Village are going to send a representative to the town just like us?"

"They will have the right to do so."

"Like us? With no difference?"

"Like us. But they may be obliged to choose a representative elsewhere than among themselves."

"Why?"

"Well, Chief, because the fact that the elected representative can get to the town fairly often won't be the end of the matter. The representative will also have to be someone educated, someone who understands politics and who—"

"What? What did you say?"

"Politics."

"And poli—, poli—. This thing, what is it?"

"To be exact, it is politics that the representatives will be engaged in when they meet."

"So they won't be speaking?"

"Yes, they will, Chief Ndengué. They will probably speak a great deal. That's what politics is all about. They talk, they talk, they talk. And then they say, good, we will build a road to Nkool, or to Palmtree Village." . . .

"My son," said Chief Ndengué at last, "don't be surprised to hear me laugh like this. The fact is that for some time I had been worrying for no reason and it's only now that I've realized my error."

"I don't understand," the Vespasian confessed.

"I will explain," replied the Chief, reverting to his normal serious manner. "This is why I am laughing. Since you began talking to me about your elections, I had become convinced that you were preparing to see someone else take my place at the head of our community, with the help, obviously, of your friends, the white Administrators. And now I see that I was stupid to imagine that. For if the poli—, poli— Oh, what did you say just now the representatives would do in the town?"

"Politics."

"Yes, that's it. If poli—, poli—. If whatever it is consists of talking and saying you're going to build a road, then it will have no effect on Effidi, seeing that we already have our road. Is that not true, my son?"

The serious tone showed that the man wished to be reassured.

"That is to say—I mean, Chief Ndengué—yes, you are right, partly," the Vespasian replied, in a somewhat embarrassed tone. "But I spoke of building a road just as an example. In fact, politics means doing lots and lots of other things."

"Ah?"

"Yes, yes, and that's why I was telling you that we must elect representatives who understand these things. And as I cannot see in Palmtree Village anybody who can claim to understand them, then I think those people will be obliged to choose a representative from outside their own community."

"How shameful for them!"

"I suppose, in fact, that they will not be very proud when they have to come to Effidi to ask if we can provide somebody to represent them in the assembly in the town."

"And if they come, my son, you who understand these things, tell me: what answer do we give these idiots?"

"I don't yet exactly know how these things will work out. But I think we shall be obliged to represent them because, in any case, there will not be a separate representative from each village."

"This business of yours is complicated, my son. I hope that you at least will be able to understand it, so that we don't make a laughing-stock of ourselves in the eyes of our neighbors. You know that they will seize on the slightest opportunity—"

"I'll take care of it, Chief."

The conversation went on into details until the time when the other villagers returned from Mass. It was the Chief's job to announce the news of the coming election, as it had been given him by Bikounou. He did this solemnly, during an evening meeting. The news was received and commented upon in almost as many ways as there were men present at the meeting, for the people of Effidi, outstandingly intelligent, at least in their own opinion, were keen to show that they had understood what they had just been told, and that they would be perfectly capable of playing the new game which was being wished on them by the town. Naturally, many chests swelled with pride at the idea that, once again, the neighboring villagers would remain in the background of the regional scene, since their sons were unable to compete with those of Effidi.

5

RUDYARD KIPLING

The White Man's Burden, 1899

This poem, written by Rudyard Kipling (1865–1936), is often presented as the epitome of colonialist sentiment, though some readers see in it a critical, satirical attitude toward colonialism. Do you find the poem to be for or against colonialism? Can it be both?

THINKING HISTORICALLY

"The White Man's Burden" is a phrase normally associated with European colonialism in Africa. In fact, however, Kipling wrote the poem in response to the annexation of the Philippines by the United States. How does this historical context change the meaning of the poem for you?

Neither fiction nor fact, a poem conveys emotions. How does this poem help us understand something about the feelings of people like Kipling? How would you describe that feeling?

Take up the White Man's burden—
Send forth the best ye breed—
Go, bind your sons to exile
To serve your captives' need;
To wait, in heavy harness,
On fluttered folk and wild—
Your new-caught sullen peoples,
Half devil and half child.

Take up the White Man's burden—
In patience to abide,
To veil the threat of terror
And check the show of pride;
By open speech and simple,
An hundred times made plain,
To seek another's profit
And work another's gain.

Source: Rudyard Kipling, "The White Man's Burden," *McClure's Magazine* 12, no. 4 (February 1899): 290–91.

Take up the White Man's burden—
The savage wars of peace—
Fill full the mouth of Famine,
And bid the sickness cease;
And when your goal is nearest
(The end for others sought)
Watch sloth and heathen folly
Bring all your hope to nought.

Take up the White Man's burden—
No iron rule of kings,
But toil of serf and sweeper—
The tale of common things.
The ports ye shall not enter,
The roads ye shall not tread,
Go, make them with your living
And mark them with your dead.

Take up the White Man's burden,
And reap his own reward—
The blame of those ye better
The hate of those ye guard—
The cry of hosts ye humour
(Ah, slowly!) toward the light:—
"Why brought ye us from bondage,
Our loved Egyptian night?"

Take up the White Man's burden—
Ye dare not stoop to less—
Nor call too loud on Freedom
To cloke your weariness.
By all ye will or whisper,
By all ye leave or do,
The silent sullen peoples
Shall weigh your God and you.

Take up the White Man's burden!
Have done with childish days—
The lightly-proffered laurel,
The easy ungrudged praise:
Comes now, to search your manhood
Through all the thankless years,
Cold, edged with dear-bought wisdom,
The judgment of your peers.

■ REFLECTIONS

Many of the selections within this chapter as well as its title point to the dual character of colonial society. There are the colonized and the colonizers, the "natives" and the Europeans, and, as racial categories hardened in the second half of the nineteenth century, the blacks and the whites. Colonialism centered on the construction of an accepted inequality. The dominant Europeans invested enormous energy in keeping the double standards, dual pay schedules, and separate rules and residential areas—the two castes.

One problem with maintaining a neat division between the colonized and the colonizers is that the Europeans were massively outnumbered by the indigenous people. Thus, the colonizers needed a vast class of middle-status people to staff the army, police, and bureaucracy. These people might be educated in Paris or London, raised in European culture, and encouraged to develop a sense of pride in their similarity to the Europeans ("me Christian, same like master") and their differences from the other "natives." Often, like the Indian Dr. Veraswami, they were chosen for their ethnic or religious differences from the rest of the colonized population.

In short, colonialism created a whole class of people who were neither fully colonized nor colonizers. They were in between. To the extent that the colonial enterprise was an extension of European social class differences, these in-between people could be British as well as "native." Orwell's Flory is only one of the characters in *Burmese Days* caught between two worlds. One of the most notorious of this class of Europeans "gone native" is the Mr. Kurtz that Conrad's crew will meet upriver. The idea that Africa becomes a setting for the breakup of a European mind might be generalized to apply to the European perception of the colonial experience. It is certainly one of the dominant themes of the European colonial novel. Even the great ones often center on the real or imagined rape, ravishing, or corruption of the European by the seething foreign unknown. This attitude also helps us understand how Kipling could be both anti-imperialist and racist. Imperialism could seem like a thankless act to those who tried to carry civilization to "sullen peoples, half devil and half child."

All the novels and poetry excerpted in this chapter are well worth reading in their entirety, and many other excellent colonial novels can be chosen from this period as well as from the 1930s and 1940s. E. M. Forster's *A Passage to India* and Paul Scott's *The Raj Quartet* stand out as fictional introductions to British colonialism in India. (Both have also received excellent adaptations to film, the latter as the series for television called *The Jewel in the Crown.*) In addition to Francis Bebey, Ferdinand Oyono and Mongo Beti address French colonialism in Cameroon. On

South Africa, the work of Alan Payton, Andre Brink, J. M. Coetzee, Peter Abrams, and James McClure, among many others, stands out.

The advantage of becoming engrossed in a novel is that we feel part of the story and have a sense that we are learning something firsthand. Of course, we are reading a work of fiction, not gaining firsthand experience or reading an accurate historical account of events. A well-made film poses an even greater problem. Its visual and aural impact imparts a psychological reality that becomes part of our experience. If it is about a subject of which we know little, the film quickly becomes our "knowledge" of the subject, and this knowledge may be incomplete or inaccurate.

On the other hand, a well-written novel or film can whet our appetite and inspire us to learn more. Choose and read a novel about colonialism or some other historical subject. Then read a biography of the author or research his or her background to determine how much the author knew about the subject. Next, read a historical account of the subject. How much attention does the historian give to the novelist's subject? How does the novel add depth to the historical account? How does the historical account place the novel in perspective? Finally, how does the author's background place the novel in historical context?

23

Westernization and Nationalism

Japan, India, and the West, 1820–1939

■ HISTORICAL CONTEXT

By the second half of the nineteenth century, the West (meaning Europe and North America) had industrialized, created more representative governments and open societies than the world had known before, and demonstrated the power of its science, technology, and military might by colonizing much of the rest of the world. For those who looked on from outside, the West was a force to be reckoned with.

Some of those observers knew the impact of the West firsthand. The Japanese had experienced Western traders and missionaries since 1543 but had controlled their numbers and influence. The Act of Seclusion in 1636 limited European contact in Japan to a small colony of Dutch traders for the next two hundred years. Not until the appearance of Commodore Perry's steam fleet in 1853 did a new policy toward the West seem necessary.

India had experienced Western colonization and trade since the early 1600s, losing coastal trading cities to various European powers until the English consolidated their hold in the eighteenth century. By 1880 all but a few princely states had come under the rule of the British Indian Empire.

We have then, in these two examples, different degrees of Western influence and penetration. Nevertheless, both of these societies were forced to confront the power of the West. In both cases, the effort to become independent of the West meant considering what might be imitated or borrowed. Broadly speaking, this meant some degree of Westernization.

How did the people of Japan and India answer the challenge of the West? What motivated some to seek to Westernize? What led others to reject Westernization entirely? And what role did nationalism play in the struggle over Westernization?

Nationalism had been a potent force in Europe since the French Revolution, with its national draft army, National Assembly, nationalization of church lands, national flag, national anthem, and celebration of French citizenship. Napoleon's armies inadvertently spread national consciousness among his enemies. Poets and politicians from Vienna to Madrid sought to create and establish the elements of their own national cultures and nation-states. European colonization ignited the same spark of national identity in Asia and Africa. Nationalism was itself a Western movement, but nationalism could be built from any indigenous or traditional culture. Extreme Westernizers might be willing to dispense with traditional ways entirely. Extreme anti-Westernizers could invoke nationalism alone. But most thoughtful subjects of Western influence between the mid-nineteenth and mid-twentieth centuries recognized the need to draw on old strengths while borrowing what worked. How did the authors of these selections face the challenge?

■ THINKING HISTORICALLY

Appreciating Contradictions

The process of Westernization, like the experience of conquest and colonization that often preceded it, was fraught with conflict and led to frequent contradictions. Often, the struggle for national independence meant the borrowing of Western practices and ideologies, both Marxist and liberal. Indeed, the idea of national self-determination was a product of the French and American revolutions, as we have seen. Even the words and languages employed in the debate reflected Western origins, as English or French was often the only common language of educated colonized peoples. Therefore, it is not surprising that contradictory behavior and ambivalent relationships were endemic in the postcolonial world, just as they had been under colonialism. These contradictions usually manifested themselves in an individual's cultural identity. How do colonized persons adopt Western ways, embrace traditional culture, and not feel as though their identity has been divided between the two? Such individuals may not fit entirely into either world and so may be torn between who they were and who they have become. The somewhat anguished experiences of these colonized people are difficult to understand. We typically want to accept one view or another, to praise or to blame. But as we have learned, the history of peoples and nations is rarely that clear. In examining some of the fundamental

contradictions in the history of Westernization, we might better understand how people were variously affected.

The historical thinking skill one learns in reading documents from
people torn between different ideals is the appreciation of contradictions. This operates on a number of levels. We learn that people can
hold two contradictory ideas in their minds at the same time; and, in
consequence, we learn to do it ourselves. This prevents us from jump-
ing to conclusions or oversimplifying the historical process. In addition,
we learn how the struggle over contradictory goals, whether internalized or expressed in group conflict, moves history forward.

1

FUKUZAWA YUKICHI

Good-bye Asia, 1885

Fukuzawa* Yukichi (1835–1901) was one of the most important
Japanese Westernizers during Japan's late-nineteenth-century rush to
catch up with the West. The son of a lower samurai (military) family,
his pursuit of Western knowledge took him to a Dutch school in
Osaka, where he studied everything from the Dutch language to
chemistry, physics, and anatomy, and to Yedo, where he studied English.
Due to his privileged background and Western schooling, he was
naturally included in the first Japanese mission to the United States in
1860 as well as in the first diplomatic mission to Europe in 1862.
After he returned to Japan, he spent many years teaching and writing
the books that would make him famous. The best known of these
was *Seiyo Jijo* (Things Western), which in 1866 introduced Japanese
readers to the daily life and typical institutions of Western society.
According to Fukuzawa Yukichi, the main obstacle that prevented
Japanese society from catching up with the West was a long heritage
of Chinese Confucianism, which stifled educational independence.

In the years after the Meiji Restoration of 1868, in which feudalism
was abolished and power was restored to the emperor, Fukuzawa
Yukichi became the most popular spokesman for the Westernizing
policies of the new government. In this essay, "Good-bye Asia," written

* foo koo ZAH wah

Source: Fukuzawa Yukichi, "Datsu-a Ron" ("On Saying Good-bye to Asia"), in *Japan: A Documentary History*, ed. David J. Lu (Armonk, NY: M. E. Sharpe, 1997), 2:351–53. From Takeuchi Yoshimi, ed., *Azia Shugi (Asianism) Gendai Nihon Shisō Taikei (Great Compilation of Modern Japanese Thought)* (Tokyo: Chikuma Shobō, 1963), 8:38–40.

in 1885, he describes the spread of Western civilization in Japan. Why does he believe that it is both inevitable and desirable? What do you make of his attitude toward Chinese and Korean civilizations?

THINKING HISTORICALLY

Fukuzawa Yukichi is an unapologetic Westernizer. How does his attitude resemble that of a religious convert? Despite his lack of doubt about the advantages of Western ways, however, he does not criticize Japanese culture. He shows how a Westernizer could at the same time be nationalistic. In what ways is his attitude also nationalistic?

Transportation has become so convenient these days that once the wind of Western civilization blows to the East, every blade of grass and every tree in the East follow what the Western wind brings. Ancient Westerners and present-day Westerners are from the same stock and are not much different from one another. The ancient ones moved slowly, but their contemporary counterparts move vivaciously at a fast pace. This is possible because present-day Westerners take advantage of the means of transportation available to them. For those of us who live in the Orient, unless we want to prevent the coming of Western civilization with a firm resolve, it is best that we cast our lot with them. If one observes carefully what is going on in today's world, one knows the futility of trying to prevent the onslaught of Western civilization. Why not float with them in the same ocean of civilization, sail the same waves, and enjoy the fruits and endeavors of civilization?

The movement of a civilization is like the spread of measles. Measles in Tokyo start in Nagasaki and come eastward with the spring thaw. We may hate the spread of this communicable disease, but is there any effective way of preventing it? I can prove that it is not possible. In a communicable disease, people receive only damages. In a civilization, damages may accompany benefits, but benefits always far outweigh them, and their force cannot be stopped. This being the case, there is no point in trying to prevent their spread. A wise man encourages the spread and allows our people to get used to its ways.

The opening to the modern civilization of the West began in the reign of Kaei (1848–58).[1] Our people began to discover its utility and gradually and yet actively moved toward its acceptance. However, there was an old-fashioned and bloated government that stood in the way of

---

[1] Refers to the Kaei era of the emperor Kōmei (r. 1846–1867). The emperor opposed Western influences but was forced to allow Dutch vaccination in 1849, admit Commodore Perry's U.S. fleet in 1853, permit coaling rights to U.S. ships in 1854, and accept the Treaty of Amity and Commerce in 1859. [Ed.]

progress. It was a problem impossible to solve. If the government were allowed to continue, the new civilization could not enter. The modern civilization and Japan's old conventions were mutually exclusive. If we were to discard our old conventions, that government also had to be abolished. We could have prevented the entry of this civilization, but it would have meant loss of our national independence. The struggles taking place in the world civilization were such that they would not allow an Eastern island nation to slumber in isolation. At that point, dedicated men (*shijin*) recognized the principle of "the country is more important than the government," relied on the dignity of the Imperial Household, and toppled the old government to establish a new one.[2] With this, public and the private sectors alike, everyone in our country accepted the modern Western civilization. Not only were we able to cast aside Japan's old conventions, but we also succeeded in creating a new axle toward progress in Asia. Our basic assumptions could be summarized in two words: "Good-bye Asia (*Datsu-a*)."

Japan is located in the eastern extremities of Asia, but the spirit of her people have already moved away from the old conventions of Asia to the Western civilization. Unfortunately for Japan, there are two neighboring countries. One is called China and another Korea. These two peoples, like the Japanese people, have been nurtured by Asiatic political thoughts and mores. It may be that we are different races of people, or it may be due to the differences in our heredity or education; significant differences mark the three peoples. The Chinese and Koreans are more like each other and together they do not show as much similarity to the Japanese. These two peoples do not know how to progress either personally or as a nation. In this day and age with transportation becoming so convenient, they cannot be blind to the manifestations of Western civilization. But they say that what is seen or heard cannot influence the disposition of their minds. Their love affairs with ancient ways and old customs remain as strong as they were centuries ago. In this new and vibrant theater of civilization when we speak of education, they only refer back to Confucianism. As for school education, they can only cite [Chinese philosopher Mencius's] precepts of humanity, righteousness, decorum, and knowledge. While professing their abhorrence to ostentation, in reality they show their ignorance of truth and principles. As for their morality, one only has to observe their unspeakable acts of cruelty and shamelessness. Yet they remain arrogant and show no sign of self-examination.

---

[2] The Meiji Restoration (1868). Meiji was a son of Kōmei (who died of smallpox in 1867). Meiji restored the power of the emperor over the Tokugawa Shogunate, a feudal council that had ruled since 1603. Meiji eagerly sought contacts with the West so that Japan would not fall behind. [Ed.]

In my view, these two countries cannot survive as independent nations with the onslaught of Western civilization to the East.[3] Their concerned citizens might yet find a way to engage in a massive reform, on the scale of our Meiji Restoration, and they could change their governments and bring about a renewal of spirit among their peoples. If that could happen they would indeed be fortunate. However, it is more likely that would never happen, and within a few short years they will be wiped out from the world with their lands divided among the civilized nations. Why is this so? Simply at a time when the spread of civilization and enlightenment (*bummei kaika*) has a force akin to that of measles, China and Korea violate the natural law of its spread. They forcibly try to avoid it by shutting off air from their rooms. Without air, they suffocate to death. It is said that neighbors must extend helping hands to one another because their relations are inseparable. Today's China and Korea have not done a thing for Japan. From the perspectives of civilized Westerners, they may see what is happening in China and Korea and judge Japan accordingly, because of the three countries' geographical proximity. The governments of China and Korea still retain their autocratic manners and do not abide by the rule of law. Westerners may consider Japan likewise a lawless society. Natives of China and Korea are deep in their hocus pocus of nonscientific behavior. Western scholars may think that Japan still remains a country dedicated to the *yin* and *yang* and five elements.[4] Chinese are meanspirited and shameless, and the chivalry of the Japanese people is lost to the Westerners. Koreans punish their convicts in an atrocious manner, and that is imputed to the Japanese as heartless people. There are many more examples I can cite. It is not different from the case of a righteous man living in a neighborhood of a town known for foolishness, lawlessness, atrocity, and heartlessness. His action is so rare that it is always buried under the ugliness of his neighbors' activities. When these incidents are multiplied, that can affect our normal conduct of diplomatic affairs. How unfortunate it is for Japan.

What must we do today? We do not have time to wait for the enlightenment of our neighbors so that we can work together toward the development of Asia. It is better for us to leave the ranks of Asian nations and cast our lot with civilized nations of the West. As for the way of dealing with China and Korea, no special treatment is necessary just because

---

[3] By 1885 China had been "opened" by Western powers in two opium wars (1839–1842, 1856–1860). Korea had been invaded by France (1866) and the United States (1871). Its isolation ended in 1885 by treaty with the United States. [Ed.]

[4] *Yin* and *yang* is a traditional Chinese duality (cold/hot, passive/active, female/male) illustrated by a circle divided by an "s" to show unity within duality. The five elements suggest another traditional, prescientific idea that everything is made of five basic ingredients. [Ed.]

they happen to be our neighbors. We simply follow the manner of the Westerners in knowing how to treat them. Any person who cherishes a bad friend cannot escape his bad notoriety. We simply erase from our minds our bad friends in Asia.

2

Images from Japan: Views of Westernization, Late Nineteenth Century

This selection consists of two prints by Japanese artists from the Meiji period of Westernization. The first print, Figure 23.1 is called *Monkey Show Dressing Room* (1879), by Honda Kinkachiro. What is this print's message? What is the artist's attitude toward Westernization?

The second piece, Figure 23.2, *The Exotic White Man*, shows a child born to a Western man and a Japanese woman. What is the artist's message? Does the artist favor such unions? What does the artist think of Westerners?

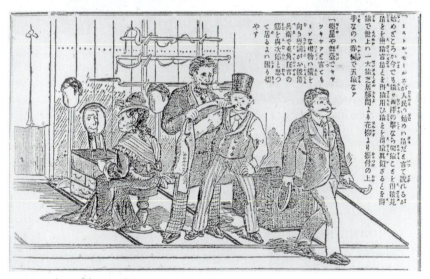

Figure 23.1   Monkey Show Dressing Room.

Figure 23.2 The Exotic White Man.
Source: Werner Forman/Art Resource, NY.

THINKING HISTORICALLY

Compare the attitudes of these artists with that of Fukuzawa Yukichi. Prints, like cartoons, are a shorthand that must capture an easily recognizable trait. What, evidently, were the widely understood Japanese images of the West? Where do you think these stereotypes of the West came from? Do you see any signs in these prints of ambivalence on the part of the artist?

3

KAKUZO OKAKURA
The Ideals of the East, 1904

Kakuzo Okakura (1862–1913) was a Japanese scholar who was responsible for the development and preservation of the arts in Japan. In addition to creating important art schools and journals, he was the director of the Imperial Art School in Tokyo. In 1890 he founded the first Japanese art academy. In later life he worked and lectured in England and the United States, serving as the director of the Chinese and Japanese department at Harvard and, after 1910, as curator of the Museum of Fine Arts in Boston. He is best known for *The Book of Tea*, which introduced the ritual beauty of the Japanese tea service to a Western audience. He also wrote for a Western audience *The Awakening of Japan* and *The Ideals of the East*, from which this selection is taken.

What are the "ideals of the East" that Okakura celebrates? What are the features of the West that he wants Japan to avoid?

THINKING HISTORICALLY

In Okakura, the contradictions abound. He was a cosmopolitan world traveler, living in Europe, the United States, China, and India, as well as Japan. Yet, at the Imperial Art School in Tokyo, he offered no courses in Western art. He spent his last years in Boston, developing the Asian art collection of an American museum. He wrote all of his major books in English, albeit to extol Asian, especially Japanese, art to the wider world. He was a modern urbanite who sought strength of identity in blood and the past.

How does he use the then popular Western idea of "race" in this selection? How does he negotiate the conflict between Japanese nationalism and a broader Pan-Asian identity? How does he combine love of monarchy with ideas of democracy? How does he reconcile tradition and individualism?

The Range of Ideals

Asia is one. The Himalayas divide, only to accentuate, two mighty civilisations, the Chinese with its communism of Confucius, and the Indian with its individualism of the Vedas. But not even the snowy barriers can

Source: Kakuzo Okakura, *Ideals of the East: The Spirit of Japanese Art* (Mineola, NY: Dover Publications, Inc., 2005), 1–4, 103–6.

interrupt for one moment that broad expanse of love for the Ultimate and Universal, which is the common thought-inheritance of every Asiatic race, enabling them to produce all the great religions of the world, and distinguishing them from those maritime peoples of the Mediterranean and the Baltic, who love to dwell on the Particular, and to search out the means, not the end, of life. . . .

For if Asia be one, it is also true that the Asiatic races form a single mighty web. We forget, in an age of classification, that types are after all but shining points of distinctness in an ocean of approximations, false gods deliberately set up to be worshipped, for the sake of mental convenience, but having no more ultimate or mutually exclusive validity than the separate existence of two interchangeable sciences. . . .

Buddhism—that great ocean of idealism, in which merge all the river-systems of Eastern Asiatic thought—is not coloured only with the pure water of the Ganges, for the Tartaric nations[1] that joined it made their genius also tributary, bringing new symbolism, new organisation, new powers of devotion, to add to the treasures of the Faith.

It has been, however, the great privilege of Japan to realise this unity-in-complexity with a special clearness. The Indo-Tartaric blood of this race was in itself a heritage which qualified it to imbibe from the two sources, and so mirror the whole of Asiatic consciousness. The unique blessing of unbroken sovereignty, the proud self-reliance of an unconquered race, and the insular isolation which protected ancestral ideas and instincts at the cost of expansion, made Japan the real repository of the trust of Asiatic thought and culture. Dynastic upheavals, the inroads of Tartar horsemen, the carnage and devastation of infuriated mobs—all these things, sweeping over her again and again, have left to China no landmarks, save her literature and her ruins, to recall the glory of the Tang emperors or the refinement of Sung society. . . .

It is in Japan alone that the historic wealth of Asiatic culture can be consecutively studied through its treasured specimens. The Imperial collection, the Shinto[2] temples, and the opened dolmens, reveal the subtle curves of Hang[3] workmanship. The temples of Nara[4] are rich in representations of Tang culture, and of that Indian art, then in its splendour, which so much influenced the creations of this classic period—natural heirlooms of a nation which has preserved the music, pronunciation, ceremony, and costumes, not to speak of the religious rites and philosophy, of so remarkable an age, intact.

---

[1] He means Central Asian Turks and Mongols. [Ed.]
[2] Traditional Japanese religion. [Ed.]
[3] Han, i.e., classical Chinese. [Ed.]
[4] City in Japan, capital 710–784 (the Nara Period). [Ed.]

The treasure-stores of the daimyos,[5] again, abound in works of art and manuscripts belonging to the Sung and Mongol dynasties, and as in China itself the former were lost during the Mongol conquest, and the latter in the age of the reactionary Ming, this fact animates some Chinese scholars of the present day to seek in Japan the fountain-head of their own ancient knowledge.

Thus Japan is a museum of Asiatic civilisation; and yet more than a museum, because the singular genius of the race leads it to dwell on all phases of the ideals of the past, in that spirit of living Advaitism[6] which welcomes the new without losing the old. The Shinto still adheres to his pre-Buddhistic rites of ancestor-worship; and the Buddhists themselves cling to each various school of religious development which has come in its natural order to enrich the soil.

The Yamato poetry,[7] and Bugaku music,[8] which reflect the Tang ideal under the régime of the Fujiwara aristocracy,[9] are a source of inspiration and delight to the present day, like the sombre Zennism[10] and No-dances,[11] which were the product of Sung illumination. It is this tenacity that keeps Japan true to the Asiatic soul even while it raises her to the rank of a modern power.

The history of Japanese art becomes thus the history of Asiatic ideals—the beach where each successive wave of Eastern thought has left its sand-ripple as it beat against the national consciousness. Yet I linger with dismay on the threshold of an attempt to make an intelligible summary of those art-ideals. For art, like the diamond net of Indra,[12] reflects the whole chain in every link. It exists at no period in any final mould. It is always a growth, defying the dissecting knife of the chronologist. To discourse on a particular phase of its development means to deal with infinite causes and effects throughout its past and present. Art with us, as elsewhere, is the expression of the highest and noblest of our national culture, so that, in order to understand it, we must pass in review the various phases of Confucian philosophy; the different ideals which the Buddhist mind has from time to time revealed; those mighty political cycles which have one after another unfurled the banner of nationality; the reflection in patriotic thought of the lights of poetry and the shadows of heroic characters; and the echoes, alike of the wailing of a multitude, and of the mad-seeming merriment of the laughter of a race. . . .

---

[5] Warlords of feudal Japan. [Ed.]

[6] Indian philosophy of wholeness and immediacy. [Ed.]

[7] Earliest Japanese poetry, seventh–tenth centuries; also period of Tang dynasty in China. [Ed.]

[8] Ceremonial dance music of elite of same period. [Ed.]

[9] Ruling clan in Heian period (794–1185). [Ed.]

[10] Japanese Zen Buddhism. [Ed.]

[11] Highly stylized Japanese dance theater. [Ed.]

[12] Indian god. [Ed.]

The Vista

The simple life of Asia need fear no shaming from that sharp contrast with Europe in which steam and electricity have placed it to-day. The old world of trade, the world of the craftsman and the pedlar, of the village market and the saints'-day fair, where little boats row up and down great rivers laden with the produce of the country, where every palace has some court in which the travelling merchant may display his stuffs and jewels for beautiful screened women to see and buy, is not yet quite dead. And, however its form may change, only at a great loss can Asia permit its spirit to die, since the whole of that industrial and decorative art which is the heirloom of ages has been in its keeping, and she must lose with it not only the beauty of things, but the joy of the worker, his individuality of vision, and the whole age-long humanising of her labour. For to clothe oneself in the web of one's own weaving is to house oneself in one's own house, to create for the spirit its own sphere.

Asia knows, it is true, nothing of the fierce joys of a time-devouring locomotion, but she has still the far deeper travel-culture of the pilgrimage and the wandering monk. For the Indian ascetic, begging his bread of village housewives, or seated at evenfall beneath some tree, chatting and smoking with the peasant of the district, is the real traveller. To him a countryside does not consist of its natural features alone. It is a nexus of habits and associations. Of human elements and traditions, suffused with the tenderness and friendship of one who has shared, if only for a moment, the joys and sorrows of its personal drama. The Japanese peasant-traveller, again, goes from no place of interest on his wanderings without leaving his *hokku* or short sonnet, an art-form within reach of the simplest.

Through such modes of experience is cultivated the Eastern conception of individuality as the ripe and living knowledge, the harmonised thought and feeling of staunch yet gentle manhood. Through such modes of interchange is maintained the Eastern notion of human intercourse, not the printed index, as the true means of culture.

The chain of antitheses might be indefinitely lengthened. But the glory of Asia is something more positive than these. It lies in that vibration of peace that beats in every heart; that harmony that brings together emperor and peasant; that sublime intuition of oneness which commands all sympathy, all courtesy, to be its fruits, making Takakura, Emperor of Japan, remove his sleeping-robes on a winter night, because the frost lay cold on the hearths of his poor; or Taiso, of Tang, forego food, because his people were feeling the pinch of famine. It lies in the dream of renunciation that pictures the Boddhi-Sattva[13] as refraining from Nirvana till

---

[13] Buddhist Boddisattva: saint; model of compassion. [Ed.]

the last atom of dust in the universe shall have passed in before to bliss. It lies in that worship of Freedom which casts around poverty the halo of greatness, imposes his stern simplicity of apparel on the Indian prince, and sets up in China a throne whose imperial occupant—alone amongst the great secular rulers of the world—never wears a sword.

These things are the secret energy of the thought, the science, the poetry, and the art of Asia. Torn from their tradition, India, made barren of that religious life which is the essence of her nationality, would become a worshipper of the mean, the false, and the new; China, hurled upon the problems of a material instead of a moral civilisation, would writhe in the death-agony of that ancient dignity and ethics which long ago made the word of her merchants like the legal bond of the West, the name of her peasants a synonym for prosperity; and Japan, the Fatherland of the race of Ama,[14] would betray the completeness of her undoing in the tarnishing of the purity of the spiritual mirror, the bemeaning of the sword-soul from steel to lead. The task of Asia to-day, then, becomes that of protecting and restoring Asiatic modes. But to do this she must herself first recognise and develop consciousness of those modes. For the shadows of the past are the promise of the future. No tree can be greater than the power that is in the seed. Life lies ever in the return to self. How many of the Evangels have uttered this truth! "Know thyself," was the greatest mystery spoken by the Delphic Oracle. "All in thyself," said the quiet voice of Confucius. And more striking still is the Indian story that carries the same message to its hearers. For once it happened, say the Buddhists, that, the Master having gathered his disciples round him, there shone forth before them suddenly—blasting the sight of all save Vajrapani, the completely-learned—a terrible figure, the figure of Siva, the Great God. Then Vajrapani, his companions being blinded, turned to the Master and said, "Tell me why, searching amongst all the stars and gods, equal in number to the sands of the Ganges, I have nowhere seen this glorious form. Who is he?" And the Buddha said, "He is thyself!" and Vajrapani, it is told, immediately attained the highest.

It was some small degree of this self-recognition that re-made Japan, and enabled her to weather the storm under which so much of the Oriental world went down. And it must be a renewal of the same self-consciousness that shall build up Asia again into her ancient steadfastness and strength. The very times are bewildered by the manifoldness of the possibilities opening out before them. Even Japan cannot, in the tangled skein of the Meiji period,[15] find that single thread which will give her the clue to her own future. Her past has been clear and continuous as a mala,

---

[14] Japanese divers. [Ed.]
[15] 1868–1912. [Ed.]

a rosary, of crystals. From the early days of the Asuka period,[16] when the national destiny was first bestowed, as the receiver and concentrator, by her Yamato genius, of Indian ideals and Chinese ethics; through the succeeding preliminary phases of Nara and Heian, to the revelation of her vast powers in the unmeasured devotion of her Fujiwara period, in her heroic reaction of Kamakura,[17] culminating in the stern enthusiasm and lofty abstinence of that Ashikaga[18] knighthood who sought with so austere a passion after death—through all these phases the evolution of the nation is clear and unconfused, like that of a single personality. Even through Toyotomi,[19] and Tokugawa,[20] it is clear that after the fashion of the East we are ending a rhythm of activity with the lull of the democratising of the great ideals. The populace and the lower classes, notwithstanding their seeming quiescence and commonplaceness, are making their own the consecration of the Samurai, the sadness of the poet, the divine self-sacrifice of the saint are becoming liberated, in fact, into their national inheritance.

But to-day the great mass of Western thought perplexes us. The mirror of Yamato is clouded, as we say. With the Revolution, Japan, it is true, returns upon her past, seeking there for the new vitality she needs. Like all genuine restorations, it is a reaction with a difference. For that self-dedication of art to nature which the Ashikaga inaugurated has become now a consecration to the race, to man himself. We know instinctively that in our history lies the secret of our future, and we grope with a blind intensity to find the clue. But if the thought be true, if there be indeed any spring of renewal hidden in our past, we must admit that it needs at this moment some mighty reinforcement, for the scorching drought of modern vulgarity is parching the throat of life and art.

We await the flashing sword of the lightning which shall cleave the darkness. For the terrible hush must be broken, and the raindrops of a new vigour must refresh the earth before new flowers can spring up to cover it with their bloom. But it must be from Asia herself, along the ancient roadways of the race, that the great voice shall be heard.

Victory from within, or a mighty death without.

---

[16] 552–645. [Ed.]

[17] 1185–1333. [Ed.]

[18] 1336–1573, Feudal period. [Ed.]

[19] Toyotomi Hideyoshi (1537–1598). A feudal lord who ended feudalism. [Ed.]

[20] Tokugawa Ieyasu (1543–1616). Founder and first shogun of the Tokugawa Shogunate (1603–1868). [Ed.]

4

RAMMOHUN ROY

Letter on Indian Education, 1823

India's Westernization was less voluntary than Japan's. While Japan successfully limited European colonialism to a few seaports in the seventeenth century and was not forced to deal with the West again until after Commodore Perry's steam-age arrival in 1853, India became increasingly colonized by England throughout the eighteenth and nineteenth centuries. Because of India's long history as a British colony, aspects of Westernization there were deeper and more complex, the most obvious being use of the English language.

A colonial and foreign tongue, English had the advantage of uniting a country with dozens of regional languages (some of which were also imposed by foreign conquerors), while at the same time providing access to universities and a body of knowledge and literature as advanced as any in the world. English instruction—rather than ancient Sanskrit or Hindi or another Indian regional language—was championed by Britons who thought it would make Indians loyal and by Indians who thought it would unite them as a nation. The Indian use of English had its detractors, too: Britons who thought it dangerous or unseemly, and Britons and Indians who thought it patronizing and demeaning.

The debate over teaching English or Indian languages was part of a larger debate about the relative value of Western and Indian culture. Increasingly, toward the end of the nineteenth century as science took center stage in English culture, Indians found themselves torn between the claim of science and the appeal of traditional Indian religious knowledge.

Rammohun Roy (1772–1833) was an Indian social and religious reformer, as well as one of the earliest proponents of English education. Roy was an accomplished linguist who knew Latin, Greek, Hebrew, Arabic, Persian, and ancient Indian Sanskrit as well as his native Bengali. Yet when the British proposed to build a new Sanskrit school in Calcutta, Roy fired off the following letter to the British prime minister. Why did Roy object to a school that taught Sanskrit, the sacred language of ancient Hindu culture? What were his reasons for preferring English education for Indians?

Source: Rammohun Roy, Letter on Indian Education, in H. Sharp, ed., *Selections from Educational Records, Part I, 1781–1839* (Calcutta: Superintendent Government Printing, 1920; reprint, Delhi: National Archives of India, 1965), 98–101.

THINKING HISTORICALLY

To effectively communicate his ideas on Indian education, Roy had to strike a delicate balance in expressing deference to the British government while asserting enough authority to be taken seriously. How did he accomplish this dual task? How did he suggest that he knew more about the issue than his superiors in the English government, without seeming arrogant or ungrateful? How does his letter show that he was an Indian who benefited from an English education but did not pose a threat to British rule? What does his letter reveal about the inherent tensions in colonial India, within individuals and the society as a whole?

To His Excellency the Right Hon'ble William Pitt, Lord Amherst
My Lord,

Humbly reluctant as the natives of India are to obtrude upon the notice of Government the sentiments they entertain on any public measure there are circumstances when silence would be carrying this respectful feeling to culpable excess. The present Rulers of India, coming from a distance of many thousand miles to govern a people whose language, literature, manners, customs, and ideas are almost entirely new and strange to them, cannot easily become so intimately acquainted with their real circumstances, as the natives of the country are themselves. We should therefore be guilty of a gross dereliction of duty to ourselves, and afford our Rulers just ground of complaint at our apathy, did we omit on occasions of importance like the present to supply them with such accurate information as might enable them to devise and adopt measures calculated to be beneficial to the country, and thus second by our local knowledge and experience their declared benevolent intentions for its improvement.

The establishment of a new Sanskrit School in Calcutta evinces the laudable desire of Government to improve the Natives of India by Education, a blessing for which they must ever be grateful; and every well wisher of the human race must be desirous that the efforts made to promote it should be guided by the most enlightened principles, so that the stream of intelligence may flow into the most useful channels.

When this Seminary of learning was proposed, we understood that the Government in England had ordered a considerable sum of money to be annually devoted to the instruction of its Indian Subjects. We were filled with sanguine hopes that this sum would be laid out in employing European Gentlemen of talents and education to instruct the natives of India in Mathematics, Natural Philosophy, Chemistry, Anatomy and other useful Sciences, which the Nations of Europe have carried to a degree of perfection that has raised them above the inhabitants of other parts of the world.

While we looked forward with pleasing hope to the dawn of knowledge thus promised to the rising generation, our hearts were filled with mingled feelings of delight and gratitude; we already offered up thanks to Providence for inspiring the most generous and enlightened of the Nations of the West with the glorious ambitions of planting in Asia the Arts and Sciences of modern Europe.

We now find that the Government are establishing a Sanskrit school under Hindu Pundits to impart such knowledge as is already current in India. This Seminary (similar in character to those which existed in Europe before the time of Lord Bacon[1]) can only be expected to load the minds of youth with grammatical niceties and metaphysical distinctions of little or no practicable use to the possessors or to society. The pupils will there acquire what was known two thousand years ago, with the addition of vain and empty subtilties [sic] since produced by speculative men, such as is already commonly taught in all parts of India.

The Sanskrit language, so difficult that almost a life time is necessary for its perfect acquisition, is well known to have been for ages a lamentable check on the diffusion of knowledge; and the learning concealed under this almost impervious veil is far from sufficient to reward the labour of acquiring it. But if it were thought necessary to perpetuate this language for the sake of the portion of the valuable information it contains, this might be much more easily accomplished by other means than the establishment of a new Sanskrit College; for there have been always and are now numerous professors of Sanskrit in the different parts of the country, engaged in teaching this language as well as the other branches of literature which are to be the object of the new Seminary. Therefore their more diligent cultivation, if desirable, would be effectually promoted by holding out premiums and granting certain allowances to those most eminent Professors, who have already undertaken on their own account to teach them, and would by such rewards be stimulated to still greater exertions.

From these considerations, as the sum set apart for the instruction of the Natives of India was intended by the Government in England, for the improvement of its Indian subjects, I beg leave to state, with due deference to your Lordship's exalted situation, that if the plan now adopted be followed, it will completely defeat the object proposed; since no improvement can be expected from inducing young men to consume a dozen of years of the most valuable period of their lives in acquiring the niceties of the Byakurun or Sanskrit Grammar. For instance, in learning to discuss such points as the following: *Khad* signifying to eat, *khaduti*, he or she or it eats. Query, whether does the word

[1] Francis Bacon (1561–1626), English philosopher often credited with developing the scientific method. [Ed.]

khaduti, taken as a whole, convey the meaning *he, she,* or *it eats,* or are separate parts of this meaning conveyed by distinct portions of the word? As if in the English language it were asked, how much meaning is there in the *eat,* how much in the *s?* and is the whole meaning of the word conveyed by those two portions of it distinctly, or by them taken jointly?

Neither can much improvement arise from such speculations as the following, which are the themes suggested by the Vedanta: In what manner is the soul absorbed into the deity? What relation does it bear to the divine essence? Nor will youths be fitted to be better members of society by the Vedantic doctrines, which teach them to believe that all visible things have no real existence; that as father, brother, etc., have no actual entirety, they consequently deserve no real affection, and therefore the sooner we escape from them and leave the world the better. Again, no essential benefit can be derived by the student of the Meemangsa from knowing what it is that makes the killer of a goat sinless on pronouncing certain passages of the Vedas, and what is the real nature and operative influence of passages of the Veda, etc.

Again the student of the Nyaya Shastra cannot be said to have improved his mind after he has learned from it into how many ideal classes the objects in the Universe are divided, and what speculative relation the soul bears to the body, the body to the soul, the eye to the ear, etc.

In order to enable your Lordship to appreciate the utility of encouraging such imaginary learning as above characterised, I beg your Lordship will be pleased to compare the state of science and literature in Europe before the time of Lord Bacon, with the progress of knowledge made since he wrote.

If it had been intended to keep the British nation in ignorance of real knowledge the Baconian philosophy would not have been allowed to displace the system of the schoolmen, which was the best calculated to perpetuate ignorance. In the same manner the [Sanskrit] system of education would be the best calculated to keep this country in darkness, if such had been the policy of the British Legislature. But as the improvement of the native population is the object of the Government, it will consequently promote a more liberal and enlightened system of instruction, embracing mathematics, natural philosophy, chemistry and anatomy, with other useful sciences which may be accomplished with the sum proposed by employing a few gentlemen of talents and learning educated in Europe, and providing a college furnished with the necessary books, instruments, and other apparatus.

In representing this subject to your Lordship I conceive myself discharging a solemn duty which I owe to my countrymen and also to that enlightened Sovereign and Legislature which have extended their benevolent cares to this distant land actuated by a desire to improve its inhabitants and I therefore humbly trust you will excuse the liberty I have taken in thus expressing my sentiments to your Lordship.

I have, etc.,

Rammohun Roy
Calcutta;
The 11th December 1823

5

THOMAS BABINGTON MACAULAY

Minute on Indian Education, 1835

Thomas Babington Macaulay (1800–1859) was a famous British historian and politician. In 1833, the British Parliament passed the Government of India Act, which authorized the British East India Company to govern all aspects of Indian life. As a highly respected statesman, Macaulay was appointed by Parliament to the governing body, the Supreme Council of India in Calcutta, on which he served from 1834 to 1838. He was particularly interested in the issue of education in India, which he addressed in the following memo, or "minute." It became the rationale for the wide use of English in Indian schools and colleges. What was Macaulay's position? Which of his arguments would you expect to be particularly persuasive to the Company? What responses would you expect from Indians?

THINKING HISTORICALLY

In what ways was the establishment of English education an aid for Indians? In what ways was it a tool of colonial control used by the English?

We have a fund to be employed as Government shall direct for the intellectual improvement of the people of this country. The simple question is, what is the most useful way of employing it?

All parties seem to be agreed on one point, that the dialects commonly spoken among the natives of this part of India contain neither

Source: Bureau of Education, Selections from Educational Records, Part I (1781–1839), ed. H. Sharp (Calcutta: Superintendent, Government Printing, 1920; reprint, Delhi: National Archives of India, 1965), 107–17.

literary nor scientific information, and are moreover so poor and rude that, until they are enriched from some other quarter, it will not be easy to translate any valuable work into them. It seems to be admitted on all sides, that the intellectual improvement of those classes of the people who have the means of pursuing higher studies can at present be affected only by means of some language not vernacular amongst them.

What then shall that language be? One-half of the committee maintain that it should be the English. The other half strongly recommend the Arabic and Sanscrit. The whole question seems to me to be—which language is the best worth knowing?

I have no knowledge of either Sanscrit or Arabic. But I have done what I could to form a correct estimate of their value. I have read translations of the most celebrated Arabic and Sanscrit works. I have conversed, both here and at home, with men distinguished by their proficiency in the Eastern tongues. I am quite ready to take the oriental learning at the valuation of the orientalists themselves. I have never found one among them who could deny that a single shelf of a good European library was worth the whole native literature of India and Arabia. The intrinsic superiority of the Western literature is indeed fully admitted by those members of the committee who support the oriental plan of education.

It will hardly be disputed, I suppose, that the department of literature in which the Eastern writers stand highest is poetry. And I certainly never met with any orientalist who ventured to maintain that the Arabic and Sanscrit poetry could be compared to that of the great European nations. But when we pass from works of imagination to works in which facts are recorded and general principles investigated, the superiority of the Europeans becomes absolutely immeasurable. It is, I believe, no exaggeration to say that all the historical information which has been collected from all the books written in the Sanscrit language is less valuable than what may be found in the most paltry abridgments used at preparatory schools in England. In every branch of physical or moral philosophy, the relative position of the two nations is nearly the same.

How then stands the case? We have to educate a people who cannot at present be educated by means of their mother-tongue. We must teach them some foreign language. The claims of our own language it is hardly necessary to recapitulate. It stands pre-eminent even among the languages of the West. It abounds with works of imagination not inferior to the noblest which Greece has bequeathed to us,—with models of every species of eloquence,—with historical composition, which, considered merely as narratives, have seldom been surpassed, and which, considered as vehicles of ethical and political instruction, have never been equaled—with just and lively representations of human life and human nature,—with the most profound speculations on metaphysics, morals, government, jurisprudence, trade,—with full and correct information respecting every experimental science which tends to preserve the health, to increase the comfort, or to expand the intellect of man. Whoever knows that language has ready access to all the vast intellectual wealth which all the wisest nations of the earth have created and hoarded in the course of ninety generations. It may safely be said that the literature now extant in that language is of greater value than all the literature which three hundred years ago was extant in all the languages of the world together. Nor is this all. In India, English is the language spoken by the ruling class. It is spoken by the higher class of natives at the seats of Government. It is likely to become the language of commerce throughout the seas of the East. It is the language of two great European communities which are rising, the one in the south of Africa, the other in Australia,—communities which are every year becoming more important and more closely connected with our Indian empire. Whether we look at the intrinsic value of our literature, or at the particular situation of this country, we shall see the strongest reason to think that, of all foreign tongues, the English tongue is that which would be the most useful to our native subjects.

The question now before us is simply whether, when it is in our power to teach this language, we shall teach languages in which, by universal confession, there are no books on any subject which deserve to be compared to our own, whether, when we can teach European science, we shall teach systems which, by universal confession, wherever they differ from those of Europe differ for the worse, and whether, when we can patronize sound philosophy and true history, we shall countenance, at the public expense, medical doctrines which would disgrace an English farrier, astronomy which would move laughter in girls at an English boarding school, history abounding with kings thirty feet high and reigns thirty thousand years long, and geography made of seas of treacle and seas of butter. . . .

And what are the arguments against that course which seems to be alike recommended by theory and by experience? It is said that we ought to secure the co-operation of the native public, and that we can do this only by teaching Sanscrit and Arabic.

I can by no means admit that, when a nation of high intellectual attainments undertakes to superintend the education of a nation comparatively ignorant, the learners are absolutely to prescribe the course which is to be taken by the teachers. It is not necessary however to say anything on this subject. For it is proved by unanswerable evidence, that we are not at present securing the co-operation of the natives. It would be bad enough to consult their intellectual taste at the expense of their intellectual health. But we are consulting neither. We are withholding from them the learning which is palatable to them. We are forcing on them the mock learning which they nauseate.

This is proved by the fact that we are forced to pay our Arabic and Sanscrit students while those who learn English are willing to pay us. All the declamations in the world about the love and reverence of the natives for their sacred dialects will never, in the mind of any impartial person, outweigh this undisputed fact, that we cannot find in all our vast empire a single student who will let us teach him those dialects, unless we will pay him. . . .

I have been used to see petitions to Government for compensation. All those petitions, even the most unreasonable of them, proceeded on the supposition that some loss had been sustained, that some wrong had been inflicted. These are surely the first petitioners who ever demanded compensation for having been educated gratis, for having been supported by the public during twelve years, and then sent forth into the world well furnished with literature and science. They represent their education as an injury which gives them a claim on the Government for redress, as an injury for which the stipends paid to them during the infliction were a very inadequate compensation. And I doubt not that they are in the right. They have wasted the best years of life in learning what procures for them neither bread nor respect. Surely we might with advantage have saved the cost of making these persons useless and miserable. Surely, men may be brought up to be burdens to the public and objects of contempt to their neighbours at a somewhat smaller charge to the State. But such is our policy. We do not even stand neuter in the contest between truth and falsehood. We are not content to leave the natives to the influence of their own hereditary prejudices. To the natural difficulties which obstruct the progress of sound science in the East, we add great difficulties of our own making. Bounties and premiums, such as ought not to be given even for the propagation of truth, we lavish on false texts and false philosophy. . . .

In one point I fully agree with the gentlemen to whose general views I am opposed. I feel with them that it is impossible for us, with our limited means, to attempt to educate the body of the people. We must at present do our best to form a class who may be interpreters between us and the millions whom we govern,—a class of persons Indian in blood and colour, but English in tastes, in opinions, in morals and in intellect. To that class we may leave it to refine the vernacular dialects of the country, to enrich those dialects with terms of science borrowed from the Western nomenclature, and to render them by degrees fit vehicles for conveying knowledge to the great mass of the population.

I would strictly respect all existing interests. I would deal even generously with all individuals who have had fair reason to expect a pecuniary provision. But I would strike at the root of the bad system which has hitherto been fostered by us. I would at once stop the printing of Arabic and Sanscrit books. I would abolish the Mudrassa and the Sanscrit College at Calcutta. Benares is the great seat of Brahminical learning; Delhi of Arabic learning. If we retain the Sanscrit College at Benares and the Mahometan College at Delhi we do enough and much more than enough in my opinion, for the Eastern languages. If the Benares and Delhi Colleges should be retained, I would at least recommend that no stipends shall be given to any students who may hereafter repair thither, but that the people shall be left to make their own choice between the rival systems of education without being bribed by us to learn what they have no desire to know. The funds which would thus be placed at our disposal would enable us to give larger encouragement to the Hindoo College at Calcutta, and establish in the principal cities throughout the Presidencies of Fort William and Agra schools in which the English language might be well and thoroughly taught.

6

MOHANDAS K. GANDHI

Hind Swaraj, 1921

Mohandas K. Gandhi (1869–1948), the father of Indian independence, combined the education of an English lawyer with the temperament of an Indian ascetic to lead a national resistance movement against the British. In the century that followed British-supported reforms to the Indian education system (in the early nineteenth century), British rule had become far more pervasive and increasingly hostile toward Indian culture. Unlike Indian educational reformers, who had embraced Western culture as a means to uplift Indians, Gandhi became extremely critical of Western culture as he witnessed the havoc British rule wreaked on his country.

Gandhi began to develop his ideas of *Hind Swaraj,** or Indian Home Rule, in 1909 while he sailed from England to South Africa, where he served as a lawyer for fellow Indians. An early version of this essay, published then, was reissued in its present form in 1921, two years after he returned to his birthplace, India, and again in 1938, in the last years of struggle against British rule.

After Gandhi's introduction, the essay takes the form of questions and answers. The questions are posed by a presumed "reader" of Gandhi's pamphlet. As "editor," Gandhi explains what he means. How does Gandhi compare life in Europe and India? What does he think of the possibility of Hindus and Muslims living together? What

* hihnd swah RAHJ

Source: M. K. Gandhi, *Hind Swaraj* (Ahmedabad, India: Navajivan, 1938), 31–33, 44–45, 58–59, 69–71.

does he mean by passive resistance or soul-force (Satyagraha)? Why does he think it is preferable to violence, or body-force? Gandhi was assassinated by a Hindu extremist in 1948 before he had a chance to shape the new nation. What kind of India would Gandhi have tried to create had he lived? Compare Gandhi's response to the West with that of Rammohun Roy in an earlier selection. In what respects is his attitude like that of his contemporary, Kakuzo Okakura?

THINKING HISTORICALLY

Some historians have argued that Gandhi's contradictory roles—Hindu philosopher espousing secular nationalism and anti-modernist revolutionary—were ultimately unbridgeable. Notice how Gandhi makes a lawyer's case for traditional Indian values. How does he combine both religious and secular goals for India? How does he combine Hindu religious ideas with respect for Muslims? Were Gandhi's contradictions a fatal flaw, or could they have been his strength?

Civilization

READER   Now you will have to explain what you mean by civilization.

EDITOR   Let us first consider what state of things is described by the word "civilization." Its true test lies in the fact that people living in it make bodily welfare the object of life. We will take some examples. The people of Europe today live in better-built houses than they did a hundred years ago. This is considered an emblem of civilization, and this is also a matter to promote bodily happiness. Formerly, they wore skins, and used spears as their weapons. Now, they wear long trousers, and, for embellishing their bodies, they wear a variety of clothing, and, instead of spears, they carry with them revolvers containing five or more chambers. If people of a certain country, who have hitherto not been in the habit of wearing much clothing, boots, etc., adopt European clothing, they are supposed to have become civilized out of savagery. Formerly, in Europe, people ploughed their lands mainly by manual labour. Now, one man can plough a vast tract by means of steam engines and can thus amass great wealth. This is called a sign of civilization. Formerly, only a few men wrote valuable books. Now, anybody writes and prints anything he likes and poisons people's minds. Formerly, men travelled in waggons. Now, they fly through the air in trains at the rate of four hundred and more miles per day. This is considered the height of civilization. It has been stated that, as men progress, they shall be able to travel in airship and reach any part of the world in a few hours. Men will not need the use of their hands and feet. They will press a button, and they will have their clothing at their side. They will press another button, and they will have their newspaper. A third, and motor-car will be in waiting for them. They will have a variety of delicately dished up food. Everything will be done by machinery. Formerly, when people wanted to fight with one another, they measured between them their bodily strength; now it is possible to take away thousands of lives by one man working behind a gun from a hill. This is civilization. Formerly, men worked in the open air only as much as they liked. Now thousands of workmen meet together and for the sake of maintenance work in factories or mines. Their condition is worse than that of beasts. They are obliged to work, at the risk of their lives, at most dangerous occupations, for the sake of millionaires. Formerly, men were made slaves under physical compulsion. Now they are enslaved by temptation of money and of the luxuries that money can buy. There are now diseases of which people never dreamt before, and an army of doctors is engaged in finding out their cures, and so hospitals have increased. This is a test of civilization. Formerly, special messengers were required and much expense was incurred in order to send letters; today, anyone can abuse his fellow by means of a letter for one penny. True, at the same cost, one can send one's thanks also. Formerly, people had two or three meals consisting of home-made bread and vegetables; now, they require something to eat every two hours so that they have hardly leisure for anything else. What more need I say? . . . Even a child can understand that in all I have described above there can be no inducement to morality.

The Hindus and the Mahomedans

READER   Has the introduction to Mahomedanism [Islam] not unmade the nation?

EDITOR   India cannot cease to be one nation because people belonging to different religions live in it. The introduction of foreigners does not necessarily destroy the nation; they merge in it. A country is one nation only when such a condition obtains in it. That country must have a faculty for assimilation. India has ever been such a country. In reality there are as many religions as there are individuals; but those who are conscious of the spirit of nationality do not interfere with one another's religion. If they do, they are not fit to be considered a nation. If the Hindus believe that India should be peopled only by Hindus, they are living in dreamland. The Hindus, the Mahomedans, the Parsis and the Christians who have made India their country are fellow-countrymen, and they will have to live in unity, if only for their own interest. In no part of the world are one nationality and one religion synonymous terms; nor has it ever been so in India.

READER   But what about the inborn enmity between Hindus and Mahomedans?

EDITOR   That phrase has been invented by our mutual enemy. When the Hindus and Mahomedans fought against one another, they certainly spoke in that strain. They have long since ceased to fight. How, then, can there be any inborn enmity? Pray remember this too, that we did not cease to fight only after British occupation. The Hindus flourished under Moslem sovereigns and Moslems under the Hindu. Each party recognized that mutual fighting was suicidal, and that neither party would abandon its religion by force of arms. Both parties, therefore, decided to live in peace. With the English advent quarrels recommenced. . . .

How Can India Become Free?

READER   If Indian civilization is, as you say, the best of all, how do you account for India's slavery?

EDITOR   This civilization is unquestionably the best, but it is to be observed that all civilizations have been on their trial. That civilization which is permanent outlives it. Because the sons of India were found wanting, its civilization has been placed in jeopardy. But its strength is to be seen in its ability to survive the shock. Moreover, the whole of India is not touched. Those alone who have been affected by Western civilization have become enslaved. We measure the universe by our own miserable foot-rule. When we are slaves, we think that the whole universe is enslaved. Because we are in an abject condition, we think that the whole of India is in that condition. As a matter of fact, it is not so, yet it is as well to impute our slavery to the whole of India. But if we bear in mind the above fact, we can see that if we become free, India is free. And in this thought you have a definition of Swaraj. It is Swaraj when we learn to rule ourselves. It is, therefore, in the palm of our hands. Do not consider this Swaraj to be like a dream. There is no idea of sitting still. The Swaraj that I wish to picture is such that, after we have once realized it, we shall endeavour to the end of our life-time to persuade others to do likewise. But such Swaraj has to be experienced, by each one for himself. One drowning man will never save another. Slaves ourselves, it would be a mere pretension to think of freeing others. Now you will have seen that it is not necessary for us to have as our goal the expulsion of the English. If the English become Indianized, we can accommodate them. If they wish to remain in India along with their civilization, there is no room for them. It lies with us to bring about such a state of things. . . .

Passive Resistance

READER   Is there any historical evidence as to the success of what you
have called soul-force or truth-force? No instance seems to have
happened of any nation having risen through soul-force. I still think
that the evil-doers will not cease doing evil without physical
punishment.

EDITOR   The [Hindu] poet Tulsidas [1532–1623] has said: "Of religion,
pity, or love, is the root, as egotism of the body. Therefore, we
should not abandon pity so long as we are alive." This appears to
me to be a scientific truth. We have evidence of its working at every
step. The universe would disappear without the existence of that
force. . . .

   The fact that there are so many men still alive in the world
shows that it is based not on the force of arms but on the force of
truth or love. Therefore, the greatest and most unimpeachable evidence of the success of this force is to be found in the fact that, in
spite of the wars of the world, it still lives on.

   Thousands, indeed tens of thousands, depend for their existence on a very active working of this force. Little quarrels of millions of families in their daily lives disappear before the exercise of
this force. Hundreds of nations live in peace. History does not and
cannot take note of this fact. History is really a record of every interruption of the even working of the force of love or of the soul.
Two brothers quarrel; one of them repents and re-awakens the love
that was lying dormant in him; the two again begin to live in
peace; nobody takes note of this. But if the two brothers, through
the intervention of solicitors or some other reason take up arms or
go to law—which is another form of the exhibition of brute
force,—their doings would be immediately noticed in the press,
they would be the talk of their neighbours and would probably
go down to history. And what is true of families and communities is true of nations. There is no reason to believe that there is
one law for families and another for nations. History, then, is a
record of an interruption of the course of nature. Soul-force,
being natural, is not noted in history.

READER   According to what you say, it is plain that instances of this
kind of passive resistance are not to be found in history. It is necessary to understand this passive resistance more fully. It will be better, therefore, if you enlarge upon it.

EDITOR   Passive resistance is a method of securing rights by personal
suffering; it is the reverse of resistance by arms. When I refuse to do
a thing that is repugnant to my conscience, I use soul-force. For
instance, the Government of the day has passed a law which is
applicable to me. I do not like it. If by using violence I force the

Government to repeal the law, I am employing what may be termed body-force. If I do not obey the law and accept the penalty for its breach, I use soul-force. It involves sacrifice of self.

7

JAWAHARLAL NEHRU
Gandhi, 1936

Mohandas K. Gandhi and Jawaharlal Nehru* were the two most important leaders of India's national independence movement. In 1936 Nehru published his autobiography, excerpted here, in which he had much to say about the importance of Gandhi in his life. Though they worked together and Nehru was Gandhi's choice as the first Indian prime minister, they expressed in their personalities and ideas two very different Indias. How would you describe these two Indias? Was it Gandhi's or Nehru's vision of the future that was realized? Who do you think was a better guide for India? Why?

THINKING HISTORICALLY

Think of Gandhi and Nehru as the two sides of the Indian struggle for independence. Did India benefit from having both of these sides represented? What would have happened if there had been only Gandhi's view or only Nehru's?

How was the debate in India about the influence of the West different from the debate in Japan?

I imagine that Gandhiji[1] is not so vague about the objective as he sometimes appears to be. He is passionately desirous of going in a certain direction, but this is wholly at variance with modern ideas and conditions, and he has so far been unable to fit the two, or to chalk out all the intermediate steps leading to his goal. Hence the appearance of

---

* jah wah HAHR lahl   NAY roo
[1] Term of endearment for Gandhi. [Ed.]

Source: Jawaharlal Nehru, *An Autobiography* (New Delhi: Allied Publishers, 1942–1962), 510–11.

vagueness and avoidance of clarity. But his general inclination has been clear enough for a quarter of a century, ever since he started formulating his philosophy in South Africa. I do not know if those early writings still represent his views. I doubt if they do so in their entirety, but they do help us to understand the background of his thought.

"India's salvation consists," he wrote in 1909, "in unlearning what she has learned during the last fifty years. The railways, telegraphs, hospitals, lawyers, doctors, and suchlike have all to go; and the so-called upper classes have to learn consciously, religiously, and deliberately the simple peasant life, knowing it to be a life giving true happiness." And again: "Every time I get into a railway car or use a motor bus I know that I am doing violence to my sense of what is right"; "to attempt to reform the world by means of highly artificial and speedy locomotion is to attempt the impossible."

All this seems to me utterly wrong and harmful doctrine, and impossible of achievement. Behind it lies Gandhiji's love and praise of poverty and suffering and the ascetic life. For him progress and civilization consist not in the multiplication of wants, of higher standards of living, "but in the deliberate and voluntary restriction of wants, which promotes real happiness and contentment, and increases the capacity for service." If these premises are once accepted, it becomes easy to follow the rest of Gandhiji's thought and to have a better understanding of his activities. But most of us do not accept those premises, and yet we complain later on when we find that his activities are not to our liking.

Personally I dislike the praise of poverty and suffering. I do not think they are at all desirable, and they ought to be abolished. Nor do I appreciate the ascetic life as a social ideal, though it may suit individuals. I understand and appreciate simplicity, equality, self-control; but not the mortification of the flesh. Just as an athlete requires to train his body, I believe that the mind and habits have also to be trained and brought under control. It would be absurd to expect that a person who is given to too much self-indulgence can endure much suffering or show unusual self-control or behave like a hero when the crisis comes. To be in good moral condition requires at least as much training as to be in good physical condition. But that certainly does not mean asceticism or self-mortification.

Nor do I appreciate in the least the idealization of the "simple peasant life." I have almost a horror of it, and instead of submitting to it myself I want to drag out even the peasantry from it, not to urbanization, but to the spread of urban cultural facilities to rural areas. Far from his life's giving me true happiness, it would be almost as bad as imprisonment for me. What is there in "The Man with the Hoe" to idealize over? Crushed and exploited for innumerable generations, he is only little removed from the animals who keep him company.

Who made him dead to rapture and despair,
A thing that grieves not and that never hopes,
Stolid and stunned, a brother to the ox?[2]

This desire to get away from the mind of man to primitive conditions where mind does not count, seems to me quite incomprehensible. The very thing that is the glory and triumph of man is decried and discouraged, and a physical environment which will oppress the mind and prevent its growth is considered desirable. Present-day civilization is full of evils, but it is also full of good; and it has the capacity in it to rid itself of those evils. To destroy it root and branch is to remove that capacity from it and revert to a dull, sunless, and miserable existence. But even if that were desirable it is an impossible undertaking. We cannot stop the river of change or cut ourselves adrift from it, and psychologically we who have eaten of the apple of Eden cannot forget that taste and go back to primitiveness.

[2] From poem by Edwin Markam, "The Man with the Hoe" (1899), which was a response to the painting of the same title by Jean Millet. [Ed.]

■ REFLECTIONS

We have looked at the conflict between Westernization and nationalism through windows on Japan and India. For the Japanese, the borrowing of Western institutions and ideas provided an escape from colonization. By the time India gained political independence in 1947, it had become partially Westernized by three hundred years of colonialism. Yet in both countries there were those who resisted Western ways, those who embraced them, and others still who developed ambivalent feelings toward the West.

This last response — often accepting the contradictions: treasuring the traditional while trying the new — may have been the most difficult, but ultimately the most useful. It must have been far easier to cast off everything Asian, as Fukuzawa Yukichi urged, or make fun of any contact with the West as monkeying around or frightful miscegenation, as the Japanese cartoons suggested. Japan may have made the most successful non-Western transition to industrial modernity because it steered a path between Fukuzawa Yukichi's prescription for wholesale cultural capitulation and the cartoonists' blanket rejection of anything new and foreign.

India, with older indigenous traditions than Japan but also a longer period confronting the influence of Western culture, approached independence in 1947 with a political elite trained in English law, liberal and Marxist political parties, a literate English-speaking middle class, and a long-suppressed hunger for economic freedom and material well-being. Gandhi feared violence, anticolonial in 1909 and anti-Muslim in 1947, more than the repressions of the old society. While he sought a new social cohesion in traditional religious spiritualism, Nehru hoped to forge a new solidarity along the Western industrial socialist model.

Some may find the nationalist vision of Okakura more unsettling. Certainly his celebration of Asian art was long overdue. Though Japanese art, especially, was well known to a Western elite of artists and collectors (Gaughin for one made it his own), most Westerners ignorantly dismissed it. It is interesting that even today many college courses in art history ignore Asian art, relegating it at best to a separate course. In introducing Asian art to the West, Okakura began a Herculean task, still not fully accomplished. But Okakura's nationalism had a sharp edge that cut aggressively in the next generation. In his eagerness to embrace a deep Asian past as his own, he adopted for Japan centuries of oppressive Asian dynasties including the Mongols, in the process turning cultural heritage into racial inheritance. The idea of race, initially a Western pseudo-science to rationalize dominion, would be turned against the West with consequences as devastating as those experienced in Europe in the 1930s and 1940s. That is not to blame Okakura for later Japanese nationalism. He merely participated in a kind of nationalism that turned lethal.

Nationalism could always turn inward or outward. Even when it turned outward, it did not have to denigrate "the other." The idea that the nation consisted of those who lived on the same soil and the idea that each nation had its own individual attributes were beliefs of what historians have come to call "liberal nationalism," the nationalist movement that prevailed especially in the first half of the nineteenth century. The antagonistic idea that national identity was in the blood, and that, therefore, not only are some nations better than others but their superiority is in their genes, were beliefs of the "ethnic nationalism" that developed along with racism at the end of the century. A belief that nations were based on blood would help spawn two world wars.

24

World War I and Its Consequences

Europe and the World, 1914–1920

■ HISTORICAL CONTEXT

The Europe that so many non-European intellectuals sought to imitate or reject between 1880 and 1920 came very close to self-destructing between 1914 and 1918, and bringing many of the world's peoples from Asia, Africa, and the Americas down with it. The orgy of bloodletting, then known as the "Great War," put seventy million men in uniform, of whom ten million were killed and twenty million were wounded. Most of the soldiers were Western European, though Russia contributed more soldiers than France or Germany, while Japan enlisted as many as the Austro-Hungarian Empire that began the war. Enlisted men also came from the United States, Canada, Australia, New Zealand, South Africa, and the colonies: India, French West Africa, and German East Africa, among others. The majority of soldiers were killed in Europe, especially along the German Western Front—four hundred miles of trenches that spanned from Switzerland to the English Channel, across Belgium and France. But battles were also fought along the borders of German, French, and English colonies in Africa, and there were high Australian casualties on the coast of Gallipoli in Ottoman Turkey.

The selections in this chapter focus on the lives and deaths of the soldiers, as well as the efforts of some of their political leaders to redefine the world around them. We examine the experiences of soldiers and how the war changed the lives of those who survived its devastating toll. We compare the accounts of those who fought on both sides of the great divide. Germany and the Austro-Hungarian Empire, joined by the Ottoman Empire, formed an alliance called the Central Powers (see Map 24.1). In opposition, England, France, and Russia, the Allied Powers, were later joined by Italy, Greece, Japan, and the United States. We compare views across the generational divide as well as from the trenches and government offices.

858

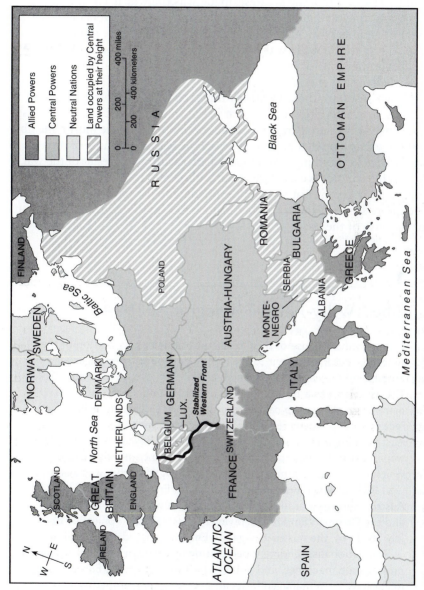

Map 24.1 Allied Powers and Central Powers in World War I.

■ THINKING HISTORICALLY

Understanding Causes and Consequences

From 1914 to 1920, the greatest divide was the war itself. It marked the end of one era and the beginning of another. Few events have left the participants with such a profound sense of fundamental change. And so our study of the war is an appropriate place to ask two of the universal questions of major historical change: What caused it? What were the consequences?

The *causes* are those events or forces that came before; the *consequences* are the results, what the war itself prompted to occur. Thus, causes and consequences are part of the same continuum. Still, we must remember that not everything that happened before the war was a cause of the war. Similarly, not everything that happened afterward was a result of the war.

In this chapter we explore specific ideas about cause and consequence. Our goal is not to compile a definitive list of either but, rather, to explore some of the ways that historians and thoughtful readers can make sense of the past.

1

The "Willy-Nicky" Telegrams, 1914

The immediate cause of the Great War was the assassination of the Archduke Ferdinand, heir to the throne of the Austro-Hungarian Empire, on his visit to the Bosnian city of Sarajevo on June 28, 1914. The assassin was a Bosnian Serb who was acting as part of a Bosnian nationalist group called "Young Bosnia," with help from recently independent Serbia, in an effort to detach Bosnia from the Austro-Hungarian Empire. The damage might have ended there if it were not for the alliances that knit Europe into competing camps, which were already armed and expecting a fight. Serbia was allied with Russia, which was, in turn, allied with England and France. Austria-Hungary was allied with Germany, as well as with Italy (briefly) and the Ottoman Empire. Following the assassination of its heir on July 28, 1914, the Austro-Hungarian Empire declared war on Serbia.

The nationalist sentiment percolating up through national armies, propaganda machines, and political parties throughout Europe might have been managed by its array of kings and emperors who had unusually international backgrounds and actually were members

Source: *The Kaiser's Letters to the Tsar: Copied from Government Archives in Petrograd, and Brought from Russia by Isaac Don Levine*, ed. Neil Grant (London: Hodder and Stoughton, 1920).

of the same extended family. But it was not managed. The ruling families of Europe contained numerous first cousins who were all grandchildren of England's Queen Victoria. Among them were Kaiser Wilhelm II of Germany and Czar Nicholas II of Russia. This selection contains the telegrams sent between Wilhelm II and Nicholas II (Willy and Nicky) from July 29 to August 1, 1914. What do they tell you about the origins of World War I?

THINKING HISTORICALLY

This selection shifts our focus to the short-term or immediate causes of the war. It also raises the question of the importance of specific individuals. Historians often disagree about the relative importance of individuals as opposed to social forces in history. What does this selection lead you to think about the importance of the individual in history?

Russian Tsar Nicholas II to German Kaiser Wilhelm II

29 July 1914, 1 a.m.
Peter's Court Palais
Sa Majesté l'Empereur
Neues Palais

Am glad you are back. In this serious moment, I appeal to you to help me. An ignoble war has been declared to a weak country. The indignation in Russia shared fully by me is enormous. I foresee that very soon I shall be overwhelmed by the pressure forced upon me and be forced to take extreme measures which will lead to war. To try and avoid such a calamity as a European war I beg you in the name of our old friendship to do what you can to stop your allies from going too far.

Kaiser to Tsar

29 July 1914, 1.45 a.m. (this and the previous telegraph crossed) It is with the gravest concern that I hear of the impression which the action of Austria against Serbia is creating in your country.

The unscrupulous agitation that has been going on in Serbia for years has resulted in the outrageous crime, to which Archduke Francis Ferdinand fell a victim. The spirit that led Serbians to murder their own king and his wife still dominates the country.

You will doubtless agree with me that we both, you and me, have a common interest as well as all Sovereigns to insist that all the persons morally responsible for the dastardly murder should receive their deserved punishment. In this case politics plays no part at all.

On the other hand, I fully understand how difficult it is for you and your Government to face the drift of your public opinion. Therefore, with regard to the hearty and tender friendship which binds us both from long ago with firm ties, I am exerting my utmost influence to induce the Austrians to deal straightly to arrive to a satisfactory understanding with you. I confidently hope that you will help me in my efforts to smooth over difficulties that may still arise.

Your very sincere and devoted friend and cousin
Willy

Kaiser to Tsar

29 July 1914, 6.30 p.m.
Berlin

I received your telegram and share your wish that peace should be maintained.

But as I told you in my first telegram, I cannot consider Austria's action against Servia an "ignoble" war. Austria knows by experience that Servian promises on paper are wholly unreliable. I understand its action must be judged as trending to get full guarantee that the Servian promises shall become real facts. This my reasoning is borne out by the statement of the Austrian cabinet that Austria does not want to make any territorial conquests at the expense of Servia.

I therefore suggest that it would be quite possible for Russia to remain a spectator of the austro-servian conflict without involving Europe in the most horrible war she ever witnessed. I think a direct understanding between your Government and Vienna possible and desirable, and as I already telegraphed to you, my Government is continuing its exercises to promote it.

Of course military measures on the part of Russia would be looked upon by Austria as a calamity we both wish to avoid and jeopardize my position as mediator which I readily accepted on your appeal to my friendship and my help.

Willy

Tsar to Kaiser

29 July 1914, 8.20 p.m.
Peter's Court Palace

Thanks for your telegram conciliatory and friendly. Whereas official message presented today by your ambassador to my minister was conveyed in a very different tone. Beg you to explain this divergency! It would be right to give over the Austro-servian problem to the Hague conference. Trust in your wisdom and friendship.

Your loving Nicky

Tsar to Kaiser

30 July 1914, 1.20 a.m.
Peter's Court Palais

Thank you heartily for your quick answer. Am sending Tatischev this evening with instructions.

The military measures which have now come into force were decided five days ago for reasons of defence on account of Austria's preparations.

I hope from all my heart that these measures won't in any way interfere with your part as mediator which I greatly value. We need your strong pressure on Austria to come to an understanding with us.

Nicky

Kaiser to Tsar

30 July 1914, 1.20 a.m.
Berlin

Best thanks for telegram. It is quite out of the question that my ambassador's language could have been in contradiction with the tenor of my telegram. Count Pourtalès was instructed to draw the attention of your government to the danger & grave consequences involved by a mobilisation; I said the same in my telegram to you. Austria has only mobilised against Servia & only a part of her army. If, as it is now the case, according to the communication by you & your Government, Russia mobilises against Austria, my rôle as mediator you kindly intrusted me with, & which I accepted at you[r] express prayer, will be endangered if not ruined. The whole weight of the decision lies solely on you[r] shoulders now, who have to bear the responsibility for Peace or War.

Willy

Kaiser to Tsar

31 July 1914
Berlin

On your appeal to my friendship and your call for assistance began to mediate between your and the austro-hungarian Government. While this action was proceeding your troops were mobilised against Austro-Hungary, my ally. [T]hereby, as I have already pointed out to you, my mediation has been made almost illusory.

I have nevertheless continued my action.

I now receive authentic news of serious preparations for war on my Eastern frontier. Responsibility for the safety of my empire forces preventive measures of defence upon me. In my endeavours to maintain the peace of the world I have gone to the utmost limit possible. The responsibility for the disaster which is now threatening the whole civilised world will not be laid at my door. In this moment it still lies in your power to avert it. Nobody is threatening the honour or power of Russia who can well afford to await the result of my mediation. My friendship for you and your empire, transmitted to me by my grandfather on his deathbed has always been sacred to me and I have honestly often backed up Russia when she was in serious trouble especially in her last war.

The peace of Europe may still be maintained by you, if Russia will agree to stop the milit. measures which must threaten Germany and Austro-Hungary.

Willy

Tsar to Kaiser

31 July 1914 (this and the previous telegram crossed)
Petersburg, Palace
Sa Majesté l'Empereur, Neues Palais

I thank you heartily for your mediation which begins to give one hope that all may yet end peacefully.

It is *technically* impossible to stop our military preparations which were obligatory owing to Austria's mobilisation. We are far from wishing war. As long as the negotiations with Austria on Servia's account are taking place my troops shall not make any provocative action. I give you my solemn word for this. I put all my trust in God's mercy and hope in your successful mediation in Vienna for the welfare of our countries and for the peace of Europe.

Your affectionate,
Nicky

Tsar to Kaiser

1 August 1914
Peter's Court, Palace
Sa Majesté l'Empereur
Berlin

I received your telegram. Understand you are obliged to mobilise but wish to have the same guarantee from you as I gave you, that these measures do not mean war and that we shall continue negotiating for the benefit of our countries and universal peace dear to all our hearts. Our long proved friendship must succeed, with God's help, in avoiding bloodshed. Anxiously, full of confidence await your answer.

Nicky

Kaiser to Tsar

1 August 1914
Berlin

Thanks for your telegram. I yesterday pointed out to your government the way by which alone war may be avoided.

Although I requested an answer for noon today, no telegram from my ambassador conveying an answer from your Government has reached me as yet. I therefore have been obliged to mobilise my army.

Immediate affirmative clear and unmistakable answer from your government is the only way to avoid endless misery. Until I have received this answer alas, I am unable to discuss the subject of your telegram. As a matter of fact I must request you to immediatly [sic] order your troops on no account to commit the slightest act of trespassing over our frontiers.

Willy

World War I Propaganda Posters, 1915–1918

Posters were the communication medium of the First World War. In an age when governments had still not taught most people how to read but increasingly needed their consent or compliance, images often spoke louder than words, but those images had to be *persuasive*.

The American poster from 1917 and the German poster from 1915–1916 (Figures 24.1 and 24.3) implore men to enlist in the army; the Italian poster from 1917 (Figure 24.2) encourages people to buy war bonds. What do you think accounts for the similar graphic style

Figure 24.1 Recruiting Poster for U.S. Army, 1917.
Source: Library of Congress, 3g03859.

Figure 24.2   Italian Poster for National War Loan, 1917.
Source: Snark / Art Resource, NY.

used in these three posters? How effective do you think they were, and why?

Another strategy for promoting loyalty, patriotism, and support for a war that was lasting far longer than anyone had anticipated was to demonize or ridicule the enemy. What feelings does the U.S. anti-German poster from 1917–1918 (Figure 24.4) attempt to provoke in viewers, and how does the scene shown achieve this?

Figure 24.3 Recruiting Poster for German Army, 1915–1916.
Source: Library of Congress, 3g11546.

Women contributed to the war in various ways. Figure 24.5 asks German women to contribute their gold. Figure 24.6 urges women in London to come to work in the munitions industry. What images of women do these posters portray? Finally, Figure 24.7 asks Americans to support Armenian refugees from the Ottoman Empire in newly proclaimed independent Armenia and Syria. What response is the image of woman and child supposed to evoke?

THINKING HISTORICALLY

When war broke out overseas in 1914, President Woodrow Wilson declared it a European matter that had nothing to do with the United

Figure 24.4   Propaganda Poster, United States, 1917–1918.
Source: Library of Congress, LC-DIG-ds-03216.

States, and most Americans agreed. Indeed, the United States did not join the war and throw its crucial weight behind the Allied Powers until April 1917. What role do you think propaganda such as Figure 24.4 played in swaying public opinion? This and the other posters illustrate both sides' efforts to promote and sustain the cause of war. What do they tell you about the causes of the war? What do they tell you about the consequences?

Figure 24.5 German Appeal to Women: Gold for the War.
Source: Library of Congress, 3g11609.

Figure 24.6 English Appeal to Women: Munitions Work.

Source: World War Poster Collection (MSS36), University of Minnesota Libraries, Archives and Special Collections, Minneapolis, MN.

YOU CAN'T LET US STARVE

2½ million women and children now starving to death.

YOUR BIT SAVES A LIFE

Send Money to

ARMENIAN and SYRIAN RELIEF

1 Madison Ave. N.Y. City

Figure 24.7 "Your Bit Saves a Life."

Source: World War Poster Collection (MSS36), University of Minnesota Libraries, Archives and Special Collections, Minneapolis, MN.

3

WILFRED OWEN

Dulce et Decorum Est, 1917

Wilfred Owen (1893–1918) enlisted in the British Army in 1915, was wounded in 1917, and was hospitalized, released, and sent back to the front, where he died on November 4, 1918, one week before the end of the war. In this poem, he describes a poison gas attack. Like the machine gun and the airplane, gas was a common element of the new mechanized mass warfare. Owen describes how physically debilitating the effects of gas were. Why was gas such an effective and deadly weapon? How, according to Owen, had the nature of war changed?

THINKING HISTORICALLY

The concluding phrase, which means "Sweet and proper it is to die for one's country," was a Latin declaration of patriotic duty that English students repeated as a lesson, not only in Latin classes but, more important, in their political education as subjects of the British Empire. How does Owen portray this lesson as a cause of the war? What does he imagine to be the consequences of fighting a war with such patriotic slogans in mind?

Dulce et Decorum Est

Bent double, like old beggars under sacks,
Knock-kneed, coughing like hags, we cursed through sludge,
Till on the haunting flares we turned our backs
And towards our distant rest began the trudge.
Men marched asleep. Many had lost their boots
But limped on, blood-shod. All went lame; all blind;
Drunk with fatigue; deaf even to the hoots
Of tired, outstripped Five-Nines[1] that dropped behind.

Gas! GAS! Quick, boys!—An ecstasy of fumbling,
Fitting the clumsy helmets just in time;
But someone still was yelling out and stumbling,
And flound'ring like a man in fire or lime. . . .

---

[1] German artillery shells. [Ed.]

Source: Wilfred Owen, *Poems*, ed. Siegfried Sassoon (London: Chatto and Windus, 1920).

Dim, through the misty panes and thick green light,
As under a green sea, I saw him drowning.

In all my dreams, before my helpless sight,
He plunges at me, guttering, choking, drowning.

If in some smothering dreams you too could pace
Behind the wagon that we flung him in,
And watch the white eyes writhing in his face,
His hanging face, like a devil's sick of sin;
If you could hear, at every jolt, the blood
Come gargling from the froth-corrupted lungs,
Obscene as cancer, bitter as the cud
Of vile, incurable sores on innocent tongues,
My friend, you would not tell with such high zest,
To children ardent for some desperate glory.
The old Lie: Dulce et decorum est
Pro patria mori.

4

Memories of Senegalese Soldiers, 1914–1918/1981–1999

Not only did the roots of the First World War lie in competing imperial claims, but some of the fighting took place along imperial divides of colonies as well. Africans in French and English colonies were mobilized to fight Africans in neighboring German colonies, and vice versa. In addition, many Africans were mobilized to fight in Europe, especially after European troops suffered heavy losses along the Western Front. Over 140,000 West Africans were recruited into the French Army between 1914 and 1918 to serve in Europe. Some 45,000 never returned. Senegal mobilized more than other colonies: 29,000, probably more than one-third of the men of military age.

Source: Joe Lunn, *Memoirs of the Maelstrom: A Senegalese Oral History of the First World War* (Portsmouth, NH: Heinemann, 1999), 40, 42, 78–79, 97–98, 102–3, 110, 137, 165–66, 172–73, 174, 108–9, 190, 230, 232–33. Headings added; individual names and footnotes deleted.

The historian Joe Lunn interviewed eighty-five of these Senegalese veterans for his book *Memoirs of the Maelstrom: A Senegalese Oral History of the First World War*, from which these selections are drawn. What do these various Senegalese voices tell you about the African experience in the First World War? How was their experience of the war different from that of European soldiers? How were Senegalese soldiers recruited, and why did they enlist? What were their expectations?

THINKING HISTORICALLY

These memories provide greater insight into the consequences than the causes of World War I. How did the war change the lives of those African troops who survived? How did it change the way the Senegalese and French thought of themselves and each other?

[Recruitment]

Many of the young men fled from the village [when the *chef de canton* came to take soldiers]. [But] they used to arrest their fathers [if] they [did not] come back. [And] often their mothers used to say to their sons [when they returned from the countryside for food]: "You know that your name has been written [down by the *chef de canton*] and [yet] you ran away. And now your father has been arrested and he will be taken [to] prison. So go and enter the army." And often they used to go and enter the army [so that] their fathers [would be] released.

In each family they only took one young man, never two. And my father decided that I should go and enter the army instead of my elder brother. Because, he told me: "If I die, your elder brother could care for the family, but you are too young for that." That's why he sent me into the army. I was not happy to go, [but] because I was very close to my father . . . I felt obliged to.

I was in Bamako [on leave] when Blaise Diagne and Galandou Diouf[1] came to recruit soldiers. [And my friend and I] attended the meeting he called for recruitment. [And] Blaise Diagne's propaganda [at] this meeting [was very effective]. Because, before he came, he had made the son of

---

[1] Blaise Diagne (1872–1934), from Senegal, became in 1914 the first black African elected to the French national parliament where he fought for and won the right of urban Senegalese to be citizens and soldiers. He was appointed by French prime minister George Clemenceau to head the recruitment drive in French West Africa during the war. Galandou Diouf (1875–1941), the first black African elected (in 1909) to the Senegalese assembly, was Diagne's assistant. They argued that military service was a vehicle to full and equal citizenship for Africans. [Ed.]

the *chef de quartier* in Bamako a lieutenant. [So] almost all the town was there, because the chief had called everybody, and there were a lot, a lot, a lot of people! The fact that Blaise Diagne had made his son a lieutenant was a very important thing for him personally, because . . . for the Bambara becoming an officer in the army was a very great honor. [And Diagne came] with many, many people—August Brunet [the lieutenant governor of Haut-Sénégal et Niger] and [other] French administrators. [And] he was [accompanied by] some Bambara soldiers too. But they were not simple soldiers; all of them had "*grades.*"[2] [And after speeches by Galandou Diouf, the *chef de quartier*, and his son, Diagne spoke.] [And although] I have forgotten almost all his speech, I remember that he told them that he was sent by the President of the Republic of France who needed [more] soldiers to go on fighting. And after [he finished], he introduced the son of the *chef de quartier* to [all] the other parents that were at the meeting. [And he told them:] "I want some other soldiers to enter the army, so perhaps they too can become lieutenants." So as soon as he said that, everybody gave him the name of his son. And the secretary was writing down their names. [And] that's why he succeeded with his recruitment mission [among the Bambara]—[because] everybody was expecting his son to become an officer one day.

[Becoming Soldiers]

We all joined the same army—the French army. . . . So we did not think about our [previous] way of living, our behavior, our [former] kingdoms. We were bound to follow the French regulations and their way of thinking about all these things. [And although] little arguments sometimes [occurred] between soldiers from the same country, [the status of a man's family] wasn't stressed. . . . There wasn't any [social] differentiation [with regard to slaves] because we were following another system—another [way of] life—which was the French one.

[Departures]

We [sailed from Dakar] on a boat called *l'Afrique* on May 9, 1916. There was a French officer with us—[a lieutenant called Oeuvre]—[who] was a very very bad man. We spent [the first] three days [being allowed to go on deck] in the boat . . . and we had a good journey. [But] when we arrived at a place called "the Gulf" [Golfe de Gascogne] . . . this French officer said that all the soldiers had to go downstairs—deep inside the ship. And he put [a guard] at the door [to prevent] any of us from going

[2] Ranks. [Ed.]

out. . . . And we [were confined for] the [next] six days in the bottom [of the boat near] the keel. [And] we suffered a lot in the bottom of the ship because there was no air. From time to time they opened the [portholes] to let some air [in, but] after that they closed them [again]. And even during meals, we were eating in the bottom of the ship. And it was very hot [there] and it was very tight.

[In France]

When we went [to the camps in France,] Diagne joined us [there] to see about our conditions. Whenever you had problems, he came and solved them. Sometimes the food was bad or insufficient, for example. [So] when Diagne came, if we said the food was not good, he called the officers together and asked [them] why. He said, "I brought soldiers to fight for you and to help you. And I don't see why you treat them like this!" So he would tear off the ranks [of insignia] of the officers and put them on the table.

We felt very proud after the attack because the French had tried many times to retake the fort, but finally, we [were the ones] that took it. . . . And when we were leaving the fort, our officers told us not to wash our uniforms even though they were very dirty and covered with mud. But we were told: "Don't wash your uniforms. Cross the country as you are so that everyone who meets you will know that you made the attack on Fort Douaumont." And we took the train [and traveled] for three days between Douaumont and St. Raphäel. And in every town we crossed, the French were clapping their hands and shouting: "*Vive les tirailleurs sénégalais!*" . . . And afterwards, whenever we were walking in the country—everywhere we used to go—if we told people that we made the attack on Fort Douaumont, the French were looking at us with much admiration.

One day I was in the [mess hall] in the camp [where] we used to eat. And often after eating, we used to drink coffee in cups. But before drinking it, we used to make "cheers" with the other soldiers. So on this day, I took my cup and I wanted to make "cheers" with a French soldier who was sitting next to me. So I made the "cheers," [but] the soldier said to me, "don't touch my cup, you are too dirty!" And [this made] me very angry. [So] I punched him and we began to fight. And when they went to get the captain, the captain told me that I was right, and he told the French soldier that he would be punished. But afterwards, I became very friendly with this same soldier.

I had a very good [French] friend—his name was Perout—[and we] were in the same unit. . . . I was his only African friend, [but] we spent a lot of time together. [And] I often went to his house [when on leave]. He invited me [there] for lunch, or dinner, and sometimes I spent the night. . . . And when his [family] came to visit him, they kissed me before they kissed him — his father, his mother, and his sisters.

"Marraine de guerre" . . . was the term used by the soldiers to say "my girlfriend"; instead of saying "my girlfriend," they said "my *marraine de guerre.*" [And] the African soldiers in France had their *marraines de guerre* too. They were not prostitutes. They were girls of good families who saw us and knew that we were [far from] our countries. [And they realized] we needed some affection and some money . . . to buy cigarettes with, to go to the movies, and so on.

[And we met them] on the street or in cafés. A French girl saw you and felt very pleased by [your appearance]. And she said to you that she wanted to take you to her house to present you to her parents. And you got [an adopted] French family in that way. [But] it wasn't necessary to have love affairs [with them]. From time to time some *marraines de guerre* fell in love with the soldiers they invited home. But generally, they were only friendly relations.

Some of the French who had never seen a "black" man used to pay to come and see us. [And the European soldiers] were making money selling tickets. [They] used to take us to a hidden place and told us: "Stay here. We are going to bring some Frenchmen who have never seen 'black' people before." [But] we didn't know they were making money in that way.

[And after they] got the money, they used to bring the *Tubabs*[3] to look at us. And [they] said: "This one is a Senegalese, this one is a Somalian, [and so forth]." And the *Tubabs* were touching us, and peeking, creeping very close to us because we [looked so different].

[Return]

One day [we were on] the ship that brought us back to Senegal from Bordeaux. . . . There were [many] Senegalese soldiers [aboard, and sometimes] they got into arguments with some of the "white" men who treated them like "dirty niggers." . . . And one of these soldiers — a citizen from Goree — was [called] a *"sale nègre"* by a "white" man. . . . I think maybe the [French]man was not well educated, or perhaps he was drunk. [And the soldier hit] him hard . . . and [they] started fighting. [And] we all [joined in] and started to give our friend some help. And we beat [the

[3] Europeans. [Ed.]

Frenchman] badly until he asked to be forgiven. He was crying and said that he would never do it again.

So what happened [afterwards]? Nothing! We were within our rights, because discrimination between people [was no longer tolerated] at that time, [and] we were French citizens like anybody else. [If] the "white" man wanted to start acting like that, we [could retaliate] and nothing happened. [But] if the same thing had happened before the war, [we] would not have done the same thing. Because we had less power then, and [we] were treated badly like this [by the French] all the time.

[The parents of those who had been killed] knew the number of soldiers who went to the war together, and they [also] knew the number of soldiers who came back. So no one [had to tell] them that their sons were dead; they guessed it [on their own]. [But afterward], we told them how they died. Those [of us who] knew their sons had died explained to their families [what had happened to them]. . . . [I had to do this once.] . . . A son [from my grandfather's family] was lost in Champagne. . . . And [they] knew that we went [to the war] together. But when I came back, they didn't see him. And after a while, they began to ask me where he was. And I told them: "He is dead; you have to make the sacrifices."

[After the War]

We went to France, we fought for France, and the French took us by force to fight for them. [But] we learned nothing [there]—[not] even the French language. They only taught us some rudimentary [commands], [in order] to use us in the war. But they didn't care about teaching us the structure and the sound of their language. So [although we] went to the war, [we] came back here without any real knowledge of the French language.

I received many lasting things from the war. I demonstrated my dignity and courage, and [I] won the respect of the people and the [colonial] government. And whenever the people of the village had something to contest [with the French]—and they didn't dare do it [themselves] because they were afraid of them—I used to do it for them. And many times when people had problems with the government, I used to go with my decorations and arrange the situation for [them]. Because whenever the *Tubabs* saw your decorations, they knew that they [were dealing with] a very important person. . . . And I gained this ability—of obtaining justice over a *Tubab*—from the war.

The war changed many, many things. At first, when we joined the army, when you had an argument or a problem with a "white" man, what happened? You were wrong; you were [always] wrong. But later, those things changed. [Then] they looked into the matter and determined who was wrong or right. [But] before that time, the "black" man didn't mean anything. So that [change] was something [very important]. [And] the respect we gained [from] the war [continued] increasing; it never [diminished]. [And this] respect [continued] increasing day to day—up until [it culminated in] the Independence Day.

5

Zimmermann Telegram, 1917

By the beginning of 1917, the war was at a stalemate. German troops were well fortified along their western front from the Ardennes Forest in northern France across Belgium to the Atlantic. Neither the Germans nor the French and English on the other side of this line could advance. A British naval blockade of Germany led to a German decision to begin unrestricted submarine warfare, hoping to force a British surrender before a likely American intervention. The United States remained neutral, but after the sinking of the ocean liner *Lusitania* in 1916, Washington threatened to become involved if there were further submarine attacks.

On January 11, 1917, German Foreign Secretary Albert Zimmermann telegrammed the German ambassador to Mexico in code. British intelligence intercepted the telegram and sent the following translation to the United States.

What did Zimmermann propose? What did he hope to gain? What were the risks?

THINKING HISTORICALLY

It is difficult to distinguish between the immediate or precipitant role of the Zimmermann telegram and the longer-term role of German expansion, especially Germany's submarine attacks in the Atlantic, in U.S. intervention. President Woodrow Wilson, reelected in 1916 because "he kept us out of war," made full use of the telegram to declare war. For him, the telegram was the smoking gun. He declared war despite the doubts of German sympathizers, who thought that

Source: U.S. National Archives Record Group 59: General Records of the Department of State, 1756–1979, National Archives and Records Administration, National Archives Identifier 302025.

the telegram was a forgery intended to provoke the United States, and despite the fact that he was prevented from proving its authenticity by the British, who did not want the Germans to know that they had broken German codes. For both Wilson and the opponents of war, the telegram was crucial.

Zimmermann saw the telegram differently. He admitted sending it, affirming its authenticity (thus inadvertently undermining the American antiwar movement) because he thought it would keep the United States out of the war. How could he have imagined the telegram would keep the United States neutral? Why is it also likely that Zimmermann thought the submarine attacks would not be a cause of war?

Berlin, January 19, 1917

On the first of February we intend to begin submarine warfare unrestricted. In spite of this, it is our intention to endeavour to keep neutral the United States of America.

If this attempt is not successful, we propose an alliance on the following basis with Mexico: That we shall make war together and together make peace. We shall give general financial support, and it is understood that Mexico is to reconquer the lost territory in New Mexico, Texas, and Arizona. The details are left to you for settlement. . . .

You are instructed to inform the President of Mexico of the above in the greatest confidence as soon as it is certain that there will be an outbreak of war with the United States and suggest that the President of Mexico, on his own initiative, should communicate with Japan suggesting adherence at once to this plan; at the same time, offer to mediate between Germany and Japan.

Please call to the attention of the President of Mexico that the employment of ruthless submarine warfare now promises to compel England to make peace in a few months.

Zimmermann
(Secretary of State)

6

V. I. LENIN

War and Revolution, 1917

One of the great casualties of the First World War was the Russian Empire, including the czar, his family, many of the members of their class, and its centuries-old autocratic system. The burden of war was simply too much for Russian society to bear. The disillusionment in the army and civilian society, along with the overwhelming costs of war, fueled uprisings among civilians and the army, and Czar Nicholas II was forced to abdicate in February of 1917. The government that emerged, under Alexander Kerensky, proved unable to satisfy the growing demands of peasants, veterans, and urban workers for "land, peace, and bread," a slogan that V. I. Lenin (1870–1924) and the communists exploited, successfully seizing power from the moderate parliamentarians in October of that year.

As a Marxist, Lenin believed that he could establish a socialist society in Russia, but he argued that Russian conditions (such as economic underdevelopment; the devastation of war; and the opposition of Europe, the United States, and Russian nobles to the revolution) made a democratic transition impossible. According to Lenin, a self-appointed government acting in the interests of the working class was the only way to a socialist Soviet Union. Lenin called this government "the dictatorship of the proletariat." Lenin delivered his "War and Revolution" address in May of 1917, during the fateful summer that followed the liberal February revolution and preceded the Bolshevik Revolution in October. How did Lenin view the First World War and Russia's continued participation in it? What did he hope to accomplish in the summer of 1917? How did he hope to accomplish it? The most important news for Russia's allies, England and France, in the summer of 1917 was the United States' entry into the war on their behalf. What was Lenin's reaction to this development?

THINKING HISTORICALLY

According to Lenin, what were the causes of the First World War? What did he believe to be the main cause of the Russian Revolution that occurred in February? What were the consequences of that revolution? What did he think would be the causes of a new revolution in Russia?

What we have at present is primarily two leagues, two groups of capitalist powers. We have before us all the world's greatest capitalist powers — Britain, France, America, and Germany — who for decades

Source: V. I. Lenin, *Collected Works*, 4th English ed. (Moscow: Progress Publishers, 1964), 24:398–421.

have doggedly pursued a policy of incessant economic rivalry aimed at achieving world supremacy, subjugating the small nations, and making threefold and tenfold profits on banking capital, which has caught the whole world in the net of its influence. That is what Britain's and Germany's policies really amount to. . . .

These policies show us just one thing—continuous economic rivalry between the world's two greatest giants, capitalist economies. On the one hand we have Britain, a country which owns the greater part of the globe, a country which ranks first in wealth, which has created this wealth not so much by the labour of its workers as by the exploitation of innumerable colonies, by the vast power of its banks which have developed at the head of all the others into an insignificantly small group of some four or five super-banks handling billions of rubles, and handling them in such a way that it can be said without exaggeration that there is not a patch of land in the world today on which this capital has not laid its heavy hand, not a patch of land which British capital has not enmeshed by a thousand threads. . . .

On the other hand, opposed to this, mainly Anglo-French group, we have another group of capitalists, an even more rapacious, even more predatory one, a group who came to the capitalist banqueting table when all the seats were occupied, but who introduced into the struggle new methods for developing capitalist production, improved techniques, and superior organization, which turned the old capitalism, the capitalism of the free-competition age, into the capitalism of giant trusts, syndicates, and cartels. This group introduced the beginnings of state-controlled capitalist production, combining the colossal power of capitalism with the colossal power of the state into a single mechanism and bringing tens of millions of people within the single organization of state capitalism. Here is economic history, here is diplomatic history, covering several decades, from which no one can get away. It is the one and only guide-post to a proper solution of the problem of war; it leads you to the conclusion that the present war, too, is the outcome of the policies of the classes who have come to grips in it, of the two supreme giants, who, long before the war, had caught the whole world, all countries, in the net of financial exploitation and economically divided the globe up among themselves. They were bound to clash, because a redivision of this supremacy, from the point of view of capitalism, had become inevitable. . . .

The present war is a continuation of the policy of conquest, of the shooting down of whole nationalities, of unbelievable atrocities committed by the Germans and the British in Africa, and by the British and the Russians in Persia—which of them committed most it is difficult to say. It was for this reason that the German capitalists looked upon them as their enemies. Ah, they said, you are strong because you are rich? But we are stronger, therefore we have the same "sacred" right to plunder. That is what the real history of British and German finance capital in the course of several decades preceding the war amounts to. That is what the history of Russo-German, Russo-British, and German-British relations amounts to. There you have the clue to an understanding of what the war is about. That is why the story that is current about the cause of the war is sheer duplicity and humbug. Forgetting the history of finance capital, the history of how this war had been brewing over the issue of redivision, they present the matter like this: Two nations were living at peace, then one attacked the other, and the other fought back. All science, all banks are forgotten, and the peoples are told to take up arms, and so are the peasants, who know nothing about politics. . . .

What revolution did we make? We overthrew Nicholas. The revolution was not so very difficult compared with one that would have overthrown the whole class of landowners and capitalists. Who did the revolution put in power? The landowners and capitalists—the very same classes who have long been in power in Europe. . . . The [February] Russian revolution has not altered the war, but it has created organizations which exist in no other country and were seldom found in revolutions in the West. . . . We have all over Russia a network of Soviets of Workers', Soldiers', and Peasants' Deputies. Here is a revolution which has not said its last word yet. . . .

In the two months following the revolution the industrialists have robbed the whole of Russia. Capitalists have made staggering profits; every financial report tells you that. And when the workers, two months after the revolution, had the "audacity" to say they wanted to live like human beings, the whole capitalist press throughout the country set up a howl.

On the question of America entering the war I shall say this. People argue that America is a democracy, America has the White House. I say: Slavery was abolished there half a century ago. The anti-slave war ended in 1865. Since then multimillionaires have mushroomed. They have the whole of America in their financial grip. They are making ready to subdue Mexico and will inevitably come to war with Japan over a carve-up of the Pacific. This war has been brewing for several decades. All literature speaks about it. America's real aim in entering the war is to prepare for this future war with Japan. The American people do enjoy considerable freedom and it is difficult to conceive them standing for compulsory military service, for the setting up of an army pursuing any aims of conquest—a struggle with Japan, for instance. The Americans have the example of Europe to show them what this leads to. The American capitalists have stepped into this war in order to have an excuse, behind a smoke-screen of lofty ideals championing the rights of small nations, for building up a strong standing army. . . .

Tens of millions of people are facing disaster and death; safeguarding the interests of the capitalists is the last thing that should bother us. The only way out is for all power to be transferred to the Soviets, which represent the majority of the population. Possibly mistakes may be made in the process. No one claims that such a difficult task can be disposed of offhand. We do not say anything of the sort. We are told that we want the power to be in the hands of the Soviets, but they don't want it. We say that life's experience will suggest this solution to them, and the whole nation will see that there is no other way out. We do not want a "seizure" of power, because the entire experience of past revolutions teaches us that the only stable power is the one that has the backing of the majority of the population. "Seizure" of power, therefore, would be adventurism, and our Party will not have it. . . .

Nothing but a workers' revolution in several countries can defeat this war. The war is not a game, it is an appalling thing taking a toll of millions of lives, and it is not to be ended easily.

. . . The war has been brought about by the ruling classes and only a revolution of the working class can end it. Whether you will get a speedy peace or not depends on how the revolution will develop.

Whatever sentimental things may be said, however much we may be told: Let us end the war immediately — this cannot be done without the development of the revolution. When power passes to the Soviets the capitalists will come out against us. Japan, France, Britain — the governments of all countries will be against us. The capitalists will be against, but the workers will be for us. That will be the end of the war which the capitalists started. There you have the answer to the question of how to end the war.

7

ROSA LUXEMBURG

The Problem of Dictatorship, 1918

Events moved very quickly in Russia in 1917. In May, Lenin insisted that the February revolution was incomplete. Remaking Russian society could not be achieved by a seizure of the state alone, but would also require mobilizing the support of a majority of the country's workers. The new Soviets, or workers' organizations, were to provide

Source: Rosa Luxemburg, *The Russian Revolution and Leninism or Marxism?* (Ann Arbor: The University of Michigan Press, 1961), 68–72. Introduction by Bertram D. Wolfe.

the foundation for this grassroots revolution. Futher, Lenin believed that workers throughout Europe needed to be liberated through revolution before peace and stability could be attained. The realities of the October revolution, however, obscured many of these original ideas. By the fall, Lenin and his Bolshevik party seized power without majority support while civil war still raged in Russia. The success of the Bolshevik Revolution in October required a new revolutionary ideology.

Rosa Luxemburg (1870–1919) was born in Russian Poland, but at the age of nineteen fled to Switzerland, where she earned a doctorate in law and political science. At twenty-five she migrated to Germany where, as a journalist and theorist, she became an impassioned and influential voice in the German democratic socialist movement. She criticized its bureaucratic leadership and excoriated its submission to war hysteria. Her opposition to the war led to frequent imprisonment. While Luxemburg was imprisoned, Lenin seized power, and she composed her thoughts on the Russian Revolution in 1918.

As a cofounder of the German Spartacus League (which later became the German Communist Party), Luxemburg believed that the Bolshevik Revolution could mean the liberation of working people throughout Russia, then Germany and the rest of Europe. But since 1904 she disagreed with Lenin's ideas of centralized control and party discipline. What objections does she make to Lenin's revolution? What do you think of her arguments?

Ironically, the apparent success of Lenin's strategy in Russia led many in the German Spartacus League to agitate for a similar seizure of power in Germany at the end of the war. Rosa Luxemburg tried to dissuade them, believing it to be suicidal. Outvoted, she joined their uprising in Berlin in January 1919 and was subsequently arrested and murdered by the police.

THINKING HISTORICALLY

Causes and consequences are often different sides of the same event. We might say that the First World War was a cause of the Russian Revolution or, conversely, that the Russian Revolution was a consequence of the First World War. Lenin argued that one of the consequences of the First World War was the particular sort of revolution he advocated, on the grounds that a democratic revolution was impossible under the circumstances. What do you think of that argument? Rosa Luxemburg disagreed that such draconian measures were necessary, and she argued that Lenin's revolutionary strategy would have its own consequences. Why did she think a dictatorial revolution could lead only to a dictatorial society?

Freedom only for the supporters of the government, only for the members of one party—however numerous they may be—is no freedom at all. Freedom is always and exclusively freedom for the one who thinks differently. Not because of any fanatical concept of "justice" but because all that is instructive, wholesome and purifying in political freedom depends on this essential characteristic, and its effectiveness vanishes when "freedom" becomes a special privilege.

The Bolsheviks themselves will not want, with hand on heart, to deny that, step by step, they have to feel out the ground, try out, experiment, test now one way now another, and that a good many of their measures do not represent priceless pearls of wisdom. Thus it must and will be with all of us when we get to the same point—even if the same difficult circumstances may not prevail everywhere.

The tacit assumption underlying the Lenin-Trotsky theory of dictatorship is this: that the socialist transformation is something for which a ready-made formula lies completed in the pocket of the revolutionary party, which needs only to be carried out energetically in practice. This is, unfortunately—or perhaps fortunately—not the case. Far from being a sum of ready-made prescriptions which have only to be applied, the practical realization of socialism as an economic, social and juridical system is something which lies completely hidden in the mists of the future. What we possess in our program is nothing but a few main signposts which indicate the general direction in which to look for the necessary measures, and the indications are mainly negative in character at that. Thus we know more or less what we must eliminate at the outset in order to free the road for a socialist economy. But when it comes to the nature of the thousand concrete, practical measures, large and small, necessary to introduce socialist principles into economy, law and all social relationships, there is no key in any socialist party program or textbook. That is not a shortcoming but rather the very thing that makes scientific socialism superior to the utopian varieties.

The socialist system of society should only be, and can only be, an historical product, born out of the school of its own experiences, born in the course of its realization, as a result of the developments of living history, which—just like organic nature of which, in the last analysis, it forms a part—has the fine habit of always producing along with any real social need the means to its satisfaction, along with the task simultaneously the solution. However, if such is the case, then it is clear that socialism by its very nature cannot be decreed or introduced by *ukase*. It has as its prerequisite a number of measures of force—against property, etc. The negative, the tearing down, can be decreed; the building up, the positive, cannot. New Territory. A thousand problems. Only experience is capable of correcting and opening new ways. Only unobstructed, effervescing life falls into a thousand new forms and improvisations, brings to light creative new force, itself corrects all mistaken attempts. The public life of countries with limited freedom is so poverty-stricken, so miserable, so rigid, so unfruitful, precisely because, through the exclusion of democracy, it cuts off the living sources of all spiritual riches and progress. (Proof: the year 1905 and the months from February to October 1917.)[1] There it was political in character; the same thing applies to economic and social life also. The whole mass of the people must take part in it. Otherwise, socialism will be decreed from behind a few official desks by a dozen intellectuals.

Public control is indispensably necessary. Otherwise the exchange of experiences remains only with the closed circle of the officials of the new regime. Corruption becomes inevitable. (Lenin's words, Bulletin No. 29) Socialism in life demands a complete spiritual transformation in the masses degraded by centuries of bourgeois rule. Social instincts in place of egotistical ones, mass initiative in place of inertia, idealism which conquers all suffering, etc., etc. No one knows this better, describes it more penetratingly; repeats it more stubbornly than Lenin. But he is completely mistaken in the means he employs. Decree, dictatorial force of the factory overseer, draconian penalties, rule by terror—all these things are but palliatives. The only way to a rebirth is the school of public life itself, the most unlimited, the broadest democracy and public opinion. It is rule by terror which demoralizes.

---

[1] In both 1905 and February/March of 1917, uprisings could not become revolutions because democracy was so thin. Only authoritarian regimes could carry out a revolution, as Lenin did in October/November 1917. [Ed.]

8

Syrian Congress Memorandum, 1919

As it became clear that the Allies would defeat the Central Powers, they began considering the nature of the peace and how they would construct the postwar world. On the issue of how to treat a defeated Germany after the war, the insistence of the French on stiff financial retribution fanned the embers for the next generation. Almost as important in the eyes of the victors was how to treat the defeated Ottoman Empire. In January 1918, President Woodrow Wilson gave a speech to the U.S. Congress in which he listed "Fourteen Points" intended to ensure a just and lasting peace. An overall theme was the need for "national self-determination."

Source: "The King-Crane Commission Report," in *Papers Relating to the Foreign Relations of the United States: Paris Peace Conference, 1919* (Washington, DC: GPO, 1947), 12:780–81.

Point XII began: "The Turkish portions of the present Ottoman Empire should be assured a secure sovereignty, but the other nationalities which are now under Turkish rule should be assured an undoubted security of life and an absolutely unmolested opportunity of autonomous development." The Arabs of the Middle East constituted at least one of these "other nationalities," and many of them expected their independence after the war. Instead the Paris Peace Conference instituted a system of "mandates" by which the victorious European powers maintained control over enemy colonies, including the Ottoman Arab territories, until the Europeans determined the colonies were prepared for independence.

This selection details the Syrians' objections to this arrangement, sent as a memorandum to the King-Crane Commission, the body responsible for overseeing the transfer of Ottoman territory. What were their objections? What evidence did they give to support their position? What did they want?

THINKING HISTORICALLY

Do you think this conflict could have been an expected consequence of the First World War? Do you think Wilson's Fourteen Points made the Syrian demands more likely? Do you think the European powers expected this response? What were the consequences of the failure of the Allies to settle these grievances?

We the undersigned members of the General Syrian Congress, meeting in Damascus on Wednesday, July 2nd 1919, . . . provided with credentials and authorizations by the inhabitants of our various districts, Muslims, Christians, and Jews, have agreed upon the following statement of the desires of the people of the country who have elected us to present them to the American Section of the International Commission; the fifth article was passed by a very large majority; all the other articles were accepted unanimously.

1. We ask absolutely complete political independence for Syria within these boundaries. The Taurus System on the North; Rafah and a line running from Al Jauf to the south of the Syrian and the Hejazian line to Akaba on the south; the Euphrates and Khabur Rivers and a line extending east of Abu Kamal to the east of Al Jauf on the east; and the Mediterranean on the west.

2. We ask that the Government of this Syrian country should be a democratic civil constitutional Monarchy on broad decentralization principles, safeguarding the rights of minorities, and that the King be the Emir Feisal, who carried on a glorious struggle in the cause of our liberation and merited our full confidence and entire reliance.

3. Considering the fact that the Arabs inhabiting the Syrian area are not naturally less than other more advanced races and that they are by no means less developed than the Bulgarians, Serbians, Greeks, and Romanians at the beginning of their independence, we protest against Article 22 of the Covenant of the League of Nations, placing us among the nations in their middle stage of development which stand in need of a mandatory power.

4. In the event of the rejection by the Peace Conference of this just protest for certain considerations that we may not understand, we, relying on the declarations of President Wilson that his object in waging war was to put an end to the ambition of conquest and colonization, can only regard the mandate mentioned in the Covenant of the League of Nations as equivalent to the rendering of economical and technical assistance that does not prejudice our complete independence. And desiring that our country should not fall a prey to colonization and believing that the American Nation is furthest from any thought of colonization and has no political ambition in our country, we will seek the technical and economical assistance from the United States of America, provided that such assistance does not exceed 20 years.

5. In the event of America not finding herself in a position to accept our desire for assistance, we will seek this assistance from Great Britain, also provided that such assistance does not infringe the complete independence and unity of our country and that the duration of such assistance does not exceed that mentioned in the previous article.

6. We do not acknowledge any right claimed by the French Government in any part whatever of our Syrian country and refuse that she should assist us or have a hand in our country under any circumstances and in any place.

7. We oppose the pretensions of the Zionists to create a Jewish commonwealth in the southern part of Syria, known as Palestine, and oppose Zionist migration to any part of our country; for we do not acknowledge their title but consider them a grave peril to our people from the national, economical, and political points of view. Our Jewish compatriots shall enjoy our common rights and assume the common responsibilities.

8. We ask that there should be no separation of the southern part of Syria, known as Palestine, nor of the littoral western zone, which includes Lebanon, from the Syrian country. We desire that the unity of the country should be guaranteed against partition under whatever circumstances.

9. We ask complete independence for emancipated Mesopotamia and that there should be no economic barriers between the two countries.

10. The fundamental principles laid down by President Wilson in condemnation of secret treaties impel us to protest most emphatically against any treaty that stipulates the partition of our Syrian country and against any private engagement aiming at the establishment of Zionism in the southern part of Syria; therefore we ask the complete annulment of these conventions and agreements.

The noble principles enunciated by President Wilson strengthen our confidence that our desires emanating from the depths of our hearts, shall be the decisive factor in determining our future; and that President Wilson and the free American people will be our supporters for the realization of our hopes, thereby proving their sincerity and noble sympathy with the aspiration of the weaker nations in general and our Arab people in particular.

We also have the fullest confidence that the Peace Conference will realize that we would not have risen against the Turks, with whom we had participated in all civil, political, and representative privileges, but for their violation of our national rights, and so will grant us our desires in full in order that our political rights may not be less after the war than they were before, since we have shed so much blood in the cause of our liberty and independence.

We request to be allowed to send a delegation to represent us at the Peace Conference to defend our rights and secure the realization of our aspirations.

9

Algemeen Handelsblad Editorial on the Treaty of Versailles, June 1919

The Netherlands remained neutral throughout the war. The Dutch newspaper *Algemeen Handelsblad*, edited by Charles Boissevain, was an influential liberal voice, neither pro-German nor pro-Entente. This is its editorial on the Treaty of Versailles. What did it think of the Treaty of Versailles? What provisions of the treaty did it question?

THINKING HISTORICALLY

On January 18, 1918, President Woodrow Wilson gave a speech in which he proclaimed "Fourteen Points" to be covered in the eventual peace treaty. These points included free trade, self-determination of nations, reductions in armed forces, and withdrawal from conquered territories. There was no punishment of Germany included: no assignment of war guilt, no claim of reparations, no imposition on the German economy (other than the proposal that all belligerents relinquish their colonies). All of these punishments, however, were included in the peace treaty the Germans were forced to sign at Versailles on June 28, 1919.

Source: *Source Records of the Great War, Vol. VII,* ed. Charles F. Horne (New York: National Alumni, 1923).

What did the editor of the *Algameen Handelsblad* see as the likely consequences of the Treaty of Versailles?

The peace conditions imposed upon Germany are so hard, so humiliating, that even those who have the smallest expectation of a "peace of justice" are bound to be deeply disappointed.

Has Germany actually deserved such a "peace"? Everybody knows how we condemned the crimes committed against humanity by Germany. Everybody knows what we thought of the invasion of Belgium, the submarine war, the Zeppelin raids.

Our opinion on the lust of power and conquest of Germany is well known. But a condemnation of wartime actions must not amount to a lasting condemnation of a people. In spite of all they have done, the German people is a great and noble nation.

The question is not whether the Germans have been led by an intellectual group to their destruction, or whether they are accomplices in the misdeeds of their leaders—the question is, whether it is to the interest of mankind, whether there is any sense in punishing a people in such a way as the Entente governments wish to chastise Germany.

The Entente evidently desires the complete annihilation of Germany. Not only will the whole commercial fleet be confiscated, but the shipbuilding yards will be obliged to work for the foreigner for some time to come.

Whole tracts of Germany will be entirely deprived of their liberty; they will be under a committee of foreign domination, without adequate representation.

The financial burden is so heavy that it is no exaggeration to say that Germany is reduced to economic bondage. The Germans will have to work hard and incessantly for foreign masters, without any chance of personal gain, or any prospect of regaining liberty or economic independence.

This "peace" offered to Germany may differ in form from the one imposed upon conquered nations by the old Romans, but certainly not in essence. This peace is a mockery of President Wilson's principles. Trusting to these, Germany accepted peace. That confidence has been betrayed in such a manner that we regard the present happenings as a deep humiliation, not only to all governments and nations concerned in this peace offer, but to all humanity.

These conditions will never give peace. All Germans must feel that they wish to shake off the heavy yoke imposed by the cajoling Entente, and we fear very much that that opportunity will soon present itself. For has not the Entente recognized in the proposed so-called "League of Nations" the evident right to conquer and possess countries for economic and imperialistic purposes? Fettered and enslaved, Germany will always remain a menace to Europe.

The voice and opinion of neutrals have carried very little weight in this war. But, however small their influence and however dangerous the rancorous caprice of the Entente powers may be to neutrals, it is our conviction and our duty to protest as forcibly as possible against these peace conditions.

We understand the bitter feelings of the Entente countries. But that does not make these peace conditions less wrong, less dangerous to world civilization, or any less an outrage against Germany and against mankind.

■ REFLECTIONS

By studying causes and consequences of world events, we learn how things change; more important, we learn how to avoid repeating past mistakes. History is full of lessons that breed humility as well as confidence. In *The Origins of the First World War*,[1] historian James Joll points out how unprepared people were for the war as late as the summer of 1914. Even after the Austrian ultimatum to Serbia was issued on July 23 (almost a month after the assassination of the Archduke Franz Ferdinand on June 28), diplomats across Europe left for their summer holidays. By August, all of Europe was at war, though the expectation was that it would be over in a month.

We could make a good case for diplomatic blundering as an important cause of the First World War. It is safe to say that few statesmen had any inkling of the consequences of their actions in 1914. And yet, if we concentrate on the daily decisions of diplomats that summer, we may pay attention only to the tossing of lit matches by people sitting on powder kegs rather than on the origins of the powder kegs themselves.

President Wilson blamed secret diplomacy, the international system of alliances, and imperialism as the chief causes of the war. On the importance of imperialism, Wilson's conclusion was the same as that of Lenin, though he certainly did not share Lenin's conviction that capitalism was the root cause of imperialism, and in 1919 neither alliances nor imperialism was regarded as un-American or likely to end anytime soon. Still, Wilson's anti-imperialism might have prevented the League of Nations from creating new empires under the guise of protective mandates. One of the consequences of a Wilsonian peace might have been the creation of independent states in the Middle East and Africa a generation earlier.

The principle of the "self-determination of nations" that Wilson espoused, however, was a double-edged sword. The fact that the war

---

[1] James Joll, *The Origins of the First World War* (London: Longman, 1992), 200.

had been "caused" by a Bosnian Serb nationalist assassin in 1914 might have been a warning that national self-determination could become an infinite regress in which smaller and smaller units sought to separate themselves from "foreign" domination.

The rise of nationalist movements and the rise of international organizations were only two consequences of the First World War. Historians have attributed many other aspects of the twentieth century to the war. Stephen O'Shea offers a striking list of cultural changes:

> It is generally accepted that the Great War and its fifty-two months of senseless slaughter encouraged, or amplified, among other things: the loss of a belief in progress, a mistrust of technology, the loss of religious faith, the loss of a belief in Western cultural superiority, the rejection of class distinctions, the rejection of traditional sexual roles, the birth of the Modern [in art], the rejection of the past, the elevation of irony to a standard mode of apprehending the world, the unbuttoning of moral codes, and the conscious embrace of the irrational.[2]

Evidence of any of these consequences is only barely visible in the accounts of a chapter that ends in 1920, but many of the developments described in the next few chapters were consequences of World War I as well.

[2] Stephen O'Shea, *Back to the Front: An Accidental Historian Walks the Trenches of World War I* (New York: Avon Books, 1996), 9.

25

World War II and Mass Killing

Germany, the Soviet Union, Japan, and the United States, 1926–1945

■ HISTORICAL CONTEXT

In some ways World War II resembled World War I. At the European core, England and France again fought Germany and Austria. As in World War I, the United States eventually came to the aid of England and France, playing a decisive role. In both conflicts Russia also fought against Germany, only until the Soviet revolution in 1917, but fiercely and at great cost as the Soviet Union from 1941 to 1945. By contrast, Japan, an enemy of Germany in World War I, became an important German ally in World War II, and the pro-German Ottoman Empire of World War I was an independent, neutral Turkey in World War II.

While the main combatants were aligned on the same sides, and both wars ended in the defeat of Germany and its allies, the causes and consequences of the two wars were significantly different. The causes of World War II are clearer than those of World War I. German aggression was a factor in both wars, but in the buildup to World War I, there was much blame to go around. World War II, on the other hand, followed the aggressive conquests of Japan and Germany. Both countries had been militarized by extreme nationalist regimes. Similar "fascist" movements took power in Italy and Eastern Europe, partly in response to the economic hardship of the Great Depression of the 1930s. These movements, like the German Nazi Party, were led by demagogues—Hitler in Germany, Mussolini in Italy—who called for dictatorial power, the expulsion or conquest of foreigners, colonial expansion, and aggressive, violent solutions to social and economic problems. Similarly, the military party that took power in Japan sought an empire in China and Southeast Asia to ensure its economic prosperity.

The aggressions of Germany and Japan unleashed forces of violence that also distinguished World War II from World War I. New technologies of warfare (machine guns, biplanes, and gas in World War I) that had been directed almost entirely at soldiers in trenches were transformed by World War II into missiles and warheads that rained down on civilian populations. Even the victorious Allies directed previously unheard of violence against civilian populations in the firebombing of cities like Dresden and Tokyo and the use of nuclear bombs on Hiroshima and Nagasaki.

Despite the pounding barbarity of the Western Front, the era of World War I still contained features of earlier gentlemanly conflict. Like chivalric jousters, aristocratic World War I pilots displayed colorful scarves and saluted their falling rivals. But the extreme nationalist and racist movements of the interwar years instilled a hatred of the enemy that eviscerated any possibility of compassion or fellow feeling. Totalitarian governments indoctrinated mass citizen armies with a hatred that sometimes made the new technologies of violence redundant. Millions of newly designated enemies—neighbors as well as foreigners—were murdered by hand.

Totalitarianism—total control by the state—was a new ideology in this period, marked by the increased reach of the modern state through advertising, mass media, and militarization and, at the same time, the failure of liberal ideals, voluntary associations, markets, and political parties to provide prosperity and security. The word originated with the rise of fascism in Italy (*totalitarismo*) and Germany (*totalstatt*) in the 1920s. By the end of World War II, the word was used to describe the state control of Stalinist Russia as well as fascist regimes. In the twenty-first century, it is sometimes used to criticize the unity of corporations and the state.

■ THINKING HISTORICALLY

Empathetic Understanding

Empathetic understanding is the kind of understanding we have when we put ourselves "in the shoes" of others and try to understand how they feel.[1] Without it we understand people only from the outside.

Empathetic understanding of people from a foreign culture or the past is difficult enough, but it is especially difficult to understand human suffering and the people who intentionally cause it—the two

---

[1] For those familiar with German or the sociology of Max Weber, I am referring to *Verstehen*. [Ed.]

conditions we encounter in this chapter as we study Hitler, the perpetrators of the Holocaust, and the victims.

To say a person is evil is a moral judgment that gives us little insight into the person's motivations or feelings. Similarly, to dismiss someone as insane excuses the person's actions and also leaves us with little understanding. To put ourselves in the shoes of the victims may be difficult to bear—nevertheless, empathetic understanding increases our knowledge of the past while it deepens our humanity in the present.

1

BENITO MUSSOLINI

The Doctrine of Fascism, 1932

Totalitarismo was a term coined in 1923 by an Italian leftist critic of fascism, Giovanni Amendola, to show how Benito Mussolini's goal of total state control was more encompassing than premodern dictatorships. The term was then adopted by the Italian philosopher of fascism and supporter of Mussolini Giovanni Gentile as a positive description of the ideology's goals. Gentile is thought to have been at least the co-author of "The Doctrine of Fascism," which has been attributed to Mussolini (1883–1945), founder and leader of the Fascist Party, prime minister of Italy after 1922, dictator (*Il Duce*) of a police state after 1925, and ally of Hitler during World War II.

What did Mussolini mean by *fascism*? What did he see as the failures of the liberal state?

THINKING HISTORICALLY

What kind of person might respond favorably to a doctrine like this? Which of its values might appeal to you or people you know?

Rejection of Individualism and the Importance of the State

Anti-individualistic, the Fascist conception of life stresses the importance of the State and accepts the individual only in so far as his interests coincide with those of the State, which stands for the conscience

---

Source: Benito Mussolini, *The Doctrine of Fascism* (Florence: Vallecchi Editore, 1935), 14–20.

and the universal will of man as a historic entity. It is opposed to classical liberalism which arose as a reaction to absolutism and exhausted its historical function when the State became the expression of the conscience and will of the people. Liberalism denied the State in the name of the individual; Fascism reasserts the rights of the State as expressing the real essence of the individual. And if liberty is to be the attribute of living men and not of abstract dummies invented by individualistic liberalism, then Fascism stands for liberty, and for the only liberty worth having, the liberty of the State and of the individual within the State. The Fascist conception of the State is all embracing; outside of it no human or spiritual values can exist, much less have value. Thus understood, Fascism, is totalitarian, and the Fascist State — a synthesis and a unit inclusive of all values — interprets, develops, and potentates the whole life of a people.

No individuals or groups (political parties, cultural associations, economic unions, social classes) outside the State. Fascism is therefore opposed to Socialism to which unity within the State (which amalgamates classes into a single economic and ethical reality) is unknown, and which sees in history nothing but the class struggle. Fascism is likewise opposed to trade unionism as a class weapon. But when brought within the orbit of the State, Fascism recognizes the real needs which gave rise to socialism and trade unionism, giving them due weight in the guild or corporative system in which divergent interests are coordinated and harmonized in the unity of the State. . . .

Fascist State as a Spiritual Force

The Fascist State, as a higher and more powerful expression of personality, is a force, but a spiritual one. It sums up all the manifestations of the moral and intellectual life of man. Its functions cannot therefore be limited to those of enforcing order and keeping the peace, as the liberal doctrine had it. It is no mere mechanical device for defining the sphere within which the individual may duly exercise his supposed rights. The Fascist State is an inwardly accepted standard and rule of conduct, a discipline of the whole person; it permeates the will no less than the intellect. It stands for a principle which becomes the central motive of man as a member of civilized society, sinking deep down into his personality; it dwells in the heart of the man of action and of the thinker, of the artist and of the man of science: soul of the soul.

Fascism, in short, is not only a law-giver and a founder of institutions, but an educator and a promoter of spiritual life. It aims at refashioning not only the forms of life but their content—man, his character, and his faith. To achieve this propose it enforces discipline and uses authority, entering into the soul and ruling with undisputed sway. Therefore it has chosen as its emblem the Lictors rods, the symbol of unity, strength, and justice. . . .

The Absolute Primacy of the State

The keystone of the Fascist doctrine is its conception of the State, of its essence, its functions, and its aims. For Fascism the State is absolute, individuals and groups relative. Individuals and groups are admissible in so far as they come within the State. Instead of directing the game and guiding the material and moral progress of the community, the liberal State restricts its activities to recording results. The Fascist State is wide awake and has a will of its own. For this reason it can be described as "ethical."

At the first quinquennial assembly of the regime, in 1929, I said "The Fascist State is not a night watchman, solicitous only of the personal safety of the citizens; nor is it organized exclusively for the purpose of guaranteeing a certain degree of material prosperity and relatively peaceful conditions of life; a board of directors would do as much. Neither is it exclusively political, divorced from practical realities and holding itself aloof from the multifarious activities of the citizens and the nation. The State, as conceived and realized by Fascism, is a spiritual and ethical entity for securing the political, juridical, and economic organization of the nation, an organization which in its origin and growth is a manifestation of the spirit. The State guarantees the internal and external safety of the country, but it also safeguards and transmits the spirit of the people, elaborated down the ages in its language, its customs, its faith. The State is not only the present; it is also the past and above all the future. Transcending the individual's brief spell of life, the State stands for the immanent conscience of the nation. The forms in which it finds expression change, but the need for it remains. The State educates the citizens to civism, makes them aware of their mission, urges them to unity; its justice harmonizes their divergent interests; it transmits to future generations the conquests of the mind in the fields of science, art, law, human solidarity; it leads men up from primitive tribal life to that highest manifestation of human power, imperial rule". . . .

But imperialism implies discipline, the coordination of efforts, a deep sense of duty and a spirit of self-sacrifice. This explains many aspects of the practical activity of the regime, and the direction taken by many of the forces of the State, as also the severity which has to be exercised towards those who would oppose this spontaneous and inevitable movement of XXth century Italy by agitating outgrown ideologies of the XIXth century, ideologies rejected wherever great experiments in political and social transformations are being dared.

Never before have the peoples thirsted for authority, direction, order, as they do now. . . .

2

ADOLF HITLER

Mein Kampf, 1926

Hitler (1889–1945) wrote *Mein Kampf* (My Struggle) in prison where he was jailed after an unsuccessful attempt to take over the German government in Munich in 1923. As he wrote in the Epilogue, included at the end of this selection, the German National Socialist Labor (Nazi) Party, banned after the attempted coup in 1923, was revived by 1926 to become a force in German politics.

We read from this rambling 700-page book today because of what happened in the years after its publication in 1926. In the context of the global depression after 1929, the Nazi Party grew to be the largest party in the German Parliament by 1932 with 37 percent of the popular vote. In January 1933 Hitler was appointed chancellor by President Paul von Hindenburg. He proceeded to concentrate all power in his hands as *Fuhrer* (Dictator), militarize the German economy, and mobilize for war. In 1938, while the rest of Europe stood by, he annexed his native Austria and German-speaking regions of Czechoslovakia. In March 1939, he added the rest of Czechoslovakia. On September 1, 1939, the German invasion of Poland triggered World War II in Europe.

During the same period, the Nazi regime imposed increasingly discriminatory restrictions on German Jews. As early as 1933, Jews were banned from government service, law practice, some medical careers, and some schools, and Dachau, the first concentration camp in Germany, was built. In 1935 the Nuremburg laws outlawed any civic life for Jews and any sexual contact between Jews and non-Jews. In the next couple of years, Jews were banned from all other occupations, Jewish children were banned from public schools, and German properties were seized. With the outbreak of war, Jews in Germany and in German-occupied countries were rounded up and put in concentration camps where they were forced to work in factories for private corporations or government producers of war materials. In 1941 the Nazis began building extermination camps, first in Poland, to annihilate Jews, Poles, and other enemies of the Nazis. These included communists, socialists, political dissenters, homosexuals, Romani (Gypsies), Slavs, and other ethnic and religious minorities. By 1945, upwards of 11 million Jews and other "undesirables" had been killed.

It would be a mistake to try to see all of this in embryo in a young artist in Vienna twenty years before, or even in the vitriolic ruminations

Source: Adolf Hitler, *Mein Kampf*, trans. Ralph Manheim (Boston: Houghton Mifflin, 1999), 11–13, 15, 20–21, 34, 51–52, 56–58, 65, 78, 126, 134–36.

of a prison inmate ten years later, but what do these selections suggest to you about Hitler's motivations and the roots of Nazism?

THINKING HISTORICALLY

To understand the unthinkable it is necessary to resist the temptation to demonize. To call someone a "Devil" or "Evil Incarnate" obviates the need to understand and learn. The English word *understand* is equivalent to the German word *Verstehen*, which social scientists have used to connote empathetic knowledge: relating to another human, putting oneself in his or her shoes. This is a technique to gain knowledge; it has nothing to do with excusing or forgiving. Try this with probably the hardest subject in history: How did that aspiring art student become Hitler? What went wrong? How did his background, environment, and experience produce a future monster?

In the House of My Parents

Today it seems to me providential that Fate should have chosen Braunau on the Inn as my birthplace. For this little town lies on the boundary between two German states which we of the younger generation at least have made it our life work to reunite by every means at our disposal.

German-Austria must return to the great German mother country, and not because of any economic considerations. No, and again no: even if such a union were unimportant from an economic point of view; yes, even if it were harmful, it must nevertheless take place. One blood demands one Reich. Never will the German nation possess the moral right to engage in colonial politics until, at least, it embraces its own sons within a single state. Only when the Reich borders include the very last German, but can no longer guarantee his daily bread, will the moral right to acquire foreign soil arise from the distress of our own people. Their sword will become our plow, and from the tears of war the daily bread of future generations will grow. . . .

I, too, while still comparatively young, had an opportunity to take part in the struggle of nationalities in old Austria. Collections were taken for the *Südmark*[1] and the school association; we emphasized our convictions by wearing corn-flowers[2] and red, black, and gold colors; 'Heil' was our greeting, and instead of the imperial anthem we sang '*Deutschland über Alles*,' despite warnings and punishments. In this way

---

[1] Another term for Austria. Apparently devised in imitation of the old imperial Marks by the *Verein für Deutschtum im Ausland*, founded in 1881 to defend the endangered nationality of Germans in the border territories.

[2] The corn-flower was the emblem of Germans loyal to the imperial House of Hohenzollern and of the Austrian Pan-Germans.

the child received political training in a period when as a rule the subject of a so-called national state knew little more of his nationality than its language. It goes without saying that even then I was not among the lukewarm. In a short time I had become a fanatical 'German Nationalist,' though the term was not identical with our present party concept.

This development in me made rapid progress; by the time I was fifteen I understood the difference between dynastic '*patriotism*' and folkish '*nationalism*'; and even then I was interested only in the latter. . . .

Did we not know, even as little boys, that this Austrian state had and could have no love for us Germans?

Our historical knowledge of the works of the House of Habsburg was reinforced by our daily experience. In the north and south the poison of foreign nations gnawed at the body of our nationality, and even Vienna was visibly becoming more and more of an un-German city. The Royal House Czechized wherever possible, and it was the hand of the goddess of eternal justice and inexorable retribution which caused Archduke Francis Ferdinand, the most mortal enemy of Austrian-Germanism, to fall by the bullets which he himself had helped to mold. For had he not been the patron of Austria's Slavization from above! . . .

Years of Study and Suffering in Vienna

When after the death of my mother I went to Vienna for the third time, to remain for many years, the time which had meanwhile elapsed had restored my calm and determination. My old defiance had come back to me and my goal was now clear and definite before my eyes. I wanted to become an architect, and obstacles do not exist to be surrendered to, but only to be broken. I was determined to overcome these obstacles, keeping before my eyes the image of my father, who had started out as the child of a village shoemaker, and risen by his own efforts to be a government official. I had a better foundation to build on, and hence my possibilities in the struggle were easier, and what then seemed to be the harshness of Fate, I praise today as wisdom and Providence. While the Goddess of Suffering took me in her arms, often threatening to crush me, my will to resistance grew, and in the end this will was victorious.

I owe it to that period that I grew hard and am still capable of being hard. And even more, I exalt it for tearing me away from the hollowness of comfortable life; for drawing the mother's darling out of his soft downy bed and giving him 'Dame Care' for a new mother; for hurling me, despite all resistance, into a world of misery and poverty, thus making me acquainted with those for whom I was later to fight.

In this period my eyes were opened to two menaces of which I had previously scarcely known the names, and whose terrible importance for the existence of the German people I certainly did not understand: Marxism and Jewry. . . .

In the years 1909 and 1910, my own situation had changed somewhat in so far as I no longer had to earn my daily bread as a common laborer. By this time I was working independently as a small draftsman and painter of watercolors. Hard as this was with regard to earnings—it was barely enough to live on—it was good for my chosen profession. Now I was no longer dead tired in the evening when I came home from work, unable to look at a book without soon dozing off. My present work ran parallel to my future profession. Moreover, I was master of my own time and could apportion it better than had previously been possible.

I painted to make a living and studied for pleasure. . . .

Today it is difficult, if not impossible, for me to say when the word 'Jew' first gave me ground for special thoughts. At home I do not remember having heard the word during my father's lifetime. I believe that the old gentleman would have regarded any special emphasis on this term as cultural backwardness. In the course of his life he had arrived at more or less cosmopolitan views which, despite his pronounced national sentiments, not only remained intact, but also affected me to some extent.

Likewise at school I found no occasion which could have led me to change this inherited picture.

At the *Realschule*, to be sure, I did meet one Jewish boy who was treated by all of us with caution, but only because various experiences had led us to doubt his discretion and we did not particularly trust him; but neither I nor the others had any thoughts on the matter.

Not until my fourteenth or fifteenth year did I begin to come across the word 'Jew,' with any frequency, partly in connection with political discussions. This filled me with a mild distaste, and I could not rid myself of an unpleasant feeling that always came over me whenever religious quarrels occurred in my presence.

At that time I did not think anything else of the question.

There were few Jews in Linz. In the course of the centuries their outward appearance had become Europeanized and had taken on a human look; in fact, I even took them for Germans. The absurdity of this idea did not dawn on me because I saw no distinguishing feature but the strange religion. The fact that they had, as I believed, been persecuted on this account sometimes almost turned my distaste at unfavorable remarks about them into horror.

Thus far I did not so much as suspect the existence of an organized opposition to the Jews.

Then I came to Vienna.

Preoccupied by the abundance of my impressions in the architectural field, oppressed by the hardship of my own lot, I gained at first no insight into the inner stratification of the people in this gigantic city. Notwithstanding that Vienna in those days counted nearly two hundred thousand Jews among its two million inhabitants, I did not see them. In the first few weeks my eyes and my senses were not equal to the flood of values and ideas. Not until calm gradually returned and the agitated picture began to clear did I look around me more carefully in my new world, and then among other things I encountered the Jewish question. . . .

Once, as I was strolling through the Inner City, I suddenly encountered an apparition in a black caftan and black hair locks. Is this a Jew? was my first thought.

For, to be sure, they had not looked like that in Linz. I observed the man furtively and cautiously, but the longer I stared at this foreign face, scrutinizing feature for feature, the more my first question assumed a new form:

Is this a German?

As always in such cases, I now began to try to relieve my doubts by books. For a few hellers I bought the first anti-Semitic pamphlets of my life. Unfortunately, they all proceeded from the supposition that in principle the reader knew or even understood the Jewish question to a certain degree. Besides, the tone for the most part was such that doubts again arose in me, due in part to the dull and amazingly unscientific arguments favoring the thesis.

I relapsed for weeks at a time, once even for months.

The whole thing seemed to me so monstrous, the accusations so boundless, that, tormented by the fear of doing injustice, I again became anxious and uncertain.

Yet I could no longer very well doubt that the objects of my study were not Germans of a special religion, but a people in themselves; for since I had begun to concern myself with this question and to take cognizance of the Jews, Vienna appeared to me in a different light than before. Wherever I went, I began to see Jews, and the more I saw, the more sharply they became distinguished in my eyes from the rest of humanity. Particularly the Inner City and the districts north of the Danube Canal swarmed with a people which even outwardly had lost all resemblance to Germans. . . .

What had to be reckoned heavily against the Jews in my eyes was when I became acquainted with their activity in the press, art, literature, and the theater. All the unctuous reassurances helped little or nothing. It sufficed to look at a billboard, to study the names of the men behind the horrible trash they advertised, to make you hard for a long time to come. This was pestilence, spiritual pestilence, worse than the Black Death of olden times, and the people were being infected with it! . . .

If, with the help of his Marxist creed, the Jew is victorious over the other peoples of the world, his crown will be the funeral wreath of humanity and this planet will, as it did thousands of years ago, move through the ether devoid of men.

Eternal Nature inexorably avenges the infringement of her commands.

Hence today I believe that I am acting in accordance with the will of the Almighty Creator: *by defending myself against the Jew, I am fighting for the work of the Lord.* . . .

Political Reflections Arising Out of My Sojourn in Vienna

The Western democracy of today is the forerunner of Marxism which without it would not be thinkable. It provides this world plague with the culture in which its germs can spread. In its most extreme form, parliamentarianism created a 'monstrosity of excrement and fire,' in which, however, sad to say, the 'fire' seems to me at the moment to be burned out. . . .

Munich

In the spring of 1912 I came at last to Munich. . . .

. . . A *German* city! What a difference from Vienna! I grew sick to my stomach when I even thought back on this Babylon of races. In addition, the dialect, much closer to me, which particularly in my contacts with Lower Bavarians, reminded me of my former childhood. . . .

Assuredly at a certain time the whole of humanity will be compelled, in consequence of the impossibility of making the fertility of the soil keep pace with the continuous increase in population, to halt the increase of the human race and either let Nature again decide or, by self-help if possible, create the necessary balance, though, to be sure, in a more correct way than is done today. But then this will strike all peoples, while today only those races are stricken with such suffering which no longer possess the force and strength to secure for themselves the necessary territories in this world. For as matters stand there are at the present time on this earth immense areas of unused soil, only waiting for the men to till them. But it is equally true that Nature as such has not reserved this soil for the future possession of any particular nation or race; on the contrary, this soil exists for the people which possesses the force to take it and the industry to cultivate it.

Nature knows no political boundaries. First, she puts living creatures on this globe and watches the free play of forces. She then confers the master's right on her favorite child, the strongest in courage and industry.

When a people limits itself to internal colonization because other races are clinging fast to greater and greater surfaces of this earth, it will be forced to have recourse to self-limitation at a time when the other peoples are still continuing to increase. . . .

For us Germans the slogan of 'inner colonization' is catastrophic, if for no other reason because it automatically reinforces us in the opinion that we have found a means which, in accordance with the pacifistic tendency, allows us 'to earn' our right to exist by labor in a life of sweet slumbers. Once this doctrine were taken seriously in our country, it would mean the end of every exertion to preserve for ourselves the place which is our due. Once the average German became convinced that he could secure his life and future in this way, all attempts at an active, and hence alone fertile, defense of German vital necessities would be doomed to failure. In the face of such an attitude on the part of the nation any really beneficial foreign policy could be regarded as buried, and with it the future of the German people as a whole.

Taking these consequences into account, it is no accident that it is always primarily the Jew who tries and succeeds in planting such mortally dangerous modes of thought in our people. He knows his customers too well not to realize that they gratefully let themselves be swindled by any gold-brick salesman who can make them think he has found a way to play a little trick on Nature, to make the hard, inexorable struggle for existence superfluous, and instead, sometimes by work, but sometimes by plain doing nothing, depending on how things 'come out,' to become the lord of the planet.

It cannot be emphasized sharply enough *that any German internal colonization must serve to eliminate social abuse particularly to withdraw the soil from widespread speculation, but can never suffice to secure the future of the nation without the acquisition of new soil.*

If we do not do this, we shall in a short time have arrived, not only at the end of our soil, but also at the end of our strength. . . .

Conclusion

On November 9, 1923, in the fourth year of its existence, the National Socialist German Workers' Party was dissolved and prohibited in the whole Reich territory. Today in November, 1926, it stands again free before us, stronger and inwardly firmer than ever before.

All the persecutions of the movement and its individual leaders, all vilifications and slanders, were powerless to harm it. The correctness of its ideas, the purity if its will, its supporters' spirit of self-sacrifice, have caused it to issue from all repressions stronger than ever.

If, in the world of our present parliamentary corruption, it becomes more and more aware of the profoundest essence of its struggle, feels itself to be the purest embodiment of the value of race and personality and conducts itself accordingly, it will with almost mathematical certainty some day emerge victorious from its struggle. Just as Germany must inevitably win her rightful position on this earth if she is led and organized according to the same principles.

A state which in this age of racial poisoning dedicates itself to the care of its best racial elements must some day become lord of the earth.

May the adherents of our movement never forget this if ever the magnitude of the sacrifices should beguile them to an anxious comparison with the possible results.

3

HEINRICH HIMMLER

Speech to the SS, 1943

Heinrich Himmler (1900–1945) was one of the most powerful leaders of Nazi Germany. He was the head of the SS, or *Schutzstaffel*, an elite army that was responsible for, among other things, running the many concentration camps. Hitler gave Himmler the task of implementing the "final solution of the Jewish question": attempted genocide of the Jewish population of Germany and the other countries the Nazis occupied. The horror that resulted is today often referred to by the word *holocaust* (literally, holy burnt offering).

The following reading is an excerpt from a speech Himmler gave to SS leaders on October 4, 1943. What was Himmler's concern in this speech? What kind of general support for the extermination of the Jews does this excerpt suggest existed?

THINKING HISTORICALLY

Psychiatrists say that people use various strategies to cope when they must do something distasteful. We might summarize these strategies as denial, distancing, compartmentalizing, ennobling, rationalizing, and scapegoating. *Denial* is pretending that something has not happened. *Distancing* removes the idea, memory, or reality from the mind, placing it at a distance. *Compartmentalizing* separates one action, memory, or idea from others, allowing one to "put away" certain feelings.

Source: Heinrich Himmler, "Secret Speech at Posen," in *A Holocaust Reader*, ed. Lucy S. Dawidowicz (New York: Behrman House, 1976), 132–33.

Ennobling makes the distasteful act a matter of pride rather than guilt, nobility rather than disgrace. *Rationalizing* creates "good" reasons for doing something, while *scapegoating* puts blame on someone else.

What evidence do you see of these strategies in Himmler's speech? Judging from the speech, which of these strategies do you think his listeners used to justify their actions?

I also want to make reference before you here, in complete frankness, to a really grave matter. Among ourselves, this once, it shall be uttered quite frankly; but in public we will never speak of it. Just as we did not hesitate on June 30, 1934, to do our duty as ordered, to stand up against the wall comrades who had transgressed,[1] and shoot them, so we have never talked about this and never will. It was the tact which I am glad to say is a matter of course to us that made us never discuss it among ourselves, never talk about it. Each of us shuddered, and yet each one knew that he would do it again if it were ordered and if it were necessary.

I am referring to the evacuation of the Jews, the annihilation of the Jewish people. This is one of those things that are easily said. "The Jewish people is going to be annihilated," says every party member. "Sure, it's in our program, elimination of the Jews, annihilation—we'll take care of it." And then they all come trudging, 80 million worthy Germans, and each one has his one decent Jew. Sure, the others are swine, but this one is an A-1 Jew. Of all those who talk this way, not one has seen it happen, not one has been through it. Most of you must know what it means to see a hundred corpses lie side by side, or five hundred, or a thousand. To have stuck this out—excepting cases of human weakness—to have kept our integrity, that is what has made us hard. In our history, this is an unwritten and never-to-be-written page of glory, for we know how difficult we would have made it for ourselves if today—amid the bombing raids, the hardships, and the deprivations of war—we still had the Jews in every city as secret saboteurs, agitators, and demagogues. If the Jews were still ensconced in the body of the German nation, we probably would have reached the 1916–17 stage by now.[2]

The wealth they had we have taken from them. I have issued a strict order, carried out by SS-Obergruppenfuhrer Pohl, that this wealth in its entirety is to be turned over to the Reich as a matter of course. We have taken none of it for ourselves. Individuals who transgress will be punished in accordance with an order I issued at the beginning, threatening

---

[1] A reference to the "Night of the Long Knives," when Hitler ordered the SS to murder the leaders of the SA, a Nazi group he wished to suppress. [Ed.]

[2] Here Himmler is apparently referring to the stalemate on Germany's Western Front in World War I. [Ed.]

that whoever takes so much as a mark of it for himself is a dead man. A number of SS men—not very many—have transgressed, and they will die, without mercy. We had the moral right, we had the duty toward our people, to kill this people which wanted to kill us. But we do not have the right to enrich ourselves with so much as a fur, a watch, a mark, or a cigarette, or anything else. Having exterminated a germ, we do not want, in the end, to be infected by the germ, and die of it. I will not stand by and let even a small rotten spot develop or take hold. Wherever it may form, we together will cauterize it. All in all, however, we can say that we have carried out this heaviest of our tasks in a spirit of love for our people. And our inward being, our soul, our character has not suffered injury from it.

4

JEAN-FRANÇOIS STEINER
Treblinka, 1967

Treblinka, in Poland, was one of several Nazi extermination camps (see Map 25.1). In these "death factories," the Nazis murdered millions of Jews as well as Roma and Sinti, communists, socialists, Poles, Soviet prisoners of war, and other people. Extermination of Jews became official Nazi policy in 1942. Extermination camps were built to supplement earlier concentration camps used to contain political prisoners, Jews, and other forced laborers (many of whom also died there). In this selection, Steiner describes some of the elaborate study and preparation that went into the design of an extermination camp, focusing on the work of Kurt Franz, whom the prisoners called Lalka. What were the problems the Nazis faced in building an extermination camp? How did they solve them? What does this level of efficiency and scientific planning tell you about the Nazi regime or the people involved?

THINKING HISTORICALLY

Try to imagine what went through the mind of Lalka as he designed the extermination process at Treblinka. How did concerns for efficiency and humanity enter into his deliberations? Do you think he

---

Source: Jean-François Steiner, *Treblinka* (New York: Simon & Schuster, 1967), 153–54, 155–58, 159–60.

Map 25.1 Major Nazi Concentration Camps in World War II.

909

found his work distasteful? If so, which of the strategies mentioned in the previous selection did he adopt?

What would it have been like to be a sign-painter, guard, or hair-cutter at Treblinka? What do you imagine went through the minds of the victims?

Each poorly organized debarkation [of deportees from trains arriving at Treblinka] gave rise to unpleasant scenes—uncertainties and confusion for the deportees, who did not know where they were going and were sometimes seized with panic.

So, the first problem was to restore a minimum of hope. Lalka had many faults, but he did not lack a certain creative imagination. After a few days of reflection he hit upon the idea of transforming the platform where the convoys [trains] arrived into a false station. He had the ground filled in to the level of the doors of the cars in order to give the appearance of a train platform and to make it easier to get off the trains. . . . On [a] wall Lalka had . . . doors and windows painted in gay and pleasing colors. The windows were decorated with cheerful curtains and framed by green blinds which were just as false as the rest. Each door was given a special name, stencilled at eye level: "Stationmaster," "Toilet," "Infirmary" (a red cross was painted on this door). Lalka carried his concern for detail so far as to have his men paint two doors leading to the waiting rooms, first and second class. The ticket window, which was barred with a horizontal sign reading, "Closed," was a little masterpiece with its ledge and false perspective and its grill, painted line for line. Next to the ticket window a large timetable announced the departure times of trains for Warsaw, Bialystok, Wolkowysk, etc. . . . Two doors were cut into the [wall]. The first led to the "hospital," bearing a wooden arrow on which "Wolkowysk" was painted. The second led to the place where the Jews were undressed; that arrow said "Bialystok." Lalka also had some flower beds designed, which gave the whole area a neat and cheery look. . . .

Lalka also decided that better organization could save much time in the operations of undressing and recovery of the [deportees'] baggage. To do this you had only to rationalize the different operations, that is, to organize the undressing like an assembly line. But the rhythm of this assembly line was at the mercy of the sick, the old, and the wounded, who, since they were unable to keep the pace, threatened to bog down the operation and make it proceed even more slowly than before. . . . Individuals of both sexes over the age of ten, and children under ten, at a maximum rate of two children per adult, were judged fit to follow the complete circuit,[1] as long as they did not show serious wounds or marked disability. Victims who did not correspond to the norms were to be conducted to the "hospital" by members of the blue commando and turned over to the Ukrainians [guards] for special treatment. A bench was built all around the ditch of the "hospital" so that the victims would fall of their own weight after receiving the bullet in the back of the head. This bench was to be used only when Kurland[2] was swamped with work. On the platform, the door which these victims took was surmounted by the Wolkowysk arrow. In the Sibylline language of Treblinka, "Wolkowysk" meant the bullet in the back of the neck or the injection. "Bialystok" meant the gas chamber.

Beside the "Bialystok" door stood a tall Jew whose role was to shout endlessly, "Large bundles here, large bundles here!" He had been nicknamed "Groysse Pack." As soon as the victims had gone through, Groysse Pack and his men from the red commando carried the bundles at a run to the sorting square, where the sorting commandos immediately took possession of them. As soon as they had gone through the door came the order, "Women to the left, men to the right." This moment generally gave rise to painful scenes.

While the women were being led to the left-hand barracks to undress and go to the hairdresser,[3] the men, who were lined up double file, slowly entered the production line. This production line included five stations. At each of these a group of "reds" shouted at the top of their lungs the name of the piece of clothing that it was in charge of receiving. At the first station the victim handed over his coat and hat. At the second, his jacket. (In exchange, he received a piece of string.) At the third he sat down, took off his shoes, and tied them together with the string he had just received. Until then the shoes were not tied together in pairs, and since the yield was at least fifteen thousand pairs of shoes per day, they were all lost, since they could not be matched up again. At the fourth station the victim left his trousers, and at the fifth his shirt and underwear.

After they had been stripped, the victims were conducted, as they came off the assembly line, to the right-hand barracks and penned in until the women had finished: ladies first. However, a small number, chosen from among the most able-bodied, were singled out at the door to carry the clothing to the sorting square. They did this while running naked between two rows of Ukrainian guards. Without stopping once they threw their bundles onto the pile, turned around, and went back for another.

---

[1] The "complete" circuit was getting off the train, walking along the platform through the door to the men's or women's barracks, undressing, and being led to the gas chamber "showers." [Ed.]

[2] Kurland was a Jew assigned to the "hospital," where he gave injections of poison to those who were too ill or crippled to make the complete circuit. [Ed.]

[3] Haircutter. [Ed.]

Meanwhile the women had been conducted to the barracks on the left. This barracks was divided into two parts: a dressing room and a beauty salon. "Put your clothes in a pile so you will be able to find them after the shower," they were ordered in the first room. The "beauty salon" was a room furnished with six benches, each of which could seat twenty women at a time. Behind each bench twenty prisoners of the red commando, wearing white tunics and armed with scissors, waited at attention until all the women were seated. Between haircutting sessions they sat down on the benches and, under the direction of a *kapo* [prisoner guard] who was transformed into a conductor, they had to sing old Yiddish melodies.

Lalka, who had insisted on taking personal responsibility for every detail, had perfected the technique of what he called the "Treblinka cut." With five well-placed slashes the whole head of hair was transferred to a sack placed beside each hairdresser for this purpose. It was simple and efficient. How many dramas did this "beauty salon" see? From the very beautiful young woman who wept when her hair was cut off, because she would be ugly, to the mother who grabbed a pair of scissors from one of the "hairdressers" and literally severed a Ukrainian's arm; from the sister who recognized one of the "hairdressers" as her brother to the young girl, Ruth Dorfman, who, suddenly understanding and fighting back her tears, asked whether it was difficult to die and admitted in a small brave voice that she was a little afraid and wished it were all over.

When they had been shorn the women left the "beauty salon" double file. Outside the door, they had to squat in a particular way also specified by Lalka, in order to be intimately searched. Up to this point, doubt had been carefully maintained. Of course, a discriminating eye might have observed that . . . the smell was the smell of rotting bodies. A thousand details proved that Treblinka was not a transient camp, and some realized this, but the majority had believed in the impossible for too long to begin to doubt at the last moment. The door of the barracks, which opened directly onto the "road to heaven," represented the turning point. Up to here the prisoners had been given a minimum of hope, from here on this policy was abandoned.

This was one of Lalka's great innovations. After what point was it no longer necessary to delude the victims? This detail had been the subject of rather heated controversy among the Technicians. At the Nuremberg trials, Rudolf Höss, Commandant of Auschwitz, criticized Treblinka where, according to him, the victims knew that they were going to be killed. Höss was an advocate of the towel distributed at the door to the gas chamber. He claimed that this system not only avoided disorder, but was more humane, and he was proud of it. But Höss did not invent this "towel technique"; it was in all the manuals, and it was utilized at Treblinka until Lalka's great reform.

Lalka's studies had led to what might be called the "principle of the cutoff." His reasoning was simple: Since sooner or later the victims must realize that they were going to be killed, to postpone this moment was only false humanity. The principle "the later the better" did not apply here. Lalka had been led to make an intensive study of this problem upon observing one day completely by chance, that winded victims died much more rapidly than the rest. The discovery had led him to make a clean sweep of accepted principles. Let us follow his industrialist's logic, keeping well in mind that his great preoccupation was the saving of time. A winded victim dies faster. Hence, a saving of time. The best way to wind a man is to make him run—another saving of time. Thus Lalka arrived at the conclusion that you must make the victims run. A new question had then arisen: At what point must you make the victims run and thus create panic (a further aid to breathlessness)? The question had answered itself: As soon as you have nothing more to make them do. Franz located the exact point, the point of no return: the door of the barracks.

The rest was merely a matter of working out the details. Along the "road to heaven" and in front of the gas chambers he stationed a cordon of guards armed with whips, whose function was to make the victims run, to make them rush into the gas chambers of their own accord in search of refuge. One can see that this system is more daring than the classic system, but one can also see the danger it represents. Suddenly abandoned to their despair, realizing that they no longer had anything to lose, the victims might attack the guards. Lalka was aware of this risk, but he maintained that everything depended on the pace. "It's close work," he said, "but if you maintain a very rapid pace and do not allow a single moment of hesitation, the method is absolutely without danger." There were still further elaborations later on, but from the first day, Lalka had only to pride himself on his innovation: It took no more than three quarters of an hour, by the clock, to put the victims through their last voyage, from the moment the doors of the cattle cars were unbolted to the moment the great trap doors of the gas chamber were opened to take out the bodies. . . .

But let us return to the men. The timing was worked out so that by the time the last woman had emerged from the left-hand barracks, all the clothes had been transported to the sorting square. The men were immediately taken out of the right-hand barracks and driven after the women into the "road to heaven," which they reached by way of a special side path. By the time they arrived at the gas chambers the toughest, who had begun to run before the others to carry the bundles, were just as winded as the weakest. Everyone died in perfect unison for the greater satisfaction of that great Technician Kurt Franz, the Stakhanovite [model worker] of extermination.

TIMOTHY SNYDER

Holocaust: The Ignored Reality, 2009

The mass killing of Jews was a policy of the Nazis fueled by long-standing anti-Semitism, aggravated by German economic collapse and propaganda that linked Jews to both communist laborer agitation and the bankers at the upper levels of finance capitalism. This anti-Semitism was not limited to Germany, however. It was especially pervasive throughout Eastern Europe, where most Jews lived. Thus, it would be a mistake, according to the author of this selection, to think of the Holocaust solely in terms of Germany and German Jews. What are the broader dimensions of the Holocaust that the author describes? Further, if the Holocaust refers only to the killing of Jews, how might a focus on this genocide alone minimize the scale of civilian casualties in World War II?

THINKING HISTORICALLY

The process of understanding without excusing is a struggle between the intellect and the emotions. No historical study can be entirely divorced from the emotions, but subjects like mass slaughter make it harder than many other subjects to be objective. Other factors might inhibit the historian's ability to get to the truth. One difficulty, for instance, lies with sources. What limitations does Snyder see in the sources that have been available to understand the Holocaust? How representative are survivors? What can we learn from the perpetrators? How do statistics help and hinder our understanding? What is gained, and lost, by distinguishing between such events as holocaust, genocide, war crimes, massacres, civilian casualties, and "collateral damage"?

Though Europe thrives, its writers and politicians are preoccupied with death. The mass killings of European civilians during the 1930s and 1940s [see Map 25.2] are the reference of today's confused discussions of memory, and the touchstone of whatever common ethics Europeans may share. The bureaucracies of Nazi Germany and the Soviet Union turned individual lives into mass death, particular humans into quotas of those to be killed. The Soviets hid their mass shootings in dark woods and falsified the records of regions in which they had

Source: Timothy Snyder, "Holocaust: The Ignored Reality," *New York Review of Books* 56, no. 12 (July 16, 2009), http://www.nybooks.com/articles/22875.

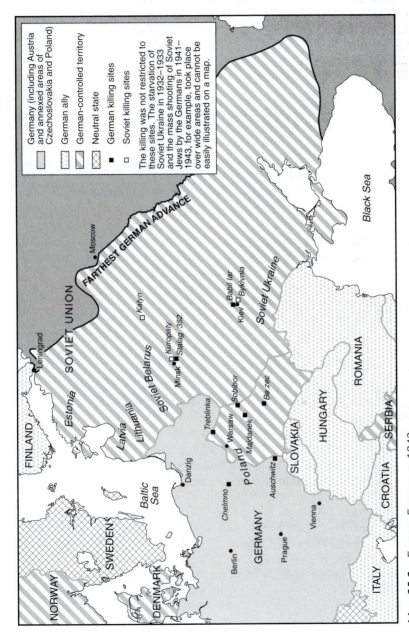

Map 25.2 Eastern Europe, c. 1942.

Source: Courtesy of the New York Review of Books.

The map legend reads:

- Germany (including Austria and annexed areas of Czechoslovakia and Poland)
- German ally
- German-controlled territory
- Neutral state
- ■ German killing sites
- □ Soviet killing sites

The killing was not restricted to these sites. The starvation of Soviet Ukraine in 1932–1933 and the mass shooting of Soviet Jews by the Germans in 1941–1943, for example, took place over wide areas and cannot be easily illustrated on a map.

starved people to death; the Germans had slave laborers dig up the bodies of their Jewish victims and burn them on giant grates. Historians must, as best we can, cast light into these shadows and account for these people. This we have not done. Auschwitz, generally taken to be an adequate or even a final symbol of the evil of mass killing, is in fact only the beginning of knowledge, a hint of the true reckoning with the past still to come.

The very reasons that we know something about Auschwitz warp our understanding of the Holocaust: we know about Auschwitz because there were survivors, and there were survivors because Auschwitz was a labor camp as well as a death factory. These survivors were largely West European Jews, because Auschwitz is where West European Jews were usually sent. After World War II, West European Jewish survivors were free to write and publish as they liked, whereas East European Jewish survivors, if caught behind the iron curtain, could not. In the West, memoirs of the Holocaust could (although very slowly) enter into historical writing and public consciousness.

This form of survivors' history, of which the works of Primo Levi[1] are the most famous example, only inadequately captures the reality of the mass killing. *The Diary of Anne Frank* concerns assimilated European Jewish communities, the Dutch and German, whose tragedy, though horrible, was a very small part of the Holocaust. By 1943 and 1944, when most of the killing of West European Jews took place, the Holocaust was in considerable measure complete. Two thirds of the Jews who would be killed during the war were already dead by the end of 1942. The main victims, the Polish and Soviet Jews, had been killed by bullets fired over death pits or by carbon monoxide from internal combustion engines pumped into gas chambers at Treblinka, Belżec,[2] and Sobitór in occupied Poland.

Auschwitz as symbol of the Holocaust excludes those who were at the center of the historical event. The largest group of Holocaust victims — religiously Orthodox and Yiddish-speaking Jews of Poland, or, in the slightly contemptuous German term, *Ostjuden*[3] — were culturally alien from West Europeans, including West European Jews. To some degree, they continue to be marginalized from the memory of the Holocaust. The death facility Auschwitz-Birkenau was constructed on territories that are today in Poland, although at the time they were part of the German Reich. Auschwitz is thus associated with today's Poland by anyone who visits, yet relatively few Polish Jews and almost no Soviet Jews died there. The two largest groups of victims are nearly missing from the memorial symbol.

[1] Primo Levi (1919–1987), Italian chemist, poet, essayist, novelist. Author of the memoir *Survival in Auschwitz*. [Ed.]

[2] Also rendered as Belżec. [Ed.]

[3] Eastern Jews (from Eastern Europe). [Ed.]

An adequate vision of the Holocaust would place Operation Reinhardt, the murder of the Polish Jews in 1942, at the center of its history. Polish Jews were the largest Jewish community in the world, Warsaw the most important Jewish city. This community was exterminated at Treblinka, Belżec, and Sobitór. Some 1.5 million Jews were killed at those three facilities, about 780,863 at Treblinka alone. Only a few dozen people survived these three death facilities. Belżec, though the third most important killing site of the Holocaust, after Auschwitz and Treblinka, is hardly known. Some 434,508 Jews perished at that death factory, and only two or three survived. About a million more Polish Jews were killed in other ways, some at Chelmno, Majdanek, or Auschwitz, many more shot in actions in the eastern half of the country.

All in all, as many if not more Jews were killed by bullets as by gas, but they were killed by bullets in easterly locations that are blurred in painful remembrance. The second most important part of the Holocaust is the mass murder by bullets in eastern Poland and the Soviet Union. It began with SS Einsatzgruppen shootings of Jewish men in June 1941, expanded to the murder of Jewish women and children in July, and extended to the extermination of entire Jewish communities that August and September. By the end of 1941, the Germans (along with local auxiliaries and Romanian troops) had killed a million Jews in the Soviet Union and the Baltics. That is the equivalent of the total number of Jews killed at Auschwitz during the entire war. By the end of 1942, the Germans (again, with a great deal of local assistance) had shot another 700,000 Jews, and the Soviet Jewish populations under their control had ceased to exist.

There were articulate Soviet Jewish witnesses and chroniclers, such as Vassily Grossman. But he and others were forbidden from presenting the Holocaust as a distinctly Jewish event. Grossman discovered Treblinka as a journalist with the Red Army in September 1944. Perhaps because he knew what the Germans had done to Jews in his native Ukraine, he was able to guess what had happened there, and wrote a short book about it. He called Treblinka "hell," and placed it at the center of the war and of the century. Yet for Stalin, the mass murder of Jews had to be seen as the suffering of "citizens." Grossman helped to compile a *Black Book* of German crimes against Soviet Jews, which Soviet authorities later suppressed. If any group suffered especially under the Germans, Stalin maintained wrongly, it was the Russians. In this way Stalinism has prevented us from seeing Hitler's mass killings in proper perspective.

In shorthand, then, the Holocaust was, in order: Operation Reinhardt, Shoah[4] by bullets, Auschwitz; or Poland, the Soviet Union, the

---

[4] Mass murder. [Ed.]

rest. Of the 5.7 million or so Jews killed, roughly 3 million were pre-war Polish citizens, and another 1 million or so pre-war Soviet citizens: taken together, 70 percent of the total. (After the Polish and Soviet Jews, the next-largest groups of Jews killed were Romanian, Hungarian, and Czechoslovak. If these people are considered, the East European character of the Holocaust becomes even clearer.)

Yet even this corrected image of the Holocaust conveys an unacceptably incomplete sense of the scope of German mass killing policies in Europe. The Final Solution, as the Nazis called it, was originally only one of the exterminatory projects to be implemented after a victorious war against the Soviet Union. Had things gone the way that Hitler, Himmler, and Göring expected, German forces would have implemented a Hunger Plan in the Soviet Union in the winter of 1941–1942. As Ukrainian and south Russian agricultural products were diverted to Germany, some 30 million people in Belarus, northern Russia, and Soviet cities were to be starved to death. The Hunger Plan was only a prelude to Generalplan Ost, the colonization plan for the western Soviet Union, which foresaw the elimination of some 50 million people.

The Germans did manage to carry out policies that bore some resemblance to these plans. They expelled half a million non-Jewish Poles from lands annexed to the Reich. An impatient Himmler ordered a first stage of Generalplan Ost implemented in eastern Poland: ten thousand Polish children were killed and a hundred thousand adults expelled. The Wehrmacht[5] purposefully starved about one million people in the siege of Leningrad, and about a hundred thousand more in planned famines in Ukrainian cities. Some three million captured Soviet soldiers died of starvation or disease in German prisoner-of-war camps. These people were purposefully killed: as with the siege of Leningrad, the knowledge and intention to starve people to death was present. Had the Holocaust not taken place, this would be recalled as the worst war crime in modern history.

In the guise of anti-partisan actions, the Germans killed perhaps three quarters of a million people, about 350,000 in Belarus alone, and lower but comparable numbers in Poland and Yugoslavia. The Germans killed more than a hundred thousand Poles when suppressing the Warsaw Uprising of 1944. Had the Holocaust not happened, these "reprisals" too would be regarded as some of the greatest war crimes in history. In fact they, like the starvation of Soviet prisoners of war, are scarcely recalled at all beyond the countries directly concerned. German occupation policies killed non-Jewish civilians in other ways as well, for example by hard labor in prison camps. Again: these were chiefly people from Poland or the Soviet Union.

The Germans killed somewhat more than ten million civilians in the major mass killing actions, about half of them Jews, about half of them non-Jews. The Jews and the non-Jews mostly came from the same part of

[5] German Army. [Ed.]

Europe. The project to kill all Jews was substantially realized; the project to destroy Slavic populations was only very partially implemented.

Auschwitz is only an introduction to the Holocaust, the Holocaust only a suggestion of Hitler's final aims. Grossman's novels *Forever Flowing* and *Life and Fate* daringly recount both Nazi and Soviet terror, and remind us that even a full characterization of German policies of mass killing is incomplete as a history of atrocity in mid-century Europe. It omits the state that Hitler was chiefly concerned to destroy, the other state that killed Europeans en masse in the middle of the century: the Soviet Union. In the entire Stalinist period, between 1928 and 1953, Soviet policies killed, in a conservative estimate, well over five million Europeans. Thus when one considers the total number of European civilians killed by totalitarian powers in the middle of the twentieth century, one should have in mind three groups of roughly equal size: Jews killed by Germans, non-Jews killed by Germans, and Soviet citizens killed by the Soviet state. As a general rule, the German regime killed civilians who were not German citizens, whereas the Soviet regime chiefly killed civilians who were Soviet citizens. Soviet repressions are identified with the Gulag, much as Nazi repressions are identified with Auschwitz. The Gulag,[6] for all of the horrors of slave labor, was not a system of mass killing. If we accept that mass killing of civilians is at the center of political, ethical, and legal concerns, the same historical point applies to the Gulag as to Auschwitz. We know about the Gulag because it was a system of labor camps, but not a set of killing facilities. The Gulag held about 30 million people and shortened some three million lives. But a vast majority of those people who were sent to the camps returned alive. Precisely because we have a literature of the Gulag, most famously Aleksandr Solzhenitsyn's *Gulag Archipelago*, we can try to imagine its horrors—much as we can try to imagine the horrors of Auschwitz.

Yet as Auschwitz draws attention away from the still greater horrors of Treblinka, the Gulag distracts us from the Soviet policies that killed people directly and purposefully, by starvation and bullets. Of the Stalinist killing policies, two were the most significant: the collectivization famines of 1930–1933 and the Great Terror of 1937–1938. It remains unclear whether the Kazakh famine of 1930–1932 was intentional, although it is clear that over a million Kazakhs died of starvation. It is established beyond reasonable doubt that Stalin intentionally starved to death Soviet Ukrainians in the winter of 1932–1933. Soviet documents reveal a series of orders of October–December 1932 with evident malice and intention to kill. By the end, more than three million inhabitants of Soviet Ukraine had died.

---

[6] A system of Soviet labor camps, many in remote locations, where political prisoners were sent and sometimes disappeared. [Ed.]

What we read of the Great Terror[7] also distracts us from its true nature. The great novel and the great memoir are Arthur Koestler's *Darkness at Noon* and Alexander Weissberg's *The Accused*. Both focus our attention on a small group of Stalin's victims, urban Communist leaders, educated people, sometimes known in the West. This image dominates our understanding of the Great Terror, but it is incorrect. Taken together, purges of Communist Party elites, the security police, and military officers claimed not more than 47,737 lives.

The largest action of the Great Terror, Operation 00447, was aimed chiefly at "kulaks," which is to say peasants who had already been oppressed during collectivization.[8] It claimed 386,798 lives. A few national minorities, representing together less than 2 percent of the Soviet population, yielded more than a third of the fatalities of the Great Terror. In an operation aimed at ethnic Poles who were Soviet citizens, for example, 111,091 people were shot. Of the 681,692 executions carried out for alleged political crimes in 1937 and 1938, the kulak operation and the national operations accounted for 633,955, more than 90 percent of the total. These people were shot in secret, buried in pits, and forgotten.

The emphasis on Auschwitz and the Gulag understates the numbers of Europeans killed, and shifts the geographical focus of the killing to the German Reich and the Russian East. Like Auschwitz, which draws our attention to the Western European victims of the Nazi empire, the Gulag, with its notorious Siberian camps, also distracts us from the geographical center of Soviet killing policies. If we concentrate on Auschwitz and the Gulag, we fail to notice that over a period of twelve years, between 1933 and 1944, some 12 million victims of Nazi and Soviet mass killing policies perished in a particular region of Europe, one defined more or less by today's Belarus, Ukraine, Poland, Lithuania, and Latvia. More generally, when we contemplate Auschwitz and the Gulag, we tend to think of the states that built them as systems, as modern tyrannies, or totalitarian states. Yet such considerations of thought and politics in Berlin and Moscow tend to overlook the fact that mass killing happened, predominantly, in the parts of Europe between Germany and Russia, not in Germany and Russia themselves.

The geographic, moral, and political center of the Europe of mass killing is the Europe of the East, above all Belarus, Ukraine, Poland, and the Baltic States, lands that were subject to sustained policies of atrocity by both regimes. The peoples of Ukraine and Belarus, Jews above all but not only, suffered the most, since these lands were both part of the Soviet Union during the terrible 1930s and subject to the worst of the German

---

[7] Period in 1930s of Stalin's purges of political rivals and anyone who voiced criticism. Here refers to 1937–1938. [Ed.]

[8] Soviet policy from 1928 to 1940 to end private property in farmland and create large farming communes. Forced collectivization of peasant kulaks led to mass starvation. [Ed.]

repressions in the 1940s. If Europe was, as Mark Mazower[9] put it, a dark continent, Ukraine and Belarus were the heart of darkness.

Historical reckonings that can be seen as objective, such as the counting of victims of mass killing actions, might help to restore a certain lost historical balance. German suffering under Hitler and during the war, though dreadful in scale, does not figure at the center of the history of mass killing. Even if the ethnic Germans killed during flight from the Red Army, expulsion from Poland and Czechoslovakia in 1945–1947, and the firebombings in Germany are included, the total number of German civilians killed by state power remains comparatively small. . . .

The main victims of direct killing policies among German citizens were the 70,000 "euthanasia" patients and the 165,000 German Jews. The main German victims of Stalin remain the women raped by the Red Army and the prisoners of war held in the Soviet Union. Some 363,000 German prisoners died of starvation and disease in Soviet captivity, as did perhaps 200,000 Hungarians. At a time when German resistance to Hitler receives attention in the mass media, it is worth recalling that some participants in the July 1944 plot to kill Hitler were right at the center of mass killing policies: Arthur Nebe, for example, who commanded Einsatzgruppe B in the killing fields of Belarus during the first wave of the Holocaust in 1941; or Eduard Wagner, the quartermaster general of the Wehrmacht, who wrote a cheery letter to his wife about the need to deny food to the starving millions of Leningrad.

It is hard to forget Anna Akhmatova: "It loves blood, the Russian earth." Yet Russian martyrdom and heroism, now loudly proclaimed in Putin's Russia, must be placed against the larger historical background. Soviet Russians, like other Soviet citizens, were indeed victims of Stalinist policy: but they were much less likely to be killed than Soviet Ukrainians or Soviet Poles, or members of other national minorities. During World War II several terror actions were extended to eastern Poland and the Baltic states, territories absorbed by the Soviet Union. In the most famous case, 22,000 Polish citizens were shot in 1940 at Katyn and four other sites; tens of thousands more Poles and Balts died during or shortly after deportations to Kazakhstan and Siberia. During the war, many Soviet Russians were killed by the Germans, but far fewer proportionately than Belarusians and Ukrainians, not to mention Jews. Soviet civilian deaths are estimated at about 15 million. About one in twenty-five civilians in Russia was killed by the Germans during the war, as opposed to about one in ten in Ukraine (or Poland) or about one in five in Belarus.

Belarus and Ukraine were occupied for much of the war, with both German and Soviet armies passing through their entire territory twice, in attack and retreat. German armies never occupied more than a small portion of Russia proper, and that for shorter periods. Even taking into

---

[9] Historian, author of *The Dark Continent: Europe's Twentieth Century* (2000). [Ed.]

account the siege of Leningrad and the destruction of Stalingrad, the toll taken on Russian civilians was much less than that on Belarusians, Ukrainians, and Jews. Exaggerated Russian claims about numbers of deaths treat Belarus and Ukraine as Russia, and Jews, Belarusians, and Ukrainians as Russians: this amounts to an imperialism of martyrdom, implicitly claiming territory by explicitly claiming victims. This will likely be the line propounded by the new historical committee appointed by President Dmitri Medvedev to prevent "falsifications" of the Russian past. Under legislation currently debated in Russia, statements such as those contained in this paragraph would be a criminal offense.

Ukrainian politicians counter Russia's monopolization of common suffering, and respond to Western European stereotypes of Ukrainians as Holocaust collaborators, by putting forward a narrative of suffering of their own: that millions of Ukrainians were deliberately starved by Stalin. President Viktor Yushchenko does his country a grave disservice by claiming ten million deaths, thus exaggerating the number of Ukrainians killed by a factor of three; but it is true that the famine in Ukraine of 1932–1933 was a result of purposeful political decisions, and killed about three million people. With the exception of the Holocaust, the collectivization famines were the greatest political disaster of the European twentieth century. Collectivization nevertheless remained the central element of the Soviet model of development, and was copied later by the Chinese Communist regime, with the predictable consequence: tens of millions dead by starvation in Mao's Great Leap Forward.[10]

The preoccupation with Ukraine as a source of food was shared by Hitler and Stalin. Both wished to control and exploit the Ukrainian breadbasket, and both caused political famines: Stalin in the country as a whole, Hitler in the cities and the prisoner-of-war camps. Some of the Ukrainian prisoners who endured starvation in those camps in 1941 had survived the famine in 1933. German policies of starvation, incidentally, are partially responsible for the notion that Ukrainians were willing collaborators in the Holocaust. The most notorious Ukrainian collaborators were the guards at the death facilities at Treblinka, Bełżec, and Sobibor. What is rarely recalled is that the Germans recruited the first cadres of such men, captured Soviet soldiers, from their own prisoner-of-war camps. They rescued some people from mass starvation, one great crime in the east, in order to make them collaborators in another, the Holocaust.

Poland's history is the source of endless confusion. Poland was attacked and occupied not by one but by both totalitarian states between 1939 and 1941, as Nazi Germany and the Soviet Union, then allies, exploited its territories and exterminated much of its intelligentsia at

---

[10] Chinese communist collectivization (1958–1961) under Mao Zedong, which failed. [Ed.]

that time. Poland's capital was the site of not one but two of the major uprisings against German power during World War II: the ghetto[11] uprising of Warsaw Jews in 1943,[12] after which the ghetto was leveled; and the Warsaw Uprising of the Polish Home Army in 1944, after which the rest of the city was destroyed. These two central examples of resistance and mass killing were confused in the German mass media in August 1994, 1999, and 2004, on all the recent five-year anniversaries of the Warsaw Uprising of 1944, and will be again in August 2009.

If any European country seems out of place in today's Europe, stranded in another historical moment, it is Belarus under the dictatorship of Aleksandr Lukashenko. Yet while Lukashenko prefers to ignore the Soviet killing fields in his country, wishing to build a highway over the death pits at Kuropaty, in some respects Lukashenko remembers European history better than his critics. By starving Soviet prisoners of war, shooting and gassing Jews, and shooting civilians in anti-partisan actions, German forces made Belarus the deadliest place in the world between 1941 and 1944. Half of the population of Soviet Belarus was either killed or forcibly displaced during World War II: nothing of the kind can be said of any other European country.

Belarusian memories of this experience, cultivated by the current dictatorial regime, help to explain suspicions of initiatives coming from the West. Yet West Europeans would generally be surprised to learn that Belarus was both the epicenter of European mass killing and the base of operations of anti-Nazi partisans who actually contributed to the victory of the Allies. It is striking that such a country can be entirely displaced from European remembrance. The absence of Belarus from discussions of the past is the clearest sign of the difference between memory and history.

Just as disturbing is the absence of economics. Although the history of mass killing has much to do with economic calculation, memory shuns anything that might seem to make murder appear rational. Both Nazi Germany and the Soviet Union followed a path to economic self-sufficiency, Germany wishing to balance industry with an agrarian utopia in the East, the USSR wishing to overcome its agrarian backwardness with rapid industrialization and urbanization. Both regimes were aiming for economic autarky in a large empire, in which both sought to control Eastern Europe. Both of them saw the Polish state as a historical aberration;[13] both saw Ukraine and its rich soil as indispensable. They defined different groups as the enemies of their designs, although the German plan to kill every Jew is

---

[11] Ghettos were urban areas in which Jews were forced to live, apart from the rest of the society. [Ed.]

[12] Revolt of Polish Jews in April 1943 in opposition to removal to Treblinka. Crushed by German troops in May. [Ed.]

[13] Polish territory had often been part of one or more larger states. [Ed.]

unmatched by any Soviet policy in the totality of its aims. What is crucial is that the ideology that legitimated mass death was also a vision of economic development. In a world of scarcity, particularly of food supplies, both regimes integrated mass murder with economic planning.

They did so in ways that seem appalling and obscene to us today, but which were sufficiently plausible to motivate large numbers of believers at the time. Food is no longer scarce, at least in the West; but other resources are, or will be soon. In the twenty-first century, we will face shortages of potable water, clean air, and affordable energy. Climate change may bring a renewed threat of hunger.

If there is a general political lesson of the history of mass killing, it is the need to be wary of what might be called privileged development: attempts by states to realize a form of economic expansion that designates victims, that motivates prosperity by mortality. The possibility cannot be excluded that the murder of one group can benefit another, or at least can be seen to do so. That is a version of politics that Europe has in fact witnessed and may witness again. The only sufficient answer is an ethical commitment to the individual, such that the individual counts in life rather than in death, and schemes of this sort become unthinkable.

The Europe of today is remarkable precisely in its unity of prosperity with social justice and human rights. Probably more than any other part of the world, it is immune, at least for the time being, to such heartlessly instrumental pursuits of economic growth. Yet memory has made some odd departures from history, at a time when history is needed more than ever. The recent European past may resemble the near future of the rest of the world. This is one more reason for getting the reckonings right.

6

DR. ROBERT WILSON

Letters from Nanking, 1937–1938

In 1946 the American-led International Military Tribunal for the Far East brought charges against the defeated Iwane Matsui, former commander of the Japanese Shanghai Expeditionary Forces, for what was already being called "the Rape of Nanking." Matsui was charged with leading an army that systematically killed 200,000 defenseless Chinese civilians, committed 20,000 cases of rape, and stole or burned much of the property in the city.

Source: *Documents on the Rape of Nanking*, ed. Timothy Brook (Ann Arbor: University of Michigan Press, 1999), 210–11, 214–17, 250–54.

Dr. Robert Wilson was one of three American medical doctors, and the only surgeon, who remained at the University Hospital in Nanking when the Chinese defenders retreated and Japanese troops occupied the city in December 1937. He wrote these letters to his family, even after he realized he wouldn't be able to mail them, as a kind of diary of events between December 1937 and March 1938.

What does Wilson's diary tell you about the Japanese occupation of Nanking? What does it tell you about Japanese forces? What are "war crimes" in the midst of war?

THINKING HISTORICALLY

It would be difficult to get into the shoes, much less the minds, of these Japanese troops from the viewpoint of a single American observer. Nevertheless, how might Robert Wilson account for their behavior? How do you make sense of it?

Tuesday, December 14

. . . On Monday morning the 13th, exactly four months after the trouble started in Shanghai, the Japanese entered the city by several gates at once. Some came in Hoping Men [Gate] in the north and some in Hansi and Kwanghua Mens in the west and south-east respectively. By night they had complete control of the city and numerous Japanese flags flew from various places including their former embassy.

The entire remaining population of Nanking, some 150 or 200 thousand individuals, were crowded into the zone I have described earlier as the refugee zone. The International Committee[1] are doing a tremendous job with them and there is no doubt but that they have saved thousands of lives by their efforts. At the last moment thousands of Chinese soldiers threw away their uniforms and equipment and donned looted civilian clothes and crowded into the zone. Handling them is a grave problem in itself. Doubly grave has it become since the Japanese have not been fooled and are rounding them up by the hundreds and shooting them, putting their bodies in the conveniently handy dugouts built for air-raid protection.

Any civilian who shows no signs of fear and goes quietly about his business in the daytime seems relatively safe. Nobody is safe at night. Last night Mr. Chi, architect for the university and left behind to look after the buildings as best he could, was only saved from shooting by the intervention of Charlie Riggs, who stoutly maintained that Chi was his

---

[1] The European (including German) and North American governors of the International Zone (non-Asian). [Ed.]

coolie.[2] They then came over to our place with another Chinese University staff man, Mr. Ku, and all three stayed the night on some cots we put up in the living room. Steele of the *Chicago Daily News* also slept there and we totalled eleven people sleeping on the main floor and up, and I completely lost track of the innumerable Chinese that slept in the basement. The servants are rightly scared to death. To finish this paragraph more or less as it began, any civilian that shows signs of fear or tries to run away is promptly bayonetted. I sewed up one severed trachea this afternoon and we have had several dozen cases of bayonetting.

This morning we were treated to a thorough though unofficial inspection by thirty or so Japanese troops with fixed bayonets. They poked into everything. [Dr. James] McCallum, [Dr. C. S.] Trimmer and I showed them around and they would jabber away in Japanese while we would jabber away in both Chinese and English and neither had any idea what the other was saying. They lined up some of the nurses and took away their pens, flashlights and wrist watches. They did a pretty good job of looting the nurses' dormitory, taking all kinds of petty things. So far there has been no physical violence done to any of our staff.

Wednesday, December 15

... The slaughter of civilians is appalling. I could go on for pages telling of cases of rape and brutality almost beyond belief. Two bayonetted cases are the only survivors of seven street cleaners who were sitting in their headquarters when Japanese soldiers came in without warning or reason and killed five of their number and wounded the two that found their way to the hospital. I wonder when it will stop and we will be able to catch up with ourselves again.

Saturday, December 18

Today marks the sixth day of the modern Dante's Inferno, written in huge letters with blood and rape. Murder by the wholesale and rape by the thousands of cases. There seems to be no stop to the ferocity, lust and atavism of the brutes. At first I tried to be pleasant to them to avoid arousing their ire but the smile has gradually worn off and my stare is fully as cool and fishy as theirs.

Tonight as I came back from supper to stay here for the night I found three soldiers had ransacked the place. Miss [Iva] Hynds had accompanied them to the back gate. Two of them arrived and the other had disappeared. He must be hiding somewhere around the place. I motioned to

---

[2] Word used for usually Chinese workers. [Ed.]

the others outside stating in no uncertain terms that this was a Beikoku Byoyen [American hospital]. How do you like that? The two that were there allowed themselves to be led out. They had taken Miss Hynds' watch and several other watches and fountain pens as well.

Let me recount some instances occurring in the last two days. Last night the house of one of the Chinese staff members of the university was broken into and two of the women, his relatives, were raped. Two girls about 16 were raped to death in one of the refugee camps. In the University Middle School where there are 8,000 people the Japs came in ten times last night, over the wall, stole food, clothing, and raped until they were satisfied. They bayonetted one little boy, killing him, and I spent an hour and a half this morning patching up another little boy of eight who had five bayonet wounds including one that penetrated his stomach, a portion of omentum was outside the abdomen. I think he will live.

I just took time out because the third soldier had been found. He was on the fourth floor of the nurses' dormitory where there were fifteen nurses. They were scared within an inch of their lives. I don't know how much he had done before I arrived but he didn't do anything afterwards. He had a watch or two and was starting off with one of the girls' cameras. I motioned for him to give it back to her and to my surprise he obeyed. I then accompanied him to the front door and bade him a fond farewell. Unfortunately he didn't get the swift kick that I mentally aimed at him. One of the earlier ones was toying around with a rather formidable looking pistol which I'm thankful he didn't use.

One man I treated today had three bullet holes. He is the sole survivor of a group of eighty, including an eleven year old boy, who were led out of two buildings within the so-called safety zone and taken into the hills west of Tibet Road and there slaughtered. He came to after they had left and found the other seventy-nine dead about him. His three bullet wounds are not serious. To do the Japanese justice there were in the eighty a few ex-soldiers.

One girl I have is a half-wit with some sort of birth injury, I believe. She didn't have any more sense than to claw at a Japanese soldier who was taking away her only bedding. Her reward was a bayonet thrust that cut half the muscles of one side of her neck.

Another girl of seventeen has a terrific gash in her neck and is the only survivor of her family, the rest of them were finished off. She was employed by the International Export Company.

As I left the hospital for supper after finishing my rounds on the 150 cases now under my care, the full moon was rising over Purple Mountain and was indescribably beautiful, and yet it looked down on a Nanking that was more desolate than it has been since the Taiping Rebellion [1853–64]. Nine-tenths of the city are totally deserted by Chinese and contain only roving bands of plundering Japanese. The remaining tenth contains almost two hundred thousand terrified citizens.

Last night [Plumer] Mills, [Lewis] Smythe and [George] Fitch went over in Fitch's car to escort Mills to Ginling [College]. Minnie [Vautrin] holds the fort there with several thousand women. When they got to the front gate they were held up by a patrol of Japanese soldiers under command of a pugnacious, impudent lieutenant. He lined the men on one side and Miss Vautrin, Mrs. Chen [Shui-fang] and Mrs. [deWitt] Twinem on the other side. He snatched the hats off the men and ordered everyone off the place including the women. Fitch told him he didn't have a place for them to stay but he insisted. They just got into the car when he ordered them back again and again harangued them for some minutes, finally sending the men back where they came from. Later we learned that while this was going on some Japanese soldiers had climbed over the wall and helped themselves to sixteen women.

The population faces famine in the near future and there is no provision for winter's fuel. It is not a pleasant winter that we look forward to. It is too bad that the newspaper reporters left on the day they did instead of two days or so later when they could have been more detailed in their reports of the Reign of Terror.

Another interruption to usher two Japanese soldiers off the premises.

As I probably won't get much sleep tonight I had better turn in dressed to get what I can.

Thursday, February 10

. . . The proportion of medical [to] surgical cases at the hospital is steadily increasing so that now Trim has about 50 patients to my 100. Today for the first time I went to our regular surgical clinic at 2 p.m., starting my operative schedule at 3:30. I shall try to continue that as the clinic certainly needs a guiding hand and there have been a lot of complaints about the way people are being treated there. This afternoon a woman came in with her face badly burned. She had returned to her home, on the orders of the Japanese, four days ago. Several Japanese soldiers promptly visited the house and demanded girls. She had only one 11 year old and one 12 year old and as these did not satisfy the soldiers they set fire to her house burning up the 11 year old girl in the building.

We are getting a large number of women from 16 to 30, most of them nice looking girls who are ridden with venereal disease from frequent raping. All of them have gonorrhea, most have syphilis and a large proportion have chancroid as well. That aspect of the clinic is certainly a heartbreaking one. It doesn't take long for any remote respect for the Japanese soldiers to evaporate permanently.

When our two cases of beri-beri showed up the other day we got immediate action and a boat is starting from Shanghai tomorrow with 100 tons of green beans. We hope to cut down any further incidence.

Yesterday I tried my first heterogeneous skin graft using pinch grafts from a father to his daughter. The graft looked fine today but it is much too early to tell. This afternoon I admitted a horribly burned little girl who has all the skin off her lower abdomen and anterior thighs. It happened six days ago and the mother had put on a concoction of mice boiled in oil and ground up. I had to give the child a general anaesthesia to clean it up. Her father had been shot offhand by the Japs about a month ago and the mother had not been able to give the child the attention she wanted to.

We get up to the tune of Jap airplanes and hear them all day long. Every now and then we think some Chinese planes come to the outskirts but we have no direct confirmation except occasional radio reports from Hankow. . . .

Sunday, February 13

. . . Last night we finally had the members of the Japanese Embassy to dinner. Three of the four came, the fourth having celebrated the previous day too vigorously. The previous day was the Anniversary of the founding of the Empire. Mssrs. Fukui, Fukuda and Kasuya were the guests. We put our excellent radio upstairs and played some classical records for them. We settled the problem of what to talk about by finding that two of them played bridge so that a bridge game was quickly organized. Fitch and Fukuda playing Riggs and Fukui. Unfortunately they stayed until ten-fifteen so that we didn't get any of the news broadcasts. Ordinarily we listen to Manila at 8:50, Hongkong at 9:30 and Shanghai at 10:10. Occasionally London at 6:00 and now and then Melbourne or some other place that happens to be giving the news.

Another cheerful tale came to my attention yesterday. Two weeks ago six Japanese soldiers entered the town of Liulangchiao some miles southwest of our town. They proceeded with their usual system of rape and looting. Some of the men in the town organized some resistance and killed three of the soldiers, the other three getting away. The three soon returned with several hundred who quickly threw a cordon around the town. A town of 500 inhabitants, it had only about 300 at the time. These 300 were all tied together in groups of six to eight and thrown in the icy river. They then leveled the town so that there wasn't a wall standing. The story was told me by a man who had gone from Nanking to Tanyangchen, a village just beyond Liulangchiao. He talked with the few terrified inhabitants of the surrounding territory and saw the ruins. Coming back he passed two soldiers on sentry duty at Yuhwatai just outside of South Gate. He was with his wife and child. They had passed the sentries about fifty yards when one of them casually shot in their direction, the bullet going through his flank but fortunately not entering the peritoneum. He is anxious to get out and return to Tanyangchen.

Only tonight four Jap soldiers came in and robbed several people in the University Library at the point of pistols of several hundred dollars. I guess the millennium is not here yet.

March 7

. . . The fall of Nanking on December 13 was immeasurably hastened by the incompetence and defection of T'ang Sheng-chih who was supposed to coordinate the defence. I shall not go into details on that here but will some day when the opportunity affords. If anyone had mentioned to us on December 12 that the entry of the Japanese would be the signal for a reign of terror almost beyond description we would have laughed at their fears. We had urged our Chinese staff to stay in the firm belief that, once the much vaunted Japanese Imperial army had taken control, lives would be safe and, while there might be some interference in the conduction of affairs, it would be only petty annoyances and that we need not be overconcerned.

When the mass murder, rapine, looting and arson began shortly after the entry of the Japanese troops we at first could not believe our eyes but were effectively convinced in a very short time. We had experienced no trouble whatever at the hands of Chinese soldiers even during the night of December 12 when tens of thousands of them streamed northward through the city to their slaughter at Hsia Kwan. It is true that they had burned some of the buildings just outside of the city walls in preparation for a defence of the walls that was never made, but outside of that and the burning of the Ministry of Communications, which burned on December 12th and therefore was presumably burned by Chinese, no destruction was carried out.

The Red Swastika Society[3] has for the last month been feverishly burying bodies from all parts of the city outside the zone and from the surrounding countryside. A conservative estimate of the number of people slaughtered in cold blood is somewhere about 100,000, including of course thousand of soldiers that had thrown down their arms. A few pitiful survivors of many of the mass murders managed to get to the hospital to tell their tale. I will record only one incident to illustrate.

At the University where the haphazard registration was going on of the twenty thousand people occupying the new library and compound and the main University buildings and compound, speeches were made urging all those that had been connected with the military to acknowledge it. They were promised that if they did so they would be made into labor gangs and their lives would be spared. If they did not acknowledge it and for any reason the Japanese suspected they had been connected with the military they would be summarily shot. About two hundred came forward

---

[3] Nazi German imitation of Red Cross Society. [Ed.]

and gave themselves up. I treated several survivors of that group. They were separated into several gangs and joined with hundreds of others picked up elsewhere. One bunch was taken into the hills beyond Ginling College, a few machine guns sprayed on them, several gallons of gasoline doused over their heads and they were set afire. Two survivors later died in the hospital burned almost beyond recognition, one not even having been hit by the machine guns, and the other having his jaw torn open.

7

AKIHIRO TAKAHASHI

Memory of Hiroshima, 1945/1986

The author of this selection, Akihiro Takahashi, was fourteen years old on August 6, 1945, when the United States bombed Hiroshima. He was standing in line with other students in the courtyard of the Hiroshima Municipal Junior High School. His and other survivors' recollections of that day and its aftermath were recorded, transcribed, and translated some forty years later by a Japanese peace project called "The Voice of Hibakusha."[1] What does this testimony contribute to your understanding of the history of mass killing?

THINKING HISTORICALLY

One of the difficulties in thinking about the unthinkable is remembering the details we want to forget. Trauma victims often repress memories that are too painful to bear. In some cases time revives memories as well as heals. Akihiro Takahashi's recollections display both a prodigious and courageous memory. How might this process of remembering and telling be helpful to him? How might it be helpful to others?

. . . [W]e saw a B-29 approaching and about fly over us. All of us were looking up the sky, pointing out the aircraft. Then the teachers came out from the school building and the class leaders gave the command to fall in. Our faces were all shifted from the direction of the sky to that of the platform. That was the moment when the blast came.

[1] Japanese term for the victims of Hiroshima and Nagasaki: literally, the "explosion-affected people."

Source: "The Voice of Hibakusha," Testimony of Akihiro Takahashi in Atomic Archive, http://www.atomicarchive.com/Docs/Hibakusha/Akihiro.shtml.

And then the tremendous noise came and we were left in the dark. I couldn't see anything at the moment of explosion just like in this picture. We had been blown by the blast. Of course, I couldn't realize this until the darkness disappeared. I was actually blown about 10 m. My friends were all marked down on the ground by the blast just like this. Everything collapsed for as far as I could see. I felt the city of Hiroshima had disappeared all of a sudden. Then I looked at myself and found my clothes had turned into rags due to the heat. I was probably burned at the back of the head, on my back, on both arms and both legs. My skin was peeling and hanging like this. Automatically I began to walk heading west because that was the direction of my home. After a while, I noticed somebody calling my name. I looked around and found a friend of mine who lived in my town and was studying at the same school. His name was Yamamoto. He was badly burnt just like myself. We walked toward the river. And on the way we saw many victims. I saw a man whose skin was completely peeled off the upper half of his body and a woman whose eye balls were sticking out. Her whole body was bleeding. A mother and her baby were lying with a skin completely peeled off. We desperately made away crawling. And finally we reached the river bank. At the same moment, a fire broke out. We made a narrow escape from the fire. If we had been slower by even one second, we would have been killed by the fire. Fire was blowing into the sky, becoming 4 or even 5 m high. There was a small wooden bridge left, which had not been destroyed by the blast. I went over to the other side of the river using that bridge. But Yamamoto was not with me any more. He was lost somewhere. I remember I crossed the river by myself and on the other side, I purged myself into the water three times. The heat was tremendous. And I felt like my body was burning all over. For my burning body the cold water of the river was as precious as a treasure. Then I left the river, and I walked along the railroad tracks in the direction of my home. On the way, I ran into another friend of mine, Tokujiro Hatta. I wondered why the soles of his feet were badly burnt. It was unthinkable to get burned there. But it was an undeniable fact that the soles were peeling and red muscle was exposed. Even though I myself was terribly burnt, I could not go home ignoring him. I made him crawl using his arms and knees. Next, I made him stand on his heels and I supported him. We walked heading toward my home repeating the two methods. When we were resting because we were so exhausted, I found my grandfather's brother and his wife, in other words, great uncle and great aunt, coming toward us. That was quite a coincidence. As you know, we have a proverb about meeting Buddha in Hell. My encounter with my relatives at that time was just like that. They seemed to be the Buddha to me wandering in the living hell.

Afterwards I was under medical treatment for one year and half and I miraculously recovered. Out of sixty junior high school classmates, only ten of us are alive today. Yamamoto and Hatta soon died from the acute radiation disease. The radiation corroded their bodies and killed them. I myself am still alive on this earth suffering after-effects of the bomb. I have to see regularly an ear doctor, an eye doctor, a dermatologist and a surgeon. I feel uneasy about my health every day. Further, on both of my hands, I have keloids.[2] My injury was most serious on my right hand and I used to have terrible keloids right here. I had them removed by surgery in 1954, which enabled me to move my wrist a little bit like this. For my four fingers are fixed just like this, and my elbow is fixed at one hundred twenty degrees and doesn't move. The muscle and bones are attached [to] each other. Also the fourth finger of my right hand doesn't have a normal nail. It has a black nail. A piece of glass which was blown by the blast stuck here and destroyed the cells of the base of the finger. That is why a black nail continues to grow and from now on, too, it will continue to be black and never become normal. Anyway I'm alive today together with nine of my classmates for this forty years. I've been living believing that we can never waste the deaths of the victims. I've been living on, dragging my body full of sickness, and from time to time I question myself; I wonder if it is worth living in such hardship and pain and I become desperate. But it's time I manage to pull myself together and I tell myself once my life was saved, I should fulfill my mission as a survivor; in other words, it has been and it is my belief that those who survived must continue to talk about our experiences. To hand down the awful memories to future generations representing the silent voices of those who had to die in misery. Throughout my life, I would like to fulfill this mission by talking about my experience both here in Japan and overseas.

■ REFLECTIONS

Short of war, the world community has adopted three strategies to counter genocide and the mass killing of civilians. The first is the trial of war criminals. At the conclusion of World War II, the victorious Allies conducted war-crime trials of leading Nazi and Japanese officials. Twelve high Nazi officials and seven Japanese leaders, including Iwane Matsui for the "Rape of Nanking," were sentenced to death. Many others served prison sentences. Critics argued that some of the alleged crimes ("wars of aggression" and "crimes against peace") were vague and that the victorious Allies might be guilty of these as well. Other charges—specifically "war crimes" and "crimes against humanity"—were devised as a response to the trials, an ex post facto (after the fact)

---

[2] Scars. [Ed.]

violation of standard procedure where prosecution must be based on criminal statutes.

The problem was that the technology and practice of warfare had largely outrun international agreements. The first Geneva Conventions, dating from 1864, were mainly concerned with the treatment of the wounded and prisoners. Therefore, the second strategy was developing and refining international laws regarding human rights and the protection of civilians. In 1948, the "Universal Declaration of Human Rights" passed by the United Nations, itself a shaper and guardian of international law, offered a recognized standard and continuing process for defining and preventing genocide, mass murder, and "crimes against humanity." A fourth Geneva Convention in 1949 added the destruction of civilian populations in time of war to the list of war crimes for which a country would be held responsible. In addition, the precedent of the "International Military Tribunal" that tried Nazi and Japanese officials led to the creation of international laws and courts for the prosecution of war crimes and mass murder. The legacy continues. In 2002, the United Nations' International Court of Criminal Justice in The Hague, Netherlands, brought President Milošević of Yugoslavia to trial for the "ethnic cleansing" of Muslims in Kosovo and Bosnia, and continued with the prosecution of others. An International Tribunal for Genocide in Rwanda similarly tried Hutu Rwandans for the mass murder of Tutsi fellow citizens in 1994.

A third strategy has emerged in recent years, largely where human rights abuses or civilian casualties have occurred within a national population. Often without the benefit of international courts or agencies, governments seeking to put past grievances aside, rather than prosecute offenders, have created "truth and reconciliation" commissions. In 1995, after decades of racist violence, the new South African government under Nelson Mandela established such a commission. Former white officials were guaranteed immunity from prosecution in return for complete and remorseful testimony of their crimes. Similarly, in El Salvador after a decade of violence in the 1980s, a new government established a Truth Commission in 1992 with United Nations assistance.

Finding the truth is the beginning of any strategy toward renewal. To promote understanding, archives must be opened, press and Internet censorship must be challenged, and laws such as the Freedom of Information Act must be used aggressively. But in addition, we must develop sensitivity to the plight of victims, knowledge of the victimizers' motives, and understanding about the ways that the horrendous can happen.

1

HEONIK KWON

Origins of the Cold War, 2010

Heonik Kwon is a modern specialist on Korean and Cold War history. He is one of a growing number of Cold War scholars who are examining the many "hot wars" that were caused by the "cold" conflict between the United States and the Soviet Union. In this selection he mentions the Korean War, but he is mainly concerned with examining the causes of the Cold War. How, according to Kwon, does the establishment of a beginning date and cause of the Cold War become a moral issue? What alternate starting dates for the Cold War does Kwon discuss? Which of these do you find most convincing? How do the ideas of George Kennan and J. Edgar Hoover help us understand the causes of the Cold War?

THINKING HISTORICALLY

One goal of propaganda is to convert rational analysis into powerful emotions, frequently fear. How do the writings included here of Kennan, Hoover, and Eisenhower do this? The line between propaganda and self-delusion can be very thin. Do you think these important people believed what they said? How did the Cold War psychology become so pervasive?

The story of the cold war, like that of any other war in human history, begins somewhere and ends somewhere. There is no consensus about the question of beginning. The origin of the cold war is an unsettled issue that continues to engender instructive debate among historians. Reflecting on the diverse ways to think about the origin of the cold war means rethinking the political history of the twentieth century and therefore considering the changing conditions of the contemporary world in new historical perspectives. However, this openness to historical reasoning and imagining does not extend to the other end of the story. There is a strong consensus in contemporary literature that the end of the cold war is a fait accompli, a universal historical reality. The question of the end has no room for diversity and generates no such positive interpretive controversies like those about the origin. The story of the cold war we tell ourselves today, therefore, has an open-ended beginning and a closed ending.

Source: Heonik Kwon, *The Other Cold War* (New York: Columbia University Press, 2010), 1–3, 70–73.

The term *cold war* refers to the prevailing condition of the world in the second half of the twentieth century, divided into two separate paths of political modernity and economic development. In a narrower sense, it means the contest of power and will between the two dominant states, the United States and the Soviet Union, that (according to George Orwell, who coined the term in 1945) set out to rule the world between them under an undeclared state of war, being unable to conquer one another. In a wide definition, however, the global cold war also entails the unequal relations of power among the political communities that pursued or were driven to pursue a specific path of progress within the binary structure of the global order. The "contest-of-power" dimension of the cold war has been an explicit and central element in cold war historiography; in contrast, the "relation-of-domination" aspect has been a relatively marginal, implicit element. The debates about the origins of the cold war contribute to disclosing how complex the great bifurcation in the project of modernity has been for both nations and communities. The origin of the cold war is not merely a question of time but also, in significant measure, a moral question: Which side of the bipolarized human community was more responsible for bringing about the global order and engendering political and military crises? The moral question is intertwined with the chronological one, and their connectedness is more apparent in places where the bipolar conflict was waged in a violent form.

Imagining the political future of Korea, for example, is inseparable from locating the origin of the Korean War. For people who date the origin of the war to 1950, the culpability for the devastating civil war rests unquestionably with the northern Communist regime, which launched, with endorsement and support from Mao Zedong and Joseph Stalin, an all-out surprise offensive against the southern territory in June of that year. For those who trace the war's origin to earlier years, the blame is apportioned equally to the belligerent, strongly anti-Communist southern regime, which instigated a series of border skirmishes and crushed domestic radical nationalist forces in a ruthless manner from 1947 to 1950. The latter measure provoked the outbreak of armed partisan activities in parts of the southern territory, which were effectively in a state of war from 1948 on. For those who associate the origin of the Korean War with the end of the Pacific War in 1945, however, the main responsibility for the civil war lies instead with the United States and the Soviet Union, which partitioned and separately occupied the postcolonial nation after the surrender of Japan. (And we should add to these divergent views the official position taken by North Korea, which continues to paint its part in the war as an act of self-defense against the unprovoked aggression from South Korea, orchestrated by the United States, despite a wealth of evidence that points to the contrary.) These diverse perspectives on the origin of one of the first violent manifestations of the bipolar global order are not merely matters of scholarly debate. They are also deeply ingrained in the society that endured what was at once a civil war and an international war, provoking heated public debate and developing conflicting political voices and forces. In this context, the origin of the cold war is largely the origin of the war-induced wounds felt in the society, thereby making the very concept of a "cold" war somewhat contradictory, so that claiming a particular version of the origin is simultaneously an act of asserting a particular vision of the nation's history and future.

In the wider terrain, too, the cold war's temporal identity continues to be revised as to the question of its origin. Conventional knowledge associates the origin of the cold war with the end of World War II and the breakdown of the wartime alliance between the Western powers and the Soviet state. However, several scholars have challenged this conventional view. For example, Melvyn Leffler retraces the origin to the period following the Russian Revolution of 1917, whereas William Appleman Williams famously argues that the seeds of the cold war were sown much earlier, during the nineteenth-century contest for global supremacy between the established European imperial powers and the newly rising American power. Each of these revisions of the cold war's origin is simultaneously an attempt to reinterpret the meaning of the global conflict in modern history. Leffler's scheme foregrounds the importance of ideology (the antagonistic view to communism as a radically alien way of life incompatible with the market-based liberal world) in the construction of the cold war global order, whereas Williams shows how the perception of the alien ideological other mirrored for the United States at the turn of the twentieth century the nation's own ideological self-image defined in terms of so-called Manifest Destiny—the idea that America, as a sole benevolent and progressive power, confronts the backward and confused world infested with imperialist excess and colonial miseries. . . .

Two important documents of the early cold war show how the ideological "other" was imagined both from within and from without. George Kennan, an American diplomat considered the "father of containment policy," wrote in his famous "Long Telegram" sent from the U.S. Embassy in Moscow to the U.S. State Department in February 1946:

> At bottom of [the] Kremlin's neurotic view of world affairs is the traditional and instinctive Russian sense of insecurity. Originally, this was the insecurity of a peaceful agricultural people trying to live on a vast exposed plain in the neighborhood of fierce nomadic peoples. To this was added, as Russia came into contact with the economically advanced West, fear of more competent, more powerful, more highly organized societies in that area. . . . For this

reason they have always feared foreign penetration, feared direct contact between [the] Western world and their own, feared what would happen if Russians learned the truth about the world without or if foreigners learned the truth about the world within. And they have learned to seek security only [in] a patient but deadly struggle for total destruction of rival power, never in compacts and compromises with it.

In September of the same year, J. Edgar Hoover, director of the U.S. Federal Bureau of Investigation, spoke at the San Francisco Conference of the American Legion:

During the past five years, American Communists have made their deepest inroads upon our national life. In our vaunted tolerance for all peoples the Communist has found our "Achilles' heel." . . . The Communist Party in this country is not working for the general welfare of all our people—it is working against our people. It is not interested in providing for the common defense. It has for its purpose the shackling of America and its conversion to the Godless, Communist way of life. . . . We, of this generation, have faced two great menaces in America—Fascism and Communism. Both are materialistic; both are totalitarian; both are anti-religious; both are degrading and inhuman. In fact, they differ little except in name. Communism has bred Fascism and Fascism spawns Communism. Both are the antithesis of the American belief in liberty and freedom. If the peoples of other countries want Communism, let them have it, but it has no place in America.

Kennan highlighted the "traditional and instinctive Russian sense of insecurity": just as their "neurotic" leaders ruthlessly destroyed all domestic oppositions to their rule, he argued, so would they act in a similar fashion toward their defined enemies abroad. Kennan's "Long Telegram" was mainly about the threats to the West's security in the international sphere, and it was Hoover who epitomized the flip side of the "two-pronged policy of containment"—the commitment to containing communism both at home and abroad. In his book *A Study of Communism,* Hoover explored what he called the biggest mystery of his time: "How anyone who enjoys the rights and privileges of American citizenship [can] bring himself to join a [Communist] movement which is such an outspoken foe of our entire way of life."

As the views of these influential state officials were circulated and were becoming a consensus in policy circles and public opinion, by the end of 1946 "the basic Cold War psychology" was taking hold of the U.S. administration. The Soviet maneuvers in northern Iran and incursions to the Turkish border in 1946 strengthened the belief in the United States that the Russians were hell bent on expansion and that only a united, preponderant counterforce could stop it. At the same time, Stalin encouraged the idea of encirclement by hostile Western forces to justify his brutal terror campaigns against his own population. The rise of the so-called cold war security culture was to a large measure, according to Mary Kaldor, a reciprocal action between opposing powers and had an "inertial logic" of mutually reinforcing external threats and internal fears. She argues that the construction of the cold war was thus a "joint venture" between the contending political blocs.

Hoover stated that "if the peoples of other countries want Communism, let them have it, but it has no place in America." It is argued in recent studies that American foreign politics in the mid-twentieth century was based on a broad bipartisan compromise between the Republican-dominated militancy against domestic labor and civil rights unrests and the largely Democrat-led initiatives to aggressively counter Communist threats in foreign soils. These studies show that although the U.S. administration perceived the threats of communism to be coming both from within the society and from overseas, the formulation of security threats was initially complicated by bipartisan politics in which contending groups lay emphasis on either the domestic dimension or the foreign dimension of containment. These two dimensions of perceived Communist threats gradually merged into a rhetorical whole; the polemics against the enemy within (such as Hoover's) and the polemics against the external enemies (such as Kennan's) became increasingly indistinguishable. In the beginning of the 1960s, therefore, Hoover advocated radical measures against overseas Communist threats to Asia and Europe, whereas Kennan lamented the lack of spiritual vigilance and moral solidarity against communism within the Western world. Hence, we should add to Kaldor's idea of "joint venture" another dimension—how the vision of the ideological enemy inside and the vision of the enemy outside colluded with each other, thereby augmenting the intensity of anti-Communist politics.

Dwight D. Eisenhower aptly summed up the emerging Manichean worldview in his inaugural speech in 1953: "The forces of good and evil are massed and armed and opposed as rarely before in history. Freedom is pitted against slavery; lightness against the dark." This anti-Communist worldview drew on an epidemiological model of society as a vulnerable organism. Hoover saw communism as "a condition akin to disease that spreads like an epidemic and like an epidemic a quarantine is necessary to keep it from infecting the nation." In 1950, an important report from the U.S. National Security Council known as NSC-68 described the Soviet Union as aiming to "contaminate" the Western world by means of its preferred technique of infiltrating "labor unions, civic enterprises, schools, churches, and all media for influencing opinion." The document argued that, in parallel with the urgency to stop domestic contagion, there was a need internationally "to quarantine a growing number of [states] infected [by the disease of communism]."

2

WINSTON CHURCHILL

Iron Curtain Speech, 1946

Winston Churchill (1874–1965) was British prime minister and an ally of President Franklin D. Roosevelt during World War II. On March 5, 1946, six months after the end of World War II and a year after the death of Roosevelt, Churchill spoke at the invitation of Roosevelt's successor, President Harry S. Truman, at Westminster College in Truman's home state of Missouri.

What changes since the end of the war does Churchill describe? Why do they concern him?

THINKING HISTORICALLY

This speech is often said to have signaled the beginning of the Cold War. As in any good speech, Churchill's words evoke emotional responses in addition to providing information. What emotional responses do phrases like *iron curtain* and *Christian civilization* evoke in this speech? How would parts of the speech have helped to create a "cold war" mentality?

A shadow has fallen upon the scenes so lately lighted by the Allied victory. Nobody knows what Soviet Russia and its Communist international organisation intends to do in the immediate future, or what are the limits, if any, to their expansive and proselytising tendencies. I have a strong admiration and regard for the valiant Russian people and for my wartime comrade, Marshal Stalin. There is deep sympathy and goodwill in Britain—and I doubt not here also—towards the peoples of all the Russias and a resolve to persevere through many differences and rebuffs in establishing lasting friendships. We understand the Russian need to be secure on her western frontiers by the removal of all possibility of German aggression. We welcome Russia to her rightful place among the leading nations of the world. We welcome her flag upon the seas. Above all, we welcome constant, frequent and growing contacts between the Russian people and our own

Source: *Sinews of Peace* (the *Iron Curtain Speech*), presented at Westminster College in Fulton, Missouri, on March 5, 1946.

people on both sides of the Atlantic. It is my duty however, for I am sure you would wish me to state the facts as I see them to you, to place before you certain facts about the present position in Europe.

From Stettin in the Baltic to Trieste in the Adriatic, an iron curtain has descended across the Continent. Behind that line lie all the capitals of the ancient states of Central and Eastern Europe. Warsaw, Berlin, Prague, Vienna, Budapest, Belgrade, Bucharest and Sofia, all these famous cities and the populations around them lie in what I must call the Soviet sphere, and all are subject in one form or another, not only to Soviet influence but to a very high and, in many cases, increasing measure of control from Moscow. Athens alone—Greece with its immortal glories—is free to decide its future at an election under British, American and French observation. The Russian-dominated Polish Government has been encouraged to make enormous and wrongful inroads upon Germany, and mass expulsions of millions of Germans on a scale grievous and undreamed-of are now taking place. The Communist parties, which were very small in all these Eastern States of Europe, have been raised to pre-eminence and power far beyond their numbers and are seeking everywhere to obtain totalitarian control. Police governments are prevailing in nearly every case, and so far, except in Czechoslovakia, there is no true democracy.

Turkey and Persia are both profoundly alarmed and disturbed at the claims which are being made upon them and at the pressure being exerted by the Moscow Government. An attempt is being made by the Russians in Berlin to build up a quasi-Communist party in their zone of Occupied Germany by showing special favours to groups of left-wing German leaders. At the end of the fighting last June, the American and British Armies withdrew westwards, in accordance with an earlier agreement, to a depth at some points of 150 miles upon a front of nearly four hundred miles, in order to allow our Russian allies to occupy this vast expanse of territory which the Western Democracies had conquered.

If now the Soviet Government tries, by separate action, to build up a pro-Communist Germany in their areas, this will cause new serious difficulties in the British and American zones, and will give the defeated Germans the power of putting themselves up to auction between the Soviets and the Western Democracies. Whatever conclusions may be drawn from these facts—and facts they are—this is certainly not the Liberated Europe we fought to build up. Nor is it one which contains the essentials of permanent peace.

The safety of the world requires a new unity in Europe, from which no nation should be permanently outcast. It is from the quarrels of the strong parent races in Europe that the world wars we have witnessed, or which occurred in former times, have sprung. Twice in our own lifetime we have seen the United States, against their wishes and their traditions, against arguments, the force of which it is impossible not to comprehend, drawn by irresistible forces, into these wars in time to secure the victory of the good cause, but only after frightful slaughter and devastation had occurred. Twice the United States has had to send several millions of its young men across the Atlantic to find the war; but now war can find any nation, wherever it may dwell between dusk and dawn. Surely we should work with conscious purpose for a grand pacification of Europe, within the structure of the United Nations and in accordance with its Charter. That I feel is an open cause of policy of very great importance.

In front of the iron curtain which lies across Europe are other causes for anxiety. . . . In a great number of countries, far from the Russian frontiers and throughout the world, Communist fifth columns are established and work in complete unity and absolute obedience to the directions they receive from the Communist centre. Except in the British Commonwealth and in the United States where Communism is in its infancy, the Communist parties or fifth columns constitute a growing challenge and peril to Christian civilisation. These are sombre facts for anyone to have to recite on the morrow of a victory gained by so much splendid comradeship in arms and in the cause of freedom and democracy; but we should be most unwise not to face them squarely while time remains. . . .

3

The Vietnamese Declaration of Independence, 1945

Although this document may predate the Cold War, it demonstrates the importance of the anticolonial struggle to create new states at the end of World War II. Vietnam had been part of French Indochina from 1887 until World War II, when it was occupied by Japan. This Declaration of Independence represented an effort by Vietnamese nationalists to prevent the French from retaking the country from the defeated Japanese.

The author of the declaration, Ho Chi Minh (1890–1969), is a prime example of the kind of new national leader torn between the appeals of Washington and Moscow. A founder of the French Communist Party in 1921 as well as the Vietnamese Communist Party in 1930, he was also the leader of the Viet Minh, the Vietnamese nationalist movement, even enjoying the secret help of the United States during World War II in the battle against Japan.

What, according to Ho Chi Minh, were the effects of French colonialism in Vietnam? What reasons does he give for Vietnamese independence?

Source: Ho Chi Minh, *Selected Works* (Hanoi, 1960–1962), 3:17–21.

THINKING HISTORICALLY

Since this document was intended as a declaration of Vietnamese nationalism, delivered in Vietnamese to the Vietnamese people, one is struck by the use of ideological language from both the U.S. Declaration of Independence and the French Declaration of the Rights of Man and Citizen. What other signs do you see that Ho Chi Minh may have been interested in attracting the favor of a U.S. or French audience? What purpose would such a strategy serve?

"All men are created equal. They are endowed by their Creator with certain inalienable rights, among these are Life, Liberty, and the pursuit of Happiness."

This immortal statement was made in the Declaration of Independence of the United States of America in 1776. In a broader sense, this means: All the peoples on the Earth are equal from birth, all the peoples have a right to live, to be happy and to be free.

The Declaration of the French Revolution made in 1791 on the Rights of Man and the Citizen also states: "All men are born free and with equal rights, and must always remain free and have equal rights."

Those are undeniable truths.

Nevertheless, for more than eighty years, the French imperialists, abusing the standard of *Liberty, Equality, and Fraternity*,[1] have violated our Motherland and oppressed our fellow-citizens. They have acted contrary to the ideals of humanity and justice. In the field of politics, they have deprived our people of every democratic liberty.

They have enforced inhuman laws; they have set up three distinct political regimes in the North, the Center and the South of Vietnam in order to wreck our national unity and prevent our people from being united.

They have built more prisons than schools. They have mercilessly slain our patriots — they have drowned our uprisings in rivers of blood. They have fettered public opinion; they have practised obscurantism against our people. To weaken our race they have forced us to use opium and alcohol.

In the fields of economics, they have fleeced us to the backbone, impoverished our people, and devastated our land.

They have robbed us of our rice fields, our mines, our forests, and our raw materials. They have monopolised the issuing of bank-notes and the export trade. They have invented numerous unjustifiable taxes and reduced our people, especially our peasantry, to a state of extreme poverty.

They have hampered the prospering of our national bourgeoisie; they have mercilessly exploited our workers.

In the autumn of 1940, when the Japanese Fascists violated Indochina's territory to establish new bases in their fight against the Allies,

---

[1] This was the rallying cry of the French Revolution of 1789. (*Fraternity* means brotherhood.) [Ed.]

the French imperialists went down on their bended knees and handed over our country to them.

Thus, from that date, our people were subjected to the double yoke of the French and the Japanese. Their sufferings and miseries increased. The result was that from the end of last year to the beginning of this year, from Quang Tri province to the North of Vietnam, more than two million of our fellow-citizens died from starvation. On March 9, the French troops were disarmed by the Japanese. The French colonialists either fled or surrendered, showing that not only were they incapable of "protecting" us, but that, in the span of five years, they had twice sold our country to the Japanese.

On several occasions before March 9, the Vietminh League urged the French to ally themselves with it against the Japanese. Instead of agreeing to this proposal, the French colonialists so intensified their terrorist activities against the Vietminh members that before fleeing they massacred a great number of our political prisoners detained at Yen Bai and Cao Bang.

Notwithstanding all this, our fellow-citizens have always manifested toward the French a tolerant and humane attitude. Even after the Japanese putsch of March 1945, the Vietminh League helped many Frenchmen to cross the frontier, rescued some of them from Japanese jails, and protected French lives and property.

From the autumn of 1940, our country had in fact ceased to be a French colony and had become a Japanese possession.

After the Japanese had surrendered to the Allies, our whole people rose to regain our national sovereignty and to found the Democratic Republic of Vietnam.

The truth is that we have wrested our independence from the Japanese and not from the French.

The French have fled, the Japanese have capitulated, Emperor Bao Dai has abdicated. Our people have broken the chains which for nearly a century have fettered them and have won independence for the Fatherland. Our people at the same time have overthrown the monarchic regime that has reigned supreme for dozens of centuries. In its place has been established the present Democratic Republic.

For these reasons, we, members of the Provisional Government, representing the whole Vietnamese people, declare that from now on we break off all relations of a colonial character with France; we repeal all the international obligation that France has so far subscribed to on behalf of Vietnam and we abolish all the special rights the French have unlawfully acquired in our Fatherland.

The whole Vietnamese people, animated by a common purpose, are determined to fight to the bitter end against any attempt by the French colonialists to reconquer their country.

We are convinced that the Allied nations which at Tehran and San Francisco have acknowledged the principles of self-determination and equality of nations, will not refuse to acknowledge the independence of Vietnam.

A people who have courageously opposed French domination for more than eighty years, a people who have fought side by side with the Allies against the Fascists during these last years, such a people must be free and independent.

For these reasons, we, members of the Provisional Government of the Democratic Republic of Vietnam, solemnly declare to the world that Vietnam has the right to be a free and independent country and in fact it already has been so. The entire Vietnamese people are determined to mobilise all their physical and mental strength, to sacrifice their lives and property in order to safeguard their independence and liberty.

4

EDWARD LANSDALE

Report on CIA Operations in Vietnam, 1954–1955

France did not cede independence to Vietnam in 1945; nor did the United States support the Viet Minh against the French. The newly declared Democratic Republic of Vietnam controlled only the north while French forces controlled the south. Ho Chi Minh and the Viet Minh forces continued their struggle against the French, finally defeating them at the battle of Dien Bien Phu in 1954. An international peace conference at Geneva called for a temporary division of northern and southern Vietnam to be followed in two years by a national election for a unified government. However, in the wake of the Chinese communist victory in China in 1949 and the American fear of its further spread in the Korean War (1950–1953), the United States increasingly saw Ho Chi Minh and the Viet Minh as part of the expansion of communism rather than a national independence movement. In 1954 President Eisenhower voiced belief in a "falling domino" theory in which the loss of Vietnam would lead to communist victories throughout Southeast Asia and beyond. Fearing that Ho Chi Minh would win 80 percent of the vote in a general Vietnamese election, Eisenhower created a separate South Vietnamese government and army in violation of the Geneva Accords, and he sent U.S. advisors and resources to make this division along the 17th parallel permanent. But one of the problems was that many pro-French

Source: Edward Lansdale, "Report on CIA Operations in Vietnam, 1954–55," in *The Pentagon Papers*, abr. ed., ed. George C. Herring (New York: McGraw-Hill, 1993), 23–36.

Catholics lived in the north where the Viet Minh were strongest, and many Viet Minh lived and operated in the south. Thus, the creation of a southern Republic of Vietnam required large-scale population transfers as well as efforts to bolster the resources and legitimacy of an untried southern government and army.

In this selection, Edward Lansdale informs his CIA superiors of some of the activities of one of the teams of advisors sent by the United States to accomplish these tasks. Lansdale was a legendary early CIA operative, known for his work in defeating a similar communist and nationalist movement in the Philippines. What did Lansdale's team attempt to do in the north? What was the purpose of the first rumor campaign? How would you judge the tactics and success of the Saigon Military Mission (SMM) team in the north? What did the CIA do in the south? How successful were its efforts?

THINKING HISTORICALLY

What do you make of Lansdale's quotation marks around "cold war"? What does Lansdale's use of the word *team* suggest to you? What does Lansdale mean by "the Geneva Agreements . . . imposed restrictive rules on all official Americans"? Notice how Lansdale uses terms such as *Vietminh* and *Vietnamese*, the "government," and "security forces." How might others use these terms? What do you think of Lansdale's praise of American reporters for giving "the U.S. an objective account of events in Vietnam"? How does Lansdale describe the differences between the Viet Minh and the "Vietnamese national army"? What conclusions does he draw from the differences between those two armies? What different conclusions could one draw?

Foreword

. . . It was often a frustrating and perplexing year, up close. The Geneva Agreements signed on 21 July 1954 imposed restrictive rules upon all official Americans, including the Saigon Military Mission. An active and intelligent enemy made full use of legal rights to screen his activities in establishing his stay-behind organizations south of the 17th Parallel and in obtaining quick security north of that Parallel. The nation's economy and communications system were crippled by eight years of open war. The government, including its Army and other security forces, was in a painful transition from colonial to self rule, making it a year of hot-tempered incidents. Internal problems arose quickly to points where armed conflict was sought as the only solution. The enemy was frequently forgotten in the heavy atmosphere of suspicion, hatred and jealousy.

The Saigon Military Mission received some blows from allies and the enemy in this atmosphere, as we worked to help stabilize the government and to beat the Geneva time-table of Communist takeover in the north. However, we did beat the time-table. The government did become stabilized. The Free Vietnamese are now becoming unified and learning how to cope with the Communist enemy. We are thankful that we had a chance to help in this work in a critical area of the world, to be positive and constructive in a year of doubt. . . .

Highlights of the Year

a. Early Days

. . . Working in close cooperation with George Hellyer, USIS[1] Chief, a new psychological warfare campaign was devised for the Vietnamese Army and for the government in Hanoi. Shortly after, a refresher course in combat psywar was constructed and Vietnamese Army personnel were rushed through it. A similar course was initiated for the Ministry of Information. Rumor campaigns were added to the tactics and tried out in Hanoi. It was almost too late.

The first rumor campaign was to be a carefully planted story of a Chinese Communist regiment in Tonkin taking reprisals against a Vietminh village whose girls the Chinese had raped, recalling Chinese Nationalist troop behavior in 1945 and confirming Vietnamese fears of Chinese occupation under Vietminh rule; the story was to be planted by soldiers of the Vietnamese Armed Psywar Company in Hanoi dressed in civilian clothes. The troops received their instructions silently, dressed in civilian clothes, went on the mission, and failed to return. They had deserted to the Vietminh. . . .

Ngo Dinh Diem[2] arrived on 7 July, and within hours was in despair as the French forces withdrew from the Catholic provinces of Phat Diem and Nam Dinh in Tonkin.[3] . . . The Tonkinese had hopes of American friendship and listened to the advice given them. Governor [name illegible] died, reportedly by poison. Tonkin's government changed as despair grew. On 21 July, the Geneva Agreement was signed. Tonkin was given to the Communists. Anti-Communists turned to SMM[4] for help in establishing a resistance movement and several tentative initial arrangements were made. . . .

[1] United States Information Service, the overseas offices of the United States Information Agency (USIA), which was created by President Eisenhower in 1953 to project a positive image of the United States in the world. [Ed.]
[2] Ngo Dinh Diem (1901–1963), a Catholic, became a favorite of the United States while in exile. He returned to Vietnam in 1954 and became first president of South Vietnam as the French withdrew; he was deposed and killed in a coup in 1963. [Ed.]
[3] Area of northern Vietnam. French Indochina consisted of Cambodia, Laos, and three areas now making up Vietnam: Tonkin in the north, Annam in the center, and Cochinchina in what is now southernmost Vietnam. [Ed.]
[4] Saigon Military Mission, the group run by Lansdale. [Ed.]

b. August 1954

An agreement had been reached that the personnel ceiling of U.S. military personnel with MAAG[5] would be frozen at the number present in Vietnam on the date of the cease-fire, under the terms of the Geneva Agreement. In South Vietnam this deadline was to be 11 August. It meant that SMM might have only two members present, unless action were taken. General O'Daniel agreed to the addition of ten SMM men under MAAG cover, plus any others in the Defense pipeline who arrived before the deadline. A call for help went out. Ten officers in Korea, Japan, and Okinawa were selected and rushed to Vietnam.

SMM had one small MAAG house. Negotiations were started for other housing, but the new members of the team arrived before housing was ready and were crammed three and four to a hotel room for the first days. Meetings were held to assess the new members' abilities. None had had political-psychological warfare experience. Most were experienced in paramilitary and clandestine intelligence operations. Plans were made quickly, for time was running out in the north; already the Vietminh had started taking over secret control of Hanoi and other areas of Tonkin still held by French forces.

Major Conein was given responsibility for developing a paramilitary organization in the north, to be in position when the Vietminh took over. . . . [His] . . . team was moved north immediately as part of the MAAG staff working on the refugee problem. The team had headquarters in Hanoi, with a branch in Haiphong. Among cover duties, this team supervised the refugee flow for the Hanoi airlift,[6] organized by the French. One day, as a CAT C-46[7] finished loading, they saw a small child standing on the ground below the loading door. They shouted for the pilot to wait, picked the child up and shoved him onto the aircraft, which they promptly taxied out for its takeoff in the constant air shuffle. A Vietnamese man and woman ran up to the team, asking what they had done with their small boy, whom they'd brought to say goodbye to relatives. The chagrined team explained, finally talked the parents into going south to Free Vietnam, put them in the next aircraft to catch up with their son in Saigon. . . .

c. September 1954

. . . Towards the end of the month, it was learned that the largest printing establishment in the north intended to remain in Hanoi and do business

---

[5] Military Assistance Advisory Group: military advisors sent to Vietnam by President Truman beginning in 1950 to train a Vietnamese national army for South Vietnam. [Ed.]

[6] To fly Catholics from the northern city of Hanoi to South Vietnam. [Ed.]

[7] A plane; Civil Air Transport was established in Shanghai in 1946 as a Chinese airline and was owned and used by the CIA after 1950. The C-46 was a military transport and cargo plane made by the Curtiss-Wright Company. [Ed.]

with the Vietminh. An attempt was made by SMM to destroy the modern presses, but Vietminh security agents already had moved into the plant and frustrated the attempt. This operation was under a Vietnamese patriot whom we shall call Trieu; his case officer was Capt. Arundel. Earlier in the month they had engineered a black psywar strike in Hanoi: leaflets signed by the Vietminh instructing Tonkinese on how to behave for the Vietminh takeover of the Hanoi region in early October, including items about property, money reform, and a three-day holiday of workers upon takeover. The day following the distribution of these leaflets, refugee registration tripled. Two days later Vietminh currency was worth half the value prior to the leaflets. The Vietminh took to the radio to denounce the leaflets; the leaflets were so authentic in appearance that even most of the rank and file Vietminh were sure that the radio denunciations were a French trick. . . .

d. October 1954

Hanoi was evacuated on 9 October. The northern SMM team left with the last French troops, disturbed by what they had seen of the grim efficiency of the Vietminh in their takeover, the contrast between the silent march of the victorious Vietminh troops in their tennis shoes and the clanking armor of the well-equipped French whose Western tactics and equipment had failed against the Communist military-political-economic campaign.

The northern team had spent the last days of Hanoi in contaminating the oil supply of the bus company for a gradual wreckage of the engines in the buses, in taking the first actions for delayed sabotage of the railroad (which required teamwork with a CIA special technical team in Japan who performed their part brilliantly), and in writing detailed notes of potential targets for future paramilitary operations. (U.S. adherence to the Geneva Agreement prevented SMM from carrying out the active sabotage it desired to do against the power plant, water facilities, harbor, and bridge.) The team had a bad moment when contaminating the oil. They had to work quickly at night, in an enclosed storage room. Fumes from the contaminant came close to knocking them out. Dizzy and weak-kneed, they masked their faces with handkerchiefs and completed the job.

Meanwhile, Polish and Russian ships had arrived in the south to transport southern Vietminh to Tonkin under the Geneva Agreement. This offered the opportunity for another black psywar strike. A leaflet was developed by Binh with the help of Capt. Arundel, attributed to the Vietminh Resistance Committee. Among other items, it reassured the Vietminh they would be kept safe below decks from imperialist air and submarine attacks, and requested that warm clothing be brought; the warm clothing item would be coupled with a verbal rumor campaign that Vietminh were being sent into China as railroad laborers. . . .

f. December 1954

... Till and Peg Durdin of the N.Y. Times, Hank Lieberman of the N.Y. Times, Homer Bigart of the N.Y. Herald-Tribune, John Mecklin of Life-Time and John Roderick of Associated Press, have been warm friends of SMM and worked hard to penetrate the fabric of French propaganda and give the U.S. an objective account of events in Vietnam. The group met with us at times to analyze objectives and motives of propaganda known to them, meeting at their own request as U.S. citizens. These mature and responsible news correspondents performed a valuable service for their country. . . .

g. January 1955

The Vietminh long ago had adopted the Chinese Communist thought that the people are the water and the army is the fish. Vietminh relations with the mass of the population during the fighting had been exemplary, with a few exceptions; in contrast, the Vietnamese National Army had been like too many Asian armies, adept at cowing a population into feeding them, providing them with girls. SMM had been working on this problem from the beginning. Since the National Army was the only unit of government with a strong organization through the country and with good communications, it was the key to stabilizing the situation quickly on a nation-wide basis. If Army and people could be brought together into a team, the first strong weapon against Communism could be forged. . . .

5

PATRICE LUMUMBA

Interview with Russian News Agency TASS, July 1960

Patrice Lumumba (1925–1961) was a founder and leader of the independence movement of the Congolese in the Belgian Congo in the 1950s and the first freely elected prime minister of the Republic of the Congo upon independence in 1960. He was a charismatic speaker and popular national leader. The U.S. ambassador, who was no friend, said Lumumba could walk into any gathering of Congolese politicians as a waiter with a tray on his head and come out as prime minister.

Source: Patrice Lumumba, *The Truth about a Monstrous Crime of the Colonialists*, transcribed by Thomas Schmidt (Moscow: Foreign Languages Publishing House, 1961), 53–55.

Belgium hoped that Congolese independence would be only symbolic. After nominally granting independence on June 30, 1960,
Belgium continued to support its colonialists, soldiers, and the very
lucrative mining company in Katanga.

In 1961, Lumumba was deposed in a coup by his former aide,
Joseph Mobutu, and then assassinated by agents of the resource-rich,
breakaway Congo state of Katanga, with the connivance of Belgium
and the United States. From 1965 to 1997, Mobutu ruled the Congo
with an iron fist. For most of those years, until the end of the Cold
War, Mobutu enjoyed the support of the United States.

According to this document, what did Belgium do to retain control? What was the response of the United Nations? How did this
power struggle become a part of the Cold War?

THINKING HISTORICALLY

Lumumba clearly knew that he was enraging the United States by giving an interview to the Soviet press while in Washington — especially a
friendly interview. What words in this transcript convey a more ideological than informative message? What parts of this interview show
Moscow and Lumumba trying to please each other? How might you
try to determine when one of the compliments is propaganda and
when it is genuine?

Question: How, in your opinion, is the U.N. Security Council decision
on the rapid withdrawal of Belgian troops from the Congo being
fulfilled?

Answer: Belgium has already proved that she has no respect for
Security Council decisions. The Belgian Government is continuing its
aggressive actions and savage reprisals against our people. It will be
recalled that as far back as July 14, the Security Council demanded in a
resolution that Belgian troops should leave the Congo; it sent U.N.
armed forces to our country to back up this decision. But since then not
a single Belgian soldier has left the territory of the Congo. Every day the
troops of the Belgian colonialists kill soldiers of our national army and
massacre hundreds of Congolese civilians. These facts are not widely
known in the world because the Belgian colonialists have got the press
of other Western countries to write as little as possible about the doings
of Belgian soldiers in the Congo.

Our government and Parliament have from the very first demanded
that Belgian troops should leave the Congo. The pertinent Soviet
proposal tabled in the Security Council was the only proposal fully conforming to our people's interests. We continue to demand and declare
that the immediate withdrawal of Belgian troops is the only way of
restoring law and order in the Congo. That is why we ask all democratic
and peace-loving countries to support our demand. The last Belgian

soldier should have left the Congo long ago. The U.N. troops, which arrived to ensure implementation of the Security Council's resolution, have now been in the Congo for over a fortnight. But the situation has not changed. I must say that the Security Council's resolutions are being fulfilled anything but properly, although the Council had already passed two resolutions—on July 14 and 22—on the need to withdraw Belgian troops from the Congo. Such a small country as Belgium allows herself to behave in this way only because the Congo now lacks the weapons to throw out the Belgian colonialists.

Question: What is the situation in Katanga? What is your opinion of Katanga's so-called secession from the Congo recently announced by Mr. Tshombe?

Answer: There has never been a Katanga problem as such. The gist of the matter is that the imperialists want to lay their hands on our country's riches and to continue exploiting our people. The imperialists have always had their agents in the colonial countries. Tshombe, in particular, is an agent of the Belgian imperialists. Everything he says and writes is not his own. He merely mouths the words of the Belgian colonialists. It is well known that Tshombe is an ex-businessman who has long since thrown in his lot with the colonial companies in the Congo. But very few people know that just recently, as a result of dishonest machinations and overdrafts, Tshombe owed Belgian companies in the Congo more than ten million Belgian francs. He was arrested and was to be tried. But in view of the situation that took shape, Tshombe was "pardoned" and released by the Belgians and since then he has been obediently carrying out all their orders.

Question: What is the Congolese people's view of the Soviet Union's stand on the Congo's struggle to attain genuine independence and territorial integrity?

Answer: The Soviet Union was the only Great Power whose stand conformed to our people's will and desire. That is why the Soviet Union was the only Great Power which has all along been supporting the Congolese people's struggle. I should like to convey the heartfelt gratitude of the entire Congolese people to the Soviet people and to Prime Minister Nikita Khrushchev personally for your country's timely and great moral support to the young Republic of the Congo in its struggle against the imperialists and colonialists. I should also like to thank the Soviet Union for the assistance in food which it is extending to the Congo.

6

United States Summary of Congo Crisis, December 1960

Africa was almost "off the map" of U.S. foreign policy in the 1950s. The French and British struggled against rising demands for independence in Africa, especially against the National Liberation Front in French Algeria and the Mau Mau uprising in British Kenya, but the United States had no African colonies and little corporate economic presence in Africa. European colonial powers were, however, allies of the United States, and many, including Belgium, were members of NATO, the military alliance that joined Europe and the United States in mutual defense against the Soviet Union and its satellites. Thus, the interests of the French (as in Vietnam), the British (as in South Africa), and the Belgians (as in the Belgian Congo) easily bled into the interests of the United States.

Almost all of Africa was still under colonial control in the 1950s, but by 1960 "the wind of change," as British Prime Minister Harold Macmillan noted, was sweeping through the African continent. Britain and France found it easier to acclimate than did Belgium. Belgian resistance to full independence for the new Republic of the Congo was at the root of what was called "the Congo Crisis" (as if Belgian decolonization were a single storm rather than a tree in a prevailing wind).

This selection is drawn from a study of the roots and meaning of the Congo crisis by the government of the United States at the twilight of the Eisenhower administration in 1960. The report is called an "Analytical Chronology" (versus a "nonanalytical" chronology consisting of a simple list of dates and events). The report concentrated on the events of 1960 in an effort to devise future policy for the incoming Kennedy administration that would inherit the issue on January 20, 1961. This selection contains a few pages from the beginning of the report, on background, and a few pages on the development of U.S. policy.

What did the authors of the report think were the important things to know? How might these concerns be different today? What does this selection tell you about how U.S. policy developed and how the Congo Crisis became part of the Cold War?

Source: "Analytical Chronology" [December 1960], National Security Files, Box 27, John F. Kennedy Library and Museum, pp. 1–3, 18–20.

The "Background" section of the selection discusses, among other things, the education and motivation of various Congo leaders, both "moderate" and "radical." How does the author's treatment of these two groups differ? What does this suggest about how one becomes a moderate or a radical?

In the section on "Development of U.S. Policy," how evenly does the author present the positions of Belgium and Lumumba?

I. Early Background

The Congo crisis has become so complicated that some of the early, rather simple facts about it are sometimes forgotten. Although basic information is found in a number of research documents . . . , it may be helpful to recall some early US planning assumptions and basic political factors.

1. Constitutional difficulties for the Congo were freely predicted because of the tribal diversity of the country, the brevity of the life of political institutions which might have developed unifying trends, the clashing personalities of the candidates for leadership, and the differing regional interests. The constitution under which the new state obtained independence was a provisional document. The Congolese parliament was at the same time a constitutional convention which was to elaborate a new constitution. The United States was informed, even prior to the independence of the Congo, of Mr. Tshombe's intention to proclaim an independent Katanga. (We discouraged him and also told the Belgians that we thought this a dangerous idea that should not be supported. At the same time, we decided to maintain friendly relations with Mr. Tshombe as far as possible since support for an independent Katanga might still become desirable some time in the future.)

2. Severe economic difficulties in the Congo were predictable, and the Department in fact worked intensively on plans to help overcome those initial difficulties. The flight of capital especially during the year prior to independence, the drawing-down of reserves by the Belgians, the advance collection of taxes to meet the growing difficulties, and the enormous public debt which the Belgians proposed to saddle on the Congo, coupled with Belgium's limited ability to assist the new country, clearly foreshadowed an economic crisis almost immediately upon the attainment of independence. Although Belgian investments in the Congo amounted to about $3.5 billion, public improvements had been largely financed by the floating of bonds, many of which had been sold in foreign money markets. Service on that debt was expected to absorb

23 per cent of ordinary Congolese budget expenditures. We estimated a gap of about $180 million between expected internal financial resources and planned Congo Government expenditures during the first year of independence, and had worked out plans to help close that gap . . . [fearing that otherwise the] Congolese government would repudiate its debt, resort to the printing press and possibly expropriate Belgian assets in order to meet its difficulties.

3. A breakdown of the internal security system was not expected, even though great internal strains were anticipated due to political, tribal and regional divergences. The "Force Publique," consisting of 24,000 African troops and 975 Belgian officers, was correctly regarded as a well-trained, non-political organ of the executive, but the Belgians (and we, who relied on Belgian information) completely misjudged the degree of loyalty of the troops to their Belgian officers. The Belgians expected that some of their women would be molested and some of their property endangered, but they saw the danger as coming from civilians—who on the whole did not misbehave—and thought that the Belgian-officered "Force Publique" would help to unify the country and protect European lives and property.

4. Even before the crisis erupted, it had become clear that the radical Patrice Lumumba would be an undesirable Prime Minister from the point of view of Belgium and that Joseph Kasavubu would be more likely to preserve friendly ties with Belgium. In the elections to the House of Representatives in May, 1960, Lumumba and his affiliates obtained 36 out of 137 seats whereas Kasavubu's Abako party obtained 12 seats. . . . The Belgians clearly showed they wanted to handicap Lumumba's government-forming mission and that they favored Kasavubu. Their plan miscarried, however. Kasavubu failed to create a coalition government, Lumumba succeeded, and as a result of this maneuvering Lumumba was even more bitter about the Belgians and Kasavubu more clearly identified with them. As part of the deals that resulted in Lumumba becoming Prime Minister, Kasavubu became President, a position that was initially thought to be largely honorific.

5. There was no known Communist among the top Congolese leadership. However, there were a number of leftist radicals. Foremost among them was Lumumba, leader of the Mouvement National Congolais (MNC), who was known as a clever anti-white rabble-rouser. In his political campaigns, Lumumba had opposed Communism but there had been reports that the Communists (as well as certain radical African leaders of other countries) had helped to finance his campaigns. Antoine Gizenga, the leader of the Partí Solidaire Africain (PSA), who subsequently also came under heavy Communist influence, was an unknown quantity for a long time except that it was known that he had been invited on a brief trip to Eastern Europe following the Brussels Round Table Conference in December, 1959. He is thus sometimes referred to

as being "Moscow (or Prague-) trained" but there is no evidence that he actually was trained or that he embraced the Communist ideology and party discipline. He returned from his Eastern European trip by way of Guinea where he picked up Madame Andree Blouin, a confirmed anti-Western Marxist. Anicet Kashamura, who was Information Minister in the Lumumba Government, was a radical anti-Belgian exponent of CEREA (Centre de Regroupement Africain), a pro-Marxist and had visited East Berlin and Prague during the Brussels Round Table Conference, and likewise became a friend of Mme. Blouin. He was also at one time eager to visit the United States. In general, the line between pro-Communism on the one hand and hyper-nationalist, anti-"colonialist," Marxist thinking on the other is very difficult to draw in the Congo or anywhere else in Africa. Events, including the kind of support and opposition they encountered subsequent to independence, no doubt influenced the thinking of the entire Congolese leadership.

Although there was no Communist Party in the Congo, accusations of Communist sympathies or loyalties were freely used already during the election campaign in May. In Katanga province, for instance, the anti-Lumumba propaganda of Moise Tshombe's Belgian-financed CONAKAT (Confederation des Associations Katangaises) party pictured Lumumba as a puppet manipulated by Moscow. Clearly, to all the parties that realized that cooperation with Belgium and with the West in general was most desirable and indeed necessary for the Congo, Lumumba was the arch-enemy. He reciprocated the sentiment by picturing his conservative enemies as stooges of the Belgians. The line between moderates (such as Bomboko, Bolikango, Sendwe, Tshombe) and radicals (such as Lumumba, Gizenga and Kashamura) was thus pretty clearly drawn before the Congo emerged onto the international scene. . . .

VI. Development of US Policy

The Department from the beginning supported the principle of a UN operation in the Congo and believed that exclusive reliance on the UN for the rehabilitation of the Congo provided the best means of keeping out Soviet assistance and its inevitable subversive accompaniments. The President issued a directive that US aid should be given through the United Nations. In implementing this policy, we placed severe restraints on our own bilateral aid operations. In this respect, our policy was clear from the beginning. On the other hand, the US position with respect to Katanga and the rate of Belgian troop withdrawal was heavily influenced by the uncertainties of the situation, the desire to keep open the possibility of alternative policies, Lumumba's violent pronouncements, and considerations of NATO solidarity.

When Premier Tshombe of Katanga asked for US recognition, we informed our Consul that "should other states recognize Katanga it is possible that the US might reconsider its position (against recognition) but under no, repeat no, circumstances will we take the lead." Tshombe himself was informed that we hoped he would feel free to continue to discuss problems with our Consul on a frank and friendly basis and that our inability to recognize his government should not be interpreted as hostility toward himself or his government (Deptel 17).

The Belgian Government consistently attempted to picture the Congo crisis in terms of the Cold War. On July 16, Foreign Minister Wigny told the US, British and French ambassadors that "Lumumba's activities of the past few days . . . have now made it clear that the Congo problems must be looked at in the context of the East-West struggle. This means that the essential thing is to get rid of Lumumba. From now on he can only be a source of trouble and an instrument for a Soviet takeover in the Congo." (Brussels 200). He argued that the UN operation would result in strengthening Lumumba's position. The Director of Political Affairs of the Belgian Foreign Ministry on the same occasion "suggested that the Western countries might withdraw recognition from the central government of the Congo and deal on a de facto basis with the actual authorities in control of the situation in the country, i.e., the six provincial governments."

Belgium did not give outright recognition to the Katanga government, but from the beginning it sought "de facto autonomy enforced by Belgian troops" (Brussels 207). Our Embassy at Brussels recommended that "the United States continue publicly to proclaim support for the maintenance of unity of the Congo as long as this objective has any chance of fulfillment. At the same time, we cannot avoid dealing on a day-to-day basis with the de facto government of Katanga province, which should protect our position for the future."

Belgian Minister of State Camille Gutt called on the Secretary on July 19 and drew parallels between the Congo situation and Korea, expressing the hope that the US reaction "would be as firm as in the Korean case." He said his Foreign Minister hoped for "full US support in the UN" and said at the same time that Belgians intended to withdraw only their "intervention forces," i.e. that Belgian troops originally stationed on the Belgian bases in the Congo would remain. He opposed the dispatch of the UN forces to the Katanga. The Secretary and Gutt discussed the possibility that the UN "presence" in Katanga might consist of only one or two civilian representatives.

On July 20, the Belgian Ambassador called on Under Secretary Merchant and asked that the US oppose, if necessary by its veto, any proposal setting a time limit for the Belgian withdrawal from the Congo. He claimed that the Congo-Belgian treaty was still alive because it had not been put to a vote by the Congolese and Belgian parliaments. Mr. Merchant urged the Ambassador to have at least some troop withdrawal take place before the Security Council met, but said the question of ultimate withdrawal could still be related to the ability of the UN to establish and maintain order (i.e., the position which had been so violently denounced by Lumumba).

The Department was disturbed about the possibility of armed clashes between the UN troops and the Belgian troops serving Premier Tshombe of Katanga, and consistently counseled caution on the part of the UN. In view of Belgian agitation over the possibility of an armed UN action against Katanga, the Department on July 27 upon recommendation of Ambassador Burden in Brussels instructed Ambassador Timberlake (Deptel 262) "as soon as possible after Hammarskjold's arrival . . . (to) seek to see him and ascertain his plans with respect to Katanga and Belgian bases. The Department has consistently felt that the best chance of working out these problems lies in the passage of time and the absence of precipitate UN action."

The British and French Governments also made demarches to Hammarskjold, urging him to "slow down" the evacuation of Belgian troops from Katanga. Hammarskjold refused, citing the UN resolutions, and urged instead that the British and French put pressure on the Belgians to see the light and comply. (Our Charge d'affaires commented: "Judged by Lumumba's press statements in the US and conversations with Congolese of various political stripes here, the Belgian troop issue is the central, all-pervading issue occupying all Congolese minds. Despite the pitiful state of almost everything, they think and talk about nothing else. The whole future of the UN mission is tied up in this issue. If the UN fails or appears to drag its feet they will very probably be asked to leave and be replaced by someone who wants Belgian troops out.")

The Belgians also frequently cited NATO interest in their bases in the Congo, but these were feeble arguments. (Any public references to such arguments, however, were eagerly seized by Radio Moscow to picture the Belgian action in the Congo as NATO-inspired and approved.) One factor in British and French support for the Belgian position on the bases was the argument that "for Belgium to withdraw from these bases under pressure of a UN decision would create a precedent which could jeopardize other foreign bases in Africa and elsewhere, particularly Bizerte" (Brussels 378). The Belgians and the French, and to a lesser extent the British, were concerned with maintenance of NATO solidarity on the Congo issue, and this, too, operated as an inhibiting factor in establishing a clear US position in favor of speedy implementation of the UN resolutions. . . .

TIME MAGAZINE

Nikita Khrushchev: "We Will Bury You," November 26, 1956

The first years of the Cold War pitted former World War II allies Soviet Premier Joseph Stalin and Presidents Roosevelt, Truman, and Eisenhower against each other. Stalin died in 1953, to be followed by two inconsequential leaders[1] and then longtime Communist Party leader Nikita Khrushchev, premier from 1955 to 1964. Khrushchev initiated the Soviet space and missile program, but he attempted to reduce the size of the army and strengthen the consumer sector of the economy. In February 1956, Khrushchev startled party members with a speech denouncing Stalin as a brutal dictator. The speech expressed long-suppressed grievances, especially in the dependent Soviet satellite states of Poland, East Germany, Romania, and Hungary.

Hungarians opposed to continued Soviet rule saw an opportunity in the new climate and took to the streets in protest in October 1956. On November 1 their leader Imre Nagy declared an independent Hungarian government and asked for UN recognition. On November 4, Soviet troops invaded Hungary, crushing the revolution by November 10. This selection is a *Time* magazine report of a routine event the following week.

On November 17 Khrushchev attended a reception at the Polish Embassy hosted by visiting Polish communist leader Wladyslaw Gomulka, who also invited representatives of Western countries. At the reception, Khrushchev compared Soviet troops in Hungary and Eastern Europe with Western troops in two areas. What are these areas? What do you think of these comparisons? What was Khrushchev's attitude toward the United States and Western capitalist countries? What was his attitude toward colonialism?

THINKING HISTORICALLY

No four words better raised the fear of a Soviet threat for Americans during the Cold War than Khrushchev's "We will bury you." Numerous American political leaders, commentators, and citizens referred to that quote in the following years to underscore Soviet aggressive intentions. With those four words, the reformist premier who

[1] Georgy Malenkov and Nikolai Bulganin.

Source: "We Will Bury You!" *Time*, November 26, 1956.

de-Stalinized Kremlin policy and later traveled through the United States arguing for nuclear disarmament and peaceful coexistence could be pictured as a dangerous belligerent.

What do you think Khrushchev meant by those four words? Why do you think *Time* magazine chose them to headline the article? How else might you summarize the evening at the Polish Embassy? What would be your headline?

At the final reception for Poland's visiting Gomulka, stubby Nikita Khrushchev planted himself firmly with the Kremlin's whole hierarchy at his back, and faced the diplomats of the West, and the satellites, with an intemperate speech that betrayed as much as it threatened.

"We are Bolsheviks!" he declared pugnaciously. "We stick firmly to the Lenin precept—don't be stubborn if you see you are wrong, but don't give in if you are right." "When are you right?" interjected First Deputy Premier Mikoyan—and the crowd laughed. Nikita plunged on, turning to the Western diplomats. "About the capitalist states, it doesn't depend on you whether or not we exist. If you don't like us, don't accept our invitations, and don't invite us to come to see you. Whether you like it or not, history is on our side. We will bury you!"

Just the day before, ambassadors of twelve NATO nations had walked out on a Khrushchev tirade that lumped Britain, France and Israel as bandits. Now Khrushchev was off again.

The Kremlin men cheered. Gomulka laughed. Red-faced and gesticulating, Nikita rolled on: "The situation is favorable to us. If God existed, we would thank him for this. On Hungary—we had Hungary thrust upon us. We are very sorry that such a situation exists there, but the most important thing is that the counterrevolution must be shattered. They accuse us of interfering in Hungary's internal affairs. They find the most fearful words to accuse us. But when the British, French and Israelis cut the throats of the Egyptians,[2] that is only a police action aimed at restoring order! The Western powers are trying to denigrate Nasser,[3] although Nasser is not a Communist. Politically, he is closer to those who are waging war on him, and he has even put Communists in jail."

"He had to," offered Soviet President Kliment Voroshilov.[4] Khrushchev turned on him and said: "Don't try to help me."

---

[2] On November 5, 1956, combined British and French forces invaded Egypt in retaliation for Egyptian nationalization of the Suez Canal, while Israel occupied the Egyptian Sinai Peninsula. [Ed.]

[3] Gamal Abdel Nasser (1918–1970), nationalist leader and president of Egypt, 1956–1970. Nasser was a socialist, was a leader of neutral "nonaligned nations," and sought help from the United States, Soviet Union, and China. [Ed.]

[4] Chairman of the Presidium of the Supreme Soviet, the head of state but a largely symbolic office compared with the premier or the head of the Communist Party, both of which positions Khrushchev held. [Ed.]

"Nasser is the hero of his nation, and our sympathies are on his side. We sent sharp letters to Britain, France and Israel—well, Israel, that was just for form, because, as you know, Israel carries no weight in the world, and if it plays any role, it was just to start a fight. If Israel hadn't felt the support of Britain, France and others, the Arabs would have been able to box her ears and she would have remained at peace. I think the British and French will be wise enough to withdraw their forces, and then Egypt will emerge stronger than ever."

Turning again to the Westerners, Khrushchev declared: "You say we want war, but you have now got yourselves into a position I would call idiotic" ("Let's say delicate," offered Mikoyan) "but we don't want to profit by it. If you withdraw your troops from Germany, France and Britain—I'm speaking of American troops—we will not stay one day in Poland, Hungary and Rumania." His voice was scornful as he added: "But we, Mister Capitalists, we are beginning to understand your methods."

By this time, the diplomats—who, in turn, have come to understand Mister Khrushchev's methods—had already left the room.

8

Soviet Telegram on Cuba,
September 7, 1962

On January 1, 1959, Cuban revolutionaries under Fidel Castro overthrew the government of U.S.-backed dictator Fulgencio Batista. The Castro government increasingly faced opposition from the United States and relied on the support of the Soviet Union. U.S. efforts to depose Castro included a failed CIA-sponsored invasion by Cuban exiles at the Cuban Bay of Pigs, April 17–19, 1961, three months after John F. Kennedy came into office. Expecting further U.S. attempts at toppling the regime, the Castro government received from the Soviet Union midrange nuclear missiles. President Kennedy learned of their existence on October 14, 1962. He demanded they be withdrawn and ordered a naval blockade of Cuban ports. The confrontation,

Source: Telegram of Soviet Ambassador to Cuba A. I. Alekseev to the USSR Ministry of Foreign Affairs (MFA), September 7, 1962 at Woodrow Wilson International Center for Scholars, Cold War International History Project, Virtual Archive: http://digitalarchive.wilsoncenter .org/document/111762. [Source: Archive of Foreign Policy of the Russian Federation (AVP RF), Moscow, copy courtesy of National Security Archive (NSA), Washington, DC; trans. Mark H. Doctoroff.]

known as the Cuban Missile Crisis, October 18–29, came dangerously close to erupting into a nuclear war. The crisis ended with
Khrushchev withdrawing the missiles and the United States pledging
not to invade Cuba and to withdraw American missiles from Turkey.

This document reveals Cuban and Soviet attitudes shortly after the
Cuban receipt of the missiles but a month before the crisis. The document is a telegram, dated September 7, 1962, from the Soviet ambassador in Cuba to the Soviet Foreign Ministry in Moscow. In it he
informs Moscow about recent events on the island. What seems to be
happening? What conclusions does the Soviet ambassador draw?
What does the ambassador want the Soviet government to do? How
well informed does the ambassador seem to be about events in Cuba,
the United States, and Latin America? Do you think President Kennedy
would have been less alarmed if he had read this telegram?

THINKING HISTORICALLY

How are the words that the Soviet ambassador uses to describe the
situation in Cuba different from the way Americans would understand it? How significant were the Soviet missiles for the ambassador? Why are the charges of aggressive activity by the United States
against Cuba more believable in this document than they would be in
a magazine article or a public speech?

Recently, the ruling circles of the USA have noticeably activated a policy
of provocation against Cuba;[1] military preparations and its political isolation. Nearly every day, the air space and territorial waters of Cuba are
violated by American airplanes, submarines and ships trying to establish
permanent control over the territory of Cuba and diverting passenger and
transport ships bound for Cuba. The landing of counter-revolutionary
bands of spies and arms has been increased.

The constant acts of provocation are carried out from the territory
of the USA base at Guantanamo, most often in the form of shooting at
Cuban patrols. Especially noteworthy among all these provocations are
far reaching acts like the August 24 shelling of the hotel in which mainly
live Soviet specialists, and also the lies published by the Kennedy Administration about the alleged August 30 attack, in international waters, on
an American airplane from two small Cuban ships. In the USA government's announcement, it is noted that in the event of a repeat of "an

[1] In November 1961, President Kennedy initiated Operation Mongoose, a secret plan to
stimulate a rebellion in Cuba, bring Cuban exiles into the U.S. army for training, undermine the
regime, and assassinate Castro. General Edward Lansdale was put in charge of operations. The
program was stepped up in the spring of 1962. The CIA also continued to support internal
resistance to Castro and engaged the assistance of organized crime figures who had interests in
Cuba to assassinate Castro. [Ed.]

incident of this type," the armed forces of the United States "will take all necessary retaliatory measures." It is entirely evident that this carries a great danger for Cuba, since it gives the most reactionary anti-Cuban authorities in the USA an opening at any moment to organize a provocation and unleash aggressive actions against Cuba.

In regard to the above two last actions undertaken by the USA, the government of Cuba came forward with corresponding official declarations signed by Fidel Castro. Both of these declarations were circulated as official documents to the UN. The goal of these declarations is to attract the attention of the appropriate international organizations and all of world public opinion to the provocative and far-reaching acts of the USA, to unmask the aggressive schemes of the United States in relation to Cuba, and to ward them off. In these declarations the government of Cuba precisely makes the point that the anti-Cuban actions and schemes of the USA present a threat not only to Cuba, but to the whole world.

The series of provocations is now accompanied by a whipped up, broad anti-Cuba campaign in the USA press, striving with all its might to convince the population of the United States of the alleged presence in Cuba of large contingents of Soviet troops and of the fact that Cuba has turned into a military base of "world Communism" which presents a grave threat to the USA and all Latin American countries. Under this pretext, the press, certain American senators and other public figures demand of the Kennedy administration the revival of the Monroe Doctrine,[2] establishment of a sea and air blockade of Cuba, the bringing into force of the Treaty of Rio de Janeiro,[3] and the military occupation of Cuba.

Following the signing in Moscow of the Soviet-Cuban communiqué in which the agreement of the Soviet government to provide assistance in strengthening its armed forces is noted, Kennedy in a public statement on September 4 pointed to the defensive nature of Cuba's military preparations and noted that Soviet military specialists are in Cuba to teach the Cubans how to use defensive equipment presented by the Soviet Union. Several USA press agencies, commenting on that part of Kennedy's statement, underline the evidence of the fact that the president of the USA obviously preferred an attempt to calm down those circles in the USA which are supporting quick, decisive actions against Cuba. Along with this, in Kennedy's statement there are contained insinuations of purported aggressive Cuban schemes regarding influence on the American continent and a threat to use "all necessary means" to "defend" the continent.

---

[2] The Monroe Doctrine (1823) warned European nations that any efforts by them to interfere in affairs of the Americas would be viewed as aggression requiring U.S. intervention. [Ed.]

[3] The Inter-American Treaty of Reciprocal Assistance (1947) held that any attack on one nation of the Americas would be viewed as an attack on them all. [Ed.]

According to certain information, the USA State Department through its ambassadors notified the governments of Latin American countries that they can expect changes in the situation in the Caribbean basin "if Castro's government does not come to its senses." More probably, in the near future the USA, using the pretext of an allegedly growing threat to the Western hemisphere, will embark on a long process of increasing the pressure on governments of the Latin-American countries and will probably convene a meeting of foreign ministers of the member-countries of the OAS[4] to work out supplementary sanctions against Cuba. One can also assume that the most wildly aggressive powers in the USA (the Pentagon, the Cuban external counter-revolution,[5] and others) will continue to exert pressure on Kennedy in order to realize the most decisive actions against Cuba.

The campaign of anti-Cuban hysteria has been conveyed via American propaganda to Latin American countries too. There the publication of articles and transmissions of radio programs of anti-Cuban and anti-Soviet content is constantly encouraged, while the external Cuban counter-revolution and local reaction put constant pressure on the governments of those countries, conduct loud demonstrations and terrorize individuals and organizations which speak out in defense of the Cuban revolution, and by means of bribery and blackmail get a range of people who have visited Cuba to make anti-Cuban statements, and so forth.

Simultaneously, the USA continues actively to conduct purely military preparations,[6] aimed at repressing possible centers of the national-liberation movement in Latin America, and, given the appropriate circumstances, the Cuban revolution itself. This is shown by such facts as the organization by the United States of schools for instruction in methods of street-fighting and anti-partisan struggle in many Latin American countries (in Panama, Peru, Colombia, Equador, Bolivia, and others); continuing intensive instruction of Cuban counter-revolutionaries in camps located on the territory of the USA, in Puerto Rico and in several Central American countries; many inspection trips to these bases, schools, and camps by responsible American military officials and the heads of the Cuban counter-revolution, including Miro Cardona;[7]

---

[4] Organization of American States. A State Department memo dated May 17, 1962, lists Operation Mongoose "Task 1" as "obtain some special and significant action within the OAS organization against the Castro-Communist regime." For this and following U.S. security memos, see http://www.globalsecurity.org/intell/library/reports. [Ed.]

[5] "External counter-revolution" refers to Cuban exiles in the United States and elsewhere, including veterans of the Bay of Pigs, who were still organized to topple Castro. [Ed.]

[6] Whether President Kennedy was willing to mount another military operation is uncertain, but active preparations were made to train exiles, prepare a blockade, and consider all options, including military. [Ed.]

[7] Jose Miro Cardona (1902–1974): briefly prime minister of Cuba in 1959; went into exile and led anti-Castro Cubans in the United States. Was to be president if Bay of Pigs invasion succeeded. [Ed.]

unflagging efforts of the USA aimed at strengthening the unity of the external Cuban counter-revolution and unity in the action of counter-revolutionary organizations active in Cuba itself, etc.

At the same time, the USA is actively continuing to conduct its efforts towards the political isolation of Cuba, particularly in Latin America. The USA is concentrating on putting pressure on the governments of Mexico and Brazil,[8] which continue to express their support for the principle of non-interference and self-determination of peoples. This pressure is applied through economic means, and also by exploiting the domestic reaction. The realization of Kennedy's visit to Mexico, following which he was to have quickly visited Brazil too (this visit was put off to the last months of the year), served the goals of determining the likelihood of attracting these two countries to the anti-Cuban plans of the USA.

Until now none of the attempts of the USA to attract Brazil and Mexico to its anti-Cuban adventures has had any success.

Under pressure from the USA, in a majority of Latin American countries the local authorities are applying the harshest measures aimed at forbidding or tightly limiting visits of any groups or individuals to Cuba, and also their contacts with Cuban delegations in third countries. People who visit Cuba or make contact with Cuban delegations in third countries are subject to arrest, repression, investigations upon return to their homeland. The USA does not lack means for organizing broad and loud provocations against Cuban delegations taking part in international quorums, as took place recently in Finland[9] and Jamaica.

Referring to the decision taken at the meeting at Punta-del-Este about the exclusion of Cuba from the OAS, the USA is undertaking all measures to deny Cuba participation in any organizations connected with the inter-American system. In particular, they recently undertook an attempt to secure the exclusion of Cuba from the Pan American Health Organization (PAHO). The unlawful denial of Cuba's application to join the so-called Latin American Free Trade Association is another example.[10] In response to the American policy towards Cuba of provocation, military threats, and political isolation, the Cuban government is intensifying its efforts on strengthening its own armed forces,

[8] Mexico and Brazil were thought particularly important propaganda targets by the United States. [Ed.]

[9] U.S. State Department memo, June 27, 1962: "it is important to work with the forthcoming youth festival in Helsinki (where there will be 2,000 Latin American students) to take the festival away from the Communists and ensure a good amount of anti-Communist propaganda emanating from this support." [Ed.]

[10] Memo from Lansdale on Operation Mongoose, July 5, 1962: "State reports that diplomatic efforts are being made to block Cuba's application for accreditation to the European Economic Community. Similarly, efforts are being made to exclude Cuba from the proposed Latin American Free Trade area." [Ed.]

struggling with the internal counter-revolution, unmasking before world public opinion the aggressive designs of the USA, and broadening its anti-American propaganda in Latin America. At the end of August, taking into account the activization of provocative actions by the USA and the possible increase in the unleashing of counter-revolutionary bands and manifestations of domestic counter-revolution, preventive arrests were carried out in the country and strengthened control was established over many registered [known] counter-revolutionary elements and the places where they gather.

The Cuban leaders are paying serious attention to the question of strengthening the devotion to the revolution of the cadres of its diplomatic missions, particularly in Latin American countries; they are taking every opportunity, as was the case with their presentation at the Latin American Free Trade Association, to widen the sphere of their activity in Latin America; they are strengthening their connections with the Latin American peoples by inviting to Cuba society delegations and individual Latin American officials; in timely fashion and aggressively, they speak at international organizations, unmasking the aggressive schemes and actions of the USA; they are striving to take part in any international forums at which there is a possibility to expose the aggressive character of American imperialism; they are strengthening Cuba's ties with African and Asian countries, etc.

The Cuban leadership believes, however, that the main guarantee of the development of the Cuban Revolution under conditions of possible direct American aggression is the readiness of the Soviet government to provide military assistance to Cuba and simultaneously to warn the USA of that fact. From this position, the joint Soviet-Cuban communiqué about [Ernesto "Che"] Guevara's visit to Moscow was greeted by the Cuban leaders and the vast majority of the Cuban people with great enthusiasm and gratitude. The Cuban leadership and Fidel Castro himself suggest that these warnings will help to prevail against those forces in the USA that are warning of the outbreak now of a world conflict, and are staving off a direct American attack on Cuba in the near future.

In our opinion, in the near future the ruling circles of the USA will continue to expand the attacks on Cuba by all the above-mentioned means: provocations, the propaganda campaign, military preparations, and actions of the domestic counter-revolution, political isolation, and so forth. Their success in drawing the Latin American countries into their aggressive actions will most depend on the positions of the governments of Mexico and Brazil.

We also suggest that the question of direct American actions against Cuba will be decided by the correlation of forces in American ruling circles which have differing approaches to questions of war and peace in the present period, and the struggle between them on these issues.

The mood of the overwhelming majority of the Cuban people is defiant, and regardless of the reality of the threat of intervention, no panic or fear before the threat which is hanging over Cuba is observed in the masses of the people. The American provocations make possible an ever-tighter unity of the Cuban workers and raise the political consciousness of the masses.

Regarding the provocations, the influence of the Soviet Union in Cuba has grown as never before, and our cooperation with the Cuban leaders has been strengthened even more.

In the interest of future productive work with our Cuban friends it would be desirable to receive from you for dispatch to the Cuban leaders information which we have about the plans of the USA government toward Cuba.

9

Telephone Transcript: Soviet Premier and Afghan Prime Minister, 1979

The Soviet war in Afghanistan (1979–1989), which eventually contributed to the dissolution of the Soviet Union itself, began, like the American war in Vietnam, with seemingly small steps on behalf of a client who lacked widespread support. This document reveals one of the first of those steps. The Soviet client was Nur Mohammed Taraki, a leader of the communist movement in Afghanistan who came to the Afghan presidency as a result of a military coup in April 1978. His ambitious program of radical social reform alienated tribal and religious leaders. After only a year of an Afghan communist experiment, he was seeking aid from Moscow—an effort captured in this document. It is a transcript of a telephone conversation between the Soviet premier Alexei Kosygin and the Afghan prime minister Nur Mohammed Taraki on March 18, 1979, about six months before the Soviets sent troops into Afghanistan. Alexei Kosygin succeeded Khrushchev as Soviet premier, serving from 1964 to 1980.

It was common in the Cold War period to speak of clients of the big powers, like Taraki, as "puppets," but historians have since recognized that such collaborators had considerable power. What are the different powers that Kosygin and Taraki exert in this conversation? How are their differences expressed and resolved?

Source: Transcript of telephone conversation between Soviet premier Alexei Kosygin and Afghan prime minister Nur Mohammed Taraki, March 18, 1979. Cold War International History Project Bulletin, Issues 8–9, Winter 1996/1997, 145–46.

THINKING HISTORICALLY

Notice that Kosygin uses different words than Taraki to describe the Afghan people. What are these differences, and how do you explain them? How did Soviet ideology hinder Soviet policy?

KOSYGIN   Ask Comrade Taraki, perhaps he will outline the situation in Afghanistan.

TARAKI   The situation is bad and getting worse.

KOSYGIN   Do you have support among the workers, city dwellers, the petty bourgoisie, and the white collar workers in Herat? Is there still anyone on your side?

TARAKI   There is no active support on the part of the population. It is almost wholly under the influence of Shiite slogans—follow not the heathens, but follow us. The propaganda is underpinned by this.

KOSYGIN   Are there many workers there?

TARAKI   Very few—between 1,000 and 2,000 people in all.

KOSYGIN   What are the prospects?

TARAKI   We are convinced that the enemy will form new units and will develop an offensive.

KOSYGIN   Do you not have the forces to rout them?

TARAKI   I wish it were the case.

KOSYGIN   What, then, are your proposals on this issue?

TARAKI   We ask that you extend practical and technical assistance, involving people and arms.

KOSYGIN   It is a very complex matter.

TARAKI   Iran and Pakistan are working against us, accordingly to the same plan. Hence, if you now launch a decisive attack on Herat, it will be possible to save the revolution.

KOSYGIN   The whole world will immediately get to know this. The rebels have portable radio transmitters and will report it directly.

TARAKI   I ask that you extend assistance.

KOSYGIN   We must hold consultations on this issue. Do you not have connections with Iran's progressives? Can't you tell them that it is currently the United States that is your and their chief enemy? The Iranians are very hostile toward the United States and evidently this can be put to use as propaganda. What foreign policy activities or statements would you like to see coming from us? Do you have any ideas on this question, propaganda-wise?

TARAKI   Propaganda help must be combined with practical assistance. I suggest that you place Afghan markings on your tanks and aircraft and no one will be any the wiser. Your troops could advance from the direction of Kushka and from the direction of Kabul. In our view, no one will be any the wiser. They will think these are Government troops.

KOSYGIN   I do not want to disappoint you, but it will not be possible to conceal this. Two hours later the whole world will know about this. Everyone will begin to shout that the Soviet Union's intervention in Afghanistan has begun. If we quickly airlift tanks, the necessary ammunition and make mortars available to you, will you find specialists who can use these weapons?

TARAKI   I am unable to answer this question. The Soviet advisers can answer that.

KOSYGIN   Hundreds of Afghan officers were trained in the Soviet Union. Where are they all now?

TARAKI   Most of them are Moslem reactionaries. We are unable to rely on them, we have no confidence in them.

KOSYGIN   Can't you recruit a further 50,000 soldiers if we quickly airlift arms to you? How many people can you recruit?

TARAKI   The core can only be formed by older secondary school pupils, students, and a few workers. The working class in Afghanistan is very small, but it is a long affair to train them. But we will take any measures, if necessary.

KOSYGIN   We have decided to quickly deliver military equipment and property to you and to repair helicopters and aircraft. All this is for free. We have also decided to deliver to you 100,000 tons of grain and to raise gas prices from $21 per cubic meter to $37.

TARAKI   That is very good, but let us talk of Herat. Why can't the Soviet Union send Uzbeks, Tajiks, and Turkmens in civilian clothing? No one will recognize them. We want you to send them. They could drive tanks, because we have all these nationalities in Afghanistan. Let them don Afghan costume and wear Afghan badges and no one will recognize them. It is very easy work, in our view. If Iran's and Pakistan's experience is anything to go by, it is clear that it is easy to do this work, they have already shown how it can be done.

KOSYGIN   You are, of course, oversimplifying the issue. It is a complex political and international issue, but, irrespective of this, we will hold consultations again and will get back to you.

TARAKI   Send us infantry fighting vehicles by air.

KOSYGIN   Do you have anyone to drive them?

TARAKI   We will find drivers for between 30 and 35 vehicles.

KOSYGIN   Are they reliable? Won't they flee to the enemy, together with their vehicles? After all, our drivers do not speak the language.

TARAKI   Send vehicles together with drivers who speak our language — Tajiks and Uzbeks.

KOSYGIN   I expected this kind of reply from you. We are comrades and are waging a common struggle and that is why we should not stand on ceremony with each other. Everything must be subordinate to this.

■ REFLECTIONS

The Cold War used to be ancient history. It ended at such breathtaking speed and with such pronounced results that few imagined tomorrow would have anything to do with yesterday. The Soviet Union collapsed in 1991, like the Berlin Wall in 1989, into an irretrievable heap of rubble. Commissars became capitalists, the USSR awoke as Russia, Leningrad turned back into St. Petersburg, and the red flag with hammer and sickle was exchanged for a French-like tricouleur of red, white, and blue stripes. Shoppers replaced placeholders as waiting lines disappeared; shelves of pricey foreign delicacies appeared fully stocked.

Whole countries cracked off along the periphery of what had been a great empire. Baltic city-states breathed their own air and minted their own money. Newly independent Central Asian countries built mosques and elected new dictators. These non-Soviet "stans" sent Russians back to Russia, from which they emigrated by the millions to Toledo and Tel Aviv. Some of those who stayed turned nationalized industries into personal possessions. Others lost their jobs, their savings, their homes, and half their life expectancies. New classes emerged—the "Russian mafia" from the KGB, the plutocrats from the bureaucrats—except they were often the same people in better clothes.

So too the view from America. Reagan's "Evil Empire" of 1983 became a partner in peace. In 1990 Mikhail Gorbachev received the Nobel Prize for ending the Cold War. *Time* magazine—the same magazine that brought America the Cold War—named Gorbachev "Man of the Year." Ex-president Nixon—the same Nixon who had made a career of anticommunism, coming into national prominence in a "kitchen debate" with Khrushchev in 1959—said Gorbachev should have been "Man of the Decade." Times had changed.

But the New World Order of nuclear disarmament, shrunken military budgets, and global cooperation that Gorbachev and Reagan envisioned never quite arrived. A CIA director became president of the United States, shortly followed by his son, and a KGB secret policeman from the old USSR became president of the new Russia. George W. Bush, the son, said he looked into the eyes of Vladimir Putin, the KGB man, and saw his soul. Putin saw a partner. That was in June 2001. In the following years, the United States became more militarized and chose to show it could fight two major wars (in Iraq and Afghanistan) at the same time, while Putin, as president and prime minister, closed down the budding democracy of Russia faster than one could say Ivan the Terrible.

From the vantage point of 2016, ghosts of the Cold War reemerge. Despite, or perhaps because of, the rise of a common enemy of terrorist organizations, a more militarized Russia and Western Europe face off along newly charged precarious borders. One hopes the lessons of the Cold War have been learned.

27

New Democracy Movements

The World, 1977 to the Present

■ HISTORICAL CONTEXT

One of the most striking developments in world history has been the recent rise in the number of democracies and the increasing consensus that democracy is desirable and achievable. Before 1945, democracy was limited to a few Western countries, many of which ruled colonial empires like despots. The end of World War II brought an end to those colonial empires. But the newly created independent states of Asia and Africa did not always opt for democracy. India, which became independent in 1947, did create what is still called today "the world's largest democracy," but elsewhere many newly independent regimes established single-party dictatorships to replace colonial rule.

In some ways the Cold War made things worse. The United States and the Soviet Union demanded loyalty above all from their client states. For the Soviet Union that meant the domination of puppet Communist parties in Eastern Europe. For the United States, the desired loyalty was to vigorous anticommunism at home and abroad. Dictators delivered better than democrats, who were often too sympathetic to popular forces, communists and socialists included. Consequently the Cold War superpowers extinguished budding national democracies and democratic movements. At least for the duration of the conflict, nondemocratic regimes in Eastern Europe, Latin America, and even much of Africa were rewarded with financial and military assistance that enabled them to continue old feuds, social conflicts, or civil wars, as long as they remained loyal to their patron.

As the Cold War came to an end in the late 1980s, the exhausted and indebted former enemies cared less about who governed in Poland, South Africa, or Argentina, thus allowing new democratic movements to rise and rule. After the Soviet Union was replaced by the Russian

Federation in 1991, independent states mushroomed throughout the Baltic region and Eastern Europe. Similarly, in Latin America, military dictatorships were replaced by democratic governments, some of which even called themselves "socialist." Before 1991, it was inconceivable that Russian or American governments would ever have allowed such a change.

In a perverse way, the Cold War had undermined the popular legitimacy of democratic movements. Since both the United States and the Soviet Union claimed to be democratic, while subverting democratic movements abroad, nationalist leaders, especially in Africa, derided democracy as an imperialist ideology. But since 1991, it has become easier to see democracy and human rights as universal goals.

Our chapter spans the Cold War and post–Cold War periods. This allows us to see how democratic movements developed in the context of the Cold War and have thrived since its end. During the last decade of the Cold War, demands for democracy were voiced *against* the clients of the Soviet Union and the United States, as we see in the protests of the "Mothers of the Plaza de Mayo" in Argentina, and *by* the leaders of those superpowers, as we see in Mikhail Gorbachev's policy of *Perestroika*. After the Cold War, countries like East Germany and South Africa were freed by their patrons to pursue their own destinies, as indicated here in the address by Nelson Mandela that is included in the chapter.

In recent years, democracy movements have continued to develop in Eastern Europe and Latin America, but the newest breakthroughs have been in the Middle East. These began in Tunisia in December 2010, when a young street vendor set himself on fire after his goods had been taken and he had been denied a hearing by government authorities. Massive street protests followed, bringing down the ruler of the country, forcing him, his family, and his aides into exile. The example of Tunisia sparked popular protests in Egypt against President Mubarak in January 2011, resulting in his resignation by February. As similar movements for popular government broke out in Bahrain, Yemen, and Libya, these and other Arab countries were swept up in what was called an "Arab Spring." This is perhaps most remarkable because the Middle East had been for so long dominated by oil-rich autocratic sheiks, super-privileged royal families, and, as a consequence of the Cold War and the creation of Israel, U.S.–supplied military regimes: Iran and Iraq at various times and Egypt throughout.

Whether the Arab Spring turns into a truly democratic summer is complicated by continued high unemployment, remaining members of the old ruling class, sectarian conflicts, and global politics, but the hunger for popular representation and responsive government, once tasted, is unlikely to disappear. A powerful model, the Arab Spring has raised democratic aspirations from China to Chile.

■ THINKING HISTORICALLY

Using Connections and Context to Interpret the Past

When historians ask about causes, as they frequently do, they look to connections with past events and the general context in which the event takes place. These are two different ways of understanding the causes of anything. To take an example from our discussion of the Arab Spring, we might ask to what extent the events in Egypt in early 2011 were connected to (that is, a continuation of or influenced by) the events in Tunisia, and to what extent the Egyptian revolution was a product of the Egyptian context (its unique problems, politics, etc.). Obviously both played a role; that is why historians frequently study connections and context together, but it is always valuable to understand which, if either, was more important.

In this chapter we will search the primary source documents for signs of connections to earlier events and for the impact of the local and immediate context of the events under discussion. An explanation of an historical event that ignores either outside influences or the internal context is almost always incomplete. We may or may not be able to conclude which was more important, but we will learn to look in both directions.

1

HEBE DE BONAFINI AND MATILDE SÁNCHEZ

The Madwomen at the Plaza de Mayo, 1977/2002

The history of Latin America is pockmarked by the rule of *caudillos*, generals, and military juntas. During the Cold War, with the blessings of the United States, anticommunist military dictatorships ruled throughout Central and South America. Since the end of the Cold War, democracies have created a new Latin America. We might date

Source: Hebe de Bonafini and Matilde Sánchez, "The Madwomen at the Plaza de Mayo," trans. Patricia Owen Steiner in *The Argentina Reader: History, Culture, Politics*, eds. Gabriela Nouzeilles and Graciela Montaldo (Durham: Duke University Press, 2002), 430–37.

the origins of these new democracies to the protests against the military juntas of the Cold War. Under some of the most brutal of these terrorist states, dedicated to repress any opposition, some people found the strength to say "no."

In Argentina between 1975 and 1978, 22,000 to 30,000 people were killed by the military. In addition to hundreds of communist revolutionaries who had already declared war on the military, tens of thousands of ordinary citizens were rounded up, interrogated, tortured, and ultimately "disappeared" with a bullet in the back of the head or the drop of a broken body into the Atlantic Ocean from an army helicopter. Infants were taken from their condemned parents and given to their torturers to be raised as their own. Students left one day for school and never returned. And so it was the mothers of teenagers and the grandmothers of infants who had suddenly disappeared who began asking for an accounting. As the women began to gather in the Plaza de Mayo of Buenos Aires, the police mocked them as the "Madwomen" of the Plaza, insinuating that they had been driven mad by misbehaved children who ran away from home. But the constant presence of these women, each Thursday afternoon in the Plaza, allowed the world to see the Mothers for who they were and listen to their stories.

Hebe de Bonafini was one of these "Madwomen," having lost two sons to the repression. Here, with the help of journalist Matilde Sánchez, Hebe de Bonafini tells what happened after she was denied information about her eldest son Jorge Omar in March 1977. What enabled her and the other Mothers to challenge the junta? Of course, the women were not asking for democracy *per se*; they were demanding the return of their children and at the very least they wanted information. But how did these demands grow to challenge an antidemocratic regime?

THINKING HISTORICALLY

We read nothing here to suggest that Hebe de Bonafini read past democratic theorists or borrowed ideas of democracy from historical sources. In fact, she says nothing about democracy. The eruption of the force of the Mothers sprang from the specific context of Argentina: foremost, the military dictatorship and the state terrorism against leftists. But the Argentine coup had connections to military planners throughout the hemisphere. Further, on a personal level, women made connections with one another. How did the forging of these connections among the women contribute to the strength of the protest? And how did connections to outside observers provide a stage and an audience much larger than could be gathered in the Plaza de Mayo?

I was beginning to notice that the faces were repeating themselves in the courts and police stations of La Plata. But I didn't say hello to the other women. And it was obvious that what had happened to me had happened to them because after a time I had exhausted all the possibilities in La Plata and absolutely had to go to Buenos Aires, where I began to run into those same faces in the courts, in the Ministry of the Interior, which was located at the time in the Casa Rosada itself. But we gave each other only shy, sideways glances. For my part, at first there was only a disguised effort to fish for a little information. Since we were all standing in the same lines, there was no need to ask questions. Each of us had to repeat her own story of the crime dozens of times to the changing faces at the little windows.

It was in April, I believe, when I first started to talk with some of the women. Our conversations were limited to the habeas corpus petitions[1] and the best way of writing them and of identifying the judges that weren't granting them. But I didn't give any of the women my name or my telephone number. We were anonymous, distrustful people, united by the paperwork and the lives we were trying to recover. Faces of mothers without children, wives without husbands or brothers. Women looking for other people, we were a precarious company in the aloneness of bureaucracy. . . .

On the train from La Plata to Buenos Aires, one of those faces that I used to see in those days in the offices of the capital was already approaching its dreadful destiny. That afternoon my steps and my itinerary matched those of that gray-haired woman with the dark circles under her eyes whom I had spotted days before on the train when I went to the First Army Corps. We both made the change to the subway at Constitución and rode together to the Plaza de Mayo, to the offices of Interior Minister Albano Harguindeguy. I greeted her. We didn't meet again for two weeks.

"We could go back on a bus if that seems like a good idea to you," the woman finally said one afternoon when we saw each other again. "It's a little more expensive, but it's a much more comfortable ride."

I agreed. We sat down in the back of the bus. We were silent. Then I began to ask myself why I had accepted her invitation if I intended to remain mute. In reality, I was wondering if she had a child missing. Perhaps her child might be sharing the cell and some meals with my son while we were sharing the bus seat, mute, not knowing how to get to know each other under such circumstances. She was the one who spoke. She didn't give her name. She was looking for her twenty-four-year-old daughter. They had taken her away five months ago. She was pregnant.

---

[1] The women were encouraged to file petitions of "habeas corpus," which would release a prisoner from unlawful detention, but the petitions were routinely denied without explanation. [Ed.]

I was overwhelmed by astonishment: her case seemed unbelievable. How could that woman go on living if her daughter was a prisoner and about to give birth? I refused to believe that things were really so harsh, so crude. I didn't know the woman's name, but I began to feel a tremendous sense of solidarity with her pain. I was beginning to think that my case was not as serious, although it was my own case that was hurting me. Yet as the bus sped along—probably late because it was leaving lines of passengers standing at every stop—I felt a bond of sisterhood with that woman. I felt understood. She went on talking about her daughter, about the paperwork she had done. But although she sounded sad, she seemed a little released from her own suffering, as if she had gotten past the moments of confusion that I was now living through myself. "We are many more than you believe," she finally said, "and we are beginning to work."

"To work?" I asked. I had no idea what that could mean in this case The woman responded that a group of mothers were doing their paperwork together and were arranging for interviews with influential people who could help them. I asked her if my presence would do any good. . . .

The woman smiled; that initial distance between us had evaporated. She said that next Thursday afternoon a group of mothers would be getting together at the Plaza de Mayo. They were going to sign a petition or meet with a priest. It wouldn't be a bad idea to come—"the more mothers, the better." I said that I'd think it over (something in me was still asking if we weren't creating too much of a scandal over nothing, over some confusion that would surely be cleared up sooner or later). The woman stood up and shook hands with me and began to walk down the aisle of the bus.

"Don't forget. Thursday at two, on the dot." . . .

I walked around; it wasn't two o'clock yet. I hadn't seen the woman from the train with the dark circles under her eyes. I was feeling nervous; I wanted to be sure she would be in the Plaza before I arrived. Suddenly I asked myself why I was afraid: what was wrong, when you came right down to it, with my joining those women? The billboards on Bolívar Street proclaimed the official slogan, "The country is advancing," in sky-blue letters on a white background, like the national flag. I followed that street back to the Plaza.

Some women were already there, near the obelisk, on the right, standing together beside a bench. There were no more than ten: the woman from the train hadn't arrived yet, but another woman walked toward me. She had brown hair and strong, attractive features. She was short, with strong arms and workers' hands, and her body made you think of a great fortress. The weather was cool for April, but she was wearing a loose cotton T-shirt. I tried to explain who I was and how I happened to be there: "A lady from La Plata told me on the bus." It was all very vague, but the woman began to smile. "Ah! Yes." she said at last. "She mentioned you. She said you'd be here. Come on over."

They all appeared extremely rushed. They were talking quickly, softly, their voices bumping into one another. They were passing around a piece of paper. "By chance we managed to get hold of a typewriter," the woman whispered to me. "We wrote a letter to President Videla pleading for our children. Now we're signing it, before we deliver it to the secretary. Sign it if you want.". . .

The women continued passing around the paper and explaining what it was about to the latest women to arrive. Behind us, the city kept on at its rhythm; it didn't seem to realize that we were there. Men were hurrying because the banks were closing; some retired men, completely indifferent, were lying in the sun. We women might well be alumnae of some school, meeting to arrange another reunion. Most of us were about my age or somewhere in their fifties; Azucena moved quickly, like a young woman, but she was a little older. She and I became friends. I agreed with the petition, and I signed. I did it with a large, clear signature so that the president would read my name and it would be engraved on his eyes. Also, so that he would know that my son's name gave me no shame.

We left saying that we would see each other again the following Thursday in the Plaza. At that time, none of us thought that our waiting without children would be longer than a couple of months or that the initial search would someday be transformed into this painful story. . . .

Toward the end of September 1977, we are already more than fifty women, and our feelings grow closer with our growing numbers. Every time there are more of us. Every time we feel stronger and less afraid. Every time we feel safer together. But every time there are more children missing. At the benches on the side of the Plaza we feel defiant, almost invincible for a few minutes. The truth is, they don't know what to do with us. If there is anything left in their hearts, it is the line from all those macho tangos about "my poor old lady." That keeps us safe for the moment. They think that we are crazed by grief, that we'll last until we get tired of standing there with all our varicose veins or until one of us has a heart attack. . . .

They dispatch the police. "This is a demonstration, and the country is under a state of siege. Move on, ladies, move on." We begin to walk together in pairs, arm in arm. Then they make us walk separately.

The Plaza is big, the pairs break up, nobody can make us out from the other women who are just out for a walk. We know that the most important thing is to keep closing the circle, but imperceptibly, a little closer to the obelisk each time, so that they don't have time to realize it. There are more of them all the time; but every Thursday there are more of us, and the police bring reinforcements. They stand in front of the obelisk and keep us from getting close to it. We walk around talking in pairs, watching the necks of the pair of mothers in front of us. . . .

September 1977: . . . Azucena said it would be a good idea for all of us to join the annual pilgrimage to Luján "because people talk a lot on the way and we can stand out." We agreed: besides, there were also many Catholic mothers with us who wanted to go to pray the rosary. The problem is that not all of them wanted to go on foot: some would meet in Haedo, others in Moreno or Castelar. "We all have to agree clearly on where we'll meet."

"I know," said Eva, a mother who usually preferred to keep quiet. "We have to wear something that can be spotted from far away so we can find each other. A kerchief on our heads, for example."

"Or a mantilla. But we don't all have mantillas. Better a kerchief."

"Yes," says another woman. "Or better still a baby diaper; it looks like a kerchief, but it'll make us feel better, closer to our children.". . .

The husbands come along that day, but they always keep a little to the side. As soon as they enter the crowd, they see many other white-headed women like their wives. The diapers leap out at the sun in the sea of people walking along: we begin to come together, first two, then three. Further on, we come across another small group. The diapers multiply and stun the rest of the pilgrims who have already ceased to see them as a coincidence. When we get to the plaza across from the basilica in Luján, we're a good-sized group. Fifteen or twenty of us come together, and, standing in a circle, we pray the rosary for the children who no longer are. For the children who have disappeared.

Naturally the word *disappeared* bursts out. What does it mean? some-one asks. The term is explicit: only someone who didn't want to understand could fail to understand. The word is multiplied many times by our mouths. It is repeated with the Ave Marias of the rosary. It embraces all the impunity of the situation. One woman, then another, comes over to talk with us. Their children are also "disappeared," they want to see us again, to pray with us, even with diapers on their heads. People look on, listening to the rosary in the plaza. In the basilica, in front of the altar, some of the devoted women are taking communion or praying for world peace. We are, in some way, the horrible worm that has wriggled out of a shining Argentina "that is advancing." Advancing toward what? Toward those graves without crosses. Toward the bottom of the river. . . .

A few days before the World Cup, a final blow struck "our family." On 25 May, in the afternoon, military forces abducted a group of women in a pastry shop in Lomas de Zamora. One of them was María Elena Bugnone, who was looking for her husband, her brother-in-law Raúl, her sister, and her sister's husband. Not one of that group of women ever returned. Later information from released prisoners indicated that María Elena was held for two years in the prison at Ezeiza. . . .

We know that the World Cup will fill the country with tourists and media professionals from all over the world. I said, "The question is how do we take advantage of those TV cameras for our own cause, to ask for our children and produce a juicy scandal for the government."

"But we don't know how to talk very well, Hebe. We know how to keep house, and we have learned how to do the paperwork, but what are we going to answer if they ask us something in English?"

"It's easy, Clarita," said a mother who had just joined but had plenty of energy. "You look at the journalist, and you say, 'We want our children. We want them to tell us where they are.'"

Our slogans and our rallying cries were being born: later on, they would shatter our silent circling of the obelisk at the center of the Plaza. But for the month of May they wouldn't let us circle: the police were there waiting punctually at three o'clock and charged whenever they saw more than three women together. But we fought them as long as we could. They threw us out one side, and we slipped back in the other. They dragged us out of one flower bed, and, after going around the block, we turned up next to the other. This game of cat and mouse that so exasperated them had for us the almost symbolic objective of occupying the obelisk, the center of the Plaza. From there people would see us better.

And the World Cup began: Argentine flags, confetti thrown from every office window. This meant the indifference of others, of all those Argentines who didn't want to know anything about death but preferred to celebrate to the end the mad fiesta power had offered them, stuffing themselves full with the four TV channels until they were sick or thoroughly brainwashed.

Meanwhile, we women worked to spread the news about our group. We sent hundreds of letters to foreign politicians, and we sought interviews with different world TV networks. Those men listened to us wide-eyed, some became indignant, and all considered us news. We had made it.

2

MIKHAIL GORBACHEV

Perestroika and Glasnost, 2000

Mikhail Gorbachev (b. 1931) was the head (general secretary) of the Communist Party of the Soviet Union (1985–1991) and president of the Soviet Union (1988–1991). He led the party and the state through the wrenching changes of its liberalization, democratization, and demise. Beginning in 1985, Gorbachev envisioned the democratic reform of the party and state. His formula was *perestroika* (restructuring) and *glasnost* (opening). In this selection from his memoir, he describes that effort.

Source: Mikhail Gorbachev, *On My Country and the World* (New York: Columbia University Press, 2000), 55–61.

In what ways was the democratization of the Soviet Union, as described here, different from that of Argentina (see the previous document)?

THINKING HISTORICALLY

In what ways does Gorbachev connect his democratization with the ideas and efforts of others? In what ways does he attribute it to the particular context of the Soviet Union and the world in the late 1980s?

There has been a continuing debate over when reform actually began in our country. Politicians and journalists have been trying to locate the exact point at which all our dramatic changes began. Some assert that reforms in Russia did not really begin until 1992.

The basis for reform was laid by Khrushchev.[1] His break with the repressive policies of Stalinism was a heroic feat of civic action. Khrushchev also tried, though without much success, to make changes in the economy. Significant attempts were made within the framework of the so-called Kosygin reforms. Then came a long period of stagnation and a new attempt by Yuri Andropov[2] to improve the situation in our society. An obvious sign that the times were ripe for change was the activity of the dissidents. They were suppressed and expelled from the country, but their moral stand and their proposals for change (for example, the ideas of Andrei Sakharov[3]) played a considerable role in creating the spiritual preconditions for perestroika.

Of course external factors were also important. Thus the Prague Spring of 1968 sowed the seeds of profound thought and reflection in our society. The invasion of Czechoslovakia, dictated by fear of the "democratic infection," was not only a crude violation of the sovereignty and rights of the Czechoslovak people. It had the effect, for years, of putting the brakes on moves toward change, although change was long overdue both in our country and throughout the so-called socialist camp. I should also acknowledge the role of such phenomena as Willy Brandt's[4] "Eastern policy" and the search for new avenues toward social progress by those who were called Euro-Communists. All this contributed to

---

[1] Nikita Khrushchev, first secretary of the Communist Party of the Soviet Union from 1953 to 1964; responsible for early de-Stalinization reforms. See chapter 26, selection 7. [Ed.]

[2] General secretary of the Communist Party of the Soviet Union from November 1982 until February 1984. [Ed.]

[3] Soviet nuclear scientist who became a human rights activist. [Ed.]

[4] Mayor of West Berlin 1957–1966, chancellor of West Germany 1969–1974, and leader of the socialist Social Democratic Party of Germany (SPD) 1964–1987. His Eastern policy was an effort to improve relations with communist East Germany, Poland, and the Soviet Union. [Ed.]

deeper reflection in our country, reflection on the values of democracy, freedom, and peace and the ways to achieve them.

Thus we see that attempts at change were made, quite a few of them in fact. But none of them produced results. This is not surprising: After all, none of these attempts touched the essence of the system—property relations, the power structure, and the monopoly of the party on political and intellectual life. The suppression of dissidence continued in spite of everything.

Clearly what was needed was not particular measures in a certain area, even if they were substantial, but rather an entirely different policy, a new political path. Since early 1985, especially after the April plenum of the CPSU Central Committee,[5] this kind of policy began to be formulated. A new course was taken.

Today, in retrospect, one can only be amazed at how quickly and actively our people, the citizens of our country, supported that new course. Apathy and indifference toward public life were overcome. This convinced us that change was vitally necessary. Society awakened.

Perestroika was born out of the realization that problems of internal development in our country were ripe, even overripe, for a solution. New approaches and types of action were needed to escape the downward spiral of crisis, to normalize life, and to make a breakthrough to qualitatively new frontiers. It can be said that to a certain extent perestroika was a result of a rethinking of the Soviet experience since October.[6]

The vital need for change was dictated also by the following consideration. It was obvious that the whole world was entering a new stage of development—some call it the postindustrial age, some the information age. But the Soviet Union had not yet passed through the industrial stage. It was lagging further and further behind those processes that were making a renewal in the life of the world community possible. Not only was a leap forward in technology needed but fundamental change in the entire social and political process.

Of course it cannot be said that at the time we began perestroika we had everything thought out. In the early stages we all said, including myself, that perestroika was a continuation of the October revolution. Today I believe that that assertion contained a grain of truth but also an element of delusion.

The truth was that we were trying to carry out fundamental ideas that had been advanced by the October revolution but had not been realized: overcoming people's alienation from government and property, giving power to the people (and taking it away from the bureaucratic

---

[5] The Central Committee of the Communist Party of the Soviet Union was the governing body between party congress meetings. [Ed.]

[6] October 1917, the Bolshevik Revolution. [Ed.]

upper echelons), implanting democracy, and establishing true social justice.

The delusion was that at the time I, like most of us, assumed this could be accomplished by improving and refining the existing system. But as experience accumulated, it became clear that the crisis that had paralyzed the country in the late 1970s and early 1980s was systemic and not the result of isolated aberrations. The logic of how matters developed pointed to the need to penetrate the system to its very foundations and change it, not merely refine or perfect it. We were already talking about a gradual shift to a social market economy, to a democratic political system based on rule of law and the full guarantee of human rights.

This transition turned out to be extremely difficult and complicated, more complicated than it had seemed to us at first. Above all, this was because the totalitarian system possessed tremendous inertia. There was resistance from the party and government structures that constituted the solid internal framework of that system. The nomenklatura encouraged resistance. And this is understandable: Since it held the entire country in its hands, it would have to give up its unlimited power and privileges. Thus the entire perestroika era was filled with struggles—concealed at first and then more open, more fully exposed to public view—between the forces for change and those who opposed it, those who, especially after the first two years, simply began to sabotage change.

The complexity of the struggle stemmed from the fact that in 1985 the entire society—politically, ideologically, and spiritually—was still in the thrall of old customs and traditions. Great effort was required to overcome these traditions, as mentioned above. There was another factor. Destroying the old system would have been senseless if we did not simultaneously lay the foundations for a new life. And this was genuinely unexplored territory. The six-year perestroika era was a time filled with searching and discovery, gains and losses, breakthroughs in thought and action, as well as mistakes and oversights. The attempted coup in August 1991 interrupted perestroika. After that there were many developments, but they were along different lines, following different intentions. Still, in the relatively short span of six years we succeeded in doing a great deal. The reforms in China, incidentally, have been going on since 1974, and their most difficult problems still remain unsolved.

What specifically did we accomplish as a result of the stormy years of perestroika? The foundations of the totalitarian system were eliminated. Profound democratic changes were begun. Free general elections were held for the first time, allowing real choice. Freedom of the press and a multiparty system were guaranteed. Representative bodies of government were established, and the first steps toward a separation of powers were taken. Human rights (previously in our country these were only "so-called," reference to them invariably made only in scornful quotation marks) now became an unassailable principle. And freedom of conscience was also established.

Movement began toward a multistructured, or mixed, economy providing equality of rights among all forms of property. Economic freedom was made into law. The spirit of enterprise began to gain strength, and processes of privatization and the formation of joint stock companies got under way. Within the framework of our new land law, the peasantry was reborn and private farmers made their appearance. Millions of hectares of land were turned over to both rural and urban inhabitants. The first privately owned banks also came on the scene. The different nationalities and peoples were given the freedom to choose their own course of development. Searching for a democratic way to reform our multinational state, to transform it from a unitary state in practice into a national federation, we reached the threshold at which a new union treaty was to be signed, based on the recognition of the sovereignty of each republic along with the preservation of a common economic, social, and legal space that was necessary for all, including a common defense establishment.

The changes within our country inevitably led to a shift in foreign policy. The new course of perestroika predetermined renunciation of stereotypes and the confrontational methods of the past. It allowed for a rethinking of the main parameters of state security and the ways to ensure it. . . .

In other words, the foundations were laid for normal, democratic, and peaceful development of our country and its transformation into a normal member of the world community.

These are the decisive results of perestroika. Today, however, looking back through the prism of the past few years and taking into account the general trends of world development today, it seems insufficient to register these as the only results. Today it is evidently of special interest to state not only *what* was done but also *how* and *why* perestroika was able to achieve its results, and what its mistakes and miscalculations were.

Above all, *perestroika would have been simply impossible if there had not been a profound and critical reexamination not only of the problems confronting our country but a rethinking of all realities—both national and international.*

Previous conceptions of the world and its developmental trends and, correspondingly, of our country's place and role in the world were based, as we have said, on dogmas deeply rooted in our ideology, which essentially did not permit us to pursue a realistic policy. These conceptions had to be shattered and fundamentally new views worked out regarding our country's development and the surrounding world.

This task turned out to be far from simple. We had to renounce beliefs that for decades had been considered irrefutable truths, to reexamine the very methods and principles of leadership and action, indeed to rethink our surroundings entirely on a scientific basis (and not according to schemes inherited from ideological biases).

The product of this effort was the new thinking, which became the basis for all policy—both foreign and domestic—during perestroika. The point of departure for the new thinking was an attempt to evaluate everything not from the viewpoint of narrow class interests or even national interests but from the broader perspective: that of giving priority to the interests of all humanity with consideration for the increasingly apparent wholeness of the world, the interdependence of all countries and peoples, the humanist values formed over centuries.

The practical work of perestroika was to *renounce stereotypical ideological thinking and the dogmas of the past. This required a fresh view of the world and of ourselves with no preconceptions, taking into account the challenges of the present and the already evident trends of the future in the third millennium.*

During perestroika, and often now as well, the initiators of perestroika have been criticized for the absence of a "clear plan" for change. The habit developed over decades of having an all-inclusive regimentation of life. But the events of the perestroika years and of the subsequent period have plainly demonstrated the following: *At times of profound, fundamental change in the foundations of social development it is not only senseless but impossible to expect some sort of previously worked out "model" or a clear-cut outline of the transformations that will take place. This does not mean, however, the absence of a definite goal for the reforms, a distinct conception of their content and the main direction of their development.*

All this was present in perestroika: a profound democratization of public life and a guarantee of freedom of social and political choice. These goals were proclaimed and frequently reaffirmed. This did not exclude but presupposed the necessity to change one's specific reference points at each stage as matters proceeded and to engage in a constant search for optimal solutions.

An extremely important conclusion follows from the experience of perestroika: Even in a society formed under totalitarian conditions, democratic change is possible by *peaceful evolutionary means.* The problem of revolution and evolution, of the role and place of reforms in social development, is one of the eternal problems of history. In its inner content perestroika of course was a revolution. But in its form it was an evolutionary process, a process of reform.

Historically the USSR had grown ripe for a profound restructuring much earlier than the mid-1980s. But if we had not decided to begin this restructuring at the time we did, even though we were quite late in doing so, an explosion would have taken place in the USSR, one of tremendous destructive force. It would certainly have been called a revolution, but it would have been the catastrophic result of irresponsible leadership.

In the course of implementing change we did not succeed in avoiding bloodshed altogether. But that was a consequence solely of resistance by the opponents of perestroika in the upper echelons of the nomenklatura. On the whole the change from one system to another took place peacefully and by evolutionary means. Our having chosen a policy course that was supported from below by the masses made this peaceful transition possible. And our policy of glasnost played a decisive role in mobilizing the masses and winning their support.

Radical reforms in the context of the Soviet Union could only have been initiated from above by the leadership of the party and the country. This was predetermined by the very "nature" of the system — supercentralized management of all public life. This can also be explained by the inert condition of the masses, who had become used to carrying out orders and decisions handed down from above.

From the very beginning of the changes our country's leadership assigned primary importance to open communication with the people, including direct disclosure in order to explain the new course. Without the citizens' understanding and support, without their participation, it would not have been possible to move from dead center. That is why we initiated the policies of perestroika and glasnost simultaneously.

Like perestroika itself, glasnost made its way with considerable difficulty. The nomenklatura on all levels, which regarded the strictest secrecy and protection of authorities from criticism from below as the holy of holies of the regime, opposed glasnost in every way they could, both openly and secretly, trampling its first shoots in the local press. Even among the most sincere supporters of perestroika, the tradition over many years of making everything a secret made itself felt. But it was precisely glasnost that awakened people from their social slumber, helped them overcome indifference and passivity and become aware of the stake they had in change and of its important implications for their lives. Glasnost helped us to explain and promote awareness of the new realities and the essence of our new political course. In short, without glasnost there would have been no perestroika.

The question of the relation between ends and means is one of the key aspects of politics and of political activity. If the means do not correspond to the ends, or, still worse, if the means contradict the ends, this will lead to setbacks and failure. The Soviet Union's experience is convincing evidence of this. When we began perestroika as a process of democratic change, we had to ensure that the means used to carry out these changes were also democratic.

In essence, glasnost became the means for drawing people into political activity, for including them in the creation of a new life, and this, above all, corresponded to the essence of perestroika. Glasnost not only created conditions for implementing the intended reforms but also made it possible to overcome attempts to sabotage the policy of change.

We are indebted to glasnost for a profound psychological transformation in the public consciousness toward democracy, freedom, and the humanist values of civilization. Incidentally, this was one of the guarantees that the fundamental gains of this period would be irreversible.

Perestroika confirmed once again that the normal, democratic development of society rules out universal secrecy as a method of administration. Democratic development presupposes glasnost—that is, openness, freedom of information for all citizens and freedom of expression by them of their political, religious, and other views and convictions, freedom of criticism in the fullest sense of the word.

Why, then, did perestroika not succeed in achieving all its goals? The answer primarily involves the question of "harmonization" between political and economic change.

The dominant democratic aspect of perestroika meant that the accent was inevitably placed on political reform. The dialectic of our development during those years was such that serious changes in the economic sphere proved to be impossible without emancipating society politically, without ensuring freedom—that is, breaking the political structures of totalitarianism. And this was accomplished. But economic change lagged behind political change, and we did not succeed in developing economic change to the full extent.

3

NELSON MANDELA

Nobel Peace Prize Address, 1993

Democracy for South Africa meant racial democracy: political equality for all South Africans regardless of the color of their skin. It meant the end of apartheid, a system of legal racial segregation in jobs, housing, and access to the political process. It meant the end of the political domination of the 80 percent of South Africans who were black by the 10 percent who were white. In practice, it meant the defeat of the white-supremacist National Party that had ruled South Africa since 1948 and the victory of the mainly black African National Congress party, led by Nelson Mandela despite his imprisonment from 1962 to 1990.

A change of this magnitude was made even more momentous by the fact that it occurred relatively peacefully when National Party

Source: Acceptance Speech of the President of the African National Congress, Nelson Mandela, at the Nobel Peace Prize Award Ceremony: Oslo, Norway. December 10, 1993, http://www.nobelprize.org/nobel_prizes/peace/laureates/1993/mandela-lecture_en.html.

leader and South African president F. W. de Klerk released Mandela from prison in 1990 and scheduled elections that would include the previously outlawed African National Congress for 1994. As a consequence, the Noble Peace Prize committee awarded the 1993 prize jointly to Mandela and de Klerk.

The Nobel Peace Prize is not, of course, a democracy prize. Still, the realization of a political democracy in black-majority South Africa is what the Nobel committee celebrated. Mandela humbly accepted the prize, knowing the challenges that lay ahead in creating a democratic state in South Africa. What did he see as the elements of the democracy he hoped to create? What were his goals? What, if any, elements of democracy did he not include? How was his vision of democracy different from that of Gorbachev?

THINKING HISTORICALLY

The end of institutional racism in South Africa came about after domestic protests, starting in the black township of Soweto in 1976, attracted international attention. Western campaigns to boycott South African goods and investments gained support during the following decade. By the end of the Cold War, the support of anticommunist white South Africa by the United States became unnecessary as well as untenable. Thus, the Nobel Peace Prize acknowledged both a national and an international achievement. How does Mandela recognize the national context of the South African democratic revolution? How does he connect the arrival of democracy in South Africa with the global development of democracy and human rights?

Your Majesty the King,
Your Royal Highness,
Honourable Prime Minister,
Madame Gro Brundtland,
Ministers,
Members of Parliament and Ambassadors,
Esteemed Members of the Norwegian Nobel Committee,
Fellow Laureate, Mr. F. W. de Klerk,
Distinguished guests,
Friends, ladies and gentlemen:

I am indeed truly humbled to be standing here today to receive this year's Nobel Peace Prize.

I extend my heartfelt thanks to the Norwegian Nobel Committee for elevating us to the status of a Nobel Peace Prize winner.

I would also like to take this opportunity to congratulate my compatriot and fellow laureate, State President F. W. de Klerk, on his receipt of this high honour.

Together, we join two distinguished South Africans, the late Chief Albert Luthuli and His Grace Archbishop Desmond Tutu, to whose seminal contributions to the peaceful struggle against the evil system of apartheid you paid well-deserved tribute by awarding them the Nobel Peace Prize.

It will not be presumptuous of us if we also add, among our predecessors, the name of another outstanding Nobel Peace Prize winner, the late African-American statesman and internationalist, the Rev. Martin Luther King Jr.

He, too, grappled with and died in the effort to make a contribution to the just solution of the same great issues of the day which we have had to face as South Africans.

We speak here of the challenge of the dichotomies of war and peace, violence and non-violence, racism and human dignity, oppression and repression and liberty and human rights, poverty and freedom from want.

We stand here today as nothing more than a representative of the millions of our people who dared to rise up against a social system whose very essence is war, violence, racism, oppression, repression and the impoverishment of an entire people.

I am also here today as a representative of the millions of people across the globe, the anti-apartheid movement, the governments and organisations that joined with us, not to fight against South Africa as a country or any of its peoples, but to oppose an inhuman system and sue for a speedy end to the apartheid crime against humanity.

These countless human beings, both inside and outside our country, had the nobility of spirit to stand in the path of tyranny and injustice, without seeking selfish gain. They recognised that an injury to one is an injury to all and therefore acted together in defence of justice and a common human decency.

Because of their courage and persistence for many years, we can, today, even set the dates when all humanity will join together to celebrate one of the outstanding human victories of our century.

When that moment comes, we shall, together, rejoice in a common victory over racism, apartheid and white minority rule.

That triumph will finally bring to a close a history of five hundred years of African colonisation that began with the establishment of the Portuguese empire.

Thus, it will mark a great step forward in history and also serve as a common pledge of the peoples of the world to fight racism wherever it occurs and whatever guise it assumes.

At the southern tip of the continent of Africa, a rich reward is in the making, an invaluable gift is in the preparation, for those who suffered in the name of all humanity when they sacrificed everything—for liberty, peace, human dignity and human fulfilment.

This reward will not be measured in money. Nor can it be reckoned in the collective price of the rare metals and precious stones that rest in the bowels of the African soil we tread in the footsteps of our ancestors. It will and must be measured by the happiness and welfare of the children, at once the most vulnerable citizens in any society and the greatest of our treasures.

The children must, at last, play in the open veld, no longer tortured by the pangs of hunger or ravaged by disease or threatened with the scourge of ignorance, molestation and abuse, and no longer required to engage in deeds whose gravity exceeds the demands of their tender years.

In front of this distinguished audience, we commit the new South Africa to the relentless pursuit of the purposes defined in the World Declaration on the Survival, Protection and Development of Children.

The reward of which we have spoken will and must also be measured by the happiness and welfare of the mothers and fathers of these children, who must walk the earth without fear of being robbed, killed for political or material profit, or spat upon because they are beggars.

They too must be relieved of the heavy burden of despair which they carry in their hearts, born of hunger, homelessness and unemployment.

The value of that gift to all who have suffered will and must be measured by the happiness and welfare of all the people of our country, who will have torn down the inhuman walls that divide them.

These great masses will have turned their backs on the grave insult to human dignity which described some as masters and others as servants, and transformed each into a predator whose survival depended on the destruction of the other.

The value of our shared reward will and must be measured by the joyful peace which will triumph, because the common humanity that bonds both black and white into one human race, will have said to each one of us that we shall all live like the children of paradise.

Thus shall we live, because we will have created a society which recognises that all people are born equal, with each entitled in equal measure to life, liberty, prosperity, human rights and good governance.

Such a society should never allow again that there should be prisoners of conscience nor that any person's human rights should be violated.

Neither should it ever happen that once more the avenues to peaceful change are blocked by usurpers who seek to take power away from the people, in pursuit of their own, ignoble purposes.

In relation to these matters, we appeal to those who govern Burma that they release our fellow Nobel Peace Prize laureate, Aung San Suu Kyi, and engage her and those she represents in serious dialogue, for the benefit of all the people of Burma.

We pray that those who have the power to do so will, without further delay, permit that she uses her talents and energies for the greater good of the people of her country and humanity as a whole.

Far from the rough and tumble of the politics of our own country, I would like to take this opportunity to join the Norwegian Nobel Committee and pay tribute to my joint laureate, Mr. F. W. de Klerk.

He had the courage to admit that a terrible wrong had been done to our country and people through the imposition of the system of apartheid.

He had the foresight to understand and accept that all the people of South Africa must, through negotiations and as equal participants in the process, together determine what they want to make of their future.

But there are still some within our country who wrongly believe they can make a contribution to the cause of justice and peace by clinging to the shibboleths that have been proved to spell nothing but disaster.

It remains our hope that these, too, will be blessed with sufficient reason to realise that history will not be denied and that the new society cannot be created by reproducing the repugnant past, however refined or enticingly repackaged.

We live with the hope that as she battles to remake herself, South Africa will be like a microcosm of the new world that is striving to be born.

This must be a world of democracy and respect for human rights, a world freed from the horrors of poverty, hunger, deprivation and ignorance, relieved of the threat and the scourge of civil wars and external aggression and unburdened of the great tragedy of millions forced to become refugees.

The processes in which South Africa and Southern Africa as a whole are engaged, beckon and urge us all that we take this tide at the flood and make of this region a living example of what all people of conscience would like the world to be.

We do not believe that this Nobel Peace Prize is intended as a commendation for matters that have happened and passed.

We hear the voices which say that it is an appeal from all those, throughout the universe, who sought an end to the system of apartheid.

We understand their call, that we devote what remains of our lives to the use of our country's unique and painful experience to demonstrate, in practice, that the normal condition for human existence is democracy, justice, peace, non-racism, non-sexism, prosperity for everybody, a healthy environment and equality and solidarity among the peoples.

Moved by that appeal and inspired by the eminence you have thrust upon us, we undertake that we too will do what we can to contribute to the renewal of our world so that none should, in future, be described as the wretched of the earth.

Let it never be said by future generations that indifference, cynicism or selfishness made us fail to live up to the ideals of humanism which the Nobel Peace Prize encapsulates.

Let the strivings of us all prove Martin Luther King Jr. to have been correct, when he said that humanity can no longer be tragically bound to the starless midnight of racism and war.

Let the efforts of us all, prove that he was not a mere dreamer when he spoke of the beauty of genuine brotherhood and peace being more precious than diamonds or silver or gold.

Let a new age dawn!

Thank you.

4

GEORGE W. BUSH

Remarks at the 20th Anniversary of the National Endowment for Democracy, 2003

Democratic change in Argentina, Russia, and South Africa were, for the most part, national stories, independent of the United States. In fact, in Argentina, the military junta had enjoyed U.S. support, as had the apartheid regime in South Africa, until President Jimmy Carter took office in the late 1970s.

President George W. Bush (president, 2001–2009) claimed the march of democracy as a product of U.S. initiative and made its spread, especially in the Middle East, a cornerstone of his foreign policy. In this selection from a 2003 address to the conservative organization National Endowment for Democracy, he made his case. By this date, he had already invaded Iraq and deposed Saddam Hussein with the stated aim of starting the spread of democracy in the Middle East. What did he mean by *democracy*? How did he expect it would spread?

THINKING HISTORICALLY

How and why did President Bush give his plan historical continuity? How did he apply it to the specific context of the Middle East?

The roots of our democracy can be traced to England, and to its Parliament—and so can the roots of this organization. In June of 1982, President Ronald Reagan spoke at Westminster Palace and declared, the turning point had arrived in history. He argued that Soviet communism had failed, precisely because it did not respect its own people—their creativity, their genius and their rights.

President Reagan said that the day of Soviet tyranny was passing, that freedom had a momentum which would not be halted. He gave this organization its mandate: to add to the momentum of freedom across the world. Your mandate was important 20 years ago; it is equally important today.

A number of critics were dismissive of that speech by the President. According to one editorial of the time, "It seems hard to be a sophisticated European and also an admirer of Ronald Reagan." Some observers on both sides of the Atlantic pronounced the speech simplistic and naive,

---

Source: "Remarks by President George W. Bush at the 20th Anniversary of the National Endowment for Democracy," National Endowment for Democracy.

and even dangerous. In fact, Ronald Reagan's words were courageous and optimistic and entirely correct.

The great democratic movement President Reagan described was already well underway. In the early 1970s, there were about 40 democracies in the world. By the middle of that decade, Portugal and Spain and Greece held free elections. Soon there were new democracies in Latin America, and free institutions were spreading in Korea, in Taiwan, and in East Asia. This very week in 1989, there were protests in East Berlin and in Leipzig. By the end of that year, every communist dictatorship in Central America[1] had collapsed. Within another year, the South African government released Nelson Mandela. Four years later, he was elected president of his country—ascending, like Walesa and Havel, from prisoner of state to head of state.

As the 20th century ended, there were around 120 democracies in the world—and I can assure you more are on the way. Ronald Reagan would be pleased, and he would not be surprised.

We've witnessed, in little over a generation, the swiftest advance of freedom in the 2,500 year story of democracy. Historians in the future will offer their own explanations for why this happened. Yet we already know some of the reasons they will cite. It is no accident that the rise of so many democracies took place in a time when the world's most influential nation was itself a democracy.

The United States made military and moral commitments in Europe and Asia, which protected free nations from aggression, and created the conditions in which new democracies could flourish. As we provided security for whole nations, we also provided inspiration for oppressed peoples. In prison camps, in banned union meetings, in clandestine churches, men and women knew that the whole world was not sharing their own nightmare. They knew of at least one place—a bright and hopeful land—where freedom was valued and secure. And they prayed that America would not forget them, or forget the mission to promote liberty around the world. . . .

And now we must apply that lesson in our own time. We've reached another great turning point—and the resolve we show will shape the next stage of the world democratic movement.

Our commitment to democracy is tested in countries like Cuba and Burma and North Korea and Zimbabwe—outposts of oppression in our world. . . .

Our commitment to democracy is tested in China. That nation now has a sliver, a fragment of liberty. . . .

Our commitment to democracy is also tested in the Middle East, which is my focus today, and must be a focus of American policy for decades to come. . . .

---

[1] President Bush meant Central Europe. [Ed.]

In the words of a recent report by Arab scholars, the global wave of democracy has — and I quote — "barely reached the Arab states." They continue: "This freedom deficit undermines human development and is one of the most painful manifestations of lagging political development." The freedom deficit they describe has terrible consequences, of the people of the Middle East and for the world. In many Middle Eastern countries, poverty is deep and it is spreading, women lack rights and are denied schooling. Whole societies remain stagnant while the world moves ahead. These are not the failures of a culture or a religion. These are the failures of political and economic doctrines.

As the colonial era passed away, the Middle East saw the establishment of many military dictatorships. Some rulers adopted the dogmas of socialism, seized total control of political parties and the media and universities. They allied themselves with the Soviet bloc and with international terrorism. Dictators in Iraq and Syria promised the restoration of national honor, a return to ancient glories. They've left instead a legacy of torture, oppression, misery, and ruin.

Other men, and groups of men, have gained influence in the Middle East and beyond through an ideology of theocratic terror. Behind their language of religion is the ambition for absolute political power. Ruling cabals like the Taliban show their version of religious piety in public whippings of women, ruthless suppression of any difference or dissent, and support for terrorists who arm and train to murder the innocent. The Taliban promised religious purity and national pride. Instead, by systematically destroying a proud and working society, they left behind suffering and starvation.

Many Middle Eastern governments now understand that military dictatorship and theocratic rule are a straight, smooth highway to nowhere. But some governments still cling to the old habits of central control. There are governments that still fear and repress independent thought and creativity, and private enterprise — the human qualities that make for a — strong and successful societies. Even when these nations have vast natural resources, they do not respect or develop their greatest resources — the talent and energy of men and women working and living in freedom.

Instead of dwelling on past wrongs and blaming others, governments in the Middle East need to confront real problems, and serve the true interests of their nations. The good and capable people of the Middle East all deserve responsible leadership. For too long, many people in that region have been victims and subjects — they deserve to be active citizens.

Governments across the Middle East and North Africa are beginning to see the need for change. Morocco has a diverse new parliament; King Mohammed has urged it to extend rights to women. Here is how His Majesty explained his reforms to parliament: "How can society achieve progress while women, who represent half the nation, see their rights violated and suffer as a result of injustice, violence, and marginalization, notwithstanding the dignity and justice granted to them by our glorious religion?" The King of Morocco is correct: The future of Muslim nations will be better for all with the full participation of women.

In Bahrain last year, citizens elected their own parliament for the first time in nearly three decades. Oman has extended the vote to all adult citizens; Qatar has a new constitution; Yemen has a multiparty political system; Kuwait has a directly elected national assembly; and Jordan held historic elections this summer. Recent surveys in Arab nations reveal broad support for political pluralism, the rule of law, and free speech. These are the stirrings of Middle Eastern democracy, and they carry the promise of greater change to come.

As changes come to the Middle Eastern region, those with power should ask themselves: Will they be remembered for resisting reform, or for leading it? In Iran, the demand for democracy is strong and broad, as we saw last month when thousands gathered to welcome home Shirin Ebadi, the winner of the Nobel Peace Prize. The regime in Teheran must heed the democratic demands of the Iranian people, or lose its last claim to legitimacy.

For the Palestinian people, the only path to independence and dignity and progress is the path of democracy. And the Palestinian leaders who block and undermine democratic reform, and feed hatred and encourage violence are not leaders at all. They're the main obstacles to peace, and to the success of the Palestinian people.

The Saudi government is taking first steps toward reform, including a plan for gradual introduction of elections. By giving the Saudi people a greater role in their own society, the Saudi government can demonstrate true leadership in the region.

The great and proud nation of Egypt has shown the way toward peace in the Middle East, and now should show the way toward democracy in the Middle East. Champions of democracy in the region understand that democracy is not perfect, it is not the path to utopia, but it's the only path to national success and dignity.

As we watch and encourage reforms in the region, we are mindful that modernization is not the same as Westernization. Representative governments in the Middle East will reflect their own cultures. They will not, and should not, look like us. Democratic nations may be constitutional monarchies, federal republics, or parliamentary systems. And working democracies always need time to develop—as did our own. We've taken a 200-year journey toward inclusion and justice—and this makes us patient and understanding as other nations are at different stages of this journey.

There are, however, essential principles common to every successful society, in every culture. Successful societies limit the power of the state and the power of the military—so that governments respond to the will of the people, and not the will of an elite. Successful societies protect freedom with the consistent and impartial rule of law, instead of selecting applying—selectively applying the law to punish political opponents. Successful societies allow room for healthy civic institutions—for political parties and labor unions and independent newspapers and broadcast media. Successful societies guarantee religious liberty—the right to serve and honor God without fear of persecution. Successful societies privatize their economies, and secure the rights of property. They prohibit and punish official corruption, and invest in the health and education of their people. They recognize the rights of women. And instead of directing hatred and resentment against others, successful societies appeal to the hopes of their own people.

These vital principles are being applied in the nations of Afghanistan and Iraq. With the steady leadership of President Karzai, the people of Afghanistan are building a modern and peaceful government. Next month, 500 delegates will convene a national assembly in Kabul to approve a new Afghan constitution. The proposed draft would establish a bicameral parliament, set national elections next year, and recognize Afghanistan's Muslim identity, while protecting the rights of all citizens. Afghanistan faces continuing economic and security challenges—it will face those challenges as a free and stable democracy.

In Iraq, the Coalition Provisional Authority and the Iraqi Governing Council are also working together to build a democracy—and after three decades of tyranny, this work is not easy. The former dictator ruled by terror and treachery, and left deeply ingrained habits of fear and distrust. Remnants of his regime, joined by foreign terrorists, continue their battle against order and against civilization. Our coalition is responding to recent attacks with precision raids, guided by intelligence provided by the Iraqis, themselves. And we're working closely with Iraqi citizens as they prepare a constitution, as they move toward free elections and take increasing responsibility for their own affairs. As in the defense of Greece in 1947, and later in the Berlin Airlift, the strength and will of free peoples are now being tested before a watching world. And we will meet this test.

Securing democracy in Iraq is the work of many hands. American and coalition forces are sacrificing for the peace of Iraq and for the security of free nations. Aid workers from many countries are facing danger to help the Iraqi people. The National Endowment for Democracy is promoting women's rights, and training Iraqi journalists, and teaching the skills of political participation. Iraqis, themselves—police and borders guards and local officials—are joining in the work and they are sharing in the sacrifice.

This is a massive and difficult undertaking—it is worth our effort, it is worth our sacrifice, because we know the stakes. The failure of Iraqi democracy would embolden terrorists around the world, increase dangers to the American people, and extinguish the hopes of millions in the region. Iraqi democracy will succeed—and that success will send forth the news, from Damascus to Teheran—that freedom can be the future of every nation. The establishment of a free Iraq at the heart of the Middle East will be a watershed event in the global democratic revolution.

Sixty years of Western nations excusing and accommodating the lack of freedom in the Middle East did nothing to make us safe—because in the long run, stability cannot be purchased at the expense of liberty. As long as the Middle East remains a place where freedom does not flourish, it will remain a place of stagnation, resentment, and violence ready for export. And with the spread of weapons that can bring catastrophic harm to our country and to our friends, it would be reckless to accept the status quo.

Therefore, the United States has adopted a new policy, a forward strategy of freedom in the Middle East. This strategy requires the same persistence and energy and idealism we have shown before. And it will yield the same results. As in Europe, as in Asia, as in every region of the world, the advance of freedom leads to peace.

The advance of freedom is the calling of our time; it is the calling of our country. From the Fourteen Points to the Four Freedoms, to the Speech at Westminster, America has put our power at the service of principle. We believe that liberty is the design of nature; we believe that liberty is the direction of history. We believe that human fulfillment and excellence come in the responsible exercise of liberty. And we believe that freedom—the freedom we prize—is not for us alone, it is the right and the capacity of all mankind.

Working for the spread of freedom can be hard. Yet, America has accomplished hard tasks before. Our nation is strong; we're strong of heart. And we're not alone. Freedom is finding allies in every country; freedom finds allies in every culture. And as we meet the terror and violence of the world, we can be certain the author of freedom is not indifferent to the fate of freedom.

With all the tests and all the challenges of our age, this is, above all, the age of liberty. Each of you at this Endowment is fully engaged in the great cause of liberty. And I thank you. May God bless your work. And may God continue to bless America.

5

NOAM CHOMSKY

"America Paved the Way for ISIS," 2015

Writing twelve years after President Bush's 2003 address to the National Endowment for Democracy, Noam Chomsky paints a very different picture of the role of the United States in the Middle East. In this selection, taken from an interview with Chomsky in 2015, he supports the view that the U.S.-led invasion of Iraq led to sectarian civil war and the rise of terrorism exemplified by ISIS (the "Islamic State of Iraq and Syria") rather than to democracy.

Chomsky foresaw these developments. In a lecture at the University of Florida in 2003, Chomsky, a philosopher, linguist, and critic on the left, echoed the warning of many others and opposed Bush's invasion of Iraq: "The United States has succeeded in turning Iraq into a haven for terrorists for the first time. It was horrible in all sorts of ways but was not involved in international terrorism before, and now it is a center of it."[1]

How and why, according to Chomsky, did the United States frustrate secular, democratic tendencies in the Middle East? Based on this and the previous reading, what were the strengths and weaknesses of the United States in spreading democracy in the world? Are we living in an age of increasing democracy or increasing disorder?

THINKING HISTORICALLY

Context is important in interpreting change. In early 2011, a series of popular revolts against dictatorial and corrupt governments spread across North Africa and the Middle East. It was called an "Arab Spring." It appeared to herald a wave of democratic movements not unlike those that had previously swept through Russia, Eastern Europe, and South America. In that context, George Bush's predictions about the spread of democracy, if not his actions, seemed more tenable.

But even by 2011, there were no actual democracies in the Middle East (only Israel claimed to be one). Enough hopeful sprouts appeared in Egypt, Libya, and even Iraq and Syria to make future democracy seem plausible, but these democratic aspirations have

---

[1] "Where's the Security in Bush's National Security Strategy?" Noam Chomsky. Delivered at the University of Florida, October 21, 2003, accessed at https://chomsky.info/20031021, October 3, 2015.

Source: Noam Chomsky, "The World of Our Grandchildren," *Jacobin*, February 13, 2015. Reprinted as "America Paved the Way for ISIS, *Salon*, October 30, 2015.

wilted for the time being. And in Iraq and Syria, the rise of ever more extremist groups has infected Muslim societies worldwide.

How does this new context, only a few years after the Arab Spring, change our evaluations of the arguments of Bush and Chomsky? How might we minimize the effects of present contexts in understanding the past and the way things are changing?

The Middle East is engulfed in flames, from Libya to Iraq. There are new jihadi groups. The current focus is on ISIS. What about ISIS and its origins?

There's an interesting interview that just appeared a couple of days ago with Graham Fuller, a former CIA officer, one of the leading intelligence and mainstream analysts of the Middle East. The title is "The United States Created ISIS." . . .

He [Fuller] hastens to point out that he doesn't mean the US decided to put ISIS into existence and then funded it. His point is—and I think it's accurate—that the US created the background out of which ISIS grew and developed. Part of it was just the standard sledgehammer approach: smash up what you don't like.

In 2003, the US and Britain invaded Iraq, a major crime. . . . The invasion was devastating to Iraq. Iraq had already been virtually destroyed, first of all by the decade-long war with Iran in which, incidentally, Iraq was backed by the US, and then the decade of sanctions.

They [the sanctions] were described as "genocidal" by the respected international diplomats who administered them, and both resigned in protest for that reason. They [the sanctions] devastated the civilian society, they strengthened the dictator [Saddam Hussein], compelled the population to rely on him for survival. That's probably the reason he wasn't sent on the path of a whole stream of other dictators who were overthrown.

Finally, the US just decided to attack the country in 2003. The attack is compared by many Iraqis to the Mongol invasion of a thousand years earlier. Very destructive. Hundreds of thousands of people killed, millions of refugees, millions of other displaced persons, destruction of the archeological richness and wealth of the country back to [ancient] Sumeria.

One of the effects of the invasion was immediately to institute sectarian divisions. Part of the brilliance of the invasion force and its civilian director, Paul Bremer, was to separate the sects, Sunni, Shi'a, Kurd, from one another, set them at each other's throats. Within a couple of years, there was a major, brutal sectarian conflict incited by the invasion.

You can see it if you look at Baghdad. If you take a map of Baghdad in, say, 2002, it's a mixed city: Sunni and Shi'a are living in the same neighborhoods, they're intermarried. In fact, sometimes they didn't even know who was Sunni and who was Shi'a. It's like knowing whether your friends are in one Protestant group or another Protestant group. There were differences but it was not hostile.

In fact, for a couple of years both sides were saying: there will never be Sunni–Shi'a conflicts. We're too intermingled in the nature of our lives, where we live, and so on. By 2006 there was a raging war. That conflict spread to the whole region. By now, the whole region is being torn apart by Sunni–Shi'a conflicts.

The natural dynamics of a conflict like that is that the most extreme elements begin to take over. They had roots. Their roots are in the major US ally, Saudi Arabia. That's been the major US ally in the region as long as the US has been seriously involved there, in fact, since the foundation of the Saudi state. It's kind of a family dictatorship. The reason is it has a huge amount of oil.

Britain, before the US, had typically preferred radical Islamism to secular nationalism. And when the US took over, it essentially took the same stand. Radical Islam is centered in Saudi Arabia. It's the most extremist, radical Islamic state in the world. It makes Iran look like a tolerant, modern country by comparison, and, of course, the secular parts of the Arab Middle East even more so.

It's not only directed by an extremist version of Islam, the Wahhabi Salafi version, but it's also a missionary state. So it uses its huge oil resources to promulgate these doctrines throughout the region. It establishes schools, mosques, clerics, all over the place, from Pakistan to North Africa.

An extremist version of Saudi extremism is the doctrine that was picked up by ISIS. So it grew ideologically out of the most extremist form of Islam, the Saudi version, and the conflicts that were engendered by the US sledgehammer that smashed up Iraq and has now spread everywhere. That's what Fuller means.

Saudi Arabia not only provides the ideological core that led to the ISIS radical extremism, but it also funds them. Not the Saudi government, but wealthy Saudis, wealthy Kuwaitis, and others provide the funding and the ideological support for these jihadi groups that are springing up all over the place. This attack on the region by the US and Britain is the source, where this thing originates. That's what Fuller meant by saying the United States created ISIS.

You can be pretty confident that as conflicts develop, they will become more extremist. The most brutal, harshest groups will take over. That's what happens when violence becomes the means of interaction. It's almost automatic. That's true in neighborhoods, it's true in international affairs. The dynamics are perfectly evident. That's what's happening. That's where ISIS comes from. If they manage to destroy ISIS, they will have something more extreme on their hands.

HAGAI EL-AD

"Israel's Charade of Democracy," 2015

Israel is often called the only democracy in the Middle East, especially in the media of Israel and the United States. In this op-ed from the *New York Times*, an Israeli human rights advocate challenges that characterization. Hagai El-Ad is the executive director of B'Tselem, the Israeli Information Center for Human Rights in the Occupied Territories. What does he see as the limitations to his government's claims to democracy? Why does he believe Israel has become more democratic or less democratic?

THINKING HISTORICALLY

Finding context in a long-term struggle like the Israel-Palestine conflict in the Middle East is something like the child's game of Who Started It? Israelis would say that we must see the context of Palestinian attacks on Israelis. Palestinians would say that such attacks are inevitable responses to colonial occupation. Israelis would say they were there first. How do we decide which context is relevant, or how far back we should go in determining "who started it?"

Israel's occupation of the Palestinian territories is nearing the half-century mark, and Israel's new right-wing government offers little hope of ending it. Nevertheless, the new government promises something else of value: clarity. And with that clarity, the opportunity to challenge the prolonged lie of the occupation's "temporary" status. For if the occupation has become permanent in all but its name, what about the voting rights of Palestinians?

Two months ago, on election day in Israel, Prime Minister Benjamin Netanyahu declared that Israel's Arab citizens were flocking to the polls "in droves"—a clear effort to cast the voting of one-fifth of Israel's citizens as a danger to be counteracted. That undermined basic democratic principles, but it paled in contrast to the status of the Palestinian population living next door in territories under direct or indirect Israeli rule. They have no say at all in choosing the government of the occupying power that is in ultimate command of their fate.

If you look at all the land Israel controls between the Jordan and the Mediterranean, that area contains some 8.3 million Israelis and Palestinians of voting age. Roughly 30 percent—about 2.5 million—are Palestinians living outside Israel under varying degrees of Israeli control—in East Jerusalem, the West Bank and the Gaza Strip. They have some ability to

---

Source: Hagai El-Ad, "Israel's Charade of Democracy," *New York Times*, May 31, 2015.

elect Palestinian bodies with limited functions. But they are powerless to choose Israeli officials, who make the weightiest decisions affecting them.

International humanitarian law does not grant a people living under temporary military occupation the right to vote for the institutions of the occupying power. But "temporary" is the operative word. Military occupations are meant to have an end. And common sense says half a century is not "temporary."

Nevertheless, that is the basis for denying Palestinians their political rights: Their status is temporary, we are told, until a political agreement with Israel allows them to vote for sovereign Palestinian institutions. Now the chances of that happening are more clear. On the eve of elections, Mr. Netanyahu promised that there would be no Palestinian state while he is in office.

Does that mean nobody in the occupied territories has a meaningful vote? No. In fact, some people do: Israeli settlers.

In August 1970, the Israeli parliament, the Knesset, discussed amending the Knesset Election Law, which stipulated that Israelis—with few exceptions like diplomats on duty abroad—had to be inside Israel to vote. The amendment sought to expand the exception to include Israelis "residing in the territories held by the Israel Defense Force." In other words, Israeli settlers could vote for the Knesset from outside Israel; their Palestinian neighbors could not participate from anywhere.

In a Knesset session discussing the amendment before it passed, one legislator and peace activist, Uri Avnery, expressed a widely held belief that peace initiatives would soon make the amendment obsolete. He expressed the hope that "it won't be long—a year, a year and a half, two at most—before the thing called 'the held territories' is no more, and the I.D.F. pulls back into Israel's borders."

More than four decades later, what has become obsolete is not the amendment, but rather the accuracy of a description of Knesset elections often heard here: general, national, direct, equal, confidential and proportional.

How can elections be "general" when millions of people under Israel's control for almost 50 years cannot take part in electing the institutions that hold sway over them? Let's face it. Only the first six of Israel's parliamentary elections—those held before 1967—were truly "general." Even though the Palestinian Arab citizens of Israel proper were under military rule inside its borders at the time, they could vote.

Settlers now have voted in their communities in 14 Knesset elections. Over time, their numbers rose from a few hundred to hundreds of thousands. Yet one thing remained constant: Millions of Palestinians could not cast a meaningful vote, even as the voting of their settler neighbors—citizens of an occupying power—helped decide the fate of the disenfranchised.

To be sure, after the Oslo Accords were signed in 1993, Palestinians in the occupied territories got to cast ballots for some institutions of their own. But Palestinian independence never came to pass, and the interim partial autonomy established in its stead underscored how "temporariness" is abused while ultimate control remains with Israel.

The Oslo Accords themselves were meant to be an interim arrangement, in effect for five years. The most recent Palestinian vote under them, in 2006, proved of little value to the Palestinians; the results were set aside after Hamas emerged as the winner in the new Palestinian parliament — whose autonomous powers in effect merely relieved Israel of responsibilities for infrastructure, health care and education.

In reality, the Palestinian Authority remains subject to the whims of the occupying power — as was demonstrated most recently when Israel froze (and then unfroze) the transfer of Palestinian tax revenues to it.

All this is shameful. And one of the occupation's most shameful aspects is the democratic facade that obscures an undemocratic and oppressive reality. Israel's use of military force against Palestinians is one variety of violence. Its patronizing disregard for millions of subjects, while boasting of its own "celebration of democracy," is violence of another kind — violence to history, reality and the truth.

A day will come when this occupation ends. It may end with one state, two states, or something else. That specific political choice is beyond the deeper question of human rights, as long as the option eventually chosen respects the human rights of all. For now, the one choice we cannot make is to continue calling the current reality democratic and the occupation temporary.

Clarity may be of value after all, if it helps bring the occupation's end sooner.

7

Occupy Wall Street, 2011

In the wake of a global financial crisis in 2008 and the following "Great Recession" that in some countries duplicated the effects of the Great Depression of the 1930s, a number of movements sprang up in opposition to what were seen as the progenitors of the crisis: Wall Street, corporations, crony capitalism, government support of big money, and economic inequality. One of the most visible of these protests, because of its location, was Occupy Wall Street. But similar groups sprang up in cities in the United States and throughout the world. Here we see a declaration from the New York group as well as images from protests on both Wall Street and in Adelaide, New Zealand.

Source: http://www.nycga.net/resources/declaration/ or http://occupywallst.org/forum /first-official-release-from-occupy-wall-street/.

Critics of the protests frequently said that it was not clear what the protesters wanted. What does the New York document tell you about the demands of the protesters? Do they seem to be all over the map, or is there a unifying theme? In what ways would the realization of these goals increase democracy?

Finally, look at the two photos. Do they suggest diverse protests across the globe or a considerable degree of consensus? Are these images from opposite sides of the world distinct or interchangeable?

THINKING HISTORICALLY

The demands in the New York declaration spring from the specific context of the financial crisis in the United States. Yet the authors reach out to connect with movements throughout the world. How does a national context become a global context? What phrases or stylistic features connect this document to other declarations or manifestos of the past?

Declaration of the Occupation of New York City

This document was accepted by the NYC General Assembly on September 29, 2011.

As we gather together in solidarity to express a feeling of mass injustice, we must not lose sight of what brought us together. We write so that all people who feel wronged by the corporate forces of the world can know that we are your allies.

As one people, united, we acknowledge the reality: that the future of the human race requires the cooperation of its members; that our system must protect our rights, and upon corruption of that system, it is up to the individuals to protect their own rights, and those of their neighbors; that a democratic government derives its just power from the people, but corporations do not seek consent to extract wealth from the people and the Earth; and that no true democracy is attainable when the process is determined by economic power. We come to you at a time when corporations, which place profit over people, self-interest over justice, and oppression over equality, run our governments. We have peaceably assembled here, as is our right, to let these facts be known.

- They have taken our houses through an illegal foreclosure process, despite not having the original mortgage.
- They have taken bailouts from taxpayers with impunity, and continue to give Executives exorbitant bonuses.

- They have perpetuated inequality and discrimination in the workplace based on age, the color of one's skin, sex, gender identity and sexual orientation.
- They have poisoned the food supply through negligence, and undermined the farming system through monopolization.
- They have profited off of the torture, confinement, and cruel treatment of countless animals, and actively hide these practices.
- They have continuously sought to strip employees of the right to negotiate for better pay and safer working conditions.
- They have held students hostage with tens of thousands of dollars of debt on education, which is itself a human right.
- They have consistently outsourced labor and used that outsourcing as leverage to cut workers' healthcare and pay.
- They have influenced the courts to achieve the same rights as people, with none of the culpability or responsibility.
- They have spent millions of dollars on legal teams that look for ways to get them out of contracts in regards to health insurance.
- They have sold our privacy as a commodity.
- They have used the military and police force to prevent freedom of the press.
- They have deliberately declined to recall faulty products endangering lives in pursuit of profit.
- They determine economic policy, despite the catastrophic failures their policies have produced and continue to produce.
- They have donated large sums of money to politicians, who are responsible for regulating them.
- They continue to block alternate forms of energy to keep us dependent on oil.
- They continue to block generic forms of medicine that could save people's lives or provide relief in order to protect investments that have already turned a substantial profit.
- They have purposely covered up oil spills, accidents, faulty bookkeeping, and inactive ingredients in pursuit of profit.
- They purposefully keep people misinformed and fearful through their control of the media.
- They have accepted private contracts to murder prisoners even when presented with serious doubts about their guilt.
- They have perpetuated colonialism at home and abroad.
- They have participated in the torture and murder of innocent civilians overseas.
- They continue to create weapons of mass destruction in order to receive government contracts.

To the people of the world,

We, the New York City General Assembly occupying Wall Street in Liberty Square, urge you to assert your power.

Figure 27.1 Occupy Wall Street, 2011.
Source: © Tomas Abad / Alamy Stock Photo.

Figure 27.2 Occupy Auckland, New Zealand, 2011.
Source: © Kim Ludbrook / epa / Corbis.

Exercise your right to peaceably assemble; occupy public space; create a process to address the problems we face, and generate solutions accessible to everyone.

To all communities that take action and form groups in the spirit of direct democracy, we offer support, documentation, and all of the resources at our disposal.

Join us and make your voices heard!

■ REFLECTIONS

This chapter has argued that democracy is new and spreading, especially in recent years and decades. But any argument has to bear the burden of a counterargument. How might we counter the argument of this chapter?

First we might point out that a claim for recent years or decades is always subject to the near-sightedness of the present. Recent events and movements that seem important now may well disappear from the longer view a hundred or five hundred years from now. A century from now, will the six years of Gorbachev's reform become a blip, possibly like the Russian Revolution of 1905 or even that of 1917, in a long history of continued Czarism from Saint Vladimir I's rule during the tenth century through Putin VI's rule in the twenty-second century? Will the Arab Spring seem like the seasonal change the term implies rather than the beginning of a new age? Has Egypt seen its last pharaoh or was Mubarak only the most recent?

This line of questioning rests, I think too much, on a belief that the past is far more continuous than it is. Many other fifty-year periods of the past experienced as many protests as our own age. Many other historical periods produced protests of the have-nots against the haves. But the ideas and vocabulary of democracy are certainly new at least to recent centuries. No peasant uprising of the ancient or medieval world called for elected representatives, universal suffrage, equality before the law, the people as source of the law, freedom of expression, belief, and religion, universal education, social justice, and human rights. These are all principles and practices that have evolved and developed over the last couple of centuries. They all have earlier roots, but taken together they form a set of hopes, expectations, and experiences that are distinctly modern. Times *do* change.

A second line of criticism might run like this. Even if democracy is a modern idea and experience, how can we certify a flowering in a couple of protests, many of which have been thwarted or defeated?

Gorbachev's democratization, after all, occurred twenty-five years ago and even Russians do not remember it fondly. Some of the democratic gains that were won by Gorbachev by 1991 receded in the following years under Boris Yeltsin, first president of the Russian Federation (1991–1999), and Vladimir Putin (president and prime minister since 1999). To take one indicator of glasnost—press freedom—since 1993 over 200 Russian journalists have been murdered, making Russia the third most dangerous country in the world for a free press. Gorbachev today calls for a new wave of democratic protests in Russia: something like the Arab Spring. And what about the Arab Spring? Five years on, the Arab Spring has turned into dark winter. In Egypt, the military old guard imposes a less forgiving police-state than the one the revolution challenged. In Tunisia, the achievement of democratic revolution, one Tunisian recently quipped, is that now "everyone is above the law."[1] In Libya, the revolution that deposed Gaddafi reverted to tribal war, the uprising in Syria led to sectarian conflict and civil war, and those of Bahrain and Yemen were crushed (with some U.S. support).

To this argument, I would respond that the Arab revolution is definitely a work in progress. It occurs in a part of the world where democracy was least expected. The same might be said of the former Soviet Union. Gorbachev started a process that unleashed democratic and national independence movements throughout the former Soviet dominions. Some of these continue to be controlled by single parties or strong men, but not all. Czechoslovakia managed a peaceful Velvet Revolution and then a peaceful divorce between the Czech Republic and Slovakia. Poland and Hungary have become viable democracies. The Baltic states—Estonia, Lithuania, and Latvia—are independent republics. Many of the former Soviet states like Ukraine, Belarus, and "the stans" are independent. And, perhaps most remarkably of all, the former East Germany became independent, then part of a unified German state, one of the most democratic in Europe. One can carp about backsliding in Russia and the rise of supernationalists in Hungary, but there is no way to dismiss the numbers of people or countries who now govern themselves. Their example and the example of even temporarily successful democratic revolutions from the Philippines to Paraguay have buttressed the expectation that self-government in a free society is the right of all.

Democracy is not a light turned on, or off. It is a process that advances, or recedes. Still the advances are more contagious and longer lasting, at least in the mind. Few want to return to the conditions of dictatorship. But the process is rarely smooth. There are those in any

---

[1] Quoted by Michael J. Totten, Dispatches, April 18, 2012, at http://www.worldaffairsjournal.org/blogs/michael-j-totten.

society who lose privilege or power in a democratic revolution. And they are, by definition, the privileged and powerful.

The Mothers of the Disappeared still gather around the Plaza de Mayo; they still seek a full accounting for the acts of state terrorism under the military junta of the 1970s. Students in Chile are fighting battles fought by their parents and grandparents. Latin Americans celebrate democratic and independence movements that go back hundreds of years, but that have still not been fully realized. Indeed, in the Americas and the rest of the world the goalposts have moved since the days when democratic states accepted enslaved Africans, invisible Indians, and colonial subjects. Recent claims for human rights, freedom from sexual or gender discrimination, and international jurisdiction over war crimes and genocide are all extensions of our democratic expectations. Failure or retrenchment can be seen as the setting of the next battle rather than a sign that democracy failed or, worse, that it doesn't work.

Democratic demands in the twenty-first century reach further than ever before. Likewise, the conditions for achieving democracy have also expanded. A democracy that was limited to white men of the propertied class could function with an educational system that ignored everyone else. A mass democracy requires a mass citizenry educated to think and participate intelligently. It requires what Franklin D. Roosevelt called "freedom from want" to allow all citizens the time and resources to participate. And it requires the level playing field, unencumbered by special interests with private agendas. The early years of modern liberal democracy heard the call for the separation of church and state. Today we hear the call for the separation of corporations and the state. The effort to create the public space where citizens can create their common world continues.

28

Globalization

The World, 1990 to the Present

■ HISTORICAL CONTEXT

Globalization is a term used by historians, economists, politicians, religious leaders, social reformers, business people, and average citizens to describe large-scale changes and trends in the world today. It is often defined as a complex phenomenon whereby individuals, nations, and regions of the world become increasingly integrated and interdependent, while national and traditional identities are diminished. Although it is a widely used term, *globalization* is also a controversial and widely debated topic. Is globalization really a new phenomenon, or is it a continuation of earlier trends? Is it driven by technological forces or economic forces, or both? Does it enrich or impoverish? Is it democratizing or antidemocratic? Is it generally a positive or negative thing?

Some limit the definition of globalization to the global integration driven by the development of the international market economy in the last twenty to forty years. Worldwide integration dates back much further, however, and has important technological, cultural, and political causes as well. In fact, all of human history can be understood as the story of increased interaction on a limited planet. Ancient empires brought diverse peoples from vast regions of the world together under single administrations. These empires, connected by land or maritime routes, interacted with each other through trade and exploration, exchanging goods as well as ideas. The unification of the Eastern and Western hemispheres after 1492 was a major step in the globalization of crops, peoples, cultures, and diseases. The industrial revolution joined countries and continents in ever vaster and faster transportation and communication networks. The great colonial empires that developed during the eighteenth and nineteenth centuries integrated the populations of far-flung areas of the world. The commercial aspects of these developments cannot be divorced from religious zeal, technological innovations, and political motives, which were often driving factors.

The current era of economic globalization is largely a product of the industrial capitalist world, roughly dating back to the middle of the nineteenth century. We might call the period between 1850 and 1914 the first great age of globalization in the modern sense. It was the age of ocean liners, mass migrations, undersea telegraph cables, transcontinental railroads, refrigeration, and preserved canned foods, when huge European empires dramatically reduced the number of sovereign states in the world. The period ended with World War I, which not only dug trenches between nations and wiped out a generation of future migrants and visitors, but also planted seeds of animosity that festered for decades, strangling the growth of international trade, interaction, and immigration.

Since the conclusion of World War II in 1945, and increasingly since the end of the Cold War in 1989, political and technological developments have enabled economic globalization on a wider scale and at a faster pace than occurred during the previous age of steamships and telegraphs. The collapse of the Soviet Union and international communism unleashed the forces of market capitalism as never before. Jet travel, satellite technology, mobile phones, and the World Wide Web have revived global integration and enabled the global marketplace. The United States, the World Bank, and the International Monetary Fund led in the creation of regional and international free-trade agreements, the reduction of tariffs, and the removal of national trade barriers, touting these changes as agents of material progress and democratic transformation. Yet these changes have also elicited wide-ranging resistance in peaceful protests, especially against the West's economic dominance, and violent ones against the West's political and cultural domination, such as the terrorist attacks on September 11, 2001.

Multinational companies are now able to generate great wealth by moving capital, labor, raw materials, and finished products through international markets at increasing speeds and with lasting impact. This economic globalization has profound cultural ramifications; increasingly the peoples of the world are watching the same films and television programs, speaking the same languages, wearing the same clothes, enjoying the same amusements, and listening to the same music. Whether free-market capitalism lifts all boats, or only yachts, is a hotly debated issue today.

■ THINKING HISTORICALLY

Understanding Process

What are the most important ways in which the world is changing? What are the most significant and powerful forces of change? What is the engine that is driving our world? These are the big questions raised at the end of historical investigation. They also arise at the beginning, as the assumptions that shape our specific investigations. *Globalization* is one of the words most frequently used to describe the big changes that are occurring in our world. All of the readings in this chapter assume or describe some kind of global integration as a dominant driver of the world in which we live. This chapter asks you to think about large-scale historical processes. It asks you to examine globalization as one of the most important of these processes. It asks you to reflect on what globalization means and what causes it. How does each of these authors use the term? Do the authors see this process as primarily commercial and market-driven, or do they view it as a matter of culture or politics? Does globalization come from one place or many, from a center outwards, or from one kind of society to another? Is globalization linear or unidirectional, or does it have differing, even opposite effects? What do these writers, thinkers, and activists believe about the most important changes transforming our world? And what do you think?

1

SHERIF HETATA

Dollarization, 1998

Sherif Hetata is an Egyptian intellectual, novelist, and activist who was originally trained as a medical doctor. He and his wife, the prominent feminist writer Nawal El-Saadawi, have worked together to promote reform in Egypt and the larger Arab world. In this presentation given at a conference on globalization, Hetata outlines the global economy's homogenizing effects on culture. Through what historic lens does Hetata view globalization? What links does he make between globalization and imperialism? What do you think of his argument?

Source: Sherif Hetata, "Dollarization, Fragmentation, and God," in *The Cultures of Globalization*, ed. Fredric Jameson and Masao Miyoshi (Durham, NC: Duke University Press, 1998), 273–74, 276–80.

THINKING HISTORICALLY

What, according to Hetata, is the main process that is changing the world? Does he think the engine of world change is primarily techno-logical, commercial, or cultural?

As a young medical student, born and brought up in a colony, like many other people in my country, Egypt, I quickly learned to make the link between politics, economics, culture, and religion. Educated in an English school, I discovered that my English teachers looked down on us. We learned Rudyard Kipling by heart, praised the glories of the British Empire, followed the adventures of Kim in India, imbibed the culture of British supremacy, and sang carols on Christmas night.

At the medical school in university, when students demonstrated against occupation by British troops it was the Moslem Brothers who beat them up, using iron chains and long curved knives, and it was the governments supported by the king that shot at them or locked them up.

When I graduated in 1946, the hospital wards taught me how poverty and health are linked. I needed only another step to know that poverty had something to do with colonial rule, with the king who supported it, with class and race, with what was called imperialism at the time, with cotton prices falling on the market, with the seizure of land by foreign banks. These things were common talk in family gatherings, expressed in a simple, colorful language without frills. They were the facts of everyday life. We did not need to read books to make the links: They were there for us to see and grasp. And every time we made a link, someone told us it was time to stop, someone in authority whom we did not like: a ruler or a father, a policeman or a teacher, a landowner, a *maulana* (religious leader or teacher), a Jesuit, or a God.

And if we went on making these links, they locked us up.

For me, therefore, coming from this background, cultural studies and globalization open up a vast horizon, one of global links in a world where things are changing quickly. It is a chance to learn and probe how the economics, the politics, the culture, the philosophical thought of our days connect or disconnect, harmonize or contradict.

Of course, I will not even try to deal with all of that. I just want to raise a few points to discuss under the title of my talk, "Dollarization, Fragmentation, and God." Because I come from Egypt, my vantage point will be that of someone looking at the globe from the part we now call South, rather than "third world" or something else.

A New Economic Order: Gazing North at the Global Few

Never before in the history of the world has there been such a concentration and centralization of capital in so few nations and in the hands of so few people. The countries that form the Group of Seven,[1] with their 800 million inhabitants, control more technological, economic, informatics, and military power than the rest of the approximately 4.3 billion who live in Asia, Africa, Eastern Europe, and Latin America.

Five hundred multinational corporations account for 80 percent of world trade and 75 percent of investment. Half of all the multinational corporations are based in the United States, Germany, Japan, and Switzerland. The OECD (Organisation for Economic Cooperation and Development) group of countries contributes 80 percent of world production. . . .

A Global Culture for a Global Market

To expand the world market, to globalize it, to maintain the New Economic Order, the multinational corporations use economic power and control politics and the armed forces. But this is not so easy. People will always resist being exploited, resist injustice, struggle for their freedom, their needs, security, a better life, peace.

However, it becomes easier if they can be convinced to do what the masters of the global economy want them to do. This is where the issue of culture comes in. Culture can serve in different ways to help the global economy reach out all over the world and expand its markets to the most distant regions. Culture can also serve to reduce or destroy or prevent or divide or outflank the resistance of people who do not like what is happening to them, or have their doubts about it, or want to think. Culture can be like cocaine, which is going global these days: from Kali in Colombia to Texas, to Madrid, to the Italian mafiosi in southern Italy, to Moscow, Burma, and Thailand, a worldwide network uses the methods and the cover of big business, with a total trade of $5 billion a year, midway between oil and the arms trade.

At the disposal of global culture today are powerful means that function across the whole world: the media, which, like the economy, have made it one world, a bipolar North/South world. If genetic engineering gives scientists the possibility of programming embryos before children are born, children, youth, and adults are now being programmed

---

[1] Canada, France, Germany, Italy, Japan, the United Kingdom, and the United States meet as the G7. [Ed.]

after they are born in the culture they imbibe mainly through the media, but also in the family, in school, at the university, and elsewhere. Is this an exaggeration? an excessively gloomy picture of the world?

To expand the global market, increase the number of consumers, make sure that they buy what is sold, develop needs that conform to what is produced, and develop the fever of consumerism, culture must play a role in developing certain values, patterns of behavior, visions of what is happiness and success in the world, attitudes toward sex and love. Culture must model a global consumer.

In some ways, I was a "conservative radical." I went to jail, but I always dressed in a classical, subdued way. When my son started wearing blue jeans and New Balance shoes, I shivered with horror. He's going to become like some of those crazy kids abroad, the disco generation, I thought! Until the age of twenty-five he adamantly refused to smoke. Now he smokes two packs of Marlboros a day (the ones that the macho cowboy smokes). That does not prevent him from being a talented film director. But in the third-world, films, TV, and other media have increased the percentage of smokers. I saw half-starved kids in a marketplace in Mali buying single imported Benson & Hedges cigarettes and smoking.

But worse was still to come. Something happened that to me seemed impossible at one time, more difficult than adhering to a leftwing movement. At the age of seventy-one, I have taken to wearing blue jeans and Nike shoes. I listen to rock and reggae and sometimes rap. I like to go to discos and I sometimes have other cravings, which so far I have successfully fought! And I know these things have crept into our lives through the media, through TV, films, radio, advertisements, newspapers, and even novels, music, and poetry. It's a culture and it's reaching out, becoming global.

In my village, I have a friend. He is a peasant and we are very close. He lives in a big mud hut, and the animals (buffalo, sheep, cows, and donkeys) live in the house with him. Altogether, in the household, with the wife and children of his brother, his uncle, the mother, and his own family, there are thirty people. He wears a long *galabeya* (robe), works in the fields for long hours, and eats food cooked in the mud oven.

But when he married, he rode around the village in a hired Peugeot car with his bride. She wore a white wedding dress, her face was made up like a film star, her hair curled at the hairdresser's of the provincial town, her finger and toe nails manicured and polished, and her body bathed with special soap and perfumed. At the marriage ceremony, they had a wedding cake, which she cut with her husband's hand over hers. Very different from the customary rural marriage ceremony of his father. And all this change in the notion of beauty, of femininity, of celebration, of happiness, of prestige, of progress happened to my peasant friend and his bride in one generation.

The culprit, or the benevolent agent, depending on how you see it, was television.

In the past years, television has been the subject of numerous studies. In France, such studies have shown that before the age of twelve a child will have been exposed to an average 100,000 TV advertisements. Through these TV advertisements, the young boy or girl will have assimilated a whole set of values and behavioral patterns, of which he or she is not aware, of course. They become a part of his or her psychological (emotional and mental) makeup. Linked to these values are the norms and ways in which we see good and evil, beauty and ugliness, justice and injustice, truth and falseness, and which are being propagated at the same time. In other words, the fundamental values that form our aesthetic and moral vision of things are being inculcated, even hammered home, at this early stage, and they remain almost unchanged throughout life.

The commercial media no longer worry about the truthfulness or falsity of what they portray. Their role is to sell: beauty products, for example, to propagate the "beauty myth" and a "beauty culture" for both females and males alike and ensure that it reaches the farthest corners of the earth, including my village in the Delta of the Nile. Many of these beauty products are harmful to the health, can cause allergic disorders or skin infections or even worse. They cost money, work on the sex drives, and transform women and men, but especially women, into sex objects. They hide the real person, the natural beauty, the process of time, the stages of life, and instill false values about who we are, can be, or should become.

Advertisements do not depend on verifiable information or even rational thinking. They depend for their effect on images, colors, smart technical production, associations, and hidden drives. For them, attracting the opposite sex or social success or professional achievement and promotion or happiness do not depend on truthfulness or hard work or character, but rather on seduction, having a powerful car, buying things or people. . . .

Thus the media produce and reproduce the culture of consumption, of violence and sex to ensure that the global economic powers, the multinational corporations can promote a global market for themselves and protect it. And when everything is being bought or sold everyday and at all times in this vast supermarket, including culture, art, science, and thought, prostitution can become a way of life, for everything is priced. The search for the immediate need, the fleeting pleasure, the quick enjoyment, the commodity to buy, excess, pornography, drugs keeps this global economy rolling, for to stop is suicide.

2

PHILIPPE LEGRAIN

Cultural Globalization Is Not Americanization, 2003

Philippe Legrain, an economist, journalist, and former advisor to the
World Trade Organization, takes aim at what he calls the myths of
globalization in the following article. What, according to him, are
these myths? What are the consequences of globalization according
to Legrain? What evidence does he cite to support his argument?
How does his view differ from that of Hetata?

THINKING HISTORICALLY

Does Legrain believe the driving force of globalization is economic
or cultural? How important does he think globalization is? How,
according to the author, is globalization changing the world?

Fears that globalization is imposing a deadening cultural uniformity are
as ubiquitous as Coca-Cola, McDonald's, and Mickey Mouse. Europeans
and Latin Americans, left-wingers and right, rich and poor—all of them
dread that local cultures and national identities are dissolving into a
crass All-American consumerism. That cultural imperialism is said to
impose American values as well as products, promote the commercial at
the expense of the authentic, and substitute shallow gratification for
deeper satisfaction.

. . . If critics of globalization were less obsessed with "Cocacoloniza-
tion," they might notice a rich feast of cultural mixing that belies fears
about Americanized uniformity. Algerians in Paris practice Thai boxing;
Asian rappers in London snack on Turkish pizza; Salman Rushdie
delights readers everywhere with his Anglo-Indian tales. Although—as
with any change—there can be downsides to cultural globalization, this
cross-fertilization is overwhelmingly a force for good.

The beauty of globalization is that it can free people from the tyranny of geography. Just because someone was born in France does not
mean they can only aspire to speak French, eat French food, read French
books, visit museums in France, and so on. A Frenchman—or an American, for that matter—can take holidays in Spain or Florida, eat sushi or
spaghetti for dinner, drink Coke or Chilean wine, watch a Hollywood
blockbuster or an Almodóvar, listen to bhangra or rap, practice yoga or

Source: Philippe Legrain, "Cultural Globalization Is Not Americanization," *Chronicle of
Higher Education* 49, no. 35 (May 9, 2003): B7.

kickboxing, read *Elle* or *The Economist*, and have friends from around the world. That we are increasingly free to choose our cultural experiences enriches our lives immeasurably. We could not always enjoy the best the world has to offer.

Globalization not only increases individual freedom, but also revitalizes cultures and cultural artifacts through foreign influences, technologies, and markets. Thriving cultures are not set in stone. They are forever changing from within and without. Each generation challenges the previous one; science and technology alter the way we see ourselves and the world; fashions come and go; experience and events influence our beliefs; outsiders affect us for good and ill.

Many of the best things come from cultures mixing: V. S. Naipaul's Anglo-Indo-Caribbean writing, Paul Gauguin painting in Polynesia, or the African rhythms in rock 'n' roll. Behold the great British curry. Admire the many-colored faces of France's World Cup–winning soccer team, the ferment of ideas that came from Eastern Europe's Jewish diaspora, and the cosmopolitan cities of London and New York. Western numbers are actually Arabic; zero comes most recently from India; Icelandic, French, and Sanskrit stem from a common root.

John Stuart Mill was right: "The economical benefits of commerce are surpassed in importance by those of its effects which are intellectual and moral. It is hardly possible to overrate the value, for the improvement of human beings, of things which bring them into contact with persons dissimilar to themselves, and with modes of thought and action unlike those with which they are familiar. . . . It is indispensable to be perpetually comparing [one's] own notions and customs with the experience and example of persons in different circumstances. . . . There is no nation which does not need to borrow from others."

It is a myth that globalization involves the imposition of Americanized uniformity, rather than an explosion of cultural exchange. For a start, many archetypal "American" products are not as all-American as they seem. Levi Strauss, a German immigrant, invented jeans by combining denim cloth (or "serge de Nîmes," because it was traditionally woven in the French town) with Genes, a style of trousers worn by Genoese sailors. So Levi's jeans are in fact an American twist on a European hybrid. Even quintessentially American exports are often tailored to local tastes. MTV in Asia promotes Thai pop stars and plays rock music sung in Mandarin. CNN en Español offers a Latin American take on world news. McDonald's sells beer in France, lamb in India, and chili in Mexico.

In some ways, America is an outlier, not a global leader. Most of the world has adopted the metric system born from the French Revolution; America persists with antiquated measurements inherited from its British-colonial past. Most developed countries have become intensely secular, but many Americans burn with fundamentalist fervor—like

Muslims in the Middle East. Where else in the developed world could there be a serious debate about teaching kids Bible-inspired "creationism" instead of Darwinist evolution?

America's tastes in sports are often idiosyncratic, too. Baseball and American football have not traveled well, although basketball has fared rather better. Many of the world's most popular sports, notably soccer, came by way of Britain. Asian martial arts—judo, karate, kickboxing— and pastimes like yoga have also swept the world.

People are not only guzzling hamburgers and Coke. Despite Coke's ambition of displacing water as the world's drink of choice, it accounts for less than 2 of the 64 fluid ounces that the typical person drinks a day. Britain's favorite takeaway is a curry, not a burger: Indian restaurants there outnumber McDonald's six to one. For all the concerns about American fast food trashing France's culinary traditions, France imported a mere $620 million in food from the United States in 2000, while exporting to America three times that. Nor is plonk[1] from America's Gallo displacing Europe's finest: Italy and France together account for three-fifths of global wine exports, the United States for only a twentieth. Worldwide, pizzas are more popular than burgers, Chinese restaurants seem to sprout up everywhere, and sushi is spreading fast. By far the biggest purveyor of alcoholic drinks is Britain's Diageo, which sells the world's best-selling whiskey (Johnnie Walker), gin (Gordon's), vodka (Smirnoff), and liqueur (Baileys).

In fashion, the ne plus ultra is Italian or French. Trendy Americans wear Gucci, Armani, Versace, Chanel, and Hermès. On the high street and in the mall, Sweden's Hennes & Mauritz (H&M) and Spain's Zara vie with America's Gap to dress the global masses. Nike shoes are given a run for their money by Germany's Adidas, Britain's Reebok, and Italy's Fila.

In pop music, American crooners do not have the stage to themselves. The three artists who were featured most widely in national Top Ten album charts in 2000 were America's Britney Spears, closely followed by Mexico's Carlos Santana and the British Beatles. Even tiny Iceland has produced a global star: Björk. Popular opera's biggest singers are Italy's Luciano Pavarotti, Spain's José Carreras, and the Spanish-Mexican Placido Domingo. Latin American salsa, Brazilian lambada, and African music have all carved out global niches for themselves. In most countries, local artists still top the charts. According to the IFPI, the record-industry bible, local acts accounted for 68 percent of music sales in 2000, up from 58 percent in 1991.

One of the most famous contemporary writers is a Colombian, Gabriel García Márquez, author of *One Hundred Years of Solitude*.

---

[1] British slang for cheap, low-quality alcohol. [Ed.]

Paulo Coelho, another writer who has notched up tens of millions of global sales with *The Alchemist* and other books, is Brazilian. More than 200 million Harlequin romance novels, a Canadian export, were sold in 1990; they account for two-fifths of mass-market paperback sales in the United States. The biggest publisher in the English-speaking world is Germany's Bertelsmann, which gobbled up America's largest, Random House, in 1998.

Local fare glues more eyeballs to TV screens than American programs. Although nearly three-quarters of television drama exported worldwide comes from the United States, most countries' favorite shows are homegrown.

Nor are Americans the only players in the global media industry. Of the seven market leaders that have their fingers in nearly every pie, four are American (AOL Time Warner, Disney, Viacom, and News Corporation), one is German (Bertelsmann), one is French (Vivendi), and one Japanese (Sony). What they distribute comes from all quarters: Bertelsmann publishes books by American writers; News Corporation broadcasts Asian news; Sony sells Brazilian music.

The evidence is overwhelming. Fears about an Americanized uniformity are over-blown: American cultural products are not uniquely dominant; local ones are alive and well.

3

MIRIAM CHING YOON LOUIE

Sweatshop Warriors: Immigrant Women Workers Take On the Global Factory, 2001

Sherif Hetata and Philippe Legrain highlight the impact of globalization on consumers, but it is also important to examine how it affects workers. Free-trade policies have removed barriers to international trade, with global consequences. An example of such change can be witnessed along the border between Mexico and the United States, especially in the export factories, or *maquiladoras*,* that are run by international corporations on both the U.S. and Mexican sides of the border. In the following excerpt, Miriam Ching Yoon Louie, a writer

---

* mah kee lah DOH rahs

Source: Miriam Ching Yoon Louie, *Sweatshop Warriors: Immigrant Women Workers Take On the Global Factory* (Cambridge, MA: South End Press, 2001), 65–71, 87–89.

and activist, interviews Mexican women who work in these factories and explores both the challenges they face and the strength they show in overcoming these challenges. What is the impact of liberalized trade laws on women who work in the *maquiladoras*? What is neoliberalism, and how is it tied to globalization? Why are women particularly vulnerable to these policies?

THINKING HISTORICALLY

According to Louie, how far back do neoliberalism and economic globalization date? How does Louie's assessment of economic globalization differ from the views expressed by Legrain? How might they both be right?

Many of today's *nuevas revolucionarias*[1] started working on the global assembly line as young women in northern Mexico for foreign transnational corporations. Some women worked on the U.S. side as "commuters" before they moved across the border with their families. Their stories reveal the length, complexity, and interpenetration of the U.S. and Mexican economies, labor markets, histories, cultures, and race relations. The women talk about the devastating impact of globalization, including massive layoffs and the spread of sweatshops on both sides of the border. *Las mujeres*[2] recount what drove them to join and lead movements for economic, racial, and gender justice, as well as the challenges they faced within their families and communities to assert their basic human rights. . . .

Growing Up Female and Poor

Mexican women and girls were traditionally expected to do all the cooking, cleaning, and serving for their husbands, brothers, and sons. For girls from poor families, shouldering these domestic responsibilities proved doubly difficult because they also performed farm, sweatshop, or domestic service work simultaneously. . . .

Petra Mata, a former seamstress for Levi's whose mother died shortly after childbirth, recalls the heavy housework she did as the only daughter:

> Aiyeee, let me tell you! It was very hard. In those times in Mexico, I was raised with the ideal that you have to learn to do everything— cook, make tortillas, wash your clothes, and clean the house—just the way they wanted you to. My grandparents were very strict. I always

---

[1] New revolutionaries. [Ed.]

[2] moo HAIR ace   The women. [Ed.]

had to ask their permission and then let them tell me what to do. I was not a free woman. Life was hard for me. I didn't have much of a childhood; I started working when I was 12 or 13 years old.

Neoliberalism and Creeping Maquiladorization

These women came of age during a period of major change in the relationship between the Mexican and U.S. economies. Like Puerto Rico, Hong Kong, South Korea, Taiwan, Malaysia, Singapore, and the Philippines, northern Mexico served as one of the first stations of the global assembly line tapping young women's labor. In 1965 the Mexican government initiated the Border Industrialization Program (BIP) that set up export plants, called *maquiladoras* or *maquilas*, which were either the direct subsidiaries or subcontractors of transnational corporations. Mexican government incentives to U.S. and other foreign investors included low wages and high productivity; infrastructure; proximity to U.S. markets, facilities, and lifestyles; tariff loopholes; and pliant, pro-government unions. . . .

Describing her quarter-century-long sewing career in Mexico, Celeste Jiménez ticks off the names of famous U.S. manufacturers who hopped over the border to take advantage of cheap wages:

> I sewed for twenty-four years when I lived in Chihuahua in big name factories like Billy the Kid, Levi Strauss, and Lee *maquiladoras*. Everyone was down there. Here a company might sell under the brand name of Lee; there in Mexico it would be called Blanca García.

Transnational exploitation of women's labor was part of a broader set of policies that critical opposition movements in the Third World have dubbed "neoliberalism," i.e., the new version of the British Liberal Party's program of laissez faire capitalism espoused by the rising European and U.S. colonial powers during the late eighteenth and nineteenth centuries. The Western powers, Japan, and international financial institutions like the World Bank and International Monetary Fund have aggressively promoted neoliberal policies since the 1970s. Mexico served as an early testing ground for such standard neoliberal policies as erection of free trade zones; commercialization of agriculture; currency devaluation; deregulation; privatization; outsourcing; cuts in wages and social programs; suppression of workers', women's, and indigenous people's rights; free trade; militarization; and promotion of neoconservative ideology.

Neoliberalism intersects with gender and national oppression. Third World women constitute the majority of migrants seeking jobs as maids, vendors, *maquila* operatives, and service industry workers. Women also pay the highest price for cuts in education, health and housing programs, and food and energy subsidies and increases in their unpaid labor. . . .

The deepening of the economic crisis in Mexico, especially under the International Monetary Fund's pressure to devaluate the peso in 1976, 1982, and 1994, forced many women to work in both the formal and informal economy to survive and meet their childbearing and household responsibilities. María Antonia Flores was forced to work two jobs after her husband abandoned the family, leaving her with three children to support. She had no choice but to leave her children home alone, *solitos*, to look after themselves. Refugio Arrieta straddled the formal and informal economy because her job in an auto parts assembly *maquiladora* failed to bring in sufficient income. To compensate for the shortfall, she worked longer hours at her *maquila* job and "moonlighted" elsewhere:

> We made chassis for cars and for the headlights. I worked lots! I worked 12 hours more or less because they paid us so little that if you worked more, you got more money. I did this because the schools in Mexico don't provide everything. You have to buy the books, notebooks, *todos, todos* [everything]. And I had five kids. It's very expensive. I also worked out of my house and sold ceramics. I did many things to get more money for my kids.

In the three decades following its humble beginnings in the mid-1960s, the *maquila* sector swelled to more than 2,000 plants employing an estimated 776,000 people, over 10 percent of Mexico's labor force. In 1985, *maquiladoras* overtook tourism as the largest source of foreign exchange. In 1996, this sector trailed only petroleum-related industries in economic importance and accounted for over U.S. $29 billion in export earnings annually. The *maquila* system has also penetrated the interior of the country, as in the case of Guadalajara's electronics assembly industry and Tehuacán's jeans production zones. Although the proportion of male *maquila* workers has increased since 1983, especially in auto-transport equipment assembly, almost 70 percent of the workers continue to be women.

As part of a delegation of labor and human rights activists, this author met some of Mexico's newest proletarians[3] — young indigenous women migrant workers from the Sierra Negra to Tehuacán, a town famous for its refreshing mineral water springs in the state of Puebla, just southeast of Mexico City. Standing packed like cattle in the back of the trucks each morning the women headed for jobs sewing for name brand manufacturers like Guess?, VF Corporation (producing Lee brand clothing), Gap, Sun Apparel (producing brands such as Polo, Arizona,

[3] Workers, especially exploited ones (a Marxist term derived from Latin for lower classes). [Ed.]

and Express), Cherokee, Ditto Apparel of California, Levi's, and others. The workers told U.S. delegation members that their wages averaged U.S. $30 to $50 a week for 12-hour work days, six days a week. Some workers reported having to do *veladas* [all-nighters] once or twice a week. Employees often stayed longer without pay if they did not finish high production goals.

Girls as young as 12 and 13 worked in the factories. Workers were searched when they left for lunch and again at the end of the day to check that they weren't stealing materials. Women were routinely given urine tests when hired and those found to be pregnant were promptly fired, in violation of Mexican labor law. Although the workers had organized an independent union several years earlier, Tehuacán's Human Rights Commission members told us that it had collapsed after one of its leaders was assassinated.

Carmen Valadez and Reyna Montero, long-time activists in the women's and social justice movements, helped found Casa de La Mujer Factor X in 1977, a workers' center in Tijuana that organizes around women's workplace, reproductive, and health rights, and against domestic violence. Valadez and Montero say that the low wages and dangerous working conditions characteristic of the *maquiladoras* on the Mexico-U.S. border are being "extended to all areas of the country and to Central America and the Caribbean. NAFTA represents nothing but the '*maquiladorization*' of the region."

Elizabeth "Beti" Robles Ortega, who began working in the *maquilas* at the age of fourteen and was blacklisted after participating in independent union organizing drives on Mexico's northern border, now works as an organizer for the Servicio, Desarrollo y Paz, AC 520 (SEDEPAC) [Service, Development and Peace organization]. Robles described the erosion of workers' rights and women's health under NAFTA:

> NAFTA has led to an increase in the workforce, as foreign industry has grown. They are reforming labor laws and our constitution to favor even more foreign investment, which is unfair against our labor rights. For example, they are now trying to take away from us free organization which was guaranteed by Mexican law. Because foreign capital is investing in Mexico and is dominating, we must have guarantees. The government is just there with its hands held out; it's always had them out but now even more shamelessly. . . . Ecological problems are increasing. A majority of women are coming down with cancer—skin and breast cancer, leukemia, and lung and heart problems. There are daily deaths of worker women. You can see and feel the contamination of the water and the air. As soon as you arrive and start breathing the air in Acuña and Piedras Negras [border cities between the states of Coahuila and Texas], you sense the heavy air, making you feel like vomiting.

Joining the Movement

Much of the education and leadership training the women received took place "on the job." The women talked about how much their participation in the movement had changed them. They learned how to analyze working conditions and social problems, who was responsible for these conditions, and what workers could do to get justice. They learned to speak truth to power, whether this was to government representatives, corporate management, the media, unions, or co-ethnic gatekeepers. They built relations with different kinds of sectors and groups and organized a wide variety of educational activities and actions. Their activism expanded their world view beyond that of their immediate families to seeing themselves as part of peoples' movements fighting for justice. . . .

Through her participation in the movement, [María del Carmen Domínguez] developed her skills, leadership, and awareness:

> When I stayed at work in the factory, I was only thinking of myself and how am I going to support my family—nothing more, nothing less. And I served my husband and my son, my girl. But when I started working with La Mujer Obrera I thought, "I need more respect for myself. We need more respect for ourselves." (laughs) . . .
> . . . I learned about the law and I learned how to organize classes with people, whether they were men or women like me.

4

ZEYNEP TUFEKCI

The Machines Are Coming, 2015

All studies of globalization emphasize the impact of technological change. Fifty years ago, historians and social commentators envisioned a future in which machines would replace human labor, drastically reducing the work week and providing abundant leisure time for all. In the same fifty years, the number of workers effectively doubled with the entry of women. Was the prediction wrong or too early? How does Zeynep Tufekci account for this failed prediction and update it?

Source: Zeynep Tufekci, "The Machines Are Coming," *New York Times*, April 18, 2015.

THINKING HISTORICALLY

The author is a techno-sociologist concerned with the impact of technologies on social change. She distinguishes between technologies used to empower people and those that are not. What social and economic processes direct technological change? How do they determine who benefits?

The machine hums along, quietly scanning the slides, generating Pap smear diagnostics, just the way a college-educated, well-compensated lab technician might.

A robot with emotion-detection software interviews visitors to the United States at the border. In field tests, this eerily named "embodied avatar kiosk" does much better than humans in catching those with invalid documentation. Emotional-processing software has gotten so good that ad companies are looking into "mood-targeted" advertising, and the government of Dubai wants to use it to scan all its closed-circuit TV feeds.

Yes, the machines are getting smarter, and they're coming for more and more jobs.

Not just low-wage jobs, either.

Today, machines can process regular spoken language and not only recognize human faces, but also read their expressions. They can classify personality types, and have started being able to carry out conversations with appropriate emotional tenor.

Machines are getting better than humans at figuring out who to hire, who's in a mood to pay a little more for that sweater, and who needs a coupon to nudge them toward a sale. In applications around the world, software is being used to predict whether people are lying, how they feel and whom they'll vote for.

To crack these cognitive and emotional puzzles, computers needed not only sophisticated, efficient algorithms, but also vast amounts of human-generated data, which can now be easily harvested from our digitized world. The results are dazzling. Most of what we think of as expertise, knowledge and intuition is being deconstructed and recreated as an algorithmic competency, fueled by big data.

But computers do not just replace humans in the workplace. They shift the balance of power even more in favor of employers. Our normal response to technological innovation that threatens jobs is to encourage workers to acquire more skills, or to trust that the nuances of the human mind or human attention will always be superior in crucial ways. But when machines of this capacity enter the equation, employers have even more leverage, and our standard response is not sufficient for the looming crisis.

Machines aren't used because they perform some tasks that much better than humans, but because, in many cases, they do a "good enough" job while also being cheaper, more predictable and easier to control than quirky, pesky humans. Technology in the workplace is as much about power and control as it is about productivity and efficiency.

This used to be spoken about more openly. An ad in 1967 for an automated accounting system urged companies to replace humans with automated systems that "can't quit, forget or get pregnant." Featuring a visibly pregnant, smiling woman leaving the office with baby shower gifts, the ads, which were published in leading business magazines, warned of employees who "know too much for your own good"—"your good" meaning that of the employer. Why be dependent on humans? "When Alice leaves, will she take your billing system with her?" the ad pointedly asked, emphasizing that this couldn't be fixed by simply replacing "Alice" with another person. The solution? Replace humans with machines. To pregnancy as a "danger" to the workplace, the company could have added "get sick, ask for higher wages, have a bad day, aging parent, sick child or a cold." In other words, be human.

I recently had a conversation with a call center worker from the Philippines. While trying to solve my minor problem, he needed to get a code from a supervisor. The code didn't work. A groan escaped his lips: "I'm going to lose my job." Alarmed, I inquired why. He had done nothing wrong, and it was a small issue. "It doesn't matter," he said.

He was probably right. He is dispensable. Technology first allowed the job to be outsourced. Now machines at call centers can be used to seamlessly generate spoken responses to customer inquiries, so that a single operator can handle multiple customers all at once. Meanwhile, the customer often isn't aware that she is mostly being spoken to by a machine.

This is the way technology is being used in many workplaces: to reduce the power of humans, and employers' dependency on them, whether by replacing, displacing or surveilling them. Many technological developments contribute to this shift in power: advanced diagnostic systems that can do medical or legal analysis; the ability to outsource labor to the lowest-paid workers, measure employee tasks to the minute and "optimize" worker schedules in a way that devastates ordinary lives. Indeed, regardless of whether unemployment has gone up or down, real wages have been stagnant or declining in the United States for decades. Most people no longer have the leverage to bargain.

In the 1980s, the Harvard social scientist Shoshana Zuboff examined how some workplaces used technology to "automate"—take power away from the employee—while others used technology differently, to "informate"—to empower people.

For academics, software developers and corporate and policy leaders who are lucky enough to live in this "informate" model, technology has been good. So far. To those for whom it's been less of a blessing, we keep doling out the advice to upgrade skills. Unfortunately, for most workers, technology is used to "automate" the job and to take power away.

And workers already feel like they are powerless as it is. Last week, low-wage workers around the country demonstrated for a $15-an-hour wage, calling it economic justice. Those with college degrees may not think that they share a problem with these workers, who are fighting to reclaim some power with employers, but they do. The fight is poised to move up the skilled-labor chain.

Optimists insist that we've been here before, during the Industrial Revolution, when machinery replaced manual labor, and all we need is a little more education and better skills. But that is not a sufficient answer. One historical example is no guarantee of future events, and we won't be able to compete by trying to stay one step ahead in a losing battle.

This cannot just be about machines' capabilities or human skills, since the true solution lies in neither. Confronting the threat posed by machines, and the way in which the great data harvest has made them ever more able to compete with human workers, must be about our priorities.

It's easy to imagine an alternate future where advanced machine capabilities are used to empower more of us, rather than control most of us. There will potentially be more time, resources and freedom to share, but only if we change how we do things. We don't need to reject or blame technology. This problem is not us versus the machines, but between us, as humans, and how we value one another.

5

POPE FRANCIS

On Care for Our Common Home, 2015

When Pope Benedict took the unheard of step of resigning the papacy in 2013 in the wake of scandals about clerical abuse, few thought the cardinals would choose an Argentine with roots among the most desperately poor to take his place. But they did. Jorge Mario Bergoglio worked as a janitor and a nightclub bouncer before enrolling in the seminary. As a priest and bishop, he served the poor of Buenos Aires. His fellow cardinals who chose him to be pope in 2013 knew they were making a break with the past.

On June 18, 2015, *Time* magazine wrote: "Pope Francis rocked the international community Thursday with the long-anticipated release of his climate encyclical, an authoritative church teaching poised to

Source: Pope Francis, "On Care for Our Common Home." © Copyright—Libreria Editrice Vaticana, http://w2.vatican.va/content/francesco/en/encyclicals/documents/papa-francesco _20150524_enciclica-laudato-si.html.

reshape the international conversation on climate change." Since its release, the 184-page document has indeed broadened the conversation about climate change and challenged the world to act.

How does the pope, who took the name Francis after Francis of Assisi, the patron saint of the poor, show that climate change is especially harmful to the poor? How does he link climate change to changes in culture and communication? How does he relate deterioration of the environment to such essentials of capitalism as private property, private profits, commerce, and markets?

THINKING HISTORICALLY

What does the encyclical suggest about the process of change that led to the current situation? When did it start? When did damage accelerate? Given this development, what does Pope Francis think can be done now? What does he urge us to do?

1. *"LAUDATO SI', mi' Signore"* — *"Praise be to you, my Lord."* In the words of this beautiful canticle, Saint Francis of Assisi reminds us that our common home is like a sister with whom we share our life and a beautiful mother who opens her arms to embrace us. "Praise be to you, my Lord, through our Sister, Mother Earth, who sustains and governs us, and who produces various fruit with coloured flowers and herbs."

2. This sister now cries out to us because of the harm we have inflicted on her by our irresponsible use and abuse of the goods with which God has endowed her. We have come to see ourselves as her lords and masters, entitled to plunder her at will. The violence present in our hearts, wounded by sin, is also reflected in the symptoms of sickness evident in the soil, in the water, in the air and in all forms of life. This is why the earth herself, burdened and laid waste, is among the most abandoned and maltreated of our poor; she "groans in travail." We have forgotten that we ourselves are dust of the earth; our very bodies are made up of her elements, we breathe her air and we receive life and refreshment from her waters. . . .

Chapter One: What Is Happening to Our Common Home

I. Pollution and Climate Change

Pollution, waste and the throwaway culture

20. Some forms of pollution are part of people's daily experience. Exposure to atmospheric pollutants produces a broad spectrum of health hazards, especially for the poor, and causes millions of premature deaths. People take sick, for example, from breathing high levels of smoke from

fuels used in cooking or heating. There is also pollution that affects everyone, caused by transport, industrial fumes, substances which contribute to the acidification of soil and water, fertilizers, insecticides, fungicides, herbicides and agrotoxins in general. Technology, which, linked to business interests, is presented as the only way of solving these problems, in fact proves incapable of seeing the mysterious network of relations between things and so sometimes solves one problem only to create others.

21. Account must also be taken of the pollution produced by residue, including dangerous waste present in different areas. Each year hundreds of millions of tons of waste are generated, much of it non-biodegradable, highly toxic and radioactive, from homes and businesses, from construction and demolition sites, from clinical, electronic and industrial sources. The earth, our home, is beginning to look more and more like an immense pile of filth. In many parts of the planet, the elderly lament that once beautiful landscapes are now covered with rubbish. Industrial waste and chemical products utilized in cities and agricultural areas can lead to bioaccumulation in the organisms of the local population, even when levels of toxins in those places are low. Frequently no measures are taken until after people's health has been irreversibly affected.

22. These problems are closely linked to a throwaway culture which affects the excluded just as it quickly reduces things to rubbish. To cite one example, most of the paper we produce is thrown away and not recycled. It is hard for us to accept that the way natural ecosystems work is exemplary: plants synthesize nutrients which feed herbivores; these in turn become food for carnivores, which produce significant quantities of organic waste which give rise to new generations of plants. But our industrial system, at the end of its cycle of production and consumption, has not developed the capacity to absorb and reuse waste and by-products. We have not yet managed to adopt a circular model of production capable of preserving resources for present and future generations, while limiting as much as possible the use of non-renewable resources, moderating their consumption, maximizing their efficient use, reusing and recycling them. A serious consideration of this issue would be one way of counteracting the throwaway culture which affects the entire planet, but it must be said that only limited progress has been made in this regard.

Climate as a common good

23. The climate is a common good, belonging to all and meant for all. At the global level, it is a complex system linked to many of the essential conditions for human life. A very solid scientific consensus indicates that we are presently witnessing a disturbing warming of the climatic system. In recent decades this warming has been accompanied by a constant rise in the sea level and, it would appear, by an increase of extreme weather

events, even if a scientifically determinable cause cannot be assigned to each particular phenomenon. Humanity is called to recognize the need for changes of lifestyle, production and consumption, in order to combat this warming or at least the human causes which produce or aggravate it. It is true that there are other factors (such as volcanic activity, variations in the earth's orbit and axis, the solar cycle), yet a number of scientific studies indicate that most global warming in recent decades is due to the great concentration of greenhouse gases (carbon dioxide, methane, nitrogen oxides and others) released mainly as a result of human activity. As these gases build up in the atmosphere, they hamper the escape of heat produced by sunlight at the earth's surface. The problem is aggravated by a model of development based on the intensive use of fossil fuels, which is at the heart of the worldwide energy system. Another determining factor has been an increase in changed uses of the soil, principally deforestation for agricultural purposes.

24. Warming has effects on the carbon cycle. It creates a vicious circle which aggravates the situation even more, affecting the availability of essential resources like drinking water, energy and agricultural production in warmer regions, and leading to the extinction of part of the planet's biodiversity. The melting in the polar ice caps and in high altitude plains can lead to the dangerous release of methane gas, while the decomposition of frozen organic material can further increase the emission of carbon dioxide. Things are made worse by the loss of tropical forests which would otherwise help to mitigate climate change. Carbon dioxide pollution increases the acidification of the oceans and compromises the marine food chain. If present trends continue, this century may well witness extraordinary climate change and an unprecedented destruction of ecosystems, with serious consequences for all of us. A rise in the sea level, for example, can create extremely serious situations, if we consider that a quarter of the world's population lives on the coast or nearby, and that the majority of our megacities are situated in coastal areas. . . .

III. Loss of Biodiversity

32. The earth's resources are also being plundered because of shortsighted approaches to the economy, commerce and production. The loss of forests and woodlands entails the loss of species which may constitute extremely important resources in the future, not only for food but also for curing disease and other uses. Different species contain genes which could be key resources in years ahead for meeting human needs and regulating environmental problems.

33. It is not enough, however, to think of different species merely as potential "resources" to be exploited, while overlooking the fact that they have value in themselves. Each year sees the disappearance of thousands of plant and animal species which we will never know, which our

children will never see, because they have been lost for ever. The great majority become extinct for reasons related to human activity. Because of us, thousands of species will no longer give glory to God by their very existence, nor convey their message to us. We have no such right. . . .

IV. Decline in the Quality of Human Life and the Breakdown of Society

46. The social dimensions of global change include the effects of technological innovations on employment, social exclusion, an inequitable distribution and consumption of energy and other services, social breakdown, increased violence and a rise in new forms of social aggression, drug trafficking, growing drug use by young people, and the loss of identity. These are signs that the growth of the past two centuries has not always led to an integral development and an improvement in the quality of life. Some of these signs are also symptomatic of real social decline, the silent rupture of the bonds of integration and social cohesion.

47. Furthermore, when media and the digital world become omnipresent, their influence can stop people from learning how to live wisely, to think deeply and to love generously. In this context, the great sages of the past run the risk of going unheard amid the noise and distractions of an information overload. Efforts need to be made to help these media become sources of new cultural progress for humanity and not a threat to our deepest riches. True wisdom, as the fruit of self-examination, dialogue and generous encounter between persons, is not acquired by a mere accumulation of data which eventually leads to overload and confusion, a sort of mental pollution. Real relationships with others, with all the challenges they entail, now tend to be replaced by a type of internet communication which enables us to choose or eliminate relationships at whim, thus giving rise to a new type of contrived emotion which has more to do with devices and displays than with other people and with nature. Today's media do enable us to communicate and to share our knowledge and affections. Yet at times they also shield us from direct contact with the pain, the fears and the joys of others and the complexity of their personal experiences. For this reason, we should be concerned that, alongside the exciting possibilities offered by these media, a deep and melancholic dissatisfaction with interpersonal relations, or a harmful sense of isolation, can also arise. . . .

Chapter Two: The Gospel of Creation

VI. The Common Destination of Goods

93. Whether believers or not, we are agreed today that the earth is essentially a shared inheritance, whose fruits are meant to benefit everyone. For believers, this becomes a question of fidelity to the Creator,

since God created the world for everyone. Hence every ecological approach needs to incorporate a social perspective which takes into account the fundamental rights of the poor and the underprivileged. The principle of the subordination of private property to the universal destination of goods, and thus the right of everyone to their use, is a golden rule of social conduct and "the first principle of the whole ethical and social order." The Christian tradition has never recognized the right to private property as absolute or inviolable, and has stressed the social purpose of all forms of private property. Saint John Paul II forcefully reaffirmed this teaching, stating that "God gave the earth to the whole human race for the sustenance of all its members, *without excluding or favouring anyone*." These are strong words. He noted that "a type of development which did not respect and promote human rights—personal and social, economic and political, including the rights of nations and of peoples—would not be really worthy of man." He clearly explained that "the Church does indeed defend the legitimate right to private property, but she also teaches no less clearly that there is always a social mortgage on all private property, in order that goods may serve the general purpose that God gave them." Consequently, he maintained, "it is not in accord with God's plan that this gift be used in such a way that its benefits favour only a few." This calls into serious question the unjust habits of a part of humanity. . . .

Chapter Five: Lines of Approach and Action

IV. Politics and Economy in Dialogue for Human Fulfillment

189. Politics must not be subject to the economy, nor should the economy be subject to the dictates of an efficiency-driven paradigm of technocracy. Today, in view of the common good, there is urgent need for politics and economics to enter into a frank dialogue in the service of life, especially human life. Saving banks at any cost, making the public pay the price, foregoing a firm commitment to reviewing and reforming the entire system, only reaffirms the absolute power of a financial system, a power which has no future and will only give rise to new crises after a slow, costly and only apparent recovery. The financial crisis of 2007–08 provided an opportunity to develop a new economy, more attentive to ethical principles, and new ways of regulating speculative financial practices and virtual wealth. But the response to the crisis did not include rethinking the outdated criteria which continue to rule the world. Production is not always rational, and is usually tied to economic variables which assign to products a value that does not necessarily correspond to their real worth. This frequently leads to an overproduction of some commodities, with unnecessary impact on the environment and with negative results on regional economies. . . .

190. Here too, it should always be kept in mind that "environmental protection cannot be assured solely on the basis of financial calculations of costs and benefits. The environment is one of those goods that cannot be adequately safeguarded or promoted by market forces." Once more, we need to reject a magical conception of the market, which would suggest that problems can be solved simply by an increase in the profits of companies or individuals. Is it realistic to hope that those who are obsessed with maximizing profits will stop to reflect on the environmental damage which they will leave behind for future generations? Where profits alone count, there can be no thinking about the rhythms of nature, its phases of decay and regeneration, or the complexity of ecosystems which may be gravely upset by human intervention. Moreover, biodiversity is considered at most a deposit of economic resources available for exploitation, with no serious thought for the real value of things, their significance for persons and cultures, or the concerns and needs of the poor. . . .

Chapter Six: Ecological Education and Spirituality

202. Many things have to change course, but it is we human beings above all who need to change. We lack an awareness of our common origin, of our mutual belonging, and of a future to be shared with everyone. This basic awareness would enable the development of new convictions, attitudes and forms of life. A great cultural, spiritual and educational challenge stands before us, and it will demand that we set out on the long path of renewal.

I. Towards a New Lifestyle

203. Since the market tends to promote extreme consumerism in an effort to sell its products, people can easily get caught up in a whirlwind of needless buying and spending. Compulsive consumerism is one example of how the techno-economic paradigm affects individuals. . . . This paradigm leads people to believe that they are free as long as they have the supposed freedom to consume. But those really free are the minority who wield economic and financial power. Amid this confusion, postmodern humanity has not yet achieved a new self-awareness capable of offering guidance and direction, and this lack of identity is a source of anxiety. We have too many means and only a few insubstantial ends.

204. The current global situation engenders a feeling of instability and uncertainty, which in turn becomes "a seedbed for collective selfishness." When people become self-centred and self-enclosed, their greed increases. The emptier a person's heart is, the more he or she needs things to buy, own and consume. It becomes almost impossible to accept the

limits imposed by reality. In this horizon, a genuine sense of the common good also disappears. As these attitudes become more widespread, social norms are respected only to the extent that they do not clash with personal needs. So our concern cannot be limited merely to the threat of extreme weather events, but must also extend to the catastrophic consequences of social unrest. Obsession with a consumerist lifestyle, above all when few people are capable of maintaining it, can only lead to violence and mutual destruction.

205. Yet all is not lost. Human beings, while capable of the worst, are also capable of rising above themselves, choosing again what is good, and making a new start, despite their mental and social conditioning. We are able to take an honest look at ourselves, to acknowledge our deep dissatisfaction, and to embark on new paths to authentic freedom. No system can completely suppress our openness to what is good, true and beautiful, or our God-given ability to respond to his grace at work deep in our hearts. I appeal to everyone throughout the world not to forget this dignity which is ours. No one has the right to take it from us. . . .

6

NAOMI KLEIN

"How Science Is Telling Us All to Revolt," 2013

Naomi Klein is a Canadian journalist, author, and social activist. This selection introduces the theme of her most recent book, *This Changes Everything: Capitalism vs. The Climate* (2014). How are the work and language of the scientists Klein discusses different from that of Pope Francis? How are their conclusions similar? How would you compare their proposed solutions?

THINKING HISTORICALLY

The climate scientists presented by Klein describe processes of change by plotting measurements of such things as carbon, sea level, and temperature precisely at regular intervals. The resulting data give them a precise history of the processes they're mapping. Normally,

Source: Naomi Klein, "How Science Is Telling Us All to Revolt," *New Statesman*, October 29, 2013.

scientists, like historians, are content with describing processes. They rarely have the confidence to make predictions, and they almost never engage in extreme political action based on predictions. Klein's scientists do both. What do you think accounts for this departure from the usual step-by-step, gradual methods of science? What makes a process of global change so important—and so certain—that extraordinary action on the part of scientists is acceptable? Is climate change such a process? Is capitalism its cause?

Is our relentless quest for economic growth killing the planet? Climate scientists have seen the data—and they are coming to some incendiary conclusions.

In December 2012, a pink-haired complex systems researcher named Brad Werner made his way through the throng of 24,000 earth and space scientists at the Fall Meeting of the American Geophysical Union, held annually in San Francisco. This year's conference had some big-name participants, from Ed Stone of NASA's Voyager project, explaining a new milestone on the path to interstellar space, to the film-maker James Cameron, discussing his adventures in deep-sea submersibles.

But it was Werner's own session that was attracting much of the buzz. It was titled "Is Earth F**ked?" (full title: "Is Earth F**ked? Dynamical Futility of Global Environmental Management and Possibilities for Sustainability via Direct Action Activism").

Standing at the front of the conference room, the geophysicist from the University of California, San Diego walked the crowd through the advanced computer model he was using to answer that question. He talked about system boundaries, perturbations, dissipation, attractors, bifurcations and a whole bunch of other stuff largely incomprehensible to those of us uninitiated in complex systems theory. But the bottom line was clear enough: global capitalism has made the depletion of resources so rapid, convenient and barrier-free that "earth-human systems" are becoming dangerously unstable in response. When pressed by a journalist for a clear answer on the "are we f**ked" question, Werner set the jargon aside and replied, "More or less."

There was one dynamic in the model, however, that offered some hope. Werner termed it "resistance"—movements of "people or groups of people" who "adopt a certain set of dynamics that does not fit within the capitalist culture." According to the abstract for his presentation, this includes "environmental direct action, resistance taken from outside the dominant culture, as in protests, blockades and sabotage by indigenous peoples, workers, anarchists and other activist groups."

Serious scientific gatherings don't usually feature calls for mass political resistance, much less direct action and sabotage. But then again, Werner wasn't exactly calling for those things. He was merely observing that mass uprisings of people—along the lines of the abolition movement, the civil rights movement or Occupy Wall Street—represent the likeliest source of "friction" to slow down an economic machine that is careening out of control. We know that past social movements have "had tremendous influence on . . . how the dominant culture evolved," he pointed out. So it stands to reason that, "if we're thinking about the future of the earth, and the future of our coupling to the environment, we have to include resistance as part of that dynamics." And that, Werner argued, is not a matter of opinion, but "really a geophysics problem."

Plenty of scientists have been moved by their research findings to take action in the streets. Physicists, astronomers, medical doctors and biologists have been at the forefront of movements against nuclear weapons, nuclear power, war, chemical contamination and creationism. And in November 2012, *Nature* published a commentary by the financier and environmental philanthropist Jeremy Grantham urging scientists to join this tradition and "be arrested if necessary," because climate change "is not only the crisis of your lives—it is also the crisis of our species' existence."

Some scientists need no convincing. The godfather of modern climate science, James Hansen, is a formidable activist, having been arrested some half-dozen times for resisting mountain-top removal coal mining and tar sands pipelines (he even left his job at NASA this year in part to have more time for campaigning). Two years ago, when I was arrested outside the White House at a mass action against the Keystone XL tar sands pipeline, one of the 166 people in cuffs that day was a glaciologist named Jason Box, a world-renowned expert on Greenland's melting ice sheet.

"I couldn't maintain my self-respect if I didn't go," Box said at the time, adding that "just voting doesn't seem to be enough in this case. I need to be a citizen also."

This is laudable, but what Werner is doing with his modelling is different. He isn't saying that his research drove him to take action to stop a particular policy; he is saying that his research shows that our entire economic paradigm is a threat to ecological stability. And indeed that challenging this economic paradigm—through mass-movement counter-pressure—is humanity's best shot at avoiding catastrophe.

That's heavy stuff. But he's not alone. Werner is part of a small but increasingly influential group of scientists whose research into the destabilisation of natural systems—particularly the climate system—is leading them to similarly transformative, even revolutionary, conclusions. And for any closet revolutionary who has ever dreamed of overthrowing the present economic order in favour of one a little less likely to cause Italian pensioners to hang themselves in their homes, this work should be of particular interest. Because it makes the ditching of that cruel system in favour of something new (and perhaps, with lots of work, better) no longer a matter of mere ideological preference but rather one of species-wide existential necessity.

Leading the pack of these new scientific revolutionaries is one of Britain's top climate experts, Kevin Anderson, the deputy director of the Tyndall Centre for Climate Change Research, which has quickly established itself as one of the UK's premier climate research institutions. Addressing everyone from the Department for International Development to Manchester City Council, Anderson has spent more than a decade patiently translating the implications of the latest climate science to politicians, economists and campaigners. In clear and understandable language, he lays out a rigorous road map for emissions reduction, one that provides a decent shot at keeping global temperature rise below 2° Celsius, a target that most governments have determined would stave off catastrophe.

But in recent years Anderson's papers and slide shows have become more alarming. Under titles such as "Climate Change: Going Beyond Dangerous . . . Brutal Numbers and Tenuous Hope," he points out that the chances of staying within anything like safe temperature levels are diminishing fast.

With his colleague Alice Bows, a climate mitigation expert at the Tyndall Centre, Anderson points out that we have lost so much time to political stalling and weak climate policies—all while global consumption (and emissions) ballooned—that we are now facing cuts so drastic that they challenge the fundamental logic of prioritizing GDP growth above all else.

Anderson and Bows inform us that the often-cited long-term mitigation target—an 80 per cent emissions cut below 1990 levels by 2050—has been selected purely for reasons of political expediency and has "no scientific basis." That's because climate impacts come not just from what we emit today and tomorrow, but from the cumulative emissions that build up in the atmosphere over time. And they warn that by focusing on targets three and a half decades into the future—rather than on what we can do to cut carbon sharply and immediately—there is a serious risk that we will allow our emissions to continue to soar for years to come, thereby blowing through far too much of our 2° "carbon budget" and putting ourselves in an impossible position later in the century.

Which is why Anderson and Bows argue that, if the governments of developed countries are serious about hitting the agreed upon international target of keeping warming below 2° Celsius, and if reductions are to respect any kind of equity principle (basically that the countries that have been spewing carbon for the better part of two centuries need to cut before the countries where more than a billion people still don't have electricity), then the reductions need to be a lot deeper, and they need to come a lot sooner. . . .

The fact that the business-as-usual pursuit of profits and growth is destabilising life on earth is no longer something we need to read about in scientific journals. The early signs are unfolding before our eyes. And increasing numbers of us are responding accordingly: blockading fracking activity in Balcombe; interfering with Arctic drilling preparations in Russian waters (at tremendous personal cost); taking tar sands operators to court for violating indigenous sovereignty; and countless other acts of resistance large and small. In Brad Werner's computer model, this is the "friction" needed to slow down the forces of destabilisation; the great climate campaigner Bill McKibben calls it the "antibodies" rising up to fight the planet's "spiking fever."

It's not a revolution, but it's a start. And it might just buy us enough time to figure out a way to live on this planet that is distinctly less f**ked.

7

Cartoons on Globalization, 2000s

The following are editorial cartoons. Each addresses economic components of globalization, and each in some way addresses the relationship between those in the most developed part of the world and those in the developing world.

Figure 28.1, "As an Illegal Immigrant," raises questions about increased labor and capital mobility, allowing the import of migrant workers and the export of capital for foreign factories. What is the point of the cartoon? How would you describe its attitude toward globalization?

Figure 28.2, "Help Is on the Way, Dude," focuses on an irony of some well-intentioned efforts to protect the environment and exploited foreign laborers. What is the irony? How might you solve the problem posed by the cartoon?

Figure 28.3, "Cheap Chinese Textiles," explores the problem of low-cost manufacturing countries flooding global markets with cheap products. What is the meaning of the comment by the representative of the European Union (EU)? What is the meaning of the cartoon?

Figure 28.4, "Keep the Europeans Out," examines a concern of North American farmers, here expressed on a placard of a Canadian farmer. What is that concern, and what is the farmer's solution? What is the point of the cartoon? What does this cartoon say about the use of tariffs, quotas, or other protectionist barriers to limit global competition? Compare this cartoon to the previous one on this issue.

Figure 28.5, "I Don't Mean to Hurry You," asks about the wishes of people in the developing world. What is the point of the cartoon?

Figure 28.1 "As an Illegal Immigrant."
Source: Gary Markstein.

Figure 28.2 "Help Is on the Way, Dude."
Source: By permission of Chip Bok and Creators Syndicate, Inc.

Figure 28.3 "Cheap Chinese Textiles."
Source: Patrick Chappatte, The International Herald Tribune / Cagle Cartoons.

Figure 28.4 "Keep the Europeans Out."
Source: Bruce MacKinnon/artizans.com.

Figure 28.5 "I Don't Mean to Hurry You."

Source: J. McGillen, www.cartoonstock.com.

THINKING HISTORICALLY

All of these cartoonists explore a process of economic globalization. What are the economic forces that bring about the globalization depicted in these cartoons? To what extent does the humor in these cartoons depend on a realization that globalization is inevitable? To what extent is that attitude shared by the authors of the other selections in this chapter?

■ REFLECTIONS

Globalization is not one process, but many. It is as technological as the Internet, smart phones, and the latest flu vaccine. It is as cultural as international film festivals, sushi, and disappearing languages. It is as political as the United Nations, time zones, and occupying armies. Perhaps most important, it is economic. People migrate for jobs, factories move for cheaper labor, and neither consumers nor corporations care about country of origin. Since the end of communism, the entire world has become a single market.

Is this a good thing? It depends on whom you ask. Sherif Hetata sees overcommercialization undermining national traditions. Philippe Legrain applauds the new menu of possibilities. Life is clearly hard for the women working in the sweatshops of international corporations, as Miriam Ching Yoon Louie points out; but is economic globalization responsible for their suffering, or does it provide women like them with new opportunities?

It is the duty of citizens, not historians, to decide what outcomes are good or bad, better or worse. But historians can help us decide by showing us where we are—by deepening the temporal dimension of our awareness.

Understanding the process of change is the most useful "habit of mind" we gain from studying the past. Although the facts are many and the details overwhelming, the historical process appears to us only through the study of the specifics. And we must continually check and revise our interpretations to conform to new information. But like a storyteller without a plot, we are lost without some overall understanding of how our world is changing.

More important, understanding change does not mean that we have to submit to it. Of the processes of globalization discussed in this chapter—trade and technological transfers, cultural homogenization and competition, commercialization and market expansion—some may seem inevitable, some strong, some even reversible. Intelligent action requires an appreciation of the possible as well as the identification of the improbable.

History is not an exact science. Fortunately, human beings are creators, as well as subjects, of change. Even winds that cannot be silenced can be deflected, harnessed, or made to chime. Which way is the world moving? What are we becoming? What can we do? What kind of world can we create? These are questions that can be answered only by studying the past, both distant and recent, and trying to understand the overarching changes that are shaping our lives. Worlds of history converge upon us, but only one world will emerge from our wishes, our wisdom, and our will.

Acknowledgments, Volume Two

Chapter 15

1   Nicholas D. Kristof. "1492: The Prequel" from *The New York Times Magazine*, June 6, 1999. All rights reserved. Used by permission and protected by the Copyright Laws of the United States. The printing, copying, redistribution, or retransmission of this Content without express written permission is prohibited.
2   Ma Huan. From *The Overall Survey of the Ocean Shores*, ed. and trans. Feng Ch'eng Chun, originally published by The Hakluyt Society, 1970. Reprinted by permission of David Higham.
4   Christopher Columbus. "Letter to King Ferdinand and Queen Isabella" from *The Four Voyages of Columbus*, ed. Cecil Jane, Copyright © 1988 Dover Publications. Reprinted by permission of the publisher.
5   Kirkpatrick Sale. Excerpt from *The Conquest of Paradise*. Copyright © 1990 by Kirkpatrick Sale. Used by permission of The Joy Harris Literary Agency.

Chapter 16

1   Bernal Diaz. Excerpt from *The Conquest of New Spain*, trans. J. M. Cohen, Penguin UK, 1963. Reprinted by permission of Penguin UK.
2   From "The Broken Spears" by Miguel Leon-Portilla, Copyright © 1962, 1990 by Miguel Leon-Portilla, Expanded and Updated Edition © 1992 by Miguel Leon-Portilla. Reprinted by permission of Beacon Press, Boston.
4   Nzinga Mbemba. "Appeal to the King of Portugal" from *The African Past*, ed. Basil Davidson. Copyright © 1964 by Basil Davidson. Reprinted by permission of Curtis Brown, Ltd.
6   J. B. Romaigne. From *Journal of a Slave Ship Voyage*, Dover Publications. Reprinted by permission of the publisher.

Chapter 17

1   Bartolomeo de Las Casas. From *The Devastation of the Indies: A Brief Account*, trans. Herma Briffault, Copyright 1974. Reproduced with permission of CONTINUUM PUBLISHING COMPANY in the format Textbook via Copyright Clearance Center.
4   Benjamin J. Kaplan. *Divided by Faith: Religious Conflict and the Practice of Toleration in Early Modern Europe*, pp. 28–32, 100–103. Cambridge, Mass.: The Belknap Press of Harvard University Press, Copyright © 2007 by Benjamin J. Kaplan. Reprinted by permission of Harvard University Press.

Chapter 18

1   Miu Family of Guangdong Province. "Family Instructions for the Miu Lineage," trans. Clara Yu, from *Chinese Civilization: A Sourcebook*, Second Edition, ed. Patricia Ebrey. Copyright © 1993 Free Press. Reprinted with the permission of Simon & Schuster, Inc.

3   Anna Bijns. "Unyoked Is Best! Happy the Woman without a Man," trans. by Krtistiaan P. G. Aercke, from *Women and Writers of the Renaissance and Reformation*, ed. Katharina M. Wilson, The University of Georgia Press, 1987.

7   Countess de Rochefort. "Diary of the Countess de Rochefort" from *Not in God's Image*, eds. Julia O'Faolain and Lauro Martines, HarperCollins Publishers. Used by permission of the author.

8   "Court Case on Marriage in High Court of Aix" from *Not in God's Image*, eds. Julia O'Faolain and Lauro Martines, HarperCollins Publishers. Used by permission of the author.

9   Mary Jo Maynes and Ann Waltner. "Childhood, Youth, and the Female Life Cycle: Women's Life-Cycle Transitions in a World-Historical Perspective: Comparing Marriage in China and Europe" from *Journal of Women's History* 12:4. Copyright © 2001 Journal of Women's History. Reprinted with permission of The Johns Hopkins University Press.

Chapter 19

1   Jack Goldstone. Excerpt from *Why Europe? The Rise of the West in World History 1500–1850*. Copyright © 2009 by Jack Goldstone. Reprinted with the permission of The McGraw-Hill Companies, Inc.

5   Bonnie S. Anderson and Judith P. Zinsser. From *A History of Their Own: Women in Europe from Prehistory to the Present*, Volume I. Copyright © 1988 by Bonnie S. Anderson and Judith Zinsser. Reprinted by permission of HarperCollins Publishers.

7   Lynda Norene Shaffer. "China, Technology, and Change" from *World History Bulletin* 4, no. 1 (Fall/Winter 1986–1987), pages 1–6. Used with permission.

8   Sugita Gempaku. From *Japan: A Documentary History*, ed. David J. Lu (Armonk, NY: M. E. Sharpe, 1997), pp. 219–220. English translation copyright © 1997 by David J. Lu. Reprinted with permission from M. E. Sharpe, Inc.

Chapter 20

7   Toussaint L'Ouverture. "Letter to the Directory, November 5, 1797" from *The Black Jacobins*, ed. C. L. R. James, Vintage Books, 1989. Reproduced with permission of Curtis Brown Group Ltd, London on behalf of the Estate of CLR James. Copyright © The Estate of CLR James.

8   Simón Bolívar, *Selected Writings of Bolivar*, Vol. I, ed. Harold A. Bierck (New York: The Colonial Press Inc.,1951), 103–121.

Chapter 21

1   Arnold Pacey. *Technology in World Civilization: A Thousand-Year History*, 1,775 word excerpt from pages 128–135. © 1990 Massachusetts Institute of Technology, by permission of The MIT Press.

2   *Sources of Japanese Tradition*, Second Edition, Volume Two: 1600–2000, ed. Wm. Theodore de Bary et. al. Copyright © 2005 Columbia University Press. Republished with permission of Columbia University Press; permission conveyed through Copyright Clearance Center, Inc.

6   T. H. Von Laue, "A Secret Memorandum of Sergei Witte on the Industrialization of Imperial Russia," *The Journal of Modern History*, Vol. 26, No. 1, March 1954. Copyright © 1954 The University of Chicago Press. Used with permission.

8   Samuel L. Bailey and Franco Ramella. *One Family, Two Worlds: An Italian Family's Correspondence Across the Atlantic*. Copyright © 1988 by Rutgers, the State University. Reprinted by permission of Rutgers University Press.

Chapter 22

2   George Orwell. From *Burmese Days*, copyright © 1934 by George Orwell and renewed 1962 by Sonia Pitt-Rivers, reprinted by permission of Houghton Mifflin Harcourt Publishing Company. All rights reserved.

4   Francis Bebey, from *King Albert*, translated by Joyce A. Hutchinson (Westport, Conn.: Lawrence Hill, 1981). Reprinted with the permission of Kidi Bebey.

Chapter 23

1   Fukuzawa Yukichi. From *Japan: A Documentary History*, ed. David J. Lu (Armonk, NY: M. E. Sharpe, 1997), pp. 351–353. English translation copyright © 1997 by David J. Lu. Reprinted with permission from M. E. Sharpe, Inc.

6   Mohandas K. Gandhi. Excerpt from *Hind Swaraj, Navajivan, 1938*. Reprinted by permission of The Navajivan Trust.

Chapter 24

4   Joe Lunn. Reprinted with permission from *Memoirs of the Maelstrom: A Sengalese Oral History of the First World War* by Joe Lunn. Copyright © 1999 by Joe Lunn. Published by Heinemann, Portsmouth, NH. All rights reserved.

Chapter 25

2   Adolf Hitler. Excerpts from *Mein Kampf*, trans. Ralph Manheim. Published by Hutchinson. Copyright © 1943, renewed 1971 by Houghton Mifflin Harcourt Publishing Company. Reprinted by permission of Houghton Mifflin Harcourt Publishing Company and The Random House Group Limited. All rights reserved.

Chapter 26

Chapter 27

Chapter 28

About the Author

Kevin Reilly is a professor of humanities at Raritan Valley College and has taught at Rutgers, Columbia, and Princeton Universities. Cofounder and first president of the World History Association, Reilly has written numerous articles on the teaching of history and has edited works including *The Introductory History Course* for the American Historical Association. A specialist in immigration history, Reilly incorporated his research in creating the "Modern Global Migrations" globe at Ellis Island. His work on the history of racism led to the editing of *Racism: A Global Reader*. He was a Fulbright scholar in Brazil and Jordan and an NEH fellow in Greece, Oxford (UK), and India. Awards include the Community College Humanities Association's Distinguished Educator of the Year and the World History Association's Pioneer Award. He has also served the American Historical Association in various capacities, including the governing council.